Not great

The Changing Experience of Childhood

Families and Divorce

Carol Smart, Bren Neale and
Amanda Wade

Polity

First published in 2001 by Polity Press in association with Blackwell Publishers Ltd.

Editorial office:
Polity Press
65 Bridge Street
Cambridge CB2 1UR, UK

Marketing and production:
Blackwell Publishers Ltd
108 Cowley Road
Oxford OX4 1JF, UK

Published in the USA by
Blackwell Publishers Inc.
Commerce Place
350 Main Street
Malden, MA 02148, USA

A catalogue record for this book is available from the British Library.

Library of Congress Cataloging-in-Publication Data
Smart, Carol.
    The changing experience of childhood : families and divorce / Carol Smart, Bren Neale, and Amanda Wade.
        p.   cm.
Includes bibliographical references and index.
    ISBN 0-7456-2399-9 (HN : acid-free paper) — ISBN 0-7456-2400-6 (pbk. : acid-free paper)
    1. Children of divorced parents.   2. Children—Family relationships.
I. Neale, Bren.   II. Wade, Amanda.   III. Title.
    HQ777.5 .S573 2001
    305.23—dc21

                                                                2001000148

Typeset in 10.5 on 12 pt Sabon
by Ace Filmsetting Ltd, Frome, Somerset
Printed in Great Britain by MPG Books Ltd, Bodmin, Cornwall

This book is printed on acid-free paper.

Contents

Acknowledgements

We wish to express our thanks to all the children who helped us with this research. We hope that they enjoyed participating in the research as much as we enjoyed meeting them.

We also wish to acknowledge the vital support of both the ESRC and the Nuffield Foundation who made these two projects possible. Sharon Witherspoon of Nuffield has been unfailingly helpful and we hope that the Trustees will continue to support qualitative research of this kind. The ESRC research project (No. L129251049) on which much of our analysis here is based was graded 'Outstanding' by peer review. Naturally we are grateful to our reviewers (whoever they may be) for being so generous in their assessment. We are also grateful to the ESRC for funding us to revisit the children during 2001 to see how things have changed for them since 1997–8. Our thanks also go to those long-suffering colleagues who sat on our advisory committee. The academics on the committee are included below, but in addition we wish to acknowledge Diana McNeish from Barnardos, Stephanie Martin (guardian *ad litem*), and Jonathon Whybrow of John Howell & Co., Solicitors. It was great fun working with them. Some organizations were also especially helpful or supportive of our research and we would like to mention the Family Court Welfare Service, National Family Mediation, Family Mediation (Scotland), One Parent Families (Scotland), Stepfamily (Scotland), UK College of Family Mediators, Parentline Plus, and Young Voice.

There are a number of scholars we would like to mention because their work has sustained us throughout this project. They are: Leena Alanen, Julia Brannen, Ros Edwards, John Eekelaar, Janet Finch,

Allison James, Kathleen Kiernan, Mavis Maclean, Jennifer Mason, Judith Masson, Berry Mayall, David Morgan, Ginny Morrow, Ann Phoenix, Christine Piper, Jeremy Roche, Selma Sevenhuijsen, Tom Shakespeare, Joan Tronto and Maureen Winn Oakley.

Finally, our thanks to Sue Cramp, Daryl Gardner and Julia Wassall, who so carefully and diligently transcribed all the interview tapes.

1

Rethinking Childhood/ Rethinking Families

[Childhood is] a period of growth, that is to say, the period in which the individual, in both the physical and moral sense, does not yet exist, the period in which he [*sic*] is made, develops and is formed . . . In everything, the child is characterised by the very instability of his nature, which is the law of growth. The educationalist is presented not with a person wholly formed – not a complete work or a finished product – but with a *becoming*, an incipient being, a person in the process of formation.

Durkheim, 1979: 150

Children can be viewed as fully social beings, capable of acting in the social world and of creating and sustaining their own culture. . . . If we see children as actors . . . we can ask how their actions constrain, facilitate, encourage and in a myriad of ways have implications for others, adults in particular.

Waksler, 1991: 23, 68

Introduction

Over the past two decades sociologists can be said to have rediscovered children.[1] This is not to say, of course, that children were ignored prior to 1980, but that we have been witnessing a transformation in thinking about the nature of childhood and the place occupied by children in a variety of social and public settings. This transformation is reflected in the two quotations above. The first, from a text originally published in 1911 and written by one of the 'founding fathers' of sociology, conceptualizes children as half-socialized beings whose childhoods must be shaped for them. They are 'unfinished products' rather than 'complete works', indicating their status as 'projects' that must be continuously managed by adults (Hallden, 1991). The second quotation, from a sociological collection on childhood published eighty years later, invites us to conceptualize children in a different way: this time as creative social and moral agents with the strengths and capabilities to shape their own childhoods. Under this new paradigm children are transformed from unfinished projects under adult control to fully social *persons* with the capacity to act, to interact and to influence the social world. This transformation in sociological thinking has generated a great deal of debate,[2] for it concerns the fundamentally important issue of the nature of childhood and where the boundaries between adulthood and childhood should be drawn. It is therefore a fitting theme for the introductory chapter to our book. Our purpose here is to draw out the salient features of this transformation in sociological thinking. In the first half of the chapter we explore the notion of children as 'projects', showing how this approach to children has grown out of the 'naturalistic' models of childhood, particularly those emanating from developmental psychology and socialization theory, and we examine the impact of this mode of thinking on perceptions of child–adult relationships and the place of children in their families. In the second half of the chapter we go on to trace the gradual assimilation of ideas about the social nature of children that accords them their personhood. We start with Ariès's notion that childhood is socially constructed and we review the recent literature that has explored children's agency and competence in a variety of settings. We conclude by considering how these new ideas on childhood have been imported into family research, and we show how developments in both of these fields have opened up the potential for a new sociology of children's family lives. In exploring these themes we will lay the theoretical foundation for our empirical study of childhood after parental divorce or separation, which we report on in subsequent chapters of this book.

'Natural' childhoods?

Questions about the nature of childhood are hardly new; they have been taxing the minds of social theorists since the days of Socrates, resulting in a proliferation of novel and sometimes contradictory sets of beliefs (Jenks, 1982; Hendrick, 1997). As Jenks notes, we have yet to reach any consensus on the nature of the child, simply because these beliefs reflect different visions of the social world held by particular theorists rather than any 'higher' truth about children themselves. Here we shall introduce four powerful images or models of childhood which continue to inform contemporary thinking among parents, professionals and policy-makers. The first of these models evokes an image of children as 'little devils' beset by 'original sin' (Jenks, 1996; James,

Jenks and Prout, 1998). They are seen as inherently evil, corrupt and wilful and in need of harsh treatment to 'beat the devil out'. This view of the child (exemplified by Hobbes's *Leviathan* (1651)) was formalized through the introduction of harsh methods of child-rearing in sixteenth- and seventeenth-century Puritan Europe, and it continues to find adherents today (Hendrick, 1997). As a variation on this theme the imagery of the 'little savage' or barbarian is also used, implying that children are not so much 'bad' as innately wild and uncivilized (Alanen, 1992). These images are countered by an equally strong image of the child as a 'little angel', a presumption that children are naturally good, pure, innocent and kind.[3] This view was propounded by Rousseau in 1762, who argued that rather than punishing children into grace we would do better to protect them, celebrate their goodness and seek to emulate the intrinsic values which they embody (James, Jenks and Prout, 1998). Rousseau's child was a child of nature. He assumed childhood goodness to be a natural (rather than a social) state, one that separates the child from the corrupt world of adults and, as such, his theories run the risk of sentimentality. But in perceiving children in a positive light with innate qualities that should be recognized, Rousseau's ideas have fed into the new styles of sociological thinking that accord children their personhood (James, Jenks and Prout, 1998). These notions of children as 'devils', 'savages', or 'angels' have become intertwined in contemporary adult thinking, reflecting a deep-seated paradox about the true condition of childhood.

Children as embryonic adults: developmental psychology

The fourth model for understanding the child is the 'embryonic' model. This is equally essentialist in assuming the child to have certain innate qualities. But rather than being seen as inherently good or evil children are presumed to be in an emergent state with unfixed natures. If they have any social characteristics at all they are said to be weak, fragile, unstable, irrational, deficient and capricious in both mind and body (and hence liable to be 'good', 'bad' or 'wild' and capable of being all three in turn (Durkheim, 1979)). This way of viewing children emerged from early developmental psychology, which ties the social nature of children firmly to their biological growth and development (Jenks, 1982; Prout and James, 1997). In this evolutionary model, children start off as little more than simple biological organisms or blank slates. They then progress, both physically and intellectually, through a series of sequentially linked phases or stages through their childhoods. As they progress they move from simplicity to complexity of thought, from incompetence to competence, from irrational to rational behaviour, gradually learning the cognitive skills involved with reasoning, logic, causality and morality until they eventually achieve the fully social state of adulthood (Prout and James, 1997). The precise details of this transition is a matter for debate: 'Freud posited five stages, Sullivan eight, Piaget six, Kohlberg six and Erikson posits eight' (Denzin, 1977: 8).[4]

Like the other models discussed above, this 'embryonic' model is presumed to be biologically determined and natural and, therefore, claims to be universal. Defining children in terms of their physical growth and psychological development means foregrounding what is common to them all, so that they become a unitary category from which any variation is perceived as 'deviance' (James and Prout, 1995). Piaget's 'child' represented all children, and in his view this universal child could be 'captured' and explained in the child development laboratory (Piaget, 1972). His developmental stages came to be regarded as benchmarks against which the 'normality' of all children could be measured. In the process, 'the child' became a somewhat generalized, hypothetical and ahistorical child, rather than an actual, embodied, biographically unique and socially differentiated child.

Of the models of childhood outlined above this 'embryonic' model, based on theories of child development, has had the most far-reaching influence on contemporary thinking and on the lives of real children. As well as having an impact on everyday, 'common sense' conceptualizations of the child, it has informed the practices of generations of educationalists, paediatricians, child-rearing experts and public policymakers. It also underpins contemporary understandings of child welfare in legal and therapeutic practice (Rose, 1989; Brannen, 1989; Jenks, 1996: 29). This is reflected, for example, in the policy of age-grading in contemporary education systems, and in the importance attached by adults and children alike to the precise chronological age of the child as a marker of social status and competence. Waksler (1991: 63) notes that children are commonly described as pre-verbal, pre-cognitive, inexperienced and immature. In other words, they became a negative category, defined in terms of *not* something (or *not yet* something) rather than as something. They are seen to be in a learning mode, at or between stages, as if they are in a permanent state of transition (Hood-Williams, 1990; Leonard, 1990). As such they are never perceived as just 'being'. Defined not as 'persons' but as 'potential persons' they are located in the margins of social life and valued more for their future potential as adults than for what they might actually be as children (Cockburn, 1998). This embryonic model of childhood has become so embedded in our everyday understandings of children that it is difficult to think outside it (Prout and James, 1997).

Childhood socialization

The models of childhood outlined above are all based on the assumption that childhood is a natural and universal condition. Childhood as a social condition was, until recently, simply not recognized, perhaps because the widespread acceptance of these naturalistic models left little theoretical space in which to explore alternative constructions of the child. Until the 1970s, the available research on children was therefore focused almost entirely on the psychological or pedagogical development of their bodies, intellects and personalities or with policy/welfare concerns about their protection or control (see chapter 2). What has been missing from the overall canon of research on childhood, however, has been a counterbalance to these concerns that recognizes children as social beings and pays attention to the social aspects of their lives. Early sociological work, which might have provided alternative models, singularly failed to do so. Few classic sociologists paid any attention to children. Preoccupied by grand theorizing about the social structures of society and the functioning of institutions within them, few of the founding fathers paid much attention to children, or indeed to the 'domestic sphere' at all. Those who did consider children relied heavily on developmental psychology and used these ideas uncritically, to inform their work. This is evident in the quotation from Durkheim above. For him, the child is simply a 'becoming' who must be socialized. In Durkheim's view: 'The child, on entering life, brings to it only his [*sic*] nature as an individual. Society finds itself, with each new generation, faced with a tabula rasa . . . on which it must build anew' (1956: 72).

Thereafter, socialization theory became the main focus of enquiry. Socialization was identified as a range of practices by which the child internalizes the values of the social system, is made to conform, and is transformed from an asocial being into a fully social adult. The aim of socialization theory was to explain how these processes transform the child, focusing in particular on the functions performed by the key institutions of community, education and the family. 'The family' in these sociological accounts came to be inextricably linked to its perceived function of socialization:

The family . . . is the most important 'primary' group in society. . . . All those values which are of the most importance for the formation of adult character are first experienced and exercised by children in the context of the family. . . . These qualities are not 'taught' or 'learned' in any straightforward . . . way, they are actually embodied in people and their behaviour [which] the child perceives . . . and appraises. . . . In this way the family is an educative group of the most fundamental kind . . . a kind of avenue through which [the child] comes gradually to an experience of . . . wider social groupings . . . to the complicated secondary groups of society . . . and to full adulthood. (Fletcher, 1962: 27–8)

In many of these accounts the actual processes of socialization were glossed over. Ritchie and Koller (1964), for example, in their *Sociology of Childhood*, described the key roles that parents play as men or women, husbands or wives, providers or homemakers, friends or enemies, workers or players and believers or sceptics. The children, they suggested, simply absorbed these key roles, partly by instruction but primarily by observing and mimicking their parents.

In the structural-functionalist writings of the 1940s and 1950s, particularly in the work of Talcott Parsons (1951), socialization assumed the character of a totalitarian system of control that gradually engulfed the child through the psychological process of 'internalization' and moulded it for its own ends. In some of these accounts the child appears as a 'barbarian' to be tamed (Parsons, 1951) while in others the child is represented as a passive object to be moulded into shape. Prout and James explain how the process was envisaged:

> The child is portrayed, like the laboratory rat, as being at the mercy of external stimuli: passive and conforming. Lost in a social maze it is the adult who offers directions. The child, like the rat, responds accordingly and is finally rewarded by becoming social, by becoming adult. . . . The socialising agents [schools and parents] teach, serve as models and invite participation. Through their ability to offer gratification and deprivations they induce co-operation and learning and prevent disrupting deviance. (1997: 13)

Theories of socialization have shed light on the pedagogic processes by which children acquire language and other skills and attributes, but they hardly constitute a rounded sociology of childhood, if only because children appear as no more than passive learners (or as deviants who resist socialization) (Thorne, 1987). By and large, socialization is not about what children themselves do or about the interaction of adult and child. Nor does it explore the meaning of institutions such as the family for the child (Prout and James, 1997; Waksler, 1991; Alanen, 1992). It is much more about what adults, including parents, do to children to prepare them for life in the adult world. There is an overriding preoccupation with the reproduction of the adult social order at the expense of the child–adult interactions that go to make up the process (Thorne, 1987: 94; Prout and James, 1997). Children themselves are made to stand in the shadow of adults (Alanen, 1992). Socialization theory has also been criticized for implying a coherent set of values and behaviours for children to be socialized into, a proposition which ill fits the pluralism of late modern societies. In Parsons's (1951) highly deterministic theory, for example, society is presented as a monolithic, well-oiled and automated machine that is fed by the compliant personalities of its members and which 'consumes' children in order to perpetuate itself (Jenks, 1982). In such writings the social worlds and moral agency of real children were relegated, on the one hand, to the confines of individual psychology and, on the other, to the dictates of the social system.

Children as 'projects'

The supposedly natural and universal models of childhood outlined above share a key feature that we have touched upon only briefly in our account. They are based on a view of the child as a 'project' that must be managed in some way by adults. The 'little devil' or 'savage' model represents a call to discipline, punish, and tame children and render them safe for their own good and the good of others. This model continues to find adherents today among those who call for 'boot camps', 'short sharp shocks' and night curfews for wayward youth, and those who condone the corporal punishment of children by their parents and childminders. 'Beating the devil out of the child for his own good' has found its modern-day counterpart in the equally incongruous notion of a 'loving smack'. More generally, this model has been translated in contemporary thinking into a 'social problems' perspective that sees children as a potential nuisance or threat that must be dealt with through firm controls (Thorne, 1987; de Winter, 1997). 'Little angels', no less than 'little devils', also constitute a project for adults in that they need protection from the corrosive influences of adult society, or, alternatively, as 'fallen angels', they need saving from corruption, abuse or poverty. Rousseau's progressive ideas about the innate qualities of children were the forerunners of contemporary perspectives on the victimization of children which led to the development of a range of protectionist or 'child-saving' strategies over the course of the nineteenth and twentieth centuries (Platt, 1969; Thorne, 1987). But it is within socialization theory, with its focus on the mechanisms for moulding children to fit adult society, that the notion of child-as-project is most fully developed. Seen as 'embryonic persons' who are continually developing and learning, all children become projects that must be managed from the moment of their birth until they achieve their full potential as adults. This view of childhood continues to be all-pervasive: 'Childhood is the most intensely governed sector of personal existence. . . . The modern child has become the focus of innumerable projects that purport to safeguard it from physical, sexual and moral danger [and] to ensure its "normal" development' (Rose, 1989: 121).

Inferior children

As 'embryonic persons' and as 'projects' children are, by definition, marginal beings. But this marginalization has further dimensions. Firstly these models are based on the presumption that children are not only different from adults but inferior to adults. This is the implicit, taken-for-granted component of the embryonic model of childhood. As 'blank slates', 'savages' or unfinished products, children are weak-willed, dependent, irrational, unstable, incompetent, deficient, asocial, amoral and, ultimately, not fully human.[5] These implied characteristics mean that to call someone 'childish' is not a neutral or descriptive observation: it is almost a term of abuse (Oakley, 1994). Of course it is adults (not children) who proffer these derogatory definitions of children's natures; and they are quick to define themselves as the very antithesis of these characteristics. These constructions of childhood are so 'adultcentric' that it has become impossible to understand the nature of childhood without reference to the nature of adulthood – they are defined in terms of each other:

> Cultures project onto infants and young children a nature opposite to the qualities prized in adults. Valuing independence, we define children as dependent: the task of socialization is to encourage independence. In the nineteenth century, when parental authority was idealised, adults defined children as wilful and the goal of socialization was to teach obedience. The Japanese, who value interdependence, define infants as too autonomous and needing to be tempted into dependence. (Thorne, 1987: 95)

As Thorne argues, adult definitions of children are bound up with notions of what kind of project they envisage the child to be, and this in turn is linked to their own idealized visions of the (adult) social world. Seeing children as essentially different and as an inferior social group has consequences for children themselves. Adults create hierarchical boundaries between themselves and children on the basis of the supposed ontological differences between the two and, in this way, maintain children in structurally powerless positions in society (Mayall, 1994; Christensen, 1998). Under these hierarchical models the subtle, everyday mechanisms through which children are dominated by adults – through controls on their bodies, voices, time, space, behaviour, activities, economic power and so on – are not open to sociological scrutiny. On the contrary such power differentials are seen as the way child–adult relationships should operate as part of the natural, 'adultocratic' order of things (in much the same way that traditional patriarchal authority over women was once seen as natural) (Hood-Williams, 1990; Alanen, 1992; Oakley, 1994).

This can be seen, for example, in the Newsons' (1976) study of child development in families, where adultocratic power relationships between children and their parents were simply taken for granted. This led them to focus on 'obedience' and 'respect' as the responses that children were presumed to owe to adults, and to interpret interactions between parent and child in terms of 'commands' and 'compliance' even where these concepts clearly did not fit their data (Hood-Williams, 1990). The perceived inferiority of children is bound up with their domination and control and is therefore a powerful reinforcer of their marginalization as persons.

Invisible children

If, in some accounts, actual children become inferior, one-dimensional beings, in other accounts they are simply eclipsed. There seems little need for children-as-projects to appear 'in the flesh' so to speak, so they are effectively rendered invisible (Alanen, 1992). Ambert's (1993) survey of classic sociological texts and North American journals revealed an absence of children, while post-war texts on the family proved hardly better. They make only passing reference to children themselves, subsuming them under the headings of Socialization, Child-Rearing or Education (James and Prout, 1996). The concepts of Family, Socialization and Childhood are 'moulded together into one piece that cannot be broken into parts for separate consideration' (Alanen, 1992: 91). In any discussion of family, of course, children are deeply implicated; they are the defining feature of familial ideology, the quintessential blood tie (Makrinioti, 1994). But, as such, children are on the receiving end of family values. They are objectified as the rationale for the (adult) 'doing' of family life, rather than seen as 'doers' of family life in their own right. Young and Willmott's (1957) classic study of family and kinship in east London, for example, explores relationships between spouses and their wider kin and the respective roles of adult family members, including the work of child-rearing. The parents talk of the gendered nature of parenting, their methods of discipline and their aspirations for their children's high-schooling and future careers. The children themselves, however, are brought into the picture only as the *raison d'être* for family life, the 'project' around which the families cohere. This tendency to submerge children in their families has been called the 'familialization' of childhood (Alanen, 1992; Makrinioti, 1994: 268–71). Children, it seems, are presumed to 'belong to' their parents. Their social identity is thought to mirror that of their parents, and when they become the targets of social approval or criticism, despite numerous intervening influences on their lives, their parents receive the credit or blame. The concept of 'family', seen in functionalist and essentialist terms, is often equated with parental agency alone. It is commonly said, for example, that 'the family is there to care for the children', as if the children were mere extensions of their parents. Statistically speaking, children do not seem to count either. They are described and examined as a by-product of the family unit rather than treated as units of observation in their own right (Qvortrup, 1997). In these ways, children have been fused with their parents into an idealized, inseparable family unit. In the process, the diverse identities and interests of individual family members have been concealed (Makrinioti, 1994: 268).

One of the consequences of this tendency towards 'familialization' is that children are rarely asked to speak for themselves about family life, for it is presumed that their parents can speak for them (Brannen, 1999). In both a research and policy context, talking to children about family life has conventionally been seen as somehow inappropriate, as if it is an intrusion into what is essentially a private sphere of life. There are underlying ethical concerns that speaking to children about personal family matters will somehow unravel, undermine or subvert the family and damage its integrity. These concerns, combined with entrenched views that children are hardly worth consulting (Brannen, 1999) have contributed to the marginalization of children in family sociology, just as they have been marginalized in other areas of research and policy. As a result we have been left with an impoverished understanding of actual children in families and of family life from the child's point of view.

'Social' childhoods: children as active and interactive persons

Childhood as a variable social construction

Challenges to these naturalistic models of childhood began to emerge during the 1970s in anthropological, social historical and feminist writings and in the interactionist and phenomenological schools of sociology. Researchers from these varied disciplines sought to establish the social condition of children's childhoods and to offer a new model of childhood based on a view of children as persons with agency (i.e. with the capacity to act, interact and influence their social worlds). These ideas were eventually consolidated into a new sub-discipline of childhood studies.[6] This new sub-discipline is not solely the preserve of sociologists of course. It is an interdisciplinary endeavour that has brought about developments in psychological, historical, pedagogical and social policy and in legal thinking about children (Brannen, 1999).[7] Perhaps the overarching feature of the new discipline is the recognition that childhood is not simply a natural or universal state arising out of children's biological condition, but also a social construct which is culturally variable (Prout and James, 1997).

The social historian Philippe Ariès (1962) was one of the first researchers to observe that while children are present in all cultures, their childhoods, viewed spatially and temporally, are perceived and practised in countless ways. To be a child in seventeenth-century England, for example, was a very different social experience from being a twentieth-century child. What a child 'is' reflects the particular sociocultural context in which the child lives. The physical facts of infancy and childhood are but the raw material upon which cultures work to fashion different versions of what it means to be a child (Jenks, 1996: 121).[8] As Frones (1993: 1) points out, 'There is not one childhood but many, formed at the intersection of different cultural, social and economic systems. Different positions in society produce different experiences.' Elaborating on the theme, James, Jenks and Prout observe:

> To describe childhood or indeed any phenomenon as socially constructed is to suspend a belief in . . . its taken-for-granted meanings. Thus though quite obviously we all know what children are and what childhood is like . . . childhood does not exist in a finite and identifiable form. . . . Childhoods are variable and intentional. In direct refutation of the pre-sociological models of childhood, there is no 'universal' child with which to engage. (1998: 27)

Clearly not all children are identical, nor do they necessarily share the same world view. Rather than reifying the child as a unitary category, the challenge is to explore the plurality of childhoods across the boundaries of age, gender, locality, ethnicity, religion and broad socio-economic and familial contexts (Woodhead, 1997).

Childhood agency and competency

This new thinking opened up a wealth of possibilities. Once the social nature of childhood was recognized it became possible to think beyond the developmental/socialization framework for understanding children. This approach became just one of many ways to conceptualize childhood, rather than the correct or only way. Children no longer had to be seen as empty vessels being passively socialized for adulthood, but could be conceptualized as active and interactive practitioners of social life. A small but growing industry of research began to explore children's agency in a variety of contexts, focusing on how children negotiate rules, roles and personal relationships; how they create autonomy and balance this with their (inter)dependence; how they operate as strategic actors in different social contexts and how they take responsibility for their own well-being and that of others.[9] In the process children have emerged as more than unspecified actors: they have become visible as workers, soldiers, consumers, carers, counsellors, and clients of a whole variety of services (Brannen, 1999). Research on children as workers, for example, has uncovered the substantial contribution that children make to modern domestic economies and to the labour market (Morrow, 1994; Solberg, 1997) and has reconceptualized children's schooling as unpaid work that they are required to undertake on a daily basis (Qvortrup, 1985). More subtly, there have been challenges to the notion of children's peer activities and daily experiences as mere 'play'. Denzin (1977) argues that the notion of play is a fiction from the adult world. His observations of the social interactions of young children show that much of this activity concerns the work of constructing social orders by developing specific modes of communication, defining morally acceptable and unacceptable behaviour, constructing rules for entry and exit into social groups and developing strategies for dealing with difficult peers and adults. 'Children see these as serious concerns and often make a clear distinction between their play and their work' (Denzin, 1977: 185). Such findings, which show a variety of ways in which children take responsibility and demonstrate their social and economic worth, have challenged conventional assumptions about the 'childishness' of children's everyday activities.

Seeing children as active and serious practitioners of social life has, in turn, prompted a fundamental shift in thinking about their intellectual and emotional status. Children are 'knowers' of the same social world that sociologists have sought to describe and explain, and they offer a novel perspective on that world (Alanen, 1992). Perhaps the most radical part of this revision concerns the transformation of a theory of childhood deficiency into a theory of childhood competency (Waksler, 1991; Jenks, 1996). While children may in a very real sense be dependent on adults for substantial periods of time, this does not preclude the development of their sense of individual identity and their social and moral capabilities. Indeed, it is one of the tenets of modern child-rearing practices that parents should help to develop these personal attributes in their children. Whether children are able to demonstrate such competencies, of course, will depend on what opportunities they are given to practise and develop their social skills (de Winter, 1997; Cockburn, 1998), but their potential to do so is no longer in doubt:

> For those researchers for whom exploring children's roles as social actors constitutes a central concern, children's competence is taken-for-granted. The question they pose, instead, is how that competence is acknowledged and expressed or disguised and controlled in and through children's everyday relationships. . . . The institution of childhood separates children off from adults in such a way as to disguise their competencies. . . . As social actors in an adult world . . . they can be revealed to be demonstrating a shared human competence. (James, 1998: pp. viii–ix)

Competence, according to this new framework, is not precisely defined by age or learned by rote but is the product of a range of life experiences, interactions and influences which may continue throughout the life course. The focus has thus shifted away from what children cannot do towards what they can do and are doing.

Rethinking child–adult relationships

Central to this new thinking has been a transformation in the construction of child–adult relationships. While children may have different competencies to adults, this no longer means that their knowledge and achievements are inferior, nor that they should be dismissed as a different order of reality. The boundaries between the two have became more fluid. Seeing children in the new ways outlined above implies that adults have to 'see' themselves in new ways in relation to children. There is a growing recognition, for example, that adults are life-long learners and that, no less than children, their competencies change according to their experiences through the life course. Nor are adults self-sufficient; they have dependencies just as children do, and relationships of interdependence with children and other adults in a range of settings. More radically there has been scrutiny of the hierarchical structures of child–adult relationships in family life and other settings. Childhood research has moved into the familiar sociological terrain of social control and power relationships as studies have sought to explore how children position themselves in the generational system (Hallden, 1994). In the process they have started to uncover the generational oppression and/or marginalization of children in a variety of contexts (Mayall, 1994; Alderson, 1994; Cockburn, 1998). As James and Prout (1997) suggest, there can be no conception of childhood that is politically neutral. Treating children as reflexive social actors is more than a theoretical perspective, for it raises questions about the whole tenor of child–adult relationships (Prout and James, 1997; Brannen, 1999).

As a consequence of these initiatives, the child of sociological discourse has been transformed from a 'project' to a 'person'. New legitimacy has been accorded to the experiences of simply being a child, as researchers have sought to understand the meaning of childhood in and of itself and not merely as an embryonic state, a preface to some more important life stage. One of the features of this new wave of research is that children are perceived in much more positive and complimentary terms. Once they are seen as persons, they no longer have to be defined as a problem. In fact, more often than not, it is the adults who come to be perceived as problems for children. In sociological discourse, actual children have at last become visible as subjects of interest in their own right. Just as feminists once demanded that ways of knowing could no longer be exclusively masculinist but should incorporate the standpoint of women, so there is concern to move beyond adult-centred understandings and to know the world from the standpoint of children (Alanen, 1992, 1994). This interest in placing children's perspectives at the centre of analysis has prompted the development of sensitive, qualitative research methods designed to create the best conditions for drawing out children's accounts and perspectives. The aim has been to do research *with* children rather than *on* or *about* them and, in the process, to give their views legitimacy (Prout and James, 1997; Grau and Walsh, 1998; Roberts, 1999; James and Christensen, 1999).

A new social construct?

We have traced the gradual transformation in sociological thinking that, over the past two decades, has shifted understandings of children from 'project' to 'personhood'. We are not suggesting, however, that this theoretical transformation in any sense mirrors a historical transformation in adult understandings of, or responses to, children. On the contrary, the varied models of childhood outlined above have, perhaps, always been juxtaposed in adult thinking and continue to coexist in a state of uneasy tension with each other. These ways of seeing children are not mutually exclusive. It would be presumptive to suggest that only one of these frameworks is legitimate or reflects children's true nature or the reality of their lives. In this book we will take as our starting point a view of children-as-persons. But in so doing we will not be denying the reality of the structural shaping of children's lives, or their emotional and material dependence on adults, particularly on their parents. As we will show below (chapter 8) an agency perspective should not obscure the very real constraints under which children live, nor should it be confused with notions of autonomy, independence or self-determination (Neale and Smart, 1998; Brannen, 1999). Similarly, we should not be too quick to dismiss a developmental perspective when this might be a useful means of understanding how children navigate their way through childhood and into adulthood. After all, personal change and biographical development are integral features of the life course. Nor should we deny that children might share some universal features with other children that unite them as a social group. Children will continue to be projects in the sense that adults will always have responsibilities for them. Children cannot simply be liberated from adults to lead autonomous lives (Brannen, 1999).

There may also be limits to our acceptance of the cultural variability of childhoods, particularly where these variables entail hardships and oppressions. Universal prerequisites for securing children's wellbeing in the fields of health and social care, education and economic provision, for example, may well be necessary (Woodhead, 1997; James and Prout, 1997). The new framework for understanding childhood presented here is, of course, no less a social construct than the old (Jenks, 1996). It is a product of late or post-modern conditions that might, in some regards, seem impossibly naïve, over-optimistic or out of touch with the realities of some children's lives (James and Prout, 1997).[10] We should therefore not start to take it for granted but continue to maintain a critical perspective.

Rethinking children and family life

Researchers were initially slow to apply these new ideas to the context of children's family lives. Indeed, families were something of a problem for childhood researchers. The domination of functionalist accounts of family socialization and the familialization of childhood explored above meant that family research offered little scope for placing children at the centre of analysis, let alone exploring their agency. Given this climate, it is perhaps not surprising that childhood researchers were initially reluctant to study children in a family context or to align themselves with family sociology as it was then constituted. They sought instead to explore children's own social worlds, concentrating on informal settings such as the street or playground that children controlled for themselves and where they could freely exercise their agency (Brannen and O'Brien, 1996; James and Prout, 1996). This strategy was designed to give the new sub-discipline some independence and intellectual integrity rather than subsuming it within existing disciplines. It also gave children some conceptual autonomy (Thorne, 1987). Just as women had had to be liberated from their families (conceptually speaking) in order to be seen and heard, this same consideration applied to children (Oakley, 1994). But this position could not be sustained for long. After all, families are one of the social settings where children live out their childhoods, develop close relationships with others, 'find' themselves and thereby find their identities as children and as 'selves' (Brannen and O'Brien, 1996; James, 1993; James and Prout, 1996: 45). Giving children conceptual autonomy from adults, either in or outside their families, would hardly allow for children's lives to be properly investigated and understood, for children share much of their lives with adults in one setting or another. In a relatively short space of time, therefore, children were 'relocated back into the bosom of the family, but this time as active subjects' (James and Prout, 1996: 45).

While childhood research was renewing its interest in the family, family research was itself undergoing a radical transformation. This was prompted by the need to take account of what might be regarded as two constant features of family life: change and diversity. The notion of 'family' is an intrinsic part of the way people think about their personal lives; it is also deeply imbued with symbolic significance. But how families are constituted and experienced varies. The image of the 'nuclear' family is extremely tenacious of course. This stereotypical family comprises a white, heterosexual, co-residential married couple and their children who are economically supported by the husband.

But in Western societies there is a growing recognition of the incongruity between this ideological construct and the rich diversity of ways in which people live (and perhaps always have lived) their family lives.[11] 'Family' was recognized as a social rather than a natural construct in much the same way as childhood is now being recognized. Family life can now be understood in ways that do not emphasize the centrality of the conjugal bond or insist on co-residence, and which may not be organized around heterosexuality, conventional divisions of labour, or ethnocentric notions of family structure. Families are fluid as well as diverse; individual families may change over the life course, for example, through geographical mobility or migration, and they are increasingly likely to change through divorce, separation, or repartnering, thereby creating a complex variety of family structures. Such diversity and change need not be interpreted in terms of decline, immorality or deviation from a norm (although family moralists continue to do this, of course). In practice, there is no longer one dominant family form that could provide a useful benchmark. Rather, change can be understood in relation to evolving employment patterns, shifting gender relations, increasing options in sexual orientation and crosscultural influences in a multi-cultural society. Families, in sociological thinking at least, are no longer expected to remain unchanged and unchanging. They are seen as transforming themselves in relation to post-industrialism and the major structural changes of late modernity, and they are also sources of change themselves that can impact on wider society and on government policy (Silva and Smart, 1999).

Once diversity and change are brought into the frame, defining families as naturalistic, bounded entities with a fixed membership and structural form no longer seems appropriate. Families 'are' what families 'do' (Silva and Smart, 1999). They appear as fluid networks of personal relationships and practices, and it seems preferable to think of them in this way rather than resorting to institutional definitions (Finch and Mason, 1993; Morgan, 1996). Kinship in Western societies is also being reconceptualized along these lines. Kin networks are no longer seen to be rooted merely in ties of blood and law but are increasingly understood to be individualized, flexible and based on ties of affection (Schneider, 1980; Strathern, 1992; Finch, 1997).

Viewing families in these more nuanced and qualitative ways makes transparent a further feature of contemporary family relationships: they are negotiated over time rather than fixed by duty, law or the positional status of family members (Finch and Mason, 1993; Finch, 1989; Giddens, 1991; Smart and Neale, 1999). While they may well be influenced by public notions of morality, they have an essentially contingent quality.[12] As reflexive agents of change, family members may or may not nurture relationships and develop commitments over time, but either way these relationships have to be worked at rather than taken for granted. This feature of family life is not new but has, perhaps, become more transparent under the conditions of late modernity, particularly in the wake of divorce legislation that has acknowledged the fallibility of marriages (Finch, 1997). The negotiated character of family relationships is particularly apparent in spousal or partner relationships, those ties that are defined by law or custom alone. Yet it appears to be a feature of all kin relationships including, for example, those between adult children and their elderly parents (Finch and Mason, 1993). Even seemingly irrevocable parent–child relationships which are rooted in a combination of ties of blood and legality, can develop in different ways, take on different forms and be fragile. Regardless of how family members are related to each other, it seems that families are not simply 'given' but are what family members make (or try to make) of them. This means not only that individual families may be constituted in a rich variety of ways but that each person's construction of their family and kin network is unique to them.

This new way of thinking about family makes transparent the different positions occupied by individual family members. We no longer have to presume that family members think or feel the same way, or that their interests and identities are merged within an inseparable or tightly integrated unit. In other words, this approach eschews the tendency towards children's familialization that we noted above, for it grants conceptual autonomy to individual family members. Within this formulation, then, children need no longer be invisible; they emerge as fully fledged family members, actively engaged in negotiating their own family practices and relationships. They no longer just belong to families; as reflexive agents of their own lives they are part of the creation of families (Mayall, 1994). These transformations in thinking about the family have created a climate in which the insights of childhood and family research can now be productively combined. This new field of research has been characterized as the study of 'children's families' rather than 'families with children' (Brannen and O'Brien, 1996), reflecting the new status that is now to be accorded to the perspectives and standpoint of children. Explorations have been made of children's values about family life; how they conceptualize family structures and membership; how they negotiate family rules, roles and relationships and engage with parents, siblings and wider kin; how, in countless ways they actively practise, contribute to and influence family life.[13] Children's lives have been explored in a variety of familial contexts and structures, including family life following divorce.[14]

This new evidence is beginning to uncover the enormous importance that children attach to family life and relationships, and the significance of family for their sense of well-being and for the formation of their identities. Family, it seems, is the setting above all others where children aspire to be treated as people in their own right (James, 1993; Moore, Sixsmith and Knowles, 1996; Morrow, 1998, 1999; Mayall, 2000). The evidence is also beginning to challenge stereotypical assumptions that prioritize one particular family form as the best way to raise children (Moore, Sixsmith and Knowles, 1996; Morrow, 1998; Mayall, 2000). Family transitions, it seems, may offer children opportunities as well as constraints (Weiss, 1979; Moore and Beazley, 1996), while post-divorce family life 'does not entail a certain kind of childhood; there are many childhoods and children participate in the making of them' (Alanen, 1992: 131). What is emerging from this new field of research is an ethnographically rich and radically different vision of family life from that generated under the socialization model of family research. Children's accounts enable family life to be understood from an entirely new perspective, one that is likely to present a fundamental challenge to conventional wisdom about family matters.

Changing childhoods and changing families

These new ideas about childhood and family life were the starting point for a small programme of research on children's family lives following parental divorce or separation. This programme comprised two projects, one funded by the ESRC and one by the Nuffield Foundation. We wanted to explore how transformations in family life in Britain might be reshaping children's lives and thereby changing the nature of childhood at the turn of the century. More specifically, we wanted to see how children themselves might shape their own childhoods in the face of family change and what this might mean for the way they practised their family lives. In a policy context, too, we wanted to explore how new ideas about childhood might transform how we 'see' and respond to children whose parents have separated or divorced. Full details of the projects, including characteristics of the sample of children and methodology employed are given in the appendix, but we draw out some salient points here. The combined study is based on the views of 117 children and young people, ranging in age from 4 to 22, who were living in a complex variety of arrangements several years on from their parents' divorce or separation. We carried out in-depth, qualitative interviews with them in their own homes or other location of their choice.

The projects shared four broad aims:

- To explore children's day-to-day experiences under a variety of post-divorce/post-separation arrangements.
- To examine children's agency within their families.
- To explore children's values about family life.
- To bring the perspectives of young people centrally into policy debates about divorce.

We did not set out to explore the moment of separation itself, nor were we concerned with measuring long-term outcomes, although these are valid lines of enquiry of course. Rather, we wanted to highlight the importance of children's experiences as children and understand more about the actuality of their lives in the here and now. We explored their perspectives through the lens of their personhood rather than in terms of a developmental or protectionist framework. Consequently we were interested in their strengths as well as their weaknesses, and in the positive aspects of their lives as well as the negative aspects.

A striking feature of the current research on children and divorce is that very little of it is based on the views of children themselves. To date, their collective views have simply not been taken into account in the area of private family law and policy. The irony of this, we quickly discovered, is that children have a lot to say if they are given the opportunity. Most of the children who took part in our study were a fount of knowledge and information about what it is like and how to cope.

In our conversations with the children we wanted to know what values and principles they held about family life and how they conceptualized and experienced their own families. These are themes that we introduce in chapter 3, where we explore the differences between exclusive and inclusive family structures and introduce children's values surrounding care and mutual respect as key dimensions of family relations. In chapter 4 we focus on how, as reflexive agents, children manage the complex business of day-to-day living in a post-divorce family, and how they approach the work of being a child within different configurations of relationships and practices. In chapter 5 we develop ideas arising from debates about the ethic of care elaborated by Sevenhuijsen (1998) and Smart and Neale (1999) and apply these ideas to the context of childhood. We explore in some detail how children use three forms of moral reasoning – the ethics of fairness, care and respect. We contribute new insights on children's moral sensibilities and relational thinking which, in a family setting, emerge through 'moral conversations' and the workings of asymmetrical reciprocity. In chapter 6 we turn to the vexed issue of children's rights and citizenship and explore the different ways in which children might exercise their citizenship in a family context. We introduce the notion of citizenship-in-context, thereby taking forward the idea of a flexible mode of citizenship for children, without simply turning them into rights-bearing individuals with the capacity for autonomy and self-determination. In chapter 7 we focus specifically on the co-parented children in our study who were being shared across two households. We explore the varied experiences of children living under this arrangement and suggest that the precise structuring of arrangements for children may be less important than the way in which they are practised and negotiated and the extent to which children are included in the negotiations. In chapter 8 we focus on a group of children from the Nuffield sample, drawing on their perspectives and those of their parents to develop the notion of multiple realities in family life. Using a number of case studies, we explore the variety of ways in which parents construct their children's childhoods and how these constructs might affect children's developing sense of 'self' in their families. In our final chapter we explore children's views and experiences of participating in legal and welfare forums and examine the implications of our findings for the construction of children as legal and welfare subjects. Before presenting our empirical findings, however, we will turn our attention to the post-war policy context of research on childhood, families and divorce.

2

Childhood and Modern Narratives of Harm

> It is children who are the real victims of divorce. One writer has dubbed
> them 'the children of Armageddon'.
> Freeman in Wallerstein and Blakeslee, 1989: 1
>
> Divorce is a disaster under any circumstance for any child.
> Baroness Faithfull, *Hansard*, HL vol. 568, col. 813, 22 Jan. 1996

Introduction

It has become almost impossible to talk or think about children in
relation to divorce or separation without doing so within the pervasive ideational framework of 'harm'. The inevitability of harm associated with 'family breakdown' has become a conventional wisdom,
and this belief has given a renewed emphasis to the idea that family
policy must be (once again) wedded to the preservation of marriage[1]
or, failing that, to the protection of the 'innocent victims' of divorce.[2]
Of course a concern with the welfare of children is far from being a
'bad thing' and in this chapter we shall give consideration to the significance of this principle as it gathered pace in the post-war period in
England. But there is more than one story to be told about the ebb and
flow of this narrative of harm. The genuine desire to improve the lives
of children is a quite separate phenomenon to the powerfully symbolic
and politically useful rhetoric of harm, suffering and innocence. We
shall argue that the 'narrative of harm' (or what we later call 'harm-
ism') and 'children's welfare' has become a form of sentimental rhetoric that can be harnessed to political agendas. This practice carries
weight because it is always based on some degree of veracity, but at
the same time it risks tarnishing the currency in which it seeks to trade
as it becomes cynically associated with narrow political goals. The
more the needs of children become harnessed to specific campaigns,
such as the desire to preserve marriage, or the goal of moving women
out of the labour market, or the rights of fathers, the less possible it is

to have a debate that starts with the standpoint of children. Adult agendas take over and children become symbols rather than real persons.

Post-war concerns over childhood

Public policy

In one respect there is no difficulty in identifying periods or occasions when children have been presented as victims: of cruelty, neglect, hunger, homelessness, war, illness, indifference, and so on. Much of the social legislation from the early nineteenth-century Factory Acts through to the Prevention of Cruelty to Children Act, 1889, the school meals and medical inspection legislation of 1906–7, the Children Act, 1948, and beyond to the Children Act, 1989, has been in part, at least, concerned with protecting children from forms of neglect and abuse in the widest sense of these words. In nearly all of the legislation the rhetoric has been that of the child as helpless, as being acted upon, usually in some kind of damaging manner. (Hendrick, 1994: 7–8)

As Hendrick suggests, it would be mistaken to present the post-war decades as 'special' in the sense that they might be seen as heralding a *new* concern over children. The history of this concern is much longer than a mere fifty or sixty years. Moreover, as he points out in his extensive writings on childhood, although there may be different tendencies in or approaches towards child saving at different times, it would be naïve to imagine that wholly discrete or 'new' concerns appeared in any given decade. Hendrick (1994) does identify a very broad shift of emphasis from a focus on the bodies of children (physical cruelty, starvation, punishment) at the start of the twentieth century towards a concern with their minds (psychological well-being, adjustment, development) between the wars and after. But even this is far from clear-cut with the rediscovery of physical and sexual abuse of children after 1960. We must therefore be careful in depicting broad historical changes that we do not oversimplify, or give the impression that our more distant forebears were not also engaged in similar debates and activities.

When one considers childhood in the post-war era in England and Wales, the first issues that emerge are the social and psychological consequences of the evacuation of children from major cities to the countryside during the war (Macnicol, 1986) and the work of John Bowlby on maternal separation (1965, 1969). Although, as Hendrick and others[3] have pointed out, the psychologization of childhood began in the 1920s with the establishment of the Tavistock Clinic in London and the spread of child guidance clinics, this movement gathered considerable strength after the war. The evacuation of children did not only reveal the awful physical condition of poor urban children, it also brought to light their psychological condition (or possibly gave rise to those psychological conditions) which resulted in some children being declared 'unbilletable'.

The growing understanding of childhood psychology and the perception that its (healthy) foundations lay in early mother–child bonding, combined with a new emphasis pursued by the emerging social work profession in the 1950s (Woodroofe, 1962; Younghusband, 1978, 1981). This emphasis was on a psychoanalytically oriented casework approach in which social workers sought to work with the whole family to resolve their problems. The modern social work profession carried forward the concern of earlier philanthropic and charitable bodies in their particular concern over the welfare of children, but as Hendrick has suggested their interest in the 1950s became focused on the psychological aspects of that welfare.

Recognizing the importance of this new profession, Bowlby addressed them directly in 1952 and argued that social work should encourage the development of social responsibility in the family by working on the ability of each parent to make stable co-operative relations with others. Social work was seen as becoming a frontline preventive service[4] in eradicating cycles of deprivation through the use of psychoanalytic diagnosis and technique (Price-Williams, 1956). Bowlby argued,

> But for every one deprived child who becomes a fully-fledged psychopathic personality, there are probably scores who are damaged in a less dramatic way and who suffer, for instance, from depression, anxiety or psychosomatic illnesses, or who become dependent characters or rolling stones. Once again they are apt to grow up to produce more children who become deprived, especially illegitimates. Others become difficult parents who are excessively possessive of their children, feeling that their children are the first things of their own they have ever had to love. (1952: 624)

What is so interesting about these remarks, spoken in 1952 but read some fifty years later, is the extent to which Bowlby's formulation could be said to 'fit' our contemporary image of the child of divorced parents. He was, of course, talking about the child of intact 'problem' families (as they were then called) and not the modern child of divorce at all. It is therefore important to be alert to the way in which definitions of welfare and harm have changed with almost every decade in the twentieth century (Théry, 1989). This is hardly surprising, but it does mean that we cannot assume that when philanthropists spoke of harm in 1920 they were talking about the same thing as Bowlby in 1950 or social workers in 1990.

It was the iconography of the 'neglected child' that began to loom large in the 1950s through to the 1970s (Frost and Stein, 1989; Daniel and Ivatts, 1998). This child was identified in the Curtis Report (1946) and then in *The Neglected Child and his Family* (Women's Group on Public Welfare, 1948). The former was a report on the placement of children in homes, and practices of boarding out children with foster-carers when their parents could not provide adequate care. The Curtis Report revealed the neglect and cruelty that children suffered when placed in institutions, and also found an alarming degree of negligence in the placement of boarded-out children. These findings were then matched by the later (informal) report on children within their own families, which sought to reveal how children could be neglected by their own parents if they were unfortunate enough to be born into 'problem families'.

Childhood was therefore clearly on the social policy agenda[5] after the war, albeit the emphasis was increasingly on the child-as-project. As we discussed in chapter 1, the core element of the child-as-project is the perception of the child in terms of the adult citizen he or she will become. The social work focus of the time was therefore on improving parenting in order that children would experience more stability and emotional security which would, in turn, prevent them from becoming future misfits. This intervention was predominantly formulated within a psychological or psychoanalytical framework that sought to normalize the deviant family through therapeutic methods. Although children born to unmarried mothers[6] or those coming from broken homes were seen as more vulnerable to the harms inherent in the 'problem family', the immediate post-war emphasis was just as much on the dysfunctional impact of poor *parents*[7] as it was on the problems generated by being a child of a lone parent. Bowlby's classic work *Forty-Four Juvenile Thieves: Their Character and Home Life* (1946), for example, focused on the quality of mother–child bonding and the issue of separation of mother and child, rather than the question of separation from the father. Indeed, a father's unemployment was more likely to feature as a cause of concern than his absence at this time, not least because a degree of father absence was still seen as perfectly normal. Of course, we should not forget that although divorce and illegitimacy rates rose steeply immediately after the war, high rates of lone motherhood had not become an established feature of the social policy landscape (Kiernan, Land and Lewis, 1998). There was a growing concern about these families, but during the 1950s and much of the 1960s they were more likely to be included as a variant of 'the problem family' than to be disaggregated as a special type or distinct social problem.

Broken homes began to move on to the centre stage of policy concerns after the 1960s. Research began to indicate that amongst populations of children in Borstals and Approved Schools there was likely to be found a high incidence of parental separation or divorce (West, 1973). The 1969 Children and Young Persons Act had blurred the distinction between 'deprived' and 'depraved' children and had sought to introduce a more humanitarian approach to children in trouble.[8] Child offenders were to be treated in the same way as neglected children and channelled towards the child-care system rather than the criminal justice system (Packman, 1981; Tutt, 1974). After 1970 the Children's Departments that had been set up to deal with neglected children following the recommendations of the Curtis Report and the subsequent Children Act of 1948 were merged with general social work practice to create a generic service. This signalled a further step towards a holistic service in which children were to be viewed as part of the family and where the causes of delinquency or other forms of anti-social behaviour were seen to reside in the quality of the family of origin.

The debate about whether 'broken homes' caused delinquency occupied the attention of researchers throughout the 1970s (e.g. Mays, 1972; Rutter and Madge, 1976). Although this question was never resolved (simply because the issues were too complex to invite a single or simple cause), the idea of a link between any kind of deviant family form (as it would have been seen in the 1970s) and delinquency entered into popular iconography. At the same time there were concerns about 'latch key children' and delinquency. The concept of the latch-key child conjured up the deviant, working mother who was not at home to welcome her children and to ensure that they were properly under her control. Latchkey children could not only have the freedom of being in their homes alone, they could go into the streets and get up to mischief after school because their mothers would not be there to monitor them.

The narrative of broken homes and delinquency is not exactly the same as the later narrative of divorce and harmed children. The main difference was that the 1970s narrative was essentially focused on working-class families. The disrupted or dysfunctional family of the 1970s was, in the popular imagination, a working-class or unemployed family. Moreover, the brokenness they suffered might not have been caused by divorce; indeed, it would have been more likely to be an informal separation simply because divorce did not start to become common throughout the social spectrum until after 1973.[9] In addition, the middle-class child was rarely depicted as a juvenile delinquent and rarely became a client of the juvenile justice system or care system. Thus the 1960s model focused on a very specific (and class-based) outcome, namely delinquency. The later narrative of divorce and harm identified a broader range of outcomes which could include poor school performance, later unemployment, later unstable marriages, or simply depression and insecurity. These outcomes were just as likely to encompass the experience of middle-class families as working-class ones and so the population 'at risk' became hypothetically much greater. Thus, we are suggesting that the narrative of 'broken homes' created a set of understandings about children and harm which itself was predicated on a previous layer of beliefs about the harm of separation. This narrative then became a fertile cultural memory that was later reactivated as a layer of conventional wisdom in debates on divorce and harm. The debate over broken homes is not the same as the contemporary debate over the harms of divorce, but the appeal of the latter owes much to the cultural resonance it has with the earlier set of beliefs.

Family policy and private law

In the immediate post-war decades, family law (in the form of divorce law and the matrimonial jurisdiction of the magistrates) did not much concern itself with children. Policy in relation to the welfare of the child was really being played out in the field of public law rather than private law. Although it is true that the 'paramountcy' principle of the welfare of the child can be dated back to the nineteenth century, the courts rarely had occasion to address themselves to this question because divorce itself was rare. When they did, they often understood welfare as being synonymous with natural paternal rights.[10] Moreover, as Piper (1999) points out, even though the 1891 Custody of Children Act incorporated powers to consult children as to their wishes when deciding upon their welfare, rarely were they consulted except in cases of wardship. So, although these principles were in existence, neither the divorce courts, nor the magistrates' courts were really concerned about children in their everyday business because their primary task was to ascertain the guilt or innocence of husbands and wives and to allocate matrimonial assets accordingly.[11] As Denning (1946) argued, the divorce courts really had no way of becoming closely involved in the fate of the children whose welfare they were meant to ensure:

We are of the opinion [that present procedure] is but poorly fitted for
the purpose [of safeguarding the welfare of children]. The principal de-
fect is that the children are rarely, if ever, separately represented before
the Court, and the Judge is never in possession of the report of an independent person as to their welfare unless it has been obtained by one of
the parents. The result is that the welfare of children is subordinated to
the interests of their parents. (1946: 17)

Denning acknowledged that the Chancery Division of the High Court
which dealt with wardship proceedings was far superior because children were represented by a guardian *ad litem* and the judge could see
the parents and children separately. But wardship proceedings were
extremely expensive and affected only a tiny proportion of disputes
between (wealthy) parents.

So, while there was a growing belief in the harm caused to children
following parental divorce in some quarters in the late 1940s, there
was a sense that private law was ill equipped to do anything about it.
Indeed, Denning argued that 'No subject has caused us greater concern than that of the welfare of children whose parents are or have
been involved in divorce proceedings' (1946: 17). In the 1950s a similar concern was expressed by the Royal Commission on Marriage and
Divorce:

> There is a wealth of testimony as to the effects on children of the break-
> down of normal family relationships. Where family life breaks down,
> there is always a risk of a failure to meet fully the child's need for secu-
> rity and affection. If in fact there is such a failure, the child may become
> so emotionally disturbed as to reject the influences of the family and
> this may result in anti-social behaviour. . . . Where divorce takes place
> it is therefore essential that everything which is possible . . . should be
> done to mitigate the effects upon the children of the disruption of fam-
> ily life. (1956: 103, paras. 361–2)

The idea that divorce gave rise to harm for children was therefore
part of these early considerations, but these concerns did not really
surface as an independent set of worries or as a discrete narrative until
much later. Indeed this specific concern does not really become a popular narrative until after the publication of research findings from the
US, where there was a much higher divorce rate and thus a much
larger population of children experiencing their parents' divorce. Although the Royal Commission referred to a wealth of *testimony* on
this matter, there was in fact no research in the UK on the effects of
divorce until much later.

The research

The newly formulated narrative of concern over children and family life originated from the US, although the first major contribution by Goldstein, Freud and Solnit (1979; originally published in 1973) reveals a continuity of concerns with the earlier work of Bowlby and Winnicott in the UK. This is perhaps hardly surprising given that one of the authors was Anna Freud, who was a contemporary of these British psychoanalytic practitioners (albeit Bowlby and Winnicott were Kleinians rather than Freudians). Anna Freud had set up one of the first child guidance clinics in the UK in Hampstead, and was author (with Dorothy Burlingham) of two significant texts on children and evacuation and on children living apart from their families (Burlingham and Freud, 1942, 1944; see also Riley, 1983). In her work with Goldstein and Solnit (both American, the former an academic lawyer and the latter a clinical psychologist) she carried forward her earlier concerns about what happens to children who are 'placed' outside or beyond their own families. Thus both *Beyond the Best Interests of the Child* (1979) and the subsequent *Before the Best Interests of the Child* (1980) were concerned with a range of placements, including adoption, fostering and institutional care. But included in this range of placements was the growing phenomenon of 'placements' with separated parents – otherwise known as custody – after divorce.

The analysis provided of children's experiences of placement was plainly psychoanalytic, and much emphasis was placed on the importance of the psychological parent and the needs of the child in relation to this parent. Most importantly this work also focused on inadequate and/or harmful parenting in intact families. In many respects it was a restatement of established psychoanalytic orthodoxy based on clinical practice rather than the result of new empirically based work. Thus these books constitute a fascinating intellectual bridge between the 1950s and the 1970s: the authors used psychoanalytical visions rooted in the 1950s to critique legal policies and practices that were developing in the US in the 1970s. The fact that the authors were unhappy with the growing fashion in the US for courts to order contact between non-resident parents even against the wishes of residential parents and of the child, pushed their work into a confrontational relationship with family law and family policy. Goldstein et al., whatever the merits of their work, were not writing from a set of concerns about parents and their rights nor from the basis of some notion of equality between parents. Their perspective was based on an analysis of children's needs as interpreted within a psychoanalytic and clinical framework. Although their work was valorized in some quarters (especially in the 'custody wars' that broke out across the US and the UK[12]) they were swimming against a tide of enthusiasm for enforced contact and compulsory shared parenting that was beginning to sweep across the US.[13]

The work of Goldstein et al. is often cited in relation to the work of Wallerstein and Kelly (1980), partly because they were contemporaries but mainly because their findings are so antithetical to one another. Wallerstein and Kelly continued the intellectual tradition of the earlier work in this field in that they were both clinicians and based their findings on a clinical sample. However, their work came to eclipse that of Goldstein et al. and was arguably much more 'in tune' with the direction of family law and family policy in the US in the 1980s. We shall discuss below whether it is possible to say that books like *Surviving the Break-Up* influenced the shape of policy, or whether it was an expression of the same developments that were framing policy at that time, but it was certainly the case that their work became much more 'popular' than that of Goldstein et al. in family law circles.[14] Because their work has been so much cited in the UK as well as the USA it is worth giving space to their findings.

Wallerstein and Kelly

This longitudinal study explored the experiences of sixty middle-class, white American families, including 131 children, who had opted into a counselling programme following the divorce of their parents. The authors reported a range of communications problems among the families. Many parents had grave difficulties in discussing the divorce with their children, and failed to provide them with proper explanations or reassurances about future arrangements. This had the result that children were confused, bewildered or reached their own fanciful and sometimes damaging interpretations of events. The parents often failed to give them adequate opportunities to express their concerns (1980: 39–40, 138). Ironically, it seems that parental fears about the harms of divorce for children only exacerbated this problem: 'Parents are apprehensive that their children might be unhappy, frightened, or angered by their decision . . . and they are profoundly worried and sometimes heartsick about the psychological, social and economic effect of their decision on their children in the present and for the future' (1980: 39).

It was not unusual for rigid visiting schedules to be set up, often through the court, without prior consultation with the children. Sub-

sequently the children felt powerless to suggest changes in arrangements or to ask for greater flexibility (1980: 139). Outcomes for children were not strongly related to whether they retained contact with a
non-residential parent. The authors noted that a cessation of contact
could benefit children who had had an oppressive relationship with
their non-residential parent.[15] At the same time, feelings of unhappiness, rejection and loneliness were reported for a substantial number
of the children who regularly saw their non-residential parent but found
the relationship emotionally empty or oppressive (1980: 241). These
feelings were intensified where, prior to the divorce, children had not
enjoyed gratifying relationships with one or both parents or had nag-
ging doubts about their parents' interest in them (1980: 49, 53).
Wallerstein and Kelly found that such parents exploited their children
(using them for their own gratification and emotional support), and
undermined or effaced them in ways that showed a marked lack of
respect for their personhood.

An example of this was the cases (over half of the sample) where
parents embroiled their children in open and intense conflicts (1980:
125–6, 141). The authors reported that 'One of the central complaints
of the youngsters in our study was the "badmouthing" or "backbiting"
of their parents' (1980: 28). Two-thirds of the parents 'openly com-
peted for the children's love and allegiance', resulting in profound conflicts of loyalty for the children (1980: 49, 70, 88). In nearly a quarter
of the cases children were subjected to and involved in constant deni-
gration of one parent by the other and forced to form an allegiance
with one parent against the other (1980: 28–9, 232). Where such
parents had entered litigation they found particularly high levels of
anxiety in the children. The children's preoccupation with the details
of the conflict and with worries about their own future affected their
ability to tackle the other tasks of their lives, and these problems could
persist over long periods of time, sometimes for years (1980: 28–30,
37).

At follow-up, five years later, Wallerstein and Kelly found that the
children who were doing exceptionally well (34 per cent of the sample) had at least one supportive parent in their lives who recognized
and responded to them as individuals (1980: 258). The children who
were faring particularly badly (a little over one-third of the sample),
and who suffered from low self-esteem, had parents who failed to
make time for them. These parents showed a marked lack of regard
for their children's wishes and changing needs, continued to exploit
them, treated them oppressively, and/or involved them in conflicts
with their former partners. These children felt neglected, ignored, or
oppressed by one or both parents. For Wallerstein and Kelly, the

quality of parenting emerged as a significant factor for children's well-being:

> It appears that the nurturance provided during earlier years will hold the child for a while, but that good, or at least 'good enough' parenting continuing over time is needed to safeguard and to maintain good developmental progress in children. More than any other constellation of factors the disrupted or diminished parenting by one or both parents was associated with the dismayingly high incidence of depression which we found at each of the checkpoints of the study and most especially at five years. (Wallerstein and Kelly, 1980: 309)

They further add,

> [I]f the children are poorly supported and poorly informed or co-opted as allies or fought over in the continuing battle and viewed as extensions of the adults; if the relationship with one or both parents is impoverished or disrupted, and the child feels rejected; if the stresses and deprivation of the postdivorce family are no less than those of the failed marriage – then the most likely outcome for the children is developmental interference and depression. (Wallerstein and Kelly, 1980: 316–17)

Writing in the cultural climate of the 1970s and 1980s, from a psychotherapeutic perspective, Wallerstein and Kelly's interpretations of their evidence were shaped primarily by protectionist concerns. They saw the post-divorce family as especially vulnerable to risk, and in this way they contributed to the increasingly prevalent notion at the time that divorce *itself* caused bad parenting. Wallerstein and Kelly's research became known for establishing a deficit model of post-divorce parenting even though their evidence was more complex than this. On the basis of this study they went on to support the idea of shared custody as the best policy in cases of divorce. It has been argued that these authors were therefore authors not only of their research but of the popularity of obligatory shared custody orders in some states in the US. Their work has also been 'used' to support similar policies in the UK.

In a later follow-up study, Wallerstein and Blakeslee (1989) clearly step back from recommending compulsory shared custody:[16]

> But there is no evidence to support the notion that 'one size fits all' or even most. There is, in fact, a lot of evidence for the idea that different custody models are suitable for different families. The policy job ahead is to find the best match for each family. Sadly, when joint custody is imposed by the court on families fighting over custody of children, the major consequences of the fighting are shifted onto the least able members of the family – the hapless and helpless children. The children can suffer serious psychological injury when this happens. I am in favour of

joint custody in many cases, where parents and children can handle it, but it is no universal panacea. We still have a great deal to learn. (1989: 319)

Kelly has also increasingly dissociated herself from the oversimplified and popularized version of their conclusions, namely that shared custody is best regardless of the circumstances. Her recent work emphasizes the harm of conflict, particularly conflict that involves children, rather than the harm of divorce (Kelly, 2000). All authors appear to have experienced the somewhat traumatic experience of having their work taken up as part of a political campaign and thus corrupted and oversimplified. However, it should not be forgotten that they did make some clear statements on policy and practice. Not only did they support the idea of shared custody as a way of preserving the child's relationship with both parents, they also argued that 'there is some evidence that legal accountability may influence and shore up psychological and financial responsibility' (1980: 310). They went on to say that legal rights were particularly important for non-custodial parents to prevent them withdrawing from their children. It was the combination of these two conclusions that fed into the assumption that shared custody should be made compulsory in a wide range of cases – in order to meet the best interests of the child.

We shall return to this difficult question of the relationship between high-profile research, politics and policy below, but first it is necessary to complete our account of the growing narrative of the harms of divorce.

Studies in the UK

Rodgers and Pryor (1998) have carried out a meta-analysis of UK research on children and divorce, focusing on the issue of 'outcomes'. In consequence we will not replicate their work here although it is perhaps worth noting that in their summary they state: 'There is no simple or direct relationship between parental separation and children's adjustment and poor outcomes are far from inevitable' (1998: 4–5). So, rather than reviewing this same literature in terms of summarizing the findings, we will examine the major theoretical strands in the work that has been carried out and will provide examples of these different tendencies in relation to our focus on narratives of harm.

In the UK two types of study based on different epistemological foundations began to appear in the 1980s. The first continued the social work or therapeutic tradition of earlier studies of problem or dysfunctional families. These studies sought to identify problems and generate a climate of awareness of the unhappiness and sometimes misery of children whose parents divorce. Examples of this approach would be Mitchell (1985) or Walczak and Burns (1984). Walczak was a social worker who was trained at the Tavistock Clinic and who subsequently became a lecturer in social work. Together with Burns, her theoretical background was an amalgam of Attachment Theory (from Bowlby) and Systems Theory, which had become the dominant framework for social work intervention in families at this time. Their interpretative framework was therefore very close to that of Wallerstein and Kelly and, of course, Goldstein et al., although they strongly favoured the former's policy recommendations over the latter's.

These were important studies in that they approached the question of divorce through children's experiences, but they also took a child protectionist perspective, which meant that children tended to be construed as the casualties of their parents' battles. In giving a voice to children[17] they did so in the context of the child as victim. Although both studies found children who were content, or even better off after their parents' divorce, these findings were often overlooked when it came to policy recommendations.

Also in this framework was the *Exeter Family Study* by Cockett and Tripp (1994). This was a quantitative study of 174 families, including 170 interviews with children and twenty-seven interviews with non-resident parents carried out by a senior paediatrician. This study compared disrupted and intact families using measures of health and educational attainment as well as self-report and psychological measures of self-esteem. They found that the children of divorced and separated parents suffered from poorer self-esteem, had more difficulties in their daily lives with health, school performance, friendships and behaviour, were likely to have reduced educational and vocational qualifications, and were more likely to form unstable relationships. Although they identified a number of caveats and complexities which might influence these outcomes, they reported that the most important 'association' with these outcomes was the loss of parenting figures from the child's life. This finding was clearly in tune with Bowlby's theory of attachment and loss, but in this case the authors did not focus solely on the mother, but gave greater emphasis to loss of a father (since it was more usual for fathers to become 'absent' parents). They made a number of very wide-ranging policy recommendations. These included more extensive mediation, a greater emphasis on reconciliation to avoid divorce where possible, the replacement of the existing ground for divorce on two years' separation with a new process based on mediation, and more advice and support for children.

These studies are clearly engaged with the policy process and in this sense follow the tradition of Bowlby, Winnicott and others of engaging directly with policy formulation and practice. In this respect they are also close to the work of Goldstein et al. and Wallerstein and Kelly. But the second type of research that has been influential in the UK has been much less prescriptive in policy terms, even though it has had an impact on policy debates. This research has largely been based on the analysis of secondary data sets, most usually the ones generated by the large-scale longitudinal studies of the 1958 UK birth cohorts known as the National Child Development Study (NCDS). These studies (for example Kiernan, 1997; Joshi et al., 1998; Joshi, Wiggins and Clarke, 2000) have tended to be more descriptive than prescriptive and rarely ventured directly into making policy suggestions. Rather, they analyse existing data using statistical methods to try to unpack the relationship between divorce and a number of different variables. As work of this kind has become increasingly sophisticated it has tended to reveal the complexities inherent in measuring and interpreting 'outcomes' and the hazards of inferring causal relationships between variables too casually. Nonetheless, their findings have at times been seized upon to support various arguments in the policy debates on the harms of divorce.

Research, policy and politics

Research on family life in Britain and elsewhere has traditionally engaged with policy and politics at some level. This is hardly surprising, especially as so many of the early family researchers were also practitioners and their research was often carried out in a clinical context. Moreover, some of the best-known post-war figures such as Bowlby and Winnicott courted publicity and used the medium of radio broadcasts to get across their 'message'. But the mere fact that certain researchers wished, or still wish, to influence policy does not account for why some ideas are more influential than others, nor does it determine the sort of influence that might ensue. We are uncomfortable with conspiracy theories that suggest that ideas are influential because they are taken up by 'powerful interests' in society (Kaganas, 1999) and prefer to try to understand how some ideas seem to gain a cultural resonance at certain historical moments. Denise Riley (1983) studied this question closely in relation to Bowlby's work, and here we will

give some consideration to her analysis. Then we will consider whether
it helps to explain the power of the 'narratives of harm' that so dominated policy and practice in the UK at the end of the twentieth century.

Bowlby and Bowlbyism

Riley talks of Bowlby on the one hand and Bowlbyism on the other.
This device of separating the person and their written or spoken words
from what those words become once let loose in the world is not uncommon. Thus we have Marx and Marxism, Freud and Freudianism,
Thatcher and Thatcherism, even Foucault and Foucauldianism.[18] The
'ism' suggests that the work has taken on a slightly different set of
meanings by being interpreted by others or by being added to by others. It also suggests that there is some kind of 'following' or, at least,
that there has been a discernible influence generated by the body of
work or ideas. Finally, before a body of work or ideas can become an
'ism' there must be some kind of foundation in which it can take root.
For Bowlby's work this was the established influence of psychoanaly-
sis and, in particular the work of Melanie Klein.

Having separated the work from its interpretation and influence,
Riley identified a number of elements that were significant to the process
of political and policy influence. Firstly Bowlby was himself an active
popularizer of his ideas, indeed he could be said to have had a mission.
He was particularly anxious to prevent what he saw as the harms of
evacuation and of institutionalizing infants. He also wanted to promote better maternal care of infants. He used the popular media, he
wrote in an accessible style, and he also sought to influence the newly
emergent social work profession by speaking at their conferences and
writing in their journals. But this coverage of his work did not, according to Riley, mean that he was influential in policy terms. She
examines the closure of the wartime nurseries to see whether his ideas
on the harm caused by separation of mother from child really did
cause the government to alter its policy. She argues that his ideas had
little influence in this specific decision. What really mattered with the
government was the economic cost of keeping the nurseries open and
its reluctance to turn an emergency measure into a routine welfare
provision.

But, as Riley points out, the fact that Bowlbyism was not 'implemented' in a specific policy enactment[19] does not mean that it was not
influential at another level. This level is defined, following the work of

the cultural theorist Raymond Williams, as 'structures of feeling' (Riley, 1983: 152). Structures of feeling result from the combination of a 'climate of opinion' with the internalization and subjectification of these meanings such that they come to feel akin to self-generated moral imperatives. Thus we know that, after Bowlby, at least two generations of mothers in England felt intensely guilty about leaving their children in order to go out to work (even if they had no choice about it at all). Structures of feeling become personal and individualized even though they are initially a social phenomenon. Moreover, such structures do not have authors, nor are they managed and directed for some rational or governmental purpose. Bowlby the person was not responsible for these structures of feeling, even if Bowlbyism was. Bowlby might have *wanted* generations of mothers to feel this guilt and to refrain from going out to work, and he might have influenced the climate of opinion, but his *wanting* mothers to stay at home was not what created the eventual outcome. There are stages between the creation of a climate of opinion and its translation into 'structures of feeling' which become internalized. These stages can really only be identified by a post hoc analysis.

Harm and 'harm-ism'

In the research field of children and divorce it is not possible to identify one individual whose name can occupy the sort of place occupied by the name Bowlby. The body of work on harm and divorce has been generated by too many disparate scholars and those few names which might stand out (such as Wallerstein) really do not lend themselves to this treatment. So we must be content with the unattractive term 'harm-ism'. Following Riley's schema, we are separating harm from 'harm-ism' in order to distinguish between two related but distinct phenomena. Harm undoubtedly occurs in families (divorced or not), and it is entirely valid for scholars to attempt to find its causes and to consider ways of preventing it. Recent studies have revealed the complexities inherent in 'measuring' harm and in attributing cause and it is clear that different theoretical approaches identify different sorts of harm. Nonetheless, these are genuine debates amongst researchers and practitioners. But 'harm-ism' is something else. 'Harm-ism' is the tendency to see only harm, even where the evidence is more complex than this. 'Harm-ism' delights in the sad stories and dismisses the others as unimportant or as distortions of the 'real' truth. 'Harm-ism' insists that the greatest harm to children is their parents' divorce; it pushes out or

minimizes considerations of poverty, domestic violence, poor housing, inadequate financial provision and the possibility that an ongoing
marriage might be worse for children than a divorce. This constella-
tion of beliefs has been, in part, fuelled by research findings, but has
now developed an independent existence and is resistant to any evidence which might modify the harm thesis. It has, in Riley's sense,
become a climate of opinion. The question is whether it also directly
influences policy and whether it has entered into structures of feeling.

Influencing policy and practice?

The rhetoric of harm was used extensively in parliamentary debates
on the Family Law Bill in 1996 and so this provides a contemporary
case study for our analysis. The *certain* knowledge that children *are*
seriously harmed was used to support calls for better mediation, more
emphasis on reconciliation, a return to fault-based divorce, a protracted
process of divorce to deter couples starting down that route, and finally to make divorce more difficult for couples with children than for
childless couples. For example, Paul Boateng stated in the debate in
the House of Commons: 'The impact on a child of its parents divorcing is considerable. The valuable research that has been carried out in
this area highlights the need for effective multi-agency intervention to
counter the negative impact of divorce on children' (*Hansard*, vol.
279, col. 591, 17 June 1996).

On the face of it, some of these arguments were successful because
the Act did provide legislation to make the process of divorce more
prolonged, and it did place a greater emphasis on mediation and in
particular on giving information to parents on the harms of divorce
for their children. Research findings (particularly Cockett and Tripp,
originally published in 1994 and reprinted in 1996) were loosely cited
in support of this certain knowledge about harm. For example, Baroness Elles stated:

> In the White Paper *Looking to the Future* there was reference to the
> research done by Exeter University . . . Paragraph 5.16 states: 'It is con-
> firmed that marital conflict is harmful to children. These findings are
> significant.' Of course they are significant. They are also common sense.
> What is even more significant is that there is no reference to all the
> other findings in the report which show conclusively that it is infinitely
> more harmful to children to be brought up separately and to go through
> not merely the trauma of the divorce but the post-divorce period where
> they suffer all the other problems . . . I regret that the White Paper did
> not tackle more honestly some of the problems caused to children who

are no longer living at home – even a home in conflict. . . . As was reported by Dr. Richards of the Cambridge Centre for Family Research, when children were asked what they would like: 'They would almost always say they only want one thing; that their parents should stay together.' (*Hansard*, HL, vol. 568, cols 808–9, 22 Jan. 1996)

Baroness Elles did not like the fact that the government seemed to be focusing only on the harm caused by conflict rather than the harm caused by divorce. She therefore dismissed the idea of conflict as the problem, in favour of a position which argued that it was divorce itself that caused the harm. In this passage one can clearly see the way in which research findings were (mis)used and harnessed to particular political positions.

However, this does not mean that 'harm-ism' was specifically influential in changing the Bill. Other factors were particularly strong, such as the Conservative government's narrow majority, and the forceful campaign against the complete abolition of matrimonial fault marshalled by the *Daily Mail*. Nonetheless, some compromises were reached[20] on the basis of the harm argument (for example, that parents should have to wait longer to start divorce proceedings than childless couples). Moreover, the widespread media coverage of the passage of the legislation brought the issue of harm back on to a broad public agenda.

There is some evidence that 'harm-ism' might have had an even more direct influence at the level of practice – for example in the decisions of judges in contested contact cases (Smart and Neale, 1997; Hester and Radford, 1996; Wallbank, 1998; Kaganas, 1999) or in the advice given by solicitors to their clients (Neale and Smart, 1997b). In the instance of judges, case law has developed the principle that courts must be reluctant to 'deprive' a child of contact with a parent. In these cases the burden of proof is now laid on the parent who objects to contact to show how terminating contact will positively benefit the child. It is no longer enough to make a case that contact might be harmful or dangerous, the child must be shown to gain a benefit: 'No court should deprive a child of access to either parent unless it was wholly satisfied that it was in the interests of the child that access should cease, and that was a conclusion at which the court should be extremely slow to arrive' (*Re H* (Minors) (Access) [1992] 1 FLR 148).

In the mid-1990s there were a number of cases where mothers were imprisoned for contempt of court because they refused to allow contact between their children and a violent father. These draconian measures were justified on the basis that more harm would be caused to a child by the cessation of contact (even with a parent they hated and were frightened of) than by being forced to see that parent. Judges reasoned that it did not matter that children were unhappy to see a parent because they would eventually benefit from having sustained their relationship: 'the court should take a medium-term and long-term view of the child's development and not accord excessive weight to what appears likely to be short-term or transient problems' (Waite, LJ, Re D (A Minor) (Contact: Mother's hostility) [1993] 2 FLR 1, 8). It is precisely this kind of situation that researchers like Wallerstein and Lewis (1998) have condemned even though it is a popularized version of Wallerstein's early research that has been used to justify these practices.

Structures of feeling

It is hard to assess the extent to which 'harm-ism' has entered into structures of feeling. Our earlier research with parents (Smart and Neale, 1999) found examples of serious concern on the part of parents about the harm that they felt would inevitably befall their children. Some parents postponed divorcing until they felt that their children were old enough to avoid these inevitable harms and some mothers put up with domestic violence for years because they were so worried about their children. Wallerstein and Kelly (1980) found similar concerns amongst the parents they interviewed. Often parents seemed to interpret the behaviour of their children as a 'sign' of harm when it might have been typical rebelliousness or due to some other cause. This worry could go to extremes:

> JIM WALTERS: I think what worries me most is that they don't seem to have shown any signs of it affecting them. I am almost looking for something. (Parent interviewed in Smart and Neale, 1999)

These anecdotes suggest that 'harm-ism' has indeed entered into structures of feeling and has been internalized by some parents. The provision of leaflets for divorcing parents which will warn them of harm that their children may experience and which alert them to the signs of harm – while well intended – may actually consolidate these structures of feeling further. However, we will not really know how influential 'harm-ism' has been at the cultural and personal level for some time. We may need retrospective studies or oral histories carried out at some time in the future before the necessary distance is achieved to allow people to become reflexive about their beliefs.

Conclusion

We have argued that it is necessary to distinguish between research on the consequences of divorce for children and the 'narrative of harm' (or 'the phenomenon of harm-ism') which suffuses contemporary public debates about divorce. Of course these two things are not unrelated to each other and we have suggested that some researchers have contributed towards consolidating 'harm-ism', even if unintentionally. However, there comes a point when academics and researchers need to reflect upon why they are carrying out yet more studies on 'outcomes' or 'harms' given that there are so many other research questions that need investigation. Rodgers and Pryor (1998), for example, point out that UK research has been skewed towards analysing the role of socio-economic factors in post-divorce family life (in particular the issue of maintenance and the distribution of family assets) and towards outcomes (usually psychological) for children. There has been little research carried out on ethnic differences, multiple family changes and different vulnerabilities and resiliences in individuals (1998: 44). They suggest that there is also a paucity of qualitative studies on divorce which look at the experiences of separation for individual family members. We regard this study as a contribution towards the latter category. In what follows we have focused on children's experiences, not outcomes and not harms. We have suspended the all-pervasive framework of harm in order to allow the children to speak of what matters to them. We have started with the framework identified in chapter 1 of treating children as persons, and have assumed that they may have a lot of experience of what it is like to be a child of divorcing parents. We explain our methodology in detail in the appendix, and what follows is intended to be a thick and textured analysis that appreciates the experiences of all the children we interviewed.

Although we seek to avoid encouraging irresponsible narratives of harm, we do not avoid the lure of making policy suggestions. This may be rash, especially as we recognize the way in which recommendations can be oversimplified or harnessed cynically to political debates. But we have come to the conclusion that 'harm-ism' has done harm and we cannot resist the temptation to try to modify these effects. The reader will judge whether we also end up doing more harm than good!

3

Children's Perspectives on Post-Divorce Family Life

HOPE (14):[1] [My family is] different from other people's families, but I don't mind because who says what a family should be like?

CLAUDIA (12): A family isn't really like blood relatives, it's just people who love each other. . . . If I didn't love my mum or I didn't love my dad then, by law, they'd be a member of my family but you wouldn't really *feel* like a family, 'cos I mean it doesn't matter if you're rich or poor, or if you live on the streets, as long as you love each other. Of course you're going to have arguments and stuff, but if you love each other it doesn't really matter, does it, what arrangement you're in?

Introduction

The ways in which children and their parents conceptualize their families may diverge in the aftermath of divorce or separation. The parents, whose intimate partnership has ended, may no longer regard each other as 'family'. For the children, however, things might be rather different. They might continue to see both parents as integral members of the family, albeit within a new configuration of household arrangements and relationships (Klee, Schmidt and Johnson, 1989; Smart and Neale, 1999). From the children's perspective, family life does not simply end with divorce or separation. It is now possible to see beyond the concept of 'breakdown' to recognize the extent to which family relationships can endure and survive structural or legal change (Maclean and Eekelaar, 1997; Rodgers and Pryor, 1998; Smart and Neale, 1999). The ways in which families endure or survive, of course, is subject to wide variation and we currently know little in the UK about how children perceive these variations. Our purpose in this chapter, therefore, is to explore the different ways in which children make sense of their families after parental separation, both in terms of their formal constructions of family and their values about family life. Laying the groundwork for our empirical study in this way is a valid sociological enterprise in its own right. But it is also a necessary precursor to exploring the policy dimensions of our research, for we cannot hope to understand 'what works' for children in post-divorce families without first acquiring a greater insight into 'what matters' to them.

As we saw in chapter 1, sociological thinking about family life has recently undergone a transformation. The norm of the 'nuclear' family is giving way to a view of family that is grounded in varied practices and relationships. This is neatly illustrated in the introductory quotations from Hope and Claudia above. Claudia drew a distinction between families as institutions rooted in ties of law (affinity) and blood (consanguinity), and families as relationships based on ties of affection. In her view it was the latter (rather than the former) that was the essence of family life. The particular form that a family takes was not the key issue. What created real bonds between people were, for her, the value-full notions of love, care and commitment. Hence the variety of family forms in evidence and the individualized ways in which family members construct their own family and kinship networks. In chapter 1 we noted another important feature of contemporary family relationships: they are subject to individual choice and negotiation over time and thus have a contingent quality. Again the quotations above would seem to bear this out. Claudia conjured up a hypothetical scenario in which a child may not love a parent. As she noted, being a family in the formal legal sense is not the same thing as *feeling* like a family. Affection is not something that can be legally enforced, nor is it an inherent feature of blood relationships, even those between a child and parent.

These ways of thinking about family, it seems, are not confined to sociologists, nor even to adults more generally, but can be part of the thinking of children too, at least, those children with experiences of family change and diversity. But we are not suggesting that these nuanced, qualitative styles of thinking can be applied unproblematically to all family members, regardless of age or generational boundaries. Currently, children are perceived to stand outside these notions, particularly notions of negotiation and contingency. They are kept as a separate category, one that is not subject to the vagaries of individual choice or renegotiation. As Funder (1991) puts it, where the ex-spouse is familiar to us, the ex-mother or ex-father is unknown. There is an implicit assumption that in an insecure emotional world where spousal/partner relationships may no longer provide enduring support and commitment, children alone remain as the last reliable sources of unconditional love. Because parent–child relationships are based on ties of blood they are presumed to be of a qualitatively different nature to those based on legal ties alone. Indeed, Beck and Beck-Gernsheim suggest that parenthood is replacing marriage as the legal backbone of the modern family precisely because spousal relationships are becoming so fragile (Beck, 1992; Beck and Beck-Gernsheim, 1995). It is children, not spouses, who are now presumed to offer a permanent emotional bond that does not have to be earned or renewed.

But how far do these rather romanticized views of children and the parent–child bond match children's own perspectives? Are these ideas about fluidity, negotiation and contingency in family relationships reserved only for adults or, as Claudia suggests above, do children also adhere to these notions and make use of them as reflexive agents of their own lives? How do children make sense of families in general and their own family in particular when they have experienced the separation and perhaps also the re-partnering of their parents? These were the sort of questions that we initially set out to explore with the children we interviewed. We investigated the criteria used by the children to construct their families and how far and in what ways they distinguished between their 'blood' and 'social' kin. More broadly we wanted to know how much importance they attached to the formal, structural features of family life (such as household membership and legal status) and how much to the more qualitative dimensions of family life identified by Claudia above. It is to these issues that we now turn.

Constructing families

At the start of our interviews we asked the young people in our study to draw a picture of their family or otherwise map out their family for us.[2] We used these visual representations in two ways. Firstly we wanted to understand who was or was not accorded family membership. Secondly, the drawings and maps gave us an insight into how children conceptualized the web of relationships in their families. We were able to discern whether they thought of themselves as having an 'integrated' or 'split' family, or one or two homes. The children were also asked to complete a circle drawing, in which they could position themselves in relation to their kin, thereby indicating varying degrees of emotional closeness to individual family members (Johnson, Klee and Schmidt, 1988; Brannen, Heptinstall and Bhopal, 2000). We were careful, of course, not to interpret these visual representations in and of themselves. Rather we used them as a way of drawing out young people's accounts about their families and we analysed the drawings and maps in conjunction with these narratives. Their visual representations reflected the complex variety of family structures and arrangements that they were living under (see the appendix) and, to a lesser extent, the qualitative differences in their kin relationships. Out of the complexities of this data, two broad constructions were discernible. We have called these 'closed' and 'open' family boundaries and will discuss each in turn below.

The notion of boundaries and how they might be used to explore children's families was raised by James and Prout:

> All social environments have implicit ways of regulating group belonging, what we term boundaries . . . there is a wide range to be found between two extremes, from social contexts which are strongly bounded and to which entry and/or exit is strictly controlled to those which have a more open access and weaker boundaries. (1996: 46)

Drawing on the ideas of anthropologist Mary Douglas, they go on to suggest that an exploration of the different constraints which structural boundaries place on children's lives might shed light on the wide variety of family forms which children live under. Our purpose here, however, is to take these ideas forward along a slightly different trajectory. Children are no doubt influenced and constrained by the family boundaries created by others, most notably by their parents. But this is not a one-way process; rather, these boundaries are continually contested and become a site for ongoing negotiations between children and their parents. Here we want to explore how children themselves structure their family boundaries and to uncover the constraints which they might place (or try to place) on others.

Closed family boundaries

BOB (12): The way I see it you can only ever have one person that's . . . like your dad, or your mum, doing dad or mum things.

At the 'closed' end of the spectrum were children who had a strong sense of a tight-knit family unit that had been neither fragmented nor extended by their parents' separation. Their visual representations of their families were hardly different from how they would have been prior to their parents' separation (see drawings 1 and 2).

Nina and Ben lived in different family arrangements. Nina (11) lived with her mother and preferred not to visit her father's small flat. But she saw him every few days when he called round to visit the family and watch TV. Ben (14) and his brother David (aged 15) were, in contrast, in a co-parenting arrangement, spending two nights a week

Drawing 1: Nina (11)

at their father's house. Yet these differences in arrangements made relatively little difference to how these young people conceptualized their families:

> NINA (11): [My family] is pretty ordinary, except that we don't see our dad as much, but we still see him. It's not a formal arrangement, it's not that we have special visiting times or anything like that.

> BEN (14): I just treat our family as it was before they split up. Except for them living apart, it's the same as normal really.

In these cases, contact with a parent was arranged in ways that preserved a strong sense of the relationship between child and parent. Ben and David visited their father and his partner fairly regularly, but their father also maintained a second small home near his sons and decamped there regularly to spend exclusive time with them. Three other families in the sample had also adopted this strategy (with significant resource implications for the parents). In other cases children saw their fathers regularly at the homes of their grandparents or, as in Nina's case, when their father called round to the home they shared with their mother. The fathers had developed a regular routine of call-

Drawing 2: Ben (14)

ing by for a social chat, to help out around the house or to bring a new half-sibling for a visit. By creating a separate space for contact or re-creating a sense of the original family in their own homes on a regular basis, the children could enjoy a relationship with their parent which did not require them to enter a new family situation. They therefore retained a strong sense of an exclusive family that had remained rela-tively untouched by the changes in their parents' lives. Their families were no longer held together by the relationship between the parents; instead their families were held together by the children's bond with each parent.

Preserving a sense of the original blood family in these ways has implications for the kind of relationship that might develop between a child and his or her parents' new partners or spouses.[3] In closely bounded families, these partner–child relationships tended to be highly contin-gent. All the children in our sample distinguished between new part-ners and what they called their 'real' parents.[4] Such distinctions were relatively easy to maintain where the parent and partner were not cohabiting. The partner–child relationship could involve a strong element of choice and flexibility, ranging from frequent interaction to none at all. But even where a partner was co-residing with the child, children maintained clear distinctions between them and their real parents. This did not mean that these partners were not valued – some were highly valued, others less so – but they were more likely to be perceived as friend or foe, or not accorded any status at all, than accorded the status of kin:

DAVID (15): [She's not] part of the family, I just think of her as dad's friend.

NINA (11): I'd like my dad to get a new partner . . . it might be easier if he had someone else to go to as well as us. . . . It wouldn't make much difference to me, it wouldn't be like a step-mum or another mum or anything like that, it would be just, like, dad's girlfriend.

ANDRIJKA (10): [Mum and dad's partners] are a big part of my life. But I don't really think of them as family and people I love, I think of them as, I don't know, friends I suppose.

MATT (15): I don't think of [the partners and their children] as family.
Q: So how do you think of them?
MATT: I don't.

JOEY (15): Dad once referred to [his live-partner and her children] as 'family' which really annoyed me. . . . We were going to do something and he said, 'It will be like doing something as a family', and I was, like, 'no it won't it's not going to be *anything* like a family because we are not a family'. And it really upset me because it felt as if he'd rejected *us* as a family and gone on to a new family. . . . He didn't mean that but that was what it felt [like].

BOB (12): [Mum's live-in partner] has always been there to help with things like my bike . . . but he's never, ever, like if I was upset, come into my room to say 'Are you OK?' . . . He's just, like, there to help with easy things.
Q: He doesn't try to be a parent?
BOB: Well, if he did, I'd tell mum that I wasn't happy living with him.

These new partners were referred to by their first names and were clearly seen to be in a relationship directly with the parent, rather than with the child. Thus there was nothing obligatory about these relationships and the children did not necessarily spend much time with them. Sometimes siblings might have different views on whether a new partner was a member of their family. It might depend quite simply on whether they liked the person or not. Tim, for example, included his dad's new wife as a member of his family and described her as 'nice', but his younger brother Ralph didn't like her and sometimes opted to stay at home rather than go to stay over at his father's house:

RALPH (8): I don't think she's a part of our family. I think she's a bit strict. And dad's got her in his life so both of them are a bit strict. . . . She's not really a mum, so I don't really talk about things with her.

The legal concept of step-parenthood was used by relatively few of the children in our study and clearly does not enjoy the status or meaning that it once had (Dimmock, 1997). Helen (8), for example, who spent most weekends with her father and his live-in partner, asked, 'What *is* a stepmother? Is it like in Cinderella?'. Where the concept was employed by children this was usually to refer to the legal tie of marriage between parent and partner. But as Helen's comment shows, it has connotations of an inferior form of relationship for the child, a legal relationship rather than a personal relationship based on affective ties (Finch, 1997). These findings show how far things have changed since the 1970s when the re-partnering of a parent was seen by adults to create a reconstituted step-family for the child, complete with a new parental figure. What re-partnering now creates is a new site for the negotiation of family boundaries between children and their parents, which for young people like Bob and Joey (above), might entail sustained efforts to maintain and defend the original boundaries.

The closely bounded families described above all had a sense of continuity about them from pre-separation days. But not all such families remained untouched by the separation or divorce. In some cases the families had been split or fragmented. Pele (10) and Quentin (13), for example, lived with their mother and visited their father either at his home with his wife, or at their grandparents' home. Pele's drawing reflected their wider kin network, which was an important part of their daily lives, but it also reflected the acrimonious relationship between the parents that had created an impervious split between the two sides of the family. Their father's wife was excluded from the drawing (they did not get on with her and kept contact to a minimum) and they located themselves and their dog Pepper[5] on the wall between the two halves of their family:

QUENTIN (13): Pepper doesn't understand what's going on, she likes everyone, and, like, me and Pele, we're in the middle of my mum and dad 'cos we don't take sides.

In a similar vein Tom (12) spent equal time with each of his parents,

Drawing 3: Tom (11)

and drew himself as if he were split in two to indicate his equal commitment to each home. In his picture (drawing 3) the two houses are shown as separated by a dividing wall, although they were in fact some miles apart. For Tom the wall represented the way in which his parents' lives were now distinct, dividing his family in two. He described the wall as being 'very big [and] thick . . . it goes right down the middle, separating them completely'. He imagined it as having a little door at the bottom 'only small enough for [me and my sisters] to get through' and certainly too small to let his parents through. He saw the connection between his parents as being severed and his own life in each household as self-contained and distinct.

In other cases, children constructed their families as small, close-knit units, based in one household that had been diminished in size by the loss or exclusion of a parent (see drawing 4). In these cases, the young people had consciously rejected a parent as a member of their family. Adrian, for example, in the process of excluding his mother's husband and their baby son (whom he felt had displaced him), had also rejected his mother – to the extent that he was unwilling to refer to her as his parent. He also excluded his father's live-in partner, whom he shared his home with. His family consisted of his dad, sister and the dog.

Drawing 4: Melanie (12)

ADRIAN (15): I don't miss seeing her [mum]. I'm glad I don't see her . . . because of her husband, and because we don't get on.

This was very much an individual choice for Adrian; as we show below, his sister Sally constructed her family in a radically different way.

Open family boundaries

CLARE (11): I've got a new brother, I've got a mum and a dad, and a step-mum and step-dad. . . . There's more of us – I've got more people.

Drawing 5: Mel (8)

Drawing 6: Roberta (10)

At the 'open' end of the spectrum were children who constructed their families in much more inclusive ways than those described above, the prime difference being the inclusion of their parents' partners (and their kin) as kin or even as parents. In effect their families had been extended as a result of their parents' separation. These 'divorce-extended' families (Stacey, 1990) were reflected in the children's drawings (see drawings 5 and 6), which were more complex in terms of numbers of people involved and the dynamics of the networks. Like Pele, Quentin and Tom (above) some of these children saw themselves as having two sides to their family, although the boundaries between the two sides were rather more permeable. Ursula, for example (drawing 7), drew her family in two halves, reflecting household membership. She located herself with her mother and brother and the dog on the left-hand side and placed her father, his new wife and their baby son in a separate group to the right. The new partner in this case had become part of the family by virtue of her relationship with Ursula's father. Her status as kin was enhanced when she became legally bound to the family through marriage, and was consolidated still further by

Drawing 7: Ursula (18)

the arrival of the new baby, for whom Ursula felt great affection and regarded as a fully-fledged sibling. But this did not make the new partner into a parent for Ursula. It merely formalized the commitment between the two adults. As Ursula explained, 'I just call her Samantha; she's not a mother, she's my dad's wife.'

In other cases children developed an emotional bond with their parent's partner over time so that they were not only integrated into the family but were eventually accorded the status of a parent. This was particularly so for some of the younger children in the sample, such as Emma (drawing 8). However, familial titles were not necessarily used, or were not used consistently. Seven-year-old Rory, for example, sometimes called his social father 'Jim' but commented, 'Nine times out of ten I call him dad'. Where children did not have a close relationship with their 'real' parent, then they had more time and perhaps more incentive to invest in a relationship with a social parent. Bobby, for example, distinguished between daddy Mel (his live-in social father) and daddy Pete (his biological father) whom he rarely saw. His extended family thus included a 'day-to-day' father as well as a more distant father. He hoped that his good relationship with Mel might be consolidated and given legal force through marriage:

> BOBBY (8): I call him Mel and I sometimes call him 'dad'. He's a sort of step-dad 'cos they might get married. He's close as well, I see him every day, except when he's working late. . . . He's good fun.

But it was not only where real parents were 'absent' that new partners could become close and be valued as a parent. Lisa (8), for example, who shared her time between two houses, viewed her father's

Drawing 8: Emma (10)

partner as a 'second' mum, although she added that she would never replace her real mum. In certain circumstances, social parents could even assume more significance than a real parent. Sally, for example, in stark contrast to her brother Adrian (discussed above), had sustained a close relationship with her non-residential mother whom she saw whenever possible, and had developed a close emotional bond with her half-sibling and her mother's husband. She viewed him as a fully fledged parent, not as a 'second' parent or step-parent:

> SALLY (12): I think of Mick more as a dad, because I love him.

In these open family structures where partners had become kin, children could not envisage returning to their old way of life prior to their parents' separation. To do so would mean 'breaking up' their families as they were now constituted and, in the process, losing valued relationships with social parents and new siblings.

We have given here a flavour of the varied and individualized ways in which children construct their families. As we have seen, siblings living in the same household might choose to construct their families in different ways and develop different relationships with a parent, a new partner or a half-sibling, in effect living different family lives. We

have drawn a distinction here between closed and open family boundaries, but we are not suggesting that these are rigid divisions nor that all
children can be neatly located in one camp or the other. Rather, there
are degrees of closure and openness that shade into each other. It is
also the case that families are not static but have shifting boundaries
that are continually being negotiated. At the closed end of the spectrum there are children who guard their family boundaries with great
vigilance. They may try to prevent a parent re-partnering or may resist
their entry into the family by positioning them as friends, or foes, or
by choosing not to define them at all. This may be the case even where
they share their daily lives with them in a shared household. We shall
explore such practices in later chapters. At the open end of the spectrum new partners can be regarded as part of an extended network of
kin or can assume significance as parents in their own right. In these
open structures, the configuration of family relationships is extended
by divorce and does not conform to the conventional 'nuclear' norm.

   One of the most consistent patterns in the children's accounts was
their recognition of blood and legal ties as the basic structural components of family life. Without exception children distinguished between
real and social kin and, regardless of how much time they spent with a
'real' parent, they were usually included in the formal representation
of the family. The exceptions were where a child had been unable or
unwilling to sustain a relationship with that parent. In contrast, relationships with new partners had a more contingent quality and this
was the case even where children worked with relatively open family
boundaries. Given this finding it might be tempting to conclude that,
unlike social ties, blood ties have fundamental significance for children and warrant policies that prioritize the preservation of these ties
after divorce (Neale and Smart, 1999). But such an interpretation would
not do justice to our data. The formal, structural features of family life
represented in the children's drawings can only give us a partial and
somewhat superficial picture of what matters to children when they
think about families, and they provide limited insight into *why* children construct their families in particular ways. In order to flesh out
the picture and gain a more balanced perspective it is necessary to turn
to an exploration of the values which children hold about family life.

Valuing family life: 'proper' families and 'proper' parents

What do children value about family life? The very act of posing this
question is a worthwhile enterprise because it immediately invites us

to move beyond the 'problems' perspective which has come to be so strongly associated with children and divorce. But such a fundamental question is also a necessary precursor to understanding why young people attempt to negotiate and practice their family lives in particular ways. The recent work of O'Brien and colleagues (1996) and Morrow (1998) provides a useful starting point for our discussion. Working in school settings, these researchers used vignettes and group discussions to tease out what children construed as a 'proper' family. Most of the children interviewed by Morrow worked with inclusive or open views of what counts as family. While the children in both studies recognized the structural features of family outlined above and the pervasive power of the 'nuclear' family, their definitions of family did not centre round biological relatedness or the 'nuclear' norm. Instead, they invoked the principles of love, care, mutual respect and support as the basis for a proper family. One 9-year-old child, echoing Claudia's reflections at the start of this chapter, pointed out, 'you don't need a piece of paper [i.e. a marriage certificate] to show you love somebody' (O'Brien, Alldred and Jones, 1996: 90). The children with divorced parents in this study, most of whom had little contact with their fathers, felt that fathers had to show evidence of wanting to see the child and of caring for them before they could be considered part of the family. A father who forgot his child's birthday, for example, did not merit inclusion (1996: 94 and 98). In the face of such crucial issues for children, considerations of the blood tie can become somewhat superfluous. These studies included children in a range of different kinds of family, but studies that have focused on children with separated parents report similar findings. It is the quality of familial relationships (not the nature of post-divorce arrangements) that assumes significance, indicating the need to look beyond the criteria of biology and law to understand children's experiences (Isaacs, Leon and Kline, 1987; Klee, Schmidt and Johnson, 1989: 125–6).

The children in our study provided ample confirmation of these findings. In their accounts they described their families in terms of relationships rather than formal kinship structures and attached importance to the quality of these relationships:

Q: When you think about families what do they mean to you?
QUENTIN (13): People that are close to you and love you and care about you, care how you feel and just want you to be happy.
Q: What do you think a good mother should be like?
QUENTIN: It's the same as, really, the family, someone who cares about you, looks after you, loves you. . . . We've got a relationship where we can tell mum everything. I can go and talk to her and she's, like, close to me.

SALLY (12): A mum needs to be loving and kind, she needs to be there, take care of you. You need to be able to talk to her. . . . For dads, it's the same sort of thing, really.

Q: What do families mean to you?
CHARLEY (13): People you·can trust.

Q: What would be an ideal family?
KARL (14): It's important to . . . be sort of open, you don't have to hold back on anything really . . . [you can] just be yourself.

CATHERINE (20): [A good parent is] someone who you can talk to and who will listen to you and won't force their opinions on you . . . but they give guidance as well. . . . My mum kind of trusted me to make my own choices really.
Q: What about a good father?
CATHERINE: The same sort of thing really . . . My stepfather, Ewen, he does more fatherly things, like he's quite happy to sit down and talk to me. He doesn't like, tell me to do things . . . he offers advice.

As these reflections show, children value good relations of care in families. Family members are there to care for, support and love each other. Such notions were articulated consistently in the children's accounts. But there is another important theme woven into these accounts: they also value good relations of respect between family members. They viewed themselves not simply as children needing care but as young people who want to talk to others and be listened to, trust others and be trusted, and engage in open and meaningful communications (Morrow, 1999). A 'proper' parent, it seems, is not only loving and caring but someone whom a child can talk to with ease and with whom they can 'be themselves' (Morrow, 1998, 1999). In other words, children value a democratic style of family life.[6] Blood ties between kin may well have formal significance, but this observation needs to be seen in a new light. It is not so much having a *real* parent that is important to children as having a *proper* parent, based on qualitative criteria of how family relationships should be conducted. The substantial numbers of children in our study who reported feeling positive about their family lives lived under a wide variety of arrangements but they shared one thing in common. Their families were characterized by good relations of care and respect:

LOUISE (9): My family is nice, friendly, kind, present-giving. I can make friends with my family. [No contact with non-residential parent]

Q: What's it like living in your family?
BOBBY (8): Good fun. . . . We laugh at quite a lot of things. We've got a

new cat, and a garden. . . . Mum laughs more . . . It's nice to be with mum and Mel and I get to see Daddy Pete in London and he phones us. . . . It's quite an ordinary family. . . . It was good when they splitted up because they used to argue a lot. . . . It's better now, lots better. [Tenuous contact with non-residential parent]

JAKE (11): It's a good family, perfectly normal – you pretty soon get used to it and it's just like normal. Lots of people live like this these days. [Regular contact with non-residential parent]

Q: How would you describe your family?
DAVID (15): It's quite a close-knit family because mum and dad, they talk to us a lot . . . I've always had a close relationship with mum 'cos she's quite understanding and she's quite loving. . . . It's a lovely family really because, like, mum and dad will always go out of their way for us to make sure we're happy. [Co-parented]

These notions about care and respect are not confined to child–parent relationships, of course, but permeate the network of family relationships. They help to explain the wide variation in children's responses to new partners. Whether children regard partners and their children as kin will depend on them being able to develop relations of mutual respect and trust over time, thereby laying the groundwork for the negotiation of a caring relationship. It is also worth noting here that these values surrounding care and respect are seen as reciprocal. Children do not see themselves merely as the recipients of care and respect (or in more conventional thinking, as recipients of care and givers of respect), but as active participants in establishing and sustaining mutually supportive relationships in their families. Below (see chapter 5) we will develop this theme, showing how these notions underpin the development of children's moral thinking and ethical practices. Our purpose here, however, is to suggest that, taken together, these notions of care and respect explain much of what children value about family life. There is wider evidence to suggest that these values are not confined to children in divorced families but may characterize the thinking of children in general.[7] They are what make a family a 'proper' family, and a parent a 'proper' parent.

Mothers and fathers

As we have seen, the young people in our study aspired to good relations of care and respect with both their parents regardless of factors such as gender or how much time they actually spent with each parent. But while children might, in principle, value their parents equally and wish to relate to them in the same way, this does not always happen in practice. Parenting continues to be gendered, both in terms of how respective children are treated and the relative responsibilities of the parents. Children's needs for direct care and someone to talk to and confide in are more usually fulfilled by their mothers, and this was reflected in many of the children's accounts (Morrow, 1998; Neale and Smart, 1999):

> NINA (11): I don't think we'd like it living with Dad. . . . Mum looks after us nearly all the time, she's better with us and she does things that I'm comfortable with and that are right for me and Dad sometimes doesn't know what to do and gets panicked. . . . I can't really talk to my dad about my feelings and stuff. . . . Sometimes there's, like, long silences. . . . But if you're comfortable with your dad as much as you are with your mum then it's fine to sleep over there.

As we saw above, Nina regarded her father as an important member of her immediate family and had included him in her 'nuclear' family drawing: But in her circle drawing (see drawing 9) she placed herself, her mother and sister in close association with each other and her father further away.

It was almost as if Nina had two families, an 'inner' circle of family which fulfilled her needs for mutual respect and emotional support, and her conventional 'nuclear' family which was re-created when her father called round to share a meal or watch a film on TV. Nina was one of a number of children who subscribed to the idea that girls need their mums (and boys, their dads), simply because this was the reality in her own family. She acknowledged, however, that there was nothing inevitable about how she related to each of her parents and that circumstances in other families might warrant different patterns of contact and residence.

The distinctions that Nina made between her parents were of a subtle nature. In other cases, children made starker comparisons between their parents. Catherine for example, had also included both parents in her family drawing, albeit split into two discrete households. She valued her relationship with her mother and stepfather (see p. 58 above), but during her teenage years she had refused to visit her father:

> CATHERINE (20): The only time I ever saw my dad really was at Christmas because I didn't really get on with him. . . . All my dad's children are controlled a lot by what he does and things. I think a lot of it is because he frightens [you], although he's not like physical, he's just kind of got that hold over you really. . . .My dad sometimes made you

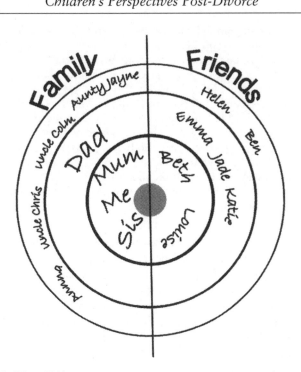

Drawing 9: Nina (11)

feel that you weren't that important, and it didn't really matter if you weren't there. . . . In some ways he's not really like a dad. . . . He's not someone I can talk to about me. . . . He's more kind of material provider, rather than the emotional side.

Besides Catherine, fourteen children in our samples had substantially reduced or broken off contact with an oppressive parent. As we saw above, Louise was very positive about her current family, but as a baby she had been physically abused by her father and put on the at risk register; Bill curtailed contact for other reasons.

Q: How do you feel about not seeing your dad?
LOUISE (9): Happy, because I didn't like him. . . . He did awful things when I was a baby . . . He didn't give you anything . . . like cards when it's your birthday, and he isn't joyful, he's moody. . . . He gave us rice to eat and . . . when I wouldn't, he threw me. . . .
Q: If a friend wanted to know what it was like after the split, what would you tell her?
LOUISE: That it would be okay, and you don't have to put up with your dad.

BILL (19): [The stepfamily] was forced upon me. It wasn't slowly drip-fed, it was, 'right, from today you have a sister . . . it's a brand new happy family so like it'. And I thought, 'Well, I don't really.' . . . We were made to feel out of place [at the new house]. Then he stopped paying maintenance. I knew he had money [but] we had to sell up and move house. He caused all this stress and trouble by lying, basically, and I knew that I could hardly go and see him at weekends and act like some big happy family. . . . I thought, 'I've got to make a stand and look after my family and protect them.' So [when I was 13] I told him, 'We don't want to come to your house any more.' . . . I don't regret it. . . . We got into a way of life where we didn't miss it. . . . If we had carried on seeing him it would have ended up worse than it is, we would have felt even more hatred.

These accounts show that, where one parent is systematically under-mining or disrupting relations of care and respect in a family, children may opt to pare down their family and put their energies into develop-ing and sustaining good family relations with their remaining kin. This does not mean, however, that the link with the other parent is irrevoca-bly broken. Several older teenagers in our samples, including Catherine and Bill, rekindled their relationships with their fathers as they ap-proached adulthood when they could do so on their own terms. The notion of an ex-mother or an ex-father, as Funder (1991) suggests, is almost unheard of, but it may be a reality for some children, at least for a part of their childhood. It seems that children might not be prepared to go on giving unconditional love, support and respect to a parent if these sensibilities are not reciprocated. At a certain point, these seem-ingly irrevocable blood ties also take on a contingent quality.

Whatever the difficulties for these particular children, they did at least have a supportive relationship with one parent to sustain them. But not all of the children in our sample found themselves in this posi-tion. Sometimes care and respect were largely absent. This appeared to be the case for two young brothers who lived with an authoritarian father. They had only sporadic contact with their mother and her hus-band, whom the boys were afraid of because of his violent behaviour. They did not have a strong notion of what family meant and their family pictures were bereft of people:

Q: Who would you include in your family, Pete?
PETE (6): Nobody.
PADDY (8): Not even me?
PETE: My brother. . . .
Q: What's it like living in your family?
PETE: Horrible.

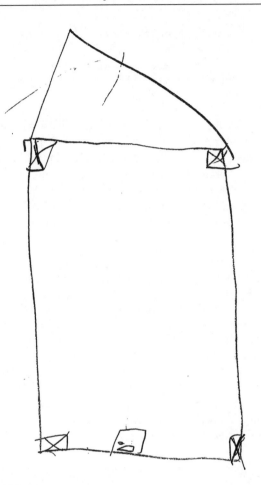

Drawing 10: Paddy (8)

Q: Can you tell me why?
PETE: Because people smack people. . . .
Q: What happens if something goes wrong?
PETE: I pay for it. . . .
Q: Are there any things you'd like to change about your family?
PETE: That we could have got on better.

We will explore this kind of experience in further detail below (chapter 8), but it is worth noting here the significant discrepancy that might exist between the ideals that children hold about family life and the reality of their own experiences.

Relationships between the parents

QUENTIN (13): I suppose when you break up because you don't love each other any more you can still be friends, I suppose I would have liked that better.

The notions of respect outlined above were also extended to how parents managed their adult relationships and their personal problems in relation to their children. The children saw their parents' divorce or separation as a way of bringing arguments to an end, and were often disappointed if the divorce failed to achieve this. The most commonly expressed regrets among the children in our sample were that their parents could not get along better. Compare the following for example:

CATHERINE (20): My dad won't speak to my mum. . . . Another reason I suppose why I didn't really like going [to see him] was because he slagged my mum off to me . . . and that was horrible because no matter what he thought about her or she about him, they were still, like, my mum and dad. . . . I mean my mum was pretty good, . . . she'd stop and realize . . . but with my dad you didn't have a choice, you just had to sit there and listen to him going on . . . and you knew he was getting at you as well. . . . It was quite hard, because you wish that even if they were divorced, that they'd just be a bit more normal, that they could at least be civil to each other.

Q: Can you tell me what your family is like?
URSULA (18): I don't know, I'd say, like, really normal, I'd say, yes, just normal.
Q: What makes it normal?
URSULA: Well, we've never had any, like, big family feuds in the street, which I would class as a bit weird. All the people in [my family] are a bit weird! – but generally as a family grouping, I think it's quite normal. . . . My mum and dad get on all right, they don't have big arguments and they don't say, 'Oh no, you cannot come in this house.' . . . They still talk and stuff. . . . There's no tension there.

The use of the word 'normal' in these accounts is instructive. Both of these young women defined 'normal' family life in terms of civil relationships between family members, and on this criterion Ursula could regard her post-divorce family as perfectly 'normal' whereas Catherine could not. Civil relations between parents were not always possible, of course, particularly where there had been sustained abuse or oppression of one parent by the other. Even where this was not the case, some ill feeling or tension might be inevitable. Children are aware of this. But what was unacceptable for the children in our study was open conflict that impacted upon them. Such conflict, no less than poor parent–child relationships, can lead to significant unhappiness for children (NFPI, 2000) and, as Catherine indicated, it is one of the main reasons why children might seek to change residence or reduce contact with a parent. At the least, children wanted their parents to contain their disputes so that they did not have to be involved, or used as emotional props, or turned into allies, spies or 'go-betweens' in a parental war. The basic premise of respect for children is the recognition that they are entitled to think and feel differently from their parents and can negotiate their own relationships. This same premise applies to other post-divorce situations as well, for example, where parents might oblige a child to visit or stay with a parent they dislike and would rather not see, or attempt to 'force' a relationship with a new partner.

Conclusion

QUENTIN (13): We're a normal divorced family.

Our findings suggest that children conceptualize family very much in terms of relationships rather than structures, and that relations of care and respect assume rather more significance for them than the particular shape and size of their family. These relational dimensions of family life influence which people they include as family members, who they want to spend time with and for how long, and to what extent they seek to modify, preserve or extend the boundaries of their family over time. What the children say here about the quality of family relationships is very much a matter of common sense; it is self-evidently true that people want to get on with others and not experience oppressive relationships. Moreover, there seems to be relatively little that is new in these accounts. The kind of reflections made by these children were also recorded in classic studies such as those by Wallerstein and Kelly (1980) and Walczak and Burns (1984). Contemporary studies of children and family life indicate too that these values are not simply confined to children with divorced parents but may have a much wider currency (Morrow, 1998). Divorce or separation, however, may serve to make these basic elements of family life more transparent for both adults and children. Certainly the reflections from the children here suggest the need to revise conventional notions about what constitutes a 'normal' or a 'proper' family.

Relationships following divorce or separation, no less than those within marriage or co-residence, may be both 'normal' and 'proper' as far as children are concerned – it depends largely on the quality of those relationships. A happy or valued family is not a 'given' but has to be created and sustained. Popular representations of post-divorce families have tended to depict them as highly conflictual and uncaring[8] and hence undesirable. But the evidence from the children in our studies does not readily support this presumption. While some children such as Catherine, for example, may have experienced their families in this way, others, such as David, clearly did not. It may no longer therefore be useful to perpetuate the unhelpful popular image of the 'dysfunctional' divorce family in opposition to the idealized married family. It may be preferable to focus instead on parenting practices, and ways in which a range of relationships can become fulfilling and sustaining. In the next chapter we look more closely at how children themselves manage and negotiate these post-divorce relationships.

4

'Doing' Post-Divorce Childhood

> While marriages can be cancelled and remade, families cannot; they live on in the persons of the children who move quietly across the boundaries of new partnerships and families.
>
> Beck and Beck-Gernsheim, 1995: 149

Introduction

This quotation from *The Normal Chaos of Love* is quite remarkable for its myopic, adult-centred understanding of the nature of post-divorce family life. While we would not dissent from the idea that families are not coterminous with marriage, we question whether the essence of family resides in the children who, it seems, flit about in a quiet fashion between the newly formed relationships generated by adults. The children in this evocative image are rendered quite passive and docile. The impression given is that they do their parents' bidding while at the same time being the receptacles of the meaning of 'family' because they inertly embody the generative product of the adults' previous union. In our two linked studies we did not find any children who could be said to move *quietly* between their parents' new relationships or households. They moved noisily, or sadly, or angrily or joyfully, but not exactly quietly. Moreover, they did not embody the meaning of family. As we saw in chapter 3, they acted out their own interpretations of family, including some people and excluding others. Some even exercised their choice not to visit one parent at all, or drove out their parents' new partners when they were sufficiently motivated to do so. Even the children who were perfectly happy did not fit this docile image: they had their own demands and wishes and were capable of making them known.

Unlike Beck and Beck-Gernsheim, we suggest that children play an active part in restructuring relationships after divorce and in redefining the meaning of family after separation. In this chapter we explore the challenges that children face in this renegotiation and in sustaining relationships with parents across separate households. This includes the ways in which the dislocations of space and the experience of parental absence implicit in post-divorce family life impact upon children's lives. We will examine changes in involvement with and connection to parents, and children's and young people's responses to the changes that occur over time as parents re-establish their lives, renegotiate relationships with former partners, and enter into or disengage from new partnerships or other forms of relationship. At the heart of this chapter is a concern with the contributions which children themselves make to the maintenance of relationships and to the complex business of living in a reorganized family. Hence our title refers to 'doing' post-divorce childhood. We start with the ontological assumption that children are sociological actors rather than passive symbols of family life. Finally, we begin to consider whether the establishment of family practices which are not coterminous with the single-household, nuclear family means that new forms of childhood are emerging in the twenty-first century.

Orienteering for children

Giddens (1991) has argued that, in post-traditional societies, individuals are increasingly obliged to work out their own solutions and moral maps when they face major transitions in their personal lives. He has suggested that this means that individuals are increasingly engaged in a reflexive project of the self in which they write their own biographies rather than following custom or tradition. With regard to the family, the transformation of traditional family forms gives rise to pioneering a new social territory and constructing innovative forms of intimate relationships. We have referred to this elsewhere (Smart, 2000) as a process of 'orienteering' without a compass in which individuals find themselves in a new cultural and moral space and need to devise a new etiquette of kinship. Following these ideas, we have been concerned to explore the extent to which this process applies to children who are increasingly navigating different forms of post-divorce family life. Even more than their parents, they have no modern cultural tradition[1] to rely on to help them find their way in the new terrain. They may have to learn to live with strangers in the form of their parents' new partners and their children, or even new half-siblings. Their expectations of their parents may have to be revised, and they may see them behaving in new and unaccustomed ways; perhaps distressed or lonely, or perhaps loving a new sexual partner, or step-parenting 'strange' children. There are no external normative frameworks available to help them with the task of forging these new relationships, and we need to understand more about how they rise to this challenge and 'do' childhood under these new conditions.

As we show in the appendix, the children in our linked studies lived in widely varying circumstances. Not only was there a complex pattern of family structures, kinship, lifestyles, and social and economic circumstances across the samples, but even where we found a close resemblance in children's backgrounds and family arrangements, their responses to and perceptions of these frequently varied. Indeed, siblings could have very different attitudes towards parents and new family members despite sharing the same pattern of residence and contact. Notwithstanding this, a number of distinct themes on the subject of the renegotiation of family relationships can be discerned in the children's accounts. Below we explore some of the key elements in 'doing' post-divorce childhood before returning to the more speculative theme of whether childhood is itself changing in certain ways.

Dealing with separation

At the core of children's and young people's renegotiation of their relationships with parents after divorce or separation is the experience of absence. Although some parents who establish civil relationships with each other may continue to do certain things as 'a family', such as spending Christmas, birthdays, or holidays together, these parents' lives do basically disengage and diverge. 'Doing' separation therefore becomes an inherent feature of children's lives; being with one parent involves them in being apart from the other. The ways in which separation is managed by children can differ widely and are affected by such things as the quality of relationships; the nature, length or frequency of the separation; its causes and predictability; the sense that children make of it; and the resources they have for responding to it.[2] We found that children with unreliable contact with a parent who seemed to make little emotional or practical investment in them could feel extremely unhappy. Yet even children with reliable contact could speak of 'missing' the parent from whom they were apart. This could be a matter of sadness even though both parents were fully involved in their lives. At the other end of the spectrum, children with an oppressive or abusive parent could find relief in never having to see that parent again. Similarly, some co-parented children, such as those having daily opportunities to see each parent and whose residence arrangements had been in place for a number of years, expressed little sense of having lost something precious as a result of their parents separating. Separation from a parent is therefore not always a problem for children; it can constitute either a loss or a gain.

These different scenarios are evidenced in the experiences of the children and young people we discuss below. Louise (9) recalled that her father's presence had caused her sadness and fear, and she was quite clear that she was happier without him around. She had made it plain to the Court Welfare Officer who interviewed her that she would not see her father under any circumstances, and as a result he was advised to drop his application for contact. Louise could be said to have been empowered by her strong stance as she stated quite firmly that no child should have to 'put up with' unsatisfactory or abusive fathers (see p. 61). In contrast, Maya felt rejected by her father and was preoccupied by his apparent lack of love and concern for her:

> MAYA (15): I don't know whether [my father] is alive or dead . . . He was horrible, really horrid because he was beating my mum . . . and he hated children. Once my mum had me he just didn't want me. . . . I think about him a lot, I suppose . . . I don't feel whole really, you know, being without a father, even though I don't like that father . . . There's sort of like a space missing . . . I've always thought that I wish I had a different father, you know, not *him* but a *proper* father. [Emphasis in original]

Maya only knew her father through her mother's accounts. His absence appeared to be disempowering, although what she regretted was not so much the loss of this relationship *per se* but that she had never had a proper father. Nor did she have other supportive relationships in her family that she could rely on. Maya and Louise therefore represent two ends of a continuum of parent–child separation: one had rejected her father and the other felt he had rejected her.

For other children parental absence was not necessarily absolute even if contact was rare, and this could give rise to the opportunity of transforming a fairly minimal relationship into something more substantial. Hector, for example, saw his father only once or twice a year because he lived abroad. Their contact was tenuous and sporadic and such meetings as they had lasted at most a matter of a few hours. During his interview Hector's most strongly voiced wish was for a closer relationship with his father:

> HECTOR (10): [My father] phoned me but my mum picked it up and there was a big argument – again. Well, not a big argument but it was a pushy argument and sort of, 'I don't see why you shouldn't come up

[here]' and 'Well, it's further for me and I don't have a car'. 'Well, you should get one then, you should make more effort'. I'd like to spend a bit more time with my dad really . . . not always just two or three hours, that's not very good. I barely know him. I've told mum I'd like to see my dad more and she said she'd like that too, and he said he'd like that too, but she says it's very hard and then he says 'Well, why doesn't she move?', and she says, 'Well, why doesn't he move?'

Hector described trying to bring about improvements in his contact with his father through the medium of email.[3] He also planned to travel independently so that he could visit his father rather than remaining dependent on his father's rare visits to Britain. At the same time, it was apparent that Hector was aware that his attempts to bring about a more satisfying relationship with his father might fail. He did not disguise from himself that contact visits appeared to be a low priority for his father, but he still wanted to improve their relationship. Hector's experiences provide an example of children's agency and how they may, on occasion, take the lead in trying to forge decent relationships.

The children we have discussed so far were dealing with long-term absence and with parents who created problems for them. But even children who had two unambiguously loving parents whom they saw regularly had to manage the emotional and physical transitions between households which can be demanded of children of divorced parents. While some grew accustomed to living in this way and became used to parting from one or other parent routinely, others experienced it as a series of separations whose repetition did little to diminish their upsetting impact:

LISA (8): [When I began to be co-parented] I thought I might miss [my mum and dad] terribly and I wouldn't want them to go, and I still don't want them to go. The boys aren't that bothered, they say, 'OK, bye', but I still make a big fuss about it. . . . [If I miss my mum and dad] I just try to get on with something nice. But it never works really because you miss the parent and you can't really stop missing them until you see them again.

Lisa faced the choice between managing these regular transitions creatively or seeing one of her parents less often. Thus where children had good relationships with their parents that they wanted to preserve, they often had to devise strategies for coping with their feelings. These involved practical measures, such as having changeovers on a school day to create a neutral territory or to interpose a diversionary activity between leaving one home and joining another. Or they might telephone one parent to exchange news while they were still staying with the other. These were strategies that parents could initiate and help to maintain, but it was striking how self-sufficient many of the children were in recognizing and dealing with their feelings. Lisa was not alone in being able to give an explicit account of the way in which she coped. Other children spoke, for example, of immersing themselves in a book as a way of entering an absorbing, imaginary world for a time, and so distracting themselves and allowing their feelings to subside. Or they spoke of the practical ways in which they dealt with their situation. While some children could turn to adults for support, it was not always available to them, and in some instances they felt that it was not appropriate to ask. In these situations children could become resilient and competent in finding their own ways to cope:

CHELSEA (8): When I go on holiday with each parent it's funny because I always miss the other one and you don't really, you can't really tell your mum and dad 'cos to them they think, 'Oh well she just wants to be with her dad or mum'. So I keep it to myself. But I send them postcards. And I normally take a picture of one of them [with me] when it's [going to be] a long time.

SABRINA (10): If I'm upset usually I'd just either ring dad or . . . I just go and sit in the dining room or sit in my bedroom and find something to do. . . . I'd just go to my room and think, think about something else and it would stop me being upset.

These strategies for coping should not necessarily be seen as burdens on children as for the most part they preferred to manage their emotions in these ways than to see less of a parent. When they did become too burdensome, however, some children did decide to opt out. We discuss some of these instances more fully in chapters 7 and 8.

Dealing with parents

Just as children's self-sufficiency and competence can be underestimated, so too their position as 'dependants' can mask their contribution to the work of sustaining relationships with other family members after divorce. This activity, which might be termed 'caring', is one of the central themes of this book. The theoretical debate on the ethic of care, and the question of whether children can be said to subscribe to such an ethic, are the subjects of chapter 5. In what follows we limit ourselves to an examination of the ways in which some children spoke of their feelings towards their parents after divorce and how this then led them to act. Finch and Mason (1993) and Mason (1996a) have suggested that caring is to do with thought, feeling and interpersonal connection as well as with activity (labour), and arises less from the structural position and kin relationship of the individuals concerned than the quality of the bond between them and the feelings of commitment which this engenders. We wanted to explore whether this proposition could be said to hold true for children and, when they were attentive to their parents' needs and circumstances, whether they acted in this way voluntarily or from a sense of obligation.

What was interesting about the accounts of the children and young people we spoke to was how many of them voiced a belief that divorce had intensified their appreciation of their parents, and their desire actively to help them. They suggested that, as a result of the divorce or separation, they no longer took their parents for granted or saw them simply as an accustomed backdrop to more immediate concerns of their daily lives. Instead, they had become more consciously aware of their attachment to their parents, perceiving the intimacy that they shared with them as potentially vulnerable, and therefore as something to which they wanted to give time and commitment.

> SELINA (16): I think I've probably got closer to mum and dad just because of the situation. . . . Like, my friends will take their parents for granted, [and say things] like 'Mum's always there when I get home' or 'Oh god, mum was moaning last night' kind of thing. But I don't 'cos when they're there I know it's only for a short time and I like appreciate them a lot more, I think. . . . My friends don't understand . . . [they'll say] 'Oh, are you coming out on Sunday?' or something and I'll be like 'Oh no, I can't because I'm going . . .' 'Oh, go on!' 'Well, no, because I won't see them for a week' kind of thing.

In some cases children simply spoke of developing a close and companionate relationship with their parents and of enjoying time spent in activities with them, or discussing subjects of mutual interest. Often, however, as in Selina's case, it was apparent that they made time to talk to their parents, and that this was an activity in which they chose to engage in preference to another.

We also found children who spoke thoughtfully about the demands made on their parents by post-divorce family life and who displayed considerable attentiveness to their feelings and circumstances. Some children, for example, recognized that their parents had to undergo regular transitions which might also be difficult. So, where a parent had not re-partnered, children could express sympathy for the one who had half a week full of children and half a week alone. Other parents might face different demands. Some, with new partners and

children, for example, had to cope with a constantly shifting population of children. Emma's mother was one such parent. As well as having Emma (10) and her baby brother Rory, she had a child by another
former partner, and was a part-time stepmother to her current partner's son Josh. Additionally, she worked as a childminder, taking in as
many as six children a day. Emma described her mother as 'Such a
busy mum, always doing anything and everything for everybody.' She
also said, 'She's like my best friend' and 'I don't mind sharing her
though 'cos she's so wonderful.' Emma's interview illustrates how she
and children like her did not simply care *about* their parents (were
solicitous for them) but cared *for* them, meaning that their attentiveness was translated into active support. She demonstrated this through
acting as a second mother to Rory and entertaining him when her
mother was busy. Her account suggested that the ways in which she
contributed towards the family were entirely voluntary and there was
no suggestion that she was burdened by her responsibilities; rather,
she was matter of fact about which tasks she could and could not take
on. Of course, parents could make it clear that they wanted children
to contribute to the running of a shared household. Clare was another
elder daughter in a large reconstituted family. She was slightly less
enthusiastic about caring in a practical way:

> CLARE (11): [Mum]'s just so busy. Because she's got four children and
> it's just really, really hard. Sometimes I feel sorry for her.
> . . .
> Q: *You're the oldest aren't you? Are there things that you have to do to
> help?*
> CLARE: Well, I do help, I don't exactly have to, but I do. . . . I get things
> for mum if she needs them, I go up to the shops if she needs something
> like milk. . . . I don't exactly like doing it, I'm usually like, 'Oh, I don't
> want to, I'm tired'. I'm just making excuses, but I usually go up there.

Clare's comments on the way she helped her mother were not volunteered, as were Emma's, but came in response to a direct question. She
did not disguise her lack of enthusiasm for household tasks and she
did not rush to offer her 'domestic services' to her mother. At the same
time, she was alert to the amount of work that her mother had to do
even if she did not particularly want to share in it.

We also found instances where boys could be just as thoughtful as
girls.[4] David, for example, like many of the children and young people
in our study with a parent who had not re-partnered, was concerned
that his mother might be lonely and so provided a degree of support
and companionship:

DAVID (15): I worry about mum ... I think my relationship with my mum has been affected because I try to speak to her more and be with her more, because she's ... got no immediate partner. ... I'll go and put the tea on and I'll try and stay in so that we can all sort of eat together.

At times, of course, children could be faced with a parent who was not coping and who was extremely needy. Parents could be vulnerable at the point of divorce and behave in ways that children found unpredictable and out of character. They could make excessive or unrealistic demands on their children for help and support. Nevertheless, in the context of ongoing family life we found that most children did not find being supportive of parents an onerous, anxiety-laden or burdensome activity, but regarded it as an everyday family practice and expression of relatedness. Interestingly, children often spoke of parents in affectionate terms that mirrored those of a parent speaking of a child. They expressed concern about whether a parent was eating properly (especially in the case of fathers living alone) and whether they were taking proper care of themselves.

BETH (14): My dad will just let people walk all over him which I'm a bit worried about. Which is probably why I'm a bit worried about leaving him when I move out, but, I don't know, he's a grown man, he should be able to look after himself by now. [laughing]
Q: Do you ever have any worries about your mum?
BETH: I think my main worry at the moment is that in like five years time her and Ian will end up splitting up or something and then she'll be really upset. I don't really worry that much about her though. She can stand up for herself. She can sort herself out. She's got a good head on her shoulders, she'll be OK.

Most of the strategies for dealing with parents that we have outlined here are 'positive' in nature. But sometimes children resorted to anger and confrontation when they felt that their parents were behaving poorly or without sufficient sensitivity to their own feelings. In these cases the children were clear that they would not put up with unacceptable behaviour on the part of a parent and were not afraid to say so:

PELE (10): Sometimes we [argue] with dad, if we know he's in the wrong. ... we made a deal that his wife wouldn't come to Quentin's bar mitzvah.
QUENTIN (13): I didn't want her there because it was my day and it wasn't right to have my mum and step-mum. But the day before he rang up to say she was coming to the 'do' afterwards.
PELE: He went back on his word and changed at the last minute.

QUENTIN: I felt very annoyed. He picked me up from school and we just sat in the car park and talked for an hour and I shouted at him. . . . I think he's got the message that we don't want her and he can at least tell the truth from the start – at least we'd know then.

Other children, in a complete antithesis to Beck and Beck-Gernsheim's image of children moving quietly, metaphorically kicked and fought to get their views across:

RACHEL (16): I had a difficult relationship with my dad for a while. I tried to move out and stuff, but that was really a bluff, I suppose. Me and my dad are both really stubborn. And we'd argue about things and it just got too much. So I packed up all my stuff and came to mum's, but I phoned him and went back the same night and sorted it out. So it may not have been the best way to go about it, but it changed after that. I have a much better relationship with him now.

And although some children came to appreciate their parents more, others were less enchanted. Their reactions could be uncomfortable for some parents, and many children were prepared to voice their anger or irritation. In other cases they might withdraw from a parent rather than shouldering the uneven struggle of trying to keep a poor relationship going.

Monitoring and managing the relationship between parents

Children were very interested in how their parents regarded each other after their separation because they could feel implicated in or worried by the dislike or hatred one parent might feel towards the other. They might also experience conflicts of loyalty. The children and young people we interviewed were quick to discern whether expressions of friendship were real or simulated for their benefit. Parents might have been willing to discuss these matters with their children, volunteering the information they thought they needed or would benefit from, but children also adopted their own strategies for testing out such information. They closely observed their parents' social interactions and noted changes in their relationships with new or established friends, or partners. Children acknowledged that this monitoring could be a form of surveillance.[5] They listened in on conversations (sometimes putting a glass to the wall), observed what letters arrived, and noted what photographs a parent carried. They were especially alert to the nuances of parents' behaviour towards each other, wanting to know 'what was going on', not only at the time of the separation but also subsequently. Given that this process of observation and evaluation was continuous, they sometimes found themselves revising their initial impressions or conclusions:

> JOEY (15): Mum and dad used to really not get on and it used to be a really sort of tight-lipped situation and now, I don't know, just gradually, and there have been times when they first started to get on it felt really strange and I sort of thought, well was dad trying to 'get back in' maybe, or is he trying to do anything. But now it just feels as though, I mean it seems to be much easier and it's just so much better. I mean he comes up at Christmas sometimes and it's just much better for them to get on and for everybody to get on as a family, because when they didn't get on it felt as if maybe we would have to take sides and I didn't want to do that. . . . I think mum sometimes used to feel as though dad and Antony and Nick and I would go off and chat because we hadn't seen each other and mum would be left in the kitchen, and sometimes she'd get quite upset about it, but now we can all get along as a family.

Joey was attentive to his mother's feelings. He also closely scrutinized the shifts in his parents' relationship and was concerned to detect whether there was a hidden agenda in his father's behaviour. Additionally, he felt relief in the re-establishment of a cordial, and possibly even friendly, relationship between them. He made it clear how much he disliked feeling caught in the middle between two alienated parents and was relieved when he no longer had to feel conflicting loyalties.

Not all parents could be civil of course, and where one (or both) parent(s) continued to be abusive, manipulative, hostile or violent children faced very difficult situations. We discuss outright manipulation of children in parental conflicts in chapter 8, but even in quite ordinary situations children could feel caught in the middle:

> MATT (15): [The arguments are] just relentless. I wish they would stop it.

It is important to recognize, however, that for some children it was their parents' divorce that allowed them to escape from the war zone:

> NICK (14): It's almost made it easier though, our mum and dad not living together, because before there were arguments and things like that and it was difficult really to live. But now that they've moved apart they're both much happier and much more relaxed. Like my mum, she comes in tense from work just 'cos her work's like that, but she comes home and she'll relax rather than before she would have come home and there probably would have been an argument about something completely stupid and irrelevant, 'cos they argued for the hell of it basically.

Both Matt and Nick tried to ignore their parents' quarrels, but sometimes children tried to act as peace makers and pacifiers.

NINA (11): Sometimes if dad doesn't like [the arrangements] then he can get me to change mum's mind.
Q: (What happens?)
NINA: He just moans, and then I talk to him on the phone and try to cheer him up.
Q: How?
NINA: I just talk to him for a while and have a joke and then it makes it easier for my mum.

ANDRIJKA (10): Sometimes dad gets a bit angry, well, not angry, but he doesn't like the way things are between the houses because they're so far away, so sometimes he tells me what he feels and I wouldn't say that in front of mum because I don't think dad would tell her how he felt, so I don't really want to tell things that dad didn't want her to know, really. . . . It's a bit upsetting because sometimes he's sort of making mum out to be a bad person when she's not and sometimes it's just, he's not actually talking about her, he's talking about the position of the houses and I feel a bit the same way about that.

The children developed a strong sense of diplomacy but also became skilful in managing difficult situations and their parents' moods. These examples reveal very clearly the emotional complexity of post-divorce childhood and the extent to which children become fluent in the new narratives of tact and sensibility.

Dealing with new partners

In chapter 3 we discussed how children viewed new partners and how this was linked to whether they operated within a model of family with closed or open boundaries. But the children could also experience their parents' re-partnering as a form of loss in that they often found that they enjoyed less parental attention than previously. This meant that they could dislike new partners out of jealousy rather than because they were intrinsically unlikeable:

THOMAS (11): I don't like mum's new partner, I'm not overly fond of what he did to us and like . . . the principle's bad, just taking someone else's partner isn't exactly the best thing to do is it? . . . Now when we go out he's always like right next to her and my brother's on the other side of her and I'm walking behind or in front of all of them and I don't get much attention now. And they're thinking of having a baby and if that happens I'll only get like a quarter of the attention and so I'm going to say that I'm going to spend a lot more time with my dad if they have a child.

HOPE (14): When mum got together with [her new partner] there were some problems at first, like I had my nose out of joint a bit having to share her, which was difficult. But we've got round that now, he's not there so much as he used to be, so we've still got our time together, which is really useful.

In some cases children acted to rid themselves of these unwelcome intruders:

CHELSEA (8): Mum had a boyfriend and he was like always really grumpy . . . I don't think I could ever like him because he was always grumpy. Whenever he came my mum always used to cook him a special, well a different, dinner than we used to have, but it was always special and I thought she liked him best but she always said, 'I don't'. But once when they were together I wrote a letter and I asked my mum to sign [it] if she loved me, so she signed. And I wrote on the letter,

> Dear Bill,
> I think it's time we split up now and got somebody else.

But my mum found out about it.

And Alex, who was 12, left notes lying around his home in prominent places which said 'JIM MUST GO'. Both he and Chelsea managed to get across to their mothers their dislike of the new men and in Chelsea's case her mother ended the relationship. In Alex's case she agreed to see him mostly when Alex was with his father.

As we saw in chapter 3, many children could form close attachments with new partners and saw them as friends or family members, if not as parents. But even where this was impossible some children were aware that even though they did not like the new partner, he or she might make their parent happy. Hope, above, for example, commented of her mother's relationship, 'They've been together for about a year and they're really close. It's really good for her.' Similarly, Beth, who spoke at length about her dislike of sharing her home with her mother's partner, when asked what wish she would like to make for her family and herself, said:

BETH (14): I'd want my mum and Ian [partner] to get on really well and stop arguing altogether. When I was little I used to be happy they argued except for the fact Ian shouted a lot, because I thought 'Oh, they might split up this time'. But I'd want them to get on well.

Clearly, re-partnering is a complex issue and some children did not feel 'free' to like a new partner because they were aware that their other parent was still alone or simply very unhappy. They could feel uncomfortable with one parent's happiness if it seemed to be based upon the other one's misery:

> JAMES (12): I haven't always liked [my dad's partner] 'cos my mum felt really unhappy. But I like her now. . . . . It's okay having her there, I'm used to it now, and I just – well, dad's happy and everything, dad's happy, and I suppose that's okay.

A major part of 'doing' post-divorce childhood seemed to involve coming to terms with the fact that parents too need happiness and that this could be valued and valuable, even if the child or young person did not much like the situation. By and large they saw the family as a network of relationships in which the needs, wishes and interests of each member had to be recognized. They knew that their feelings of dislike might not be shared by others and some recognized that their antipathy was born of jealousy rather than being based on an 'objective' evaluation of the new partner. Hope, above, described herself as initially being acutely jealous of her mother's new partner and as only beginning to acknowledge this after reaching a point in her arguments with her mother where she ran off to her father. James could only allow himself to like his father's new partner after a passage of time. What we are suggesting, therefore, is that re-partnering is a major event that prompts children to think about their families in new ways and that gives rise to a variety of strategies of management and negotiation.

An altered self?

So far we have talked about the ways in which divorce can alter children's relationships. However, there is also a sense in which it separates or distances children from their parents. If divorce changes parents, it also can make children aware that they too have to change:

> Q: Do you think [your parents' separation] has changed you at all?
> TOM (12): Don't know really. Maybe. . . . I'm very sort of cautious about criticism from people now, [more] than I would have been I think. . . . And I think I sort of get in major stresses now and again which I don't think I used to before.
>
> Q: Do you think it's changed you at all, living in a family like yours?

CHARMAINE (11): Yes, I think it's maybe made me a bit more mature. Yes, I think it's got me a bit more used to dealing with things that maybe I didn't want to happen.

What stands out for a number of children was that they felt they had become more independent of their parents. Selina, for example, recognized that she had, of necessity, become less dependent upon her parents:

SELINA (16): It was really funny when we went to Holland on the hockey tour. A couple of my friends were really missing their mum and dad. We were only there for ten days and . . . I didn't like, miss either [of my parents] because . . . well, every week I'm without one of them. In a way . . . I don't miss them at all because . . . I'm used to not having them around. . . . I suppose, due to everything, I'm a lot more independent than a lot of [my friends]. . . . And Nat's [brother] the same. We're very independent and we had to grow up a lot faster than a lot of other people. . . . Because we've had to manage really.

This newly acquired sense of independence was not restricted to the emotional sphere but could extend to the social sphere as well. Children often felt they had more autonomy and were less subject to parental oversight, even where they were making a great deal of effort to spend time with both parents. When parents lived in separate households they were not always well positioned to oversee children's day-to-day lives and could find it difficult to impose a routine or sometimes discipline. Some children experienced very different routines and/or attitudes in each home and could, as a consequence, enjoy a greater sense of freedom:

RYAN (10): I think my mum probably worries about me being at my dad's 'cos he lets me do loads of things that she wouldn't let me do.
Q: What sorts of things?
RYAN: Well, things that are more dangerous and stuff like that [physical activities such as climbing and sledding]. He lets me stay up later . . . like at weekends [mum] makes me go to bed at like ten past ten on Friday and he lets me stop up 'till about two o' clock on Saturday.
. . .
Q: If you could have a wish for the future, for you and your family, what wish would you make?
RYAN: I wouldn't wish 'em to get back together 'cos I wouldn't really like that anyway, but probably [live] a bit closer to friends and stuff like that.
Q: When you said you wouldn't like it if they got back together, what wouldn't you like?

RYAN: Well, my mum would be there to tell me not to do things.
Q: *Yes? So, some of the things that you're able to do when you're at dad's house, you wouldn't be able to do?*
RYAN: No.

Moreover, new partners did not always diminish this greater sense of freedom because they did not have the same authority as a parent:

BETH (14): It means you can get away with more, I think . . . because both my parents work late and there's only Ian [mum's partner] and he couldn't tell me what to do if he wanted to, well, he can tell me 'Please will you make your . . . why can't you wash up?' or something, but he couldn't like say, 'Right, that's it, you're staying in, you're not going out.'
Q: *Right, so that's not part of his role in the house?*
BETH: No, he can't like, boss me about, tell me how to live my life.

The post-divorce family is clearly very much a new terrain for children in which they can actively negotiate new norms and/or new styles of relationships with both parents and new partners. They are faced with new opportunities (whether welcomed or not) and in this process can change themselves and can challenge previous assumptions about how children and adults should relate. Some children began to question their parents' attitudes, values and expectations – perhaps before they might otherwise have done so as a normal part of growing up. In this sense they are clearly engaged in a form of 'orienteering' through a landscape of intimate relationships.

Changing childhoods?

Selina's belief that she had had to grow up faster than her friends (Weiss, 1979) was echoed by several of the children we interviewed, and the way they articulated their feelings demonstrates this. Divorce confronts children with experiences which make them think differently about their family practices and re-evaluate their relationships. This process gives them the opportunity to take an active, independent stance and to experience themselves as autonomous persons. Sometimes reassessing their families in this way led them to the conclusion that they did not like one parent very much, or it encouraged them to try to sustain contact with a parent. In these cases children exercised the choice which they felt they had about their family ties and could increase, reduce or even sever contact. Other children came to place more value on their parents than they once did. They became attentive to the feelings and circumstances of other family members and were responsive to opportunities for contributing to the well-being of those for whom they cared. As we have seen, they might make tea for a tired parent, offer companionship or, where parents were involved in ongoing conflict with each other, they acquired skills in empathy or mediation.

Once children begin to think for themselves about their place in their family it is not surprising that they should want to have more say in matters that affect them. Moreover, children with parents who live apart are almost invariably aware of having choices available to them about where and how they live. Some, of course, have more scope than others for negotiating the structure of their family arrangements or the nature of their day-to-day activities. Parenting styles, and the personal and social resources upon which they are able to draw, are important factors in increasing or diminishing their ability to exercise choice. Nevertheless, for many, divorce can be said to open up new areas of social experience which can offer (or demand of) children enhanced independence and autonomy. They may have to manage emotional transitions between two separate households, get used to travelling long distances to maintain contact with a parent, adapt to living intimately alongside new adults and children, or adapt to not seeing one parent at all.

It does not require a divorce for children to become active practitioners of family life who negotiate individualized relationships with different family members, value their parents or balance caring for others with their own self-interests. Doing family life in the context of divorce, for some children at least, will not be substantially different from doing family life in co-residential families. Indeed most contemporary children may be growing up a little faster in a context where both parents may work outside the home and where attitudes towards children and parenting are beginning to change. Many of the children in our study, particularly those who were living substantially in one home, spoke of their family lives with some complacency, indicating that they were not constantly acting against a background concern about the contingency of relationships but were getting on with their perfectly ordinary childhoods.

JAKE (11): It seems ordinary now, this pattern, because it's been happening like this for a long time. Basically I take things as they come and I just get on with it.

PELE (10): You get on with your life and then when something comes up, just try and cross that bridge when you come to it.

If divorce alone does not bring about this process of changing childhoods and changing families, it does contribute in quite specific ways and is probably one of the most significant catalysts in bringing into being new forms of childhood. It necessarily alters children's perception of 'family' and the relationships that this entails and, crucially, makes it impossible for children to take family ties for granted. As we discussed in chapter 1, kinship in the UK has always been substantially personal, flexible and affective (Finch, 1997) in that it is based more on the degree of liking and affection between kin than the positional relationships which exist between them. The ties between children and parents have, however, always been regarded as an exception to this and have been seen as less flexible and less voluntaristic than those between other kin. Changes in family structures and attitudes seem, however, to be bringing about more optionality in the parent–child relationship – at least for some children.[6] It is noticeable how often the children and young people in our samples spoke of 'liking' or 'not liking' individual parents. They may have felt that their parents hold a unique position in their lives which could not be taken over in any absolute sense by other adults, but they no longer felt bound to them in the same way. We found that respect and liking significantly influenced the commitment as well as the closeness they felt towards them. In facing up to the restructuring of their family lives and being confronted by the contingent nature of contemporary human relationships, it seems that some children may now be thinking much more explicitly about their relationships and what 'family' means to them. In the next chapter we turn to the ethical frameworks which form the backdrop to these issues.

5

Do Children Care? Childhood and Moral Reasoning

Introduction

Debates about children and moral reasoning are hardly new. In a range of disciplines from philosophy to literature and, more recently, developmental psychology there have flourished debates on children's capacities to reason morally, their existential condition as either innocent or evil, and their abilities to acquire a conscious sense of right and wrong at specific ages. Given the depth and extent of these huge volumes of literature and knowledge, we inevitably feel we must tread cautiously since we do not approach our topic as trained philosophers, pedagogues, psychologists or poets. However, it is our intention in this chapter to raise the question of children's moral agency within the specific context of family transformation and change. Our concern is not so much whether children *can* be morally self-reflexive, nor whether teenagers are more or less inclined to have clear views on what is good or bad about family relationships than 7-year-olds, nor indeed whether boys and girls reason differently; rather, our focus is grounded in the specifics of how children seek to resolve 'newly emergent' dilemmas and problems which arise as a consequence of changing patterns of parenting and family life.

We chose to look at this issue for two main reasons. The first, which we have discussed more fully in chapter 2, is our discomfort with the dominant conceptualization of children and childhood invoked by popular debates on divorce in the 1990s. These debates constructed the child as the inevitable victim of his or her parents' divorce to such an extent that the 'child of the broken home'[1] became the symbol of a

whole range of social ills – from predicted poor educational performance and delinquency to a measure of adult selfishness – at the end of
the twentieth century. The very term divorce became almost synonymous with harm to children. Under the weight of this imagery, *actual*
children began to vanish.

The second reason also relates to the invisibility of children, but
within a different discourse. In this chapter we will rely very heavily
on ideas originally generated by Carol Gilligan (1982) and so we must
acknowledge the importance of her contribution at the start. But there
has been a myopia in the vision generated by others who have taken
her work forward. Gilligan was a psychologist who worked with children on moral reasoning, and her specific research question was on
whether girls and boys reasoned in different ways. Her work was in
the tradition of Piaget and Kohlberg except that she turned the significance of gender difference on its head. From her work with children
she developed general models of gendered moral reasoning which entered into the domains of philosophy, jurisprudence, political theory
and feminist thought. When her work was taken up in these disciplines, her starting point with children as beings who reason morally
was simply left aside. The debate she generated focused on whether
men and women reason differently or, in a more sophisticated formulation, whether there are gendered modes of reasoning that have become institutionalized in state forms of justice and welfare provision.
Although Gilligan continued to work on research with children and
young people, her ideas about an 'ethic of justice' and an 'ethic of
care' became the possession of adults and institutions, not of children.

In one arena therefore, the idea of children had become central, but
these were children construed as passive child victims without a voice,
capacity to act, or ability to influence events. In the other arena, ideas
of moral reflexivity and moral reasoning marched on without acknowledging the significance of children in the generation of this way of
thinking or as possible moral actors in the larger picture. It was this
lack of congruity that led us to bringing these two sites together.

A digression on moral reflexivity and reasoning

Thus far we have been using terms like 'ethic of care' or 'moral reflexivity' as if their meaning was clear and as if there was no contest over
their meaning or significance. This is unsatisfactory to the extent that
not everyone is familiar with the discursive traditions in which these
ideas have arisen, and for many the concept of the 'ethic of care' in

particular is unpopular because of its apparent association with care as service provision or as an act which creates dependency in others. Some are critical of the concept because it sounds like an idealization of mothering skills or because they imagine that the sensibilities associated with an ethic of care are (either in actuality or ideologically) feminine attributes. This has given rise to accusations of bias (against caring men) or of essentialism (resurrecting the idea of maternal instincts). These criticisms are largely based on an incorrect reading of Gilligan's (1982) original work and also fail to take account of the extensive development of these ideas in the two decades following its publication.[2] There is not the space to detail these debates here, but it is perhaps important to outline the trajectory of which this work is a part.

Starting with Gilligan, we suggest that one of the most important contributions that she made was to bring questions about moral reasoning outside the confines of philosophy or developmental psychology and into everyday life. Her impact was considerable because it transgressed disciplinary boundaries and, arguably, put questions of moral reasoning back on to a wider political, sociological and policy agenda. Put very simply, she argued that Western culture had prioritized one form of moral reasoning over another and that this had had important consequences for society. Priority was given to objectivity, equality, autonomy and impartiality; this reached its pinnacle in our systems of justice, but could also be found in everyday life. She argued that other forms of moral reasoning were not seen as ethical at all but as partiality, subjectivity, interdependence and unfairness. She gave a label to these denigrated forms of moral reasoning and called them an 'ethic of care'. Thus the mode of resolving moral dilemmas which ensures that everyone has a little of what they need, rather than creating winners and losers, or a style that prioritizes the avoidance of hurt over equality, was identified as legitimate and as a necessary counterbalance to the ethic of justice.

These ideas were further developed by Joan Tronto (1993), who expanded the concept of care as a political ideal and as something to guide political philosophy and policy. Both Tronto and Sevenhuijsen (1998) clearly associated an ethic of care with feminist philosophy and its broad critique of Kantian and Cartesian thought. But their work entwines with that of other feminist thinkers such as Benhabib (1992), M. Griffiths (1995) and Young (1997), who do not work so directly within the ethic of care framework, but whose ideas build on and give further substance to this way of thinking. In particular these authors have dealt extensively with ideas of interdependence, moral reflexivity, mutual respect and how to act ethically in modern communities or even under 'post-modern' conditions.

Griffiths emphasizes the need for an autonomous self as the basis of moral agency, but her concept of autonomy is based on the idea of a self that is formed in a web of connections with others, not in isolation. Her concept of autonomy also acknowledges fluctuations in conditions of dependence and independence, in that no one can live outside the need for and demand for care and support at various stages in their lives. Benhabib also revises traditional moral philosophical concepts, rejecting the universalist tradition of Kant and others to produce a 'moral point of view' which works as a form of 'moral conversation' which is 'local' rather than a set of abstract principles with are a constant point of reference in a transcendental mode. She is to a certain extent developing Habermas's theory of communicative ethics, with its emphasis on the crucial importance of mutual respect and where debate and conversation provide the method of arriving at a moral consensus. Like Young, however, she is critical of Habermas for his attempts to produce a universal moral code and for maintaining the idea of the social contract as the basis of his conversational ethics. The social contract presumes a society or community of equals who can then converse on the basis of this equality, but, as Pateman (1988) has argued, the freedom to sign up to this social contract has always been limited to a particular sector of the (white, male, middle-class) community, and women (and children and others) have been excluded from its terms of reference. The difficulty for Benhabib, and particularly for Young, is how to incorporate difference or inequality into the basically useful concept of the moral conversation. One solution is to ensure that everyone does have a voice so that their point of view can be heard; this in turn requires the existence of both mutual respect and reciprocity.

Young develops these ideas through the concept of 'asymmetrical reciprocity', which she finds more useful than the basic proposition that inequality can be attended to by the practice of 'standing in the shoes of the other' (otherwise known as symmetrical reciprocity). Extrapolating from her argument to the situation of children and adults, Young would suggest that adults have difficulty in putting themselves in the shoes of children because they project on to children what they remember of their own childhood. So they do not see the child in question, but an image of themselves as children. She would also argue that for an adult to put themselves in the shoes of a child can often mean that the adult transposes their own class position, ethnic identity and so on, thus obliterating the significance of these important material and cultural differences. In a sense, Young is arguing that symmetrical reciprocity is impossible and so it is better to acknowledge this and keep it in the foreground of our thinking rather than pretend that we have overcome inequalities. The term asymmetrical reciprocity (cumbersome though it is) is a reminder that adults should not fool themselves that they know what children think or want by pretending that they can really take the standpoint of children. Young states that 'Participants in communicative interaction are in a relation of approach. They meet across distance of time and space and can touch, share, overlap their interests. But each brings to the relationships a history and structured positioning that makes them different from one another, with their own shape, trajectory, and configuration of forces' (1997: 50). From our perspective this notion of asymmetrical reciprocity is useful because it also means that linguistically we do not fall into the trap of 'speaking' of children as if they are socially equal to adults when we know that they are not. Our language does not ignore these differences, while at the same time we can reflect upon children as competent moral agents whose voices should be accorded respect.

These ideas are, of course, open to perpetual argumentation, particularly where moral philosophy seeks to provide actual guidelines for behaviour. But it is not necessary for us to follow these labyrinthine debates closely, because our task here is different. We are concerned to explore the extent to which children operate with transcendental or universalistic moral principles (in the Kantian sense), the way in which they might engage in other forms of moral reasoning (in the Gilligan sense), and the extent to which they are able to engage in moral conversations (in Benhabib's sense). As Gilligan herself recognized, an ethic of care and an ethic of justice are not mutually exclusive; they do coexist, even though one has usually been denigrated in favour of the other. Moreover, she argued that we need to find ways in which both can be brought together more successfully. We should not be surprised, then, that children have recourse to both of these forms of reasoning. But engaging in a moral conversation requires more than this, because it requires that the child is treated with respect and as a member of a moral community (even if they are acknowledged to be structurally unequal).[3] It also requires parents and others to acknowledge (implicitly or explicitly) that they are part of this moral conversation. As we shall see, we found that some children were quite comfortably located in the conditions conducive to moral conversation; others were fighting for the 'right of entry', while others had no knowledge that such a place existed yet, or even that it could exist. Through our research we sought to explore how readily children could engage in these moral conversations in a post-divorce context. We traced what the children had to say by presenting them with vignettes, hypothetical scenarios which typified the problems that children of divorced or separated parents have to resolve. The discussion is divided into four sections: an ethic of fairness, an ethic of care, an ethic of respect, and moral conversations. In our conclusion we shall start to raise questions about how moral conversations can be supported or facilitated in the policy arena – points which will be pursued further in our final chapter.

Children's moral reasoning on post-divorce family life

An ethic of fairness

We use the idea of an ethic of fairness rather than a fully fledged ethic of justice because we did not require the children to range as widely over issues which would have been pertinent to such a concept. The ethic of fairness is, however, a major component of any ethic of justice in that it presumes a sense of equality: it rests on the idea that different parties are equally entitled in principle and that there should be some objective measure of the distribution of goods or assets.

> *Q: Is there anything that you might like to change?*
> ROSIE (9): Yes. For there to be *eight* days in the week. That's the only thing.
> *Q: What difference would that make?*
> ROSIE: Four days with both people.

Rosie's way of ensuring complete equality was to wish for a more easily and equally divisible week so that there could be complete fairness for her parents and for herself. It was interesting that many of the children who were being co-parented in both our samples saw themselves as having to give equal amounts of themselves to each parent and as being almost arbiters in what was fair and equal treatment. They felt that they benefited too though:

> PETER (11): [The co-parenting arrangement] is fair I think.
> *Q: So what makes it fair?*
> PETER: Well mum likes to get shot of me every now and again . . . and so does my dad.
> *Q: OK, and what do you think are the best things about it for you?*
> PETER: That I can see everybody all the time and they get a fair share of seeing me.

One of the vignettes we used tapped directly into this issue of fairness. This vignette was based on a story about a child who lived most of the time with their mother and saw their father on alternate weekends. We chose this to use with the children who were being co-parented, but we restricted its application to older children because it was concerned with financial issues. The question was based on whether it was fair for a residential mother to insist that a child's father should pay for the swimming lessons that he wanted. In this vignette we made it clear that the boy in question was not being co-parented although he saw his father regularly. Half of the children (eight out of fifteen) said that the parents should split the costs equally between them.

> LOUISE (14): I think they should pay half each actually 'cos it's like they both lived with the child. I think they should both pay half each. It's only fair.

> JAMES (12): I don't know. They really should like both pay, pay alternative weeks or something.

Three of the children thought it would only be fair if the mother paid for the swimming lessons because the child lived with her and so was her responsibility, not the father's.

> KARL (14): Well, you don't really know the full story, but I mean, it's nothing to do with his dad is it really?

The remaining four children thought that one had to take more things into account before it was possible to judge what would be fair. These four moved away from strict equality towards the more rounded notion of equity:

> MATT (15): It depends how much she gets paid. It depends how much he gets paid and who gets Child Benefit.

> FRANCES (12): It depends. The mum has to pay . . . if she only goes [to her father's] on alternate weekends then the mum has to pay for feeding her and buying clothes and things, more than the dad does and so if it's just swimming lessons on Wednesdays then it would probably make up for not buying food and things and clothes.

What was so interesting about these responses is the way they reflect the positions available in the wider (adult) social debate about child support. The children who thought that the costs should be shared equally gave priority to the equal moral responsibility of mothers and fathers which gave rise to an equal financial responsibility. The ones who thought that the residential parent should pay saw her as having moral and de facto responsibility for the child – and indeed the benefit of having the child living with her – and so they thought that it followed that she should pay the costs incurred. The last group took it for granted that parents shared a moral responsibility, but then added the element of means assessment to make it financially equitable rather than simply equal.

These days it is unlikely that a majority would agree with the children who said that the residential parent alone should pay, and Karl's assertion that it was nothing to do with the father[4] would certainly be frowned upon by many, especially policy-makers. But Sam (11) captured the essence of this argument when he said, 'Her mum gets more time with him so she should pay for him.' In this perspective the child is a source of pleasure and value to the parent and, on a credit and loss calculus, the residential parent is seen as having the benefit of most of the child's company and should therefore shoulder the costs. It was a straightforward balancing of time and money, where the child in this case did not value money more highly than time.

Fairness, then, was a relative concept which could be used in a variety of ways and applied to a wide range of situations. Whether something was fair or not depended on the specific context combined with the experiences available to the children to draw upon. While some co-parented children and young people attached importance to the fairness of arrangements, this did not always mean a strict equality between the parents or an even 'sharing out' of the children. It could also mean an equitable approach which entailed taking into account the practical circumstances and emotional needs of all those likely to be affected. On this basis children could regard it as perfectly fair to spend more time with one parent than another if one of them put a disproportionate amount of effort or time into caring for the child. So if one parent was 'unfair' then an uneven distribution of time was seen as being fair across the board:

> BETH (14): Dad doesn't feel it's fair me spending more time at mum's but it does work out fairly because he's got all his meetings to go to and I'd be really fed up and wanting to go home or see my friends. It means I don't have to spend too much time with my dad, but I've still got him, I still see him.

This last quotation shows how important it ultimately is to combine understandings of how children reason ethically from both vignette, or hypothetical, questions and from questions that tap into their actual experiences.

An ethic of care

Q: If you had a wish for your family now, what would it be?
SELINA (16): Mmm, that's really hard because they both are so happy now. Dad's really happy with Gill and mum's really happy with Paul. They've both changed a hell of a lot and they've both got their own lives. And, you know, they're both really happy. But in another way, I'd love it if they got back together just so that I didn't have to move house every week. It's like putting your life into a couple of carrier bags every week and I'd love not to have to do that. I'd really love to not have to do that. It's not about them being together. That's not the important thing . . . I'd love to have one permanent base and have mum and dad living there because I want to spend my time with those two people. But I love Paul and I love Gill as well and . . . fitting them into it . . . [laughs] . . . wouldn't work. . . . And I'd rather have this and them both be happy. And I'd much prefer this moving house every week, and them to be happy than to have it the other way.

Two of the core elements of Gilligan's ethic of care were the notions of connectedness and of the avoidance of harm/hurt. Both of these elements are present in the quotation above. For Selina what was important was that she retained a strong relationship with both parents (and their new partners) and she was prepared to sacrifice some quality of life in order to preserve this. But, equally, she did not want those people to sacrifice or compromise their happiness to resolve her own dilemma. She valued their happiness, not just her own.

Jennifer Mason has argued strongly that in conceptualizing an ethic of care we need to move beyond seeing it as 'simply' activity or 'simply' affection/love. She argues that we need to pay attention to the significance of thinking and feeling in the activity of care. She therefore uses the terms *sentient activity* and *active sensibility*. Examples of sentient activity in relation to care and responsibility for family and kin might be, she suggests, 'attending to the well-being of others', 'being attuned to the individuality of others', 'interpreting the moods of others'. In addition it might embrace 'thinking through, organising or orchestrating relationships between oneself and others'. Mason has developed these arguments because of her concern that sociological work on 'care' focused too much on the labour of care rather than its thoughtfulness. Thus, for example, she would argue that a person who cares for another would not simply buy and cook the food that the other might need for sustenance, but would think through the menu and the person's preferences and would select and prepare food according to these sensibilities.

Her work is particularly important when considering the position of children. Although children may sometimes be physical carers in the sense of looking after disabled family members or taking on certain tasks for the benefit of the household, it is not expected that they should take on much of this kind of work in normal circumstances. This means that it is assumed that parents care for children, but that children do not care for parents. Mason's reformulation (which was not based on work with children) actually allows us to see the extent to which children do engage in active sensibility and sentient activities.[5] It was with this formulation in mind that we posed specific vignettes to the children and young people we interviewed that would allow for expressions of these active sensibilities. One of the hypothetical problems we asked the co-parented children to solve concerned a child who lived with their mother and was due to go to stay with their father one weekend when they received an invitation to go to Alton Towers with a friend instead. We posed this dilemma to the children under 14 years old as we thought it would be more meaningful to them.

The largest group (twelve of the thirty-eight children we asked) felt that if the child did not see the father very often that they should sacrifice the trip, or at least rearrange it so that they would not miss the weekend with the father. This was based on their understanding that the child did not see the father very frequently, although some children asserted that fathers were more important than friends and so gave us to understand that they should always take precedence. The remaining twenty-six children found a range of solutions. Eleven of them sought some kind of compromise which might entail taking the father to Alton Towers as well, especially if the friend's parents were going.

ELIZABETH (9): I think I'd rather go to my dad's if I only see him on weekends. I love him more than I love Alton Towers. Or I would ask my dad to come with me, so I would see my dad and I would go there as well.

CLARE (11): Well I think it might be nice if he stays with his father, because he's part of his family and he'll be really upset if he doesn't go. But his father could get a ticket to Alton Towers and go with them really. And that would be even nicer because they'd be able to be together and he'd be able to be with his best friend at Alton Towers.

Some of the children, especially the older ones, thought it would be too embarrassing to take their fathers along too, and so they had to think of more complex solutions. This one by Claudia was a classic example of moral reasoning from a care perspective:

CLAUDIA (12): I'd see what I was doing and then I'd try and work a way round it so I'd get to see . . . I'd get to go out with my friend but I also see my dad, like I could go and see my dad first, then go out with my friend, like see if I could come home a bit earlier or leave a bit later so then it's only a bit of a gap, then I'd get my dad back a souvenir or something and say, 'It was fun', and I'd tell him what happened and stuff, like have a nice conversation.

Claudia involved her father in the hypothetical event so that he did not feel excluded and she proposed to cut down on the time she would be away to lessen his feelings of hurt. She saw this sort of situation as an extremely hard moral dilemma and drew on her own experiences of when she had not seen one of her parents for a long time because they had been on holiday. So she knew what it was really like to want to see one of her parents and for them to want to see her. Hers was perhaps a perfect example of active sensibility.

Such compromise solutions were not only available to older children:

ROBERT (5): I think he should go to Alton Towers and then the next day he can go to dad's house.
Q: *Right, so how could he arrange that?*
ROBERT: If he could say to his dad, 'Dad is it all right if I come to your house tomorrow and go to Alton Towers with my friends?'
Q: *And what would his dad say?*
ROBERT: He'd say, 'As long as you're quite early in the morning when you get to my house.'

As a 5-year-old, Robert gave his account in a rather different way to Claudia, but it appears that he was aware of the relative value of the time spent with the father. He was fully aware that the compromise arrangement would require that he got to his father's house early the next day in order to make up for some of the lost time. He was less in control of the situation than Claudia, but he came to a similar compromise solution – although he put the words of this solution into the mouth of the adult.

Only five of the children said that the child in the vignette should simply go to Alton Towers with their friend because it was such a wonderful offer. But this was because some of the children found this situation of conflicting commitments commonplace and so did not see that there was much of a dilemma to resolve. They were used to altering their arrangements with their parents and assumed that this would be easy for all children. This reminds us again that we cannot understand the way children reason morally without understanding the context in which they have faced dilemmas and the resources they can call upon to help them resolve such problems. But this does not mean that the children could not reflect upon their own context nor that they simply responded to it without awareness. A particularly important element was, of course, how they expected parents to react to the situation.

With some of the children the ethic of care operated in a dimension that we had not anticipated. We had imagined that the children would respond in ways which centred on how the child in the vignette would deal with the situation. We did not expect that some would 'recast' the moral dilemma as one in which adults should participate. In other words some children felt that although they could see solutions, parents as adults had a duty to lighten their children's burden by adopting an ethic of care themselves.

> JAMES (12): I think his dad should let him go and then he'd be able, 'cos his dad should want him to be happy. . . . I suppose he can like see him later and can see him the next day.
> Q: *Right, but if it was really important to him to go to Alton Towers with his friend, you think his dad should let him go?*
> JAMES: I think his dad should let . . . respect that and let him go, yes, if it means that much to him.

> ELLA (14): I think his dad should understand that he wants to go to Alton Towers, he probably won't get another chance very quickly.

> TOM (12): I mean, if the dad's nice to her and sort of loves her and stuff, he should do the best for her and say, 'if you want to go, go, don't worry about me, I'll do something else.' I mean it is not as if she is going to be away the whole weekend.

Adam, quoted below, combined two elements of the ethic of care. He initially thought that how the father would respond was dependent upon his qualities as a father – either kind or not kind. But he then added a further dimension in which he showed that he could understand that the extent to which a father might miss his child interacts with his willingness to let his son be away for a day. He drew on his own experience of missing his father and also revealed that, when he had missed his father in the past and was waiting to see him, he did not ask his friends to come round to play, presumably so that his time with his father was not shared or diluted in any way.

> ADAM (6): He should ask his dad if he could go there. . . . If he was a kind daddy he would say 'yes'. If he wasn't he'd say 'no'. . . . So, hasn't Jordan seen his daddy for a long time?

Q: Mmm, probably a week or two weeks.
Adam: So he'll probably say 'no' then. If [it was] a week he'll probably say 'yes' but two weeks . . . 'Cos he hasn't seen him for ages, like me, but I don't see my daddy for ages and I wait and I wanted to see him, but I didn't ask for a friend round or anything.

An ethic of respect

An exclusive focus on an ethic of care can produce an interpretation of accounts in which children are perceived as unduly concerned with the welfare of others and lacking a sense of self-interest or autonomy. In other words, they can look too good to be true. Philosophical debates on the ethic of care would deny that this overweening altruism is a necessary corollary, and debates on moral agency and moral action are usually founded upon clear assumptions about the individual as having a sense of self and a degree of autonomy. M. Griffiths (1995), for example, focuses in considerable detail on the idea of the 'self' and the need for autonomy in order to be able to be 'free' to make moral decisions. However, these concepts of 'self' and 'autonomy' are not the isolated, individualistic forms found in most versions of liberal democratic thought (see also Sevenhuijsen, 1999). Rather, the formation of the self, according to Griffiths, takes place in a web of relationships and interdependencies, and autonomy can only be achieved through fluctuating degrees of dependency on others at various stages of the life course.

One of the reasons that we find it hard in Western cultures to appreciate children as moral actors is because they are seen as so dependent upon their parents. They are both emotionally and economically dependent to varying degrees for a considerable time. This 'truth' is partial, however. These necessary dependencies do not preclude the development in the child of a sense of self and autonomy, indeed it is one of the tenets of modern child-rearing that this is one of the objectives of parenting. But it is also a partial 'truth' because such an observation leaves unsaid the extent to which adults are also dependent on others, including children, for emotional and material support. Thus we operate with binary assumptions about children as dependent and adults as independent. There are, of course, important differences between adulthood and childhood, but we suggest that it is problematic to effect a closure on the possibility of children's moral agency by a simple and blanket reference to their presumed dependency. Theirs is a particular form of dependency on adults which, taken in the round, is actually part of the wider web of interdependence of family and civil life.

In our interviews with the children in both our samples we attempted
to tap in to this question through vignettes based on whether or not
children should be able to decide which parent they would live with.
In this section on an ethic of respect we shall focus once more on the
ESRC sample, but we shall move to the Nuffield sample in the next
section on the concept of moral conversations which further develops
these ideas. The vignette posed a situation in which, on the separation
of their parents, two sisters decided that they were happy to move
back and forth between their parents on a 50-50 basis while their
older brother, 'Jack', said that he would not do this and that he wanted
to stay living with his father rather than moving back and forth. We
did not give ages to the children in this vignette because that might
have led the children to place a specific sort of attention on age when
we wanted them to be free from our cultural presumptions that the
ability/right to make decisions comes at a certain age. We posed this
vignette to forty-one children. Only five children replied that 'Jack'
should be more or less obliged to do the same as his sisters, and this
was mainly because they thought that he was probably making the
wrong decision and that he would realize this in time.

> Tom (12): Yes, well [his age] would make a difference in my opinion
> anyway, because if he's too young, he's making the wrong decision I
> would say, but it depends like, if he's over 13 or something it's sort of
> his decision really. But being me I would, if I was the dad or something,
> I wouldn't want that because you can't really have a life without both
> parents really, because the mum's meant to be there and the dad's meant
> to be there. That's how we've come to be a big civilization us humans.
>
> Rosie (9): Well I think Jack's making a completely wrong decision. . . . I
> mean, seeing as he's spent the whole of his life with his mum so far, he's
> going to miss her loads.

All of the other children thought that Jack should be allowed to do
what he chose if he was determined and serious about it. Eight of these
thirty-six children said that he should try moving back and forth between his parents for a while before he rejected the idea, but said that
if he still felt determined to live full-time with his father he should be
allowed to do so. None of the children suggested that his wishes were
immaterial, but they varied on how strong a stance they took in relation to the status of a child's wishes. Thus some said that his parents
should let him do what he wanted to do – up to a point. In particular,
many said that 'Jack' should be allowed to choose to live full-time
with his dad, but that he really should visit his mother and even stay
with her occasionally because he would discover that he missed her.

Few of these children could imagine a situation in which a child might hate or dislike, or even be fearful of, a parent, and so the idea of not seeing one of them was not attractive in any way.

In this category these responses are typical:

CLAUDIA (12): I mean his mum will be a bit upset . . . I think he should go and visit his mum anyway, but I suppose it depends if she's really horrible to him or something, but I think it really should be what he wants to do because it's OK for the parent to say, 'Oh well Jack can come here Monday, Tuesday and Wednesday and Thursday and like the rest of the time being with so and so' but I mean if Jack doesn't want to do that then he won't be happy.

COLETTE (13): I think they should just do what they want. Like I think he should stay with his dad.
Q: Would it make a difference, do you think, how old Jack is?
COLETTE: It depends, like if he was really young they'd just be [saying] 'Oh, we're organising it for you' or 'You don't really know what you want blah, blah, blah, you're young', 'cos that's what my dad's always saying. . . . Everybody's going to say to you, aren't they, 'Oh I know what I want to do', but then every adult's going to say, 'Oh no you don't, you're only this age'.

While the majority of the children focused either on the idea that children should experiment before rejecting the proposal or emphasized that ultimately the child's happiness was the key issue, a group of about fifteen co-parented children conceptualized the problem in rather different terms. The former could be said to be adopting a kind of paternalistic welfare approach. But the latter leant more towards a perspective which saw the child as having the capacity and legitimacy to make his own choices and to have these choices respected. These children did not exactly adopt a rights approach, but something more subtle which is perhaps akin to the idea of the child as a participating citizen in the forum of the family. Not only did they think that the child should be in a position to articulate his views, they felt that – as long as the conditions were right – those views should carry weight.

HOPE (14): I think Gina and Penny should do what they want to do and do what I do, but I think what Jack wants to do should be respected.

KARL (14): Well, I think it would be, you know, it's really their choice, it's the children's choice what they want to do, I mean, well I suppose legally it isn't but sort of morally it is really.

BETH (14): I think it really should be his decision, but I think they should try to persuade him just to spend an hour . . . because otherwise it will be really hard on his mum.

ANDRIJKA (10): Well, I don't think it should be up to the parents to decide if they wanted to split equal times or wanted to spend one time with one person, I don't think it should be up to them. I think Jack should be able to choose, but I still think it would be a bit hurtful to his mum.

What was particularly interesting about these comments was that these children felt that 'Jack' should have the choice, even if he made the wrong decision. They could also weigh up the importance of his having the choice to make the wrong decision against the fact that his mother would be upset. Most of them assumed that, given time and more experience of his new situation, he would come to realize that he had made the wrong decision, but they were prepared to allow him to come to that realization rather than to force him. They were also inclined to think that the disappointed parent should handle their own hurt rather than inflicting it on the child.

ROSIE (9): [His mother would be] very put out. Yes. I mean, obviously, she'd respect his point of view. But . . . quite put out anyway.

In this respect, some of the children are at considerable variance with the way in which English family law currently operates. Although there is a congruence between ideas about the significance of age when it comes to taking decisions, these children were apparently more willing to accept the idea that children should be able to make 'wrong' decisions. It is much harder for courts and welfare officers to allow children to make what are perceived to be 'wrong' decisions. If decisions are seen as wrong the child is too easily demoted from being the asymmetrical citizen of the family to the immature child who needs others to make the 'right' decision for him or her.

Moral conversations

The Nuffield vignette on residence was framed slightly differently from the ESRC vignette. In this one we suggested that a child whose parents were separating is worried because her parents want her to choose who she will live with and she does not know which one to choose. Where necessary a prompt was given on whether the child should actually choose or whether it should be someone else. Forty children were given this vignette and their answers covered the same ground as with the ESRC sample: for example, they thought the age of the child involved was important, but they were more likely to raise issues of how kind and/or caring each parent was or to focus on practicalities such as how close each parent lived to school (fourteen children out of forty). This emphasis might have been a consequence of how the vignette was framed rather than anything else, but it shows that practical realities are important to children.

> CHELSEA (8): Well she should live with her mother, because she sees her more than her dad.

> QUENTIN (13): I'd ask him like why they're getting divorced and which one he thinks would be more sensible to stay with, and which one's like nearer to the school, 'cos if they're moving away it will affect his social life.

> TIM (10): I think he should live with his mum. That's because I live with my mum and I think it's best if I live with my mum because my mum puts more money in than my dad, because girls are like that more than boys, but my dad puts in quite a lot of money into things, like £135 every month to look after us.

> SABRINA (10): Who he gets on with, and who's close to his school and things like that, who's got a big house, whether he's got his own bedroom.

Other children put affective ties higher than material or practical considerations (thirteen out of forty), concentrating on how the child got on with his or her parents or how kind and caring each parent was. Of course the two issues of affective ties and practicalities cannot always be easily separated, especially when children are thinking of the care they receive from their parents. For some the primary carer was the obvious choice:

> MARK (15): I mean, if I had had to choose between my mum and my dad, I would have gone for my mum 'cos she was more there for me than my dad was really. My dad was there and we had some good fun at times, but he never really bothered, he was more away at work sort of thing. I remember being a lot more with my mum than my dad.

The children and young people in the Nuffield sample were also highly attuned to the problem of having to make a choice which would upset one parent. This issue was slightly more apparent with this group, we suspect because the vignettes asked the children to focus on making a decision whereas the ESRC vignette on residence focused on a boy who had already made up his mind. Basically these children were fully aware of the potential consequences of 'choosing' one parent over the other.

QUENTIN (13): But if he chooses his dad, his mum will be in a mood thinking you love your dad more than me, and if you choose your mum your dad will think it.

In order to get around this problem some of the children said that the child should split the time equally between the parents; this was the response of children who were not being co-parented as well as those who were.

BEN (14): Well I'd sort of tell him to go and live with both his mum and dad, because if you go to live mainly with one, unless you hate the other a lot, then you'll miss the other parent, and so he's better off, going and living with both of them at alternate times.

What emerged from the discussions around this vignette, however, was that the children also found another solution to the problem of having to choose between parents. This was the apparently simple expedient of talking to both of their parents about the situation, or even of having a family conference to talk over the issues. This solution allowed everyone to be involved in the decision process, but took the responsibility of making invidious choices away from the child. It was the children themselves who introduced the distinction between being *involved* in a decision and *making* a decision or choosing (our emphasis throughout).

NINA (11): Well *she should be involved in sorting it out* but I don't think her parents should actually make her choose, or anything.
Q: Why?
NINA: Because she is going to feel awful if she sees one parent and lets the other down, and they shouldn't make her do that.

QUENTIN (13): *I think you should like have a debate* so you can say, like, why you'd choose your mum 'cos she's got more time for them and she can cook for them, and your dad could say 'Well, I've got a step-mum', but then the mum could say, 'Well, they really don't like it and they wouldn't be happy with her', say to the judge or someone . . .

MARK (15): I think he should have an opinion, I don't think he should necessarily decide, *he should get a say in it, he shouldn't just be left out*, I mean it's his life as well, he shouldn't be stuck with someone he didn't want to be with.

RALPH (8): Well, he should choose but he can discuss it with his mum and dad as well.
Q: Who should decide then?
RALPH: *All discuss it together.*

JAKE (11): I think there should be some kind of agreement between him and his parents as to what should happen, rather than him just deciding who he wants to live with. . . . I think the people who are involved should get to decide, not by themselves, but by *helping each other to reach some kind of agreement* as to what would be best.

The emphasis placed by the children on joint discussions and negotiations is instructive. They recognized that it would often be a huge burden to place on a child, especially a young child, to expect them to choose between parents, but only the very youngest in our sample felt that the decision should only be taken by the mother and father because it would be too hard for the child. The others thought that the child should either be able to choose themselves (some were adamant about this) or they wanted a group decision in which the child's views could be aired and taken into account.

Jake's suggestion that there should be a way of 'helping each other to reach some kind of agreement' is particularly telling. It presumes that no one automatically knows what is best, but that it will emerge from negotiation and discussion in which everyone participates. Even those children who did not use the terms 'debate' or 'discussion' would suggest that the child should speak to both their parents to tell them how they feel. All these children appear to be assuming that children have a right to some degree of participation in family life and how it is organized, especially in relation to something as momentous as divorce. They were also working with an assumption of – to use Young's terminology – asymmetrical reciprocity. That is to say that, while they took for granted (in principle at least) that children can have views and can voice them, they did not assume that parents and children are the same, nor that they have the same knowledge or resources.

A moral conversation of the sort that these children were 'advocating' presumes a number of basic elements. It presumes that children have a 'stake' in the family and in their futures, that they can deal with difficult issues, that they can participate and, ultimately, that other parties will actually listen and place value on what is said. They took for granted that they would be entitled to be involved, although research suggests that parents in general are actually unlikely to involve their children or even fully inform them of what is going on (Smart and Neale, 1999). As Mark, quoted above, said, 'I mean it is his life as well', suggesting that this recognition should establish at least a basic principle of participation.

Moral conversations are therefore constructed from elements of an ethic of fairness, of care and of respect. Young's notion of asymmetrical reciprocity allows us to see that, even where there are inequalities and differences, it is possible for moral conversations to take place. In the case of a parent and child, it does not mean that the parent treats the child as an adult, and it seems that many children are in any case fully aware that they – as children – should not have to shoulder the full weight of family problems, particularly where they concern arguments between adults. They were also acutely aware of the significance of age and the idea that participation rights relate to a degree of maturity and knowledge. But asymmetrical reciprocity requires respect, fairness and care, not exclusion and secrecy. The perspective that the children had on issues of residence and contact seemed to transcend the thorny problem of whether children should be involved or not in the divorce process and it had no difficulty in distinguishing between participation in a decision and being required to choose. For most the latter was simply unfair because it gave them too much responsibility and because it meant hurting one of their parents. Only where there was abuse or real hatred, or where one parent clearly would not care properly for the child, was it seen as really legitimate for a child to make such a decision in isolation. If forced to choose they often came up with practical or emotional measures by which to decide, or they came up with a compromise of sharing their time between both parents. All of these elements would, of course, be introduced in an open family discussion which would allow children to voice their concern over living with a stranger (i.e. new step-parent), moving away from school and friends, being looked after by a parent who works full-time, being an adolescent girl who feels she needs her mother and so on.

The idea of moral conversations is of course premised upon some notion of a democratic family, rather than collusive, repressive or emotionally damaging families, or families where violence is inflicted on the children or the mother. We shall discuss further the idea of democracy in families in the next chapter, but it is important to recognize that even where children lived in less than ideal circumstances, they often held in their imaginations the idea of a fairer, more egalitarian household. But just because all these children did not experience the full conditions which make moral conversations truly feasible, there is no reason to reject their vision. The questions that are posed by this are, firstly, whether adults can assume the responsibility of engaging in asymmetrical reciprocity, care, respect and fairness and, secondly, whether the system of family law can facilitate such a development. We shall address the latter problem in our final chapter.

6

Children, Citizenship and Family Practices

It is important to realize that separation and divorce do give rise to serious conflicts between the interests of parents and children. . . . But it is not enough simply to recognize the conflicts. They need resolution. The children's interests cannot be characterized as rights if they are equated with, or subservient to, those of the adults. Nor can they be so treated if the resolution of such conflicts is abandoned to the uncontrolled discretion of adjudicators.

Eekelaar, 1986: 173–4

Once we move away from an exclusive concern with state–individual or state–civil society relations and consider a more horizontal dimension of citizenship, which looks at relations within civil society and how children are positioned, then new relations are revealed and new questions of power, requiring justification, emerge.

Roche, 1999a: 476

Introduction

In the fields of law, political theory, sociology and philosophy, a great deal has been written on the related questions of citizenship and rights. Recently this literature has been extended to include discussions of children and the extent to which they can be deemed to be citizens and rights-bearing individuals. As the first quotation above suggests, one impetus to these new approaches has been divorce, which has allowed for a greater recognition that children and parents may have different interests and that children should perhaps have ways of expressing their views and being recognized as separate legal 'entities' even in routine situations. The second quotation alerts us to a more general shift in thinking towards considering the importance of rights and power relations between and across individuals in the sphere of civil society rather than thinking of rights solely as a bulwark for the individual against the state. These two developments have meant that 'the family' has become an increasingly legitimate site for further debate on the rights and standing of all its members, including children. In this chapter we cannot review the whole of the literature on this subject (see Squires, 1999), but we do want to take a subset of this emerging approach to children as our starting point.

A preoccupation with rights?

As Roche (1999a) has pointed out, much of the work on citizenship which has followed the original contribution of T. H. Marshall (1950) has adopted the idea that citizenship is inevitably founded upon the possession of rights (civil, political and social). Civil rights pertain to the legal domain and entail such rights as the freedom of speech or association. Political rights concern participation in the formal processes of democracy such as the right to vote. Social rights are those that safeguard the welfare of the individual and enable them to achieve a decent quality of life. Typically, children have not been included in discussions of citizenship because the only rights that are seen as appropriate for children have been a subset of social rights, such as the right to an education. Even the idea of a right to 'freedom from want', which is clearly something of significance to children as much as to adults, tends to have been construed as a duty on the parents (or the state) rather than a right of the child.

So, although children may be seen to be bearers of *some* rights, because these limited social rights are usually seen as subservient to civil and political rights, children are not defined as citizens. It has tended to follow, therefore, that to bring children into citizenship it is presumed that they must have more rights. This line of argument is not unique to children of course, and minority status groups such as women, disabled people, and people from ethnic minorities have all claimed the full array of rights in order to take their legitimate place amongst the citizenry of modern democracies. Historical precedent might suggest that this route will be a fruitful one, but there are clear problems associated with the assumption that it will also serve children.

Progress through rights?

There are two levels on which to assess the value of legal rights in relation to citizenship. One level concerns rights as a kind of rhetorical strategy with the aim of getting certain issues on to a political or policy, or even media, agenda. Rights talk is powerful because it can condense issues into a number of clear 'demands' and because in liberal democracies there is a tendency to feel that (almost) any lack of rights is a source of injustice. To claim rights is therefore to claim (potentially) a moral high ground almost prior to the debate commencing. This strategy can work towards changing a particular climate of opinion as long as it does not incur a backlash which associates rights claims with selfish individualism and thus sees them as socially harmful. It can also empower those who lack rights and produce a political identity which is affirmative. The importance of this should not be underestimated. The process of claiming rights and indeed the experience of having them (even if few are exercised), confers a sense of dignity, personhood and agency. This is why the idea of losing rights (no matter how archaic or irrelevant) can cause so much anger and dismay. Making rights claims need not result in legal reforms in order to have a beneficial effect, and sometimes the reforms achieved may be inadequate to the task, but even so the very act of claiming them can turn individuals or groups into visible 'citizenship material'. This may be very significant in terms of gradual cultural change which can impact on people's quality of life.

However, the power of rights rhetoric would soon evaporate if there was no substance behind the claims. This brings us to the second level, namely the consolidation of rights claims through various legal mechanisms, thus moving beyond claims in general to the possibility of individual redress. Legislation against various forms of discrimination or in favour of such things as equal pay or maternity rights in the last quarter of the twentieth century are of course examples of this. However, once one moves into this substantive legal forum, specific problems of precise definition occur and endless legal arguments and procedures begin to unfold (Franklin, 1986; Smart, 1989). One moves from a philosophical sphere into the sphere of legal practice where the individual's sense of dignity, agency, and personhood can quickly be erased by negative, debilitating and alienating experiences.

The daily practice of law and the idealized principles of citizenship do not always sit easily together. Even in the modest attempt to 'ascertain the wishes and feelings of the child' in proceedings under the Children Act 1989, English law has not yet found a satisfactory way of involving actual children or hearing directly what they may have to say (Sawyer, 1995). Judges do not want children to join legal proceedings, solicitors want to protect them from the negative effects of going to law, and children who become involved do not find it particularly gratifying (Masson and Winn Oakley, 1998). Once we move to the level of implementation a Pandora's box opens and valuable principles falter at the point of becoming practice (Freeman, 1997).

It may, of course, be a box that should be opened, especially if it could lead to a greater degree of critical reflection by a legal system that is currently so 'user-unfriendly' that any child or young person who comes into contact with it is at risk of being harmed. It may also be essential if rights claims by children are going to be taken seriously, or if they are to benefit from longer-term cultural change attendant upon such claims. But the point of our argument here is that there are costs associated with transforming these claims into individually enforceable rights, and it is therefore misleading to present legal rights as if they are solutions. They bring their own problems. This means that in the process of thinking about enlarging citizenship it is essential to attend to the problem of how these individual rights are activated. It is also necessary to think just as actively about other ways of achieving what the process of claiming rights for excluded or disadvantaged groups (rather than the enforcement of individual rights) can sometimes achieve. There need to be parallel strategies that will influence cultural change which work in tandem with more legally focused strategies.[1]

Conceptualizing the child as an autonomous legal subject

Many of the arguments centred on granting children more rights in order that they should be recognized as citizens harbour a particular vision of this citizen. For example, Freeman argues, 'The question we should ask ourselves is: what sort of action or conduct would we wish, as children, to be shielded against on the assumption that we would want to mature to a *rationally autonomous adulthood* and be capable of deciding on our own system of ends as free and rational beings?' (Freeman, 1997: 38, emphasis added). The problem here, of course, is, firstly, the assumption that children will want to mature into this epitome of liberal individualistic philosophy, and, secondly, that such an individual is socially desirable. Feminist philosophers have pointed to the fallacy of the idea that adults are rational, autonomous and free (Benhabib, 1992; M. Griffiths, 1995; Sevenhuijsen, 1998; Squires, 1999; Tronto, 1993; Young, 1997) and we have rehearsed some of these arguments in the previous chapter and elsewhere (Smart and Neale, 1999). Briefly, such a vision of the adult overemphasizes the autonomy of individuals by downgrading the network of intersubjective relationships in which individuals are nurtured, supported and formed throughout their lives. It overstates independence (freedom) and loses sight of the extent to which both adults and children are interdependent (caring for, as well as being responsible for, others). It is also a vision which celebrates a society where the basic social unit is the individual rather than a collectivity of some sort, no matter how small. In a society conceived in such a way, real children would have a hard time while waiting to grow up and join the ranks of the free and autonomous adult beings. As Minow argues, 'I find something terribly lacking in rights for children that speak only of autonomy rather than need, especially the central need for relationships with adults who are themselves enabled to create settings where children can thrive' (Minow, 1987: 1910). Although we might choose to frame this sentiment less in terms of 'need' than Minow does, we share her concern about a conception of rights which robs the individual of their context and removes any notion of the importance of intersubjective life.

But not only is this vision of society and social relationships limited, it may be misplaced to assume that this is what adults should project into the longings of children. As adults, we may interpret the solution to the problems we had when we were children as being housed in a package of legal rights akin to those we can exercise as adults, but actual children, during the course of their childhood, may not share this interpretation. Adults may want to 'have their day in court' for example, but children may not.

It is important here to be clear what we are saying because it may be interpreted as being an argument against children's rights and for leaving children to the benevolent (or otherwise) intentions of their families and others (Franklin, 1986). We are not suggesting that nothing should change. Rather, we suggest that to argue a case for recognizing interdependence is to argue for rights based more on an ethic of care than simply on an ethic of justice (Gilligan, 1982; Sevenhuijsen, 1998). It is not an argument for no rights at all. It is also to recognize that rights should be seen as one strategy and not the only method that can be deployed in the process of allowing children to enter into citizenship. As we argued in chapter 5, what children seem to want is social recognition, respect and inclusion rather than simply legal rights. They do not appear to want to be free, autonomous individuals, but persons in their own right in the context of a set of relationships. These persons in their own right should not simply be mistaken for the autonomous rights-bearing individual so familiar to liberal philosophy. It may be that in Western liberal democracies we can only become persons in our own right if we have the full array of legal rights, but this is a reflection of our culture of legal individualism rather than an ontological given. We would argue that the notion of personhood contained within the concept of a person in her own right is a much fuller entity than the anticipatory, litigious, rights-bearing subject of the law.

It may also be, as Roche (1999a) has pointed out, that there are different routes into citizenship as well as different degrees of citizenship. Drawing on arguments by Walby (1997) he points out that men and women may have had different pathways into citizenship, with men achieving first their social and civil rights, followed by their political rights; while women won first their political rights (the vote) before achieving social and civil rights. It may be that children will gain first their social rights, then their civil rights, and later their political rights. But he also points to the useful concept of 'partial citizenship' (Bulmer and Rees, 1996) which recognizes that citizenship is not a zero-sum concept with individuals either being citizens or non-citizens. He points out that some groups may be 'part in, and part out, of citizenship' and also that the character of citizenship is always uneven and contested. Partial citizenship is not promoted here as something to aspire to; rather, the concept is seen as a more adequate description of the reality of citizenship for most people.

There may of course be problems with this flexible and partial concept, particularly if it becomes prescriptive rather than descriptive. Governments may argue that certain minority groups, such as for example, travellers or refugees, do not need to be 'full' citizens and that they should be content with a few social rights. This is why we prefer to think in terms of citizenship-in-context. This idea acknowledges that citizenship is contested, but it avoids the problem of implying that partial citizenship is sufficient for some categories of people (a kind of second-class status) while insisting that citizenship is practised in a context for *all* citizens. However, there are hostages to fortune even in this formulation, not least because where children are concerned the overdetermining context is nearly always perceived to be chronological age. Thus, if citizenship-in-context for children came to mean that very young children enjoyed few benefits, with an expanding array as they grew older, then there would be no progress at all on our current position. This linear, chronological interpretation of 'context' would not challenge our understanding of the child's relationship to citizenship at all. It is true that English law has moved slightly beyond simply using age as a marker and now includes 'understanding'[2] or 'maturity'.[3] In the legal forum it is therefore no longer assumed that understanding and competence are directly related to chronological age. But although this has meant that children younger than 16 can be assumed to be competent, there is still an overarching presumption that they pass through developmental phases in an identifiable and measurable fashion. As a consequence, as Sawyer (1995) has pointed out, it is usually medical professionals who are called upon to assess how 'mature' or competent a child is. As we argued in chapter 1, the idea that children acquire an adult level of understanding or reasoning about the world in a smoothly linear fashion is now contested (Cockburn, 1999). Children's understanding is increasingly seen to be related to context and experience. Thus children may come to understand personal relationships at a very early age, even though they have little knowledge of world politics, or social institutions. Moreover, the sorts of experiences children may have had (rather than simply the quantity over time), influences their understanding. This relates to our discussion in chapter 4 on how the children of divorced or separated parents may have developed a deeper insight into relationships than other children and how they may grow up a little faster than others.

Harré (1986) has also argued that the *same* child can display different levels of understanding depending on the context he or she is in. So, for example, a parent or teacher or other adult who sees a child as immature and as having nothing of interest to say may simply convey to that child that it is inappropriate for them to display their actual depth of understanding. The same child, when spoken to in a different way, in a different context, may display very different levels of comprehension (see also James and Prout, 1996). 'Maturity' is therefore not a steady state; it may be context-dependent. Such insights as these reveal the catch-22 situation that children are caught in if they strive to be treated as citizens in the legal sphere. The law requires a child to demonstrate maturity or understanding before he or she can (in principle) participate, and yet an alien legal, or quasi-legal, forum may be the worst context in which to expect a child to reveal the depth and breadth of his or her understanding – particularly in cases of conflict between family members where much is at stake. Unfortunately, if a child cannot display 'maturity' in this public sphere, they are seen as ill equipped to take on the mantle of citizenship, because this notion of citizenship is disembodied and context-free. Indeed, a child, who cannot articulate complex feelings and ideas in a clear narrative form and in response to clearly 'loaded' questions in a strange or artificial environment, is seen as poor material for a serious legal subject and an unreliable witness.[4] An alternative approach might instead offer children increased opportunities to experience a range of contexts so that they could become equipped to participate as citizens. As Cockburn puts it: 'Central to my argument lies a critique of lay notions of experience and maturation. I suggest that there is no point in waiting for maturation without experience; it is experience that enables maturation' (1999: 7).

Of course, one of the most important contexts in which children gain experience and mature is within families. The problem, therefore, for the question of children and the acquisition of the status of citizenship resides predominantly with forms of family practice. Are children able to be citizens of their families? This is not a question of the rights of children versus the rights of parents, in which an equalization of the scales would produce the child citizen. It is a matter of how adults allow for the possibility of children becoming citizens within that most private of spheres, the home.

Opportunities to participate in family life

We already know that there exist a wide range of different parenting practices, some of which encourage children to participate in decision-making and to take responsibility for the quality of family life and communal living (Brannen and O'Brien, 1996; James, 1999; Gorrell-Barnes et al., 1998; Borland et al., 1998; Jamieson, 1998). There may even be wider cultural and demographic trends in Britain which will provide the foundation for widespread changes in parent–child relationships (Hendrick, 1997; Clarke, 1996). What is less certain is whether (and how) this participation works when parents are divorcing or separating. We cannot necessarily read off from one situation to another. Ackers (2000) has explored these issues in relation to decisions about moving home in the context where a parent (usually the father) might have a job or promotion prospects which require children to move to different countries and/or to different schools. She suggests that in these cases, where the interests of the most economically powerful adult are diametrically opposed to those of the child, the notion of participation becomes 'strained'. Her study showed that parents and children might hold 'family meetings', but these were designed to inform the children of the impending move, rather than to discuss whether it should happen or not. Children were sometimes offered the 'choice' to stay behind with relatives or at a boarding school, or were given the 'choice' to return home when they were older, but children certainly could not veto the decision for the family to move. By analogy, it is perhaps unlikely that parents would want to be so 'democratic' that they would allow children to veto their decision to divorce.[5] However, a degree of participation which would provide children with full information on what was likely to happen to them and which could allow for modifications to take into account their wishes and preferences, is not at all unthinkable. Yet there is some evidence to suggest that parents are reluctant to discuss even these practical issues with their children (Richards and Stark, 2000) and that they prefer them to know little about what is going on in the belief that this will minimize worry. Of course, parents themselves will not always know what is going to happen and, as Richards and Stark (2000) argue, parents may not pass on information for 'good' reasons. For example, they may not know whether the matrimonial home will have to be sold, whether they will have to move, how much money they will have and so on. The decision to separate may also be very sudden or dramatic, as in instances of violence or where one partner announces that they are leaving. Parents may not share their plans with each other, let alone their children. But this does not necessarily mean that in principle and in practice children cannot participate at all; that they cannot be treated as people in their own right; nor that they cannot be accorded the respect of being seriously listened to.

During the course of this research we often speculated on whether post-divorce family life might create greater rather than fewer opportunities for children to become active participants in their families' destinies. As we argue in chapter 4, divorce seems to change children's perceptions of their parents, and this may give rise to a slight shift in 'power' relations between the child and the adult. But this may be counterbalanced by feelings of insecurity, loss of material well-being and even by the behaviour of parents who feel that they need to become more authoritarian (or even more permissive) in the face of predicted delinquency or other reported harms that are likely to befall their children. We are therefore not making any claims that the post-divorce family is more (or less) democratic than the cohabiting family. We would suggest, however, that the cultural phenomenon of divorce has focused attention on children in such a way that post-divorce parent–child relationships can no longer be taken for granted in the way that relationships in cohabiting families may still be. The very fact that these relationships have been problematized means that there is a cultural space available in which change, reflection and redefinition can occur.

We shall explore these issues through three main case studies which exemplify different ways in which children can start to develop their own sense of agency and hence struggle to become participating members of their families, rather than simply objects of parental authority and care. How 'family democracy' manifests itself can vary greatly, and it is far from being an easily identifiable set of procedures (such as voting on decisions) that each family must go through in order to be democratic. Rather, it is, first, a matter of the extent to which a child is recognized as a person in their own right, with a voice and independent emotions and desires. Second, it is a matter of how other members of the family accommodate and compromise in the face of these considerations. These elements can vary greatly, and it is important to recognize that there are different routes into what we refer to as citizenship-in-context.

Three case studies

Lyra's story

Lyra's situation was not typical in that there were three parent figures in her life rather than two, but in every other respect her situation epitomized a particular style of democratic family life which can be said to be associated with progressive forms of parenting and a professional, but 'alternative', family background which is far from uncommon in metropolitan sectors of large cities. She was 11 years old when we interviewed her, and her mother (Mary) was a part-time social worker who had never been married to, or lived with, Lyra's father. Because of her status as a 'single mother', Mary decided to ask her then partner, Chris, to become Lyra's legal guardian. They lived together for several years, both sharing the care of Lyra. But Mary and Chris separated and, when Lyra was approximately 3 years old, she learned of the existence of her biological father, Tom. Thus, by the time we interviewed her some eight years later, Lyra had three parents and was spending time with both of her biological parents and with her guardian in three different households. What was particularly interesting about this story was the extent to which it was Lyra who decided she wanted to establish an ongoing, meaningful relationship with her father. As she explained:

> LYRA (11): But see, most of the time I'm at my mum's house I'm spending with my friends 'cos I don't get to go with my friends at my dad's house and at Chris's house I usually go out somewhere bike riding.
> *Q: So how did this arrangement get set up? I mean has it always been like this, or has it ever been different?*
> LYRA: Well yes, it has been different because, well my dad didn't know I was born until I was 3, which is why I had a guardian and my mum and Chris used to live in a house together, and then they moved into different houses . . . and I never used to stay at my dad's house, I just went on Fridays. So as the years have gone by I've got more time with my dad which I wanted.

Lyra referred to the first meeting with her dad as 'cool' although she did not remember a great deal about it given that she was only 3 years old. It would seem that Lyra's mother had decided at the time when her relationship with Chris was ending that she should give Lyra's father the opportunity to get to know his daughter and that Lyra had the right to know her biological father. It became the 'proper thing to do'. Lyra was very clear that, as she got to know Tom and to share his interests in music and other things, she wanted to stay with him more.

Q: So how did you arrange to see more of him?
LYRA: Well, I'm not really sure actually 'cos it all happened, I don't really know. They just told me, 'Would you like to see more of him?' and I said 'Yes'. They said, 'How much more?' and I said, 'As much as possible', so . . .

This account suggests a number of things. Firstly, her mother and former partner were willing to accommodate a third parent into their arrangement if that was what Lyra wanted. This had clearly not been their original intention because Lyra's birth had not been communicated to Tom. Yet over time Mary and Chris had begun to think differently and were willing to see their daughter as an independent person with the right to form her own relationships. When asked how she thought that all the adults in her life viewed the slightly complex arrangements that had been set up, Lyra was very clear about what the adults thought and wanted:

LYRA: I think . . . well, my mum likes it, I think she thinks it's quite good. And I think she thinks it's getting a bit hectic, but I'm not sure, 'cos it's like I think she thinks that I should spend a lot of time here and that it will be too unsettling for me, which is not what I think. I think Chris is OK with it, and Tom just wants to spend more time with me.

She went on to say that from her perspective it was 'as good as it gets'. At each house she got something different and she shared different interests and activities with each adult. She regarded her mother's house as her 'main' house or base. At Chris's house she could spend time watching TV and had access to chocolates, which her mother would not allow. She clearly did not feel it was necessary to spend her time intensively with Chris. But with Tom, because they had the least amount of time together, she spent all her time doing things with him. It is clear from the quoted passage above that Lyra felt that she could be perfectly open about her feelings and that she discussed things with her parents so that she was aware of their views. There appeared to be a great deal of openness, and Lyra was regularly asked whether she was happy with things.

LYRA: My mum asks me whether I like it and we usually have a big debate about [the fact that] I want to see Tom more. 'You can't, there's not enough time in the week', but they've raised it a bit so it's quite good. Yes, my mum's always, or sometimes, asking me, 'Do you like it the way it is?' and I say 'Yes'.

All three parents were involved in her decision about her secondary school and, according to Lyra, when she wanted something she would tell her mum, who would phone Chris for a view, and then would phone Tom to see if there was general agreement. If there was a problem 'they work something out'.

From this account it would seem that Lyra did feel herself to be a person of equal worth in her family, with a voice and with the expectation that her views would be taken into account. Negotiating Tom back into their lives could not have been easy for Mary or Chris, but it was accomplished slowly and with Lyra in a position of some control over events. Tom, it would seem, was wise enough not to demand a relationship with her nor to threaten legal action against her mother and, as a consequence, Lyra did not become a pawn in the adults' battle, but a player herself in the unfolding family story.

Louise's story

Lyra's story can be said to fit a certain ideal model of family life, based on consensus, discussion, reason and order. Her family had all the building blocks of a democratic lifestyle in place, including a commitment to children's participation and to sustaining relationships. But not all families are like this. Not all have the material resources to manage some of the problems, the quality of some relationships is poor, there are different cultures of family living, and sometimes some personalities clash. The important issue that needs to be addressed, therefore, is whether the idea of citizenship for children in families can only exist where there is consensus and 'harmony' or whether it can exist in different ways in very different sorts of family arrangements.

Louise was in a very different situation to Lyra. She was 14 when we interviewed her and her parents had separated four years previously. Both had re-partnered. She had one brother, two step-siblings and two half-siblings. Her 'real' brother, Damian (16) lived with her mother and the two new half-siblings (who were babies). She lived with her father, his wife and her stepbrother Dean (8). Her stepsister Becky (13) lived with her biological father in Sussex, but was in the process of moving back to live with her mother and Louise's father. Louise's story was full of conflict, hostility and, in the case of her mother and stepfather, violence.

LOUISE: [My parents] split up when I was 9 and I decided I wanted to live with my dad.
Q: What made you decide that?
LOUISE: Well I didn't like my mum's boyfriend and I thought it would be better living with my dad 'cos my mum had my brother, so my dad had one of the children and mum had the other one. It's a bit more fair.

Louise also made it clear that she did not get on with her brother at that time and that they wanted 'a bit of space without each other'. At the time we interviewed her they were getting on well. When her parents first separated her father went back to live with his mother until he could buy another place, and during that time Louise saw a lot of him. He had his new house for about six months before she decided that she wanted to live there. Her mother had met another man about two months after the divorce and he had moved in. But Louise said she was frightened of him at first, and even when she got to know him she did not like him. She said that she worried about her mother a lot because of 'what her boyfriend is doing to her' and the fact that being a woman meant that she could not defend herself. But her brother stayed with her mother and she felt that this offered her some protection and also provided an economic resource to her now that he was working.

When Louise's father first met his second wife (Sheryl) and she moved in with her two children, Louise objected. She argued with Becky and with Sheryl until things got so bad that Sheryl moved out. However, there was a reconciliation and Louise identified two important elements in this transformation of relationships.

LOUISE: Well when she came to live with us a second time, we started getting on better 'cos me and Becky used to get on better. And my dad and Sheryl got engaged and everything so it helped a bit. Me and Sheryl started talking properly without arguing . . . so it helped a lot. And then my mum says for me not to argue too much and I always listen to my mum.
Q: So you were able to talk to your mum were you?
LOUISE: Yes, 'cos when she was younger her real dad left her and she had an adopted dad and then my nan and my mum's adopted dad got divorced and she went on to somebody else and my mum went through a lot, so she understood. But with my dad's parents still being together, I couldn't talk to him.

Louise was not only able to use her mother as a resource, but also her grandmother and a close friend of hers at school who had had similar experiences. She talked through her problems openly, although she found her father a less useful resource in this process. However, she recognized how upset he was when Sheryl moved out and she explained that he wanted her to get help to stop her arguing with Sheryl and Becky all the time. It would seem that he was willing to defer his own personal needs and desires to give his daughter some time to adjust. It was a year and a half before Sheryl moved back in.

Louise had not expected her parents to split up, but it became apparent that there had been a lot of arguments in her family. Four years after the separation, her parents had little to do with one another and Louise was glad about this because it meant that there was no opportunity for arguments. She nonetheless spent a lot of time with her mother and saw a lot of her brother, who often stayed with her and her father. As she said, 'I got my say and I've been happy since I've lived here. And Damian's been happy since he lived at my mum's. He did live here for a while but then he went back to my mum's. If I hadn't had my say I would still be living with my mum and I wouldn't have been happy at all.'

Louise's family situation was not exactly harmonious: her parents did not have extensive material resources and it was clear that she had been through periods of considerable unhappiness and conflict. But she had a voice and her views were accommodated to a considerable extent. She had people she could discuss things with who did not draw her into taking sides as if she was merely an extension of their own emotions and desires. She was allowed to make choices, as was her brother. They were also allowed to change their minds. She was aware that parents could manipulate their children because her stepsister Becky had decided to move to live with her father when Sheryl married Louise's father. But having lived with him and his new wife for a year she had decided to return to her mother, only to find herself the object of her father's attempts to persuade her to change her mind. Louise therefore felt herself to be fortunate that she had choices and influence, even though these might not be exercised in circumstances exactly of her choosing.

Karl's story

Karl's situation was quite different again to that of Louise and Lyra. Karl was 14 and his parents, who were both middle-class professionals, had separated when he was 10. Their divorce had been acrimonious and they had remained actively hostile to one another, incurring frequent returns to court over contact and maintenance. Indeed they were still fighting over maintenance because his father wanted to reduce the amount he paid following the increase in his level of contact with Karl. At the time of the interview Karl spent more or less half his time with each parent. Neither parent had re-partnered and they lived in the same city, albeit some distance apart. Karl had a sister who was at university, but prior to that she had lived with their mother and only visited their father occasionally. He had no grandparents.

Because Karl's arrangements varied each week he talked about how complicated it was for him to organize his sporting commitments and his evening job. He kept the clothes his father bought him at his father's house, and the clothes his mother bought him at her house. His greatest difficulty in the practical sense was that his computer was at his mother's house and his father did not have one he could work on. His father also used his bedroom as his office and ran a very different regime to the more laid-back style of his mother's house. As he said,

> KARL: [My father] won't just let me do a simple thing and cook it myself, he sort of tells me how to do it whatever it is, even if I know how to do it, even if I've done it before loads of times. He tells me how to do it every time. . . . . It's sort of more rigid what we do, kind of thing.

Karl felt he had been caught between his parent's battles, particularly their battles over him. He felt they both tried to persuade him to live with them and he also revealed that they both 'shared' with him their dislike of their former spouse. His parents communicated only by letter, and we asked how this affected him:

> KARL: Well that on its own doesn't really worry me too much, but my mum says things about my dad, and my dad says things about my mum, you know, sort of, that's not very nice really for me. My mum's always going on about how annoying he is or whatever and my dad does the same.

Karl felt that he had a certain amount of choice in his situation, for example he could swap weekends around if he gave his parents notice. However, it was clear that he did not feel – even at the age of 14 – that he could do anything more radical. He did not communicate a great deal with his father, but spoke more to his mother. She was the one who would pay for extras and school trips and so on, even though Karl was aware that his father had substantial savings. Karl had got used to 'putting up' with things or letting himself 'get used' to them. So, for example, he would not ask his father for something if his mother, who was much less well off, could not afford it.

This does not mean that Karl was without his own resources of course. At the time when his father took his mother back to court to try to increase contact, his father arranged for him to have his own solicitor. The solicitor was concerned, however, that Karl was being manipulated and Karl himself said that he was subjected to 'quite a lot of pressure around that time'. We asked him what he did in response to this:

> KARL: Well, I think one thing I did, you know, if my dad or my mum said something, I would tell my solicitor what they'd told me and then, so that she knew what I'd been told to say, you know. I'd say, 'My mum says I should . . .' or 'My dad says I should do this', and it was easier to say what I wanted then 'cos she knew what my parents wanted, so it was a bit easier then.

It is possible to see from this passage that Karl was not only aware that both his parents wanted to influence him, but that he found a very good way of circumventing this pressure in his conversations with the solicitor. Moreover he did this in a subtle and tactful way which displayed loyalty to both his parents, without him losing his own sense of agency.

When we asked Karl what he thought what, in general terms, the best arrangement for post-divorce parenting might be his answer was instructive:

> KARL: Well I don't know. Well, the least disturbance would be if one of the parents ran away, I think actually, from the child's point of view, that would actually be, you know, the nicest, if they never saw their other parent at all to be honest.

This comment perhaps reflects the extent to which Karl felt that he shouldered the burden of his parents' problems, inflexibility and hostility. His sister had opted out of it all, but he felt that he had to be fair to both of his parents even though this was at considerable cost to himself. But he implied his own unhappiness in a very subtle way while never actually being critical of his parents.

> *Q: What would be an ideal family?*
> KARL: I think it's sort of important to do things together, not just have the home as a place where you all meet and go off in different directions, sort of you're only there for meals or whatever. And it needs to be open, you can do what you like and you don't have to hold back on anything really, you're just at ease. You don't have to keep up your reputation or anything, you can just be yourself and sort of just relax.

We got the impression that Karl found it difficult to voice his own wishes because of the level of conflict between his parents. Yet Karl was by no means the least fortunate of all the children and young people we interviewed and he showed considerable resourcefulness and dignity. Some had far fewer choices, had much worse relationships with one or both of their parents or step-parents, felt completely unloved and ignored, and some had even been physically abused. But we have not chosen Karl's story because it was 'horrific', but rather because it was, in many ways, quite routine and ordinary. Karl could not achieve a feeling of being a citizen of the family because the situation he was in meant that he did not feel he could easily express his own views and needs. It was not that his parents did not love him, nor that they were unaware of his unhappiness, it was simply that he felt so constrained by their ongoing conflict. Most of his physical, material and educational needs were well met, but he felt he had little power or influence in his home life. He felt he could not say openly what he thought because it might mean becoming embroiled in, or exacerbating, those conflicts.

In situations like Karl's there seems to be little basis for participation between parents and children – even though his particular parents were not against the idea in principle. This is why these are not always problems that can be solved by a resort to legal rights, or courts or solicitors. Karl, after all, had a solicitor. Problems of the sort that Karl experienced may be due to interpersonal dynamics or even a familial culture in which the wishes and desires of parents (unintentionally) take precedence over those of the children without there being any space for the 'moral conversations' or 'asymmetrical reciprocity' that we discussed in chapter 5. It is for these reasons that we need to look further than legal rights if we are interested in pursuing the idea of children's citizenship-in-context.

Conclusion: enlarging citizenship

Very few of the children and young people we interviewed were interested in having a voice in legal proceedings unless they felt that they had no voice in their family. Very few wanted the privacy of their families opened up to professional intervention and none spoke in terms of legal rights. But many did want to be able to participate in decisions, they wanted fair and caring arrangements and relationships, they wanted respect and dignity too. The question that arises, therefore, is whether the summation of their preferences can be read as a demand for specific legal rights within the family.

In her research with children on the UN Convention of the Rights of the Child, Lyon and her colleagues (1998) concluded that children did indeed want more rights and that they felt cheated that they had not received more information about the rights that the UN Convention was encouraging in respect of children. Her results suggest that rights are the way forward and that children are eager to become legal subjects. Our findings are more ambivalent. This may be a consequence of very different methodologies and, of course, very different contexts. Lyon et al. were working with classes of schoolchildren who were given information on the UN Convention first and then asked what they knew about, or felt about, their rights. We were talking to children about their experiences of post-divorce family life and we did not introduce the concept of rights in a direct fashion at all. Our interviews were one to one and were reflexive and in-depth. We tried to let the children talk openly about their experiences and we were not concerned to learn what they 'knew' about the legal system or their rights. Notwithstanding these differences, both studies, in their different ways, have revealed that children want information and to have the choice of whether or not to participate. For Lyon this signalled a need for children to have a more clearly stated range of rights as well as the right to separate representation.

While we do not dissent from this conclusion, we suggest that this is too narrow an approach to achieve the rounded complexity of the enlarged notion of citizenship-in-context that the children we interviewed were implicitly articulating. Very often what the children wanted was flexibility in contact arrangements, a degree of autonomy and control in their lives, ways of resolving differences without extinguishing love and affection, ways of maintaining relationships without losing their sense of selfhood. Sometimes they did not expect things to change, but they still wanted to have a voice. They often just wanted parents to know how difficult things were for them or they wanted to be free of feelings of conflict of loyalty that parents could impose. These important ingredients do not add up to legal rights, yet for many children they were the essence of good family life. The problem, therefore, is how to achieve these less tangible and less measurable indicators of citizenship.

One approach has been to challenge the idea that parents have rights over children. To a large extent English family law has been trying to achieve this for some decades. The Children Act 1989 is quite clear that parents have responsibilities for, not rights over, children. The UN Convention on the Rights of the Child 1989 (ratified in England and Wales in 1991) also stresses this emphasis on responsibilities, including the responsibility of parents to allow children to participate in family life (Children's Rights Office, 1995). Yet there are countervailing influences which sustain the popular image of the parent as patriarch, in particular the right of parents to withdraw their children from sex education or the right of parents to inflict corporal punishment on children. As James and James (1999) argue, 'Many parents believe, rightly or wrongly, that they *do* have rights over their children and that it *is* their right to make decisions about their children's future when they divorce. Such a view makes the assertion of children's agency and *their right* to be heard much more difficult to accommodate' (1999: 204). This suggests that much more needs to be done to challenge parents' views of their children, and this might indicate the need for the sort of cultural campaigns that have accompanied struggles to improve the social status of women, black people, disabled people, gay people and so on. Such campaigns often focus on the need to 'give voice' to disadvantaged groups. Williams (1999) has argued in relation to welfare principles that what is more important than rights is the ability for people to be able to voice their diverse needs and for these to become formulated into collective claims rather than individual demands (Fraser, 1995). These ideas are particularly important where children are concerned. Thus what needs to be heard is not only the expression of the rights of individual children so much as the kind of things that children in general have to say about what constitutes 'good' family life.[6] We suggest that once such voices can be heard two things can start to happen. First, children's experiences could become more widely disseminated and available to parents in general in such a way that the private realm of parenting could become more open to a range of different ideas. Parents could also hear what children in general, and in their diversity, think and feel without it having to be distilled into a specific conflict with their own child. Second, the terms of policy debates concerning children could begin to be influenced. No longer need it be only experts and judges whose views frame or influence policies or guidelines.

This would be a slow process of cultural change in which legal rights played an important part in redefining the status of children but where this enlarged concept of citizenship requires changes to the quality of intimate relationships. In our final chapter we will explore more closely some of the policy developments which need to work in parallel with legal rights and which might be useful in creating a practical form of democracy for children in families. However, we want to stress that all these ideas need to reflect the diversity of children's lives and to be alert to the fact that not all children want the same thing. We have argued in this chapter that quite different kinds of families can provide children with respect, dignity, and the opportunity to participate and to be appreciated in their own right. This ground-up, research-based process is quite different to one based on theorizing a 'common good' for all children and then imposing it in a downwards fashion. This means that we cannot provide a blueprint for family democracy other than identifying values of participation, respect, fairness and care. We also recognize that there are many different ways in which children can be acknowledged (or ignored) and respected (or undermined). There are also many forms of participation (or exclusion) as well as acknowledging that children have many different strategies for dealing with these situations. The case studies we have discussed in this chapter show these complexities and also reveal that parents who might never have given a thought to children's rights nonetheless provide very democratic foundations, while sometimes those who speak most vociferously of rights may do little in practice to nurture them. In the next two chapters we will look more closely at how some of these incongruous realities, expectations and aspirations between parents and children, are played out in different post-divorce families.

7

Children's Experiences of Co-Parenting

Divide the living boy, and give half to one, and half to the other.

1 Kings 3:25

Introduction

It may seem to be something of a cliché to refer to the judgement of Solomon as a way of introducing the issue of co-parenting after divorce, but co-parenting (defined as 'apportioning' a child on a 50-50 time-share basis) really does appear to be the modern equivalent of this radical biblical solution. Elsewhere Smart and Neale (1999) have defined co-parenting as a model of post-divorce parenting in which children move between their parents' homes in order to preserve routine and everyday interactions between them and *both* their parents. The precise arrangement may vary from family to family, depending on their circumstances and location(s). The children may spend an equal amount of time in each home, moving day by day, or week by week, or may make their weekday or term-time home with one parent and stay with their non-resident parent for weekends or school holidays. Invariably, however, parental care (the day-to-day physical and emotional work involved in raising children) and parental authority (the responsibility for decisions about the way in which children are raised) are the responsibility of both of the parents. Both remain actively and visibly involved in their children's lives and, to varying degrees, reach decisions about their upbringing jointly.

It is impossible to measure whether co-parenting after divorce is increasing because such arrangements need not be officially recorded and because there is no exact definition that can be safely imposed upon the range of flexible arrangements that parents and children adopt over time. Even though we started our research with a clear idea of what co-parenting was, we quickly found that one parent might think he or she was sharing child care on a 50-50 basis while the other parent did not think so at all. We also found that children did not necessarily measure co-parenting in terms of time. A child who spent two days a week with one parent might 'feel' just as much co-parented as the child who spent three and a half days a week with each parent. Co-parenting, we discovered, is a measure of the quality of relationships, not just a measure of time and place. Indeed, we became increasingly worried that, as the idea of co-parenting seemed to be becoming more and more popular, it was being interpreted as a simple and easily imposed splitting of time. Just as Solomon suggested an easily imposed splitting of the child's body to provide equal parts to the competing mothers, so our modern version might actually become a detrimental splitting of the child's time to provide equal parts to competing parents.

The Children Act has clearly provided legitimacy to this model of post-divorce parenting. Section 11(4), which deals with shared residence, provides for children to live in more than one household. However, the guidance accompanying the Act was quite specific that it was not intended that shared residence orders should become the norm, stating explicitly that 'most children will still need the stability of a single home' (Department of Health, 1991: para. 2.28). Brenda Hoggett (1989), then a Law Commissioner and one of the originators of the Act, makes a similar point, explaining that she did not expect the new private law provisions to lead to a significant increase in fathers' participation in children's upbringing. Instead, she hoped for 'small improvements in how people feel' about their different roles as parents. Joint parenting, as envisaged by the Children Act, was about contact and the minimization of conflict rather than a sharing of the day-to-day care of children. Since the implementation of the Act there has been something of a change in judicial attitudes towards co-parenting, however, and it is no longer regarded as, in principle, wrong. Nevertheless it continues to be viewed with caution (Harty and Wood, 1991; Conway, 1995; White, Carr and Lowe, 1995).

Advocates of co-parenting suggest that it provides children with the security of a 'normal' relationship with both parents (as opposed to the artificiality of a contact – or 'access' – relationship). They argue that it prevents the burden of practical care from falling on one parent and that it promotes gender equality and an ideology of sharing (Baker, 1996; Burgess, 1998; Parton, 1997). Opponents, however, question the wisdom of such arrangements and express concern that it is a solution which suits parents more than children. Bridge (1996: 17), for example, claims that parents are motivated to establish co-parenting arrangements from self-interest or from the need to achieve agreement with a hostile spouse. In this negative formulation it can be seen as a way of lessening feelings of loss and guilt and of retaining control without losing out to the other parent. Of course there are valid points to be made on both sides of this argument and in our research we found instances of all of these elements. However, because our project was focused on what children had to say about their experiences of being co-parented we find that this debate actually misses the point. In talking to children and young people we found that the issues were much more complex than this two-sided debate would allow. One child might value being co-parented while her brother might not; one might hate having to move about while the other might enjoy it. The arrangement might be fair for the parents, but the children might also find it fair. Equally they might find it valuable while they were under 12 but find it tedious once they became teenagers. We found that co-parenting, from the perspective of children and young people, was not intrinsically better or worse than living with one parent and seeing the other regularly, occasionally or never. What mattered to them was the quality of their relationships.

However, our account is running ahead of itself and so, in this chapter, we propose to explore what the co-parented children in both our ESRC study and our Nuffield study had to say about their lived, everyday experiences of cross-household parenting. In the ESRC sample all sixty-five children were being, or had been, co-parented because this project was originally devised to study this new form of post-divorce family life. In the Nuffield sample of fifty-two, twelve children were co-parented. Here we propose to examine the children's experiences of moving between different homes, how they handled both the practical and emotional transitions – including positive and negative experiences, whether they found it a sustainable form of family life and how they might have tried to change it.

Practicalities

ROSIE (9): It must be a bit *boring* for children who don't have separated parents. Well, obviously, unless their parents are separati*ng*. Because then it's obviously a bit confusing and a bit scary. But I mean, go to school, go home, just do whatever you do and then it's the same *every day*. Whereas with me, I get to go to a different place half the week.

Q: Thinking about your family . . . what do you think is the best thing about having two houses?

RORY (7): I'd say that you can just like move around, like a journey, not being stuck in the same house all the time.

One of the things that the children had to adjust to was having two homes and, of course, routinely travelling between them. Where these homes were close this might not cause any significant practical difficulties because older children at least could pop back and forth if they needed to. Indeed for some children like Rosie and Rory they experienced this as an exciting expansion of their horizons. Yet, as Rosie acknowledged, the shift in children's home life to living in two places can be frightening at first and required a period of adaptation. Many spoke about how difficult it was initially, but how they 'got used to it' over time so that it became simply routine.[1] But they also spoke about the careful planning that was required, particularly when they could not pop back and forth:

> SELINA (16): It gets to about five o'clock on Sunday and I get like a really awful feeling and then . . . aah, packing up again . . . I don't complain about it. That's just the way it is. There's no *point* complaining about it, nothing's going to change. . . . [But] usually on a Sunday around that time . . . we're upset because we're having to move and everyone's temper's . . . you know, you get quite irritable . . .
> Q: *Are there any things that you can do to make it a bit easier for yourself?*
> SELINA: Planning. A hell of a lot of planning, and thinking ahead. That is like the main thing – thinking ahead. Like, hockey fixtures can come up at the last minute and . . . obviously, I have my kit because I'm training every week, but my *game* kit, my proper socks, shirt, that's all at one place. And it's like 'Aargh'. . . . But planning ahead is the main thing that I have to try and do . . . just to organize myself. And I have a lot of files and you know, things like that, to keep things organized.

Some young people had jobs like paper rounds that were very difficult to sustain if they were in different places half the week. Younger children found it a problem if they left favourite toys at one place or simply lost track of them altogether between school and their two homes. Clothes could also be a major practical problem:

> NICOLA (9): Right at the moment dad's got all of my clean trousers there and these are too small for me, I got them when I was 5, so that gets quite annoying.
> Q: *How come all your clean trousers are over there?*
> NICOLA: Because I stayed a week with dad so I took quite a lot of clothes over there [and] none of them came back. And yesterday I wore some leggings and I just spilled bean juice on them and so I've got to wear

these and the other ones are really too small and feel uncomfortable.
Q: Did you leave your things at dad's so he could wash them or . . .?
NICOLA: Well no, I just made a mistake.

Living in two places therefore required major organizational skills, either on the part of the children or their parents. These practical problems could be exacerbated if parents were hostile towards one another or if they placed obstacles in the way of children taking things back and forth. Sometimes, of course, it was simply impractical to move items every few days or each week. A major problem mentioned by boys was the immobility of computers. Few parents could afford to have two for each child and this could be a serious problem for some young people, particularly if their computer was their main source of entertainment or a necessary requirement for homework.[2]

In addition to these material practicalities, children had to adapt to different regimes in their different homes. Parents might have different rules about what time children had to go to bed, or about what they could watch on television. Some parents might welcome friends into the home and others might not. Some children had to get used to eating very different things at different houses, as well as having to share bedrooms with their step-sibling for half a week while having their own bedroom for the rest of the time. This could require an astonishing amount of flexibility, especially if one parent was much 'stricter' than another, or if parents had very different styles of parenting:

Q: Is it difficult to remember what to do at each house?
LISA (8): No, not really, 'cos they're different places and they look very different, as soon as you walk in you think 'Ah, late night tonight, stories, cornetto' and at mum's house you think, 'Ah, nice early night tonight, nice little bowl of cereal and some lovely hot chocolate'.

Some of the older children came close to expressing the experience of what Goffman (1967) described as role adaptation or role conflict. Because they moved between two very different regimes they became adept at behaving quite differently in their different homes. They responded to their parents differently and almost became different people when they switched environments:

KARL (14): When I'm here I don't, sort of [say], 'Hang on, what am I doing? Why am I doing this, I don't normally do this', you know, I just sort of, wherever I am I just sort of do whatever it is. *I'd get really confused if my mum and dad swapped places, that would just totally confuse me.* I'd be doing all the wrong things at the wrong house! [Our emphasis]

Others found the transitions between households more difficult and had to make a conscious effort to adapt:

> RACHEL (16): You sort of change, depending what house you're at. I don't know about other people, but *I find that I'm a different person at different houses.* 'Cos the different environment and . . . my parents react differently to different things. Difficult to explain. So I adapt to my environment, I suppose. . . . I mean, my core personality doesn't change, I suppose. But the way I behave does. . . . [and] because we like change a bit, who we are, what we do and stuff, it takes a while to settle in, to being . . . the other person. I mean, it's getting shorter, but it used to take a couple of days. And then when there was short times, and I'd only be somewhere a couple of days, it was a bit disconcerting. But it's getting better now. [Our emphasis]

Switching roles and virtually becoming 'different' people is, of course, something children do when they pass from home to school (Mayall, 1994), or from school to holiday jobs and so on. The difference for these young people though, was that what one 'is' at home is often experienced as a 'core' identity (Allat, 1996), and so in having two homes their sense of ontological security could be upset – as in Rachel's experience.

This experience of dissimilarity and ontological insecurity could lead to children becoming reflexively aware of family life as something which did not simply 'happen' but which was created, managed and negotiated. They might have to become sensitive to their parents' feelings as they moved from one house to the other, learning what to say and what not to say in order to avoid causing upset. Moreover, they might have to do this in a context in which there were no guidelines for them to follow and perhaps no one in whom to confide. Sometimes it was hard for children to manage those moments when both sides of their lives might come together. When Selina was in a school play, for example, she arranged for her parents and their respective partners to see the performance on different nights, trying, at the same time, to avoid them becoming aware of the manoeuvring which this involved.

Emotions

Positive emotions

For some of the children we interviewed, being co-parented was experienced as almost the same as being parented by married, cohabiting parents. Some parents had either stayed friends after they divorced, or had managed to set aside their antipathy to such an extent that they shared Christmases and even went on holiday together. These were cases where parents had not re-partnered and usually where they had made a conscious decision to give priority to an ongoing shared parenting project rather than finding new relationships. Sometimes this friendship could confuse children and could lead to an expectation that their parents would get back together but this was not always the case:

> HANNAH (11): When mum comes to collect us from my dad's house she sometimes stays for lunch and we go out somewhere or something . . . say my mum was at work, my dad would just have us that time and then my mum would have us later on or something. . . . And we had a couple of holidays together . . . it's quite good . . . I'm sure they enjoy it more . . . 'cos if me and [my sister] are doing some sort of children's thing . . . they've got company, and it's quite nice having them both there.

Some of the children learnt that it was possible for parents to remain fond or respectful of one another and some voiced their appreciation of parents who were trying hard to set their conflicts aside, or at least to manage them in private.[3] Children in this situation (which of course need not be peculiar to co-parenting parents) were spared any sense of split loyalties or that worrying feeling that the dislike that parents might have for each other might also be felt towards the child:

> TOM (12): It's worked out really well. I don't think there could be any better arrangement than this.
> *Q: So what is it that you think makes it work so well?*
> TOM: I think it's because even though mum and dad don't love each other they're still very kind to each other and they get on really well, even when we swap over and things.

Co-parenting could offer children a sense of continuity of shared parenting, particularly if both parents had been equally involved in child care prior to divorce or separation.[4] It could mean that the children felt fully involved in the lives of both their parents and this provided a tangible and demonstrable experience of being loved and included in two families:

> ROSIE (9): I've read books about children who only see their parents sometimes. And it . . . I mean, like, say the mother starts another relationship, and then so does the father. And like . . . she's with her mother

all the time . . . then the child will just feel sort of *completely* unloved. Completely unwanted. So it'll be absolutely terrible. Like, whereas, if you see them both all the time, you get a chance to really get to know the mother's partner or the father's partner. But . . . it's more sharing, it's more sharing of time, love, money, everything. . . . I am quite lucky really, 'cos my dad and my mum aren't .. rivals or anything. They're just not together.

Rosie and children in her situation expressed considerable happiness and were clearly strong advocates of co-parenting. However, the experiences of other children in the two studies would suggest that it is unwise to draw the conclusion that it is co-parenting *per se* that gives rise to such satisfying outcomes. These successful outcomes may depend far more upon the characters, personalities, resources and values of the parents and children involved than in one particular form of post-divorce parenting.

Negative emotions

Some children, especially as they grew older, found having two homes really problematic. For them it was not like having two homes; rather it was like having no home at all.

> COLETTE (13): Everyone thinks I'm lucky 'cos I can go where I want, if I fall out with one parent I can just go to the other house, but it's, I hate it, everyone goes, 'Oh, you get two Christmases and two birthdays', and stuff, no I hate it, I really hate it . . . I just want to be normal . . . it feels like I haven't got a proper home really . . . whenever anyone asks me for my phone number or address or something I always give them two and they're like, 'Which one do I phone?' and I don't know and they're like, 'Well which one are you at the most?' and I don't know that either . . . 'cos they've got this stupid thing that . . . most of the week at one house and the next week the most of the week at the other house . . . and I always have to ask them where I'm going to be . . . I've always hated it. I always get in trouble at school as well 'cos I don't have the right books sometimes and stuff. But I can also use it as an excuse, that's why I haven't got the right books and why I didn't do my homework.

Colette found it really hard that her friends never knew where she was and she felt that her semi-nomadic lifestyle marked her out as different or 'not normal'. She obviously felt out of control of her everyday life because she had to ask her parents where she would be each week and this felt like an impediment to growing up. Colette was clear that she wanted her parents to get back together and she was very angry at the disruption their separation had caused. She was therefore resistant and resentful and appeared to be on the verge of giving up on the arrangement. But it was not always easy for young people to do this. In Matt's case he had been co-parented for five years and, because his parents were still extremely hostile towards one another, his arrangement was based on spending alternate nights with each parent. Although he was unhappy with it, he did not feel he could do anything about it:

MATT (15): It's just a drag really for me.
Q: What's the worst thing about it?
MATT: Just not being able to settle down in one place for longer than one night. . . . It's just my room. Really it doesn't ever feel lived in as it would if I was at one house all the time, that's it really. . . .
Q: If you had a completely free choice, what would you like to do?
MATT: I'd like to stay in one place. [When mum and dad were together] it was more settled, it just seemed more calm and peaceful. . . .
Q: How do you think [your mum and dad] would react if you said 'Can we try something different?'
MATT: I don't know, they'd probably like go mental about the amount of time I was spending at each house. . . . I'd just feel under pressure not to say anything. . . . They'd fight over every day. . . . They argue over like, whoever had had like one *long* day or something. It's just relentless. I wish they would stop it I suppose.

In cases like these what appears to have happened is that parents have agreed that they want to share the care of their children, but their children have not felt able to express their own feelings on the arrangements. In these cases co-parenting can be just as debilitating for children as those cases where one parent refuses to allow children to see the other parent or to spend meaningful time with them.

But even in cases where there is a much more democratic basis for post-divorce parenting, children and young people can find being co-parented has heavy emotional costs. In Selina's case she was quite clear that she would rather be co-parented than anything else. She was also clear that she loved her parents equally and they all got on well together. But she still found it very hard to manage the transitions between her two homes each week:

SELINA (16): I find on Sunday evening I always *miss* where I've just come from. Either way. It's not like I miss mum more than dad or anything like that. When I get here and I've been at mum's all week I miss mum and I miss Paul [step-dad] and I miss *that* – 'cos it's two different families and two different ways of doing things. You know, even things like

clearing the table, whatever. . . . I always come on Sunday night and I
start unpacking all my stuff, whatever, if I've come from mum's, and I'll
start just to miss mum a bit 'cos I've had her all week. . . . And then by
Monday I go to school and by Monday night it's just 'I'm at dad's now'
and I'm in that mood. . . . It's just Sunday evenings really that make me
. . . and sometimes if I'm going . . . if I *get* upset about it, it's always on
a Sunday night. Like, I have a cry or whatever. Or write it down. I
always write stuff down. Just like, a thought book. I just write things in
it when I need to. And then . . . I'm all right again by Monday.

We have discussed in chapter 4 the sense of loss that children and young
people could feel, even when they saw their parents regularly. Co-
parenting can be described as a series of mini-bereavements for some
children and, even if they were prepared to do it, it obviously had its
costs. Selina was looking forward to going to university because it offered her a way out of the emotional see-saw she felt she was on.

Sometimes children went as far as to suggest that co-parenting was
really good for parents rather than for children.

Q: Who do you think this arrangement works best for?
LISA (8): Both of them [parents]. I don't like it. There are good advantages and bad advantages . . . but I don't like living away from the two
of them.

CHARMAINE (11): I think it's probably a lot easier for my parents because
they're not swapping around all the time. . . . But it's fine now because
it's been about four years so I've got used to it.

SELINA (16): I mean, they've still got their house, haven't they? They're
not moving. And I don't think they realize how hard it is. I don't think
they understand how hard it is! But then no one would until they actually did it themselves.

It may not be possible to predict which children will experience co-
parenting as an enlarging experience which provides two homes and
those who will experience it as a diminishing experience depriving
them of any sense of home at all. For many children co-parenting must
feel like going back and forth to boarding school – some will love it
and some will hate it, quite regardless of whether it is a decent school
or not. Because their reaction can be so personal it was not surprising
to find that siblings could respond quite differently to the same situation. Sometimes one sibling 'opted out' of the arrangement, although
this could make it much harder for a remaining child to opt out later:

CHRISSIE (19): At first all three of us would go routinely to see dad at
weekends and if there was something different we'd ring him. And then

it changed so that I wouldn't be going as the routine and now it's got to the stage where Bob will be going unless he rings and James [the middle child] is sort of in the change because . . .

BOB (12): He, only recently, had a problem with sleeping here.

CHRISSIE: I'm not sure if it's just an excuse because he's finding it difficult to tell my dad he doesn't want to come or if he really does, I mean he has quite a bad spider phobia. . . . I remember finding it difficult when I had to come to terms with the fact that I didn't want to come every week and had to tell my dad, which was quite hard, and we did go through quite a few months of it being awkward. You know, my dad wanted to know why I didn't want to come all of a sudden and I had a boyfriend which I used as my excuse and I think James is consciously trying to make it easier. . . . I mean, it's just he's got an active social life and weekends are the only time he can go out with his friends and things. . . . It is really just, I think simply because of the distance. I think if mum and dad lived closer we'd be able to be at either place and keep the social lives going but because of the distance, certainly James, and Bob actually, all their friends are out near my mum, and it's very difficult.

The problem that Chrissie and Bob identified was that their father might interpret their reluctance to stay with him every weekend as a form of rejection. They were worried about him becoming lonely, especially as they felt that his life had become relatively empty since the divorce. Yet they had their own needs as they were growing into young adults.

Too much parenting?

Many of the children and young people we spoke to were involved in a wide range of outside activities such as football, climbing, ice-hockey, drama, music lessons, jazz dancing, choral singing, delivering newspapers or rehoming stray animals. But others felt they had to (or wanted to) limit such pastimes in order to spend time with their parents. The routines of co-parenting often made substantial inroads into children's time, in addition to which the complex schedules of children who were cared for at after-school clubs or by childminders until parents returned home from work meant that many had little free time once they had had an evening meal and completed their homework. Little wonder that some children talked longingly of the times when they felt peaceful and relaxed, or when they had time just to 'chill out'. Co-parenting could be said to steal time away from letting children just 'be' children.[5] If each parent insists on quality time with their children and if children feel guilty about going out with friends rather than keeping company with their parents then co-parenting might actually begin to diminish the freedoms of childhood and deny children the experience of independence.

> HAROLD (12): I like my family . . . I think you should spend an equal amount of time at your mum and dad's . . . We sleep Mondays, Wednesdays, Fridays and Sundays at our mum's and Tuesdays, Thursdays and Saturdays at our dad's . . . I see them both every day. I come back to mum's after school and then round to my dad's for an hour or so.
> *Q: If a friend invited you out for the day and you had arranged to be with dad, what would you do?*
> HAROLD: I haven't got [many friends] . . . I wouldn't go on the trip really, I wouldn't want to, I'd prefer to stay with mum or dad . . . I wouldn't like them to [have new partners] because I wouldn't like to spend time with the other person.

It seems hardly surprising that Harold did not have many friends since his parents seemed to fill every minute of his life that was not taken up by school. His mother had wanted to remarry at one stage, but Harold and his younger brother objected so much that the relationship ended. Subsequently both parents had agreed that they would not have any other relationships until the children had grown up. So although this was a divorced family, it seemed to be tightly woven together with Harold, the eldest son, acting as a kind of cement. While for children like Rosie, who we discussed above, divorce had actually extended her family and her horizons, Harold's horizons had shrunk to the space around his parents. He never seemed to do anything that did not involve one parent and he was not interested in achieving greater independence. Indeed, like Colette, Harold was one of the co-parented children we interviewed who saw the way forward as being to get his parents back together so that he could see them both at the same time.

The potential problem of having too much of one's parents' time and attention was identified in various ways by a number of children. Frances (who we mention in chapter 5) captured this nicely. Her commitments – especially if she was to have time with friends – seemed to require that she be cloned so that she could be the dutiful daughter, and yet still have some space for herself and her friends.

> *Q: If you had a wish for yourself and your family, what would your wish be?*
> FRANCES (12): [That] there was two of me, then I could be with mum and I could be with dad at the same time and I could see my friends.

When co-parenting fails

Most of the children we spoke to made it clear that being co-parented was not an easy option, even though many thought that they preferred it to the alternative of living with one parent and seeing the other less often or only occasionally. Many of the problems they faced were structural (for example they did not have enough time or they had to travel long distances) or were to do with missing parents or missing friends. However, in some cases the problem that children had to negotiate took the form of a parent. It was extraordinarily hard for children who were being co-parented when they did not like a parent, or when they were frightened of one of them or when one parent constantly tried to manipulate them. In these cases the children really did want to reject one of their parents – at least to a degree. This was a rather different situation to those instances where children were simply growing up and wanting more time apart from parents. In the three instances we outline below the children had either never been really happy with the idea of being co-parented in the first place, or had agreed to it because they felt that it would stop their parents arguing. In each case, therefore, the co-parenting had been more for the benefit of the parents – even though the parents might have genuinely believed that co-parenting was 'a good thing' for children whether they wanted it or not.

In Alistair's case his mother had insisted on a co-parenting arrangement because she wanted her children to 'know' their father properly. However, Alistair was frightened of his father, who had been violent towards him and who was very punitive in his whole approach to his son. Alistair had not been given a choice, however, because his mother insisted that, at the age of 9, he was too young to know what was best for him and felt he would be glad later that he 'knew' his father. Alistair was really unhappy with the arrangement and, by the time we interviewed him, he had persuaded his mother that he should spend less time with his father. So the contact was reduced, and as a consequence Alistair had become happier and also felt that his relationship with his father had improved considerably.

Q: What's it like when you're going off to dad's?
ALISTAIR (11): Well it depends whether he's been nice to me the week before. Sometimes I want to go but not usually. . . . I like mum the most. . . . I didn't like it when I was seeing dad more. I never saw my mum at weekends. So I asked for it to change. Now it's much better. Dad used to be much nastier than he is now, especially to mum. He

shouts at me, he used to give me smacks a lot, but he's better than he was.

In this case it became clear that the *quantity* of time spent with a parent could reduce the *quality* of that relationship. Put simply: more does not necessarily mean better.

Tom's experience was similar to Alistair's, except that Tom's father was not violent. Nonetheless he picked on Tom and found fault, thus making Tom feel belittled and incompetent. In this case too it had been Tom's mother who was committed to co-parenting.

> TOM (12): Usually dads visit in the evening or on every other weekend or something. *My mum didn't want to do that* because she's too fair – I think, anyway. I used to split my time really sort of evenly [between them] but I find my dad quite a prat, to put it bluntly, so I've sort of been taking away days from him and coming to mum's instead because I don't like being depressed. . . . My dad always seemed to criticize me about my homework and boss me around and tell me to do things over and over again and not let me do anything in my own time or anything. So I told mum and she said 'Well, we can't have that' so we first of all saw a . . . well mum went and saw a solicitor to just ask what would be the consequences and stuff . . . and the lawyer person said that it wasn't worth going to court because my dad would have no chance, because I have the say, he doesn't, basically. So we didn't take it to court. We were on holiday and we sent him a letter saying why and how we wanted to change it, my mum wrote a letter and I wrote a letter and we both sent them and they ended up at dad's and we gave dad about a week while we were on holiday to just sort of cool off, because if we didn't he'd get in a bit of a strop. Putting that mildly! I didn't feel very well, though, for about a week after. [Our emphasis]

In both of these cases Tom and Alistair would have been trapped into very unhappy relationships if their mothers had not changed their minds and supported them. Both boys were much happier with the more 'conventional' arrangement of living with their mothers and seeing their fathers regularly but not on an equal time-share basis.

The final example involves a young woman whose parents' separation had been acrimonious and over whom there were lengthy legal proceedings over residence and finance. She had been interviewed by both a Court Welfare Officer and a judge and had said that she wanted to be co-parented:

> CAROLINE (17): I wanted to split [my time between my parents] because I wanted to keep my mum happy still and I wanted to keep my dad happy. So I thought a week each, but my mum didn't want that. It

didn't work . . . she wouldn't let me bring anything to my dad's house, nothing at all. When you're that young you have teddy bears and all stuff like that, I had no books, no clothes. I kept asking her if I could take my stuff. . . . The only way I could get things out [was] by just hiding them. I kept trying to take [a photograph] with me, I'd put it in my bag, and then mum would find it and take it out and I kept on doing it, so eventually she just sort of ripped them up so I couldn't take them any more. I could never talk to her properly, we just always argued . . . or I just had to hold it in. . . . I just cried a lot and had lots of anger . . . I really did dislike her for what she was doing.

This co-parenting arrangement might have worked if Caroline's mother had not been so determined to prevent it from doing so. Just because there is conflict between parents it does not necessarily mean that co-parenting cannot work for the children, even if it is more difficult. But in this case Caroline's mother deliberately made it hard for her daughter and kept the conflict going through her every time she left to see her father. Eventually, after eighteen months, Caroline decided that she could not take any more. So she moved in with her father on a full-time basis and steadily reduced contact with her mother from that point onwards. When we interviewed her she had been living with her father for five years and had not seen her mother for seven months. She regretted this, but felt that she had worked hard to sustain contact with her mother but that her efforts had not been reciprocated. She had come to terms with the situation and felt that the arrangement she had was the one that worked best for her.

Children can, of course, face these same problems in other post-divorce parenting regimes (see chapter 8) but with co-parenting their difficulties can be magnified simply because they have to spend half their childhood with a problematic parent. In these cases the transitions are particularly hard because the child is leaving a preferred parent to go to live with the abusive or bullying parent. Moreover, when they are with the problem parent, their other parent is not there to mediate their relationship as they would have been before the divorce. In this sense the children can become much more vulnerable, especially to violence. Clearly then, co-parenting should not be regarded as a panacea.

Conclusion

ANNA (16): I'm just so used to it I can hardly imagine it any other way. I *can't* imagine it any other way. I mean, there's a good side and a bad side to it, as there is with everything. I'm just used to it. And I get on with my life, I quite enjoy it!

In considering whether co-parenting can 'work' for children, it may be worth reminding ourselves of Winnicott's (1964) assertion that life is inherently difficult and that no child, however kindly or understanding a home they have, will escape showing some evidence of this. What children need, Winnicott suggests, is to develop their own methods and resources for living in the world through having a sufficiency of good experiences to balance the negative ones that they will inevitably encounter. In this context, the role of the family is to be 'satisfactory enough' rather than perfect, since the latter could not equip children for the real world.

Our two studies were not designed to 'measure' whether co-parenting was a better form of post-divorce parenting than any other, nor indeed whether post-divorce parenting is better or worse than cohabiting parenting. Our aim was to elicit children's views and experiences and to discover how they developed 'their own methods and resources' for living in the world of their families. We can be quite clear, however, that while co-parenting was a source of security and emotional warmth for some children, especially younger ones, it could equally be a source of unhappiness and a prolonging of internecine misery for others. For most children it was simply 'satisfactory enough'. Thus in this chapter we have tried to present a rounded picture of their experiences and to point to attitudes and practices by parents that make life particularly hard or valuable for children who are regularly moving between households. We have tried to show the 'good side' and the 'bad side' (as Anna would say). We have also tried to shift thinking away from seeing co-parenting as a new form or structure for post-divorce life (like a template that can be imposed to produce specific results) towards seeing it as an interaction or a relationship between family members. The ideas introduced in chapter 1 about conceptualizing contemporary family life in terms of practices (Morgan, 1999) are particularly relevant here. Morgan states, 'In this alternative approach, family was to be seen as less of a noun and more of an adjective or, possibly, a verb. "Family" represents a constructed quality of human interaction or an active process rather than a thing-like object of detached social investigation' (Morgan, 1999: 16). For Morgan it is important to move away from understanding the family as a structure or 'thing' which would be rigid and based on formal blood or marriage ties. He sees the family as taking many shapes while retaining an important (although not predetermined or fixed) meaning for all the participants in family life. We saw in chapter 3 how some children also shared this interpretation of contemporary family life and we have shown in subsequent chapters how children devise strategies and develop resources to deal with changing and fluid situations – while still maintaining strong bonds with other family members they love and like. To a certain extent it is the co-parented children who routinely have to manage this micro-change and flux (albeit for some it became routine and 'normal'). These children are most clearly engaged in new 'practices' of family relationships (although of course this must be true to some extent of all children of divorced or separated parents). What mattered most to them was the quality of these relationships, not their structure.

If we start to think of co-parenting as one example of a family practice, rather than as *the* prescription or formula for 'proper' or desirable post-divorce family life, then it may be able to take its place alongside the full range of family practices that family members might deploy. It would be unfortunate if, because of the highly politicized context in which research on family life is conducted in Britain, children's complex and varied experiences of co-parenting were pressed into the service of a narrow campaign to force all parents and children into a particular model of post-divorce family life.[6] We pursue further the idea that it is the quality of relationships that is the most important thing for children in the next chapter, which will explore the competing understandings and values held by parents and children who have experienced divorce.

8

Children and their Parents: Different Perspectives

Introduction

The Nuffield study[1] from which we have derived much of the data in this book provided us with a unique opportunity to interview children whose families we had already met. In the mid-1990s Smart and Neale (1999) carried out a research project on sixty divorced parents which had focused on how they dealt with issues of residence and contact, as well as exploring their concerns and plans for their children. The Nuffield follow-up study allowed us to return to these parents to ask them if we could interview their children. This meant that we had already gathered data on the views of the parents on post-divorce childhood to which we could 'add' the views of children.[2] But not only could we offer a range of parents' views to set along side a range of children's views, we were in the position to look at the same history from two or three different perspectives. Parents and children do, of course, have different standpoints and different understandings. The same event may be trivial for a parent, but of huge emotional significance to a child. Similarly, a minor event for both parent and child may have very different consequences for both parties. So, in bringing together accounts from parents and children we do not seek to reveal a more accurate 'truth' of events or of feelings. Rather we want to give voice[3] to children's accounts so that *we* (as readers, parents, researchers, policy makers and so on) can better recognize that children have accounts of family life which may be at variance with, or which share common understandings with, parents. In addition we seek to provide a place for these accounts in the way that parental accounts of family life are automatically given space. It is usually only the parents' voices that are heard in the public sphere (or specifically in the divorce process), and no matter how caring and considerate a parent may be, the child will have a story too which may reveal different priorities and experiences. The subsuming of children's accounts into those of their parents in the public sphere is an unintentional way of silencing children and denying their accounts both validity and independent existence.

As researchers we went through a process of 'recognition' when we moved from interviewing parents to interviewing children. Just as Jessie Bernard (1978) had pointed out that within marriage there is the husband's marriage and the wife's marriage and that they might be very different, so we came to recognize that there are adults' families and children's families. Moreover, it was quickly apparent that all the children in a family will not see family life alike.[4] Even where children and parents saw events in broadly similar terms, it was a revelation to hear the story from the standpoint of the child who would often stress different aspects or who would foreground different emotions. Thus we began to appreciate certain aspects of the children's daily lives which could not be gleaned in any other way. Children clearly do not speak with their parents' voices; rather, they occupy their own biographical and sociological positions and speak from these.

In chapter 5 we explored the extent to which children could be viewed as moral agents within the context of family life. We discussed the extent to which they deployed (or expected) an ethic of fairness, of care and of respect in their relationships, and we developed the idea of 'moral conversations' in which children – albeit asymmetrically positioned – could participate in family discussions and planning. We made the point that not all families were sufficiently open or democratic for this to be feasible, and there is possibly a long way to go before the majority of parents in Britain view their children in this way. An important subset of the children we interviewed could not talk to their parents, or had tried and given up. Their parents were not necessarily 'bad' or 'uncaring' people of course. Sometimes they were too preoccupied with their own problems, sometimes they thought it would be genuinely harmful to involve their children, sometimes they simply did not think children had a 'right' to participate in such a fashion, and sometimes they were not interested in their children's views. It was the children who felt that they could not talk to their parents at all and who felt that their parents' agenda took no interest in or notice of their distinct or separate interests or feelings who seemed to us to be the most unhappy. In these situations they felt that they could not influence events and they experienced the ebb and flow of their parents' misery, anger, hatred or depression with a sense of helplessness and powerlessness. In this chapter we will therefore be exploring some of the more distressing experiences that children might have to face. However, we shall also try to indicate how hard it is for parents to 'get the balance right' between ignoring the wishes of children completely, involving them *too* much, manipulating them, talking to them so that they are informed, and protecting them from some of the realities of adult relationships. There are no rules about how much children should be involved or 'aware', but we hope that the following cases will show how it is a complex interplay between trust, protection, openness, selfishness, sensitivity and insensitivity to others.

This chapter is organized into four sections. Each of these will elaborate upon a core theme, introduced by the children, which resonates with, or provides an alternative account to, the one provided by the parent whom we had interviewed previously. In this way we seek to reveal that it is the interaction between parents and children that is the crucial element, rather than guidelines or rules on what 'all' parents should do on divorce. The first section deals with the problem for children of dealing with a parent who comes to rely too heavily on them for emotional support and who treats them almost as a 'friend'. The second deals with situations of overt manipulation where the child is utilized as an ally in a war with the other parent. The third invokes the situation of domineering parenting in which children are denied almost all moral agency and moral autonomy. The final section explores the nuances of decisions about what to tell children and the fine ethical line between 'being open' with children and 'offloading' onto them.

Children as friends: feigned equality

URSULA (18): Some people want to be your mother *and* your friend. I don't agree with that. You've got friends to confide in, for example, but your mother should be your *mother*. I think a *friend* for me is totally different. . . . [A friend] couldn't say, 'You shouldn't do that because . . .'. My dad is going through a mid-life crisis. I think he's trying to regain his youth. He goes, 'Hello chaps' and I think, 'Oh no!' . . . A dad shouldn't say, 'Oh, yeah, all mates together' 'cos I don't really think that's what it's all about. You've got to be – you've got to teach what is right and wrong, really, and you can't do that if you're saying, 'Lets go down the pub and get drunk'!

Ursula's condemnation of parents who try to be friends is uttered from a position of some confidence and critical reflexivity. She sees it as plainly inappropriate behaviour in which parents jeopardize their moral authority and the respect that is owing to them. However, for less self-assured children or young people it was much harder to develop a critical perspective while remaining more or less unaffected by their parents' apparently inappropriate behaviour.

In the case of Charlie (14) the fact that his mother treated him like a friend for a period after her separation proved to be a major problem. Charlie's mother had experienced a great deal of loneliness when her husband suddenly left her and her young son (then aged 8) and thereafter disappeared out of their lives. She had little family of her own and she found it very hard to be a single parent without another adult to confide in or rely on. Initially she felt she had not focused on her young son at all. She had mechanically dealt with his material needs but was too wrapped up in her own problems to care for him properly. Then this changed. Despite his young age, Charlie's mother quickly came to rely on Charlie to fill the gap in her life and she leaned on him quite heavily for emotional support. What the divorce did was bring about a reversal in the usual pattern of parent–child care. Charlie's mother did not spare Charlie the details about the problems in her marriage or his father's failings, both as a husband and father. She often kept Charlie up late so that she did not feel lonely in the evenings, and he played a full role in caring for her in a practical sense. They also moved house several times as Charlie's mother tried to settle into a new life. At the time we interviewed her she expressed some guilt, looking back, that at that time in their lives her young son had had to grow up so fast and, as his mother's constant helper and emotional prop, had not had much stability or formed many friendships of his own.

This rather intense relationship continued for some years until Charlie's mother became involved in a permanent adult relationship. Her new partner moved in with her, they quickly had a child together, and thereafter they married and moved to yet another neighbourhood. The mother now had another adult to share her thoughts and feelings with and to share the responsibility of raising her children. Charlie had initially been enthusiastic about these changes in his life because he really wanted a 'proper' father:

CHARLIE (14): At first I thought, 'Oh God, at last, I've actually got a father', but then, when [he moved in] I don't know – it's not quite the same. . . . [before] I got more attention . . . because there was like just me and my mum but now . . . mum's always occupied really, so I'm sort of left out.

His mother was aware that Charlie felt excluded and that she had less time for him, but could not see that there was a solution to the problem, especially as she was working full-time and attending to the new baby. From Charlie's perspective however, he had been emotionally abandoned when he still needed his mother's companionship. Moreover, he found that his new stepfather did not seem terribly interested in him, there were frequent family arguments and he felt isolated in his new home:

> *Q: How does your family compare with other families?*
> CHARLIE: I don't know really, the mothers always seem a lot kinder. I have this image of these really nice parents . . . but our family definitely isn't like that. . . . It's stressful because nobody really gets on. Sometimes I wish I had a different family. My mum isn't really that close. We don't really do anything together. She doesn't listen. . . . Whenever I try to talk to mum or something or try to ask her something it sort of conflicts. I don't really talk to mum [about my feelings] because I suppose she wouldn't really want [to know] . . . I try to keep things to myself. . . . When I'm upset, you know . . . mum's always telling me to stop shouting and then we end up having an argument. . . . I'd like a nice mum, you know, who will actually talk to me and listen if I'm upset, instead of sort of shouting back. . . . Mum's always going on at me and saying, 'I'll send you back to your father.' It's horrible. And Ray [the stepfather] doesn't really treat me like I'm his son, you know. I'm scared of him a bit, I'm someone he can get at. He can be really horrible. . . . It's just like I'm a person who just lives here, sort of like a tenant.

Listening to Charlie's account of post-divorce parenting we could see that the standpoints of the child and of the mother could not have been more different. The mother had turned her parenthood into a form of friendship with her son (Smart and Neale, 1999; Ribbens et al., 2000). This meant, for example, that she did not stay home to look after Charlie when he was ill, support him in getting to school on time when he was late, or help him with homework. By her own account, she had not spared Charlie the intimate details of the marriage breakdown, nor from knowing that his biological father had never cared for him. She was also quite open about the way in which she had relied on Charlie for emotional support and had cast him in the role of a 'grown up'. Charlie's perception of himself merely as a tenant in the household is particularly telling because he felt he wanted 'proper', supportive parents. Any attempt by Charlie to ask for some support for himself apparently brought censure from his mother or stepfather, leaving him feeling lonely and rejected. The more extreme his pleas for support or attention, the more he experienced his mother's reaction as one of exasperation.

Charlie's version of his life with his mother did not actually differ a great deal from his mother's account. His mother was perfectly candid about how she had treated her son, and both agreed that he had been 'promoted' to his mother's best friend, only to be 'demoted' when his mother's life became full again. The narratives of both mother and son in this case were broadly similar, yet when viewed from the standpoint of the child it became possible for us to see how different the consequences were for him as compared with the mother. Charlie reported considerable unhappiness and loneliness as well as a sense of powerlessness over the direction and meaning of his life. At the time we interviewed him he wanted to leave home and could not see any solutions to his problems.

Children as allies: clear manipulations?

It can be very easy to accuse parents (particularly mothers) of manipulating their children. Indeed, it has almost become routine with the growth in popularity of ideas like 'parental alienation syndrome' which seeks to explain children's expressed dislike or fear of one parent as due to the manipulations of the other (Kaganas, 1999). But although the blanket assumption that any child who voices these views must have been deliberately manipulated is clearly wrongheaded, this does not mean that parents never manipulate their children. By manipulation here we mean persistent attempts to turn children into allies and to provide them with limited and partial accounts of events that they can have no way of independently verifying. But it is always important that the full context is considered. As R. D. Laing (1971) pointed out, manipulation can be incredibly subtle: it can reside in contradictory messages, or even the contradictions between verbal messages and body language. In the context of parental relationships (whether parents are divorced or co-resident) using children as allies in conflict, or as messengers and go-betweens, is usually seen as inappropriate manipulation. We did not find many examples of this relatively clear form of manipulation, but where we did, the children we interviewed found it a damaging experience.

In the case of Max and Miriam (aged 11 and 13 at the time of the separation), their father had told us quite candidly that he had regularly 'set them straight' on things between him and their mother. According to his account both he and his former wife instructed the children to carry messages back and forth, and when the children returned with a different version of events provided by the mother, he

would 'correct' the story and send them back again to the mother. He
provided a very vivid description of how passionate he was that the
children should know the truth and that they should see through their
mother's manipulations. The children's accounts showed that both
parents were equally involved in engaging the children to take sides in
their personal war.

When they first separated the children both lived with their father
because the mother had suddenly left the family home and had nowhere to take the children. But after two years the son was showing
signs of disturbed behaviour and the mother wanted the children to
live with her. Miriam (by her account) had to do all the housework
and look after both her father and her older brother. Both children
returned to their mother, but this arrangement did not prove any better for the arguments continued. Max then returned to his father's
house, leaving Miriam on her own with her mother. Max eventually
stopped contact with his mother, while Miriam stopped contact with
her father. Both children left home when they were 17. It is, of course,
important to realize that the problems that this family faced did not
start with the divorce,[5] although it appears that it exacerbated the
conflict.

Q: What sort of family was it?
MIRIAM (19): It wasn't much of one really, it just didn't seem like a
family really, just arguments everywhere. It were all one big mess really.
. . . It didn't get any easier after [the divorce] because they used to argue
even more. If they spoke to one another it would end up in an argument, so basically they didn't speak to each other. I used to try and
please both, and try to keep quiet and not tell them things . . . but I was
sort of passing messages backwards and forwards, like, what time we
had to be back and if we were going anywhere. . . . And then, if [dad]
used to say he wanted [me] a bit longer I used to go back [to mum] and
pass the message on and then we'd end up arguing and I used to get it
taken out on me. . . . It was hard because [they] used to get at me all the
time.

As Miriam explained it, it appeared that the children were never allowed to be 'their own people', they were always required to take
sides against the other parent. They could never step outside the role
of 'go-between' because their parents could not be civil to each other
and they had to rely on the children to pass messages. From Miriam's
account it appears that neither parent gave the children the intellectual or emotional space to form their own views; the children were
simply supporting players in their parents' endless conflict. In the process the parents – at least from Miriam's standpoint – destroyed their

relationships with their children and made their children's lives harder than they needed to be.

> MIRIAM: If it could have been resolved between them I wouldn't have been involved and I would have got on with [them] better. . . . I suppose I wanted to go back to being a little kid and not have anything to do with it but because I was older I had to and I felt I was doing a lot of stuff around the house and for Max. I did need somebody [to help me], but they used to think I was old enough to do things myself. But it did affect me badly, you know, at school.

Miriam felt that she got no support from either parent; moreover, the fact that she was constantly required to choose between them ultimately affected her relationship with her brother. Because he 'chose' his father, and she 'chose' her mother, they could no longer sustain their sibling relationship. There was no middle ground or neutral territory between the parents on which the children could thrive.

> MIRIAM: Max still gets into lots of trouble. Dad told Max things which weren't true and when mum told him different he wouldn't accept it. . . . He'd have rows with mum and say, 'It's not true.' There were a lot of things which dad said to Max and me and I then found out they weren't true. . . . [Ideally] you should keep in touch with both [parents] regularly, try to see both sides and not take a view from one to the other, but it is hard. . . . Mums and dads should be the same really, so if one tells you off, then the other one sticks by it, but that wasn't happening in ours. *I felt as though I'd been used. I was in the middle,* sort of thing, and it was difficult not to take sides. [Our emphasis]

In this family it seems that there was little space for an ethic of fairness, of care, or of respect and certainly little hope of moral conversations taking place. Yet as she grew older Miriam was able to reflect upon the shortcomings of the parenting she had experienced and to develop ideas about how post-divorce family life should be conducted. When children are still dependent upon their parents it is usually more difficult for them to adopt such a reflexive stance, unless their parents can give them the space to do so.

Children as chattels: parenting as domination

Our third case study concerns a father and his son Sandy, aged 11 at the time we returned to the family. Sandy's older brother Cameron

(14) had declined to take part in the study. The father had told us that he had been forced to leave the marital home at the time of the separation, but his wife had then 'fallen to pieces' and had not been able to cope with looking after the two boys (then aged 8 and 11). While the mother was hospitalized with depression he had taken the children to live with him, and although the mother subsequently contested residence, they had been 'awarded' to him and his new partner (whom he eventually married). The mother had had to settle for contact, and without any financial support was forced to sell the family home and return to live with her parents, who were retired. The father explained that the children rarely stayed overnight with their mother because of the cramped conditions in which she lived with her parents. He also reflected that, as a traditional workaholic father, the chore of taking on the children might have been too much for him but his new partner had stepped in to take over the housekeeping side of things (although subsequently she had begun to resent this), leaving him to deal with the discipline. This residence arrangement seemed to suit Sandy's older brother but it appears that it was devastating for Sandy, who wanted to live with his mother. At the time of the interview Cameron was having sporadic contact with his mother while Sandy saw as much of her as possible and continued to harbour hopes of living with her and his grandparents.

The father in this family was quite candid about his views on children as egotistical beings who needed firm control. But he also saw them as devious and unreliable and easily susceptible to bribery. He felt that their mother and grandparents were weak and ineffectual in raising the boys for they let them 'get away' with too many things, and his aim, therefore, was to foster obedience in them through firm discipline, rather than engaging with them on an emotional level.[6] He relied on his traditional authority to exert control over his children and resorted frequently to physical punishment, although this strategy no longer worked with Cameron who was now bigger than his father and could be equally threatening.

Sandy's account showed that he and his brother viewed their parents in very different ways. Cameron had sided with his father over the divorce and wanted to be his father's favourite. Sandy, on the other hand, was unhappy about the way he was treated by his father:

SANDY: My dad tells me what to do, he doesn't leave me to do it. He's always telling me to tidy up or wash my PE kit . . . he decides where I have my birthday, what days I spend with my mum, he just decides everything. I just get my life ruled by him. I get told off, smacked and blamed for things. He used to smack me a lot. Once . . . when I hadn't finished my homework he smacked me so hard I had bruises all over my face and arm. It was just horrible.

From the father's perspective he was adopting a 'tough' style of parenting which had clear boundaries, but from Sandy's perspective it seemed as if he was uncaring and ineffectual in his moral guidance.

SANDY: My dad doesn't sit and listen like my mum. The other day I was trying to tell him about something going on at school and he started talking to Cameron. . . . In the end I just walked out of the room. My dad has no control over Cameron. . . . I think he should be making sure we don't get into trouble and he should always ask where we are and what we're doing. But he doesn't seem to mind about [those things]. . . . He doesn't have a clue.

Part of the reason for Sandy's rejection of his father's style of parenting was that he had an alternative and, from his standpoint, much more rewarding model of parent–child relationships to draw upon:

SANDY: My mum doesn't tell me what to do, she leaves me to work things out for myself. . . . I think of my grandad as more of a father than my dad because of the way he talks to me. . . . He doesn't shout at me and my dad does. He doesn't talk to me like I'm thick. My dad does and I'm not thick. And he doesn't raise his voice, he's kind, he does things for me and helps me with my homework and we did up my bike together.

Sandy's father regarded the mother and her parents as bad influences on Sandy but, from Sandy's perspective, in his mother's home he felt valued, respected and cared for. But Sandy had another reason for feeling oppressed at home. This was because his older brother shared many of his father's views and had adopted his father's tough style of dealing with Sandy. He seemed to see Sandy as a rival for his father's attention. Sandy told us that his older brother bullied him in a variety of ways, not infrequently hitting or kicking him, physically dominating him and taunting him. He had also got him into trouble by hiding his school books, and on one occasion by implicating Sandy in an incident of shoplifting. Sandy therefore felt very isolated and quite desperate when he was at home.

At the time of our interview with him, Sandy was trying to find ways of changing residence so that he could be with his mother and grandparents. He was trying to pluck up the courage to phone Childline to get some advice on where to go for help. He had not told his father that he was planning to do this because he feared that he could not talk to him or explain his feelings. He worried that his father would simply see him as disloyal. But he was also weary of his brother's abusive behaviour and tired of being the target of his aggression. Although his father asserted that he was providing a stable, disciplined family life, Sandy did not see it this way. In fact he saw quite the opposite, with a violent father who failed to provide any moral guidance and who was only interested in his obedience, not the increasingly autonomous person that he felt himself to be.

Children as family members: an ethical balancing act

The three sets of accounts we have outlined above have one main factor in common, namely the parents' belief that their children were merely appendages rather than members of their family. If we take the standpoint of the child it would seem that none of the parents discussed above were able to see their children as separate beings with (growing) rights to autonomy of thought, emotions or action. But these cases are very stark and the children we interviewed were very unhappy. Of the children cited above all but Charlie – who was too young to try to leave home – had succeeded in leaving the parental home as early as possible, or were trying to do so when we interviewed them.

Many of the other children we interviewed experienced some of the same elements found in these children's parent–child relationships, but usually they experienced them with less intensity, less relentlessness, and/or in a context of greater trust, give and take, or mutual respect. Other children might find themselves 'caught' in the middle, but had more resources or better relationships and so were able to deal with the situation with less distressing outcomes. Thus we are not implying that it is always 'wrong' for parents to disclose their feelings to their children, neither do we assume that parents should never tell their children about the circumstances of their divorce. Rather, we see such judgements as matters of fine balance. Sometimes it is much easier to see where the balance may have gone wrong (especially with the benefit of hindsight) than it is to get it 'just right'. Take, for example, this discussion generated by Quentin (13) and his brother Pele (10):

PELE: We're in the middle of my mum and dad because we don't take sides. . . . Mum is in a completely different position and dad is in a completely different position. Sometimes it's hard [being] in the middle of things. Mum might tell you something about your dad and your dad might tell you something about your mum.

QUENTIN: You get both sides of the story. . . like, if I say, 'Why did you get divorced?' mum says it's because dad was having an affair, but dad says it's because mum was driving him mad and they couldn't get on and *then* he had an affair because of that. If I say to mum, 'Well, dad's got a point' she might say, 'No he hasn't!'
Q: *How do you feel about [your parents] doing that?*
QUENTIN: I don't know, I like to know how they feel, so I can be nice to them. . . . I worry whether mum's OK, when she's annoyed or when she cries a lot.
PELE: It's good in our family 'cos at least we know what's happening.
QUENTIN: We've got like a relationship where we can tell [mum] every-thing. Like if mum got a boyfriend and we didn't like him, me and Pele, we'd tell her straight away. . . . In our case, mum's very close, she, like, brought us up. . . . [But] *they don't like tell me what to do, they don't make decisions for me or about me*, they let me live my life sort of how I want it. [Our emphasis]

The important difference between Quentin and Sandy or Miriam, is that Quentin's parents seemed to be able to tolerate the idea that their children might see things differently from them. They seemed to be able to accept the idea that their sons loved both of them and were not seek-ing to destroy their bond with the other parent. Even though, by her own 'admission', Quentin's mother felt that she had let her sons 'know too much', she recognized how important their father was to them.

An important consequence of this approach was that the children could, at quite a young age, distinguish between their parents' prob-lems and their own emotional loyalties in the family. They were not swamped by a great sea of emotional hostility but could reflect upon problems that arose with a sense of being able to cope with them. They were able to develop a resilience because (it would seem to us) the quality of their relationships with their parents was sufficiently strong and rewarding that the 'mistakes' their mother felt she made in telling them too much were not disastrous for them.

QUENTIN: [I'd like] them to get more friendly. I think mum and dad should accept the fact that they're divorced and they're not going to do anything [about it] so they might as well just be friends, just for me and Pele, and they have been trying. When dad used to come round they used to always get into a fight about something but now they can at least talk to each other a bit more. . . . We do talk to mum [about being in the middle]. She knows. She doesn't mean to put us in the middle. It's just how the situation is. . . . [We're] a normal divorced family. . . . I mean, we've got some problems but we're all right really.
PELE: You get on with your life and then when something comes up, we'll cross that bridge when we come to it.

While Quentin and Pele's parents did 'disclose' their feelings about their former spouses to their children, other parents felt strongly that adults should *never* do this. In these cases the parents held to a strong notion, that many would share, that the intimate parts of parents' lives were private. Many parents felt that some things should be kept out of parent–child discussions. These decisions about where to draw the line between what to tell and what not to tell were difficult ones for parents. Sometimes one parent might think that it was not their place to talk about the other parent's reasons for leaving and that it was up to their former partner to explain things to the children. Others felt that they would tell their children later on when they had a greater understanding of adult relationships or of sexual matters. Thus some parents were 'economical with the truth' about the reasons for their divorce in order to save their children from distress or in order to protect the relationship that their children had with the departing parent. Often this approach was based on a strong sense of altruism. Some parents even undertook to hide their own emotions in order to protect children and could sometimes create a sense of harmony in order to avoid any trace of emotional blame or manipulation. It was in this spirit that the parents of Daniel and Bob (aged 10 and 8 when their parents separated) approached the issue. The mother told us that they had agreed that they would not 'use' the children either as weapons or as proxy confidants or supporters. Indeed this mother took care to show only kindness and respect for her former spouse. Of course, not all parents could or would have the same degree of control over their emotions as this and it was clear that it was a difficult strategy to maintain when there were new tensions or particular disappointments.

But the boys in this family were not expected to choose between their parents, nor were they told the detailed reasons for their parents' divorce. Neither were they particularly aware of the tensions that arose from time to time. What arguments the parents had were kept apart from the boys and they felt that they could move easily between their two homes. They appreciated the fact that there were no apparent tensions between their parents.

> DANIEL (16): It's quite enjoyable [in our family], we all like each other really, we still see each other quite a lot. Mum and dad talk to each other, they're still close and there's no real tension there. Mum and dad are there if I need someone, but I don't necessarily use them. . . . They worry about school and what I'm doing after school . . . and not getting up to anything I shouldn't and things like that – the usual parent sort of things.

Daniel and Bob both felt supported and loved, and they also felt that they were the beneficiaries of an ongoing parenting project without it feeling unduly oppressive.

Not all parents would want to shield their children so much from the realities of their lives and from their feelings, but the mother in this family wanted her children to experience ongoing parental love without any complications. Daniel and Bob's family life was perhaps an example of an asymmetrical partnership between parents and children. The boys felt respected and able to talk to both parents, they felt cared for and felt that their parents still cared for each other. But their parents did not treat them as if they were the same as adults, nor did they allow them into the interior of their emotional lives. They felt that their children needed a particularly altruistic form of love for the duration of their childhood. This meant that they opted to safeguard their children from the burden of 'knowing too much'. This is, of course, a hard decision for parents. Telling too much can be a burden, but in another case giving such a sanitized version of events might have been conducive to secrets and lies and a sense of manipulation. The fact that it worked in this family does not mean that this is a blueprint for all families. Quentin and Pele, who did know the reasons for their parents' divorce, did not fall to pieces and seemed to accept it with equanimity. But it was an approach that was working for Daniel and Bob, who seemed to be just as content with family life as Quentin and Pele.

Conclusion: learning from the standpoint(s) of children

It is hard to refrain from making judgements about parenting styles and capacities when recounting these narratives, especially when some of the children reported themselves to be very unhappy. Usually the researcher and/or the reader will have strong feelings about things like the physical punishment of children, or the emotional exploitation of young people, and we are no exception to this rule. But we have *tried* to avoid making judgements here, and have remained as faithful to the spirit of the interviews as possible. But in linking these stories we have attempted to demonstrate how children may experience their parents' behaviour after divorce as more of a problem than the divorce itself.

We argued at the start of this chapter that it is usually only the adults' narratives of events and relationships that are given voice and legitimacy in the public sphere. This raises the question of why it is that a greater range of children's narratives and experiences has not become part of the public discourse too. As we suggested in chapter 2,

there may be a willingness to take up the 'sad' stories in order to further a political or policy goal, but in general it is not children's voices
we hear. We do not raise this because we see children's accounts as
correctives to adult accounts, nor do we suggest that they have a greater
veracity. Rather, we see them as accounts constructed from the
standpoint(s) of children, and if family policy is to proceed from an
ethical stance these standpoints also need to be included. The moral
terrain of post-divorce family life is complex and insufficiently charted,
but in developing a clearer understanding of the peaks and troughs it
seems rather odd to omit children's accounts from the picture. Just as
it is no longer ethically acceptable to devise policy for disabled people
without (at the minimum) consultation, so it is increasingly unacceptable to exclude children and young people from such discourses.

Young has argued, in relation to the need to hear various narratives
or accounts, that

> First, narrative reveals the particular experiences of those in social loca-
> tions, experiences that cannot be shared by those situated differently
> but that they must understand in order to do justice to the others. . . .
> Second, narrative reveals a source of values, culture, and meaning. . . .
> Through narrative the outsiders may come to understand why the in-
> siders value what they value and why they have the priorities they have.
> (1997: 72)

Put simply, and by analogy, Young is suggesting that in order to treat
children ethically we need to be able to hear what it is they value and
to be able to see how they make sense of the social world. She stresses
that it is particularly important to hear these narratives where one
group is less powerful, more marginalized, or somehow more disen-
franchised than the other. Her argument is that conversation can change
things because it provides the basis for understanding across difference. Seen in this light, the silencing of children in discussions about
family life (whether these discussions take place within the family group
or outside) is an obstacle to the ethical treatment of children. Young
does not apply her ideas to children, but the logic of her argument
would suggest that it is not good enough for adults to speak for children, or simply to imagine that they know what children think and
feel by virtue of once having been a child or by virtue of being a parent. Children have standpoints which are not the same as adult standpoints; moreover, they know a great deal about parenting and its
consequences as the case studies we have discussed above show. As
Masson and Winn Oakley (1998) have argued in relation to looked-
after children, being able to see arrangements from the point of view
of children quite simply changes everything.

9

Implications

Introduction

The recent growth in academic interest in participating with children in research on childhood and social life (discussed in chapter 1) is a development which is paralleled by a growing interest in finding ways of allowing children to participate more in a range of legal and social affairs. The UN Convention on the Rights of the Child has been a significant catalyst for this interest, seeing, as it does, the child as an active participant in matters that concern him or her, rather than solely as an object of concern (K. Marshall, 1997). The idea that the child is a new focus of attention *per se* would, of course, be erroneous. As we have shown in chapter 2, much research and policy formulation in the twentieth century centred on 'the child', creating a veritable industry of guidelines and practice manuals. The difference between this long-standing set of interests and concerns and the more contemporary development is precisely in the growing amplification of emphasis on the child as a reflexive, participating agent in the unfolding story of his or her own childhood. Newer, more participatory or empathetic research methods are part of a process of 'revealing' children's knowledge and wisdom in a different way.[1] In particular, this new wave of research has insisted that the knowledge thus gleaned should become part of the policy process – whether this be designing urban spaces or managing the divorce process – as well as possibly informing professional practice.

As we have noted, in the field of family law and divorce a genuine desire is growing to 'hear the voice of the child', or to 'ascertain the wishes and feelings of the child' in more appropriate ways. Clearly, research on children who have experienced their parents' divorce and are living in post-divorce families with varying degrees of success and happiness is highly relevant to these initiatives. However, we need to be attentive to the questions of how research findings should be 'used' in other contexts and, of course, whether the methods used in research are portable into other professional practices. In some ways doing research with children is easier than acting as an officer of the court with the remit to ascertain the child's wishes and feelings. The researcher can offer confidentiality and the child knows that there will be no personal ramifications arising from the research. The researcher has no duty to report back to parents what their child has said, nor need they extract only the legally relevant issues. In research the child's narrative is subject to the same analysis as that of an adult, with the research agenda set by the researchers (often in combination with children) rather than by formal legal entities or guidelines. Depending on the methodology of the research, the child can lead the interview, can decline to answer some questions and can control exactly how much they say and on what subject. This is likely to produce a very different narrative to the ones produced in formal interviews, where some professionals cannot offer complete confidentiality and where the child knows that what they say may have important personal consequences which are beyond their control once their views have been expressed. It would be pointless therefore to suggest that professionals could encourage greater participation by children simply by resorting to the methods used in qualitative research, since the epistemological and ethical foundations of this sort of research may be rather different from those of the professional interview.

This realization means that it would be naïve to rally to the call for greater participation by children in the divorce process as if this would transform children into 'open books' from which the professional could read in order to determine a 'better' outcome. Talking to children may not always be an unmitigated good, and it is vital to acknowledge that children's accounts will be highly context-dependent. Poor contexts may produce impoverished accounts which leave the professional no wiser and the child no more satisfied. The child who says that he or she is 'not bothered' may be highly bothered, but may wish to escape what is perceived to be an interrogation which seeks to get them to betray loyalties. It is not unusual for solicitors, Court Welfare Officers and Mediators to be attentive to the fact that a child is under pressure from parents to give tailored accounts, but there is less discussion of the extent to which professionals too may be part of the pressure that the child experiences. A genuine desire on the part of individual professionals to encourage openness and participation may be undermined by existing 'rules of engagement' which deny children privacy and confidentiality.

In this chapter we shall explore some of these problems and will give consideration to different levels or sorts of participation by children in the divorce process. At times our discussion will seem impossibly idealistic. Indeed, we acknowledge that it may seem fanciful to talk of participation where some children live in fear of their parents and where abuse robs some children of the potential for an independent or authentic voice of their own. But the central issue is how to progress ideas about participation in step with concerns about welfare, not in opposition to those concerns. In chapter 5 we discussed the idea of asymmetrical reciprocity. This idea requires the more powerful party in a moral conversation to be constantly aware of their power, which gives them a specific responsibility to be attentive to others. This means that the adult is not freed from responsibilities towards children at the point when children start to participate and voice their own views. Rather, it means reformulating those responsibilities so that they do not obliterate the child's agency. It is in this context that the following discussion should be read.

Asking children about professional involvement

As part of our research with children, we wanted to explore under what circumstances they would take a problem outside their immediate family and to whom they would talk if they did. As with several of the other sensitive issues we raised, we tackled this question both through hypothetical scenarios in which children were asked to imagine a situation, and through direct questioning of children who had actually had experiences of talking to professionals. Approximately 20 per cent of the fifty-two children and young people in our Nuffield study had had experience of legal, mediation or therapeutic services. However, most had only vague recollections of the process and we often learnt about this contact from parents rather than children. In the ESRC sample we did not interview the parents and so our data on this is much less reliable because we could not be sure that the children could accurately recall the 'official' personnel they may have encountered briefly. We suspect that where the children had forgotten the encounter it was because they were likely to have met these 'officials' only once or twice some years prior to our interview. Thus it should not be surprising that for some the memories were vague. Our research

may well therefore underestimate the amount of contact between professionals and children. It may also understate those encounters that
had been uneventful for the child, since these would be less likely to
feature in an interview some years later. We cannot be definitive, but
it seems likely that children will remember these encounters where
they continued over a period of time or where they were stressful or
unsatisfactory.

Taking problems outside the family

In exploring the issue of outside support we gave the Nuffield sample
of children a vignette about a child who wanted his parents to stop
arguing over contact but was unsure what to do about it. For most
children their preferred strategy in this hypothetical situation was self-
evident, namely that the child should talk to his parents and ask them
to stop.[2] We then asked what they would advise if this strategy did not
work. Their replies reflected a preference for talking to other members
of the wider family or close friends:

> ALISTAIR (11): Well, I wouldn't [talk to an outsider] 'cos it's more of a
> family thing.

> BEN (14): He could talk to his granny or one of his mum's friends. I
> mean if he, sort of, went to talk to someone outside his family then it
> would probably get around and make the situation worse.

> QUENTIN (13): [He should go to] someone in his family [then] they can
> talk to his parents . . .
> PELE (10): 'Cos his parents might not listen to a child as much as an-
> other adult.

> SALLY (12): She could talk to a friend because then she wouldn't tell
> anyone . . . Last year I talked to my friend Joanna and she helped me a
> lot . . . she convinced me to tell my teacher. . . . So friends are a lot of
> help.

There was a marked preference for keeping family problems within
the immediate family wherever possible. Preserving family privacy in
this way was seen as part of the moral code of family life – as long as
someone in the family was actually listening to the child. Going beyond the family usually meant turning to informal sources of support
such as wider kin or friends.[3] While kin could be useful advocates,
friends were highly valued for their non-judgemental, egalitarian support. They could be accessed independently and at a time to suit the

child, they offered an opportunity to share experiences and they usually offered confidentiality or a 'safe space' in which to discuss a problem. Friends could help clarify thinking about what, if anything, needed to be done. This might be all that was needed for children to feel that they could manage a problem by themselves or, alternatively, it could be an empowering process, enabling them to work out what the next step might be and take it at their own pace. Others have suggested that peer support schemes, internet chat lines and counselling services like Childline, which also offer independent access and confidentiality (as well as anonymity), are highly valued by children as a first step in taking a problem outside the family. As Cooper observes, 'We can only be sure "what children want" if we create conditions under which children are able to find out what they think about their predicaments and this is not something which courts have been designed to facilitate' (1999: 156). The point is that children and young people, like adults, do not always know exactly what is best in a difficult situation, often because they do not know what is possible, or sometimes because they have not had the opportunity to test out fledgling ideas. With friends, siblings and kin they can test out ideas and reprise them or set them in context. They can draw on wider experience in a context of trust. Indeed the children often remarked that it was particularly useful to have friends whose parents had already divorced as there was a basis for shared understanding.

The children in the Nuffield sample who had met with professionals were less positive about these experiences than they were about talking to friends and family. Below we set out four examples of the kind of problems that the children encountered.

Enforced participation

Alex had been referred to a counsellor because his mother was worried about him and thought that he was disturbed as a consequence of the divorce.

> ALEX (12): When they first split up there was this counsellor at school and mum arranged for me to meet her every Monday but that was annoying because I had to miss PT . . . I really didn't like her. She just, basically asked questions, like you're doing but she didn't put them in the same way. She didn't, like, make me *think* about stuff, she made me *tell* her stuff. [Emphasis in the original]

He was required to turn up at a time that did not suit him in a school setting where his peers would inevitably know of the referral. He also felt as if he was 'made to tell' his private thoughts to a stranger. This inevitably influenced his experience such that he found the whole process demeaning and unhelpful. He stopped attending after two sessions. His experience reflects the problems associated with well-meaning attempts to help children, and to hear what they have to say, but overlooking their right to choose whether or not to participate in the process.

Overlooking the child as a person in their own right

As we argued in chapters 5 and 6, the children in both our samples thought it was important to be allowed to be their 'own person' and to have their views respected, even if they were not shared or adopted. If professional interventions merely seemed to confirm their non-person status, then children could find them extremely negative experiences:

> MAYA (15): [When] I got sort of really upset and freaked out mum took me to the doctors and said, 'Oh there's something wrong with you Maya'. . . . Then, it's sort of like this child psychologist stuff, but I don't know, it's just the approach that they had, it just made me cry more. I feel more comfortable talking to you because I know there's nobody staring at me. . . . There was about seven of them [behind the mirror]. It felt weird 'cos you don't know what they're doing and most of the time I was just sitting there, you know, and with my step-dad there as well, he didn't agree with anything I was saying, he was saying, 'No, no, it's not like that, it's like this, blah, blah, blah.' He's always so decisive. . . . I didn't really find it helped. . . . I just didn't really talk much because, I mean, the other people around me, it's just including my mum and step-dad, you know.

This therapeutic intervention was experienced as a denial of privacy and dignity and was an effacing encounter for Maya in that it seemed to reproduce the oppressive treatment she was receiving at home. She was dealt with as part of her family and not given a chance to speak confidentially about herself as a person in her own right. The problem had been presented to her by her mother as a problem of her own making and so the therapy was defined in advance as an opportunity to sort Maya out. The number of professionals involved and their covert methods intimidated her, and she had no one to help her formulate or express her views and no space in which to do so. Similar experiences have been reported for children attending family meetings at court and those interviewed under the children's panel system in Scotland (Trinder, 1997; A. Griffiths, 1998).[4] In these situations, although the child is given the opportunity to speak, they are often silenced by the setting and its procedures. Such experiences are not only a problem for the child, they can confirm for professionals the idea that there is little point in involving children or trying to ascertain their views.

Losing control

One of the things that the children and young people disliked about their encounters with the legal system was the feeling that they could not control the way in which their views were represented. Nor could they enjoy a discussion with court officials that would not be reported back to the court and to their parents. Molly, who was one of the few adults at the time we carried out the interviews, had endured years of legal dispute between her parents over residence and contact. The problem, as she defined it, was less the issue of where she lived or how long she spent with each parent but rather the nature of the dispute itself and the impact it had on her relationship with her parents. Because of the extreme hostility between her parents, she was inevitably drawn into the legal dispute over residence.

> MOLLY (22): The Court Welfare Officer . . . didn't really know the family. I don't think it helped talking to her. I didn't see why everybody should ask all these questions and when you do tell them certain things it doesn't go in the report . . . I only really told them what they wanted to hear . . . I really had no one to talk to, so I just made up my mind [about which parent to live with] and that was it. . . . Somebody else to be involved would be a good idea, who isn't going to go straight back to court and say 'Well this and this', but just get them sat down and sort of talk between them.
> *Q: In confidence?*
> MOLLY: Yes, and then if you *do* want them to pass it on, they would.

Molly felt that she could not be frank and that what she said was used selectively. She felt she had no confidential space in which to explore her view of the problem or how it might be resolved. The narrow legal focus on the issue of residence did not resolve her parents' conflicts, and her decision to live with her father only intensified her problems with her mother. In a case like Molly's it is clear that the Court Welfare Officer was doing her duty in ascertaining the wishes and feelings of the child. But the context was so fraught and emotionally charged that Molly needed the chance to have a confidential and exploratory discussion of the problems she faced before being required to give her views.

Legal proceedings in the context of divorce remain heavily oriented towards parents and 'families' rather than the children. Children might have their own way of defining the problems in their families and of defining possible solutions to the problems, but the child's agenda may not match the adults' or the court's agenda. It seems that legal solutions that denigrate or ignore children's own perceptions of the problem might be perceived as no solution at all by children themselves (Lyon, Surrey and Timms, 1998).

Powerlessness

One of the most significant features of the experiences recounted above is that the children had been referred to these agencies without any choice on their part. Consequently they saw these encounters not so much as 'support' but more as 'interventions', even to the point of 'interrogations'. This was so even where the purpose of the encounter was therapeutic rather than investigative. At the same time, children who did seek support for themselves outside the family found that there were significant barriers to access, particularly if they wanted to access help independently of their parents and maintain their confidentiality. It seems that most counselling services require parental permission before they can see a child, while the difficulties of securing legal help are well documented (Sawyer, 1997, 1999b). The children seemed to be in a kind of catch-22 situation. Some felt forced to talk to people they did not want to talk to while others who did want to talk to people outside their immediate circle of friends and family could not find a way of doing so that ensured confidentiality. Consequently, very few children in our two samples sought help by themselves.

> VICTORIA (10): I wrote to a solicitor. . . . I just wanted to know how I could get something done about going to live with my mum. That's what I wrote. . . . It was a relief to do something about it. . . . I didn't tell my dad [about the letter]. I had tried to talk to him but he wouldn't listen.

In this case Victoria's mother was very supportive and she applied for a change to the residence order. However, in the face of opposition from her father and a refusal by the solicitor to represent her in her own right, Victoria gave in. Her efforts to get independent help failed and her attempt to act autonomously was regarded suspiciously and put down to manipulation by her mother. Doubts were cast on her personal integrity and she found herself in a worse position because her problems with her authoritarian father were ignored.

The four types of experience recounted above reveal a mismatch between the kind of professional support children might need and what is provided. Our data is limited of course,[5] but there is other evidence to suggest that children do not generally perceive adults beyond the boundaries of their families as reliable sources of support, help or empowerment.[6] In fact, they are more likely to be viewed as dismissive, intrusive, intimidating, patronizing, judgemental, coercive, untrustworthy, and as reinforcing their superiority to children (Williamson and Butler, 1995; Cantwell, 1996; Morrow, 1999). Overall, these children and young people saw professional support as a last resort.

One of the main obstacles to talking to 'outsiders' is the perception that family issues are best kept in the family and the justified fear that, by taking them to professional agencies, children are somehow being disloyal or escalating problems so that they seem insurmountable or out of control. Children might also feel a sense of stigma about professional interventions in their lives and those of their parents. Moreover, where children cannot talk to a parent they may have real fears of repercussions if that parent should find out that they have turned to outside agencies for help or have otherwise 'undermined' their parent's position (Childline, 1998). These fears may be well founded in a system that cannot provide children with confidential, independently accessible support when they need it.

So, is it always good to talk to children?

The conception of children as inadequately socialized future adults still retains a powerful hold on the social, political, cultural and economic landscape. (James and Prout, 1997: p. xiv)

The Children Act has acknowledged one of the key dimensions of children's citizenship by according them the right to participate in private law proceedings. Yet there are a number of constraints on turning this principle into practice. Children's right to be separately represented is conditional upon proof of competence, defined by Lord Scarman in the Gillick[7] case as 'sufficient understanding and intelligence to enable him or her to understand fully what is proposed' and combined with 'sufficient discretion to enable him or her to make a wise choice in his or her own interests' (Freeman, 1997: 217).[8] This is a hard test to satisfy, however, which means that children are effectively prevented from becoming legal actors in their own right (Roche, 1996). Lord Scarman's judgement on the competency of minors has not in any case been consolidated in subsequent case law, while Article 12 of the UN Convention has so far had relatively little impact on either legislation or professional practice in the UK. Solicitors and judges are reticent about talking to children. Even among family mediators and Court Welfare Officers there remains a great deal of uncertainty over what it means to ascertain the wishes and feelings of the child or, indeed, whether their wishes and feelings should be ascertained at all.[9]

Whether children should be allowed more of a voice in private proceedings is a contested issue. Those who defend current policy and practice argue that it is not necessarily in children's best interests to be involved in decision-making or to voice their views in ways that set them apart from or even in opposition to their parents. This in itself is deemed to be harmful to children, placing undue burdens of responsibility and guilt on them at too young an age and compromising their loyalties. The private law provisions of the Children Act are, in part, based on the notion that family integrity should not be threatened, and so it remains hard to disaggregate children from their parents in most cases. There are also real and justified fears that children could become the target of parental manipulation and resentment. Assumptions about children's lack of competence in making measured choices and doubts about their ability to act with moral integrity (not telling lies or allow themselves to be manipulated) also support this position. Rather than forcing them to express a view, it is argued that they should retain their right to 'act like children' and let others decide for them (Law Commission, 1988: 3.23; Cantwell and Scott, 1995). Moreover, on a practical level, it is hard enough to negotiate a settlement between two parents without adding another two or three to the negotiating table, especially when this will take more time and financial investment. On the other hand, critics of current legal practice argue that children have a right to participate and may be emotionally harmed if they are excluded from decision-making, particularly in a context where they cannot necessarily rely on parental support.[10]

The problem with this debate resides in the extent to which it is still primarily concerned with the issue of harm (see chapter 2). It remains philanthropic in nature, committed to doing good,[11] and thus fights shy of the risks inherent in the application of equally important values such as respect, integrity and dignity. As K. Marshall (1997) argues, it is extremely difficult for adults to allow children to 'choose' risky or dangerous options, if only because they fear that they will be accused of abdicating their duty of care. This preoccupation with protection also means that adults are very apprehensive of giving children anything approximating to power because they are not seen as having the commensurate responsibilities that give rise to a wise use of that power. The whole shift towards citizenship is therefore seen as a slippery slope ending in the chaos of irresponsibility and harm. Yet, as we discussed in chapter 6, it may be more appropriate, and less alarmist, to think in terms of citizenship-in-context which can accommodate elements of all these concerns. Below we suggest several steps on the way to a realignment of the balance between an overarching concern with welfare and a concern to establish children's citizenship.

Recognizing the diversity of children's lives

Perhaps the most obvious finding from our research is that we cannot assume that all children are alike or want the same things. We found some brothers were happy with arrangements while their sisters were not, or that a younger sibling might be content with contact while an older sibling was not. It was not uncommon for two children in the same family to have different parenting arrangements in place, depending on how they each got on with their parents. We cannot therefore assume that all children will benefit from the same processes or solutions. The idea of the welfare of 'the child' may be unhelpful simply because it implies that general principles can be devised that can be applied in a blanket fashion – a kind of 'one size fits all' approach. A more flexible approach which takes into account the individuality of each child in a family might embrace more elements of citizenship, while also attending rather more to the well-being of each child.

Promoting citizenship within families

Our findings have suggested that most children want a voice in important family matters and that they feel excluded and disregarded if they are denied access to any form of participation. It seems clear, however, that most children want to have these 'conversations' with their parents rather than with outsiders. This will entail a cultural shift in parenting practices which children themselves may already be helping to initiate. It would also entail a greater sharing of experiences about post-divorce family practices and a sharing of knowledge about how to anticipate and resolve common problems. Children's collective voices can be a useful and powerful resource here, and this is a particularly relevant use for research findings based on qualitative and participatory research methods. Parents may be more willing to absorb and learn from the insights of children in general than from their own children, while children's claims for public recognition may also be enhanced through the greater prominence of children's views.[12] In these ways the experiences of post-divorce families could become the focus of a range of informative and positive debates. It becomes pos-sible to think of these collectivized experiences as a form of 'cultural capital' that can become a resource beyond the individual family. Smart and Neale (1999) found that the divorced parents they interviewed often drew on their own private experiences of being a child of divorced parents as a way to guide their own behaviour. They tended to say that they wanted to manage post-divorce life better than their parents had done, and thus turned the experiences they had had as children into a moral resource for their adult actions. It is perhaps the collectiv-izing of these insights from childhood that needs to become part of new 'structures of feeling' around post-divorce family living (see chapter 2).

There may also be other ways of promoting a wider understanding of ideas about democratic styles of parenting and childhood citizen-ship. The resource pack developed by Miller (1999), in collaboration with the Children's Rights Alliance, is an example of how the princi-ples of the UN Convention on the Rights of the Child can be made more accessible for parents. The symbolic power of law could also be used in positive ways to promote a shift in cultural values. For exam-ple, definitions of parental responsibility which include respect for children and their views could be built into the substantive principles of English law, just as they have been in other jurisdictions (Children's Rights Office, 1995; Children (Scotland) Act 1995). Giving children a voice in a variety of public spaces might also have a transformative effect on adult perceptions of children and hence on parent–child rela-tionships. Of course, children and young people need to be given op-portunities to learn how to participate (or to decline to participate) before they can be expected to do so in a meaningful or public context (Cockburn, 1998). This is especially the case if we expect them to participate at times of crisis or stress such as when their parents are divorcing.

Avoiding the slide into increased intervention

Our findings suggest that not all children will want a 'legal' voice in their parents' divorce, particularly if this means having their feelings and wishes 'ascertained' in an instrumental fashion by strangers. Being consulted in an artificial manner at the point of divorce, when no one was interested before nor likely to be afterwards, may give some children the impression that they are mere negotiation 'fodder'. A clear distinction therefore needs to be maintained between inviting children to participate and requiring them to do so. If children feel they cannot decline to be interviewed by a Court Welfare Officer or by a counsellor, the original well-intentioned desire to 'hear children's voices' simply becomes a form of intervention or, as Roche (Lim and Roche, 2000) calls it, enforced intimacy. Indeed, it is possible to envisage a new industry being established which could be experienced as a new form of erosion of children's privacy and also as an additional stigma if it were operational only at the point of divorce. This means that it may be important to encourage a wide range of independent services for children, including those provided by children themselves.

Pathways and flexible provision

The key question that needs to be addressed is how professional, voluntary and self-help agencies can provide a range of support and advocacy services that children can access independently and in confidence, as and when they need to. A flexible range of services would be needed to meet children's varied needs. For example, some children might want nothing more than good-quality information provided in imaginative formats (written, videos, CD-ROMs and so on) so that they can reach a better understanding of what happens or may happen when parents divorce. They might want initially to tune into an internet/TV/radio chat line to gain some insight into other people's problems and solutions, or call into a school resource or high-street drop-in centre to get some direct advice without necessarily compromising their anonymity. They might prefer to discuss their problems, in confidence, with a counsellor using a range of media or face to face. Alternatively, they could share their experiences/problems in a peer support group.[13] They might want to work in partnership with their parents and a support team to resolve family problems over time, or use a mediation, therapeutic or legal setting to try to resolve a specific problem with a parent in the short term. They might need an advocate (such as a solicitor or the new family court adviser) to put their point of view directly to their parents or to the courts or, alternatively, a facilitator who will help them to put their *own* views across (K. Marshall, 1997). They might value being able to collaborate with their adviser/advocate over how their case is managed or what goes into 'their' section of a court report,[14] or they might want independent legal representation in a full court hearing. Other forms of participation might also be appropriate. The point would be to remain responsive to children's wishes and needs in the development of flexible provision.

These different pathways would allow for different forms of, or combinations of, participation. Children could determine for themselves how far they would wish to go, or what was appropriate. In cases where there was a threat of harm or violence, professional intervention would not be excluded, but this would be a matter of judgement in individual cases. Envisaging participation for children in this multi-faceted and responsive way might be a better way forward than trying to determine in advance who needs what kind of help and when. Professional and other agencies would need to work in partnership with children, helping them to decide what kind of participation is necessary or appropriate in their particular case and guiding them to relevant agencies. No one agency could provide all of the above services, of course. The confidential counselling and independent access which children are likely to value as a first step in taking a problem outside their family, for example, is outside the remit of Court Welfare Officers, who have to make recommendations to the courts.[15] Nor will it fit the remit of the new family court advisers under CAFCASS (the Children and Family Court Advisory and Support Service). The supportive and responsive strategy outlined here relies on inter-agency collaboration and appropriate referrals between agencies. It also relies on adults acknowledging that children have the competence to assess the quality of their relationships and to have a valid perspective on potential solutions. This strategy would also require material resources and hence considerable political support.

Facilitating child-friendly professional practice

If they are to be fully effective, professional services will need to develop more child-focused ways of interacting with children. At one level this might mean making professional procedures and environments more child-aware, for example by using straightforward, age-appropriate language, shorter sessions, flexible timetables and so on (Masson and Winn Oakley, 1998). In some situations it might also mean cultivating a more supportive and less directive culture of professional practice. Listening to children and responding to their agendas means keeping an open mind, being prepared to learn from children, and consulting with them *before* strategies have been decided so that their views can influence thinking. It also means that there should be greater flexibility around arrangements for children so that different strategies can be tested out but then renegotiated at a later date if they are not working or if the child's circumstances change.

In some cases individual professionals may wish to adopt these child-focused practices, but they may find themselves working within structures and guidelines which actually prevent this. In other cases, individuals themselves may be unwilling or unready to see children as citizens. The Court Welfare Officers who took part in Trinder's (1997) study, for example, described their child clients as 'immature', 'lacking understanding', having a 'child-like' logic and 'living in their own emotional world'. Similarly, the solicitors who were interviewed by Murch and colleagues saw children as 'potential manipulators or the victim of manipulation at the hands of parents, whose stories were therefore not to be given much credence' (1998: 152). It seems that some legal and welfare professionals still endorse a traditional view of childhood even though many are starting to change.

Recognizing children as persons in their own right and respecting their views, of course, poses difficulties for a system of family law and welfare practice that appears to operate on the basis of formulaic ideas about what is best for children. While the Children Act was not designed to operate in this fashion,[16] the current, overriding view espoused by the English courts[17] that contact with both parents is always good (unless there is strong evidence to the contrary) takes no cognizance of the views of individual children who may have good reasons not to wish to see or stay with a parent. Ironically, the idea that contact is a right of the child has espoused a rigid solution to residence and contact disputes which is in no way attentive to the idea of the child as a citizen with valid views of his or her own. There appears to be little sensitivity to children's problems arising from poor-quality parent–child relationships, emotional neglect, lack of respect, or open conflict between parents. The current legal climate, in which the definition of the problem and the preferred outcome in favour of contact have been already been decided in advance, leaves little room for alternative ways of thinking about the issues. This has given rise to situations where children have been forced to see a parent against their will.[18] Such 'solutions' do more than simply ignore children's views; they reduce them to possessions to be parcelled out among adults with little respect for their dignity.[19]

Conclusion

JAKE (11): I think there should be some kind of agreement between [the child] and his parents as to what should happen, rather than him just deciding himself. . . . I think the people who are involved should get to decide, not by themselves, but by helping each other to reach some kind of agreement as to what would be best.

Jake's vision for family citizenship is founded on mutual respect, inclusion, participation, negotiation and compromise. In this vision the child is recognized as a valued member of the family and the goal is to achieve a level of communication in which all participants have a voice. He also implies that these family members are attentive to each other, not simply fighting for their own view to prevail. His vision clearly dilutes the interpersonal power that parents in traditional or authoritarian families have presumed to be a natural right of parenthood. But he is not promoting a new form of tyranny by children, nor is he undermining the basis of family life by importing highly legalistic or unrealistic principles into everyday living. Many of the children we interviewed felt that they had this kind of relationship with their parents, and those who did spoke very positively about their families. Such relationships prefigure a greater democratization of the family. But as we have argued in previous chapters, this does not mean that childhood is being abolished nor that parents are abdicating responsibilities for their children. Rather, these changes represent different ways of raising children as citizens of the family, allowing them to take certain responsibilities and to gain experience of participation and decision-making.

Ackers (2000) has argued that we need to be attentive to the level of participation that seems appropriate in different contexts. Most of the discussion about children's participation is formulated in the context of the public sphere rather than within the family. Hart (1992), who developed the notion of a 'ladder' of participation, has suggested that this ladder comprises seven levels. He suggests that at the bottom rung of the ladder children are made to fit in to adult agendas in a way that gives them no influence or voice. Their presence is mere tokenism, or, even worse, the product of adult manipulation. Further up the ladder he suggests that children participate more actively in adult-led agendas, with their voices controlled to varying degrees. Nearer the top of the ladder they are treated as equal participants who can work collaboratively to produce an agenda or even set their own agendas with varying levels of adult support. Hart therefore operates with the idea that it is always better to be at the top of the ladder. However, children themselves may not always want to be at the top of the ladder, any more than adults do. It is possible to imagine a tyranny of enforced participation that could become extremely oppressive and counterproductive. This is why Ackers suggests a more subjective approach. She argues that the level of participation that is appropriate may not be one that is determined by the 'facts' of the case but by the quality of the relationships in the family, and by a recognition of existing power relationships in the family. For example, it is perhaps unlikely that parents would think it was desirable for children to participate in their decision to divorce. Not only would this seem inappropriate for the children, but parents also have a claim to privacy, dignity and respect. It would also be unrealistic to imagine that parents do not have more power than children. Parents can implement decisions in ways that children often cannot, and children are aware of this inequality and necessarily take it into account. In such situations it is also worth noting that one or both of the parents may have little choice in the matter either. Participation is therefore always set in a context. Moreover, participation does not eradicate power differences, even though it may allow for some power-sharing in interpersonal relationships. Participation is, of course, only one element of the process of democratization of adult–child relationships. It may not even be the most important one. The children we interviewed were just as likely to speak about respect, being allowed to 'be themselves', being cared for and being treated fairly. How these elements are combined may be more significant than the exact degree of participation achieved, or the extent to which children are informed of their legal rights.

It has been a major argument in this book that there is more than one story to be told about children's experiences of their parents' divorce. Not all the stories are happy ones but many are about resilience, transformations, growing self-reflexiveness, and the development of a new set of perspectives on parenting and family practices. The growth in the divorce rate in the second half of the twentieth century dramatically changed children's experiences of childhood. Even those children whose parents stay together will know children whose parents are divorced. This does not make divorce easy for children, but it changes the landscape of childhood into one in which these personal transformations become highly probable. In this context children need to acquire new skills (both practical and emotional) to navigate this new moral terrain (Smart, 2000). Although the rate of increase of divorce has now decelerated, it seems highly unlikely that we will witness a return to the sort of family life associated with Britain in the 1950s. Children therefore need the cultural capital that will help them to manage the personal and social transformations associated with family change. We have argued that in seeking to create family policies more suited to the 2000s than the 1950s, we need to import different ethical guidelines, as well as starting to attend more closely to what children say. This book – flawed as it may be – is part of such a project.

Appendix

Researching Children's Family Lives after Divorce

Introduction

The findings reported in this book are based on two qualitative research projects which were funded by the Nuffield Foundation and the Economic and Social Research Council. The Nuffield project was designed to explore the perspectives of children living under a variety of post-divorce or post-separation arrangements, while the ESRC project focused on exploring the varied experiences of co-parented children (i.e. those being 'shared' across two households). The projects ran concurrently over a thirty-month period from 1997 and were housed at the Centre for Research on Family, Kinship and Childhood at the University of Leeds. For the purposes of this book we have combined the two projects into one study. Our theoretical and policy-related rationales for undertaking the research are set out in our introductory chapters. Here we set out our methodology and describe the characteristics of our samples of children.

The principles of qualitative research

The style of research reported in this book is known as qualitative research. This is a systematic, rigorous and theoretically sound method for investigating and understanding the social world, but currently it seems to be little understood, particularly in the arena of public policy. We draw directly on the work of Mason (1996b) to explain the basic principles of our approach. Firstly, qualitative research is grounded in the interpretative tradition in that it is concerned with how the social world is interpreted, understood, experienced and produced. Our aim in this book has been to explore how children with divorced parents interpret and experience their families and how they practise family life and contribute to the creation of families. However, qualitative research goes beyond mere description. It usually embodies a particular intellectual puzzle that requires explanation, and from which generalizations can be made that will have a broad utility and value. In this case the intellectual puzzle was to examine how we (as adults, sociologists, policy-makers and professionals) should understand and respond to children whose parents have separated or divorced and, in the process, to produce new forms of knowledge about the changing nature of childhood and family life. Secondly, qualitative research embodies a particular approach to generating data: one that is flexible and sensitive to the social context in which the data is produced, so enhancing its validity. We say more about this below when we discuss the in-depth conversational interviews that we used to generate our data. Thirdly, qualitative research is based on methods of sampling, analysis and explanation that accept and seek to work with complexity, detail, diversity and difference. Our aim was to produce rounded explanations based on rich, detailed, contextualized data that would allow for the diversity of children's perspectives to be taken into account.

We will be saying more about these sampling and analytical strategies and how they differ from quantitative methodologies below. But it is worth pointing out here that qualitative methodologies are often dismissed as unrepresentative or anecdotal in comparison to quantitative methods. These different methodologies produce different forms of knowledge, but they have equal validity and need not be seen as incompatible. Where quantitative research can generate patterns across broad, representative samples, qualitative research can shed light on processes and meanings and can capture the complexities and multiple realities of family life. The need for some synergy between these two forms of methodological enterprise has recently been recognized in the field of research on children and divorce (Rodgers and Pryor, 1998; Hetherington and Stanley-Hagan, 1999).

Theoretical or purposive sampling

Of all the detailed and systematic techniques of qualitative research, that of sampling (deciding whom to interview and how many interviews to conduct) is perhaps the least understood. In any empirical enquiry researchers have to think about what kind of relationship their sample will have to the wider population, particularly if they wish to make generalizations or wider claims for their findings. Standard quantitative modes of sampling are based on a logic that is derived from the laws of statistics and probability. Conventional probability sampling aims to be representative, i.e. the sample should display characteristics (such as age, gender or class) in similar proportions and patterns to those found in the wider population. This is assuming, of course, that these broader patterns can be accurately known and that they are meaningful for the purposes of the study. Statistical conventions are then used to calculate the probability that the patterns observed in the sample will exist in the wider population. This is the most commonly understood form of sampling logic, yet it is probably the least commonly used logic in qualitative research. Representative sampling is not the most effective way of generating qualitative data. It usually requires the construction of very large samples that cannot then be researched with the depth or sensitivity required for qualitative analysis. Qualitative research therefore uses 'purposive' or 'theoretical' sampling techniques. These are equally rigorous but founded on an altogether different logic (Finch and Mason, 1990; Mason, 1996b). In this approach the sample is not representative of the wider population and does not therefore have to be of a sufficient size to be representative or to be analysed in terms of numbers conforming to particular patterns. Instead it is designed to provide a *relevant range* of cases or examples, incorporating different experiences or processes, which allows the researcher to make detailed comparisons between cases and to test and develop specific theoretical propositions. The proposed sample size usually has to be estimated in advance to meet the requirements of research funding bodies, but the estimate is harnessed to the need to achieve a robust range of cases. New insights and explanations can then be based on analysis of a full range of circumstances and experiences.

Characteristics of our sample

Based on the principles set out above, our strategy was to produce a theoretically driven sample of children that would allow for an exploration of a range of experiences and parenting arrangements (rather than being representative of all such experiences and circumstances). We recruited fifty-two children (from thirty-two families) into the

Nuffield project and sixty-five (from forty-seven families) into the ESRC project, giving us a total of 117 children for our presentation in this book. The figures given below are based on the combined sample. Most of the 117 children were from the Yorkshire region, although twelve were living in widely scattered locations throughout the UK. The focus of our interest was on children's day-to-day experiences under the prevailing conditions of post-divorce family life (rather than at the time of the divorce or separation itself). Consequently well over 100 of the children had at least three years' experience of post-divorce family life, including eighteen who had lived for most of their lives in such arrangements and four whose parents had never lived together. The sample included seventy-eight siblings and four step-siblings (from forty families). Siblings were included wherever possible because we wanted to explore the individualized ways in which they might experience their families. The sample was fairly evenly split between those whose parents had formerly been married (and were now separated or divorced) and those with parents who had been in non-marital relationships (ranging from stable, long-term partnerships through to tenuous relationships that ended around the time of the child's birth).

The sample was evenly split in terms of the gender of the children (fifty-eight girls and fifty-nine boys) and reflected a wide age range. We have set out the ages of the children and clustering of age groups in table 1.

The young adults who took part in the study were included because they had younger siblings who had been invited to participate. They were able to reflect back upon their families and on how things had changed over time. Three of those aged over 18 were living away at college but returning home for the holidays, while another two had set up their own homes in localities close to their parents.

In terms of socio-economic background the Nuffield sample was diverse and reflected a range of incomes and living environments. Twenty of the children were living in relatively poor socio-economic circumstances, with their families on state benefits or living in social housing. The ESRC sample was less differentiated. Approximately three-quarters of the sample were from middle-class or 'alternative' families; by 'alternative' we mean families who espoused values associated

Table 1

Age 4–7	Age 8–11	Age 12–15	Age 16–19	Age 20–22
16	55	32	11	3

with educational achievement and liberal or progressive views, but whose material resources were limited. In other words, they tended to accumulate cultural capital rather than economic capital. Ten children were of mixed parentage. However, our research questions and sampling procedures were not designed to explore cultural variations, and the experiences, values and concerns of these children were not sufficiently differentiated from the rest of the sample to warrant a separate analysis here.

Residence and contact arrangements with parents

The patterns of residence and contact with parents across the two samples are set out in table 2. At the time of interview forty-four children shared a home with their residential parent who took the main responsibility for their care (thirty-six with mothers, eight with fathers). They had varied contact arrangements with their non-residential parent, ranging from reliable contact (twenty children) to tenuous contact (twelve children), through to no contact at all (twelve children). The remaining seventy-three children were being co-parented, in other words, their mothers and fathers were sharing parental care and authority. Of these, thirty-five children were in 'uneven' time-share arrangements, the most typical being where the child spent weekdays with one parent and weekends with the other. The remaining thirty-eight children were being shared on a 50-50 basis, which meant that they split their time evenly between households, usually over two weekly cycles.

These patterns of contact and residence need to be understood in the light of the following observations. Firstly, combining our two samples for the purposes of this book means that our overall sample is weighted towards co-parented children. However, we have taken care in the analysis and interpretation of our data to give equal weight to the perspectives of children across different family arrangements and with different experiences of family relationships.[1] Secondly, while many arrangements were long-standing several children, particularly in the Nuffield sample, had moved residence or changed contact arrangements, or were

Table 2   Patterns of contact for 117 children

No contact	Tenuous contact	Reliable contact	'Unevenly' shared	'Evenly' shared
12	12	20	35	38

planning to do so at the time of interview. Subsequently we learnt of further changes where contact was resumed or stopped, or where co-parenting arrangements were modified. These arrangements, then, represent no more than a snapshot picture of family life.[2] Thirdly, the categories used here are based on adult understandings of arrangements. We have used them because they reflect dominant thinking in family law and policy, but we found that they were not necessarily meaningful from the children's point of view. For example, in terms of their day-to-day experiences there appeared to be little difference between the children who were in reliable contact arrangements and those who were being shared unevenly across two households.

Arrangements with new 'kin'

In addition there was a complex variety of arrangements with new 'kin', ranging from well-established extended families complete with new children, through to small family units which had remained unchanged or had diminished in size following the divorce (see table 3).

The majority of the young people in our study had at least one parent who was co-residing with a new partner. Many of these parents had remarried and/or produced new children. In a minority of cases neither parent was cohabiting; some had established a long-term relationship with a non-cohabiting partner, while others had not re-partnered or had done so only sporadically or fleetingly. Added to this complexity, different patterns of re-partnering were often in operation across the two households, giving rise to highly complex patterns of family life across the two samples.

Family relationships

As well as reflecting a variety of parenting and re-partnering arrangements the samples were diverse in terms of the children's day-to-day

Table 3 Living arrangements with new partners for 117 children

Lives full-time with new partner(s)	Lives part-time with new partner(s)	Does not live with new partner(s)	Neither parent currently re-partnered
25	48	16	28

experiences of family life. Relationships with parents and new family members ranged from highly supportive through to difficult and oppressive. The relationships between the two parents also varied, from amicable through to conflictual. Some children in oppressive or conflictual relationships had been planning to leave home or change residence at the time of interview because of such difficulties. There was no discernible correlation between type of family arrangement and the quality of relationships. Approximately 20 per cent of the children across the two samples had used therapeutic and legal services as part of resolving family problems or had been the subject of legal disputes between their parents, resulting in court orders for residence or contact. In twenty-one families (twenty-nine children) the parents had been (or were still) involved in legal disputes over residence, contact or maintenance. Among these, thirteen children (from nine families) had had some direct involvement with the Court Welfare Service and two had consulted a solicitor. Six further children had been referred to a school counsellor, the child psychological service or to family therapy, while another two children had social work support with occasional placements in foster-care. In ten families the parents had gone to mediation, although none of the eighteen children had been directly involved. These figures may underestimate the amount of contact that children may have had with professional agencies (we discuss the reasons for this in chapter 9).

Overall the sample was extremely rich in reflecting the complexities of contemporary childhood at a time when family transformations are increasingly common. We regard this as extremely important because children are not a unitary group who can be presumed to react either 'well' or 'badly' to divorce; rather, they live in highly diverse family circumstances, requiring varied solutions and strategies for managing their lives.

Fieldwork: recruitment and interviewing

Fieldwork was conducted over an eighteen-month period, from summer 1997 to winter 1998. Seven young people were recruited directly into the study (with parental permission sought once they had expressed an interest) while the remainder were recruited via their parental 'gatekeepers'. For the ESRC sample we used a variety of recruitment methods including contacts through voluntary agencies, support groups and professional services, press adverts, local leafleting, personal contacts and snowballing. Acquiring a sample of co-parented children with a broad enough range of experiences was something of a challenge that took longer than we had anticipated. Within the Nuffield sample of fifty-two children, eight children were recruited using personal contacts. But the remaining forty-four children were recruited from a 'ready-made' sample of 109 children (from sixty families) whose parents had previously taken part in our study of post-divorce parenthood (Smart and Neale, 1999). Using our links with these families made the process of recruitment a relatively straightforward one and gave us a valuable opportunity to explore the perspectives of children alongside those of their parents. However, we recruited fewer children than we had originally anticipated. Despite our prior links with the parents and their initial interest in the childhood research, nearly 50 per cent of the parents declined to consent to their children taking part, and we eventually recruited 40 per cent of the potential pool of 109 children into the study. The reasons for the reluctance of parents to allow us to talk to their children were not always clear. Some felt that their children were unsettled following the divorce (or might become unsettled as a result of talking to us) and were reluctant to have issues raised which they felt might distress their children. This may be indicative of the pervasive notion of harm which influences how divorced parents think about – and worry about – their children. In other cases it seemed that the research might become a focus of conflict between the parents and place the children in a difficult situation. We tried to circumvent this problem by working with and seeking consent from one parent rather than both (the ethics of this are discussed in Neale and Smart, 1998). While this proved to be a workable and effective strategy in many cases, several children were lost to the project because of issues of parental conflict. We also suspected that some parents were reluctant to run the risk of their children disclosing intimate details about their families that they wished to keep private.

Working through the parents in drawing a sample does have some drawbacks. Difficulties in recruiting children and poor sample sizes are widely reported problems in this field of research. Using an alternative strategy – through schools for example – might have been a quicker way to achieve a sample. However, parental permission would still have been needed for the qualitative style of interviews that we wished to carry out. Our home-based setting also offered some advantages over an institutionalized, school-based study. It meant we were able to interview the children in the relaxed setting of their own homes or other locations of their choice (our own office or homes, for example), and in most cases in relative privacy.

A potentially more significant issue arising from our method of recruitment concerns the power of veto which parents hold over their children's participation. We were not always able to gain direct access to children to give them an informed choice about participating. While some parents refused without even consulting with their children, others accepted the invitation on their children's behalf in a way that made the child's consent seem somewhat superfluous. Of course, 'self-selection' by research participants which, in this context, includes parental gatekeepers, is essential if sociological research is to be undertaken ethically, but even so there is some debate about whether it skews the nature of the sample towards certain kinds of experiences. It is certainly the case that a substantial majority of the children in our sample were positive about their families, appeared to be doing well in their own lives and did not feel stigmatized about their parents' divorce in the way that children apparently did twenty years ago. Whether this is a reflection of wider social trends, or merely an effect of our method of recruitment, is a matter for debate. However, the nature of the children's accounts and the varieties of post-divorce lifestyles included in our sample indicates a change in children's perceptions of post-divorce family life over the past two decades. We seek to explain this in chapter 4, where we suggest that it may be linked to the process of 'normalizing' divorce. It needs to be stressed, however, that our sample did include children who were unhappy or had experienced problems in their families, and their perspectives form an integral part of our analysis. As we have seen, some parents refused consent on the grounds that their children were or might become unsettled. But equally, some parents were keen for us to speak to unsettled children in the hope that the process might help them. Where children themselves opted in or out of the research, their motives were equally varied. Some took part, for example, precisely to communicate their positive feelings about their families, while others saw the interview as an opportunity to talk through their problems.

The interviews

We conducted in-depth qualitative interviews with the children and young people, in most cases on a one-to-one basis. Fifteen children opted to be interviewed with their siblings while two children chose to have a friend with them. Partial interviews were conducted with ten children. Some of the youngest participants engaged with the process for a short-time span and took frequent breaks for play. Seven children were inhibited by parents who chose to be present or within earshot for all or part of the interview. We used a child-friendly, conversational style of interview, supplemented by some written activities (drawings of family membership, 'emotional closeness' maps, and tick charts for 'who does what' in families and 'who decides'). We used these activities to focus the children's thinking about certain issues and to draw out their verbal reflections. Although they were time-consuming the children enjoyed these activities, and for the younger ones they provided a break from the intensity of conversation. However, we analysed these pictorial representations and written activities in conjunction with the children's commentaries about them, rather than on their own. As well as documenting concrete day-to-day practices and relationships we also explored the children's general attitudes and values about family life and their views on family decision-making. We did so through direct questioning and through the use of vignettes, where we posed a hypothetical moral dilemma and asked the children how they would resolve it (Finch, 1987; Barter and Renold, 1999). In this way we were able to explore children's moral agency and reach a better understanding of why families operate in such diverse ways. The full interviews took approximately an hour and a half to complete and were tape-recorded and fully transcribed.

Interpretive analysis

The process by which research data is analysed and interpreted depends in large part on what kind of sampling strategy has been used and the nature of the intellectual puzzle that has guided the research in the first place. A qualitative approach based on purposive sampling is usually followed through with a systematic, 'interpretive' analysis of the data. This involves scrutinizing the data for both descriptive and conceptual themes and categorizing them into 'blocks' or 'slices' of data that can then be organized into thematic files. Taking one theme or slice of data at a time, the analysis involves moving back and forth between the 'everyday' meanings, interpretations, motives and intentions of the research participants and the theoretical concepts which guided the initial research design. The data is interrogated against the theoretical underpinnings of the research to explore where initial ideas hold ground and where they need modification. Using a grounded theory approach the data can also be interrogated for new concepts and expressions of world views. Analysis of particular 'slices' of data in this way is usually complemented with the analysis of each interview seen as a whole, allowing for the use of both cross-sectional and case-study data in writing up the findings (Mason, 1996b). Analysis is not necessarily a discrete stage of the research process, following on tidily from the fieldwork stage. In practice the analytical process occurs alongside, as well as beyond, the collection of the data and may influence how the fieldwork progresses. Analysis may, for example, uncover new, relatively unexplored perspectives and warrant an extension of the range of cases in the sample.

The method of analysis described above is less well known and understood than the 'variable' method of analysis which usually goes hand in hand with representative sampling in quantitative research. In the 'variable' approach different features across a sample (for example, age or gender of child, and parenting arrangements) are seen as variables and the task is to make inferences about the apparent connections and associations between the variables, such as causal links, or direction and degree of influence. In the process, details are turned into numbers for statistical manipulation, resulting in the production of statistical trends, patterns and correlations between the variables. Quantitative research of this sort privileges the *incidence* of certain patterns of behaviour or experiences. What might hold significance in this style of research, for example, might be the number of children living in particular family patterns and holding similar views, and this will then be reflected in the way the results are presented. In our research, by contrast, we use numbers only to describe the basic characteristics of our sample. They do not generally form part of the analysis or explanation of our data. To specify the numbers of children engaged in similar practices or sharing certain experiences would not aid explanation because our method of purposive sampling simply does not lend itself to this kind of analysis; nor would it be particularly meaningful. Our qualitative analysis and reporting, like our sampling, privileges the *range* of experiences and processes under study rather than their incidence. Individualized experiences do not need to be buttressed by numbers to achieve validity; they can assume significance even if they are unique, simply by virtue of the fact that they represent another kind of experience or process and, therefore, offer a new way of understanding the issues at hand. This is a significant principle to grasp, given that we have argued in this book for the validation of the individual experiences of children and the need to recognize and draw out the differences between them.

Children-as-persons in the research process

One of the central themes of this book is the issue of listening to children. Undertaking this project was, in itself, an exercise in this. We set out to conduct research *with* children rather than *on* them, and in a variety of ways our research methods reflected our commitment to respect the personhood and agency of the children. This meant, for example, that once we had negotiated access to the children we prioritized their informed choice, privacy and confidentiality. We produced child-friendly leaflets about the research, setting out clearly what the process would entail, our obligations to the children and their right to opt in or out as they chose. We consulted with them over the conditions of the interview (timing, location and who they wished to be present) and we gave them unconditional guarantees of confidentiality.[3] The children also chose pseudonyms for themselves that we have used in our writings to protect their confidentiality. Using the children-as-persons premise in an interview setting presents the researcher with several challenges. It involves developing a healthy disregard for the child's age and minimizing power imbalances by adopting the mode of 'learner' rather than slipping into the role of 'educator', 'protector' or 'controller'. It also relies on a conversational style of interviewing and simple, direct methods of questioning based on shared understanding and openness about the purpose of the interview, rather than using indirect methods of eliciting information, which children might find disquieting or even demeaning. It depends, too, on the researcher being non-judgemental and non-intrusive, allowing the children to pace the interaction and express themselves in their own words, to raise issues of importance to them, and to say as little or as much as they choose. We found ourselves, for example, validating children's own experiences and opinions, reassuring them that there were no right or wrong answers and encouraging them to trust their own judgements. In these ways, the children were treated as social equals in the conversations and as co-producers of knowledge and meaning.

Our use of the children-as-persons premise was amply justified in this study. The majority of the children, including those as young as 5, were enthusiastic and perceptive commentators on their families and their childhoods. Not all of them participated in this way, of course, for these are skills that require practice. We suspected that some of the children in the study had had very limited experience of expressing their views, let alone having their views respected, observations which, in themselves, constituted data about the lives of these particular children. Overall however, any qualms we may have initially had about whether children could or would engage in meaningful conversation with relative strangers were quickly dispelled. We found that we learned a great deal from them. They did not simply tell us what they thought we wanted to hear, but provided honest and sometimes compelling accounts of their family lives and their values about relationships. Overall they displayed a great deal of wisdom and insight into their own situations and those of their parents. We hope we have managed to convey something of this in the presentation of our findings.

Notes

Chapter 1   Rethinking Childhood/Rethinking Families

1   Following standard conventions (Chisholm et al., 1990) we distinguish between children of primary school age and under, and young people of secondary school age and over. However, we also use the generic term 'children' when referring to both groups.

2   See, for example, Thorne, 1987; James and Prout, 1997; Waksler, 1991; Alanen, 1992; Mayall, 1994; Jenks, 1996; James, Jenks and Prout, 1998. See also Archard (1993), who distinguishes between a 'caretaker' and 'liberationist' view of children. Our discussion of the nature of childhood in this chapter draws, in particular, on these texts.

3   These representations of childhood continue to be used today. Some of the parents in Newson and Newson's study of child-rearing (1976), for example, described their children in the following terms: 'He's such a little devil', 'She's on the fiendish side', 'His behaviour is diabolical', while others described their children as people (p. 280). Ribbens (1994), in her study of child-rearing, discerned three typifications used by the mothers: 'little innocents', 'little devils' and 'small people'. This latter view is aligned with the social model of childhood described later in this chapter. See also Daniel and Ivatts (1998), who distinguish between children as threats, victims and investment.

4   See Freud (1959), Sullivan (1953), Piaget (1972), Kohlberg (1969) and Erikson (1950).

5   There are parallels between this deep-seated polarity between adult and child and that which was once presumed to exist between 'civilized' and 'savage' societies (Jenks, 1982). The 'primitive mentality' of the savage was often equated with the pre-logical thinking of children, and the relationship between the civilized man and his primitive counterpart was

conceived of in much the same way as that between child and adult: as one of benevolence or tolerance on the part of the 'superior' being (Levy-Bruhl, 1923; Tylor, 1871; Freud, 1950).

6 See, for example, Ariès (1962), Hardman (1973), Mackay (1991), Denzin (1977), and Jenks (1982) for early writings, and Thorne (1987), Waksler (1991), Chisholm et al. (1990), Qvortrup (1994), Mayall (1994), Jenks (1996), James and Prout (1997), and James, Jenks and Prout (1998) for works which consolidated the new approach.

7 See, for example, the psychologically oriented work of Richards and Light (1986), Dunn (1988), Woodhead (1997) and Moore, Sixsmith and Knowles (1996); in the pedagogic tradition, de Winter (1997); in the policy field Daniel and Ivatts (1998); and selected contributors in Hutchby and Moran Ellis (1998).

8 Ariès's work has been critiqued, for example, by Pollock (1983) for painting an overly grim picture of childhoods in past times, but this has not dented the force of his central thesis.

9 See the findings from the ESRC Children 5–16 programme (to be published in a series of volumes by Falmer Press), which focused on children's agency in a variety of contexts. Also the contributions in Qvortrup, 1994; James and Prout, 1997; Mayall, 1994; Hutchby and Moran Ellis, 1998. In the context of family life see Alanen, 1992; Andanaes and Haarvind, 1993; Mayall, 1994, 2000; Brannen and O'Brien, 1995; 1996; Brannen and Edwards, 1996; Andanaes, 1996; Dahlberg, 1996; Morrow, 1998.

10 As an example of this, the new framework stresses the cultural diversity of children's lives, but parts of the new discourse appear to be no less ethnocentric than the old. Woodhead (1997) and Boyden (1997), for example, point out that the global standards of rights for children set out in the UN Convention on the Rights of the Child are based on Western and, in particular, Christian notions of children's interests which simply may not be transferable to other cultures. In the developing countries of the South, for example, young people may assert the right to work to support themselves and their families, and resent being prevented from doing so on the basis of Westernized notions of how children should be spending their time (Boyden, 1997). For a critique of the concept of rights for children, see chapter 6 below.

11 For recent commentaries see Makrinioti, 1994; Morgan, 1996; O'Brien, Alldred and Jones, 1996; Smart and Neale, 1999; Silva and Smart, 1999.

12 See, for example, Giddens, 1992; Beck, 1992; Beck and Beck-Gernsheim, 1995; Jamieson, 1998; Silva and Smart, 1999; Smart and Neale, 1999.

13 See, for example, Mayall, 1994, 2000; Brannen and O'Brien, 1995, 1996; Brannen and Edwards, 1996; Moore, Sixsmith and Knowles, 1996; James and Prout, 1996; Morrow, 1998.

14 See, for example, Weiss (1979), Alanen (1992, 1998), Andanaes and Haarvind (1993), Andanaes (1996), Levin (1995), O'Brien, Alldred and Jones (1996); Moore and Beazley (1996); also Morrow (1998) and Mayall (2000), who explore a variety of families, including those where there has been a divorce.

Chapter 2   Childhood and Modern Narratives of Harm

1 The Labour government's consultation document *Supporting Families* (1998) stated: 'But marriage is still the surest foundation for raising children and remains the choice of the majority of people in Britain. We want to strengthen the institution of marriage to help more marriages to succeed' (Home Office, 1998: 4). The Children Act 1989 gave greater emphasis to parenting than marriage, but this idea seems to have been taken over by the emphasis on preserving marriage not only in the Green Paper but in the Family Law Act 1996.

2 So pervasive is this idea of harm that the authors have had considerable difficulty in explaining that the research for this book was not another study of degrees of harm but rather a study of children's experiences. On one occasion a particularly resistant radio interviewer was told that we were not 'measuring' harm but talking to children about their views. She responded, 'Oh, okay, what did the children have to say about harm then?' We have all experienced the incongruity of being introduced at public events as researchers who have come to talk about the 'suffering of children' or the harm of divorce. This expectation seems so pervasive that we are beginning to think that there is now only one legitimate story about divorce that people want to hear.

3 Rose (1989), Donaldson (1996), Pinchbeck and Hewitt (1973).

4 The first family caseworker was appointed by Oxfordshire Children's Department in 1952. This was seen as the first initiative in preventative work (Younghusband, 1978).

5 Of course there were far more policies designed to improve childhood than the few we have mentioned here. There was a whole raft of new education policies, free school milk and vaccination programmes, health provisions under the NHS and improved housing and sanitation.

6 See Spensky (1992) for an excellent example of this process of normalization in the context of mother and baby homes in England in the 1950s. She also points out that in England there was a growing tendency to see the unmarried mother as pathological and as likely to be a bad mother. This generated a policy in favour of the adoption of illegitimate children rather than one of supporting the lone mother to keep her child. See also Kiernan, Land and Lewis (1998: ch. 4).

7 Indeed Bowlby in 1940 remarked that rather than using the term 'broken home' he preferred to use the term 'broken mother–child relation' (see Riley, 1983: 94). His emphasis was therefore on the significance of the child–mother bond for later psychological problems, not on the mother–father bond, which came to be synonymous with the term 'broken home'.

8 See Home Office (1968).

9 It is widely acknowledged that, in practice, until the close of the 1970s there were three systems of family law: the divorce courts for the middle classes, and the magistrates' courts and social security for the working classes. See Smart (1982) and Finer (1974).

10   There were of course some notable cases where the courts did exactly this. For example, In re Agar-Ellis, Agar-Ellis v. Lascelles [1883] 24 Ch. D. 317. In this case, however, the judges decided that the welfare of the daughter (aged 16) was catered for by requiring her to abide by the natural law of paternal authority, and they refused to allow her to see her mother against her father's wishes.

11   One exception to this was Claud Mullins, who was a reforming stipendiary magistrate in London. In cases of contested custody he would always see the children in a private room, and he gave evidence to the Royal Commission on Marriage and Divorce that it was always advisable to consult with the children (Mullins, 1954).

12   In fact Goldstein et al. were not against ongoing relationships between children and their non-residential parents. What they objected to was enforced contact, which they saw as extremely harmful to the relationship between the child and the custodial parent, and hence to the child's ontological security.

13   In the Epilogue to *Beyond the Best Interests of the Child*, Solnit recounts his experience of giving evidence in a case of contested contact. His evidence was dismissed as 'novel and startling' by the judge, and as potentially stripping the court of its role in safeguarding the welfare of children. The judge stated, 'Consequently, the Court totally rejects the specious notion so ingenuously urged by Professor Solnit and his co-authors that the custodial parent should have the sole right to determine in the name of the best interests of the child whether the noncustodial parent should be permitted or denied association with his own child'. Sadly in this case it would seem that the judge would have done better to have followed Professor Solnit's advice, because the non-residential father proceeded to 'kidnap' his daughter and has not been heard from since.

14   Goldstein et al. were influential in the field of social work practice and adoption, however.

15   Children who 'were poorly treated, verbally or physically abused, or sexually misused by fathers they feared, and children who had frequently witnessed the father's cruelty to the mother . . . were freed from the psychopathology and burdening of a corrosive relationship' (Wallerstein and Kelly, 1980: 218). The authors also report that where children had rejected a parent themselves they did not feel deserted. They drew their self-esteem from good-quality relationships with others, including their residential parent, and by making a conscious decision to define themselves as different from their fathers (1980: 250–1).

16   See also Wallerstein and Lewis (1998).

17   In fact Mitchell only interviewed 'children' between 16 and 18 because she felt that if they were younger they could not give informed consent to the interview. Walczak and Burns interviewed 100 'children', but twenty-three of these were 18 or over, and twenty-seven were over 25 years old. Many of the accounts were therefore retrospective and their parents must have divorced in the 1960s and early 1970s.

18   Sometimes there is serendipity in this process. It is for example helpful to

have the sort of name that can accommodate an 'ism' attached to it. Thus Bowlby became Bowlbyism: although this is ugly, it works in a way that 'Winnicottism' surely would not have done!

19   It is also possible to see the influence of Bowlby on the Curtis Report of 1946 which recommended fostering over institutional care for children. However, the children's homes were not closed and still have not closed, even though we still 'know' how harmful they can be.

20   Ultimately, though, these recommendations came to nothing because the relevant sections of the Act were never implemented by the subsequent Labour government.

Chapter 3   Children's Perspectives on Post-Divorce Family Life

1   We use pseudonyms chosen by the children to protect their anonymity. After their names we give their ages in brackets.

2   This technique has been used by other researchers to capture children's constructions of their families. We build here on the work of Isaacs and Levin, 1984; Isaacs, Leon and Kline, 1987; Johnson, Klee and Schmidt, 1988; Klee, Schmidt and Johnson, 1989; Funder, 1991; Levin, 1995; O'Brien, Alldred and Jones, 1996; Ottosen, 1997; Morrow, 1998; and Brannen, Heptinstall and Bhopal, 2000.

3   Henceforth we usually refer to these 'kin' simply as partners or new partners, although we sometimes refer to them as spouses if they have married the parent, or as 'social' parents if they have taken on a parenting role.

4   Henceforth 'biological' parents are referred to simply as 'parents', although in some places we take our lead from the children and refer to them as 'real' parents.

5   Pets were regarded as important family members for those children who had them, and they often featured in family drawings. As Morrow (1998, 1999) shows, they are useful confidants and can give unconditional, non-judgemental love. We found that they could provide continuity and a source of comfort to children by accompanying them from house to house, particularly where they were being co-parented.

6   Family life may be characterized by a range of parenting styles: authoritarian, permissive, absent and authoritative. What distinguishes these in the main is the form of discipline used. Authoritative parenting directs a child's activities in a rational, issue-oriented manner, and exerts firm control when needed, but uses encouragement rather than punitive reactions and restrictive practices. This form of parenting has been associated with the development of social competence in children. In contrast, authoritarian (punitive or domineering) or permissive (neglectful) styles have negative effects. See the review in Sweeting, West and Richards (1998) and Miller (1999) for a description of what might be called positive or democratic parenting, which shares similarities with an authoritative style.

7   See, for example, Morrow, 1998, 1999; Brannen, Heptinstall and Bhopal, 2000; Katz and Buchanan, 1999; Mayall, 2000; and NFPI, 2000. However, our findings here are based on a predominantly white sample of children and may not reflect the values of children from different cultural or religious backgrounds. Morrow (1998), for example, found that Muslim children held strong values about the respect owed to parents by children, and this assumed rather more significance for them than the notion of mutual respect.

8   Joanna Trollope's book *Other People's Children* (1998) is one such example.

Chapter 4   'Doing' Post-Divorce Childhood

1   Of course children do have access to fairy stories and children's literature, and the increasingly popular soaps. Much traditional literature is rather negative when it comes to children's experiences of step-parents, however, and even the immensely popular Harry Potter books are negative about the experiences of living with kin who are not biological parents. One has only to think of the dreadful Dursleys and their ghastly son Dudley who had poor Harry living in a cupboard under the stairs for nearly eleven years to be reminded that children get rather negative images of life apart from their biological parents.

2   For example, as early as 1980 Wallerstein and Kelly made the point that parental absence which was chosen by a child was quite different in its consequences and psychological impact to parental absence chosen by an adult who appeared to reject the child.

3   The use of this new technology to improve father–son relationships is very interesting; we found an instance of this in our research for *Family Fragments?* (Smart and Neale, 1999).

4   We raise this because there is a strong assumption following Gilligan (1982) that it is really only girls who do this kind of emotional work. We were not attempting to test this hypothesis in this research, but we certainly found many examples of boys being attentive and caring.

5   As Rachel (16) said, 'I always knew quite a lot about what was going on between mum and dad because I've always made it my business to know quite a lot about everything. Which can be a bit annoying sometimes – Ha! – for other people.'

6   It is important to acknowledge that not all children can take advantage of these developments. In chapters 7 and 8 we identify circumstances and examples of post-divorce childhoods which are less 'open' and democratic than this.

Chapter 5   Do Children Care? Childhood and Moral
.   Reasoning

1   Of course the 'problem' of children from broken homes was not discovered in the 1990s as there had been various panics over lone motherhood and delinquency almost every decade since the Second World War. But it was in the 1990s that the idea that divorce harms every child who experiences it grew to these proportions. Thus what had been a concern to criminal law and social work practice moved into the family law domain.

2   See Benhabib (1992), Gilligan (1982), Larrabee (1993), Mason (1996a), Sevenhuijsen (1998), Smart and Neale (1999), Tronto (1993), Young (1997).

3   Iris Young (1997) argues that where there is inequality or difference it is mistaken to assume that a moral conversation is based on equivalence or sameness. She therefore uses the term 'asymmetric reciprocity' to foreground that difference and ensure that it is not ignored or subsumed by the more powerful voice.

4   In this instance it is particularly useful to be able to put Karl's remarks into a broader context. Elsewhere in the interview he made it plain that his mother always paid for extra school trips and so on, and that his father always refused to do so. If his mother could not afford to pay, he would not ask his father to do so. His parents were still embroiled in legal disputes over financial matters several years after their divorce. Of course, it is equally important to put all the children's 'hypothetical' comments derived from the vignettes into the fuller context of their interview narratives which were based on 'actuality'. To make sense of the utterances of each child it is methodologically important to have both accounts. However, in this chapter we are focusing on the vignettes and this needs to be read in the context of the whole book.

5   Examples of sentient activity can be found in chapter 4, but in this chapter, which is based on the data derived from vignettes, we tap more into active sensibility because we are dealing with hypothetical situations rather than descriptions of what the children actually do to help or to care for their parents.

Chapter 6   Children, Citizenship and Family Practices

1   We are conscious there are compelling arguments in favour of continuing to prioritize rights for children. Roche (1999b) for example has argued that the concept of rights carries with it a presumption that the rights-bearer is an active agent rather than a passive recipient of benevolence and that this is particularly important for children. Moreover there are clearly rights that children do not have which, arguably, they

should have. We accept these points, but would still insist that the debate
needs to be taken forward on a broad set of issues and that it would be a
mistake to focus too exclusively on legal rights. See also Lim and Roche
(2000).

2　The Children Act 1989 section 1(3)(a).

3　Gillick v. West Norfolk and Wisbech Area Health Authority [1985] 3
All ER 402.

4　This issue has been much discussed in the field of criminal law where
children are called to give evidence as witnesses to crimes, in particular
assaults against themselves – often by parents. In these cases the legal
system has allowed for modifications to the adversarial procedure including different forms of interview to form the basis of a child's evidence. However, these developments, which are as yet far from perfect,
are not necessarily what is required in divorce proceedings.

5　The idea of children vetoing their parents' divorce is perhaps not so unthinkable. Many parents already postpone divorce in the interests of their
children and the classic notion of 'staying together for the sake of the
children' is a kind of veto – but one based on welfare criteria rather than
democratic participation. It may therefore be possible to envisage such
discussions in some contexts.

6　One example of this is the book that was produced from this research
which was designed to be accessible to children and parents and which,
quite simply, gave voice to what the children said about what was good
and what was bad about living through divorce and post-divorce family
life (see Neale and Wade, 2000).

Chapter 7　Children's Experiences of Co-Parenting

1　These are some examples of the comments made by some of the children
and young people:

RACHEL (16): [At first] it was confusing. I'd worry I'd go to the
wrong house at a certain time or something. . . . But it's just like
second nature now. I've been doing it so long I can hardly remember what it was like before.
FRANCES (12): It was different at first, but I've got used to it now, so
its just like normal.
NICK (14): [It] was odd at first but I got used to it . . . it's like a
pattern, you just sink into it after a while.
JAMES HENRY (12): I've sort of accepted it more and got used to it,
adjusted.

2　　TOM (12): My friends like my dad's house better [than mum's] because up there there's a CD-ROM with all the computer games on
it and down here mum's only got a Macintosh and it's slightly less
advanced . . . so they always want to come to my house at dad's,

but on days that I'm at mum's house almost no-one comes over apart from the occasional best friend that likes to play with the stuff over there.

Q: *Do you miss your friends not coming so much, or is that not important?*

TOM: I just think they're a bit cheeky to like one house better than the other, they're both equally good.

3   Joe Jenkins' (9) situation was a good example of this degree of co-operation. He had been co-parented for four years and saw both of his parents every day. Although his mother and father had felt considerable bitterness towards each other when they first separated, they had come to work as a team in parenting Joe and provided each other with considerable support. They lived in the same area, each dropped in to the other's home when Joe was there, and they often shared meals and had holidays together. When interviewed, Joe described his parents as 'good friends'. He illustrated this in a story he wrote which recounted a family outing when his father discovered he had accidentally locked himself out of his house. The situation was rescued by Joe's mum, who climbed through a window and unlocked the door from the inside. Afterwards the parents decided to each keep a key to each other's home in case this should happen again. Joe saw his parents as having different personalities, interests, and abilities, but he emphasized the links which they retained with each other and their shared common purpose in providing for him. He regarded his two homes as much the same, with little to distinguish one from the other, and valued the fact that the boundary between them was permeable, enabling him to retain a sense of his family as a unit.

4   It is important of course to recognize that for many children fathers might have been been fairly distant or even almost absent figures before the divorce. For these children there might have been a sense of continuity after divorce if they continued to live with their mothers and saw their fathers occasionally. So we are not suggesting that it is only co-parenting arrangements that can provide this continuity. Indeed for some children who were co-parented after divorce, but where their fathers had been somewhat remote, it was difficult to get used to being cared for by their fathers.

5   See Ennew (1994). This is part of a broader trend towards the increased curricularization of childhood and a devaluing of time and space for children to engage in their own activities. Ennew raises the issue of whether 'quality time' for children might be seen as time for the adult rather than the child.

6   As researchers we have already experienced requests from pressure groups as well as from individuals to provide them with the 'evidence' that co-parenting is best for children. Of course, we cannot control how some people might choose to misread our findings, but we can at least make clear that we do not feel that our research supports any particular model of parenting. Nor would we support any policy measure that attempted

to impose co-parenting willy-nilly on all divorcing parents and their children. Such measures have nothing to do with listening to children.

Chapter 8 Children and their Parents: Different Perspectives

1 See the appendix for full details of the sample of children in this study.
2 Bringing the accounts of parents and children together raised some difficult ethical problems. The most obvious one was the increased possibility of recognition, either of the parent or of the children. For this reason we have drawn 'from' the accounts we were given rather than presenting them factually and we have changed a range of factors to ensure anonymity. Equally sensitive was the possible sense that either parents or children might feel that we were bringing accounts together to check them for truthfulness or accuracy. We hope that we have dispelled this idea in the text because we feel most strongly that different people will always have different accounts and interpretations of even a simple event – let alone something as complex as family life. Moreover, inasmuch as children do not stand in the same position as adults, it could hardly be assumed that they will see the world in the same way. We hope that these stories (since this is surely what they have now become) will serve to reveal the extent to which children's views and experiences cannot be subsumed into those of their parents – no matter how caring and attentive those parents might be.
3 See chapter 6 for a discussion of the importance of voice.
4 This will appear to be self-evident to most parents of course, but in policy terms it remains important to stress that not all children are alike and that 'one size' does not fit all when it comes to designing policy.
5 The father and the daughter in this family told us long stories of the conflict and violence that had characterized the marriage.
6 Cf. our discussion in chapter 1 of the model of children as little devils and the harsh methods presumed to be needed to keep them under control.

Chapter 9 Implications

1 The fact, for example, that Mitchell (1985) only interviewed young people over 16 because she felt that 'children' younger than this could not give informed consent is a marker of how far we have come in fifteen years.
2 This does not mean that all these children could talk easily to their own parents of course. The vignette taps into ideas about what should be done in principle, whereas elsewhere in our interviews we were able to gain insights into what the individual children themselves did when faced with certain difficulties.

3 For empirical evidence on this theme see Neale (2001). For further evidence on the importance of peers see H. Smith (1999) and C. Smith (2000).

4 A. Griffiths (1998) reports that only a small minority of the children brought before the Scottish children's panel entered into meaningful dialogue with the panel members. The rest used a variety of strategies (over-compliance, rebellion, or dogged silence) to avoid engaging in the process.

5 Innovative professional agencies and services do exist, although the children in this sample had not benefited from them. New child-centred counselling, peer support and mediation-based services are developing in piecemeal fashion around the country, although they are poorly funded. The pioneering Childline service is difficult to access because it is so oversubscribed. For discussions of child-centred support see Davie, Upton and Varma, 1996; Childline, 1998; Smith, 1999; Cantwell, Roberts and Young, 1999; Smith, 2000.

6 See, for example, Williamson and Butler, 1995; Masson and Oakley, 1998; Morrow, 1999; Lyon, Surrey and Timms, 1998.

7 Gillick v. West Norfolk and Wisbech Area Health Authority, [1986] AC 112. See Eekelaar (1994) for a discussion of this case.

8 See Freeman (1997: ch. 11) for a full discussion of legal interpretations of 'sufficient understanding' and the Gillick case.

9 For a review of recent evidence on this see O'Quigley (2000). Court Welfare Officers are currently reviewing their practice in preparation for their amalgamation with Guardians in CAFCASS. Mediators have also recently revised their policy so that in future they will be required to consult with parents about 'the different ways in which children may be involved or consulted, including, when appropriate, offering opportunities for them to take part directly in discussion with the mediator/s' (UK College of Family Mediators, 2000: 1).

10 Timms, 1997; Sawyer, 1997; Lyon, Surrey and Timms, 1998.

11 Which is, of course, much preferable to being committed to doing evil.

12 See Neale and Wade (2000) for a recent example in the context of divorce.

13 Some peer support services give options for children to express their views individually or collectively through written outputs or other creative means. A school-based programme in Exeter, for example, involves children in the production of a magazine at the centre of which the children develop a fictional story about a separated family.

14 This is a common practice among Guardians (Ruegger, 2000).

15 The limitations of the court welfare role and the need for inter-agency collaboration were issues raised by the Court Welfare Officers who took part in a one-day seminar, 'Listening to Children', at the Centre for Research on Family, Kinship and Childhood, University of Leeds, in June 2000.

16 The Act was designed to avoid a narrowly prescriptive approach by allowing for a fresh consideration of the needs of each individual child (Law Commission, 1986).

17 In Sawyer's view, 'The judiciary has control over court welfare officers
    and is able to influence ideas of welfare in a way which is deeply political
    and . . . founded on parents' rights. . . . The judiciary has actively resisted
    movements towards giving children greater rights or representation and
    has re-interpreted welfare, and legislation, to justify it. . . . Without a
    clear discussion of the differences between welfare and rights to repre-
    sentation . . . which entails the right to dissent . . . there can be no chil-
    dren's rights [and] also no method of presenting resistance to the authority
    of a court or to the opinions of experts. . . . This raises serious questions
    about the treatment of children within this society [and] the nature of the
    democratic society' (Sawyer, 1999b: 330).

18 See, for example, Johnston (1993). For children forced to accompany a
    Court Welfare Officer despite being 'violently unwilling' to do so, see F.
    v. F. (1996) 13 May (Court of Appeal (unreported)), cited in Maidment
    (1998). For children taken into local authority care for several weeks
    and then forced to see a physically violent parent, A. v. N. (Committal:
    refusal of contact) [1997] 1 FLR 533; for children with a surrogate par-
    ent referred to a psychologist in order to be told about their biological
    parentage and introduced to their 'real' father, Re R (a minor) (contact)
    [1993] 2 FLR 148; and for children forced against their will to have
    contact with sexually abusive fathers, Re H (minors) (access: appeals)
    1989 2 FLR 174 and the reviews in Weyland (1995), Freeman (1997)
    and Fortin (1998).

19 See critiques in Fortin (1998) and Roche (1999a). Also from the judici-
    ary, see Hall (1997), who denigrates such harsh measures and stresses
    that children's views should not be misinterpreted or overridden in these
    ways.

Appendix

1 The ESRC sample of co-parented children was probably less typical than
   the Nuffield sample. The dominance of co-parented children across the
   study as a whole reflects our sampling strategy rather than being indicative of a widespread pattern of post-divorce parenting in the UK, although it appears to be growing in popularity. Statistical evidence is not
   available, but based on large-scale American studies it would seem that
   conventional custodial-style arrangements built on mother residence continue to predominate (Buchanan, Maccoby and Dornbusch, 1996; Neale
   and Smart, 1997a; Thompson and Amato, 1999).

2 Sometimes arrangements are bound up with financial considerations on
   the part of parents. For example, a father is entitled to pay less maintenance if he has his child to stay for two nights per week, and does not have
   to pay maintenance at all if the care of the child is shared. Being residential can also give a parent a legitimate claim to the family home (Neale
   and Smart, 1997a, forthcoming).

3 For a discussion of the issue of confidentiality and how this fits with child protection issues see Neale and Smart (1998) and Roberts (1999). For more details of how we sought to prioritize children's agency in the research process see Neale and Smart (1998).

References

Ackers, L. (2000) *From 'Best Interests' to Participatory Rights: Children's Involvement in Family Migration Decisions*, University of Leeds: Centre for Research on Family, Kinship & Childhood, Working Paper 18.

Alanen, L. (1992) *Modern Childhood? Exploring the 'Child Question' in Sociology*, Research Report No. 50, Finland: University of Jyvaskylä.

Alanen, L. (1994) 'Gender and Generation: Feminism and the "Child" Question,' in J. Qvortrup (ed.) *Childhood Matters*, Aldershot: Avebury.

Alanen, L. (1998) 'Children and the Family Order: Constraints and Competencies', in I. Hutchby and J. Moran-Ellis (eds), *Children and Social Competence: Arenas of Action*. London: Falmer Press.

Alderson, P. (1994) 'Researching Children's Rights to Integrity', in B. Mayall (ed.), *Children's Childhoods Observed and Experienced*, London: Falmer Press.

Allatt, P. (1996) 'Conceptualising Parenting from the Standpoint of Children: Relationship and Transition in the Life Course', in J. Brannen and M. O'Brien (eds), *Children in Families: Research and Policy*, London: Falmer Press.

Ambert, A. (1993) 'The Place of Children in North American Sociology', in P. Alder and P. Alder (eds.), *Sociological Studies of Child Development*, Greenwich, Conn.: JAI Press.

Andanaes, A. (1996) 'Challenges and Solutions for Children with Two Homes in the Nordic Countries', in J. Brannen and R. Edwards (eds.), *Perspectives on Parenting and Childhood*, London: South

Bank University.

Andanaes, A. and Haarvind, H. (1993) 'When Parents are Living Apart', in A. Leira (ed.), *Family Sociology: Developing the Field Report* 93:5, Oslo: Institute of Social Research.

Archard, R. (1993) *Children: Rights and Childhood*, London: Routledge.

Ariès, P. (1962) *Centuries of Childhood*, London: Cape.

Baker, A. (1996) 'Post-Divorce Parenting: Rethinking Shared Residence', *Child and Family Law Quarterly*, 8(3): 217–27.

Barter, C. and Renold, E. (1999) 'The Use of Vignettes in Qualitative Research', *Social Research Update*, 25.

Beck, U. (1992) *Risk Society: Towards a New Modernity*, London: Sage.

Beck, U. and Beck-Gernsheim, E. (1995) *The Normal Chaos of Love*, Cambridge: Polity.

Benhabib, S. (1992) *Situating the Self*, Cambridge: Polity.

Bernard, J. (1978) *The Future of Marri*age, New York: Bantam Books.

Borland, M., Laybourn, A., Hill, M. and Brown, J. (1998) *Middle Childhood: The Perspectives of Children and Parents*, London: Jessica Kingsley Publishers.

Bowlby, J. (1946) *Forty-Four Juvenile Thieves: Their Character and Home Life*, London: Ballière, Tindall & Cox.

Bowlby, J. (1952) 'The Development of Social Responsibility within the Family', *Social Work*, 9(1): 623–7

Bowlby, J. (1965) *Childcare and the Growth of Love*, 2nd edn, Harmondsworth: Penguin.

Bowlby, J. (1969) *Attachment*, vol. 1 of *Attachment and Loss*, London: Hogarth Press.

Boyden, J. (1997) 'Childhood and the Policy Makers: A Comparative Perspective on the Globalisation of Childhood', in A. James and A. Prout (eds.), *Constructing and Reconstructing Childhood*, 2nd edn, London: Falmer Press.

Brannen, J. (1989) *Working Mothers: Ideologies and Experiences*, Thomas Coram Research Unit, University of London: Institute of Education.

Brannen, J. (1999) 'Reconsidering Children and Childhood: Sociological and Policy Perspectives', in. E. B. Silva and C. Smart (eds), *The New Family?*, London: Sage.

Brannen, J. and Edwards, R. (eds.) (1996) *Perspectives on Parenting and Childhood: Looking Back and Moving Forward*, London: South Bank University.

Brannen, J. and O'Brien, M. (eds.) (1995) *Childhood and Parenthood*, University of London, Institute of Education.

Brannen, J. and O'Brien, M. (eds) (1996) *Children in Families: Research and Policy*, London: Falmer Press.

Brannen, J., Heptinstall, E. and Bhopal, K. (2000) *Connecting Children: Care and Family Life in Middle Childhood*, London: Falmer Press.

Bridge, C. (1996) 'Shared Residence in England and New Zealand: A Comparative Analysis', *Child and Family Law Quarterly*, 8(1): 12–27.

Buchanan, C., Maccoby, E. and Dornbusch, S. (1996) *Adolescents after Divorce*, London: Harvard University Press.

Bulmer, M. and Rees, A. M. (1996) *Citizenship Today: The Contemporary Relevance of T. H. Marshall*, London: University College Press.

Burgess, A. (1998) *The Complete Parent*, London: IPPR.

Burlingham, D. and Freud, A. (1942) *Young Children in Wartime*, London: Allen & Unwin.

Burlingham, D. and Freud, A. (1944) *Infants Without Families: The Case For and Against Residential Nurseries*, London: Allen & Unwin.

Cantwell, B. (1996) 'Children's Voices into the Adult World', *Representing Children*, 9(3): 150–4.

Cantwell, B. and Scott, S. (1995) 'Children's Wishes, Children's Burdens', *Journal of Social Welfare and Family Law*, 17(3): 337–54.

Cantwell, B., Roberts, J. and Young, V. (1999) 'Presumption of Contact in Private Law: an Interdisciplinary Issue', *Family Law*, 29 (April): 226–32.

Childline (1998) *Unhappy Families, Unhappy Children*, London: Childline.

Children's Rights Office (1995) *Building Small Democracies*, London: Children's Rights Office.

Chisholm, L., Buchner, P., Kruger, H. and Brown, P. (eds) (1990) *Childhood, Youth and Social Change: A Comparative Perspective*, London: Falmer Press.

Christensen, P. (1998) 'Difference and Similarity: How Children's Competence is Constituted in Illness and its Treatment', in I. Hutchby and J. Moran Ellis (eds.), *Children and Social Competence: Arenas of Action*, London: Falmer Press.

Clarke, L. (1996) 'Demographic Change and the Family Situation of Children', in J. Brannen and M. O'Brien (eds), *Children in Families: Research and Policy*, London: Falmer Press.

Cockburn, T. (1998) 'Children and Citizenship in Britain', *Childhood*, 5(1): 99–117.

Cockburn, T. (1999) 'Children and the Redefinition of Citizenship in Britain', paper presented at the Rethinking Citizenship conference,

University of Leeds, June 1999.

Cockett, M. and Tripp, J. (1994) *The Exeter Family Study*, Exeter: Exeter University Press.

Conway, H. L. (1995) 'Shared Residence Orders', *Family Law*, 25: 435–7.

Cooper, A. (1999) 'With Justice in Mind: Complexity, Child Welfare and the Law', in M. King (ed.), *Moral Agendas for Children's Welfare*, London: Routledge.

Curtis Report (1946) *Report of the Care of Children Committee*, London: HMSO Cmd 6922.

Dahlberg, G. (1996) 'Negotiating Modern Child Rearing and Family Life in Sweden', in J. Brannen and R. Edwards, (eds.), *Perspectives on Parenting and Childhood*, London: South Bank University.

Daniel, P. and Ivatts, J. (1998) *Children and Social Policy*, Basingstoke: Macmillan.

Davie, R., Upton, G. and Varma, V. (1996) *The Voice of the Child: A Handbook for Professionals*, London: Falmer Press.

de Winter, M. (1997) *Children as Fellow Citizens: Participation and Commitment*, Oxford: Radcliffe Medical Press.

Denning, A. (1946) Committee on Procedure in Matrimonial Causes.

Denzin, N. (1977) *Childhood Socialisation*, San Francisco: Jossey-Bass.

Department of Health (1991) *The Children Act 1989 Guidance and Regulations*: vol. 1, *Court Orders*, London: HMSO.

Dimmock, B. (1997) 'The Contemporary Stepfamily', *Adoption and Fostering*, 21(4): 49–56.

Donaldson, G. (1996) 'Between Practice and Theory: Melanie Klein, Anna Freud and the Development of Child Analysis', *Journal of the History of the Behavioral Sciences*, 32(2): 160–76.

Dunn, J. (1988) *The Beginnings of Social Understanding*, Cambridge, Mass.: Harvard University Press.

Durkheim, E. (1956) *Education and Sociology* [1911], translated with an introduction by Sherwood D. Fox, Glencoe, Illinois: The Free Press.

Durkheim, E. (1979) 'Childhood' [1911], in W. F. Pickering (ed.), *Durkheim: Essays on Morals and Education*, London: Routledge.

Eekelaar, J. (1986) 'The Emergence of Children's Rights', *Oxford Journal of Legal Studies*, 6(2): 161–83.

Eekelaar, J. (1994) 'The Interests of the Child and the Child's Wishes: The Role of Dynamic Self Determinism,' in P. Alston (ed.), *The Best Interests of the Child*, Oxford: Clarendon Press.

Ennew, J. (1994) 'Time for Children or Time for Adults?,' in J. Qvortrup (ed.), *Childhood Matters*, Aldershot: Avebury.

Erikson, E. (1950) *Childhood and Society*, New York: Norton.

Finch, J. (1987) 'The Vignette Technique in Survey Research', *Sociology*, 21: 105–14

Finch, J. (1989) *Family Obligations and Social Change*, Cambridge: Polity.

Finch, J. (1997) *The State and the Family*, lecture to inaugurate the annual theme of the Institute of International Social Sciences, University of Edinburgh, 30 October 1996. Edinburgh: Institute of International Social Sciences.

Finch, J. and Mason, J. (1990) 'Decision Taking in the Fieldwork Process: Theoretical Sampling and Collaborative Working', in R. Burgess (ed.), *Studies in Qualitative Methodology*, vol. 2, Greenwich, Conn.: JAI Press.

Finch, J. and Mason, J. (1993) *Negotiating Family Responsibilities*, London: Tavistock/Routledge.

Finer, M. (1974) *Report of the Committee on One Parent Families*, vols 1 and 2, London: HMSO Cmnd 5629.

Fletcher, R. (1962) *The Family and Marriage in Britain*, Harmondsworth: Penguin.

Fortin, J. (1998) *Children's Rights and the Developing Law*, London: Butterworth.

Franklin, B. (ed.) (1986) *The Rights of Children*, Oxford: Blackwell.

Fraser, N. (1995) 'From Re-distribution to Recognition? Dilemmas of Justice in a "Post-Socialist" Age', *New Left Review*, 212: 68–92

Freeman, M. (1997) *The Moral Status of Children*, The Hague: Martinus Nijhoff Publishers.

Freud, S. (1950) *Totem and Taboo: Some Points of Agreement between the Mental Lives of Savages and Neurotics* [1913], London: Routledge & Kegan Paul.

Freud, S. (1959) 'Beyond the Pleasure Principle', in J. Strachey (ed.), *The Standard Edition of the Complete Psychological Works of S. Freud*, vol. 18, London: Hogarth Press.

Frones, I. (1993) 'Changing Childhood', *Childhood*, 1: 1.

Frost, N. and Stein, M. (1989) *The Politics of Child Welfare*, London: Harvester Wheatsheaf.

Funder, K. (1991) 'Children's Constructions of their Post-Divorce Families: A Family Sculpture Approach', in K. Funder (ed.), *Images of Australian Families*, Cheshire: Longman.

Giddens, A. (1991) *Modernity and Self Identity: Self and Society in the Late Modern Age*, Cambridge: Polity.

Giddens, A. (1992) *The Transformation of Intimacy*, Cambridge: Polity.

Gilligan, C. (1982) *In a Different Voice*, London: Harvard University Press.

Goffman, E. (1967) *Interaction Ritual*, New York: Anchor Books.

Goldstein, J., Freud, A. and Solnit, A. (1979) *Beyond the Best Interests of the Child*, 2nd edn, New York: Free Press.

Goldstein, J., Freud, A. and Solnit, A. (1980) *Before the Best Interests of the Child*, London: Burnett Books.

Gorrell-Barnes, G., Thompson, P., Daniel, G. and Burchardt, N. (1998) *Growing Up in Stepfamilies*, Oxford: Clarendon Press.

Grau, M. and Walsh, D. (1998) *Studying Children in Context: Theories, Methods and Ethics*, London: Sage.

Griffiths, A. (1998) *Including Children in the Process? Glasgow's Children Panel*, Paper delivered at the Socio-Legal Studies Association annual conference, Manchester Metropolitan University, April.

Griffiths, M. (1995) *Feminisms and the Self: The Web of Identity*, London: Routledge.

Hall, V. (1997) 'Domestic Violence and Contact', *Family Law*, 27 (December): 813–18.

Hallden, G. (1991) 'The Child as Project and the Child as Being: Parents' Ideas as Frames of Reference', *Childhood and Society*, 5(94): 334–56.

Hallden, G. (1994) 'The Family: A Refuge from Demands or an Arena for the Exercise of Power and Control? Children's Fictions on their Future Families', in B. Mayall (ed.), *Children's Childhoods Observed and Experienced*, London: Falmer Press.

Hardman, C. (1973) 'Can there be an Anthropology of Children?', *Journal of the Anthropological Society of Oxford*, 4(1): 84–99.

Harré, R. (1986) 'The Step to Social Constructionism', in M. Richards and P. Light (eds), *Children of Social Worlds*, Cambridge: Polity.

Hart, R. (1992) *Children's Participation: From Tokenism to Citizenship*, Florence: UNICEF Innocenti Essays no. 4.

Harty, M. and Wood, J. (1991) 'From Shared Care to Shared Residence: Perspectives on Section II of the Children Act 1989', *Family Law*, 21: 430–3.

Hendrick, H. (1994) *Child Welfare: England 1872–1989*, London: Routledge.

Hendrick, H. (1997) *Children, Childhood and English Society 1880–1990*, Cambridge: Cambridge University Press.

Hester, M. and Radford, L. (1996) *Domestic Violence and Child Contact Arrangements in England and Denmark*, University of Bristol: Policy Press.

Hetherington, E. and Stanley-Hagan, M. (1999) 'The Adjustment of Children with Divorced Parents: A Risk and Resiliency Perspective', *Journal of Child Psychology and Psychiatry*, 40(1): 129–40.

Hoggett, B. (1989) 'Joint Parenting Systems: The English Experiment', *Journal of Child Law*, 6(1): 8–12

Home Office (1968) *Children in Trouble*, London: HMSO Cmnd 3601.

Home Office (1998) *Supporting Families: A Consultation Document*, London: HMSO.

Hood-Williams, J. (1990) 'Patriarchy for Children: On the Stability of Power Relations in Children's Lives', in L. Chisholm et al. (eds.), *Childhood, Youth and Social Change: A Comparative Perspective*, London: Falmer Press.

Hutchby, I. and Moran Ellis, J. (eds.) (1998) *Children and Social Competence*, London: Falmer Press.

Isaacs, M. and Levin, I. (1984) 'Who's In My Family? A Longitudinal Study of Drawings of Children of Divorce', *Journal of Divorce*, 7(4): 1–21.

Isaacs, M., Leon, G. and Kline, M. (1987) 'When is a Parent Out of the Picture? Different Custody, Different Perceptions', *Family Process*, 26 (March): 101–10

James, A. (1993) *Childhood Identities: Self and Social Relationships in the Experience of the Child*, Edinburgh: Edinburgh University Press.

James, A. (1998) 'Foreword', in I. Hutchby and J. Moran-Ellis (eds.), *Children and Social Competence*, London: Falmer Press.

James, A. (1999) 'Parents: A Children's Perspective', in A. Bainham, S. Day Sclater and M. Richards (eds.), *What is a Parent?*, Oxford: Hart.

James A. and Christensen, P. (eds.) (1999) *Research with Children*, London: Falmer Press.

James, A. and James, A. (1999) 'Pumping up the Volume: Listening to Children in Separation and Divorce', *Childhood*, 6(2): 189–206.

James, A. and Prout, A. (1995) 'Hierarchy, Boundary and Agency: Towards a Theoretical Perspective on Childhood', in A. Ambert (ed.), *Sociological Studies of Childhood*, New York: JAI Press.

James, A. and Prout, A. (1996) 'Strategies and Structures: Towards a New Perspective on Children's Experiences of Family Life', in J. Brannen and M. O'Brien (eds), *Children in Families: Research and Policy*, London: Falmer Press.

James, A. and Prout, A. (eds) (1997) *Constructing and Reconstructing Childhood*, 2nd edn, London: Falmer Press.

James, A., Jenks, C. and Prout, A. (1998) *Theorizing Childhood*, Cambridge: Polity.

Jamieson, L. (1998) *Intimacy: Personal Relationships in Modern Societies*, Cambridge: Polity.

Jenks, C. (ed.) (1982) *The Sociology of Childhood: Essential Readings*, London: Batsford.

Jenks, C. (1996) *Childhood*, London: Routledge.

Johnson, C., Klee, L. and Schmidt, C. (1988) 'Conceptions of Parentage and Kinship among Children of Divorce', *American Anthropologist*, 90(1): 136–44.

Johnston, J. (1993) 'Children of Divorce who Refuse Visitation', in C. Depner and J. Bray (eds.), *Non Residential Parenting: Vistas in Family Living*, New York: Sage.

Joshi, H., Cooksey, E., Clarke, L., Wiggins, D. and McCullock, A. (1998) *Family Disruption and the Cognitive and Behavioural Development of Children in Longitudinal Data from Britain and the USA*, London: Centre for Longitudinal Studies, NCDS Working Paper 50.

Joshi, H., Wiggins, D. and Clarke, L. (2000) 'The Changing Home: Outcomes for Children', *Children 5–6 Research Programme Briefing*, No. 6, Swindon: ESRC.

Kaganas, F. (1999) 'Contact, Conflict and Risk', in S. D. Sclater and C. Piper (eds), *Undercurrents of Divorce*, Aldershot: Ashgate/Dartmouth.

Katz, A. and Buchanan, A. (1999) *What Sons Say*, East Molesey, Surrey: Young Voice.

Kelly, J. (2000) 'Legal and Psychological Interventions for Families in Custody and Access Disputes', paper delivered to the 10th world conference of the International Society of Family Law, Brisbane, 9–13 July.

Kiernan, K. (1997) *The Legacy of Parental Divorce: Social, Economic and Demographic Experiences in Adulthood*, CASE paper 1, London: London School of Economics.

Kiernan, K., Land, H. and Lewis, J. (1998) *Lone Motherhood in Twentieth Century Britain*, Oxford: Oxford University Press.

Klee, L., Schmidt, C. and Johnson, C. (1989) 'Children's Definition of Family Following Divorce of their Parents', *Journal of Divorce*, 13(2–3): 109–27

Kohlberg, L. (1969) 'Stage and Sequence: The Cognitive-Developmental Approach to Socialisation', in D. Gozlin (ed.), *Handbook of Socialisation Research and Theory*, Chicago: Rand McNally.

Kohlberg, L. (1984) *Essays on Moral Development*, vol. 2: *The Psychology of Moral Development*, New York: Harper & Row.

Laing, R. D. (1971) *The Politics of the Family*, London: Tavistock.

Larrabee, M. J. (ed.) (1993) *An Ethic of Care*, London: Routledge.

Law Commission (1986) *Custody*, Working Paper No. 96, London: HMSO.

Law Commission (1988) *Report on Guardianship and Custody Law*, No. 172, London: HMSO.

Leonard, D. (1990) 'Persons in their Own Right: Children and Sociology in the UK', in L. Chisholm et al. (eds), *Childhood, Youth and Social Change: A Comparative Perspective*, London: Falmer Press.

Levin, I. (1995) 'Children's Perceptions of their Family', in J. Brannen and M. O'Brien (eds), *Childhood and Parenthood*, London: University of London, Institute of Education.

Levy-Bruhl, L. (1923) *Primitive Mentality*, London: Allen & Unwin.

Lim, H. and Roche, J. (2000) 'Feminism and Children's Rights', in J. Bridgeman and D. Monk (eds), *Feminist Perspectives on Child Law*, London: Cavendish, 227–49.

Lyon, C., Surrey, E. and Timms, J. (1998) *Effective Support Services for Children and Young People when Parental Relations Break Down: A Child-Centred Approach*, Liverpool: Centre for the Study of the Child, the Family and the Law, University of Liverpool, UK.

Mackay, R. (1991) 'Conceptions of Children and Models of Socialisation' [1974] in F. Waksler (ed.), *Studying the Social Worlds of Children: Sociological Readings*, London: Falmer Press.

Maclean, M. and Eekelaar, J. (1997) *The Parental Obligation: A Study of Parenthood across Households*, Oxford: Hart.

Macnicol, J. (1986) 'The Effect of the Evacuation of Schoolchildren on Official Attitudes to State Intervention', in H. L. Smith (ed.), *War and Social Change*, Manchester: Manchester University Press.

Maidment, S. (1998) 'Parental Alienation Syndrome: A Judicial Response?', *Family Law*, 28 (May): 264–6.

Makrinioti, D. (1994) 'Conceptualisation of Childhood in a Welfare State: A Critical Re-Appraisal', in J. Qvortrup (ed.), *Childhood Matters*, Aldershot: Avebury.

Marshall, K. (1997) *Children's Rights in the Balance*, Edinburgh: Stationery Office.

Marshall, T. H. (1950) *Citizenship and Social Class*, Cambridge: Cambridge University Press.

Mason, J. (1996a) 'Gender, Care and Sensibility in Family and Kin Relationships', in J. Holland and L. Atkins (eds), *Sex, Sensibility and the Gendered Body*, Basingstoke: Macmillan.

Mason, J. (1996b) *Qualitative Researching*, London: Sage.

Masson, J. and Winn Oakley, M. (1998) *Out of Hearing: Representing Children in Care Proceedings*, London: Wiley.

Mayall, B. (ed.) (1994) *Children's Childhoods Observed and Experienced*, London: Falmer Press.

Mayall, B. (2000) 'Negotiating Childhoods', *Children 5–6 Research Programme Briefing*, No. 13, Swindon: ESRC.

Mays, J. B. (1972) *Juvenile Delinquency, the Family and the Social Group*, London: Longman.

Miller, J. (1999) *All Right at Home? Promoting Respect for the Human Rights of Children in Family Life: A Practical Guide for Professionals Working with Children*, London: Barnardos, Children's Rights Office, The Children's Society, NCH Action for Children, NSPCC, Save the Children.

Minow, M. (1987) 'Interpreting Rights: An Essay for Robert Cover', *Yale Law Journal*, 96(8): 1860–2017.

Mitchell, A. (1985) *Children in the Middle: Living through Divorce*, London: Tavistock.

Moore, M. and Beazley, S. (1996) 'Split Family Life', in M. Moore, J. Sixsmith and K. Knowles, *Children's Reflections on Family Life*, London: Falmer Press.

Moore, M., Sixsmith, J. and Knowles, K. (1996) *Children's Reflections on Family Life*, London: Falmer Press.

Morgan, D. (1996) *Family Connections*, Cambridge: Polity.

Morgan, D. (1999) 'Risk and Family Practices: Accounting for Change and Fluidity in Family Life', in E. B. Silva and C. Smart (eds.), *The New Family?*, London: Sage.

Morrow, V. (1994) 'Responsible Children? Aspects of Children's Work and Employment outside School in Contemporary UK', in B. Mayall (ed.), *Children's Childhoods Observed and Experienced*, London: Falmer Press.

Morrow, V. (1998) *Understanding Families: Children's Perspectives*, London: National Children's Bureau.

Morrow, V. (1999) ' "We Are People Too": Children's and Young People's Perspectives on Children's Rights and Decision Making in England', *International Journal of Children's Rights*, 7: 149–70.

Mullins, C. (1954) *Marriage Failures and the Children*, London: Epworth Press.

Murch, M. (1980) *Justice and Welfare in Divorce*, London: Sweet & Maxwell.

Murch, M., Douglas, G., Scanlon, L. et al. (1998) *Safeguarding Children's Welfare in Uncontentious Divorce: A Study of Section 41 of the Matrimonial Causes Act: Report to the Lord Chancellor's Department*, Cardiff: Cardiff Law School.

Neale, B. (2001) 'Dialogues with Children: Children, Divorce and Citizenship', *Childhood*.

Neale, B. and Smart, C. (1997a) 'Experiments with Parenthood?', *Sociology*, 31(2): 201–19.

Neale, B. and Smart, C. (1997b) ' "Good" and "Bad" Lawyers? Struggling in the Shadow of the New Law', *Journal of Social Welfare and Family Law*, 19(4): 377–402.

Neale, B. and Smart, C. (1998) *Agents or Dependants? Struggling to Listen to Children in Family Law and Family Research*, University of Leeds: Centre for Research on Family, Kinship and Childhood, Working Paper No. 3.

Neale, B. and Smart, C. (1999) 'In Whose Best Interests? Theorising Family Life after Parental Separation or Divorce', in S. D. Sclater and C. Piper (eds), *Undercurrents of Divorce*, Aldershot: Ashgate/ Dartmouth.

Neale, B. and Smart, C. (forthcoming) 'Caring, Earning and Changing: Parenting and Employment after Divorce', in A. Carling, S. Duncan and R. Edwards (eds), *Analysing Families: Morality and Rationality in Policy and Practice*, London: Routledge.

Neale, B. and Wade, A. (2000) *Parent Problems!* London: Young Voice.

Newson, J. and Newson, E. (1976) *Seven Years Olds in the Home Environment*, London: Hutchinson.

NFPI (National Family and Parenting Institute) (2000) *Teenagers' Attitudes to Parenting*, MORI, London: NFPI.

O'Brien, M., Alldred, P. and Jones, D. (1996) 'Children's Constructions of Family and Kinship' in J. Brannen and M. O'Brien (eds), *Children in Families: Research and Policy*, London: Falmer Press.

O'Quigley, A. (2000) *Listening to Children's Views: The Findings and Recommendations of Recent Research*, York: Joseph Rowntree Foundation.

Oakley, A. (1994) 'Women and Children First and Last: Parallels and Differences between Children's and Women's Studies', in B. Mayall (ed.), *Children's Childhoods Observed and Experienced*, London: Falmer Press.

Ottosen, M. (1997) *Reconstituted Families: New Ways of Thinking Kinship?*, paper presented at the European Sociological Association Conference, University of Essex, August.

Packman, J. (1981) *The Child's Generation*, 2nd edn, Oxford: Basil Blackwell and Martin Robertson.

Parsons, T. (1951) *The Social System*, London: Routledge & Kegan Paul.

Parton, J. (1997) 'The Joint Residence Issue', *Family Law*, 27: 775.

Pateman, C. (1988) *The Sexual Contract*, Cambridge: Polity.

Piaget, J. (1932) *The Moral Judgment of the Child*, London: Kegan, Paul, Trench, Trubner.

Piaget, J. (1972) *Psychology and Epistemology*, translated by P. Wells, Harmondsworth: Penguin.

Pinchbeck, I. and Hewitt, M. (1973) *Children in English Society*, vol.

2, London: Routledge & Kegan Paul.

Piper, C. (1999) 'The Wishes and Feelings of the Child', in S. D. Sclater and C. Piper (eds), *Undercurrents of Divorce*, Aldershot: Ashgate/ Dartmouth.

Platt, A. (1969) 'The Rise of the Child-Saving Movement', *Annals of the American Academy*, 381: 21–38.

Pollock, L. (1983) *Forgotten Children*, Cambridge: Cambridge University Press.

Price-Williams, D. R. (1956) 'The Place of Psychology in Social Work III: Psycho-analysis', *Case Conference*, 3(4): 110–13.

Prout, A. and James, A. (1997) 'A New Paradigm for the Sociology of Childhood?', in A. James and A. Prout (eds), *Constructing and Reconstructing Childhood*, 2nd edn, London: Falmer Press.

Qvortrup, J. (1985) 'Placing Children in the Division of Labour', in P. Close and R. Collins (eds.), *Family and Economy in Modern Society*, London: Macmillan.

Qvortrup, J. (ed.) (1994) *Childhood Matters*, Aldershot: Avebury.

Qvortrup, J. (1997) 'A Voice for Children in Statistical and Social Accounting', in A. James and A. Prout (eds.), *Constructing and Reconstructing Childhood*, 2nd edn, London: Falmer Press.

Ribbens, J. (1994) *Mothers and their Children: A Feminist Sociology of Childrearing*, London: Sage.

Ribbens McCarthy, J., Edwards, R. and Gillies, V. (2000) *Parenting and Step-Parenting: Contemporary Moral Tales*, Centre for Family and Household Research Occasional Paper 4, Oxford: Oxford Brookes University.

Richards, M. and Light, P. (eds) (1986) *Children of Social Worlds: Development in a Social Context*, Cambridge, Polity and Cambridge, Mass.: Harvard University Press.

Richards, M. and Stark, C. (2000) 'Children, Parenting and Information Meetings', *Family Law*, 30: 484–8.

Riley, D. (1983) *War in the Nursery: Theories of the Child and Mother*, London: Virago.

Ritchie, O. and Koller, M. (1964) *Sociology of Childhood*, New York: Meredith.

Roberts, H. (1999) 'Listening to Children: And Hearing Them', in P. Christenson and A. James (eds), *Research with Children*, London: Falmer Press.

Roche, J. (1996) 'The Politics of Children's Rights', in J. Brannen and M. O'Brien (eds), *Children in Families: Research and Policy*, London: Falmer Press.

Roche, J. (1999a) 'Children: Rights, Participation and Citizenship', *Childhood*, 6(4): 475–93.

Roche, J. (1999b) 'Citizenship: The Burdens but not the Benefits for Children', paper delivered to the seminar on Affect Ethics and Citizenship, University of London, 23–4 September.

Rodgers, B. and Pryor, J. (1998) *Divorce and Separation: The Outcomes for Children*, York: Joseph Rowntree Foundation.

Rose, N. (1989) *Governing the Soul: The Shaping of the Private Self*, London: Routledge.

Royal Commission on Marriage and Divorce (1956), *1951–1955 Report*, London: HMSO Cmnd 9678.

Ruegger, M. (2000) 'Children's Experience of the Guardian *ad litem* Service and Public Law Proceedings', *Seen and Heard*, 10(2): 41–53.

Rutter, M. and Madge, N. (1976) *Cycles of Disadvantage*, London: Heinemann.

Sawyer, C. (1995) 'The Competence of Children to Participate in Family Proceedings', *Child and Family Law Quarterly*, 7(4): 180–95.

Sawyer, C. (1997) 'The Mature Child: How Solicitors Decide', *Family Law*, 27: 19–21.

Sawyer, C. (1999a) 'Conflicting Rights for Children: Implementing Welfare, Autonomy and Justice in Family Proceedings', *Journal of Social Welfare and Family Law*, 21(2): 99–120.

Sawyer, C. (1999b) *Rules, Roles and Relationships: The Structure and Function of Child Representation and Welfare within Family Proceedings*, University of Oxford: Centre for Socio-Legal Studies.

Schneider, D. (1980) *American Kinship: A Cultural Account*, Englewood Cliffs, NJ: Prentice Hall.

Sevenhuijsen, S. (1998) *Citizenship and the Ethics of Care: Feminist Considerations about Justice, Morality and Politics*, London: Routledge.

Sevenhuijsen, S. (1999) *Caring in the Third Way*, University of Leeds: Centre for Research on Family, Kinship & Childhood, Working Paper No. 13.

Silva, E. B. and Smart, C. (1999) 'The "New" Practices and Politics of Family Life', in E. B. Silva and C. Smart (eds), *The New Family?*, London: Sage.

Smart, C. (1982) *The Ties that Bind*, London: Routledge & Kegan Paul.

Smart, C. (1989) *Feminism and the Power of Law*, London: Routledge.

Smart, C. (2000) 'Divorce and Changing Family Practices in a Post-Traditional Society', in *Family Matters*, Melbourne: Australian Institute for Family Studies.

Smart, C. and Neale, B. (1997) 'Arguments Against Virtue: Must Contact be Enforced?', *Family Law*, 28: 332–6.

Smart, C. and Neale, B. (1999) *Family Fragments?*, Cambridge: Polity.

Smith, Claire (2000) *Young People and Family Change –Their Shout*, London: Parentline Plus.

Smith, Heather (1999) *Children, Feelings and Divorce*, London: Free Association Books.

Solberg, A. (1997) 'Negotiating Childhood: Changing Constructions of Age for Norwegian Children', in A. James and A. Prout (eds), *Constructing and Reconstructing Childhood*, 2nd edn, London: Falmer Press.

Spensky, M. (1992) 'Producers of Legitimacy: Homes for Unmarried Mothers in the 1950s', in C. Smart (ed.), *Regulating Womanhood*, London: Routledge.

Squires, J. (1999) *Gender in Political Theory*, Cambridge: Polity.

Stacey, J. (1990) *Brave New Families*, New York: Basic Books.

Strathern, M. (1992) *After Nature: English Kinship in the Late Twentieth Century*, Cambridge: Cambridge University Press.

Sullivan, H. (1953) *The Interpersonal Theory of Psychiatry*, New York: Norton.

Sweeting, H., West, P. and Richards, M. (1998) 'Teenage Family Life, Lifestyles and Life Changes', *International Journal of Law, Policy and the Family*, 12: 15–46.

Théry, I. (1989) ' "The Interest of the Child" and the Regulation of the Post-Divorce Family', in C. Smart, and S. Sevenhuijsen (eds), *Child Custody and the Politics of Gender*, London: Routledge.

Thompson, R. and Amato, P. (1999) *The Post-Divorce Family: Children, Parenting and Society*, London: Sage.

Thorne, B. (1987) 'Revisioning Women and Social Change: Where are the Children?', *Gender and Society*, 1(1): 85–109.

Timms, J. (1997) 'The Tension between Welfare and Justice', *Family Law*, 27: 38–47.

Trinder, L. (1997) 'Competing Constructions of Childhood: Children's Rights and Children's Wishes in Divorce', *Journal of Social Welfare and Family Law*, 19(3): 291–305.

Trollope, J. (1998) *Other People's Children*, London: Bloomsbury.

Tronto, J. C. (1993) *Moral Boundaries*, London: Routledge

Tutt, N. (1974) *Care or Custody*, London: Darton, Longman & Todd..

Tylor, E. (1871) *Primitive Culture*, vol. 1, London: John Murray.

UK College of Family Mediators (2000) *Children, Young People and Family Mediation*, London: UK College of Family Mediators.

Waksler, F. (ed.) (1991) *Studying the Social Worlds of Children: Sociological Readings*, London: Falmer Press.

Walby, S. (1997) *Gender Transformations*, London: Routledge.

Walczak, Y. and Burns, S. (1984) *Divorce: The Child's Point of View*, London: Harper & Row.

Wallbank, J. (1998) 'Castigating Mothers: The Judicial Response to "Wilful" Women in Disputes over Paternal Contact in English Law', *Journal of Social Welfare and Family Law*, 20(4): 357–76.

Wallerstein, J. and Blakeslee, S. (1989) *Second Chances*, London: Bantam Press.

Wallerstein, J. and Kelly, J. (1980) *Surviving the Break-Up*, London: Grant McIntyre.

Wallerstein, J. and Lewis, J. (1998) 'The Long-Term Impact of Divorce on Children: A First Report from a 25-Year Study', *Family and Conciliation Courts Review*, 36: 368–83

Weiss, R. (1979) 'Growing Up a Little Faster: The Experience of Growing Up in a Single Parent Household', *Journal of Social Issues*, 35(4): 97–111.

West, D. J. (1973) *Who Becomes Delinquent?*, London: Heinemann.

Weyland, I. (1995) 'Judicial Attitudes to Contact and Shared Residence since the Children Act 1989', *Journal of Social Welfare and Family Law*, 17(4): 445–59.

White, R., Carr, P. and Lowe, N. (1995) *The Children Act in Practice*, London: Butterworth.

Williams, F. (1999) 'Good-enough Principles for Welfare', *Journal of Social Policy*, 28(4): 667–87.

Williamson, H. and Butler, I. (1995) 'Children Speak: Perspectives on their Social World', in J. Brannen and M. O'Brien (eds), *Childhood and Parenthood*, University of London: Institute of Education.

Winnicott, D. (1964) *The Child, the Family, and the Outside World*, Harmondsworth: Penguin.

Women's Group on Public Welfare (1948) *The Neglected Child and his Family*, London: Oxford University Press.

Woodhead, M. (1997) 'Psychology and the Cultural Construction of Children's Needs', in A. James and A. Prout (eds), *Constructing and Reconstructing Childhood*, 2nd edn, London: Falmer Press.

Woodroofe, K. (1962) *From Charity to Social Work*, London: Routledge & Kegan Paul.

Young, I. M. (1997) *Intersecting Voices*, Princeton, NJ: Princeton University Press.

Young, M. and Willmott, P. (1957) *Family and Kinship in East London*, Harmondsworth: Penguin.

Younghusband, E. (1978) *Social Work in Britain: 1950-1975*, London: George Allen & Unwin.

Younghusband, E. (1981) *The Newest Profession: A Short History of Social Work*, Surrey: Community Care/IPC Business Press.

Index

Martyrdom in Islam

In recent times Islamic martyrdom has become associated with suicide missions conducted by extremists. However, as David Cook demonstrates, this type of martyrdom is very different from the classical definition, which condemned suicide and stipulated that anyone who died as a believer could be considered a martyr. Ideas about martyrdom have evolved to suit prevailing circumstances, and it is the evolution of these different interpretations that Cook charts in this fascinating history of the role of suffering and people's willingness to die as a testimony to their faith. The book covers the earliest sources, including those from the Jewish and Christian traditions, discussions about what constituted martyrdom, differences in attitudes between Sunnis and Shi'ites, the role of martyrdom in conversion and the literary manifestations of romantic martyrdom. A concluding section discusses martyrdom in today's radical environment. There is no other book which considers the topic so systematically, and which draws so extensively on the Arabic and Persian sources, as well as on Muslim literature from across the world. This will be essential reading for students of Islamic history, and for those looking for an informed account of this controversial topic.

DAVID COOK is Assistant Professor in Religious Studies at Rice University. He has written *Studies in Muslim Apocalyptic* (2002), *Understanding Jihad* (2005) and *Contemporary Muslim Apocalyptic Literature* (2005).

THEMES IN ISLAMIC HISTORY comprises a range of titles exploring different aspects of Islamic history, society and culture by leading scholars in the field. Books are thematic in approach, offering a comprehensive and accessible overview of the subject. Generally, surveys treat Islamic history from its origins to the demise of the Ottoman Empire, although some offer a more developed analysis of a particular period, or project into the present, depending on the subject-matter. All the books are written to interpret and illuminate the past, as gateways to a deeper understanding of Islamic civilization and its peoples.

Editorial adviser:
Patricia Crone, *Institute for Advanced Study, Princeton University*

Already published:
Chase F. Robinson, *Islamic Historiography*

Jonathan P. Berkey, *The Formation of Islam: Religion and Society in the Near East, 600–1800*

Michael Cook, *Forbidding Wrong in Islam: An Introduction*

Martyrdom in Islam

David Cook

Rice University

CAMBRIDGE UNIVERSITY PRESS
Cambridge, New York, Melbourne, Madrid, Cape Town, Singapore, São Paulo

Cambridge University Press
The Edinburgh Building, Cambridge CB2 2RU, UK

Published in the United States of America by Cambridge University Press, New York

www.cambridge.org
Information on this title: www.cambridge.org/9780521615518

First published 2007

Printed in the United States of America

A catalogue record for this publication is available from the British Library

Library of Congress Cataloguing-in-Publication Data
Cook, David, 1966–
Martyrdom in Islam / David Cook. – 1st edn.
p.   cm. – (Themes in Islamic history)
Includes bibliographical references and index.
ISBN-13: 978-0-521-85040-7 (hardback)
ISBN-13: 978-0-521-61551-8 (paperback)
1. Martyrdom–Islam.   2. Muslim martyrs.   3. Islamic fundamentalism.   4. Islamic
law.   I. Title.   II. Series.
BP190.5.M3C66   2007
297.2'3–dc22   2006026058

ISBN-13 978-0-521-85040-7 hardback
ISBN-10 0-521-85040-1 hardback

ISBN-13 978-0-521-61551-8 paperback
ISBN-10 0-521-61551-8 paperback

Dedicated to Professor Fred M. Donner

Appreciated by all who have studied with him,
an example to all in our field.

Contents

Acknowledgments

I would like to thank a number of people who have helped me out with this book by reading and critiquing it: my closest friend, Deborah Tor, read the text with her usual thoroughness and incisiveness. My parents, W. Robert and Elaine Cook, both read over the manuscript, in addition to having provided me with the encouragement to study Islam over the years. My colleague, Paula Sanders, with whom it is a pleasure to work, also read the manuscript. My research assistant, Olivia Allison, read over the first draft. She also helped me immensely in my research throughout the Muslim world (in Africa, the Middle East and Central Asia), and exhibited unique patience with me during numerous difficulties. Several of my best students, including Noorain Khan and Saira Karim, read over the manuscript. I received help and advice from Bakhtiyar Babajanov, Betul Cavdar (for translations from Turkish), Peter Dorman, April DeConick, Rich Haeder, Mas'ud Khalili (with whom I spent several pleasant evenings and learned first-hand about the martyrdom of Ahmad Shah Mas'ud), Joshua Lingel, Badrus Sholeh and Elizabeth Urban. I would like to thank Muhammad Iysa Bello of the State University of Lagos, Nigeria, for discussing martyrdom with me and for providing intellectually stimulating conversations. My colleagues at the Department of Religious Studies, Rice University have been very helpful and supportive, especially Elias Bongmba. Thanks are also due to Etan Kohlberg of the Hebrew University of Jerusalem, from whom I first learned about the subject of Islamic martyrdom. During the process of research and writing, my work was supported by a grant from the Smith Richardson Foundation and the Baker Institute for Public Policy. Many books to which I would not have otherwise had access were purchased by funds supplied through the Jon R and Paula Mosle Research Funds. Appendix II (b) is reprinted with the permission of CNN. An especially big thanks goes to Marigold Acland, the editor at Cambridge University Press, who has helped me quite a lot during the past years and to my copy-editor on this book, Adrian Stenton. It goes without saying that all remaining mistakes are solely my responsibility.

Glossary

Arabic diacritics follow the style used in the *Encyclopedia of Islam* with standard modifications as used in the *International Journal of Middle East Studies*.

In Arabic names, Abdallah b. al-Mubarak may also be given as Ibn al-Mubarak.

'Ajami any non-Arabic language, in the classical period usually Persian
Allahu akbar! "God is greater!" (popular Muslim exclamation)
ana al-haqq "I am the Truth" or "I am [one with] the Truth" (saying associated with al-Hallaj)
al-a'raf "The Barrier" mentioned in the Qur'an
Ashab al-ukhdud the Companions of the Pit, from Qur'an 85:4–9
ashrat al-sa'a the Portents of the Hour of Judgment
ayyam al-'Arab the heroic stories and poetry of pre-Islamic battle-days
baraka blessing that is bestowed by Sufi holy men and women (often after death)
darwish (in English, *dervish*) virtually synonymous with Sufi
du'a al-mazlum the prayer of the wronged person
fatwa a legal opinion given by a qualified expert
hadith the record of the sayings and actions of the Prophet Muhammad
hajj the pilgrimage to Mecca
hijra emigration (usually the emigration to Medina, but also one of the stages of *jihad*)
hijri the lunar calendar based upon the date of the *hijra* from 622
houris (in Arabic *al-hur al-'in*) the women of paradise given to the martyrs for their pleasure
al-Isra' wa-l-mi'raj the Night Journey and Ascension into Heaven by the Prophet Muhammad
Ithna' 'ashariyya (also vocalized *Isna 'Ashariyya*) the Twelver (majority) branch of Shi'ism
jihad divinely sanctioned warfare with the objective of either expanding Islam or defending it

x

jizya the poll tax to be paid by non-Muslims (Jews and Christians) in a
Muslim state

kafir/kuffar/kafirun infidels, non-Muslims

Khuda (Persian) God

Mahdi the Muslim messianic figure

Malfuzat literally, dictations

Maqatil literature literature recording prominent violent deaths or
martyrdoms

al-maqtul the one who was killed

mihna the tribulation, historically the period between 833–47 in which the
Mu'tazila interrogated prominent Sunnis as to their belief in the doctrine of
the creation of the Qur'an

al-Mu'allaqat the seven pre-Islamic Odes supposedly suspended on the Ka'ba

muhtasib the town censor, who regulated the public domain to make sure
Islamic norms were upheld

mujahid(in) fighter(s) in the *jihad*

murabit one who guards the boundaries of Islam in a *ribat*

mustada'fun oppressed

mustakbirun proud, arrogant, haughty

nikaya terror

qadi a judge

raka'a prostration (in the Muslim prayer)

ribat a location on the borders of Islam used for the purposes of guarding

sa'alik vagabonds, used pejoratively of Sufis

sabr patience, submission to the will of God

Salam peace, the greeting Muslims exchange between each other

sati the Hindu practice of widow immolation

sayyid al-shuhada' the lord of martyrs (traditionally Hamza)

siddiqin truthful people

shahada the Muslim confession of faith "There is no God but Allah and
Muhammad is the Messenger of Allah"

shahid, (plural *shuhada'*) a martyr, one who testifies to something

shari'a the Divine Law of Sunni Islam

shirk associating other beings or creatures with the one God, the primal sin in
Islam

shuhada' al-mahabba the martyrs of love

sunna the Way of the Prophet Muhammad, the basis for Sunni Islam

sura a section of the Qur'an

talib al-'ilm a student, a seeker of knowledge

al-Tawwabun The Penitents, historically a group that appeared in 683

ta'ziya a passion play in Shi'ite Islam to commemorate the martyrdom of
al-Husayn

topoi literary tropes that are understood for their symbolic value and are not
    to be taken literally
'ulama the religious leadership of Islam
umma the community of all Muslims
wali a friend (of God), mainly in the Sufi tradition
zalimun tyrants
zuhd asceticism

Chronology

ca. 305–70 BCE, the Selucid Empire

ca. 167 BCE, the martyrdom of Eleazar and the beginnings of the Maccabean revolt

ca. 70 BCE–475 CE, the Roman Empire

ca. 30 CE, the crucifixion of Jesus Christ

115, the martyrdom of Polycarp

ca. 300–1453, the Byzantine Empire

ca. 610–22, the beginnings of the ministry of Muhammad in Mecca

622, the *hijra* to Medina

624, the Battle of Badr

625, the Battle of Uhud (martyrdom of Hamza)

627, the Battle of the Khandaq

630, the conquest of Mecca

632, the death of Muhammad

634–732, the great Muslim conquests

661, the assassination of ʿAli

661–747, the Umayyad Dynasty (ruling from Damascus)

680, the martyrdom of al-Husayn

682, the martyrdom of ʿUqba b. Nafiʾ by the Berbers

747–1258, the ʿAbbasid Dynasty (ruling from Baghdad)

754, the murder of Abu Muslim

833–47, the *mihna*, during which Ibn Hanbal was beaten

922, the martyrdom of al-Hallaj

1031, the raids on India by Mahmud of Ghazna

1131, the martyrdom of ʿAyn al-Qudat al-Hamadani

1191, the martyrdom of Shihab al-Din al-Suhrawardi

1273, the death of Jalal al-Din al-Rumi

thirteenth through fifteenth centuries, the foundation of the great Sufi brotherhoods

1490s (?) Kabir active in India

1490–1500 (?) Siti Jenar active in Indonesia

1492, the formal expulsion of Jews and Muslims from Spain

ca. 1517–1924, the Ottoman Dynasty (ruling from Constantinople, Istanbul)

1529–43, the Ethiopian *jihad*

1592–93, the murder of the scholars of Timbuktu

1609–14, the final expulsion of the Moriscos from Spain

1658–1707, Aurengzeb rules India

1804–12, the Fulani *jihad* in northern Nigeria under Shehu Usuman Dan Fodio

1881–85, the Mahdi in the Sudan

1948, the foundation of the state of Israel

1967, the Six-Day War

1979–92, the Afghan *jihad*

1980–88, the Iran–Iraq War

1987–93, the First Intifada of the Palestinians

1992–95, the Bosnian–Herzegovinian War

1999–, the Chechen War

2000–04, the Second Intifada of the Palestinians

September 11, 2001, attack on New York and Washington, DC, by al-Qa'ida

1   Martyrs in religions

Samson said: "Let me die with the Philistines!" Then he pushed with all his might, and down came the temple . . . Thus he killed many more people when he died than when he lived.
Judges 16:30

When he opened the fifth seal, I saw under the altar the souls of those who had been slain because of the word of God and the testimony they had maintained . . . each of them was given a white robe, and told to wait a little longer, until the number of their fellow servants and brothers who were to be killed was completed.
Revelation 6:9, 11

Martyrdom means witness. Witness is the most powerful form of advertisement, because it communicates personal credibility and experience to an audience. Therefore, it is not surprising that the world's missionary religions have developed the art of the promotional martyrdom into a process that is identifiable and fairly constant through different faiths. Before dealing with the specific commonalities of Islamic martyrdom (Chapter 2) we will first examine the narrative progression that historically attested martyrs and stories of their martyrdoms have laid down for us: the portrayals of the enemy, the nature of the audience participation and subsequent commitment expected from it, and the form of the martyrdom narrative, which is the method of eternalizing the act and its pathos.

For martyrdom to succeed there must be a martyr.[1] This is an absolute necessity, and all martyrdoms and their narratives can be boiled down to the fact that we are talking about a person (sometimes as part of a larger group, but even so with individuality) who will choose suffering or death in order to demonstrate an absolute commitment to a cause. Usually, the martyr is given some reality through the hagiographical accounts of his or her suffering that allow the audience to relate to this suffering. In other words, the martyrdom must have communicative force within the context of the society in which the martyrdom is taking place. The martyr must have belief in one belief system and possess

---

[1] Eugene and Anita Weiner, *The Martyr's Conviction*, p. 9 includes three basic types of martyrs: 1. choosing to suffer or die rather than give up one's faith or principles; 2. being tortured or killed because of one's convictions; 3. suffering great pain or misery for a long time.

1

a willingness to defy another belief system. He or she will stand at the defining point where belief and unbelief meet – however these two categories are constructed in the minds of the martyr, the enemy, the audience and the writer of the historical-hagiographical narrative – and define the relationship between the two. In this sense the martyr creates a boundary with his or her life that may or may not have previously been apparent.

Therefore the martyr himself/herself becomes a living definition of the intrinsic nature of the belief system for which he or she was willing to die. The martyr's defining role is most helpful when that particular belief system is under attack, is in a minority position or is not in a politically or culturally dominant position within a given geographical location. At those times there may be out-conversion or dilution of the core values of the belief system (however those are assessed, from the outside or the inside) such that many believers may not see worth in it at all. Attacks on the martyr's belief system can be coordinated and systematic or sustained by the all-encompassing nature of what is commonly perceived to be a superior belief system. (Occasionally it is possible that this dominant belief system does not even perceive itself to be leveling such an attack; merely its omnipresence creates the situation of a siege for other, subordinate belief systems, who then can be in need of a martyr-figure in order to preserve their independence or self-image.)

The martyr changes that equation (whether he or she is willing or unwilling). First of all, by making a statement, he or she creates a boundary between two belief systems. Second, he or she creates an example, a standard of conduct by which to judge other fellow believers. By demonstrating publicly that there is something in the subordinated or persecuted belief system worth dying for, the value other believers place upon it is augmented, and that belief system is highlighted. And third, by creating boundaries and examples, the martyr also creates cohesion and substance where previously there had been drift and lack of definition (at least according to the perception of the martyr and his or her hagiographer). However, in order to accomplish all of these things, the martyr must see the process through to the end (usually death). This includes a series of events which have come to be identified with martyrdom: suffering on the part of the martyr, the obvious and apparent injustice of the enemy, some type of communication of defiance on the part of the martyr and ultimately his or her death. While in some martyrdom paradigms these events do not have to be specifically directed at the martyr – for example, the suffering of the martyr or the injustice inflicted by the enemy may be indirect or even impersonal in nature – ideally all of these components would be present.

There must also be an audience. The audience need not be physically present at either the pre-martyrdom suffering or the act of martyrdom, but must have access to information concerning them. If the audience is personally a witness to the martyrdom, then it needs to coalesce around a collective memory of this emotional and traumatic event. But if the audience is not an immediate witness to the martyrdom event, then there has to be a communicative agent, who will either shape the narrative or narrate the events to one who will transmit them to the outer, secondary audience. This stage of the martyrdom is of crucial importance, perhaps even more crucial than the actual suffering and martyrdom itself. The reason for this importance lies in the shaping of the historical memory that takes place at this stage, during the course of which the traumatic events are molded into the most emotionally powerful narrative that the transmitter is capable of composing. In a way the writer or hagiographer-figure is also part of the audience, but one that has a greater interpretive role in portraying the events. After this time, the audience will rely upon this initial interpretation of the martyrdom event in order to continue to build a tradition, often vastly expanding upon the initial narrative and perhaps even creating a whole cycle or series of cycles of stories that sometimes bear little relation to the initial event.

Ideally, for the martyrdom to succeed there must be an absolute evil upon which the audience can focus their revulsion.[2] This defining aspect of martyrdom is not always physically present at the moment of martyrdom, but it must be looming in the background or have some corporeal presence against which the martyr, his or her cause, and the eventual audience make their stand. This evil can be a ruling power, the representative of a ruling power, or a system that is alien and oppressive by nature (at least according to the perception of the other participants in the martyrdom narrative). It is frequently important that the enemy be made, during the course of the martyrdom narrative, to recognize, at least tacitly, its own essential illegitimacy or perhaps evil, and the essential good of the martyr. In this way the martyr is granted stature and nobility out of the mouths of his or her own persecutors and enemies.

There are also those who acquiesce to the martyrdom. These people attempt to stand on the side, to remain spectators or emotionally uninvolved. It is not unusual in the more carefully shaped martyrdom narratives to find this group especially singled out for emotional and polemical abuse by all sides. The reason for this abuse is clear: this is the group that can be mobilized to join one side or the other. In a martyrdom narrative, this group ideally should suffer guilt for their lack of involvement, for their unwillingness to stand up for the wronged martyr, or for their fear of the consequences of confrontation with evil. In the end, the guilt that is produced among this spectator audience is capable of generating a large-scale movement that can use the martyrdom as its standard, its rallying point and its magnet for converts.

Conversion is ultimately the goal of the martyrdom narrative (though not all martyrs die in order to convert other people). Its ability to advertise the cause of the martyr is the crucible upon which the effective martyrdom narrative

---

[2] This is what Weiner and Weiner (ibid.) define as the "martyrological confrontation."

is to be judged. In reading over history's rejected narratives, the reasons for their failure become clear. These reasons include insufficient pathos, inability to communicate or connect with an audience, an unreceptive audience or an inappropriate time for a given theme of martyrdom. Sometimes martyrdom narratives fail to be effective because the market is saturated with blood and gore, too jaded to be shocked, or unable to identify with the situation portrayed in the narrative. Thus, while there are many martyrs to be found in history, few are chosen to be representative of a given movement, belief system or people. Of those few, even fewer speak across cultural boundaries and become global in their reach. But those stories that have become global are among the most moving and dramatic that humanity has produced and continue to inspire people, generation after generation.

In the end martyrdom is about blood and suffering. There is no question that the stories of martyrs are horrifying, and they focus upon the pain that so many humans have inflicted upon each other. More than occasionally a martyrdom narrative can be so elongated, so focused upon the blood and suffering, that the audience can simply be overcome by exhaustion or, as previously stated, become jaded. For this reason some martyrdom narratives focus upon brevity, make every word count, and try to achieve the level of horror through the imagination. Since the words of the narrative are few, the audience demonstrates its participation by imagining the entire scene, by filling out the missing details through the process of continual recreation of the events as they are retold to audience after audience. However, it is more common for the bloody details to be spelt out in detail, and for the audience to be brought up to the moment of collective guilt and repentance through the ritual of recitation of the endless torments of the martyr. This process of recitation in itself constitutes a collective expiation of the sin of indifference, especially in those rituals like the Good Friday–Easter sequence in Christianity or the 'Ashura' (10th of Muharram) commemoration of the martyrdom of al-Husayn in Shi'ite Islam that are repeated each year. Details of these martyrdom narratives are often known by the audience, and in many cases are expanded through the retelling of the events and the emotional need of the audience to participate in them.

While the above lists some of the cardinal binding narratives of martyrdom as they can be seen from a broad historical perspective, not all narratives have every single one of these themes, nor are all carefully crafted with all of these necessities in mind. Audiences and circumstances among religious and political groups vary widely, and the development of the theme of martyrdom is an ongoing process that continues today. Since the variables around the basic theme are practically infinite – in accord with the number of possible martyrs and audiences – it is not surprising that the theme of martyrdom is one of great intricacy and historical depth. So as to understand this historical depth, let us begin with the earliest martyrdom narratives that continue to influence our world.

Jewish martyrdom

From a historical point of view, the earliest defining moments of martyrdom have been those of the Jewish people, especially those which occurred during the period of the Hellenization of the Middle East (330s BCE onwards) after the conquest by Alexander the Great. Alexander's successors, especially the Selucid Empire (305–*ca.* 70 BCE), emphasized the Greek pantheon over and above the local Near Eastern cults (such as the Judaism of that time). This religious policy had strong political and cultural ramifications as well, since the Selucid Empire, like most of the successor states to the empire of Alexander the Great, was a heterogeneous mixture of peoples and religions ruled by a Greek aristocracy. This ruling group sought to create some type of unity within the empire, especially after the Battle of Magnesia (190 BCE), when it became clear to the Selucids that they would need to confront the growing power of Rome in the eastern Mediterranean basin.

It is by no means obvious that the Jews would be the ones to resist. As a group they did not fit into the paradigms presented above. During the Selucid period, Judaism was not a missionary religion (although during the Maccabean period that followed it, peoples surrounding the Jews in the area of Palestine, such as the Idumeans and others, were forcibly converted). However, in other ways, the paradigm holds true. The leadership of the Jewish people at the time, especially the priesthood, was highly Hellenized and thus alien to the common folk. Jews had a highly literate culture, centered around the holy books (later to become the Hebrew Bible). These books detail a long struggle between royal and priestly/prophetic elites for the right to interpret the will of God that were frequently written from the point of view of the latter elites. This demonstrates a willingness to stand up against royal prerogatives and in some cases to die for them (e.g., Elijah in I Kings 18; and Jeremiah in Jeremiah 20–21, 26, 28). Other popular heroes, such as Samson (cited at the beginning of this chapter), were also said to have been willing to die for their beliefs in order to kill their enemies.

The later books of the Hebrew Bible are filled with these types of stories. Thus, the Jews had a highly developed culture ready for martyrdom. However, even the most willing martyr needs a cause for which he or she can die. This cause was unwittingly supplied by the Selucid monarch, Antiochus IV Epiphanes (175–163 BCE), whose desire to unify the various cults of his divided realm was an understandable one. Antiochus was facing Rome, which had a highly unified belief system and the capability to project force into distant lands, and he needed to unify his realm. The obvious choice for this unity was the Greek pantheon, since he was Greek by culture and it had enough variety to supply all of the putative needs of his subjects. Politically, this process of unification made sense, but the Jews and other cults and peoples chose to resist it, ultimately causing the downfall of the Selucid Empire about fifty years later.

Despite their Hellenized and compromised leadership, some of the Jews were unwilling to accept Antiochus' religious reforms. The reasons for this revolt are described in the book of Daniel 11:31–35:

His[3] armed forces will rise up to desecrate the temple fortress and will abolish the daily sacrifice. Then they will set up the abomination that causes desolation. With flattery he will corrupt those who have violated the covenant, but the people who know their God will firmly resist him. Those who are wise will instruct many, though for a time they will fall by the sword or be burned or captured or plundered. When they fall, they will receive a little help, and many who are not sincere will join them. Some of the wise will stumble, so that they may be refined, purified and made spotless until the time of the end, for it will still come at the appointed time.[4]

From this biblical selection it is easy to see what the stakes are in the earliest martyrdom accounts. Because the Temple cult in Jerusalem had been defiled there was a necessity to resist Antiochus. This defilement was coupled with a betrayal by the Jewish political and religious elite, who had been corrupted by Hellenization according to the understanding of the biblical writer. Therefore, it was necessary to create examples – those who would die by the sword or be burned, etc. – who could resist and galvanize the population. The end result of this process is the refinement, the purification of the Jewish people, that the apocalyptic writer describes in the final verse.

Not surprisingly the Maccabean revolt (167–40 BCE) started in a conservative area to the northeast of Jerusalem, when agents of the king came to this region to compel the Jews of the area to offer sacrifices under the new religious system. When one Jew came forward to offer this sacrifice, the ancestor of the Maccabeans killed him. This revolutionary action was preceded and followed by numerous martyrdoms, the most famous and paradigmatic of which was that of Eleazar. This man was said to be a sage, and of advanced age, and was repeatedly forced to eat pork. "He, however, preferred death with glory to life with defilement," as the writer of II Maccabees puts it.[5] Different inducements were offered to him: tortures, deception, kindly advice to acquiesce from those who had already succumbed to temptation, and appeals on the basis of his age. All of these temptations were refused; on the contrary, Eleazar told his tormenters to

send him off to the netherworld without delay. "Such pretense is unworthy of my advanced age. My pretense for the sake of a brief transitory span of life would cause many of the younger generation to think that Eleazar at the age of ninety had gone over to the gentile way of life, and so they, too, would go astray because of me, and I would earn the defilement and besmirching of my old age. Indeed, even if I should be released

---

[3] Either Antiochus or in a broader sense the Selucids as a whole.
[4] Translation from the *New International Version*.
[5] Jonathan Goldstein, *II Maccabees*, p. 281 (II Maccabees 6:19).

for the present from punishment at the hands of men, alive or dead I would not escape the hands of the Almighty. Therefore, if I now bravely give up my life, I shall show myself worthy of my old age, as I leave to the young a noble example of how to go eagerly and nobly to die a beautiful death in the defense of our revered and sacred laws."[6]

He was then whipped to death. This is probably one of the earliest examples of martyrdom as it came to be understood in the monotheistic traditions of Judaism, Christianity and Islam. The martyr was willing to die for something that for others was inexplicable. Consumption of pork, for Eleazar's tormenters, was far from being something for which one should die. Even in orthodox Judaism consumption of pork is allowed in order to save one's life (the principle of *pikkuah nefesh*). But for Eleazar it was more important to set a complete example of his faith for others than it was to prolong his life or to give up any part of the Law. (Indeed, later Jewish martyrologies usually focus upon much more crucial elements of the Law, such as the breaking of the Sabbath or the rite of circumcision.) Although we have no way of knowing whether the speech put into his mouth by the writer of II Maccabees is authentic (and it probably is not, a fact that is common to almost all of the martyrdom narratives to be discussed in this book) it expresses perfectly the manner in which the idealized martyr should proceed to his or her death. For Eleazar, the priorities are clear: his life as an example to others, his responsibility before God and most especially his need to place himself physically between orthodoxy and the process of easy assimilation to the dominant culture.

For classical martyrdoms Eleazar is paradigmatic. He died for a cause that sets his faith apart from all others (at least at that time). Eleazar embraced death with the specific purpose of exalting his faith and keeping himself pure. He confronts his tormenters squarely and states clearly what the stakes are – that he does not care about life, that it is more important to think about his future judgment at the hands of God, and the example he will set for others – and goes willingly to die a horrible death. The tortures that bring about his death – the whip – are graphically described so that the reader feels that he or she is personally present and receives the full emotional impact of the scene. At the end we are left with a deep respect for Eleazar. Because he was willing to die for the Law, his death is a dignified one, and his tormenters are reduced to insignificance.

Martyrdom in Judaism during the millennia after Eleazar became increasingly important as many Jews, both willingly and unwillingly, followed in his footsteps. Since the majority of these martyrdoms were inflicted upon the Jewish people by Christians (or at least Europeans such as Adolf Hitler coming from a Christian or post-Christian environment) and not Muslims, for the most part later Jewish martyrdom is irrelevant for the purposes of this book.

---

[6] Ibid. (II Maccabees 6:24–28).

Christian martyrdom

Undoubtedly the most famous Jewish martyr was Jesus Christ. With the story of his martyrdom, immortalized as one of the foundational stories of Christianity, the art of the martyrdom narrative comes to maturity. Taking the account in the Gospel of Luke[7] as a basis for the analysis, and focusing upon Chapter 23, we see that Jesus is passive throughout the entire story. He is taken prisoner at the Garden of Gethsemane in the previous Chapter (22), betrayed by his closest disciples and friends and mocked by the soldiers and guards, all of which serves as the backdrop for the actual story of the crucifixion. At the beginning of Chapter 23, Jesus is led into the presence of the Roman governor, Pontius Pilate, after it is made clear to the reader that the Jewish leaders who have arrested him have no valid basis for accusing him.

Pilate's position is an unenviable one: in verse 4 he says, "I find no basis for a charge against this man," but it is clear this statement is very unpopular with the crowds. When Pilate finds out that Jesus is not a citizen of Judea, but a Galilean, he sends Jesus to the local ruler, Herod, to be questioned. Herod is unable to provoke Jesus into giving any answers and obviously thinks that he is harmless or at least not worthy of death. Throughout the entire martyrdom story Jesus either does not answer his accusers or gives passive, ambiguous answers. This silence gives Jesus stature and nobility that his accusers do not share. The calls on the part of the Jewish leaders and crowd, however, are unambiguous in their message that Jesus must die.[8] Pilate, therefore, is in a quandary expressed in verses 13–16:

Pilate called together the chief priests, the rulers and the people, and said to them, "You brought me this man as one who was inciting the people to rebellion. I have examined him in your presence and have found no basis for your charges against him. Neither has Herod, for he sent him back to us; as you can see, he has done nothing to deserve death. Therefore, I will punish him and then release him."

However, the pressure of the crowds was clearly wearing Pilate down, and in the end he acceded to their demands to have Jesus crucified.

The crucifixion itself is also drawn out, and emphasis is placed upon the suffering and humiliation that Jesus endured at the hands of the soldiers, the crowds and even one of the two criminals crucified alongside him. However, Jesus maintains his stature by forgiving his enemies and continuing his silence towards the specific insults hurled at him. Probably the most heart-wrenching sequence in the entire crucifixion narrative is the conversation between the two

---

[7] The Gospel of Luke is usually seen as the most historical of the four Gospels, but of course, like the others, contains the full range of the martyrdom of Jesus.

[8] This portrayal of the Jewish responsibility for Jesus' crucifixion has had wide-ranging consequences for the history of the Jewish people under Christian rule, including numerous pogroms, accusations and ultimately the Holocaust.

criminals, one of whom attacks Jesus, while the other one affirms his innocence and says, "Jesus, remember me when you come into your kingdom," to which Jesus replies, "I tell you the truth, today you will be with me in paradise" (verses 42–43). The actual death of Jesus is dramatic and given cosmic significance as darkness shadows the land and the curtain of the Temple is torn (verses 44–45). The centurion witnessing this entire sequence of events testifies to the innocence of Jesus, and finally even his detractors are reduced to silence in the face of such events.

The Jesus martyrdom narrative has all of the classical elements necessary for pathos: the obviously unjust sentence, the patently evil persecutors, the indifferent governor, the drawn-out vignettes of suffering and the affirmations from various unlikely sources (Pilate, the second criminal, the centurion) of Jesus' innocence and even superiority. It is a story very carefully woven together, and given in four (slightly) different accounts, all of which focus upon differing elements of this martyrdom.

Most of the immediate followers of Jesus, as documented in the book of Acts and other martyrological histories preserved from early Christianity, died martyrs' deaths. Most of the church traditions have massive collections of martyrs and martyrs' days upon which calendars are built.[9] These martyrdoms have almost the same format as that of Eleazar above and are extremely repetitious. Of all these martyrs perhaps two can be chosen to represent the Christian tradition: Stephen and Polycarp. Stephen's martyrdom is described in the book of Acts 6:8–15, 7:1–60, and is extremely dramatic. Being a charismatic preacher of the gospel during the period immediately following Jesus' departure, Stephen was the focus of determined opposition. At every point in the martyrdom we are given evidence of Stephen's special relationship with God. He is said to have looked like an angel (6:15), and spoke boldly before the Sanhedrin, demonstrating to them his belief that Jesus was the messiah. At the end of his sermon,

Stephen, full of the Holy Spirit, looked up to heaven and saw the glory of God, and Jesus standing at the right hand of God. "Look," he said, "I see heaven open and the Son of Man standing at the right hand of God."   (Acts 7:55–56)

At this point, having roused the fury of the Sanhedrin, Stephen has crossed over the boundary into certain death. As a token of that fact, he is granted a vision of heaven not given to others, since he is about to depart from the world. However, Stephen's death, by stoning, is not given the usual graphic detail that martyrologies favor and is merely used as a transition into the upcoming career of Paul of Tarsus.

---

[9] Some of the collections are Paul Bedjan (ed.), *Acta martyrum et sanctorum Syriace*; Irfan Shahid (ed. and trans.), *The Martyrs of Najran*; *Martyrologium romanum: ex decreto sacrosancti oecumenici Concilii Vaticani II instauratum auctoritate Ioanis Pauli PP II promulgatum*; and John Foxe (d. 1587), *Foxe's Book of Martyrs*.

Polycarp, who was Bishop of Smyrna (*ca.* 155 CE), was famous as a figure who claimed to have personally known the apostle John, and as such had great authority in the church in Asia Minor. The epistle dedicated to his martyrdom (in the form that has come down to us probably written by the historian Eusebius) sets the tone for later martyrologies. It praises the constancy of the martyrs and states,

and truly, who can fail to admire their nobleness of mind, and their patience, with that love towards their Lord which they displayed? Who, when they were so torn with scourges, that the frame of their bodies, even to the very inward veins and arteries, was laid open, still patiently endured, while even those that stood by pitied and bewailed them.[10]

Polycarp was betrayed by an apostate – contrasting his constancy with the faithlessness of the traitor – and while hiding from the authorities was granted a vision of his future end: he was to be burned alive. When he was found hiding, he had the chance to flee, but like Jesus refused to take it, saying: "Let the will of God be done." The authorities tried to persuade him to sacrifice to Caesar, but Polycarp resisted and went forward, eagerly to the stadium where he was to face his death. Like Eleazar, Polycarp took refuge in his age when called to revile Christ, and stated: "Eighty and six years have I served him, and he never did me any injury: how then can I blaspheme my king and my Savior?"[11] Threats and torments did not sway Polycarp, and he was then sentenced by the Romans to be burned alive. After a last prayer, Polycarp entered the fire, but like Shadrach, Meshach and Abed-Nego in Daniel 3, the flames did not touch his body. "Moreover, we perceived such a sweet odor [coming from the pile], as if frankincense or some such precious spices had been smoking there." Since his body could not be burned, Polycarp was then dispatched by a dagger. All of these elements (the pre-martyrdom speech, the incorruptibility of the body, etc.) will become important, if not essential, in the classical Christian (and later Muslim) martyrdom narrative. Martyrdoms continued throughout the Roman Empire until the Emperor Constantine legalized the Christian faith. Many other martyrologies focused upon the sufferings of Christians outside the Roman Empire, in the Persian Empire, orthodox Christians persecuted by the Arian Christians, and many stories of missionaries who were martyred during the course of their ministry. This long history of martyrdom remains an integral part of Christianity, even to the present day.

These martyrs laid down the essential characteristics of the Christian martyrdom: the passivity towards the process, the role of the exhortation, the demonization and ultimately the irrelevance of the persecutors, the fact that the

---

[10] "The Encyclical Epistle of the Church at Smyrna concerning the Martyrdom of the Holy Poly-carp," trans. Alexander Roberts and James Donalson, *The Ante-Nicene Fathers*, i, p. 39.

[11] Ibid., p. 41.

martyrs usually forgive their tormenters prior to their own deaths, and the long-drawn-out sequence of death with blood and gore described in excruciating detail. Martyrologies were extremely popular teaching devices throughout the Christian world, where, as previously stated, they served as one of the bases for the calendar. The prestige acquired as a result of constant martyrdom formed one of the causes for the conversion of the Roman Empire to Christianity, although of course there were others as well. When the Islamic conquests came, a large amount of this material passed into Islam and continues to be preserved in the *hadith* (tradition) and ascetic literature. We will have occasion to note several borrowed martyrdoms that are of significance to Islam.

Ultimately martyrdom is an attempt to rescue some type of meaning and dignity from death. Since all humans die, often unexpectedly, many in agony or horror, martyrdom represents a control over the uncontrollable. It does not seek to avoid death, but gives meaning to it by embracing the process and making it significant for the other faithful and also for prospective converts. By recounting in excruciating and oftentimes gory detail this death process the martyrology makes death comprehensible and familiar, even enticing to some people.

2   Martyrdom in the genesis of Islam

Allah has bought from the believers their lives and their wealth in return for paradise; they fight in the way of Allah, kill and get killed. This is a true promise from Him . . . and who fulfills His promise better than Allah? Rejoice then at the bargain you have made with Him; for that is the great triumph.[1]

Qur'an 9:111

Muslim martyrdom defies easy categorization. From the genesis of Islam at the time when the first revelations came to the Prophet Muhammad (approx. 610 CE) Muslims have been certain that suffering for the faith constituted a powerful testimonial. Although Muhammad was largely immune to the persecutions described in the Muslim historical texts personally,[2] many of those who first converted to Islam were not. Muhammad preached a radical and exclusive brand of monotheism that was in stark contrast to the fairly easy-going polytheism of the town of Mecca. Mecca had come to some prominence during the century prior to Muhammad's time (born *ca.* 570) as a result of pilgrimage to the local holy place, the Ka'ba (at that time an unroofed, square building), and some form of trade. Despite this, it was still largely homogeneous in population. Most of the inhabitants were of the tribe of Quraysh, which considered itself to be a merchant aristocracy, with a minority of transients – usually those who were married to Qurashi women or who had taken refuge in the vicinity of the holy place as a result of criminal actions – and a community of slaves. Many of the latter were Ethiopian and were originally Christians.

Muhammad's first public preaching to his hometown was not successful. For approximately three years after receiving his first revelations he had proclaimed the nascent form of Islam to his close relatives and friends with some success. His preaching to the larger community, however, resulted in rejection, social isolation, ostracism and finally in threats against him. But it was not from the Prophet Muhammad's personal experiences – which are detailed in certain cases

---

[1] All Qur'anic translations are from Majid Fakhry, *The Qur'an: A Modern English Version*.

[2] It is irrelevant to deal with the question of whether these historical texts are actually based upon the events they purport to describe or accurately convey a picture of early seventh century Mecca; the picture described here is the way the Muslim community (the audience) remembered the events.

in the Qur'an, such as *sura*s 108, 111 – that the collective Muslim memory of martyrdom was derived. This memory was focused upon the experiences of the truly weak and helpless, usually the slaves, in Meccan society. Muhammad, for the most part, was under the personal protection of powerful (usually non-Muslim) members of his tribe or clan. Slaves in Meccan society, however, lacked all protection and were expected not to offend their masters' beliefs.

Early Islam was, from the point of view of the pagan Meccans, an offense. One of the early definitive statements of belief was in *sura* 109: "Say: O unbelievers (*kafirun*), I do not worship what you worship, nor do you worship what I worship." This is a personal statement signifying the dislocation between the pagan pantheon and the worship of one God (Allah). While the pagan pantheon was assimilative in nature, in that it tended to accept diverse deities and integrate them into the belief system, Islamic monotheism is exclusive. It cannot accept the presence of other deities nor integrate or even tolerate their existence. Deities other than Allah must be satanic or demonic in nature and cannot stand any relation to the one God. *Sura* 112, another definitive statement in this regard, states: "Say: He is Allah, the only One, Allah, the Everlasting. He did not beget and is not begotten, and none is his equal." Although today this *sura* is often used in polemic against the Christian belief in the Trinity, it is clear that it is equally effective against the creation of a pantheon or the adoption of the new Muslim version of Allah (since Allah was a deity that pre-dated Islam) into a pre-existing one.

Ultimately this exclusivity created the pre-conditions for the first Muslim martyrdom experiences. Since Mecca was a consensus-driven society, and Muhammad and the Muslims were unwilling to fit into the consensus, there had to be conflict. The later *sura*s of the Qur'an portrays the early Muslim community as weak and oppressed (*mustadaʿfun*, e.g., 4:75, 8:26), though of course this was descriptive only of those Muslims who lacked all family ties in Mecca (slaves and transients). Many Qur'anic verses speak of arrogant oppressors (*mustakbirun*, e.g., 35:43, 37:35, 63:5), those who are unjust (*zalimun*), and other descriptive titles given to the pagans of Mecca. References to these diametrically opposite situations set the stage for the appearance of martyrdom stories.

Probably the best-known martyr story from the Meccan period of the Prophet Muhammad's life is that of the Ethiopian slave, Bilal. This man was persecuted for his belief in Islam. His master would take him out into the blazing sun and lay him down on his back with a heavy stone on his chest, saying to him "You will continue like this until you die or you deny [the god of] Muhammad and worship al-Lat and al-ʿUzza."[3] Eventually, however, Abu Bakr, one of the

---

[3] Ibn Hisham, *al-Sira al-nabawiyya*, i, pp. 339–40. Al-Lat and al-ʿUzza were two of the primary deities of pagan Mecca.

earliest converts to Islam and later the successor to the Prophet Muhammad, bought him and freed him from slavery. Although he did not die, Bilal became one of the paradigmatic first martyrs because of his suffering for the sake of Islam. Others were equally tormented by beatings and heat exposure, as well as by the deprivation of food and water.

It is interesting to note that the first martyr who actually died for the faith was a woman, Sumayya bint Khayyat, who like Bilal was one of the servile Muslims (a *mawla* [client] to the wealthy clan of Banu Makhzum). She was confronted by Abu Jahl (one of the harshest anti-Muslim leaders of the Quraysh), who began to slap her face and abuse her, and then stabbed her in her abdomen. Although few details of this martyrdom are given, and Sumayya's name has never become one of the common names known to Muslims, because she was the mother of the proto-Shi'ite[4] figure 'Ammar b. Yasir, her sufferings are remembered and noted in the literature.[5]

Despite the presence of martyrdom stories from the Meccan period, the outside observer is struck by the comparatively minor level of the persecution against the emerging Muslim community. What persecutions did go on were directed against a fairly small section of the group, and only one person is said to have died. The tortures that were inflicted upon Bilal and Sumayya were individual rather than institutional in nature and were not sustained over a lengthy period of time. However, for the early Muslim community itself there is no doubt that these experiences were traumatic and ultimately led to the emigration (*hijra*) of the community to the oasis town of Medina, approximately 150 miles north of Mecca. In Medina a number of the local tribesmen had converted to Islam, and they invited the Prophet Muhammad and his followers to establish themselves there in 622.

This decision was fateful for the Muslim community. From this time until the present day Islam has only rarely been divorced from power, and for the most part the Muslim paradigm of martyrdom has departed radically from other faiths which were either deprived of worldly success for their formative period of existence (like Buddhism and Christianity) or for long periods afterwards (like Judaism). For the duration of Muslim history Muslim martyrs were not usually helpless. In Medina Muhammad and his followers quickly managed to establish a functional political-religious community (*umma*) that attracted

---

[4] Shi'ites were those who supported the political and religious rights of the Prophet Muhammad's family (see Chapter 4); since Shi'ism as a coherent religious group did not come into being for several centuries after the beginning of Islam it is possible to speak of early figures as "proto-Shi'ites" (or proto-Sunnis as well).

[5] Al-Shibli, *Mahasin al-wasa'il fi ma'rifat al-awa'il*, p. 195; and see the modern rendition (loosely based upon the historical accounts) of Hanan Lahham, *Sumayya bint Khayyat: al-shahida al-ula*, p. 31f.

numbers of converts. Within five years of the *hijra* almost everyone in the oasis of Medina was Muslim – a process that was accomplished both through preaching and the application of force.

However, the Muslim domination of Medina and its environs created the conditions for war with their former hometown of Mecca, which was largely dependent upon trade routes passing nearby for its existence. Given the fact that the Muslims had been persecuted by the Meccans, it is hardly surprising that the former felt themselves entitled to attack the latter. According to Qur'an 22:39–40:

Permission is given to those who fight because they were wronged. Surely Allah is capable of giving them victory. Those who were driven out of their homes unjustly, merely for their saying: "Our Lord is Allah." Had Allah not repelled some people by others, surely monasteries, churches, synagogues and mosques, wherein the name of Allah is mentioned frequently, would have been demolished.

Although of course it is debatable whether, according to the Muslim histori- cal accounts, the Muslims were "driven out of their homes" (since in the end it was their free choice to make the *hijra* from Mecca), it is clear that this verse is an initial manifestation of a change in Islam and in the Islamic con- cept of martyrdom. Henceforward this conception would depend upon a much more active quest for justice to create the examples needed for martyrdom narratives.

Part of that quest was the restitution, at least according to the Muslim perspec- tive, of what the emigrants to Medina had lost, as well as a political-religious victory over the pagan Meccans. This first came to a head at the Battle of Badr in 624. When Muhammad and the Muslims arrived in Medina, according to the traditional accounts, they were largely without worldly possessions, having, as the Qur'an stated, been "driven out of their homes" without belongings. Since Medina is located some 150 miles up the coast of the Red Sea from Mecca along the caravan route to Syria–Palestine the Muslims were in the position to put a choke-hold over the trade Mecca needed for its existence. Badr was fought in order to protect a Meccan caravan from the Muslim raiders who threatened it, and the battle turned out to be a complete victory for the Muslims (although the caravan got away), who slaughtered a number of their Meccan opponents.

For the next six years the Muslim community, led by Muhammad, fought a series of engagements with the pagan Meccans. Although Badr was a Muslim victory, it was not exploited by the Muslims, since they lacked the manpower to follow it up. In 625 the Battle of Uhud, fought just outside Medina, resulted in a Meccan victory in which a number of prominent Muslims were killed. Further battles in 627 and an attempted pilgrimage to Mecca in 628 (seen by the Meccans as an attempted invasion) were inconclusive, and Muhammad sought to gain the upper hand over his pagan enemies by subduing or terrorizing the Bedouin tribes surrounding Medina and Mecca, and by attacking and conquering the largely Jewish settlements to the north of Medina. By 629 Muhammad was clearly in a strategically superior position and in 630 he entered Mecca peacefully and his pagan opponents converted to Islam. Further battles during that year resulted in more Muslim victories and, according to the sources, a large number of the tribes of Arabia submitted to Islam and acknowledged Muhammad's authority. Muhammad died two years later in 632.

Qur'anic teaching about martyrdom is fairly diverse and, as is usual with the Qur'an, disorganized and undeveloped. It is clear that the word *shahid* (plural, *shuhada'*), meaning both witness and martyr, is influenced by the Syriac *sahido*, which is the word that is used to translate key Christian concepts concerning martyrdom in the Syriac Bible, the Pshitta (for example, Acts 1:8).[6] With a few exceptions the word *shahid* appears in the Qur'an only with the sense of "witness." Some important verses that show this meaning are given below:

And strive for Allah as you ought to strive. He elected you, and did not impose on you any hardship in religion – the faith of your father Abraham. He called you Muslims before and in this [Qur'an] that the Apostle may bear witness against you and you may be witnesses against mankind. So, perform the prayer, give the alms and hold fast to Allah. He is your Master; and what a blessed Master and a blessed Supporter! (22:78)

The idea of either Muhammad or the Muslims being witnesses "against" (or perhaps "over," "unto") other groups is fairly common throughout the Qur'an. This sense of bearing witness is both active and passive: the Muslims should be living testimony towards the rest of humanity, but can also be called upon to bear testimony against them at the time of the Day of Judgment, should there be the need. This universal message is emphasized by Qur'an 2:143: "And thus We have made you a just nation, so that you may bear witness unto the rest of mankind, and that the Apostle [Muhammad] may bear witness unto you." Sometimes the truth being conveyed, however, is so awesome that the only witness can be God Himself: "It is He [God] who sent forth His Apostle with the guidance and the religion of truth, that He may exalt it above every other religion. Allah suffices as a witness" (48:28).

These verses summarize the primary use of the word *shahid* in the Qur'an. However, there are several verses that, while perhaps ambiguous within the context of the Qur'an, do convey the meaning of "martyr" that would become much more important in later Islam. Probably the most comprehensive of these is the sequence of Qur'an 3:138–42:

---

[6] Arthur Jeffrey, *The Foreign Vocabulary of the Qur'an*, p. 187; for Ibn Qutayba, *Ta'bir al-ru'ya*, p. 105 the word *shahid* means that "they will behold the kingdom of heaven."

This is a declaration for mankind, a guidance and admonition for the God-fearing. Do not be faint-hearted and do not grieve; you will have the upper hand, if you are true believers. If you have been afflicted by a wound, a similar wound has afflicted the others. Such are the times; We alternate them among the people, so that Allah may know who are the believers and choose martyrs [*shuhada'*] from among you. Allah does not like the evildoers! And that Allah might purify the believers and annihilate the unbelievers. Or did you suppose that you will enter Paradise before Allah has known who were those of you who have struggled and those who are steadfast. You were yearning for death before you actually met it. Now you have seen it and are beholding it.

This series of verses is to be dated to the Battle of Uhud (625), the one serious reverse in battle that the early Muslim community suffered, according to the traditional Muslim chronology. In this battle, as we will note below, the Prophet's beloved uncle Hamza, along with a number of other prominent Muslims, was killed and the community suffered from a serious depression (mostly caused by exaggerated expectations after the victory at Badr the previous year). Whether this is true or not, the close juxtaposition of the word *shuhada'* with the idea of entering Paradise and yearning for death makes it certain that we have moved away from the meaning of merely "witness" and arrived at "martyr" (as Majid Fakhry translates it above). Although the verb "chose" in 3:140 is still ambiguous, the phrase seems a fairly obvious euphemism for death.

All of the Muslim exegetes understand this verse sequence as referring to martyrdom.[7] Qur'an 3:138–42 raises a number of questions about the Muslim view of martyrdom. In the early part of the sequence the Muslims are enjoined to recall the equality of suffering that existed between them and their pagan Meccan enemies, according to the exegetes, because of the trade-off between Badr and Uhud. This equality is said to have been Allah's choice; yet, it is unclear how precisely this manifests divine will for Islam's victory (the exegete al-Razi [d. 1209] states that the reason for this is that if God aided Islam inordinately there would be no free choice between belief and infidelity). Other questions could be raised as to how the choosing of martyrs mentioned in verse 140 purifies the believers and annihilates the unbelievers in verse 141 (this point was not raised by Muslim exegetes). Additionally, given the fact that Allah is all-knowing, why is the selection of martyrs necessary in order to demonstrate which of the Muslim community have struggled and which are steadfast in verse 142 (rationalists like al-Razi gloss "knowing" with "making clear")? Presumably, since this sequence was designed to comfort the Muslim community in its time of shock at this defeat, it is questionable to what degree people were actually "yearning for death," as verse 143 states. If that were true

---

[7] Exegesis from al-Tabari, *Jami' al-bayan*, iv, pp. 100–10; Muqatil b. Sulayman, *Tafsir*, i, pp. 303–04; al-Mawardi, *Tafsir al-Mawardi*, i, pp. 425–26; Ibn Kathir, *Tafsir*, i, p. 386; al-Razi, *al-Tafsir al-kabir*, ix, pp. 11–19; al-Surabadi, *Tafsir*, i, pp. 342–45; and the Shi'ites al-Qummi, *Tafsir*, i, 131–33 and al-Tusi, *al-Tibyan fi tafsir al-Qur'an*, ii, pp. 599–603.

then one assumes that deaths incurred in battle would not have been viewed with such dismay. Other verses in the Qur'an oftentimes actually emphasize the unwillingness of the early Muslim community to fight (e.g., Qur'an 2:216, 246). Despite these questions, Qur'an 3:138–42 provides us with the beginnings of a Qur'anic martyrology.

Description of the dogma of martyrdom continues with Qur'an 3:169–70, which is probably the most famous and often-cited verse dealing with the subject:

And do not think those who have been killed in the way of Allah as dead; they are rather living with their Lord, well-provided for. Rejoicing in what their Lord has given them of His bounty, and they rejoice for those who stayed behind and did not join them, knowing that they have nothing to fear and that they shall not grieve.

Since this verse has a number of different ramifications, it will be continually referred to throughout this book. Like the previous selection, it is usually associated with the Battle of Uhud and was designed to make certain that the Muslims who had lost loved ones did not grieve inordinately or worry about their fate. The verse specifies those "killed in the way of Allah," which has been a euphemism for battle, *jihad*, and throughout the Qur'an and all Muslim literature since that time, the reference has been assumed to be to martyrs. The nature of their post-mortem status and the rewards they will enjoy will be covered in the next chapter.

Most of the Qur'anic doctrine of *jihad* is expounded in *sura*s 8–9.[8] Tradition holds that *sura* 8 was revealed in the wake of the Battle of Badr. It is key in helping the believers to see God as a personal participant in the fighting process. God is said to have granted victory "so that He may cause the Truth to triumph and nullify falsehood, even though the wicked sinners dislike it" (verse 8). In the following verses angels are said to have assisted the Muslims (verse 9), and the latter were not alone in the fighting – throwing of weapons – but God joined them: "It was not you who slew them, but Allah; and when you threw it was actually Allah who threw, so that He might generously reward the believers" (verse 17). The believers are promised that God is completely on their side, and will reward them with victory.

Much of the *jihad* teaching in the Qur'an deals with the fact that, as Qur'an 2:216 says, the early Muslim community was reluctant to fight at all and had to be encouraged. This encouragement was accomplished by the knowledge of God's complete support for their cause, their ability to win against all odds (detailed in 8:65), and the fantastic rewards to be given to those who fight. Many of these rewards are detailed in *sura* 9, where the foundational idea of *jihad* as encapsulated in the following contract is found (9:111):

---

[8] For my formulation on the subject see *Understanding* Jihad.

Allah has bought from the believers their lives and their wealth in return for Paradise; they fight in the way of Allah, kill and get killed. This is a true promise from Him in the Torah, the Gospel and the Qur'an; and who fulfills His promise better than Allah? Rejoice then at the bargain you have made with Him; for that is the great triumph.

Rightly this verse is cited at the head of many collections on the subject of *jihad*,[9] and can be seen to have contributed directly to the centrality of the subject of fighting within the Muslim community, and perhaps even indirectly to the success of the great Muslim conquests of the century following the death of Muhammad in 632. Other verses in *sura* 9 provide guidance as to which peoples can be fought, what are the bases for fighting them and how the Muslims should treat those of their blood-relatives who are either on the side of the pagans or are lukewarm in their attachment to Islam. All in all, *sura*s 8 and 9 of the Qur'an provide us with a coherent doctrine of fighting that would later come to be known as *jihad* in the path of God. This type of warfare is seen as divinely sanctioned, with the promise of either victory or death with the rank of martyr as the inducement to fight.

Compared to the Bible, the Qur'an does not detail martyrdom extensively. Most of the stories of biblical prophets do not focus upon their martyrdoms – and very few of those biblical martyr figures in the Qur'an actually died violent or persecuted deaths. Jesus, whose martyrdom is the focus of the Gospels, is specifically said to have not been killed or crucified (Qur'an 4:157–58):

And their [the Jews'] saying: "We have killed the Messiah, Jesus, son of Mary, and the apostle of Allah." They neither killed nor crucified him; but it was made to appear so unto them. Indeed, those who differ about him are in doubt about it. Their knowledge does not go beyond conjecture, and they did not kill him for certain. Rather, Allah raised him unto Him.

Thus, the act of Jesus' martyrdom, which is so central to Christianity, in which the humiliation and suffering of the story are ultimately seen as uplifting and redemptive, are seen in a completely different light in Islam. The fact that Jesus was one of God's noble messengers precludes any possibility that he could have been made to suffer such humiliation and suffering, let alone for them to have any redemptive value. From this we see that a martyrdom account can be read and understood in diametrically opposing ways by different religious and cultural traditions. John the Baptist, whose death according to the New Testament was that of a martyr, is not mentioned as such in the Qur'an. However, there are a few figures who have attracted the status of martyr. One of those is the mysterious "believer from the family of Pharaoh" mentioned in passing in Qur'an 40:28–29. When Pharaoh wanted to kill Moses for challenging him, the believer had intervened:

---

[9] For example, that of al-Bukhari, *Sahih*, Kitab al-jihad.

Then a believing man of Pharaoh's folk, who kept hidden his belief, said: "Will you kill a man for saying: 'My Lord is Allah,' when he has brought you the clear proofs from your Lord? . . . O my people yours is the dominion today, supreme in the land, but who will protect us against Allah's might, if it should smite us?'

This statement falls clearly into the category of the *jihad* of the person who speaks a word of truth to a tyrannical ruler. Clearly this particular believer was fearful of revealing his belief prior to this time and was suffering for his faith, but at a crucial moment he chose to speak out in favor of Moses and reminded Pharaoh that his judgment at the hands of God was imminent. The texts are vague as to whether this believer was actually killed for his statement. Some commentators even say that this believer was a woman, and that she was stretched to death or thrown into an oven, while others leave the issue opaque.[10] The fact that this believer is not named makes it difficult for the scholar to assess the affinities of this story.

Another group that seems to have been martyred are the equally mysterious Companions of the Pit (*Ashab al-ukhdud*), mentioned in Qur'an 85:1–9:

By the heaven of the many constellations, and by the promised Day, and by every witness and what is witnessed. Perish the Companions of the Pit, the fire well-stoked; while they sat around it, and were witnessing what they did to the believers. They did not begrudge them except that they believed in Allah, the All-Mighty, the All-Praiseworthy, to Whom belongs the dominion of the heavens and the earth.

If it were not for the fact that this selection is so elliptic, this sequence would be the best evidence for a Qur'anic martyrology. It seems possible, as some of the commentators and "stories of the prophets" writers suggest, that the reference here is to the Christian martyrs of Najran (today in northern Yemen), who were martyred by the Jewish monarch Dhu al-Nuwas during the early sixth century.[11] Here there are believers, the nature of whose belief is clearly stated, tortured and killed for the sake of their belief. What is even more interesting is the use of the root *sh-h-d* (to bear witness, to be a martyr) in verse 3 "by every witness and what is witnessed." This may be an early allusion to the future use of this root, later to be the Arabic word for "martyr." Here it is probably best translated as "witness," but clearly the witness is that of someone whose testimony is his own life. Unfortunately, there is no agreement among the exegetes as to whether the Companions of the Pit are the ones killed or doing the killing. Although the above translation seems to indicate the latter, this is not clear in the Arabic text.

Reading the whole Qur'an, one can see that the idea of being tortured or killed for one's faith is not a central theme. Proclamation, rejection of the message and

---

[10] See al-Tabari, *Jami' al-bayan*, xxiv, pp. 58–60; Ibn Kathir, *Qisas al-anbiya'*, pp. 317–18; al-Tha'labi, *'Arai's al-majalis*, pp. 189–90; see Brannon Wheeler, *Prophets in the Quran*, p. 192.

[11] Al-Tabari, *Jami' al-bayan*, xxx, pp. 131–32; al-Razi, *al-Tafsir al-kabir*, xxxi, pp. 117–18; al-Tha'labi, *'Ara'is al-majalis*, pp. 439–42.

judgment by God are much more common sequences. These few martyrdom sequences all have to be fleshed out in the "stories of the prophets" literature and their allusions even today are unclear. Martyrdom in the Jewish and Christian sense simply did not leave a strong imprint upon the holy text. And yet, from this early period Muslims are heir to a rich heritage of martyrs. These martyrs can be grouped into several categories. First, there are those martyrs such as Bilal above who suffered passively but specifically because they were Muslims. In other words, the sole reason for their suffering was their adhesion to Islamic beliefs and their refusal to compromise those beliefs upon command. This type of martyr is most easily compared to the Jewish and Christian paradigms of martyrdom described in Chapter 1.

Another type of martyr is one who is tortured or killed because of his or her identification with the Muslim community, but not specifically because of his or her beliefs. Probably the paradigmatic example of this type of martyrdom was that of Khubayb b. ʿAdi. Khubayb was captured by the Lihyan clan of the Hudhayl tribe in approximately 625, and taken in revenge for those Qurashis slain at Badr (624). His story is described in detail in the *hadith* literature and needs to be analyzed in detail.

The Messenger of Allah sent ten spies, and gave the command over them to ʿAsim b. Thabit al-Ansari (who was the grandfather of ʿAsim b. ʿUmar b. al-Khattab) until they were in a declivity between ʿUsfan and Mecca. This came to the attention of a clan of [the tribe of] Hudhayl called Banu Lihyan, and they dispatched close to 100 men who were shooters [of arrows] . . . and they surrounded them [the Muslims], and said: "If you come out and surrender yourselves then you will be under the treaty and the agreement that we will not kill any of you." ʿAsim said: "O people, we will not surrender to the protection of an infidel; O God – bring news of us to Your Prophet," and they shot arrows and killed ʿAsim.

Three [of the Muslims] surrendered according to the treaty and the agreement: Khubayb, Zayd b. al-Dathna and another man. When they were helpless, they [the Banu Lihyan] took the strings of their bows and tied them up. The third man said: "This is the beginning of treachery; by Allah, I will not accompany you, since I have an example [cf. Qurʾan 33:21] in these" meaning those who had been killed, so they dragged him and struggled with him, but he refused to accompany them, and so they left with Khubayb and Zayd b. al-Dathna until they sold them both of them after the Battle of Badr.

Banu al-Harith b. ʿAmir b. Nawfal bought Khubayb, since it was Khubayb who killed al-Harith b. ʿAmir at the Battle of Badr, and so Khubayb stayed with them as a prisoner until they decided to kill him. He asked for a razor from one of the daughters of al-Harith, so that he could shave with it, and she loaned it to him. [Thereafter] one of her young sons wandered off when she was not paying attention and came to him [Khubayb], and she found him sitting on his thigh when the razor was in his hand. She said: I was terrified and Khubayb knew it, so he said: "Are you afraid that I will kill him? I would not do such a thing." She said: "I have never seen a better prisoner than Khubayb. By Allah, one day I found him eating a bunch of grapes – though he was bound in iron – even though there was no fruit in Mecca." She would say later that it was sustenance from Allah given to Khubayb.

When they took him out from the Haram[12] to kill him in the area outside, Khubayb said to them: "Allow me to pray two raka'as [bowing for prayer]," and they left him, so he prayed two raka'as, and said: "By Allah, if it were not for the fact that they would think that I am apprehensive, I would have prayed more." He said: "O Allah! Count them each one, kill them separately and do not leave one of them!" Then he said: "I do not care what part my struggle for Allah was, since I am being killed as a Muslim, Since this is part of the essence of godhood; if He wills, He can bless the severed members of [my] body!"

Abu Saru'a 'Uqba b. al-Harith went up to him and killed him. Khubayb was an example to every Muslim who has been killed in a state of helplessness.[13]

The story of Khubayb has many of the classical elements of martyrdom. Khubayb himself was an innocent, who although he was part of a spying party sent out by Muhammad, chose to believe the amnesty offered by the Banu Lihyan and was betrayed. The two other people in the story, 'Asim b. Thabit and the unnamed man who refused to be taken alive, also provide us with paradigmatic examples, but they are not the focus of the martyrdom. After his capture, Khubayb remained in a state of purity as exemplified by the story of the razor and the little boy. Khubayb must have known that he was going to be killed in revenge for the head of the clan al-Harith whom he had killed at Badr the year before. He could have rationalized that killing the little boy who was an infidel Meccan and part of the clan that was going to kill him was the right course to take. But he put this possibility aside. It was beneath a Muslim's level to murder a little boy. However, unlike the story of Bilal, it does not appear that Khubayb was tortured in any way prior to his martyrdom.

All of these elements, however, only set the stage for the finale. Khubayb's final moments are consumed by prayer of two distinct types: the normative Muslim piety and a call for vengeance. This latter prayer, the du'a al-mazlum (the call of the oppressed, or the one treated unjustly), has great power in Islam. This idea is affirmed by traditions stating that one should "fear the prayer of the oppressed for it is answered [for certain]."[14] These ritual curses are usually rhymed and invoke the power of God to exact either justice or vengeance for the person wronged. Khubayb's martyrdom is that of the innocent Muslim who dies pure in his faith, as a testimony to the truth of Islam, without besmirching his beliefs in any way. Although this is a standard martyrdom narrative it still has a great deal of emotional power.

---

[12] The central area of Mecca, the area around the Ka'ba.
[13] Bukhari, Sahih, v, pp. 15–16 (no. 3989).
[14] E.g., al-Bukhari, Sahih, iv, p. 41 (no. 3059); al-Tabarani, Kitab al-du'a, iii, pp. 1413–16 (nos. 1313–21).

Yet another type of martyrdom is the fighting martyr. This type of martyr is almost unique to Islam, for the most part. Although both Christianity and Buddhism allow for martyrs to be aggressive in certain ways, such as in actively attempting to persuade people to join the faith or undertaking dangerous missions from which there is the possibility that the missionary might not survive, the element of a fighting martyr is missing in both of these other missionary religions. Because both Jesus and Buddha never personally took up arms (and early followers of Christianity and Buddhism were persecuted), every attempt by later theologians and sometimes by political leaders to make religious warriors – whether medieval Christian knights or Zen Buddhist fighting monks – into martyrs with true spiritual rank foundered or met with severe opposition.

This was not the case in Islam. Because Muhammad's career after the *hijra* was that of a political, military and religious leader all rolled into one, this element of actively seeking out martyrdom on the part of the believer is central to the faith. Although Muhammad did not personally seek out martyrdom, he participated in numerous battles and initiated many more (usually estimated at a total of more than eighty), as well as being on record for encouraging death in battle. (Whether these statements are historical or not is irrelevant. They exist within the collective memory of the Muslim community and are seen by substantial numbers of it as spiritually authoritative.) For this reason actively seeking martyrdom is much more central to Islam than it is to the other great missionary religions.

Early on, with the victory at the Battle of Badr, these tendencies appear. As described above, Badr was a rout of the pagan Meccans during the course of which a number of their most prominent leaders were either killed or taken prisoner. At the beginning of the battle, Muhammad reportedly stated:

By the one who holds the soul of Muhammad in His hand, every man who fights today and is killed, demonstrating patience, seeking a reward from God, going forward without going backward God will take him into paradise.

The story says that 'Umayr b. al-Humam, one of the clan of Banu Salima, had some dates in his hand, was eating them, and said "Really, now! Nothing is between me and entering paradise other than killing those [infidels]!?" and then he threw the dates aside and took up a sword, went out and fought until he was killed.[15] This story is one of the most famous of the Battle of Badr. It expresses cause and effect – Muhammad making a promise and watching someone believe him and die for it – as well as a casual attitude towards death. This is in close accord with the self-portrayal of the early Muslim community as exemplified by the Qur'anic verse 2:96: "Indeed, you will find of them [Jews] the

---

[15] Ibn Hisham, *Sira*, ii, pp. 267–68; other versions in Muslim, *Sahih*, vi, p. 44; Wensinck, *Concordance*, s.v. *tamarat*.

most attached to life, even more attached than those who associated other gods with Allah. Every one of them wishes to live for one thousand years. This long life, however, will not spare them the punishment." The Muslim community distinguished itself by the lack of attachment to life, and the Qur'an associates this love of life with infidelity.

However, despite the fact that the victory at Badr is important to early Muslim identity, for the purposes of discussing martyrdom the defeat at the Battle of Uhud (625) is more important. People are killed in almost any military engagement, but a defeat tends to bring out the desperation associated with martyrdom. One of the reasons that that was the case for the Muslims was the fact that the Qur'an placed an exaggerated level of importance upon the victory at Badr (cf. Qur'an 8:17). For political and theological reasons from Badr until the present day, Islam has been very closely wedded to victory on the battlefield (fed also by the great Islamic conquests of the next hundred years).

Uhud exemplified this trend. Badr had bred over-confidence in the Muslim community, and had made the Meccans more respectful of the Muslim's abilities. The Muslims in Medina were divided between those who fully followed Muhammad (in the Qur'an called the believers) and those who were uncommitted Muslims (called the hypocrites), and at a strategic juncture the latter departed from the battlefield of Uhud. The Muslims chose a bad position for battle, charged into the Meccan lines in an undisciplined manner and fell into a classic encirclement trap. Although in the end the Meccans avoiding giving a knockout blow to the Muslims – which they clearly could have, since the Muslims foolishly placed themselves away from the entrance to Medina, which contained their unprotected wives and families – Uhud was a severe embarrassment to the new faith. Much of the Qur'anic *sura* 3 deals with the problems created by this defeat, and many of the verses in this *sura* are foundational for Islamic martyrdom.

The best-known martyr of early Islam died at Uhud. Hamza, one of the Prophet Muhammad's youngest uncles and earliest converts, was a champion of Islam. During the Battle of Badr he was one of the mainstays of the Muslim victory, killing one of the leaders of the Meccans. Since Hamza had killed a number of prominent Meccans during this battle, this prompted what today would be called a "bounty hunt." One of the relatives of a slain Meccan offered an Ethiopian slave called Wahshi his freedom if he would kill Hamza. The opportunity to accomplish this came during the Battle of Uhud, where once again Hamza was one of the champions of the Muslim side. Since Hamza was the Muslim champion he was quite exposed; on the other hand Wahshi was able to conceal himself and throw a spear at Hamza, which in his own words "passed through his abdomen."[16] No doubt this was an excruciating death for

---

[16] Al-Bukhari, *Sahih*, v, p. 44 (no. 4072); also Ibn Hisham, *Sira*, iii, pp. 15f.

Hamza, although Wahshi's account does not dwell upon that fact. But even worse for Hamza was the fact that the Muslims were not able to recover his body immediately after his death (because they were retreating), and had to watch Hind, the wife of the Meccan leader Abu Sufyan (and mother of the future fifth caliph, Mu'awiya b. Abi Sufyan), mutilate his body. This she did by cutting him open, taking out his liver and chewing it, for which her descendants were ever afterwards referred to as "Children of the Liver-Eating Woman."[17]

Hamza's death topically is much closer to the traditional non-Muslim martyrdom. It was personal, accomplished to a large extent because of actions he took as a result of his belief in Islam (although there are those who would say it was more of a blood-vengeance issue), and the mutilation of his body stands out even in the overall gore of battle. Muslims, as will be seen in Chapter 3, place a great deal of weight upon the treatment of the body, both before and after death. The mutilation of Hamza's body, given his champion status, was an indignity that had to be matched by a rank among martyrs. Thus he is usually referred to as *sayyid al-shuhada'*, the leader or noble one of the martyrs. This title was accorded to him not because he was the first martyr – a title that arguably should go to Bilal or one of those killed at earlier battles[18] – but because his life and death exemplified what a martyr should be. He demonstrated the qualities of a hero, fought bravely for the sake of Islam and died in a noble manner.

Another later type of fighting martyr is Ja'far al-Tayyar, who was the younger brother of 'Ali b. Abi Talib (son-in-law of the Prophet Muhammad, and afterwards fourth caliph [ruled 656–61], and the ancestor of all of Muhammad's descendants). Ja'far is best known for his part in the ill-fated raid upon the town of Mu'ta, today in southern Jordan, which happened in 629. This raid was one of the first that Muhammad had sent to this area, which had recently seen the return of the Byzantines after a nearly fifteen-year absence. Mu'ta was the first time that Muslims had attempted to challenge larger, non-tribal entities like the Byzantine Empire (although it is questionable whether those who opposed the Muslims were formally Byzantine soldiers). The Battle of Mu'ta was a failure for the Muslims, however, because of their leadership. Muhammad appointed four leaders, three of whom were militarily incompetent (though long-time Muslims). The last one was the brilliant commander Khalid b. al-Walid, who afterwards was responsible for some of the most impressive Islamic conquests. Ja'far was the second of the incompetent commanders, each one of whom took the Prophet Muhammad's flag to lead the Muslims, and was killed. Khalid, to whom the command eventually devolved, did the prudent thing, which was to withdraw.

---

[17] Ibn Hisham, *Sira*, iii, pp. 41–44.

[18] In al-'Askari, *al-Awa'il*, p. 157 it is said that the first martyr in battle was al-Harith b. Abi Hala (the Prophet Muhamamd's step-son), and that the first martyr was Sumayya bint Khayyat (about her see Hannan Lahham, *Sumayya bint Khayyat: al-shahida al-ula*, and further Chapter 8).

The battle is best known, however, for the martyrdom of Ja'far. The Muslims at Mu'ta were the first who were martyred while fighting against non-Arabs, the Byzantines, and thus form something of a link with the age of the great Muslim conquests, which was to begin shortly thereafter. Ja'far is one of the main links. His martyrdom is described, as him fighting from horseback until his horse was hamstrung, then he continued fighting on foot, until both of his arms were cut off. Initially he took the banner in his right hand, until it was cut off, then in his left until it was cut off and he bled to death while uttering a war poem. When the remnants of this disastrous raid returned to Medina, the Prophet Muhammad told the Muslims he had seen Ja'far in heaven with two wings given to him by God in place of the arms he had lost in battle. Hence his name of Ja'far al-Tayyar (Ja'far the flyer).[19] Ja'far was one of the last of the "heroic" generation of Muslim commanders; after his time most commanders did not personally fight in battles and only lost their lives through gross incompetence or other unusual circumstances.

Of course there are numerous other examples of Muslim martyrs from the time of the Prophet Muhammad. But the examples listed above give us a good idea of the categories of martyrdom available from the classical pre-conquest period of Islam. These fighting martyrologies are closely akin to the genre of the "battle-days of the [pre-Islamic] Arabs" (*ayyam al-'Arab*), in that the heroism is personal, poetry is an essential part of the martyrdom and fighting is romanticized. Although many of the conquest martyrologies would continue employing these general themes, gradually after the first century of Islam (seventh–eighth centuries) they would die out.

Immediately after the death of the Prophet Muhammad in 632 the Muslim community initiated the process of the great Islamic conquests lasting approximately between 634–732. These conquests initially covered the regions immediately adjacent to the Arabian Peninsula: Yemen, Syria–Palestine, Egypt and Iraq. According to the sources these regions were conquered during the caliphate of 'Umar b. al-Khattab (634–44), who was assassinated by a Christian slave he had beaten. Two further periods of conquest followed: one under Mu'awiya b. Abi Sufyan (661–80), the dynamic governor of Syria, who became caliph after winning a civil war (656–61) against Muhammad's son-in-law 'Ali b. Abi Talib and the Muslim community of Iraq. Mu'awiya initiated conquests toward the heartlands of the Byzantine Empire (today the country of Turkey), further into North Africa and deep into the Iranian plateau. After yet another civil war, the caliphs 'Abd al-Malik (685–705) and his four sons, al-Walid I (705–15), Sulayman (715–17), Yazid II (720–24) and Hisham (724–43), continued the conquests, adding the rest of North Africa, Spain, southern France, the Caucasus Mountain region, Central Asia and parts of the Indus River Valley to the

---

[19] Ibn Hisham, *Sira*, iii, pp. 433–35; and see al-Tirmidhi, *Al-Jami' al-sahih*, v, p. 320 (no. 3852).

Muslim empire as well as mounting major failed expeditions against the Byzantine capital of Constantinople (the period 717–20 was ruled by the pacifistic caliph 'Umar II). Although there were local conquests that followed this period (such as the conquest of Sicily and southern Italy in the ninth century), these early conquests established the core Muslim area.

Culturally this core Muslim area became a unity and was over a long period of time converted to Islam. Arabic became the predominant language, except in the Iranian plateau and Central Asia where Persian regained dominance after the tenth century. During the formative first three centuries of Islam, Muslims built up an impressive religious and literary high culture. The religious focus of this high culture was the *sunna* (the way) of the Prophet Muhammad contained in the vast *hadith* (tradition) literature.[20] All of the *hadith* literature, which takes the form of statements by Muhammad or purported eye-witness reports concerning his actions, is retrojected back to this earlier time period, and made to seem as if the issues and controversies of later times were already hashed out centuries beforehand. The *hadith* literature, thus, is the basis for the *sunna*, and upon these traditions rests the equally vast edifice of the *shari'a*, the Divine Law, which is the supreme legal expression of medieval Islam. This classical Muslim civilization is the fountainhead of all contemporary Muslim societies.

The period of the great Islamic conquests was the last time when there was some doubt about whether Islam would succeed as a religion. All the ancestors of every Muslim sect and division participated in these conquests, and today all continue to look towards them with pride, knowing that the conquests demonstrated the truth of the revelation of the Qur'an. For this reason, the Muslim martyrs who died during this period can still be considered to be pan-Islamic (as opposed to the sectarian martyrs examined in Chapter 4). Several different types of martyrs can be isolated from this period. The dominant group is similar to that from the time of Muhammad: those Muslims who died in battle. Although there are many figures who fit into this category, one of the paradigmatic martyrdoms was that of the Prophet Muhammad's Companion Abu Ayyub al-Ansari, who, according to the legends surrounding him, fought and was martyred beneath the walls of Constantinople (today Istanbul). Most of the stories concerning him are concerned with the question – more fully discussed in Chapters 3 and 7 – about the degree to which it is possible to seek one's death, and the identification of the line at which seeking martyrdom becomes actual suicide.

Abu Ayyub's story is closely connected to the interpretation of Qur'an 2:195 "Spend [money] for the cause of Allah and do not cast yourselves with your own hands into destruction, and be charitable. Surely Allah loves the charitable." At a critical moment during the siege of Constantinople (presumably in 674–78), one

---

[20] This focus is upon those groups that would later become Sunnis; those who would later be called Shi'ites had a different source of authority (traditions from the Imams).

of the Muslim soldiers was said to have single-handedly attacked the Byzantine enemy. His action was met with disapproval by his fellow soldiers, who cited this verse, "do not cast yourselves with your own hands into destruction." However, Abu Ayyub clarified the issue, and stated that this verse in actuality meant to avoid excessive charity that would (or could) lead to bankruptcy. Then Abu Ayyub himself fought on until he was killed and buried outside of Constantinople[21] where his tomb is still revered to this day. Although the exact circumstances of Abu Ayyub's martyrdom are not mentioned, the implication of his comments is that he approved of single-handedly fighting the enemy and was willing to (perhaps) die in that manner.

Another group of martyrs, those who died by plague, is entirely new to the Islamic period. The early Muslims were either nomadic or semi-nomadic Arabs, whose knowledge of the deadly plagues that swept the Fertile Crescent after 540 CE was limited. Immediately after the initial conquest of Syria–Palestine in approximately 637 there was a plague, usually called the Plague of Emmaus (in Arabic, 'Imwas), which killed off a substantial percentage of the Muslim army and its leadership.[22] For the victims of plague or those exposed to it there arose the need to decide whether to stay in the afflicted region or to leave it. The most compelling choice for anyone is to flee, but from a medical point of view this option only spreads the plague to previously unafflicted regions. However, it is very difficult to make people who have been possibly exposed to the plague want to stay in the same area together with the victims, because the chance that any healthy people might die is great. Obviously the moral dilemmas created by the (apparently) indiscriminate death meted out by the unseen force of the plague are great. Therefore, plague victims have achieved martyrdom status.

The means by which this happened are two: the first was the popularization of the tradition "Whoever dies stabbed (tu'ina) or in a plague (ta'un) is a martyr"[23] (other ramifications of these and like traditions will be discussed in Chapter 3), and the second was the creation of the paradigmatic plague martyr Mu'adh b. Jabal. Mu'adh was a comparatively late convert to Islam, usually associated with the Syrian Muslim community, and was highly respected as an ascetic. His name appears frequently in the early ascetic literature of Islam. However, for our purposes, he was part of the conquering Muslim army located in southern Syria–Palestine, and rose to leadership for a brief time after his predecessor Abu 'Ubayda died from the plague. Some Muslims advised that people should leave the stricken area, but Mu'adh exhorted the people to stay, since the plague was "a blessing from your Lord, the prayer of His prophet and the manner in which the righteous ones prior to you have died." Then he is said to have prayed:

---

[21] See al-Tabari, *Jami'*, ii, pp. 203–06 (on 2:195).

[22] E.g., see Michael Dols, *The Black Death in the Middle East*; and Lawrence Conrad, "Die Pest und ihr soziales umfeld in Nahen Osten in frühen mittelalters."

[23] Cited in al-Suyuti, *Abwab al-sa'ada*, pp. 40–43; and see Wensinck, *Concordance*, s.v., *ta'un* (many citations).

"O God, Give Mu'adh and the family of Mu'adh the most generous portion of this plague, since You are capable of everything."

This prayer was granted, because Mu'adh's son, 'Abd al-Rahman b. Muljam al-Muradi, was the next to fall victim to the plague, and as he was at his son's side when he died he, too, soon caught the plague. All of the Muslims in the area repeatedly visited him, and were exhorted by him in his last extremity (which no doubt served to spread the plague even further).[24] Since Mu'adh's final exhortations are cited at some length it is important to note the role of the final exhortation in martyrology. These messages are highly stylized sermons that are designed to impart the truths the martyr (or more probably the redactor of this account) want to portray as the most important for the living. In a Muslim context these invariably take the style of chiding the heedless, reminding them of death, the gravity of life, the unexpected time of one's passing, the futility of worrying about worldly success and the transient nature of earthly possessions. The death process in the case of Mu'adh is only briefly referred to, although periodically he is said to have fainted or fallen quiet for a time. Unlike Christian martyrologies there are no descriptions of his actual sufferings, and although the scene is set in a plague house, Mu'adh could just as well have been dying from old age. We are not given access to any visions of his bodily sufferings or disfigurements.

Plague victims were frequently to avail themselves of being called martyrs, because there were to be many plagues throughout Muslim history. Probably the most famous are the numerous variants of the Black Plague that struck Egypt during the fourteenth century. At that time the famous jurisprudent al-Subki (d. 1355) was asked to explain in a *fatwa* (a legal opinion) the reasons why plague victims were martyrs, which he did at great length.[25] One beneficial side effect of the creation of plague martyrdom, and of the example of Mu'adh b. Jabal who did not flee from the plague, was a tradition of quarantine that probably minimized the deadly effects of the plague in the Muslim world more than in other areas.

Another and much smaller category of martyr is the one who was tortured for his beliefs by a non-Muslim state. As was previously stated, the number of times this happened among Muslims after the initial Meccan phase of the Prophet Muhammad's ministry was comparatively small. Muslim legal opinion was very strongly against the idea of Muslims living under non-Muslim rule, and although Muslims traveled frequently as merchants, for the most part they were not molested on account of being Muslims (of course, this does not mean that Muslim travelers were safe; it just means that when they were targeted it was not because they were Muslims or in order to force them to renounce their religion).

---

[24] Account from Ibn A'tham al-Kufi, *Kitab al-futuh*, i, pp. 310–26.
[25] Al-Subki, *Fatawa*, ii, pp. 339–54; and see al-Suyuti, *Ma rawahu al-wa'un fi akhbar al-ta'un*, pp. 150–53.

There were few strong states bordering upon the classical Islamic world that had anti-Muslim political or religious elites who sought to forcibly convert Muslims to another religion. The Christian states of Europe and especially the Byzantine Empire were the exception to this rule. Several *jihad* books list off stories of Muslims who were taken prisoner by the Byzantines and offered release if they would convert to Christianity. One describes tortures such as a boiling pot of oil into which reluctant prisoners would be thrust, while another tells of being forced to choose between hunger and eating the flesh of swine.[26]

However, these stories are extremely rare. Muslims usually were redeemed in prisoner exchanges or by paying a ransom or they disappeared into the slave markets of Byzantium and Europe where presumably they were converted to Christianity.[27] (The *jihad* writer Ibn al-Nahhas says that many were seduced from their faith in this manner.) Compared to either Judaism or Christianity, the number of Muslim martyrs forced to choose between conversion and death are few, and it is significant that even the writers of formal martyrologies cannot find more than a few examples. Even the story of the Byzantines and their pot of boiling oil ended with the Christians and the Muslim making a compromise: the Muslim agreed to kiss the Christian's head, and was freed together with all of the other Muslims who were waiting to be boiled.

The classical Muslim framework of martyrology is different from that of other faiths. Although the initial Meccan phases involve some physical violence against Muslims for the sake of Islam, this became nothing more than a historical memory. Overwhelmingly, perhaps because of the very success of the faith, Islam had to seek other conceptions of martyrdom. These have been most obviously filled by those martyrs killed in battle – a category comparatively lacking in other faiths – and to some extent those killed in plagues (and other categories to be discussed in Chapter 3). The Muslim ideal for a martyr became that person – usually a man – who through his active choice sought out a violent situation (battle, siege, guarding an unstable frontier, etc.) with pure intentions and was killed as a result of that choice. Ideally his actions expressed courage and defiance of the enemy, loyalty towards Islam and the pure intention to please God, since the acceptable manner of *jihad* was to "lift the Word of Allah to the highest" (Qur'an 9:41). In general, this type of martyrdom did not involve an extensive process of dying, unlike in Christian martyrologies, but required the martyr to speak out prior to his death. These dying words – sometimes prayers, sometimes a death poem and occasionally general words of defiance – were his immortal contribution to Islam.

---

[26] Ibn al-Nahhas, *Mashari' al-ashwaq*, i, p. 582 (no. 979), citing Ibn al-Athir; al-Tamimi, *Kitab al-mihan*, p. 383.

[27] P. S. van Koningsveld, "Muslim Slaves and Captives in Western Europe during the late Middle Ages."

3 Legal definitions, boundaries and rewards of the martyr

> *'Abdallah b. Ghalib said when he challenged the enemy: Why would I want to converse with this world – for the perceptive there is no good in it. By God, if it were not for my love of facing sleeplessness, laying on my bed with my forehead to You, walking between the platoons and the squadrons during the night, and seeking Your reward and the in-dwelling of Your favor, I would desire to depart from this world and its people. Then he broke the sheath of his sword, advanced and fought until he was killed.*
>
> Al-Tamimi, Kitab al-mihan, 232

Because of the disorganized nature of the Qur'anic martyrological doctrine, there are questions about the definition of who precisely could be counted as a martyr and what their reward would be.[1] The most decisive verse specifying the martyr's reward was Qur'an 3:169–70:

And do not think those who have been killed in the way of Allah as dead; they are rather living with their Lord, well-provided for. Rejoicing in what their Lord has given them of His bounty, and they rejoice for those who stayed behind and did not join them, knowing that they have nothing to fear and that they shall not grieve.

As previously stated, this verse provides one of the most direct proofs that there is a special place prepared for martyrs, or at least for those killed in *jihad*, because for the most part the Qur'an does not single out martyrs. Clearly the two verses are designed to promise eternal life in the presence of God with amenities that are not specified. The secondary point of the verse selection is to extend special comfort to those bereaved by the death of the martyr. In general, mourning over the dead is either forbidden in Islam or at least not encouraged. But this verse portrays the martyrs as rejoicing in their fate, and holds out this sense of happiness to loved ones at a time of obvious loss.

Further, from the Qur'an there are verses that appear to rank those blessed in heaven. For example, 57:19 states: "And those who believe in Allah and His messengers are truly the pious and the martyrs (*shuhada'*) in their Lord's sight. They shall have their wage and their light; but those who disbelieve and deny Our

---

[1] On these issues see *EI²*, "*shahid*" (Etan Kohlberg); and Bernard Freamon, "Martyrdom, Suicide, and the Islamic Law of War: A Short Legal History."

31

signs, are truly the Companions of Hell." However, there remains some question as to the correct translation of the word *shuhada*' in this verse; given the fact that the Qur'an specifies "witnesses" so often (as described in Chapter 2), there is no necessity to see this as a reference to "martyrs" exclusively. This is also the case with Qur'an 4:49, which states: "Those who obey Allah and the Apostle will be in the company of those whom God has favored of the prophets, the saints, the martyrs (*shuhada*') and the righteous people. What excellent companions they are!" Again, later Muslim exegesis would uniformly understand this to refer to the "martyrs" (as Fakhry translates it), but this conclusion is not absolutely certain.

In the Qur'an there are a great many passages that promise wonderful visions of the Hereafter to the blessed. There is no sense that the passages describing these pleasures are graded in any way, other than through a very biased reading of those two verses above, and they appear to be for the plurality of Muslims rather than specifically for martyrs. Some of these verses, however, must be examined, since they are repeated quite frequently throughout the *jihad* literature. For example, Qur'an 56:10–38 states:

And the outstrippers [those of the highest rank in heaven], the outstrippers; those are the favored ones, in the Garden of Bliss; a throng of the ancients, and a small band of the latecomers. Upon beds interwoven with gold; reclining upon them, facing each other. While immortal youths go round them, with goblets, pitchers and a cup of limpid drink. Their heads do not ache from it and they do not become intoxicated. And with such fruits as they care to choose; and such flesh of fowl as they desire; and wide-eyed houris [women of paradise] like hidden pearls; as a reward for what they used to do. They do not hear therein idle talk or vilification; only the greeting: "Peace, peace!"

As for the Companions of the Right; and behold the Companions of the Right? They are in the midst of thornless Lotus Trees, and braided acacias, and extended shade, and overflowing water, and abundant fruit, neither withheld nor forbidden, and uplifted mattresses. We have formed them originally; and made them pure virgins, tender and unaging, for the Companions of the Right.

The Companions of the Right are the blessed of heaven, as opposed to the Companions of the Left who are the damned and are described immediately afterwards. This Qur'anic selection gives us a concentrated view of what paradise looks like for the Muslim. It is a place of rest and relaxation, free from pain and suffering and full of plenty. However, the part of the selection that usually attracts the most attention is the mention of houris. These are the women of paradise, who are oftentimes adduced by anti-Muslim polemicists in order to present Islam as a sensual religion. This fact has made the issue of houris a very sensitive one for Muslims, and some Muslim apologists have taken an intellectually dishonest route and even claimed that houris are not women.[2] This allegation cannot be supported by the texts, and the balanced scholar, while obviously rejecting lurid polemical pictures against Islam, cannot go to the other extreme and deny the existence of sexual themes in both the Qur'an and the *hadith* literature as part of the visions of paradise. It is impossible to find any classical Muslim exegete who understood the verses concerning the houris as anything other than references to women whose purpose was to provide sexual pleasure for the blessed in heaven.

Other Qur'anic verses continue to specify rewards for the Muslims in paradise. Qur'an 44:50–54 states: "However, the God-fearing are in a secure place; in gardens and well-springs. They wear silk and brocade facing each other. Thus it will be; and We gave them wide-eyed houris in marriage. They call therein for every fruit in perfect security." Other selections such as 52:18–27 have very similar descriptions, sometimes containing new details such as the types of decorations in paradise, the verdancy of the fruit, the beauty of the location and the ease in which the believers take their rest. However, it is important to note that all of these descriptions, while appearing in the *jihad* literature, within the context of the Qur'an are for believers as a whole and are not limited merely to martyrs. There are no verses in the Qur'an, other than those cited at the beginning of the chapter, that single out the martyr for special treatment in heaven.

In the transition from the Qur'an to the *hadith* (traditions) literature, the situation changes completely. Inside the *hadith* literature, the figure of the martyr is delineated and described in great detail as a unique person set apart from all other Muslims. The first problem that arises is who precisely could be counted as a martyr (*shahid*) in Islam. For most canonical *hadith* collectors, it was important to emphasize that it is impossible for anyone other than God to say precisely who is and who is not a martyr. But some of the circumstances that would make being a martyr inevitable were delineated. The early *hadith* reflect a process of widening the definition of martyrdom to the point where it began to lose all meaning and simply came to cover anyone who had died a worthy death and should be admitted immediately into paradise. This is best exemplified in the work of Jalal al-Din al-Suyuti (d. 1505), who although comparatively late, collected all of these traditions into one booklet, *Abwab al-sa'ada fi asbab al-shahada* (*The Gates of Happiness Concerning the Circumstances of Martyrdom*). Al-Suyuti cites the most popular tradition expanding the number of possible cases of martyrdom:

. . . the Messenger of Allah [Muhammad] said: God Most High has established [the martyr's] reward according to his intention. What do you count as the circumstances of martyrdom? They said: Dying in the path of Allah [jihad]. The Messenger of Allah

---

2 Christoph Reuter, *My Life is a Weapon*, pp. 126–27, citing Mather Hathout (in refutation, Ibn al-Athir, *al-Nihaya fi gharib al-hadith*, i, p. 458 defines houris as "women of paradise").

said: There are seven categories of martyr other than being killed in the path of Allah. The one who dies of a stomach complaint is a martyr, the one who drowns is a martyr, the one who dies of plague is a martyr, the one who dies in a structural collapse is a martyr, the one who dies in a fire is a martyr, the one who dies of pleurisy, and the woman who dies in childbirth is a martyr.[3]

It is fairly obvious that the whole point of this tradition is to move the focus of martyrdom away from its most basic sense: that of dying in battle. Although the issue of dying in a plague (covered in Chapter 2) could have some relevance for fighters forced to garrison an afflicted territory, and conceivably the one who drowns could be aiding or participating in sea battle, the other categories are completely without relevance to fighting. The issues of the stomach complaint, the collapse and the fire, seem to suggest a settled lifestyle and a death that is happenstance. All of them seem topically removed from death in battle, other than the death by drowning, which would suggest a person who (perhaps) seeks out danger.

The other interesting personality on this list is the woman who dies in child-birth. In general women are not participants in *jihad*. The foundational tradition in this regard is cited by al-Bukhari, who quotes 'A'isha (the Prophet Muham-mad's favorite wife) asking: "O Messenger of Allah, since we see that *jihad* is the best of actions, can we [women] not fight? He answered: For you [women] the best type of *jihad* is a righteous *hajj* [pilgrimage to Mecca]."[4] A number of other traditions are available that exclude women from the process of fighting, and it is rare to find Muslim women who fought actively in battle during the pre-modern period, although there are a few exceptions to that rule. But the above tradition opens the process of martyrdom to women and is extremely important, especially when one remembers that the percentage of women who died giving birth during the pre-modern period was extraordinarily high. Also, the childbirth martyrdom would glorify the act of giving birth, which does serve to augment the number of Muslims in the world (and presumably future fighters as well).

Al-Suyuti also lists a number of other circumstances of martyrdom: the trav-eler who dies away from his home, the one who dies of fever, someone who is thrown from his mount while going to fight and dies, someone who guards (*murabit*) the frontiers of Islam, someone who dies in defense of his/her prop-erty, someone who is eaten by wild animals, someone who is denied justice and dies from it, someone who is killed by an unjust ruler after he enjoins

---

[3] Ibn al-Mubarak, *Jihad*, pp. 63–64 (no. 68); also al-Bukhari, *Sahih*, iii, p. 278 (nos. 2829–30); Muslim, *Sahih*, vi, p. 51; and al-Suyuti, *Abwab al-sa'ada*, pp. 36–37 (no. 2); in al-Baghawi, *Sharh al-sunna*, iii, p. 511 the version containing the woman who dies in childbirth is glossed as "a woman who dies untouched by a man" (this gloss seems to be related to the category of "martyrs of love" who are usually chaste).

[4] Al-Bukhari, *Sahih*, iii, p. 264 (no. 2784).

the latter to righteousness, someone who is bitten by a venomous creature (a snake or a scorpion) and dies from it, whoever dies of sickness, whoever dies of lovesickness, as well as whoever dies of seasickness. The categories become very broad after this: any believer who dies, any woman who resists being jealous, anyone who says: "O Allah, bless me in my death and what follows my death" and then dies, whoever prays the pre-dawn prayers, fasts three days out of every month and does not forget the supererogatory prayers whether at home or traveling, whoever is a student (or a seeker after knowledge, *talib al'ilm*) and dies, whoever is a righteous merchant and dies, whoever brings food to one of the border towns, whoever treats his wife and children rightly, whoever lives as a friendly person, and the righteous *muhtasib* (town censor). Some categories are unusual: a man who washes himself ritually in snow and dies from it, and someone who when his head is shaved for the *hajj*, and has a pustule on his head, and the barber shaves him and accidently cuts him, he dies from it.

A number of martyrs obtain their status through saying various ritual prayers or blessings numerous times: for example, whoever blesses Muhammad 100 times, whoever says when he wakes up: "I take refuge in Allah, the Hearer, the Knower from the rejected Satan," and reads the three final verses from *surat* al-Hashr (59), whoever reads *surat* al-Hashr, whoever dies on Friday (the Muslim day of prayer) and, finally, whoever asks truthfully of God that he be a martyr and then dies (without actually fighting at all) even if he dies on his bed.[5]

It is clear that the first tradition limiting the number of non-fighting martyrs to a total of seven – which is probably an early tradition – opened the door to a large number of other traditions along similar lines that all seek to widen the number of possible martyrs as much as possible. One of the variants of the first tradition gives us a clue why that would be the case; when Muhammad was told that the only circumstance of martyrdom was dying in battle, he is said to have replied: "Then the number of martyrs in my community would be small." After the period of the initial conquests that would indeed have been the case. By that time the status of "martyr" within the Muslim community was so high that many sought to attain it without the inconvenience of actually going out to fight. As was the case with the seven possible cases of martyrdom tradition summarized above, most of the circumstances adduced by al-Suyuti reflect a more settled society. People tended to die from attacks by wild animals rather than by being attacked by non-Muslims. Disease and snake-bites are more prominent as causes for martyrdom, together with the danger of women dying in childbirth. Proactive prayers and fulfillment of rituals in dangerous situations are also enough to make one a martyr.

---

[5] This selection follows al-Suyuti, *Abwab al-sa'ada fi asbab al-shahada* all the way through the booklet in the order in which the traditions are given. See Abu Da'ud, *Sunan*, ii, p. 87 (no. 1520) for an example of asking God for martyrdom and being counted as a martyr.

Some of the above categories are so broad as to make the title of martyr almost meaningless. For example, anyone who dies a believer would seem to include most Muslims. And if one can ask truthfully of God that one be a martyr, and then be considered to be one, even if the one who asks dies on his bed, then presumably this could include anyone. The same global aspect appears to be present in categories such as treating one's wife and children rightly, being a friendly person and being a student. The well-known tradition about dying of lovesickness will be dealt with in Chapter 6. In short, although many of these traditions might be looked upon with some suspicion by the Muslim community – since they clearly contain questionable narratives – when taken as a whole they represent a widespread effort by the community to open the doors of martyrdom to anyone who wanted it badly enough.

Jihad literature contains a vast amount of material about the martyr and helps to answer many of the basic questions about martyrdom left uncovered by the Qur'an. This literature began to appear in the late eighth and early ninth centuries, largely at the hands of two great scholars: Ibn al-Mubarak (d. 797) and Abu Ishaq al-Fazari (d. 802–03). Both of these scholar-warriors wrote significant works, but for the purposes of discussing martyrdom, Ibn al-Mubarak is paramount. He gives us the earliest discussion of the importance of motivation for the martyr:

The slain [in *jihad*] are three [types of] men: a believer, who struggles with himself and his possessions in the path of God, such that when he meets the enemy [in battle] he fights them until he is killed. This is the tested martyr (*shahid*), [and is] in the camp of God under His throne; the prophets do not exceed him [in merit] except by the level of prophecy. [Then] a believer, committing offenses and sins against himself, who struggles with himself and his possessions in the path of God, such that when he meets the enemy [in battle] he fights until he is killed. This cleansing wipes away his offenses and his sins – behold the sword wipes [away] sins! – and he will be let into heaven from whatever gate he wishes . . . [Then] a hypocrite, who struggles with himself and his possessions in the path of God, such that when he meets the enemy [in battle] he fights until he is killed. This [man] is in hell since the sword does not wipe away hypocrisy.[6]

This tradition helps us to understand that not just anyone who wants to die – whether in battle or otherwise – can be considered to be a martyr. The true martyr is distinguished by his or her pure intentions, especially during the time just prior to death. Many of the sources, both *hadith* and *jihad*, specify other traditions saying that someone who fights for this world, or for the sake of fame or a (worldly) woman merely gains what he was fighting for; the true *mujahid* (fighter) fights only to raise the Word of God to the highest (cf. Qur'an 9:41; and compare Matthew 6:2). There is an element of expiation inside the process of fighting and dying in *jihad* that will be explored further in Chapter 7.

---

[6] Ibn al-Mubarak, *Kitab al-jihad*, pp. 30–31 (no. 7); al-Tabarani, *Musnad*, ii, pp. 116–17 (no. 1023); Ibn Hanbal, *Musnad*, iv, pp. 185–86; and al-Bayhaqi, *Sunan*, ix, p. 164; *idem, Shu'ab al-iman*, iv, p. 29 (no. 4262).

The rewards for the martyr described by the Muslim *jihad* literature are very lurid. Although it is popular in anti-Muslim polemic to concentrate upon the sexual rewards of the martyr – and there can be no question that these are important – it is interesting to note that probably the most frequently cited tradition listing these rewards is entirely devoid of such content:

When your brothers were struck at [the Battle of] Uhud, Allah placed their spirits in the insides of green birds, who go to the rivers of paradise, eat from its produce, and then alight upon candles of gold in the shadow of the Throne. When they [the martyrs] realize the goodness of their drink and food, and the beauty of their rest, they say: "Would that our brothers knew what Allah has done with us, so that they too would devote themselves to *jihad*, and not abstain from battle." Allah most high says: "I will tell them of you."[7]

Other versions of this tradition emphasize the martyrs' dwelling-places as being in green meadows, their palaces being under green domes, etc. These traditions describe a paradise that is comparatively sexless, and concentrated upon fertility, verdancy and rest. The personal connection to God is equally important. But even more importantly, this tradition specifies unique treatment that will be accorded only to the Muslim martyr and not to other Muslims.

However, no one who reads the *jihad* and martyrdom literature can avoid the frequent and graphic descriptions of the sexual delights of paradise. Although it is impossible to be certain, the fact that this material is so well attested and descriptive suggests that along with the spiritual aspects of being a martyr, there was a strong sexual pull as well. In the canonical *hadith* collections this is not too blatant. The women are spoken of as being beautiful, very bright and having a good smell (usually that of musk). Obviously there are other rewards specified as well, such as the martyr being lifted 100 levels up into paradise, being in the shadow of the Throne of God or standing on pulpits of rubies guarding the Throne, and living on a dune (*kathib*) of musk.[8] But they are not as common. In the collection of al-Tirmidhi the following definitive tradition is given:

In the sight of God the martyr has six [unique] qualities: He [God] forgives him at the first opportunity, and shows him his place in paradise, he is saved from the torment of the grave, he is safe from the great fright [of the Resurrection], a crown of honor is placed upon his head – one ruby of which is better than the world and all that is in it – he is married to 72 of the houris, and he gains the right to intercede for 70 of his relatives.[9]

The special qualities of the martyr, therefore, can be grouped into several categories: personal forgiveness as well as the ability to obtain forgiveness

---

[7] Muslim, *Sahih*, vi, p. 37; al-Tabari, *Jami'*, iv, pp. 170–71, cited in Wensinck, *Concordance*, s.v. *tayr*; and compare Ibn Qutayba, *Ta'bir al-ru'ya*, p. 30.

[8] This is a summary from al-Bukhari, *Sahih*, iii, p. 267 (no. 2796), Muslim, *Sahih*, vi, pp. 37, 43, 51; Ibn Maja, *Sunan*, ii, pp. 929 (no. 2780, specifying 70,000 houris for those defending the northern Iranian city of Qazwin), 926 (no. 2799); al-Hindi, *Kanz al-'ummal*, iv, pp. 397–414.

[9] Al-Tirmidhi, *Al-Jami' al-sahih*, iii, p. 106 (no. 1712); see also Ibn Maja, *Sunan*, ii, p. 1452 (no. 4337); and al-Hindi, *Kanz al-'ummal*, iv, p. 397f who cites many similar traditions from the entire *hadith* literature.

for his loved ones, the certainty of paradise and protection from the torments of hell, honor and distinction, and exaggerated sexual powers (in other traditions said to be either the power of 70 or 100 men).

These sexual aspects of martyrdom are all the more apparent once the *jihad* literature and the descriptions of paradise from the early historical sources are examined. All of the *jihad* literature without exception lists the rewards of paradise; especially descriptions of the women. Already in Ibn al-Mubarak's early book of *jihad* there are rites such as graphic exhortations concerning the sexual pleasures of paradise and battlefield marriages to houris. For example, Yazid b. Shajara, the commander of the caliph Mu'awiya's (661–80) armies, is cited giving a speech in which he describes the descent of the houris to the battlefield, and how they encourage the soldiers to fight and scold them when they are cowards. Immediately upon the death of one of the soldiers, two of them come to him, and tell him that they are for him. Others told stories of seeing houris just before battle and describe them in graphic detail.[10] Al-Sarraj's (d. 1106–07) detailed book on the tribulations of lovers (*Masari' al-ushshaq*) lists a number of those who were in love with the houris or had relations with them via dreams or out-of-body experiences.[11] Due to these detailed accounts, a number of them quite explicit concerning the sexual features of the houris, there can be no doubt that the women of paradise were a factor in the desire of the classical Muslim warrior to achieve martyrdom.

According to this *jihad* literature, converts can also achieve a high level of martyrdom. For example, again from Ibn al-Mubarak, during a raid on the Byzantines, the Muslim soldiers were surprised when one of the Byzantines came down from the fortress that they were besieging and joined them. He said:

This morning I ate swine's flesh, drank wine and had intercourse with my wife, and while I was sleeping two men came and washed my belly and married me to two women, neither of whom was jealous of the other, and they said to me: "Convert to Islam!" So I am a Muslim. He had no sooner said this than we were attacked [. . .], and he began to stumble since he was hit above his neck, [singled out from] among the people. Fadala cried: "*Allahu akbar*; he did little but was rewarded greatly. So pray for your brother," and we prayed for him.[12]

---

[10] Ibn al-Mubarak, *Jihad*, pp. 38–39 (no. 23); 117–18 (no. 143); Ibn al-Jawzi, *'Uyun al-hikayat*, pp. 327–28, 402–03.

[11] Al-Sarraj, *Masari' al-ushshaq*, i, pp. 194–202; for other accounts of dream marriages with houris, Ibn Abi al-Dunya, *Kitab al-manam*, pp. 99–100 (nos. 169–70), 114–15 (no. 197), 121 (no. 204); for abundant descriptions of the houris and the graphic sexual attributes ascribed to them, see the literature on paradise: Ibn al-Sari, *Kitab al-zuhd*, i, pp. 52–64, 86–89; al-Sulami, *Wasf al-firdaws*, pp. 55–57, 61, 63–72; al-Bayhaqi, *al-Ba'th wa-l-nushur*, pp. 211–24; al-Isfahani, *Sifat al-janna*, pp. 122–23; al-Suyuti, *al-Budur al-safira*, pp. 554–71; and 'Abd al-Rahim al-Qadi, *Daqa'iq al-akhbar fi dhikr al-janna wa-l-nar*, pp. 68–69; also Wensinck, *Concordance*, s.v. *hur al-'in*.

[12] Ibn al-Mubarak, *Jihad*, pp. 124–25 (no. 150); the lacuna is in the text.

This story of last-minute repentance is apparently facilitated by a mystical experience that the Byzantine Christian had while still inside the enemy fortress. His wicked ways just prior to his conversion to Islam are emphasized, but then he is chosen, presumably by angels, married to two women, who are presumably houris, and then goes out of the fortress to meet his new comrades and is killed with them. Although there is no evidence that this story is historical, it demonstrates the powerful effect that this type of story can have (cf. Luke 23:40–43).

Other stories have a similar sexual content. From Ibn Abi Zaminayn's *Qudwat al-ghazi* there is a man named Nujayh, wounded by a stone thrown from a mangonel while besieging a fortress in Sicily. The story says that he passed out, and while he was in a state of unconsciousness he first was laughing and then was crying. After he came back to his senses, he told the other soldiers that he had been taken to a room made of a single red ruby with a woman in it. This woman told him of the preparations being made for him and the women he could expect to have so he laughed, and stretched out his hand towards her, but she said suddenly: "Are you going back to the world?" And so he woke up and told his story. With the setting of the sun that day he died.[13] It is striking that both of these stories involve men whose fighting experience was comparatively limited. Both the new Byzantine convert and Nujayh (who was hit by a fragment of rock) were not participants in the fighting at all, but almost spectators who achieved martyrdom.

Historical accounts of martyrs or would-be martyrs frequently detail their visions of houris or their hopes of marriage to them. For example, there is an anecdote from one Qasim b. 'Uthman who saw a man circumambulating the Ka'ba in Mecca, saying "My God! My God!" Qasim asked him why he didn't say anything else, and he said:

We were seven souls from different places who joined together, and we raided the land of the enemy. We were taken prisoner, all of us, and they took us aside on the road to a place where they could kill us. I looked to the heavens, and behold! There were seven gates open, and on each one of the seven a houri maiden. One of us was brought forward and they struck off his head, and I saw a maiden with a cloth in her hand descend to the earth, until all six had been beheaded, and only I was left. One gate was left, and I was brought forward to have my head cut off when one of the men [the enemies] asked for me, and they gave me to him. I heard her say: "What [it is] you are missing, O protected one!" and the gate closed. I, O brother, am devastated because of what I missed.[14]

Graphic visions like these recall that of Saint Stephen in Acts 7:55–56, just prior to being stoned. They represent the creative and fantastical side of martyrdom.

---

[13] Ibn Abi Zaminayn, *Qudwat al-ghazi*, pp. 241–42 (no. 111).
[14] Ibn al-Jawzi, *'Uyun al-hikayat*, pp. 235–36.

Beyond any doubt the most detailed *jihad* book available from the classical period is that of Ibn al-Nahhas al-Dumyati (d. 1411), who was a Syrian living in Egypt during the period of the later Crusades. (Although the Crusaders were expelled from Palestine in 1291, they continued to occupy the island of Cyprus and periodically raided the Egyptian and Syrian coastlands.) Ibn al-Nahhas wrote a very detailed book on fighting (discussed in later chapters), and was himself killed during a Crusader raid. His book contains a great many of the traditions cited by earlier writers, as well as comprehensive legal discussions of issues pertaining to martyrdom. There is no need to go over the stories he brings out concerning the pleasures of heaven; for the most part they conform to the patterns established by Ibn al-Mubarak and other popular *jihad* writers. But Ibn al-Nahhas overwhelms the reader with a huge variety of them, culled from historical as well as religious texts.

There is a striking difference between the popular *jihad* literature described above and the formal Islamic legal literature. Lurid descriptions of the rewards of the martyr are entirely absent from the legal literature, which consists of discussions of definitions of what constitutes a martyr and what describes the legal boundaries of a martyr's actions. Probably the most tangled legal question arising from martyrdom is the question of whether a martyr can or should proactively provoke his own death. In this legal discussion there are several different categories that should be distinguished. Because parts of the fighting process were fairly ritualized during the period when the *jihad* literature was crystallized, there were certain events that could be confused with suicide, such as the process of single combat.[15] But most scholars accepted that there is no real element of suicidal attack in a single combat and focused upon behavior that could be called suicidal, namely whether a single soldier or a small group of soldiers can legitimately attack a much larger group when the former have little chance of surviving the attack. It is fairly self-evident that there is an element of seeking death present throughout the *jihad* literature – for example, Qur'an 3:142 "You were yearning for death . . . " and the practice of praying that God grant the *shahada* (Muslim confession of faith) to a given person.[16] This element is difficult in some cases to separate from actual suicide, which is strictly forbidden in Islam (Qur'an 4:29). Therefore, it was necessary for both *jihad* writers and legal specialists to differentiate between the two categories.

Much of the legal discussion starts with the Qur'anic verse 2:195: "Spend [money] for the cause of Allah and do not cast yourselves with your own hands

---

[15] Single combats where one soldier went forward to symbolically challenge the entire enemy army usually preluded formal fighting and were answered by single champions on the other side who would do the same.

[16] E.g., al-Wasiti, *Fada'il al-Bayt al-Maqdis*, p. 23 (no. 29); Muslim, *Sahih*, vi, p. 49; Ibn al-Nahhas, *Mashari' al-ashwaq*, ii, pp. 661–92; al-Tamimi, *Kitab al-mihan*, p. 272; Ibn al-Jawzi, *'Uyun al-hikayat*, p. 329; but actually desiring death is forbidden, al-Baghawi, *Sharh*, iii, pp. 437, 506.

into destruction, and be charitable." Although the contemporary translation of Fakhry adds in the word "money" after the word "spend" in accordance with the manner in which this verse is popularly interpreted today, the original sense is far more ambiguous. It could have the meaning of "spending oneself" such as in fighting and expending energy through *jihad*, with the second part of the verse indicating a restriction: one should not actually bring about the manner of one's death deliberately. The Muslim exegetes confronting this line of thought usually cite the story of Abu Ayyub al-Ansari and his attack on the walls of the Byzantine capital of Constantinople (see Chapter 2) and come to the conclusion that inordinate bravery in battle that leads to almost certain death does not constitute suicide.[17]

Other verses that were cited in this discussion were 2:249: "How many a small force has overcome a numerous force, by the permission of Allah's" (taken from the Qur'anic story of David and Goliath), and 2:207: "And some people sell themselves for the sake of Allah's favor." Both of these verses are more important in the discussion about suicide attacks. Ibn al-Nahhas is the only major classical writer on *jihad* who discusses this topic in depth (although jurisprudents usually bring it into their compendia). He cites a number of historical accounts in which various fighters took what could be called suicidal risks in battle; however, for the purposes of discussing suicide attacks this material is not necessarily helpful. Quite a number of the examples he cites actually survived these attacks, so they cannot be properly called suicidal.

Ibn al-Nahhas cites one example of a man who rushed out of the battle lines and charged the enemy – but was not killed – and was condemned by the other Muslims for doing this. When his commander heard of this action, he cited Qur'an 61:4: "Allah loves those who fight in His cause arrayed in battle, as though they were a compact structure."[18] This condemnation seems to be both for the man's action as well as for the idea of breaking ranks (and presumably discipline) merely to seek martyrdom. Qur'anic exegetes of this verse also cited this problem, and a number of them have ruled that because the essence of *jihad* is a group activity in which individuals should be anonymous, their actions known only to God, and rewarded solely by Him, the individual attack should not be allowed.[19] The rationalist theologians, the Mu'tazilites, also tended to believe that one should not desire martyrdom.[20]

In the end, the question of whether, in seeking martyrdom, one is committing suicide comes down to the intention of the doer. Ibn al-Nahhas cites the great

---

[17] Ibn Hubaysh, *Ghazawat*, ii, p. 259 uses the phrase with more of a meaning of "do not fight a hopeless battle for nothing."

[18] Ibn al-Nahhas, *Mashariʿ al-ashwaq*, i, p. 536 (no. 938).

[19] For example, Ibn al-ʿArabi, *Ahkam al-Qurʾan*, iv, pp. 1800–01; al-Qurtubi, *al-Jamiʿ li-ahkam al-Qurʾan*, xviii, pp. 73–74.

[20] E.g., al-Yafiʿi, *Dhikr madhahib al-firaq al-thanatayn wa-sabaʿin al-mukhalifa li-l-sunna wa-l-mubtadiʿin*, p. 81.

Sufi scholar al-Ghazali (d. 1111) to say that if one commits this action with the intention of creating terror (*nikaya*) in the hearts of the enemy, then it is acceptable. But if the fighter is incapable of creating terror – al-Ghazali gives the example of a blind man – then the action cannot be undertaken to achieve martyrdom.[21] Other scholars tended to agree with al-Ghazali, and the general consensus was that if such actions were beneficial to Muslims in general, then they can be undertaken. It is unfortunate that Muslim scholars did not seriously discuss this question of whether a martyr can actually go too far in seeking out circumstances under which martyrdom can be achieved.

Treatment of the dead body, and importantly, the status of the martyr's family and relatives both in this world and the next are also the principal legal discussion topics. The subjects of funerary practice and the treatment accorded to the dead are of the utmost importance to Muslims everywhere, so it is not surprising that, given the martyr's unique status, his body should receive special treatment. This is apparent when we consider the five unique qualities that the Qur'anic exegete al-Qurtubi (d. 1272–73) specifies with regard to the martyr:

The Messenger of Allah said: God has ennobled the martyrs with five blessings never given to any of the prophets, even me: One, all of the prophets' spirits were taken by the Angel of Death, and he will take me [as well], but as for the martyrs, God is the one who will take their spirits in a way He wills and will not allow the Angel of Death to have power over their spirits. Two: all of the prophets were washed after their death, and I will be washed [as well], but the martyrs are not to be washed, since they have no need of what is in this world. Three: all of the prophets were wrapped [in linens], and I will be wrapped [as well], but the martyrs are not wrapped, but buried in their clothes. Four: all of the prophets when they die are called "dead," and when I die, it will be said "He died," but the martyrs are not referred to as "dead." Five: all of the prophets have the ability to intercede on the Day of Resurrection, as I do as well, but the martyrs have the ability to intercede every day that there is intercession.[22]

This tradition, although completely unknown from other sources, clearly indicates that certain Muslim groups believed that the martyrs should actually be granted a status higher than the prophets. Some commentators also saw the martyrs as those who would judge the other Muslims, and stand on the *a'raf* (the boundary walls between heaven and hell, alluded to in Qur'an 7:46–47) to guard the people of paradise.[23] This high status was reflected in the manner in which they died and were buried.

From a very early period it became the norm in Muslim legal literature and actual practice that the body of the martyr should not be washed, in

---

[21] Al-Ghazali, *Ihya 'ulum al-din*, ii, pp. 314–15; Ibn al-Nahhas, *Mashari' al-ashwaq*, i, p. 557; and see Fakhr al-Din al-Razi, *al-Tafsir al-kabir*, v, p. 137.

[22] Al-Qurtubi, *al-Jami' li-ahkam al-Qur'an*, iv, p. 269 (commentary to Qur'an 3:171); Ibn al-Nahhas, *Mashari' al-ashwaq*, ii, pp. 739–40 (no. 1149).

[23] Fakhr al-Din al-Razi, *al-Tafsir al-kabir*, xiv, p.

contradistinction to the normative Muslim practice.[24] Usually this custom is ascribed to the way the Prophet Muhammad treated the dead Muslims after the disastrous battle of Uhud (625). For this reason, the martyr's body will be taken in this unwashed state, left in whatever clothes he was wearing and placed directly into the grave. Ibn Abi Zayd al-Qayrawani (d. 996–97), says:

> Martyrs from battles should be buried with their blood and in their clothes as the Prophet did, but all of their weapons should be taken from them, together with belts, spurs, armor, helmet, arm-shields and other types of weapons. But their turban, robe, undergarments, shift, pants and the like should not be taken from them – this is generally agreed upon. But scholars have differed concerning hats, shoes, furs and overcloaks; most of our scholars say that these are not to be taken.[25]

Apparently the importance of this is that the inner clothing of the martyr, which would tend to be the locus of most of the blood and gore, would stay with him in the grave, but that the outer implements of war that could be reused should be taken from him. The most important element of this custom is probably for the sake of the torment of the grave: the martyr whose remains demonstrate graphically the manner of his death will not be tormented by the angels Munkar and Nakir (the angels of death) after he dies. Perhaps as a token of faith in the martyr's certain entrance into heaven, and in contradistinction to normative Muslim practice, many scholars (usually Malikis, Shafi'is and Hanbalis are specified) held that one should *not* pray over the martyr's body. Again, this is a graphic statement that there was no need for any prayers since the martyr would go directly to heaven.

The major legal issues brought out by scholars are all variants on the above. Some scholars asked what should be done about a martyr whose body could not be recovered either because of the confusion on the battlefield, or the impossibility of ascertaining the correct identity of the body or because of death at sea. Others asked whether a martyr who died in a state of major ritual impurity was still a martyr. Yet others asked how long after a battle finished can a person who expires as a result of his wounds be considered to be a martyr. For example, if they die some time after the fact as a result of wounds received on the battlefield, is the person still to be considered to have been a martyr? In general, the Muslim legal authorities show little interest in expanding the definitions of martyrdom and do not cite the more extravagant traditions mentioned by al-Suyuti at the beginning of this chapter.

For the most part, the Shi'ite legal material does not differ significantly from the Sunni discussions on martyrdom. This sectarianism will be the topic of

---

[24] E.g., al-Shaybani, *Kitab al-athar*, ii, pp. 253–312.

[25] Ibn Zayd al-Qayrawani, *al-Nawadir wa-l-ziyadat*, iii, p. 289; for the other legal schools see al-Fayruzabadi, *Muhadhdhab*, iii, pp. 282–83; al-Mawardi, *Hawi*, iii, pp. 33–38; Ibn Rushd, *Bayan*, ii, pp. 209, 250–51; al-Samarqandi, *Fiqh*, i, p. 317–19; Ibn Qudama al-Maqdisi, *Mughni*, ii, pp. 528–36.

Chapter 4. One separate category is that of the Muslim martyred together with the family of the Prophet Muhammad, who is said to receive seven levels (presumably in heaven), and will be able to intercede for seventy of his own family.[26] Given the fact that in general Shi'ite *jihad* and martyrdom focused upon sacrifice and death at the hands of the Sunni majority, it is only natural that the rewards which in Sunni literature go to the fighter, here go to the one who accompanies the family of the Prophet into death.

Classical Muslim scholars and exegetes took the subject of *jihad* and martyrdom very seriously and made a serious effort to categorize and define this difficult subject. In general, their tendency was to err on the side of caution when discussing martyrdom. They left the fighting martyr a substantial degree of freedom to seek what he desired, but sought to direct him away from foolishly throwing his life away. Although the *hadith* literature as summarized by al-Suyuti seems to widen the definition of *shahid* to the point of meaninglessness, the jurisprudents never seem to have been distracted by these secondary definitions. For them, always, the martyr was one who died in battle or as a result of wounds incurred in fighting. Always they focused the violence of the *jihad* outwards against non-believers. But this was unrealistic. For almost immediately following the first conquests Muslims began to fight and kill each other. Since one's opponent – whether Muslim or not – was invariably considered to be an infidel, didn't that make those who died in sectarian battles martyrs, too?

---

[26] Al-Barqi, *Kitab al-mahasin*, i, p. 135 (no. 170).

4   Sectarian Islam: Sunni, Shiʿite and Sufi martyrdom

A man of Banu Tamim said: I saw in this castle [Kufa] a marvel. I entered in upon ʿUbaydallah b. Ziyad as he was reclining upon an elevated seat, with two ranks of men, and upon his right was a shield with the head of Husayn b. ʿAli in it, and then I entered upon al-Mukhtar in this hall, also on this elevated seat, with the people in two ranks around him, on his right a shield with the head of ʿUbaydallah in it, then I entered in upon Musʿab in this hall and upon that elevated seat with the people in ranks around him, and to his right a shield with the head of al-Mukhtar upon it. Now I enter into ʿAbd al-Malik in this very hall, and upon that elevated seat, while the people are in ranks, and to his right a shield with the head of Musʿab.[1]

After the early Islamic conquests and the trauma of the first caliphs the Muslim community split irrevocably into two categories: those groups who upheld the hypothetical election of a caliph and supported the dynasties of caliphs that took control after 661 (the Umayyads [661–747], the ʿAbbasids [747–1258] and the Ottomans [ca. 1517–1924]), and those who did not. Of those groups that did not accept the legitimacy of these caliphal dynasties the most important were the Shiʿites (the Sunnis did support the caliphs). Since that time the Shiʿites have upheld the rights of the family of the Prophet Muhammad to rule the Muslim community and have refused to accept the legitimacy of any other political system that did not proceed from the starting point of this familial basis. Because of this divide, which has only widened since that time, sectarian martyrologies must be separated from those pan-Islamic martyrs dating from the time of the Prophet Muhammad and early Islamic conquests. This earlier group of martyrs are held in esteem by all Muslims, and for the most part died as a result of actions taken against them by non-Muslims or in battle against non-Muslims. But the sectarian martyrs – whether Sunni, Shiʿite or other – are those martyrs who are not accepted as martyrs by the entire Muslim community and for the most part were killed by those calling themselves Muslims.

[1] Ibn Hamdun, *Tadhkira*, ix, p. 217.

Quite a number of traditions detail the idea that when a Muslim kills another Muslim, both are said to be in hell.[2] This doctrine presents a problem with regard to the earliest generation of Muslims after the time of the Prophet Muhammad. The most problematic sequence for the doctrine of Muslims going to hell concerns the internecine battles fought during the caliphate of ʿAli (656–61). It is also problematic for the assassination of the caliph ʿUthman (d. 656) because this exclusively involved Muslims. Even further, almost all of those involved in these groups of events were actually Companions of the Prophet Muhammad, a group that has a very high and unimpeachable status in Sunni Islam (although not in Shiʿism). There was a natural tendency on the part of Sunnis to accord these figures the title of martyr, it was equally true that their killers were almost all veteran Muslims and for this reason would be in hell (or at least not allowed to go directly to paradise together with other martyrs). This dilemma has never been adequately resolved in Sunni Islam (although some merely avoid the issue and leave it to God to sort out), and is reflected in the early dream book of Ibn Abi al-Dunya, where some of the dead at the Battle of the Harra (a battle in 683 in Medina between the Syrian army and the Medinese, both Muslim) are described:

I saw . . . Aflah b. Kathir . . . who was killed at the Battle of the Harra, and I knew that he was dead, and that I was sleeping, and that this was just a vision, so I said: Haven't you been killed? He said: Of course. I said: And what was done with you? He said: Good. I said: Are you martyrs? He said: No, when Muslims fight each other and are killed, they are not martyrs.[3]

Despite pronouncements like this one, many sectarians would not accept this absolute exclusion of the rank of martyr from their sectarian dead, and started to grant them that title nevertheless. At a later period in Islam it became standard and even necessary in order to define one's absolute opposition to a sectarian enemy to refer to one's own dead as martyrs.

Given the sensitive issue of Muslims killing Muslims there can be no accurate or absolute definitions as to who precisely is to be counted as a martyr. Whereas Chapter 3 listed possible groups that could be considered martyrs, when considering the sectarian martyrologies anyone the aggrieved community feels is a martyr will be counted as one. Some absolute standards could be applied with regard to the earlier pan-Islamic martyrs that would either expand or limit the numbers of martyrs or the circumstances of their deaths, but that is not the case with the sectarian martyrs. In addition to this definitional problem, the narratives of martyrdom are inevitably challenged by the enemies of

[2] Al-Bukhari, *Sahih*, i, p. 16 (no. 31); cf. Qurʾan 49:9; and a number of traditions in ʿAbd al-Ghani al-Maqdisi, *Tahrim al-qatl wa-taʿzimihi*, p. 99f; and also Wensinck, *Concordance*, s.v. *qatil*, *maqtul*.

[3] Ibn Abi al-Dunya, *Kitab al-manam*, pp. 36–37 (no. 56).

the martyr's politico-religious group. This means that martyrs esteemed by a certain sect will often be demonized or held in contempt by its opponents, who may try to actively defame the memory of the deceased, destroy the relics of their bodies or act in other ways to diminish the importance of their martyrdom. Often these malevolent tendencies on the part of enemies will cause the adherents of the aggrieved sect to be the more flagrant in order to show their loyalty to the group and their rejection of their opponents. With this type of partisan loyalty, it is often impossible to tell truth from fiction – not that it was easy in the pan-Islamic martyrologies – and so we will have to suffice with presenting both sides without choosing to enter into questions of historical fact.

Sunni narratives

Sunnis do not usually think of themselves as sectarian. Being the majority sect in Islam, with about 85 percent of world Muslims, and because they have always been in the majority position with the exception of one period in Muslim history (the so-called Shi'ite century, the tenth century), they are characterized by certain feelings of majoritarianism. This majoritarianism means that Sunnis often conflate Sunnism with Islam as a whole and do not wish to accord any legitimacy towards those who are not Sunnis. Because of this preponderance of numbers in favor of Sunnis this is not difficult for them to do, but this bias should be understood before dealing with these martyrs venerated by Sunnis. This narrow understanding of martyrdom does not have importance within Sunnism since Sunnis have hardly ever been in the situation where they were oppressed (compared for example to Shi'ites); for this reason they have tended to focus on those martyrs from the time of the Prophet Muhammad and the early conquests.

However, there are a few figures that need to be mentioned for their place as Sunni martyrs. No doubt the first and foremost of them is the Caliph 'Uthman, whose star-crossed reign (644–56) ended with his assassination at the hands of Muslims from the city of Kufa (southern Iraq) and Egypt. 'Uthman, although protected from serious Muslim historical critique by virtue of the fact that he was a Companion of the Prophet and an early convert to Islam, has always been a controversial figure. Unlike his predecessors Abu Bakr (632–34) and 'Umar (634–44), whose status in Sunni Islam is not far lower than that of Muhammad, 'Uthman is recognized to have been a comparatively weak caliph. During his reign, according to the Muslim sources, the social tensions created by the massive conquests under the caliphate of 'Umar came to a head. 'Uthman was universally acknowledged to have been a pious personality, but was also a weak ruler and relied upon his Umayyad relatives for support and favored them unduly. It is difficult to say whether this is the full historical truth, but this discussion will not address that issue. During the final years of his reign

'Uthman had to deal with open opposition from many of Muhammad's surviving Companions, including the Prophet's influential youngest wife, 'A'isha, and his cousin and son-in-law, 'Ali b. Abi Talib. These leaders undermined 'Uthman's legitimacy and incited opposition against him.

But true violent opposition came from outside the capital of Medina, from Iraq and Egypt. Both of these regions sent delegations to protest various grievances to him.[4] When some of these protests turned violent, 'Ali and the other Companions in Medina sent guards to protect 'Uthman's house (including both of 'Ali's sons, al-Hasan and al-Husayn). Although this protection was temporarily effective, the Egyptian delegation, which had departed for home, believed that it had been betrayed by 'Uthman, who they suspected of sending a letter by private courier to the governor of Egypt so that the delegation would be arrested upon their return. Enraged, they came back to Medina and besieged 'Uthman's house, denying him food and water. After a number of days of this siege, the Egyptians heard that troops from Syria – ruled by 'Uthman's relative and supporter Mu'awiya b. Abi Sufyan (afterwards caliph 661–80) – were approaching, and so stormed the house and murdered the caliph while he was reading a copy of the Qur'an.

Undoubtedly this was a traumatic moment in early Islam. Although 'Uthman's predecessor 'Umar had also been assassinated, this latter assassination was at the hands of an aggrieved Christian slave who commanded no popular support. By contrast, 'Uthman's assassination had the active support of large numbers of the Muslim community in Iraq and Egypt and the passive support of many others, including some of the Prophet Muhammad's closest Companions. No one is recorded to have helped 'Uthman in any tangible manner. It is clear, however, that although 'Uthman was not liked throughout the Muslim world, the manner in which he was killed was reprehensible. There was no honor or glory in a mob of Muslims killing a man, usually said to have been eighty years old, reading the Qur'an after having been besieged in his home for some time prior to that. Therefore, a backlash against the assassins was inevitable, and even some glorification of 'Uthman among those groups that would eventually form the core of Sunnism. This glorification of 'Uthman reached its peak under the Umayyad dynasty (661–747), which to a large extent rose to power on the strength of the slogan "Vengeance for 'Uthman" and continued in Islamic Spain under the Umayyad dynasty that relocated there (754–1031).

Some of the basic themes of this martyrdom must be recounted.[5] The story of his death begins when the returning Egyptian mutineers cut down the man

---

[4] The accounts from the Muslim sources are contained in Tabari, *Ta'rikh*, iv, 365–96; and in al-Maliqi, *al-Tamhid wa-l-bayan fi maqtal al-shahid 'Uthman*. Martin Hinds summarizes and analyzes these accounts in "The Murder of the Caliph 'Uthman."

[5] This account is according to al-Maliqi, *Tamhid*, pp. 136–44; see also al-Tabari, *Ta'rikh*, iv, pp. 365–96; and al-Isfahani, *Kitab al-aghani*, xvi, pp. 348–53.

standing in front of the door of 'Uthman's house, al-Mughira b. al-Akhnas. The tale gains an ominous tone, when as an aside, one of the assassins sees a vision in which he is told that the killer of al-Mughira would be in hell. Other prominent Muslim figures, such as 'Abdallah b. Salam (an early Jewish convert), appear and warn the Egyptians of the consequences of their actions:

Do not kill him! For God has lifted the sword of tribulation (*fitna*) from between you since the time when our Prophet Muhammad was sent, and it will not remain lifted if you kill your imam ['Uthman]. [First,] if you kill him, God will draw the sword of tribulation against you, and it will not be lifted from you until Jesus son of Mary appears. Secondly, your city [Medina] has been surrounded by angels since the time when the Messenger of God settled in it, and if you kill him they will be lifted from around it and you will not be surrounded by them until you meet God.[6]

However, their response was to curse him and shove him out of the way.

As the assassins came into the house, they approached 'Uthman, who was reading the Qur'an (according to tradition "If they believe in what you have believed, they will be well-guided: but if they turn away, they are indeed dissenting, and Allah will protect you against them, for He is All-Hearing, Omniscient" [2:137]), and his wife Na'ila bint al-Farafisa threw herself around him (in some versions his head was on her lap). She tried to pick up a sword, but one of the assassins cut her hand off, and then Muhammad b. Abi Bakr (son of the first caliph, who was the leader of the group) grabbed 'Uthman's beard, and tugged his head forward. 'Uthman calmly asked Muhammad b. Abi Bakr to let go of his beard, and one of the other assassins behind him pushed 'Uthman's head down onto the text of the Qur'an that he had been reading. 'Uthman was stabbed nine times, and his blood soaked this copy of the Qur'an, which in the future was preserved by the Umayyad and the 'Abbasid caliphs until the Mongols destroyed it (presumably) in 1258. The assassins then looted 'Uthman's house and left.

Even a cursory reading of this story gives a strong feel for the symbolism involved. Every attempt is made to ensure that the reader senses that 'Uthman is old, helpless and pious, while the assassins are young, brash and impious. In later times, the Umayyad dynasty propagandists compared the martyrdom of 'Uthman to that of Jesus (although according to the Qur'an, strictly speaking, Jesus was not martyred), such as in the following anecdote associated with the Umayyad governor of Iraq, al-Hajjaj b. Yusuf al-Thaqafi (ruled 692–715):

On the authority of 'Ata' b. al-Sa'ib: I was sitting with Abu al-Bahtari al-Ta'i while al-Hajjaj was speaking [in Kufa], and he said "Jesus son of Mary in the eyes of God is like 'Uthman . . . and cited: I will cause you to die, will lift you up to Me, purify you from those who have disbelieved and place those who followed you above those who have disbelieved, till the Day of Resurrection." [Qur'an 3:55][7]

---

[6] Al-Maliqi, *Tamhid*, p. 140. [7] Ibn Abi Shayba, *Musannaf*, vi, p. 195 (no. 30609).

Citation of such a verse, praising 'Uthman as a type of Jesus, and glorifying those Muslims who followed him (the Umayyads and their supporters) over those who opposed him (everyone else) was quite inflammatory. Just as with Khubayb (Chapter 2), there are stories about the power of the prayers uttered against the assassins. The man who lifted 'Uthman's head, for example, is said to have heard 'Uthman's wife Na'ila curse him: "May God dry up your hand, may He cause your sight to go blind, and may He not forgive you your sins!"[8] Such is the power of the prayer of the wronged person that all of these things are said to have afflicted this unnamed man. (Most of the other assassins listed in the historical sources died violently as well.)

After the martyrdom of 'Uthman, Sunnis as a group have only very rarely been oppressed enough to create large groups of martyrs. There were, however, individual Sunni heroes who experienced martyrdom or were persecuted and accorded martyr status. This was because of the weakness of the Sunni community in a given period or place or because their convictions placed them outside the mainstream and in opposition to whatever ruler or government they confronted. Probably the best example of this type of martyrdom is that of Ahmad b. Hanbal (d. 855), who was an example of a martyr-figure who did not actually die, but suffered for his belief in the uncreated nature of the Qur'an (see below). Ibn Hanbal's suffering has become paradigmatic for Sunnis, especially those of the Hanbalite legal school who follow his teachings.[9] Lacking other martyrs, Sunnis have had to suffice with those like Ibn Hanbal who were persecuted but did not actually die for their beliefs.

During the middle period of the 'Abbasid dynasty (ninth century) certain of the caliphal family, especially al-Ma'mun (813–33) and his brother and successor al-Mu'tasim (833–42), championed some of the dogmas of the Mu'tazilite sect. Among this sect's doctrines were the idea that the Qur'an was created.[10] These two caliphs sought to impose these beliefs upon the religious leadership of Islam. To a large degree they succeeded because most of these religious leaders were willing to support the doctrine of the created Qur'an; however, a few such as Ibn Hanbal were not willing to change their beliefs

---

[8] Ibn Abi al-Dunya, *Mujabu al-du'a*, pp. 67–68 (nos. 29–31).

[9] There are four historical legal schools in Sunni Islam: Maliki (today in North and West Africa), Hanafi (throughout the Middle East, Central Asia, Pakistan and India), Shafi'i (East Africa and Indonesia–Malaysia), and Hanbali (Saudi Arabia). But the Hanbalites are influential because of the importance of Saudi Arabian money and education throughout the Muslim world today.

[10] The Mu'tazilite sect held to the idea that the Qur'an was created in order to forestall the idea that the Qur'an (the Word of God) had been eternally co-existent with God, and also to preclude predestinationist beliefs. Eternal co-existence of a being other than God was seen by the Mu'tazilites as possibly detracting from the absolute unity of God (*tawhid*), and creating a being with a function similar to that of Jesus in Christianity. As a result of Ibn Hanbal's suffering, eventually the 'Abbasid rulers abandoned their association with the Mu'tazilites, and the doctrine of the uncreated nature of the Qur'an became dogma in Sunni Islam (along with predestination).

upon the caliph's orders and at his whim. For remaining constant in his belief, Ibn Hanbal is credited with creating a sense of religious authority separate from that of the caliph. (The truth is that this sense of a separate religious authority within proto-Sunnism had been growing for the previous century, but Ibn Hanbal's legacy crystallized this tendency, pushing it into its maturity at the time of his taking a stand on the issue of the uncreated Qur'an.)[11]

Al-Ma'mun championed Mu'tazilism only during the last years of his life, so it was left to his comparatively unintellectual brother and successor al-Mu'tasim to enforce belief in the doctrine of the creation of the Qur'an (al-Mu'tasim himself did not care much for theological disputes). Thus, Ibn Hanbal was tortured during al-Mu'tasim's reign. The stories of his sufferings are contained in his son's, Salih b. Ahmad b. Hanbal, *Sirat al-Imam Ahmad b. Hanbal* (*The Life of the Imam Ahmad b. Hanbal*) and in most of the hagiographical literature associated with the Hanbalite rite. Ibn Hanbal is usually described as being taken to the court, where he was questioned and urged to abandon the idea of the uncreated Qur'an. In some accounts Mu'tazilite scholars are brought in to argue with him on this subject. Because the accounts that we have are uniformly hostile to the Mu'tazilites, Ibn Hanbal is able to destroy their arguments. In the end, the question is reduced to force, and Ibn Hanbal is first threatened, and then taken to a location where he can be beaten. (In some cases, that is also the caliph's court, but in other accounts he is taken to a prison cell.) He is usually said to have received twenty-nine lashes to the back. At this time Ibn Hanbal would have been in his middle fifties, although even ten lashes to the back could seriously injure a mature man.

One account narrates the situation as follows:

The Amir al-Mu'minin came and sat on his chair, and then Ahmad b. Hanbal was brought, and he said to him: By my close kinship with the Messenger of God I will have you beaten with the lash if you do not say as I do [concerning the creation of the Qur'an]. Then he turned to the flogger, and said: Take him to you, and he took him. When he beat him with one lash, he [Ibn Hanbal] said: In the name of God, when he beat him with the second lash, he said: There is no might or power save in God, and when he beat him the third time, he said: The Qur'an is the word of God, uncreated. When he was beaten with the fourth, he said "Nothing will befall us except what Allah has decreed for us."[12] [Qur'an 9:52]

Blood flowed from his shoulders and back, and the flogger ceased flogging Ibn Hanbal when he saw that there was blood on his neck (probably meaning that

---

[11] For a full discussion of these theological issues, see Josef van Ess, *Theologie und Gesellschaft im 2. und 3. Jahrhundert Hidschra: Eine Geschichte des religiösen Denkens im frühen Islam*, iii, pp. 446–81.

[12] Account from Ibn al-Jawzi, *Manaqib al-Imam Ahmad b. Hanbal*, pp. 330–31; extensive descriptions of these beatings are given in Ibn Hanbal, *Sirat al-Imam Ahmad b. Hanbal*, pp. 35–47; al-Tamimi, *Kitab al-mihan*, pp. 435–41; Ibn Abi Ya'la, *Tabaqat al-Hanabila*, i, pp. 4–20; and al-'Ulaymi, *Minhaj al-ahmad fi tarajim ashab al-Imam Ahmad*, i, pp. 23–31.

there was some danger that he would die). However, Ibn Hanbal was said to have had a hair of the Prophet Muhammad with him in one of his pockets for protection, and it aided him as he went through this trial.[13] The theological disputes went on, but Ibn Hanbal refused to concede. Eventually the ʿAbbasid rulers were forced to let him go, or the punishments they inflicted upon him would have put their cause in a negative light. At the moment that Ibn Hanbal was being beaten, the prominent Sunni scholars, Abu ʿUmar al-Mukharrami and Saʿid b. Mansur were said to have been at the Kaʿba in Mecca. They are said to have heard a voice shout out: "Ahmad b. Hanbal has been beaten today!"[14] Thus, there is cosmological significance to this theological dispute that is felt even at the Kaʿba, and Ibn Hanbal's resistance to the doctrine of the creation of the Qurʾan is connected to the most holy site of Islam.

The martyrologies list a number of other scholars, all of them prominent in the first centuries of Islam, who were beaten and tortured in various ways (e.g., Malik b. Anas, Sufyan al-Thawri). Since these scholars had sought to influence the political world (although the political and religious spheres are not separate in classical Islam) and had either passively or in some cases aggressively supported revolts aimed at reforming Islam, they cannot be counted as true martyrs. From the perspective of the Umayyad or the ʿAbbasid dynasties, these scholars were merely rebels and were largely treated as such. Unlike ordinary rebels, however, they were usually just terrorized and not executed. After the first three centuries of Islam, it became comparatively rare for Sunni religious figures, who were by that time usually closely associated with the ruling dynasty or state, to involve themselves in political rebellion. Those who were tortured or executed during this period – from Ibn Hanbal's time until the rebirth of activist Islam in the nineteenth century – were usually victims of the caprices of the rulers or other causes. This did not give them a martyr's status.[15] Thus, Sunnism as a whole, without its Sufi component (see below), is somewhat lacking in a consistent martyrology spanning the entire length of Islamic history. Where Sunnism lacks martyrs, however, Shiʿism has a rich martyrdom history.

Shiʿite martyrologies

Shiʿites have contributed more than any other single group in Islam towards martyrology. The history of Shiʿites – those groups who supported the rights of the Prophet Muhammad's family to rule the Muslim community and most especially his immediate family – is a sad one. Abu al-Faraj al-Isfahani (d. 967), although he was not Shiʿite,[16] wrote a martyrology of the family of

---

[13] Ibn al-Jawzi, ibid., p. 326.   [14] Ibid., p. 335.

[15] For an exception, see Thiery Bianquis, "Ibn al-Nablusi: un martyr Sunnite."

[16] It is possible that he was a Zaydi, a sect of Shiʿism in which hostility towards Sunnis is not emphasized.

the descendents of Muhammad. He lists a total of 189 people who were killed up until his time. The emotional power conveyed by the stories of these martyrs has provided the Shi'ites with significant propaganda that has impressed many Muslims throughout the centuries, even those who never became Shi'ite. Reading over the stories of these martyrs, individually recounted in all of their pathos, martyrdom's status as a central feature for the Shi'ite community is evident, and the powerful propaganda element of martyrdom has influenced conversion to Shi'ism.

Shi'ism originated with the idea that the Prophet Muhammad's charismatic authority and his political-religious authority – but not his prophetic status – should devolve upon his genealogical descendents who were the recipients of mystical knowledge and some part of his essence that gave them the right to rule. This idea took some time to germinate, since for the early Muslim community it was by no means clear who precisely should be the beneficiary of such loyalty. Muhammad had four daughters who reached maturity, but only the youngest, Fatima, married to 'Ali b. Abi Talib (who was Muhammad's first cousin, ward and one of his earliest converts), supplied him with blood descendents who themselves reached maturity. 'Ali's innate right to rule was not acknowledged by the Muslim community in the immediate wake of Muhammad's death in 632; others were seen as having either superior or at least equal rights of succession. Although 'Ali was married to one of the Prophet Muhammad's daughters, all of the early caliphs were related to Muhammad in some way (two were his fathers-in-law, while 'Uthman had married two of Muhammad's daughters). After the assassination of 'Uthman, 'Ali was granted the caliphate by some elements of the Muslim community. Others contested his rights, feeling that he had played too prominent of a role in 'Uthman's assassination. (In fairness to 'Ali, although he had clearly incited against 'Uthman, he also sought to protect him from the rage of the mob that eventually assassinated him, and is never said to have called for his murder. Accusations against 'Ali were raised because of his needlessly close association with the real assassins – who afterwards he appointed to high office – rather than any involvement in the actual assassination.)

'Ali had a star-crossed caliphate (656–61), in which he never managed to gain control over more than half of the Muslim world. One by one he defeated his enemies, first at the Battle of the Camel in 656 (against Medinese opponents, including prominent Companions), then at the Battle of Siffin in 657. This latter, against the Syrians, ended in a draw, and led to a process of arbitration between 'Ali and the governor of Syria, Mu'awiya b. Abi Sufyan Mu'awiya, who was the son of Muhammad's enemy Abu Sufyan and a close relative of 'Uthman, waged a brilliant propaganda war in which 'Ali was linked to 'Uthman's assassination, and Mu'awiya took on the role of avenger. Eventually 'Ali was himself assassinated in the mosque at Kufa (now in southern Iraq) in 661. Had he not been assassinated, he would probably have been quickly defeated.

His actual murder came at the hands of a Kharijite. This group, feared and hated by most Muslims of this early period, was drawn from those who had originally supported 'Ali's claims. However, they had turned against him because of his unwillingness (or inability) to press his victory at the Battle of Siffin. The groups that would later be called Kharijites felt that not to finish off the battle, and to allow a process of arbitration to take place, was to deny the will of God as it would have been manifested on the battlefield. This belief made the Kharijites 'Ali's most ferocious enemies, and he had to fight them at the Battle of Nahrawan in 658, where he defeated them. But the romantic association of numerous tribes and individuals to Kharijism – strikingly similar to others' attachment to Shi'ism during future centuries – continued, and relatives of those Kharijites killed at Nahrawan longed to kill 'Ali.

Thus, 'Ali's assassination is placed within the context of a romantic story of one 'Abd al-Rahman b. Muljam al-Muradi, the assassin, who is said to have fallen in love with a daughter of one of those killed at Nahrawan. In return for agreeing to marry her, she demanded that he bring her the head of 'Ali (compare Mark 6:22–25, Matthew 14:6–8).[17] 'Ali is said to have been assassinated in the following manner:

> 'Ali went out and called *Allahu akbar* for the prayer, and then recited from *surat al-anbiya'* (no. 21) 11 verses, and then Ibn Muljam struck him from the row [of worshippers] on his head, and the people fell upon him and took him, and wrested the sword from his hand while they were standing for prayer. 'Ali bowed and then prostrated himself, and I saw him move his head from place to place because of the blood; then he rose for the second [prayer] . . . and then he sat and proclaimed the *shahada* and said the *salam*, and leaned his back against the wall of the mosque.[18]

This differs from other accounts in which 'Ali was attacked outside the mosque. Although the wound was not a serious one, apparently the sword was poisoned, and 'Ali lingered for several days before expiring. Ibn Muljam was tortured to death by 'Ali's relatives.

The symbolism of 'Ali's assassination, like that of 'Uthman above, is very strong. He is killed either while praying or at least calling the people to prayer, and he recites from the Qur'an at the time of his attack. Symbolism attached to the assassin Ibn Muljam is no less strong, although no accounts favorable to

---

[17] This was Qatam of the Banu Taym (Ibn Abi al-Dunya, *Maqtal Amir al-mu'minin*, pp. 33 [no. 18], 34 [no. 20]); however, according to the sources there was also a tripartite assassination attempt on Mu'awiya, 'Amr b. al-'As, the governor of Egypt and 'Ali of which Ibn Muljam was a part. These two stories make an improbable fit.

[18] Ibn Abi al-Dunya, *Maqtal Amir al-mu'minin*, pp. 30–31 (no. 15); for other versions, see Ibn Shahrashub, *Manaqib Al Abi Talib*, iii, pp. 308–18; Abu al-Faraj al-Isfahani, *Maqatil al-Talibiyyin*, pp. 39–56.

him have been preserved. He is said to have recited Qur'an 2:207, "And some people sell themselves for the sake of Allah's favor . . . " (which, as will be discussed in Chapter 8, is the verse usually cited to support suicide attacks in contemporary radical Islam), implying that his action was solely for the sake of God.[19]

Although 'Ali's actual assassination marked the end of the only time that the Prophet's immediate family actually achieved political power during the first three centuries of Islam, it did not end the belief of the groups that would eventually become Shi'ite (which will be called proto-Shi'ites for the purposes of this book) from believing in the rightness of their cause. Indeed, the rights of the Prophet Muhammad's family became the most important and popular political-religious cause in early Islam. Every ruler had to confront this cause, and most had to define their legitimacy to rule either by using it or by opposing it. The denied rights of the Prophet's family refused to go away, despite the killing of Muhammad's descendents, despite the hopeless ineptitude of their attempts to revolt, and despite the weakness and incoherence of the doctrines supporting those rights. There was a romantic and tragic element that adhered to the Prophet Muhammad's family through these centuries that is difficult for an outsider to comprehend. At all times, many within the Muslim community – even those in power or the intellectual elite – were susceptible to supporting the Prophet Muhammad's family in their quest for power. When these numerous revolts failed and political oppression intensified against any who would support the rights of the Prophet's family, intellectuals found their oppositional outlet in wildly exaggerated claims about the objects of their adoration (ironically, for most of them, without actually converting to Shi'ism). Thus, from being a defeated group, by the eighth and ninth centuries the Prophet Muhammad's immediate descendents were lifted into superhuman positions, with their deaths having cosmological significance.

Without a doubt the power of the martyrology contributed mightily to this metamorphosis. These martyrologies form a major theme in Islamic literature because for many frustrated intellectual and religious leaders the only outlet for their opposition to the Umayyad or 'Abbasid dynasties was their fixation upon the martyrdoms of 'Ali and his descendents. The number of treatises describing them is virtually without end, and in this work of limited scope I cannot hope to summarize more than a few basic themes.

'Ali's own death, significant though it is in Islamic literature (both Sunni and Shi'ite equally), is left in the shadows when compared to that of his younger son al-Husayn, who was martyred in 680 at the southern Iraqi site of Karbala. After 'Ali's assassination his elder son al-Hasan allowed Mu'awiya to take the caliphate and the unchallenged rule of the Muslim world. Al-Hasan died a short

---

[19] Al-Mubarrad, *al-Ta'azi wa-l-marathi*, p. 224.

time later, after having been (according to Shiʿite accounts) poisoned. But al-Hasan's unwillingness to fight for his rights has colored his conduct with a faint odium and he is not given a very prominent place in Shiʿite martyrologies. His younger brother al-Husayn remained quietly in Medina until the death of Muʿawiya in 680, and then was invited by the inhabitants of Kufa to come and visit them. This "visit" was probably intended to have political significance. Certainly the Umayyad governor saw it that way. However, al-Husayn's trip across the Arabian Desert to Kufa, during which he was accompanied by his immediate family, including women and children, along with a small number of supporters, does not suggest a military operation.

Despite that fact, the Umayyad governor saw this visit as being a far from innocent occasion, and after quashing a budding revolt designed to welcome al-Husayn into Kufa, he sent a detachment of troops to find al-Husayn and his party. The troops found al-Husayn close to the Euphrates River at Karbala on October 10, 680 (better known as the 10ᵗʰ of Muharram, or the 'Ashura' in the *hijri* calendar). After the Umayyad governor's troops surrounded them and negotiated with them for a time, the situation degenerated into a series of single combats similar to those favored by the Arabs prior to the rise of Islam. Obviously the Umayyad troops were much better equipped to handle this than al-Husayn and his party, and since the former heavily outnumbered the latter, they pressured the small band until one by one they all fell. Al-Husayn was among the last to die, and all of his children, except one son (through whom all of his later descendents came), were killed.

In order to gain some of the emotive force that Shiʿites (and many Sunnis) feel when this story is recounted we need to look at same of the accounts.[20] Al-Husayn and his party had been traveling across the desert from Medina, and so naturally sought the banks of the Euphrates River in order to replenish their supplies of water. The Umayyad troops, under the command of ʿUmar b. Saʿd b. Abi Waqqas, were careful not to allow them to obtain the water they needed, and so al-Husayn and his group suffered from thirst in the hot Iraqi desert during the last days of their lives. The scenes of battle open with the killing of ʿAli al-Akbar, al-Husayn's eldest son (ironically his mother was Maymuna, who was an aunt of the caliph Yazid, hated by the Shiʿa). Overall, the martyrdom of al-Husayn is presented by the proto-Shiʿite accounts as a group event. Each member of al-Husayn's family and followers stands forth, recites poetry and then is slaughtered. Dreams and visions abound on this battlefield; frequently al-Husayn sees the person entering paradise, or the Prophet Muhammad appears to some of those about to be slain and informs them or others of their future in

---

[20] This material is taken from Abu Mikhnaf, *Kitab maqtal al-Husayn*, p. 120f; al-Isfaraʾini, *Nur al-ʿayn fi mashhad al-Husayn*, esp. p. 27f; al-Tamimi, *Kitab al-mihan*, pp. 142–47; al-Isfahani, *Maqatil al-Talibiyyin*, pp. 85–121; Ibn Shahrashub, *Manaqib Al Abi Talib*, iv, pp. 84–111; and al-Kashifi, *Rawzat al-shuhada'*, p. 442f.

heaven.[21] Just as with 'Ali, callers from the heavens announce his tragic death to the Muslim world, especially in Mecca, and in places (such as Jerusalem) his blood wells up from the ground.[22]

Al-Husayn is presented as the paradigmatic heroic figure, who cares for his fallen children, tries to obtain water for the non-combatant women and young ones, and fights nobly until the end. When he dies, he is said to have received at least thirty-three wounds and killed a number of the enemy. His body is treated ignobly; he was trampled under the hooves of the horsemen, and his head was cut off and presented to 'Ubayduallah b. Ziyad, the Umayyad governor, and eventually to the caliph Yazid in Damascus. (From there it either went to the Umayyad Mosque in the center of Damascus or to the Mosque of Sayyidna al-Husayn in Cairo, according to two stories.) Those who fought against al-Husayn are doomed to perdition; the face of one is said to have turned black as a punishment for killing al-'Abbas, a son of al-Husayn.[23] The event of Karbala was a defining moment for Islam: it is difficult to be neutral about it. Those who fought for al-Husayn are among the saved, while those who fought against him are irredeemably damned.

The trauma of the martyrdom of al-Husayn for Muslims of the time and since can hardly be overestimated.[24] 'Ali's assassination can be understood as the work of one man, Ibn Muljam, or at worst the result of the plotting of a small group of fanatical Kharijites. The sources present the killing of al-Husayn, on the other hand, as the result of a deliberate policy on the part of the Umayyad governor that was carried out by a high-ranking Muslim ('Umar b. Sa'd b. Abi Waqqas, whose father Sa'd had been the initial Muslim conqueror of Iraq and one of the earliest converts to Islam). While Shi'ites would find the comparison offensive, the closest analogy would be to the murder of 'Uthman previously described because 'Uthman was also killed by a large group of Muslims, led by Muhammad b. Abi Bakr (son of the first caliph), who represented a groundswell of hatred towards him. Both killings were the result of a large group of Muslims actively seeking to harm these individuals, and they were successful because of the indifference of the larger Muslim community.[25]

But there are several reasons the martyrdom of al-Husayn was the more powerful of the two stories, capturing the imagination of the Muslim world and provoking sufficient guilt among its Shi'ites as to initiate their sectarianization. Al-Husayn was the blood descendent of the Prophet Muhammad. His

---

[21] E.g., al-Tabari, *Ta'rikh*, v, p. 416.   [22] Al-Tamimi, *Mihan*, pp. 152–53.

[23] Al-Isfahani, *Maqatil*, p. 118; see another similar story in al-Tamimi, *Mihan*, pp. 154–55.

[24] For a full discussion, see Mahmoud Ayoub, *Redemptive Suffering in Islam*, p. 120f.

[25] According to al-Tabari, *Ta'rikh*, v, p. 412 'Ubaydallah b. Ziyad, the Umayyad governor of Iraq, wrote to 'Umar b. Sa'd telling him to interpose himself between al-Husayn and his group and the Euphrates River, "so as not to allow them to taste a single drop as they did to the righteous pure wronged 'Uthman." However, al-Husayn was not really involved in the murder of 'Uthman (also Ibn Shahrashub, *Manaqib Al Abi Talib*, iv, p. 97).

martyrdom epitomized the essential illegitimacy of the Umayyad rulers, who contrasted unfavorably with his pious lifestyle (of course, some of that portrayal is probably hagiographical in origin, but it certainly impressed some Muslims at the time). The poet al-Farazdaq said to al-Husayn prior to his departure: "The hearts of the people are with you, but their swords are with the Umayyads."[26] This statement epitomizes the division that grew throughout the Muslim community as a result of the martyrdom of al-Husayn and others of the Prophet Muhammad's family. While the authorities held the power, they did not hold the legitimacy or the love of the people. In addition to this, the sources present the manner of al-Husayn's death, together with most of his wives, children and close relatives, in a way designed to arouse deep emotion and guilt on the part of the reader. In some of the sources, al-Husayn's death is connected to that of other prophets, most notably John the Baptist. Just as a reluctant Herod gave orders to kill John the Baptist in order to satisfy his wife (Mark 6:17–28), so the Umayyad caliph Yazid is presented as having reluctantly ordered his governor in Iraq to capture al-Husayn, and supposedly wept upon learning that he had been killed. The comparison between these two tyrannical rulers is often made in the sources.[27]

Even beyond these comparisons, there were profound theological implications to the martyrdom of al-Husayn that continue to divide Sunnis and Shi'ites to this day.[28] Virtually all Muslims felt (and feel) horror at the murder of al-Husayn. However, among Shi'ites, especially the dominant Twelver Shi'ites this horror is transformed into a type of guilt that has lasting ramifications for believers. The blood of al-Husayn is such that the guilt for its shedding cannot be entirely expiated. The 10th of Muharram, the anniversary of his martyrdom, is a time of profound mourning and demonstrations of loyalty to al-Husayn and the other Imams that followed him. This exaggerated focus upon the death of al-Husayn has been the characteristic of all Shi'ites since the period immediately following his martyrdom, and most especially since the ninth century when the mourning for him became institutionalized. Although there are a number of doctrinal differences between Sunnism and Shi'ism, for Sunnis this focus upon al-Husayn is disturbingly reminiscent of the Christian focus upon Jesus and his redemptive sacrifice (which is rejected in the Qur'an). For this reason, the mourning for al-Husayn is one of those elements which serves to drive the two groups apart.

There are other social ramifications to the martyrdom of al-Husayn for Shi'ism. Unlike the attitude toward martyrdom in Sunnism, where the martyr is seen as a victorious personality, whose death is greeted by joy rather than

---

[26] Ibn Shahrashub, *Manaqib Al Abi Talib*, iv, p. 95.

[27] E.g., Ibn Shahrashub, *Manaqib Al Abi Talib*, iv, p. 85.

[28] Some of these are apparent in the definitions of martyrdom by al-Shaykh al-Mufid, *Awa'il al-maqalat*, pp. 114–15.

sorrow (with the exception of certain early martyrs such as 'Uthman), in Shi'ism the dominant attitude towards martyrdom is grief. Most martyrs that are venerated by Shi'ites were in fact killed by other Muslims, usually Sunnis. This is also unlike Sunnism, where as stated previously, the status of a Muslim killed by another Muslim is problematic, even if that other Muslim is schismatic. Concentration upon the divisive history of martyrdom that dominates Shi'ite history perpetuates ancient grievances between Sunnis and Shi'ites, and ensures that the rift in the Muslim community will not be easily healed (if ever). It also serves to focus the Shi'ite community upon its Sunni opponents more than any other target. While Sunnis usually do not pay much attention to Shi'ites, the latter are completely fixated upon the former, and have only occasionally been able to rip their gaze away to convert non-Muslims to the faith or to expand the lands of Islam.

Beyond the martyrdoms of 'Ali and al-Husayn, the history of the family of the Prophet Muhammad is one of martyrdom. Not all descendents of Muhammad adhered to proto-Shi'ism, let alone its majority branch, the so-called Twelver Shi'ites (*Ithna' 'ashariyya*). This latter group venerated the most immediate progeny of al-Husayn through his one surviving son, 'Ali Zayn al-'Abidin, through whom a further eight Imams (leaders of the proto-Shi'ite community, believed to have been possessed of the Prophet Muhammad's special knowledge and charisma) down to 874 CE were descended. Most of the Imams were said to have been martyred or died unnatural deaths, usually at the hands of the ruling 'Abbasid dynasty. The last several Imams were kept in special prisons that effectively denied them access to their followers, and the final one, Hasan al-'Askari (d. 873) passed away without apparent issue. However, the Twelver Shi'ites believed that he had had a son, Muhammad al-Mahdi, who had gone into occultation in 874, and would reappear to establish the messianic age at the end of the world.

Other members of the Prophet Muhammad's family were persecuted as well. The most famous martyrology in Arabic, Abu al-Faraj al-Isfahani's (d. 967), *Maqatil al-Talibiyyin* (*Slaughter of the Talibites*)[29] lists close to 200 descendants of Muhammad through both the Hasanid and Husaynid lines who came to gruesome ends during the period up to 925 (when the book was completed).[30] The vast bulk of these martyrs were slain during the period prior to the ninth century, however, when the Umayyad and 'Abbasid dynasties viewed the members of the Prophet's family as their direct competitors and as possibly undercutting their legitimacy to rule the Muslim empire. That the 'Abbasids at best could only claim descent from an uncle of the Prophet Muhammad

---

[29] Talibites were the descendents of Abu Talib, the father of 'Ali, and included the families of 'Ali's brothers.

[30] See the survey of this literature by Sebastian Gunther, "*Maqatil* literature in medieval Islam."

('Abbas), whereas the family of 'Ali could claim prophetic ancestry from both an uncle and Muhammad's daughter Fatima was a major problem. This problem was solved by interning the members of the Prophet's family during the ninth century or keeping them effectively under house arrest. Alternatively, descendants of Muhammad who fled to distant corners of the empire (Morocco, Yemen) or to territories outside the political control of the caliphate were assassinated. After the end of the ninth century, however, a number of Shi'ite or sympathetic dynasties came to power, and since that time the descendents of the Prophet Muhammad have mostly been revered.

The result of this atmosphere of paranoia concerning the Prophet Muhammad's family was the large number of martyrs documented by al-Isfahani. His book begins with the story of Ja'far al-Tayyar (brother of 'Ali, who was killed at the Battle of Mu'ta in 629 in what is today southern Jordan), and gives the most detail concerning the major figures of proto-Shi'ism, such as 'Ali and al-Husayn. Al-Isfahani's usual presentation gives us a succinct account of the circumstances of a given figure's death, then some details of whatever movement or revolt they were associated with, then a more detailed picture of their deaths, and finally some hagiographical details about them. However, al-Isfahani was not actually a Shi'ite (see footnote 16), and he does not single out important or revered personalities for excessive treatment (such as al-Husayn) in the manner that a Shi'ite would do. For example, Twelver Shi'ites doctrinally believe in the assassination of each of the Twelve Imams until 874 (when the last of them went into occultation according to the accounts): Al-Isfahani does not mention a number of the later Imams in his martyrology (e.g., 'Ali al-Hadi or Hasan al-'Askari). Also, a number of the martyrs, like Ja'far above, were killed by infidel pagans, not by Sunnis, and thus are topically not a part of Shi'ite martyrology. For al-Isfahani, the overall theme is the suffering of the entire family of the Prophet whatever the cause, rather than the specific focus upon one branch of this family.

In general, al-Isfahani's martyrology maintains a factual tone, and does not give us many supernatural details – dreams and visions are comparatively rare in his text.[31] In addition to this fact, he very rarely dwells upon the bloody or gory aspects of martyrdom. Although many of the methods used to kill the descendents of the Prophet Muhammad were gruesome, such as beheading or crucifixion, al-Isfahani passes over these details fairly quickly. Death scenes for him are not given a special prominence in his description, and for all of the sufferings of the Prophet's family, there is little feeling of vengeance contained within the text.[32] Although this martyrology has a characteristically

---

[31] A few exceptions to this rule are in al-Isfahani, *Maqatil al-Talibiyyin*, pp. 139, 367, 491.

[32] For example, the prayer on p. 393 is a general prayer for the downfall of tyrants, not of vengeance for suffering.

tragic feeling, there is not very much of a political call to action, or the call is too generalized to be of much use for any one branch of the family.

The Prophet Muhammad's family, however, were not the only ones who were martyred during this early period. Also killed were many proto-Shiʻites of one sort or another and those who took part in pro-ʻAlid revolts.[33] Probably the figure of Hujr b. ʻAdi al-Kindi, killed in 671 in Kufa, is the paradigmatic example of a follower of the Prophet's family who was willing to die for his beliefs. Hujr had been one of the most prominent supporters of ʻAli, and after ʻAli's assassination in 661 continued to be vocal in his opposition to the Umayyad regime. He was well-known for opposing the Umayyad policy of vilification of the Prophet Muhammad's family, and the glorification of ʻUthman. He is said to have stated:

"O believers, be upholders of justice, witnesses for Allah, even if it be against yourselves." [Qurʾan 4:134] I bear witness that the one you condemn is more deserving of merit than the one you praise [ʻUthman] and that the one you claim is pure is more deserved of blame than the one you vilify.[34]

With this type of open opposition, it is not difficult to see why Hujr was a marked man. After a short while, he revolted with a pathetic group of ʻAlid sympathizers that was easily suppressed by the Umayyad governor. Hujr and his twelve followers were taken to Syria where he was executed at Marj ʻAdhraʾ (ironically said to have been a town he himself had conquered years previously during the conquests).[35]

After each failed proto-Shiʻite or Shiʻite uprising during the first 200 years of Islam, a large number of those people who felt that they should have supported a given descendent of the Prophet Muhammad felt intense guilt over having failed that person. For example, after the massacre at Karbala, a movement called *al-Tawwabun* (The Penitents) appeared, whose sole goal was to expiate their own personal guilt over having failed to come to the aid of al-Husayn in his hour of need. This group, composed largely of people from Kufa, attacked the Umayyad army, and annihilated itself seeking this type of expiation.[36] From this group and others like it (although none were quite so large or single-minded), it is possible to see that the purpose of the martyrology is the process of guilt and expiation. The proto-Shiʻites, who were a comparatively small group, and the pro-ʻAlids, a much larger group, were both passive supporters of the rights of the family of the Prophet Muhammad who often failed to deliver on their promised support at key moments. But the literary

---

[33] Pro-ʻAlids were non-Shiʻites who were sympathetic to the sufferings of the Prophet Muhammad's family or who supported their claims to a limited degree because of their hostility towards the ʻAbbasid dynasty.

[34] Al-Isfahani, *Kitab al-aghani*, xvii, pp. 137–38; al-Baladhuri, *Ansab al-ashraf*, iv, pp. 243–44 for other versions.

[35] Al-Baladhuri, *Ansab*, iv, pp. 257–66; al-Isfahani, *Aghani*, xvii, p. 152.

[36] See *EI*[2], s.v. "Tawwabun" (F. M. Denny).

legacy of their feelings has lived on in the form of martyrologies that continue to move people to grief and guilt.

Kharijite martyrs

Another group, the sect of the Kharijites, was largely unmoved by guilt. This group, which was described above, were hated and feared by both proto-Sunnis and proto-Shiʻites. The absolute nature of their doctrines – which in some manifestations stated that any Muslim who committed a sin automatically became a non-Muslim and had to be fought – created an aggressive and militant group that had strong fissiparous tendencies. In general, their revolts were quickly suppressed, and adherents of Kharijism were killed down to the last man (and sometimes women). However, just as with Shiʻism, Kharijism attracted adherents because of its romantic aura, even as most Muslims reviled the actions of the sect. With their tendency to embrace death, their romantically fatalistic poems and their uncompromising doctrines, the Kharijites continued a tradition that is similar to the pre-Islamic Arab ethos.

The Kharijites were best-known because of their poetry.[37] Their paradigmatic leader, Qutari b. Fujaʻa al-Mazini (d. 697), is said to have fought governor after governor in Iraq for about twenty years, and composed several poems in which he expresses a contempt for death. One of the best known of these is:

> I say to her [the soul], when it has flown like rays from the heroes: "Woe is you! You will never pay attention.
> If you asked to stay for an extra day over the limit given you, you would not obey.
> Patience! In the arena of death, patience! Attaining eternity is not for the one asked to obey.
> Nor is the garment of staying [in this world] worth the garment of glory, so turn away from the lowly, the coward.
> The way of death is the goal of all living; its caller calls to the people of the world.
> Whoever is not slaughtered becomes disgusting and aged; the fates hand him over to the finale.
> Man has nothing better in life than when he is prepared (for death) by contempt for (worldly) goods."[38]

This type of poem shows how the ethics of the pre-Islamic Arabs have been absorbed into Islam. Rightly this poem is included in the *Diwan al-Hamasa*, a collection of poems from the ninth century otherwise dedicated to pre-Islamic poets, celebrating courage and nobility.

---

[37] See Ihsan ʻAbbas, *Diwan shʻir al-Khawarij*.
[38] Al-Tibrizi, *Sharh Diwan al-Hamasa*, pp. 24–25; Ibn Hamdun, *al-Tadhkira*, ii, p. 405 (no. 1033).

In many of the stories about the Kharijites and their opponents there are themes of bravery and cowardice. Despite the loathing that both Sunnis and Shi'ites share for the Kharijites, they are usually described as inordinately brave, reckless and capable of defeating numbers far larger than their own. This last characteristic is often used to belittle the incompetent or self-seeking commanders opposing them. For example:

[It is related concerning] Aslam b. Zur'a al-Kilabi, who had gone out to fight Abu Bilal Mirdas b. Udiyya al-Khariji, one of the Banu Rabi'a b. Hanzala, at the head of 2,000, when Mirdas had 40, that the former was defeated by the latter. Ibn Ziyad [the governor] said to him: "Woe is you! You go out leading 2,000 and are defeated by 40??" Aslam would say: "It is better for Ibn Ziyad to condemn me when I am alive than for him to praise me while I am dead."[39]

These absolute values were no longer held by very many other Muslims, and for this reason the Kharijites stood out as perhaps the only representatives of this tradition. Despite their apparent Islamic values, few of their poems actually allude to Islamic martyrdom.

Not all of the martyrs of the early Islamic period were political and religious rebels, however. Some were the ancestors of Sufism that would become so prominent within Islam over the next millennium.

Sufi martyrs from the classical period

Probably the most unusual forms of martyrdom within an Islamic context are those Sufi martyrs, who were so overwhelmed with love for God and humanity that they were willing and in some cases even anxious to demonstrate that love through death. These martyrs oftentimes have suffered at the hands of other Muslims, especially the political and religious elite, who have not understood their motivations. Sufism began to appear as a distinctive movement within Islam during the ninth century. As a belief system, it was heir to the vast tradition of asceticism that was common to both Christianity and Islam (the *zuhd* tradition in Islam). This ascetic tradition was created by the numerous holy men and women of the first centuries of Islam whose collected sayings and deeds form its basis. Gradually, towards the end of the eighth century, a system of mystical interpretation of Islam began to develop among groups closely associated with the waging of *jihad* along the borders – mainly with Byzantium, but also in Central Asia – as well as those solitary ascetics and holy men who lived in close proximity to Christian monks.

However close Muslim asceticism is to that of Christianity, and however intellectually dependent, there are certain differences. Muslim asceticism and

---

[39] Ibn Hamdun, *Tadhkira*, ii, p. 397 (no. 1011).

the early Sufism that followed it did not promote chastity, nor did it encourage complete isolation from civilization. Instead, it fostered community, usually around the border posts (*ribat*) or in urban settings where ascetics withdrew from the temptations of civilization by emphasizing personal denial (of sleep, food, etc.), spiritual exercises, continual dependence upon God and meditation and other activities such as weeping and silence. But the goals of Christian and Muslim asceticism – achieving mystical union with God – are similar, and the methods are in many cases parallel. In addition to this similarity, both types of ascetics were open to an antinomianism that more than occasionally put them into conflict with the religious elites.

Sufism owes many of its early martyrs to this antinomianism. In general, these people saw themselves as having transcended the need for the law. While in Christianity one could argue for antinomianism because of the critical attitude of the New Testament to the Jewish Torah (and Talmud), in Islam the centrality of the *shari'a* is not as easily dismissed. For the Muslim religious leadership the early Sufis were vagabonds (*sa'alik*, *darwish*) and beggars (*fuqara'*) whose presence was often detested by those around them and whose interpretation of Muslim spirituality included these elements that disregarded the *shari'a*. However, there is another side to early Sufism. The early ascetics were also fighters and participated gladly in the *jihad* against the infidel Byzantines and Turks. These proto-Sufis could also be found together with the Hanbalis defending the integrity of the *sunna* (the Way of the Prophet Muhammad) against the speculative theology of the Mu'tazilites in such cases as the *mihna* (the so-called "inquisition" of the Mu'tazilites) described above in connection with Ibn Hanbal.[40]

One of the most famous of the proto-Sufi martyrs was Ibrahim b. Adham (d. 778), who was originally from the province of Khurasan in eastern Persia (today Central Asia and Afghanistan), and, like many of the other ascetics, eventually migrated to Syria where he fought against the Byzantines. Ibrahim's early life was one of privilege, coming from a noble Arab tribe, and his conversion story is among the most dramatic of all the proto-Sufis. He heard a voice calling out one day, while he was hunting, "You were not created for this, you were not commanded to do this!"[41] Ibrahim took this remonstration to heart, left his earlier life, and migrated to Syria, where he is said to have lived in the area of Ashqelon (today south Israel) as a farmer moving from place to place. At this period the coastal region of Syria–Palestine was subject to regular Byzantine raids, as the Byzantine navy was dominant in the adjacent Mediterranean Sea.

---

[40] Christopher Melchert, "The Hanabila and the Early Sufis."
[41] Al-Isfahani, *Hilyat al-awliya*, vii, p. 426; for a slightly different version al-Sulami, *Tabaqat al-Sufiyya*, p. 37.

Ibrahim b. Adham was known for his disdain of worldly things and his desire to embrace poverty. He is said to have said to his friend Shaqiq al-Balkhi (described below): "O Shaqiq, since God has given grace to the poor, he will not ask them on the Day of Resurrection concerning charity, the *hajj*, *jihad* or maintaining relations of kinship, he will only ask those wretches, meaning the rich."[42] Despite this apparent disregard of *jihad*, Ibrahim was one of the warrior ascetics. His asceticism was that he was careful not to take his share of the spoils nor to take any of the goods of the Byzantines.[43] At least one of these raids took place at sea, and there Ibrahim fulfilled the function of a holy man; like Jonah (Jonah 1) he was able to calm the seas and save his ship.

Ibrahim owes his martyrdom to these raids against the Byzantines. He is said to have seen a dream in which paradise was opened up to him, and he saw in it two cities: one of white rubies and the other of red rubies. Ibrahim was told that these two cities were actually heavenly prototypes of earthly cities, and he was commanded to go and live in one of them. He searched through the frontier fortresses of Khurasan (then on the front lines of the battles against the Turks), and looked at Qazwin (in northern Persia, then on the front line against the mountain-dwellers of Daylam), but none of these cities were the ones he saw in his dream. Then he came to Syria, and saw the city of Tyre, and when he saw the "inscriptions that Solomon son of David had inscribed"[44] he knew that was the city for him. (The text says that the other ruby city was Ashqelon, previously mentioned.) From this location Ibrahim joined the Muslim fleet, and was killed in battle, and taken back to Tyre to be buried.[45]

Virtually no details of his actual death are given in the sources, but Ibrahim b. Adham is a paradigmatic first martyr for the proto-Sufi movement. Others that are listed in the sources include Shaqiq al-Balkhi (d. 810), who like Ibrahim came from the area of eastern Persia. He was known for his encounters with the Turks and he became a martyr fighting against them. Ironically, the story of his conversion is that he met with a Turkish holy man (not a Muslim) while on a trip as a merchant in Central Asia. According to the story, Shaqiq confronted the holy man, and told him that he was worshipping idols and that his actions were pointless, but the man turned the tables on Shaqiq and told him that his own actions were hypocritical, and that if he truly believed in God he would depend upon Him entirely for his own subsistence. This conversation caused Shaqiq to leave his life as a trader, and abandon all of his worldly goods.[46]

From that point forward, like Ibrahim b. Adham, Shaqiq al-Balkhi was a wandering mendicant, but one who specialized in preaching to non-Muslims.

---

[42] Al-Isfahani, ibid., p. 427, and other similar statements on pp. 427–29.

[43] Ibid., p. 446, also p. 451; for a full discussion see Richard Gramlich, *Alte Vorbilder des Sufitums*, i, pp. 183–87, for his death 279–82.

[44] Perhaps the inscriptions at the Dog River just to the north of Beirut.

[45] Al-Isfahani, *Hilyat al-awliya*, viii, pp. 8–9.   [46] Al-Isfahani, ibid., viii, p. 63.

Because of his ability to speak *A'jami* (a language that was probably Persian, but possibly Turkish) he converted many. The other aspect of his life was fighting the Turks, and of that we are given a glimpse:

Hatim al-Asamm [*ca*. early ninth century][47] said: We were with Shaqiq al-Balkhi raiding the Turks . . . while we were between the two lines [of battle], Shaqiq said to me: "What do you think, Hatim? I think this is like the night in which your [heavenly] wife will be escorted to you." I said: "No, by God, but today is a day of which during its night my wife will be escorted to me." Then he [Shaqiq] slept between the two lines, while his shield was beneath his head until I heard him snoring. I heard one of our companions that day crying, and I said: "What is the matter with you?" He said: "My brother has been killed." I said: "The fate of your brother has gone to Allah and His favor." He said: "Silence! I am not crying because of grief over him or because of his death, but I am crying because I know of his submission (*sabruhu*) towards God as the sword fell upon him." Hatim said: "That day a Turk took me, and forced me down so that he could slaughter me, but my heart was not focused upon him; instead my heart was focused upon God, watching what God would permit him to do. While he was searching for a knife in its sheath, a stray arrow took him, killed him and he fell away from me."[48]

Early proto-Sufis like Ibrahim b. Adham and Shaqiq al-Balkhi practiced their warfare against the infidels just as they lived the rest of their lives: in complete submission to the will of God. Although we are not given a description of Shaqiq's martyrdom, he is said to have been killed by the Turks. Many other early Muslim ascetics, like Fudayl b. 'Iyad (d. 803) and Ibn al-Mubarak (d. 797), both of them also from the area of eastern Persia, followed in the footsteps of these two but were not granted the title of martyr. They are considered paradigmatic as warrior-ascetics. The warrior tradition in Sufism never completely died out, and Chapter 5 will detail its manifestations throughout the later Muslim world.

Gradually during the later ninth century, Sufism became less and less associated with *jihad*, and its early connections with Hanbalism (and normative Sunnism) weakened.[49] Although there were always Sufis that were considered to be more "orthodox" than others (such as al-Junayd), by this period there were also those who were preaching the absence of separation between the Sufi lover and God, and other teachings that de-emphasized the importance of the law (or interpreted it mystically). These types of teachings were completely unacceptable to most of the Hanbalite religious elite that controlled the mob in Baghdad and had a great deal of influence at the 'Abbasid court.

---

[47] For biographical information on him, see Gramlich, *Alte vorbilder*, ii, pp. 63–94; for his definitions of martyrdom and *jihad*, see Farid al-Din 'Attar, *Tadhkirat al-awliya'*, p. 302.

[48] Al-Isfahani, *Hilyat al-awliya*, viii, pp. 67–68; also Ibn al-Jawzi, *Sifat al-safwa*, iv, p. 392; also Gramlich, *Alte Vorbilder*, ii, pp. 13–14.

[49] Christopher Melchert, "The Transition from Asceticism to Mysticism at the middle of the Ninth Century CE."

All of these differences came to a head with the mystic Husayn b. al-Mansur al-Hallaj who was executed in 922 as a result of court intrigues fueled by the pressure of the mob. Al-Hallaj was a peripatetic preacher, a man of some charisma who wrote at least fifty works and who had a wide following as a result of his powerful teachings of universal love and union with God. He is said to have prayed in the graveyard of the martyrs, and some of his prayers have been preserved:

I [Qadi Ibn Haddad] went out one night in the moonlight to pray at the tomb of [Ahmad] Ibn Hanbal and I saw there, from a distance, a man standing, turned towards the *qibla*. I came up to him without his seeing me, and I saw that it was Husayn b. Mansur Hallaj. He was weeping, and saying: "O You, who have intoxicated me with Your love, and let me wander through the esplanade of Your nearness, You are the Only One, in the loneliness of eternity, You are the Only One to witness You, from the height of 'the throne of truth' . . . I beseech You, out of respect for this sacred possession that You bestow upon me and for the even higher degrees I am asking from You, do not return me to myself, after having robbed me of myself; do not show me my soul now that You have robbed it from me; increase the number of my enemies in Your cities, and the number of those among Your faithful who clamor for my death!"[50]

It seems clear that part of al-Hallaj's desire to be unified with God was to provoke his own death, and perhaps it was to that end that he spoke so publicly of his love for God, and his union with the divine. Al-Hallaj's most famous saying, *ana al-haqq* (I am the Truth, or I am one with the Truth) is indicative of that union.[51] But union of this nature, for many Muslims, compromised the absolute nature of Islamic monotheism and was unacceptable.

Even given his provocative statements, al-Hallaj had his supporters. Qadi Ibn Haddad above, for example, was himself a Hanbalite, and given the close historical links between classical proto-Sufism and Hanbalism described above, it is by no means certain that al-Hallaj would have been executed, had it not been for the court intrigues of the vizier Hamid, who orchestrated a series of attacks upon the former in order to strengthen his own position at the court. These attacks were initiated in 913 by the arrest and first trial of al-Hallaj, after which he was exposed upon a pillory for a day. After this treatment, al-Hallaj was returned to prison for eight years, then given a second trial after which he was crucified. Accounts of his crucifixion are problematic, but the basic facts are that al-Hallaj was led out of prison in the face of a hostile mob, and sentenced to be lashed 1,000 lashes. However, the number of lashes was reduced to 600, since even 500 can be fatal. As he was escorted through the mob to be whipped he recited his famous last poem:

[50] Louis Massignon, *The Passion of al-Hallaj* (trans. Herbert Mason), i, pp. 277–78.
[51] See Carl Ernst, *Words of Ecstasy in Sufism*, pp. 63–72.

> The One Who invites me, so as not to seem to wrong me,
> Bid me drink from the cup He drank from: like the Host who serves a guest;
> Then when the cup was passed around, He called for the leather (execution) whip and the blade.
> Thus does it befall the one who drinks the Wine with the (zodiacal) Dragon in summer.[52]

After this public whipping, "they cut off one of his hands, then a foot; then the other hand, followed by the other foot. He then had to be hoisted in full view, on a stake. His head was cut off, then his body, in which there was still a trace of life, was hurled to the ground from the flagellation platform. And the trunk was burned wrapped in his mantle."[53] It is not at all surprising to find that al-Hallaj's followers compared his martyrdom to that of Jesus. As in the New Testament, the last words of al-Hallaj are carefully recorded, and like Jesus (Luke 23:34), al-Hallaj is said to have forgiven those who were about to kill him. A number of al-Hallaj's followers are said to have believed that he would return from the dead after a period of forty days.

Al-Hallaj was the first high-profile Sufi to be executed in such a prominent manner by a Muslim government. Although it seems obvious that his execution was directly as a result of his own actions and sayings, and that he was to some extent a willing participant in his martyrdom, the manner of his death and its pathos has had a profound effect upon Sufism, especially its Persian and Turkish varieties. In these two traditions he is remembered as something of a Husayn- or Jesus-like figure whose death was entirely the result of an evil government and vile mob working together against a blameless holy man. Al-Hallaj's spiritual devotion, his single-minded desire to join his Beloved, without counting the cost of this joining, has raised him to martyr status. But there remain many Muslims, who, when confronted with the type of utterances associated with him, are convinced that killing him was just.

Controversy surrounded certain Sufi martyrs like al-Hallaj. But his death did not cause the controversy to cease; it merely postponed the next engagement for around two centuries. During this period Sufi groups had begun to coalesce into the beginnings of the great Sufi orders. By the middle of the twelfth century 'Abd al-Qadir al-Jilani had founded the most widespread of all the Sufi orders, the Qadiriyya. To a large degree, as a result of the foundation of the Sufi orders, Sufism became normative within Sunni Islam. For the following centuries even the harshest critics of Sufism (e.g., Ibn Taymiyya) were either themselves Sufis or at least incorporated elements of Sufi spirituality into their lives. As a result of the Sufi orders, Islam spread far beyond the territories politically controlled by Muslims, to India, Central Asia, Africa and Indonesia (see Chapter 5).

---

[52] Massignon, *The Passion*, p. 583.
[53] Massignon, ibid., pp. 569–70, from the account of al-Zanji (trans. Massignon).

At the same time as 'Abd al-Qadir was founding the Qadiriyya, the last two famous martyrdoms of prominent Sufis, those of 'Ayn al-Qudat al-Hamadani (d. 1131) and Shihab al-Din al-Suhrawardi (d. 1191) occured. Both of these seminal figures were done to death by Sunni dynasties: al-Hamadani by the Turkish Seljuqs ruling in Iraq and Persia, and al-Suhrawardi by the Kurdish Ayyubids ruling in Egypt and Syria. Like al-Hallaj above, their doctrines were speculative and offensive to normative Sunni Islam, and both of these dynasties depended upon the defense of the *sunna* for their own legitimacy. Hence their willingness to execute Sufis.

'Ayn al-Qudat followed very closely in the footsteps of al-Hallaj in his willingness and even desire for self-annihilation. He was a close disciple of Ahmad al-Ghazali (d. 1126), the brother of the great Abu Hamid Muhammad al-Ghazali (d. 1111), who synthesized much important Sufi doctrine. Ahmad al-Ghazali, although not as well-known, was in some ways far more influential over the course of Sufism as a whole because of his mentoring of the founder of an important Sufi order, the Suhrawardiyya (not connected to Shihab al-Din al-Suhrawardi). He preached a doctrine of universal love that leads to the annihilation of the lover in the beloved (God).[54] From this doctrine 'Ayn al-Qudat took his own intense desire to annihilate himself. Like al-Hallaj, he is said to have had premonition of his coming martyrdom well before the fact. Since he knew of a *fatwa* that had been issued against him, he welcomed it, saying (four years before his arrest):

> If they ask for a *fatwa* from you, my friend, deliver them one . . . as for myself, I pray for such a death (*qatl*) but alas! The time is still distant! When will it happen? Ah! "That is surely no great matter for God."[55] (Qur'an 14:20)

His actual death was quite barbaric and tragic, as he was skinned alive and hung up to die, so that at the age of thirty-three one of the most brilliantly creative minds produced in classical Islamic times was snuffed out.[56] However, a number of researchers have emphasized that this martyrdom was not the result of anti-Sufi animus, but again, as with al-Hallaj, the outcome of court struggles in which 'Ayn al-Qudat was a helpless pawn.

Another similar figure was Shihab al-Din al-Suhrawardi, usually called Suhrawardi *al-maqtul* (the one who was killed) in order to differentiate him from a number of other important figures by the same name who lived at that time. This Suhrawardi was the founder of the school known as the *Ishraq*

---

[54] For a translation see Nasrollah Pourjavady (trans.), *Sawanih: Inspirations from the World of Pure Spirits*.

[55] L. Lewinsohn, "In Quest of Annihilation: Imaginalization and Mystical Death in the *Tamhidat* of 'Ayn al-Qudat al-Hamadhani."

[56] For assessments, see "'Ayn al-Quzat" in *Encyclopedia Iranica* (G. Böwering); and Hamid Dabashi, *Truth and Narrative: The Untimely Thoughts of 'Ayn al-Qudat al-Hamadani*, p. 586f.

(Illuminationist) school of theosophy. The religious jurisprudents under the Sunni Ayyubid dynasty of al-Malik al-Zahir (ruled Aleppo, 1191–1216, son of the famous Saladin) strongly disliked this type of speculation, questioned him and then declared him to be an infidel. The famous Qadi al-Fadil (friend to the Jewish rabbi-philosopher Maimonides) signed his death warrant. There are conflicting accounts as to the type of death he suffered:

> It appears . . . that people are in disagreement as to how he was killed. Some claim that he was imprisoned and denied food; others say he starved himself until he died. Some say he was strangled with a cord, while others say he was put to death by the sword. It is said that [his body] was thrown down from the citidel and burned. In a vision that Shaykh Jamaluddin al-Hanbali had, the Prophet of God [Muhammad] was seen gathering bones and placing them in holes (or, as is also said, in a sack) and saying: "These are the bones of Shihabuddin."[57]

Al-Suhrawardi's doctrine of Illumination was destined to be quite influential within the context of Sufism, especially Persian and Turkish Sufism, where his memory is revered. Like 'Ayn al-Qudat before him, he was extraordinarily prolific for one executed so young (he was approximately thirty-eight when he died). Unlike 'Ayn al-Qudat, al-Suhrawardi did not apparently cultivate the doctrine of annihilation or seek it out. But both of these martyrs' suffering can be understood within the context of the court struggles of the time, as well as the hardening attitude of certain influential Sunni scholars and jurisprudents towards speculative Sufism. In essence, the martyrdoms of 'Ayn al-Qudat and al-Suhrawardi established what for Sunni scholars were the boundaries of this type of speculation. Later Sufis were either more circumspect or stood firmly within the mainstream of Islam.

Beyond the period of these two final martyrs, Sufi doctrine becomes so diffuse that it is impossible to quantify. Sufism spread throughout many different regions of the world, and both influenced them and was influenced by them at the same time. Some of these trends will be described in Chapter 5. However, the great figure of Jalal al-Din Muhammad Mawlana al-Rumi (d. 1274) can be considered here. Even though al-Rumi did not die as a martyr, his thoughts and writings on the subject are a logical continuation of the doctrines of Ahmad al-Ghazali, 'Ayn al-Qudat and al-Suhrawardi in their use of martyrdom symbolism. Al-Rumi's primary language was Persian (though today he is revered equally by the Turks). He had fled before the Mongol invasions of the thirteenth century to Anatolia (modern Turkey) where the Turkish Seljuq dynasty ruled (even though this dynasty was submissive to the Mongols). He wandered for some years until

---

[57] Wheeler Thackston, *The Mystical and Visionary Treatises of Suhrawardi*, p. 3 (trans. of Shahrazuri, *Nuzhat al-arwah wa-rawdat al-afrah*); for further details see, Ibn Abi Usaybi'a, *Tabaqat al-atibba*', ii, pp. 273–80; and Mehdi Amin Rizvi, *Suhrawardi and the School of Illumination*, pp. 1–26.

in 1244 he met with his spiritual guide, Shams al-Din al-Tabrizi, through whom he came to understand the ecstatic attachment of the lover to God.

Rumi's works cannot be detailed here, but in a great many of them we find the important theme of martyrdom and self-annihilation. In his monumental work *Masnawi al-maʿnawi* (*Couplets of Meaning*) (composed roughly 1260–73), early on in book 1 he retells the story of the *Ashab al-ukhdud* (Companions of the Pit) from *sura* 85 (described in Chapter 2). This story is without a doubt one of the primary *loci* for discussion of dramatic martyrdom in Islam, and is most probably influenced by the stories of the Christian martyrs of Najran.[58] The story is of a Jewish king who desires for his subjects to bow down to an idol (improbable as that might seem). One woman who had a child was taken to the fire, and after the king cast the child into it, the woman was about to bow down to the idol. But from within the fire, the child spoke to her, saying:

Verily, I am not dead. Come in, O mother: I am happy here, although in appearance I am amidst the fire. The fire is a spell that binds the eye for the sake of screening (the truth) . . . Come in, mother, and see the evidence of God, that thou mayst behold the delight of God's elect.[59]

From this statement, the child then expands upon a comparison between the pain of the birth process, and how he dreaded leaving his mother when she gave birth to him, but then the world was so much more than the prison of the womb. He then compares the earthly world to the prison of the womb, "since in this fire I have such rest." He calls upon all of the other people around to come and join him, since without passing into the fire one could never taste the delights of the next world. He says:

Thou hast seen the power of that cur [the king]: come in, that thou mayst see the power of God's grace. Tis (only) out of pity that I am drawing my feet (hither), for indeed such is my rapture that I have no care for thee. Come in and call the others also, for the King has spread a (festal) table within the fire. O true believers, come in, all of you: except this sweetness, all is torment.[60]

The people then threw themselves into the fire in groups. Finally, even the king's servants had to restrain the crowds from jumping into the fire. This is an example of a classical martyrdom in the Christian and Jewish sense, and should be compared with the version given in the *hadith* and exegetical literature (translated in Section I of the Appendix). It is interesting to see that the only literary attestation of such a phenomenon in Islam is in this story.

In later passages from the *Masnawi*, al-Rumi tells us the story of the Prophet Muhammad's uncle Hamza (detailed in Chapter 2), who is portrayed as someone

---

[58] For a translation of the primary Muslim account of this martyrdom, see Appendix, No. 1.

[59] R. Nicholson (trans.), *The Mathnawi of Jalaluddin Rumi*, i, pp. 44–45; text *Mathnavi*, p. 35.

[60] Ibid., p. 45; text, p. 36.

seeking martyrdom. Although the historical evidence for the descriptions given of Hamza are weak, he is said to have gone to the Battle of Uhud "like one intoxicated" without wearing any chain mail for protection, and even naked of clothes. According to al-Rumi's version the other Muslims remonstrated with Hamza, citing the Qur'anic verse: "Do not cast yourselves with your own hands into destruction" (Qur'an 2:195).

Hamza then responds with another classic homily on martyrdom. He says that in his youth, prior to his conversion, he never sought out death. But at the time of the battle because of the revelation of Islam, he is not part of this world. Therefore, according to him, the proper verse to be cited is not, "Do not cast yourselves . . . into destruction," but " . . . hasten to forgiveness from your Lord [and a Paradise as wide as the heavens and the earth, prepared for the God-fearing]" (Qur'an 3:133). Hamza further says: "Your fear of death in fleeing (from it) is (really) your fear of yourself,"[61] and he then gives a lengthy soliloquy about how fear of death hampers one's spiritual status, and digresses into a description of the wretchedness of this life. While these themes are closely related to similar ones developed in the ascetic proto-Sufi literature discussed above, as well as the obsessive meditation upon death that characterizes early Sufism, Hamza differs because he is actually seeking death. He gives us reasons not only to seek out death, but also to avoid taking normal precautions against its early occurence. The elements, for example, of Hamza going to battle without any defensive mail and even naked, are unique to this line of Sufi martyrdom.

Rumi does not stop there, but goes on to tell us of the story of Majnun and Layla, about which we will expand in Chapter 6. From his accounts of martyrdom Rumi stands in the mainstream of classical Sufism, and has – with some exceptions – abandoned the doctrine of literal annihilation that characterized certain Sufis during this early formative period of Sufism. Rumi speaks of his beloved, the intinerate holy man Shams al-Din al-Tibrizi, a great deal in his works. For him, love for Shams was the earthly example of love for the divine, and after Shams' death (or disappearance) in 1247, Rumi was consumed with grief. He writes:

> Die now, die now in this Love die; when you have died in this Love, you will all receive new life.
> Die now, die now, and do not fear this death, for you will come forth from this earth and seize the heavens.
> Die now, die now, and break from this carnal soul, for this carnal soul is as a chain and you are prisoners.[62]

However extreme this sentiment is, it stands out as an exception within the overall context of Rumi's poetry. The balance of his work is expressive of an

---

[61] Ibid., iii, pp. 192–93; text, pp. 468–69.
[62] Arberry (trans.), *Mystical Poems of Rumi*, i, p. 70 (no. 80).

extreme and ecstatic love for the beloved (Shams, God), but unlike with al-Hallaj or ʿAyn al-Qudat, Rumi is not enamored with death or annihilation of one's humanity in favor of complete union with the beloved.[63] He is content to sing the beloved's praises but rarely goes further than that. In this manner, Rumi and his contemporaries left the ecstatic annihilation aspect of Sufism behind, and consequently the number of Sufis martyred for their beliefs by other Muslims goes down sharply after the twelfth century. But more than that, Rumi represents a turning point in Sufism overall, as he has successfully changed the passion of the martyrs into a universal love for God. This change enables these martyrs to speak to others beyond the realm of Islam, and enhances the power and appeal of Islam as a missionary faith with a universal message. Major martyrs like Hamza, the Prophet Muhammad's uncle, are no longer shown as fighters but as sacrificial figures, much like Jesus. Other fighters such as Fudayl b. ʿIyad, who never died as a martyr, are made to proclaim their devotion to the so-called greater *jihad* of fighting the lower inclinations of the soul, instead of reciting their feats on the battlefield.[64] In this way Islam's spiritual force is universalized, and its martyrs are given a broader message to proclaim.[65]

All of these martyrs associated with sectarian movements or causes had compelling reasons for choosing death (or in the case of Ibn Hanbal suffering) over life. But in the end their sacrifices are revered by a certain group of Muslims, and are usually demonized by their opponents. However, there are also paradigmatic martyrs, usually Sufis but occasionally others, whose sacrifices were sectarian, but for the greater good of Islam. These were missionaries to the non-Muslim peoples on the borders of Islam or warriors who fought with the infidels.

---

[63] Some exceptions can be found in *Mystical Poems*, i, pp. 31, 102; and *Mystical Poems*, ii, pp. 11, 26; also see Chittick, *Sufi Path of Love*, pp. 185–86, 188–93, 225–26.

[64] Nicholson, *Mathawi*, v, pp. 227–28. On the problems with the "greater *jihad*" see my *Understanding Jihad*, Chapter 3.

[65] E.g., John O'Kane (trans.), *The Feats of the Knowers of God*, pp. 92–93, 203, 249–50 (conversion of a monk), such that on p. 144 we read his philosophy: "You drew me from Khurasan to mix among the Greeks so that I would produce a good religious path."

5 Martyrs: warriors and missionaries in medieval Islam

Red blood gives no sound; suddenly the red blood became clear and changed into white blood; it spread a pleasing odor and recited a dhikr[1]: *There is no God, save Allah; Muhammad is the Messenger of Allah. This was the* dhikr *of that blood. The body disappeared, the blood was no longer seen.*

From the martyrdom of Siti Jenar, Indonesia[2]

Sufis, more than any other single group in Islam, have been responsible for large-scale conversions to Islam, and have often paid for their boldness with their lives. They were (and still are) often venerated after their deaths by the descendents of the very people who martyred them in the first place. For the most part these Sufi holy men and women were either fighters or wandering mendicants, who through their performance of miracles, especially of a healing nature, and their saintly lives, devotion to God and communicative abilities were able to convert peoples on the boundaries of Islam. These peoples were varied: from the largely Hindu population of India; to the shamanists, Buddhists and Nestorian Christians of Central Asia; to the Christians of Anatolia (Turkey) and southeastern Europe; to the pagans of West and East Africa, and the Indonesian islands (some Hindus). Sufis in general worked very closely with Muslim traders. It was primarily along trading routes, connected with the great Indian Ocean trade, the salt/gold/slave trade of Western Africa, the Silk Road of Central Asia, and the arteries of the Indus and Ganges rivers that Islam spread.[3] Some of this conversion to Islam was accompanied by conquests (such as in India, and later in West Africa), but much of it was peaceful, and almost unnoticed by the history books.

However, what has been unnoticed by history books was noticed by hagiographical accounts of missionary activity, conversion stories of prominent kings and local rulers, and/or martyrdoms of Sufis who preached to these societies. Sufi missionaries in many of the above regions used inoffensive methods in

---

[1] Remembrance of God. [2] D. A. Rinkes, *Nine Saints of Java* (trans. H. Froger), p. 23.
[3] Note that according to some accounts, the merchant who dies protecting his goods is a *shahid*, a martyr (al-Suyuti, *Abwab al-sa'da*, pp. 48, 59 [nos. 21, 43]; and see al-Khallal, *al-Hathth 'ala al-tijara wa-l-sina'a wa-l-'amal*, pp. 56–57).

74

order to communicate their message. In general, they worked to dilute boundaries between various faiths, concentrating upon the commonalities that Islam – at least in its Sufi interpretation – has with even the most obviously pagan or polytheist system. Since Sufi holy men and women had a great deal of spiritual prestige they could speak across those boundaries, and sometimes blur the lines such that Islam could through a gradual process receive converts. Over a period of generations, then, those formerly pagan, then partially Muslim converts, would gradually become more and more Islamized. This is the pattern in India, West Africa, Indonesia and parts of Central Asia. Much of the syncretistic form of Islam practiced in these locations today is the result of this gradual conversion process.

Gradual conversion to Islam produced martyrs among the Sufis – it is impossible for there to be such a cross-cultural exchange without some loss of life – but there were also more dramatic attempts at conversion. Certain less tolerant Sufi orders did not approve of a gradual method of conversion, for example the Naqshbandiyya (in India) and other more militant orders such as the Qadiriyya or some of the Tijaniyya in West Africa, or the Qadiriyya and the Naqshbandiyya in the Caucasus Mountains (south of Russia). These groups felt that the lines drawn between Islam and unbelief (paganism usually but, within the context of India, Hinduism) should be absolute and not blurred. The result of this clash, then, was *jihad* against unbelievers that was waged in several areas and which produced martyrologies.

The martyrologies that were produced of some of these prototypical saints cannot conceal on occasion their weak ties to Sufism overall and sometimes to a given order of Sufism. For example, it is not unusual for various holy figures, sometimes fighters or wandering mendicants, to be "Sufized" after their deaths. This process involves the back-projection of Sufi traits upon a given historical or semi-historical figure, and then the establishment of a cult around the place of his death. As this cult becomes more and more prominent, the population surrounding it will be gradually converted to Islam or at least Islamized. Thus, even a fighter who is martyred and does not actually convert anyone during his lifetime can in fact be a very potent catalyst for missionization and conversion after his death.

India

No region of the world has been the recipient of Muslim missionary efforts more than India. This is not surprising, given the close geographical proximity between the central, core areas of Islam (the Middle East) and India, but also given the fact that India's huge population is a draw for prospective missionaries. Until the present time, taking all of geographical India (including Pakistan,

Bangladesh and Sri Lanka as part of that term) into account, approximately a third of the total population has converted to some form of Islam. Today this represents the largest block of Muslims in the world (although as far as a single country is concerned, Indonesia has more Muslims than any other). There are several possible explanations for how so many Indians converted to Islam. One of these explanations is that conversion was the result of the *jizya* tax – the tax that non-Muslims have to pay for their "protection" according to the *shari'a*. This explanation is one that is popularly used for conversion in the Middle East. However, there is little evidence that the *jizya* tax was ever imposed upon India as a whole – even when it was almost fully controlled by the Muslim Moghul dynasty during the latter part of the seventeenth century. (Only Aurengzeb, who ruled between 1658–1707, imposed Islamic norms upon Indian society, and with limited success.)

Another interpretation is somewhat Marxist in nature, which assumes that conversion to Islam came largely from the Hindu untouchables and other lower castes who saw the possibility of liberation from an otherwise intolerable social order. There is equally little evidence for this model of conversion, and there is some evidence that the caste system continued to affect converts to Islam in a number of cases. Yet another model, already alluded to, employs the possibility that Sufi holy men and women mixing with Hindu holy men and women could over a long period of time have effected the blurring of the lines between the two faiths that eventually led to widespread conversion. Combined with the early presence of Muslim traders in the Indian Ocean already during the ninth and tenth centuries and periodically settling along the Indian coastline, these last Sufis provide the most plausible model of conversion.

However one sees this conversion pattern – whichever model eventually becomes accepted among historians – the presence of Sufi holy men and women in India at a very early stage cannot be denied. The most prominent martyr whose cult has survived down to the present day is actually a warrior, who posthumously was turned into a Sufi saint not only by Muslims but by Hindus who revered him as well. Salar Mas'ud Ghazi is said to have been a warrior in the armies of Mahmud of Ghazna (d. 1031), and his cult is centered in Bahraich (today Uttar Pradesh, India, near Ayodhya).[4] Mahmud of Ghazna was the great Muslim conqueror of the eleventh century, whose regular raids from the heights of Afghanistan upon the region of the Indus Valley and beyond made the empire of the Ghaznavids wealthy, and began the process of the political dependency of various Muslim states. But Mahmud was best known for his mass slaughters

---

[4] See Tahir Mahmood, "The Dargah of Sayyid Salar Mas'ud Ghazi in Bahraich: Legend, Tradition and Reality."

of Hindus and pillaging of Hindu holy sites, such as the famous temple at Somnath in 1025. Thus, this particular martyr, who is said to have taken part in the sacking of Somnath, was actually a fighter.

According to the legends developed by the Chishti Sufi order, Salar Mas'ud was a descendent of the Prophet Muhammad and had noble status. He was educated by a famous scholar, Sayyid Ibrahim Bara Hazari, and although he fought in the wars of Mahmud of Ghazna, he was repelled by the slaughter at Somnath. After it, Salar Mas'ud is said to have gone to Ajmer, which several hundred years later became the home of the founder of the Sufi Chishti order Mu'in al-Din Chishti, and preached Islam in the region. He then went on beyond Delhi to the region of Bahraich, where he attracted a large number of Sufis and warriors, and fought against the local Hindu rulers. During one of those battles in 1033 (when he was just nineteen years old), he was killed.[5]

It seems clear that this legend was at least partly developed by the Chishtis, as the source of information concerning Salar Mas'ud is Shaykh 'Abd al-Rahman Chishti's *Mir'at-i Mas'udi* (*Mas'ud's Mirror*) in the seventeenth century, in order to give a Muslim pre-history to their holy city of Ajmer. Early Turkish rulers, such as Muhammad b. Tughluq (1325–51), had performed pilgrimages to the site by 1340. Suvorova in her research on the Muslim saints and shrines of India has noted that the cult of this martyr is one that is common to both Muslims and Hindus, and that there may be an identification of the personality of Salar Mas'ud with Krishna on the part of some Hindus.[6] If this is indeed the case, then it is a fascinating remake of a formerly Muslim warrior who has managed to bridge the gap between Muslim and Hindu, presumably facilitating conversion. Salar Mas'ud's remake into a Sufi is also indicative of the importance of Sufism in Indian Islam.

While there are a number of other warrior saints like Salar Mas'ud, most of them are not martyrs. Kabir was probably the best known of all of the figures who blurred the lines between Muslims and Hindus – since he is acknowledged by both – in pre-British India. It is very uncertain when precisely Kabir lived (sometime during the fourteenth or fifteenth century most probably) and details of his life and religious affiliation are hotly debated both among scholars and between Hindus and Muslims. Apparently he was either born to a mixed union between a Muslim and a Hindu or at least grew up in a highly syncretistic environment. His doctrines were most definitely syncretistic, as is exemplified in some of his poetry:

---

[5] Details from Mahmood, "Sayyid Salar Mas'ud Ghazi," pp. 26–29; Rizvi, *History of Sufism in India*, i, 312–14; and see also Anna Suvorova, *Muslim Saints of South Asia*, pp. 157–58; compare his martyrdom to that of Shah Ismail Ghazi in G. H. Damant, "Risalat ash-Shuhada of Pir Muhammad Shattari," *Journal of the Asiatic Society of Bengal* 1874, pp. 215–40.

[6] Suvorova, *Muslim Saints*, p. 159.

The Hindu died crying: "Ram!" the Mussulman [Muslim] crying: "Khuda!" [God]. Kabir, that one will live, who keeps away from them both! Now the Kaaba has become Kasi,[7] Ram has become Rahim [name of God]: Coarse meal has become fine flour, and Kabir sits down to enjoy it![8]

Many other verses associated with him attest to an antinomian frame of reference, and to his contempt for orthodox doctrine from either Muslims or Hindus. Kabir was also quite familiar with the Hallajian desire to achieve union with the beloved, and often compared it to the familiar Hindu practice of *sati* (widow immolation). This fascination was not, however, translated into sensuality in this world. Kabir, in fact, demonstrates a good deal of misogyny in his poetry, comparing women to black cobras, and saying: "woman ruins everything, when she comes near a man: devotion, salvation and divine knowledge no longer enter his soul."[9] But the type of burning devotion for which Kabir longed was similar to the devotion of the *sati*, and he pictures the union with God, and the process of leaving this world in these terms:

> That death which the world dreads is joy for me:
> When shall I die? When shall I behold the One who is Plentitude and Joy supreme?
> Climbing the pyre, the Sati calls and cries: Listen, O my Friend, Masan [evil Hindu goddess]
> All the people, as passers-by, have gone away, only you and I remain at the end! . . .

> Kabir, towards that House of Love, the path is rough, impassable:
> Cut off your head, put it under your feet, if you wish to taste Love's flavor! . . .

> The Sati has taken the path of fortitude, surrendering her body and soul:
> She has applied the *mahaula* [cosmetic dye] for her Husband, and the burning ground sings her praises![10]

Many other poems ascribed to Kabir are similar in their concentration upon death as the means by which one attains the beloved.[11]

The circumstances of Kabir's life were such that he attracted the attention of the orthodox Muslim religious leadership (the *'ulama*) who encouraged the ruler Sikandar Lodi (*ca.* 1494) to kill him. According to the hagiographical accounts about him, he was said to have "abandoned the customs of the Muslims, and broken the touchability rules of the Hindus" along with many other charges.[12] According to the legend, after Sikandar's troops brought him to the court, the

---

[7] The Kaʿba is the holy site for Muslims in Mecca; Kasi is the holy site for Hindus at Benares.

[8] Vaudeville, *Kabir*, p. 263. See also G. H. Westcott, *Kabir and the Kabir Panth*, p. 37f.

[9] Vaudeville, *Kabir*, pp. 295–99, esp. 296. For his portrayal of the *sati* see Vijay Mishra, "Suffering in Union: Kabir's Burning Bride."

[10] Vaudeville, *Kabir*, pp. 219–27, at nos. 2–3, 15, 41.   [11] E.g., ibid., pp. 257–60.

[12] David Lorenzen, *Kabir Legends and Ananta–Das's* Kabir Parachai, p. 107.

qadi told Kabir to bow down to the ruler, but the latter refused. Thereupon Sikandar became enraged and ordered Kabir to be killed. First, the *qadis* tried to have him stoned, but Kabir managed to accuse them of being infidels, which made Sikandar even angrier, so he had Kabir chained and thrown into the Ganges. However, the chains came loose, and Kabir floated on the river.

Then Sikandar had Kabir tied up, and put him into a house which was set on fire. But Kabir survived that, thanks to the intervention of the god Narayan. Since Sikandar only became angrier after this miraculous survival, he called for Kabir to be trampled by a frenzied elephant. However, the elephant fled from Kabir, and would not attack him. "Kabir had not fear. He stayed there absorbed in the love of Ram."[13] In the end, Sikandar repented of his hatred of Kabir, and asked forgiveness from him, and proclaimed him to be greater than all of the *qadis*. Kabir did not die a martyr, according to the legends, but died on his bed surrounded by his Hindu and Turk (Muslim) followers, who quarreled about what to do with his body after his death. Fortunately, the choice as to whether to burn him (as the Hindus wanted) or to bury him (as the Muslims wanted) was taken away from them:

When Kabir became an immortal, he did not abandon his body. Kabir left this world taking his body with him. The devotees were astonished. When they saw that the flowers [were all that remained] they went home.[14]

Kabir is a type of the Hindu-Muslim, Muslim-Hindu martyr of the Indian sub-continent, not necessarily a common phenomenon but uniquely influential. His fame is great in both traditions, and neither one is certain to whom he belonged. Ambiguity is the key to his fame. It remains an open question, however, to what extent Kabir and the many lesser-known saints like him facilitated the conversion of Hindus to Islam. Kabir was a bridge, but a bridge to what?

This question is not an easy one to answer. Much of the Islam that developed in India was highly syncretistic, but some elements bound Muslims together. There were other Muslim Sufi martyrs that were much less ambiguous. These include the warrior saints from the middle period of Islamic conquest, especially the seventeenth and eighteenth centuries, when the great Moghul ruler Aurengzeb (ruled 1658–1707) was attempting to unify India under Muslim rule. Aurengzeb was the only Moghul ruler who was closely identified with normative Sunni Islam and who made a serious attempt to enforce the *shari'a* throughout the sub-continent.[15] Although he was able to conquer most of geographic India – a feat not repeated until the time of the British raj in the middle

---

[13] Ibid., pp. 110–12; see also Muhammad Hedayatullah, *Kabir: The Apostle of Hindu–Muslim Unity*, pp. 186–93; and Vaudeville, *Kabir*, p. 31f.

[14] Ibid., p. 126.

[15] Also contributing to the growth of Sikh martyrology, which was appearing at this time: Louis Fenech, *Martyrdom in the Sikh Tradition: Playing the Game of Love*, Chapters 3–4.

of the nineteenth century – the divisive nature of his religious edicts sowed the seeds of the collapse that occurred almost immediately after Aurengzeb's death.

During the time of Aurengzeb it is possible to discern two major trends in martyrdom. One is that of Muslims like Husayn b. al-Mansur al-Hallaj and 'Ayn al-Qudat, who died for their universal love that was difficult to distinguish from syncretism or in some cases pantheism. Like Kabir above, a number of Muslims had adopted an ascetic approach that was very similar to that of Hinduism. This attitude was offensive to Aurengzeb, who singled out one Sarmad Kashani, who was originally a Jew from Iran, and who converted to Islam. Sarmad, however, sought through his ascetic emulation of Hindu masters, to follow the way of Kabir.[16] There was a certain amount of political maneuvering in Aurengzeb's persecution of Sarmad; since the latter was under the protection of Aureng-zeb's older brother Dara Shikoh (executed 1658) and rival for the throne.

However, it is also possible that the persecution of Sarmad was because of the overall hostility of Aurengzeb to the syncretistic Sufis, and his intention to impose normative Sunni Islam within the Indian society. Like al-Hallaj, Sarmad was viewed within the context of Sufi antinomianism[17] and is said to have debated a number of times with court jurisprudents. Aurengzeb had Sarmad arraigned and forced a death sentence against him (charges of infidelity are punishable with mandatory death) which was carried out almost immediately. Like Kabir, however, he is still seen as a bridge figure within the multi-religious context of India. As a former Jew, a syncretistic Muslim and as a friend to Hindus and Christians, many of whom greatly admired him, he was in a perfect position to represent everything that Aurengzeb loathed.

Another side of Aurengzeb was his passion for conquest. As previously stated, he alone among the Moghul rulers of India (1500–1759) managed to conquer nearly all of the Indian sub-continent. This conquest was achieved with the aid of a large number of Sufis, some of whom became martyrs. Stories about these colorful characters are related in the *Malfuzat-i Naqshbandiyya* (translated by Simon Digby as *Sufis and Soldiers in Aurangzeb's Deccan*) dating from approximately the eighteenth century. In this collection of stories concerning various holy men, we first follow the adventures of one Baba Palagposh (d. 1699) and Baba Musafir (d. 1714). Neither of these two achieved martyrdom, although both fought for Aurangzeb. But several figures around the two of them did attain martyrdom. One of these was a figure named Mir Mahmud, who was a companion of Baba Musafir. Mir Mahmud repeatedly stated that he was going to be a martyr, to the general disbelief of his companions (but Baba Musafir is said to have believed him). In the general chaos that followed

---

[16] Christiane Tortel, "Loi islamique et haine impériale: Sarmad Shahid Kashani, poète mystique et martyr (m. 1659)."

[17] Some of his pronouncements can be found in Ibn Isfandiyar, *Dabistan-i mazahib*, ii, pp. 214–15.

Aurangzeb's death in 1707 (the beginning of the end for the Moghul empire), Mir Mahmud attached himself to a minor courtier named Khwajim-Quli Khan. While accompanying him, after settling his debts (important for a would-be martyr), Mir Mahmud is said to have proclaimed: "Tomorrow I shall reach the rank of martyrdom!" The next day,

the Marathas [Hindu enemies of the Muslims] came, and the khan [Khwajim-Quli Khan] rode out to fight them and went into battle. The mir came forward from out of the force of the khan and, spurring his horse on, passed into the ranks of the enemy. Here and there the horse pulled up, and the mir passed into meditation. There was a mighty fight between the two sides, but the khan's men were put to flight, and the mir was still in meditation in the midst of the army of the enemy. On all four sides the Maratha horsemen struck the mir with lances and swords and wounded him.[18]

He died in 1707 as a result of this encounter, and the author notes that the place of his martyrdom in Karnul is still well-known.

Shah Qalandar was another companion of Baba Musafir. He incurred the wrath of a person named Allah-Yar Birqa, who was in the habit of treating his wife and mother-in-law cruelly. The wife and mother-in-law came to Shah Qalandar to obtain justice from him, and he duly reprimanded Birqa. However, Birqa did not take this well, and continued to beat the two women severely, and cut off his mother-in-law's nose. So Shah Qalandar was able to obtain a separation for the wife from her abusive husband, who thereafter bore a grudge against Shah Qalandar. The latter is said to have seen a dream in which "a large yellow ant stung my big toe, and I crushed it with that toe and killed it. Then many ants gathered around me."[19] Shortly thereafter, in 1730, while Shah Qalandar was meditating after all of his followers had left him for the day, Birqa stayed with him and then

Birqa drew a knife from its sheath and stuck it in the shah's belly. As soon as the knife struck, he said: "Allah!" and placing his hand upon the wound leant forward in the posture of meditation. Birqa got up from there and went out with the naked blade in his hand.[20]

Shortly thereafter Birqa was beaten to death by the followers of Shah Qalandar, but the latter was already dead.

Other martyrdoms in the *Malfuzat* include that of a Sufi who was a martyr of love. He had fallen in love with a boy, who did not reciprocate his affections. The boy was embarrassed at the attention that the Sufi would pay to him, and finally "out of excess of rage, stabbed him in the belly with a dagger, and the darwish [Sufi] surrendered his soul to God, attaining the rank of martyrdom."[21] Baba Palangposh was able to deal with this situation and proclaimed the slain

---

[18] Digby (trans.), *Sufis and Soldiers in Aurangzeb's Deccan*, pp. 178–79 (at 179).
[19] Ibid., p. 205.   [20] Ibid., p. 206.   [21] Ibid., pp. 80–81.

Sufi a martyr of love, and calmed the angry Sufis who wanted revenge upon the boy. He also compelled the boy to participate in the funeral of the Sufi and pray over his gravesite every Friday and weep for this man. All of these stories, no doubt only a small selection of the reality of martyrdom for the Muslim community in India during this period, are very colorful and represent local beliefs in action. For example, at the same time as Baba Palangposh and his associates were operating in the Deccan, Shah 'Inayat Shahid, a radical Sufi who preached social justice in the region of Sind (today southern Pakistan), was being martyred (1718).[22] He had offended the local absentee landowners by gathering a mass movement that refused to pay tribute to the owners of the land on the basis that the tributes they extorted were wrong. Eventually he gathered a mass following that had to be confronted by force, and Shah 'Inayat was betrayed and had his head cut off.

Other groups of martyr saints in India are those from the early period of the British conquest, closely associated with the *jihad* movement of Sayyid Ahmad Shahid and Isma'il Shahid (both d. 1831).[23] Starting in 1816 Sayyid Ahmad Shahid began proclaiming in a peripatetic series of missionary tours to the Muslim masses the rejection of British rule. This rejection posed a dilemma for the Muslim community of India. Long accustomed to ruling or dominating the Indian sub-continent, mostly at the expense of the Hindus, by the beginning of the nineteenth century the Muslims were a dominated minority. This fact was fundamentally unacceptable to many of the Muslim community, and Sayyid Ahmad was one of the first to actively promote fighting the British. Other Muslim leaders had made declarations concerning the loss of hegemony, and even the need to migrate (make *hijra*) from India. However, these latter proclamations were problematic: how was a community so large and divided as that of the Muslims of India supposed to migrate?

The other option was to fight the British. However, this was also problematic because the Muslim community lacked a solid geographical base. Muslims were spread out all over the sub-continent, and with the exception of the extreme northwest (today parts of Pakistan) there was no obvious area of Muslim majority or, as in the case of parts of Bengal (today Bangledesh), this geographic concentration was not militarily defensible.[24] Sayyid Ahmad Shahid and his group decided to try to carve out a region in the northwest which they could use as a base for *jihad*. But another very powerful group, the Sikhs, also had claim on that territory, and in 1831 they fought Sayyid Ahmad, and defeated his group,

---

[22] Mumtaz Husain Pathan, "Sufi Shah 'Inayat Shahid of Sind."

[23] See Mohiuddin Ahmad, *Saiyid Ahmad Shahid: His Life and Mission*, pp. 113–21, 395–96; also, A. S. Buzmee, "Sayyid Ahmad Shahid in the Light of his Letters"; and Freeland Abbott, "The *Jihad* of Sayyid Ahmad Shahid."

[24] In frustration some Muslims did use suicide, see Stephen Dale, "Religious Suicide in Islamic Asia: Anticolonial Terrorism in India, Indonesia and the Philippines," at pp. 48, 54.

making him a martyr. His last stand at Balakot (today in northern Pakistan) was one of personal bravery. He is said to have led a charge against the Sikhs across a valley, and suffered multiple wounds from hand-to-hand combat.[25] Sayyid Ahmad Shahid's death was a disaster for his cause; he had been the charismatic leader of these *mujahidin* and scholars from all over the Indian sub-continent. Not for another twenty-five years until the "Indian Mutiny" of 1857 were the Muslims able to raise such a serious movement to fight the British domination of India. It is obvious that only a small fraction of the saints and martyrs of Muslim India – with all of their tangled legends and cults – can be covered here. Yet these figures were extremely significant for their role in localizing Islam, in some cases melding it with Hinduism, creating the unique flavor of Indian Islam that continues to this day. With all of these Sufi saints, however, it is necessary to remember that the conversion of India to Islam was only partial, and that to some extent the syncretism produced by this cultural fusion hindered the conversion process as well as facilitating it. But this was not the case in other places in the Muslim world.

Turkish martyrs in Central Asia, Anatolia and Southeast Europe

Almost at the same time as Mahmud of Ghazna was raiding down into the plains of India, the Turkish peoples were beginning their great trek from the wide spaces of Central Asia through the fertile settled areas of eastern and central Persia to the mountainous area of Kurdistan before finally debouching out onto the broad central plains of Anatolia. Only after defeating the Christian Byzantines at the Battle of Manzikert in 1071 did this way become clear for them, and the process begin by which the region of Anatolia – Greek-speaking and Christian for almost 1,000 years prior to that time – became Muslim. However, the Turks, as they entered the Muslim world at the beginning of the eleventh century, were already Muslims. Unlike the similarly nomadic Mongols, whose invasions of the eastern Muslim world 200 years after that time laid waste to the civilization of the region, the Turks came supporting Islam, especially Sunni Islam. The mini-states that the Turks established in Anatolia, especially the Sultanate of Rum, that is centered on what is today central Turkey, were centers of Islamic culture. It was to this region, for example, that Jalal al-Din al-Rumi came, fleeing the Mongol invasions. Other equally great Sufi mystics were attracted by the Turks, and willingly settled in Anatolia during the thirteenth through the fifteenth centuries.

With the collapse of the Byzantine state during the fourteenth century, the small frontier warrior group of the Ottomans established itself as a major power. Conquering first Byzantine territory along the Aegean Sea and then through the

[25] Ahmad, *Saiyid Ahmad Shahid*, pp. 282–83.

Balkans, and then finally Constantinople in 1453, the Ottoman state expanded rapidly over all Anatolia, and then ultimately over most of the eastern Mediterranean basin by the end of the sixteenth century. This rapid conquest left large numbers of non-Muslims under the rule of the Ottomans. At the same time as the conquest of the Byzantine Empire was taking place and the formation of the Ottoman state was being achieved, the large-scale conversion of Anatolia to Islam was taking place. (However, this fact does not mean that there were not always large populations of Christians, both Greek-speaking and Armenian-speaking, in Anatolia until they were either massacred or exchanged in the early twentieth century.) As one might expect, this conversion was effected by Sufi holy men, some of them martyrs.

The major Turkish martyred figure was that of Baba Ilyas, who lived in the early part of the thirteenth century (prior to 1240) in Anatolia. Baba Ilyas was said to have been a preacher, and to have made rather exaggerated claims about his abilities:

> In the Seljuq of Rum during this year was a Turkman called al-Baba [Ilyas], who claimed prophecy, and about whom people said: "There is no god but Allah and al-Baba is the friend [*wali*] of God." A great many people gathered to him, and the ruler of the Rum sent an army against him, and approximately 4,000 were killed, among them this Baba.[26]

According to the Turkish hagiographical book *Menakib ul-kudsiyye* (composed approximately 1358–59), Baba Ilyas' disciple, Baba Ishaq, rose in revolt against the Sultans of Rum, and was decisively defeated. After this debacle, Baba Ilyas (who had not accompanied Baba Ishaq to war and had actively discouraged him from rebelling) mounted a white horse and ascended up into the heavens.[27] Other rumors indicated that he had ascended to obtain the support of angels for his cause, although precisely what this cause was is unclear. The movement of Baba Ilyas and Baba Ishaq probably would not be that important (other than their proselytizing activities) were it not for the fact that one of their disciples was Haji Bektash, the founder of the Bektashi Sufi order.[28] But overall, the role of martyrs (as opposed to Sufi holy men) within Turkish history does not appear to have been that great. This was equally true across the Mediterranean Sea, where Spanish Islam was coming to an end as Baba Ilyas ascended into heaven.

---

[26] Ibn Taghribirdi, *al-Nujum*, vi, p. 339; also Ibn al-Jawzi, *Mira'at al-zaman*, viii, p. 733; al-Maqrizi, *Suluk*, i, p. 307; and the sources listed in Ahmad Karamustafa, "Early Sufism in Eastern Anatolia," i, 179–83 (curiously, Karamustafa does not seem to be aware of the Arabic sources).

[27] Elvan Celebi, *Menakibu'l kudsiyye fi menasibi'l unsiyye*, pp. 44–60, and especially p. 65 (thanks to Betul Cavdar for helping me understand these sections).

[28] John Birdge, *The Bektashi Order of Dervishes*, p. 45; and note the connection between the martyrology of Jalal al-Din al-Rumi and that of both Baba Ishaq and Haji Bektash in O'Kane (trans.), *The Feats of the Knowers of God*, pp. 263–64, where the example of the story of Majnun and Layla (see Chapter 6) is adduced (at p. 264).

The last Spanish Muslims

In general, since the Meccan period of Islam until the last century there have been comparatively few examples of Muslims being persecuted for their faith by an alien or hostile regime. One example of a lack of tolerance is to be found when the Spanish rulers Ferdinand II of Aragon (1479–1516) and Isabel I of Castile (1474–1504) conquered the last Muslim enclave of Granada on the Iberian peninsula in 1492. Ferdinand and Isabel inherited a very large Muslim minority population that included not only the region of Granada, but large Muslim populations in both of their kingdoms as a result of the some 700-year Muslim presence on the peninsula.[29] In general, the policy of previous Christian conquerors with regard to Muslims had been to give them some type of agreement with which they could continue to live their lives, or to encourage them to emigrate to Muslim territory. Large numbers of them did take this latter alternative, which meant that by the time the two Catholic monarchs conquered this last bastion of Muslim rule on the peninsula, they had a substantial minority of Muslims under their control with no place – other than North Africa – to go.

The story of the fall of the city of Granada is not accompanied in the sources by large numbers of martyr narratives,[30] although the fighting was very fierce. Each Muslim fortress resisted the Christian advance bitterly, and Granada was no exception. Afterwards, however, as the Christianization of the region of Granada proceeded, the Muslims made a number of final stands, especially during the period of 1498–99. Some of the villages around the city fought to the bitter end, after the conquest of Granada, but no personal stories are told of these fights, nor are the dead called martyrs.[31]

Gradually during the sixteenth century the policy of the Spanish government towards the minority of Muslims, the Mudejars, and the Muslim converts to Christianity, the Moriscos (who were widely suspected of being crypto-Muslims),[32] became harsher and harsher. This harshness was not only towards the Muslims (then converts) of Granada, but towards those Muslims that had been settled for centuries in the territories of Castile and Aragon. Large communities of Muslims, perhaps up to 5 percent of the total population of the two kingdoms, still lived under Christian rule at this time.[33] After the revolt of the Granadans there were a series of forced conversions in 1500 and 1566–71 (after

---

[29] See Joseph O'Callaghan, "The Mudejars of Castile and Portugal in the Twelfth and Thirteenth Centuries"; and especially Jose Hinojosa Montalvo, *Los Mudéjares: La voz del Islam en la España cristiana.*

[30] Occasionally in the *Akhir ayyam Gharanata: Nubdhat al-'asr fi akhbar muluk Bani Nasr*, the phrase *ustushhida* (to become a martyr) is used, e.g., p. 102.

[31] Ibid., 110.

[32] L. P. Harvey, "Crypto-Islam in 16th Century Spain"; and A. G. Chejne, *Islam and the West: The Moriscos*, pp. 1–17.

[33] L. P. Harvey, *Muslims in Spain 1500–1614*, pp. 12–13.

another revolt in Granada) and then a final explusion of Moriscos in 1609–14. It is surprising, however, that there are no prominent martyrs during this period. Although the Granadan villages fought the Castilian troops to the bitter end in 1498–99, there are no records of martyrdoms, nor is the revolt even called a *jihad* in the Arabic sources. Moreover, when the final explusion orders came 100 years later, the crypto-Muslims, the Moriscos, left without fighting, and without the creation of martyrs for their cause.

It is interesting to compare the responses of the crypto-Muslims during this period to those of the Christians under the early Muslim rule. During the period 850–59 Christian monks voluntarily sought martyrdom in the capital of Cordoba in order to highlight the differences between Christianity and Islam, to shore up the weakening boundaries between the two religions and to forestall conversions. This they accomplished by publicly insulting the Prophet Muhammad, an act which they knew would bring the death penalty. Some fifty monks and lay Christians took part in this action, which proved to be effective for the goals for which it was intended, and after the short period of seven years the movement ceased.[34] However, there is nothing similar for the Muslims of Spain, no galvanizing action to rally the believers to stand firm. Probably the reason for this lies in the close identification of martyrdom with fighting in Islam, that left few practical examples as to how martyrdom in such circumstances could be best utilized or whether it should even be carried out. As Harvey notes, the crypto-Muslim community after the fall of the kingdom of Granada was a depressed community, without any obvious leadership (unlike the Christian community during the ninth century), and perhaps could not summon up the will for martyrdom. For whatever reason, they left Spain peacefully when expelled in 1609–14.

West Africa

As Islam was gradually being extirpated in Spain by the Christian reconquest of the peninsula, further to the south it was advancing through the coastlands of West Africa, the Sahel region (today Mali and northern Ghana) and the Sudanic central part of West Africa (today Niger, northern Nigeria and Chad). The process by which this was accomplished was a combination of the two forms of missionization detailed above: Sufi holy men and women converted large numbers of pagan black Africans in all of these regions, but there was also the significant role of the *jihad* starting in the seventeenth and eighteenth centuries, and continuing until colonial conquest in the late nineteenth century.

---

[34] Edward Colbert, *The Martyrs of Cordoba 850–59: A Study of the Sources*, Chapters 9–11, 14; and see also James Waltz, "The Significance of the Voluntary Martyrs of Ninth-Century Cordoba"; for a translation, see Donald Atwater, *Martyrs*, pp. 86–88.

This process, however, was not monochromatic. It involved the establishment of Islamic centers of learning throughout Africa, but mainly during the pre-colonial period focusing on western Africa and the coastlands of East Africa. Islam spread together with traders, nomads, slavers and Sufi holy men.

For a paradigmatic black Muslim martyr, many Africans look to Bilal, the Ethiopian slave who suffered for his faith in Islam during the Meccan period of the Prophet Muhammad's ministry, and was later the first muezzin (Chapter 2). However, the first Muslim martyr associated with Africa itself is usually said to have been the early conqueror ʿUqba b. Nafiʿ al-Fihri, who, according to the legends, conquered all the way from the region of present-day Tunisia to Morocco, and reached the Atlantic Ocean. He was said to have been killed in 682 by the Berber tribes he had partially subdued. After marching all the way to the Atlantic, one of the Berber leaders followed him, attacked his army and killed him in the Sus Mountains (today northern Morocco) at Tahuda. Later accounts have him shouting out that he wanted martyrdom as he was fighting, although as all of his men were slain with him, it is difficult to know how this piece of information came to be known. Before leaving for North Africa, as a premonition of his upcoming martyrdom, he was supposedly told by one of the Muslim leaders: "O ʿUqba, maybe you will be one of the army that will enter paradise on their mounts" because of the fact that he would be killed fighting. Many other traditions support the idea that he desired martyrdom.[35] ʿUqba was, and continues to be, venerated throughout North Africa as a martyr and as the first major Muslim figure to be martyred in the region, and a number of tribes that would become important during later times claimed descent from him (including the Fulani).

After the death of ʿUqba b. Nafiʿ the Berber tribes converted in their entirety, but embraced Kharijism rather than a more normative form of Islam. Gradually, though, over a period of centuries through the great revivalist movements of the Almoravids (al-murabitun, 1091–1145)[36] and the Almohads (al-muwahhidun, 1171–1212) Islam began to spread further to the south.[37] As it did, great kingdoms such as Mali (ca. thirteenth–fifteenth cen.) and Songhay (1438–1591) were founded, mostly along the upper regions of the Niger River (present-day Mali and Niger). These kingdoms became rich on the trade in slaves, gold and salt that reached across the Sahara Desert. Many of the rulers of these two

---

[35] Ibn ʿAbd al-Hakam, *Futuh Ifriqiya wa-l-Andalus*, pp. 59–61; other accounts in Ibn ʿIdhari, *al-Bayan al-mughrib fi akhbar al-Andalus wa-l-Maghrib*, i, pp. 28–32; and al-Tamimi, *Mihan*, pp. 276–81.

[36] For the martyrdom account of their Mahdi, ʿAbdallah b. Yasin al-Gazuli (slain in battle 1059), see N. Levtzion and J. F. P. Hopkins (eds), *Corpus of Early Arabic Sources for West African History*, p. 244 (citing Ibn Abi Zarʿ, *Kitab anis al-mutrib bi-rawd al-qirtas fi akhbar muluk al-maghrib wa-taʾrikh madinat Fas*).

[37] Sometimes with martyrs, such as Sidi ʿUmar al-Shaykh, who was murdered in 1552; see H. T. Norris, *The Arab Conquest of the Western Sahara*, p. 241.

kingdoms waged *jihads* against the pagan blacks to the south of their territories, and converted them to Islam or enslaved them (and sometimes both).

However, the wealth of these kingdoms attracted the attention of the Moroccan state and in 1591 the latter invaded the region and conquered Timbuktu, the capital of Mali, and many other adjacent regions. This conquest spelt the end of the glorious period of Timbuktu, and its scholars, who until that point had led the region in learning and spread Islam through West Africa, bore the brunt of the attack. Al-Sa'di's account of the butchery of the scholars of Timbuktu gives us a picture of martyrdom as it occurred in West Africa. These murders happened within the context of resistance against the Moroccan occupation. In 1592, one of the leaders of Timbuktu, Qadi 'Umar, had sent his assistant to tell another leader, 'Umar al-Sharif, to avoid attacking the Moroccans. However, the assistant changed the message to say that Qadi 'Umar had proclaimed a *jihad* against the invaders, and so the people rose up, but were defeated decisively. Naturally, the Moroccans were vindictive against the leaders of this revolt:

Pasha Mahmud b. Zarqun . . . sent word to *Qa'id* al-Mustafa to execute the two *sharif*s, Shaykh Muhammad b. 'Uthman and Baba b. 'Umar, grandsons through daughters of the *sharif* Ahmad al-Saqalli. This he did in the market place in the most brutal fashion. The execution was carried out . . . cutting off their hands and feet with an axe and leaving them there to die in agony – to God we belong and to Him we shall return! . . . The two men were from the House of the Prophet – and they died as martyrs. The executioner's hands became paralyzed until the day of his death. The Virgin [Fatima] will be their [the Moroccans'] adversary on the morrow before God.[38]

This slaughter, however, was just the beginning. When the Pasha Mahmud returned to Timbuktu a year later, he arrested the scholars of the city, and during the course of their arrest there was an altercation during which fourteen of the prominent scholars were killed.[39] The rest were interned in Morocco.

Although this, to a large extent, spelt the end of the heyday of Timbuktu, Islam continued to spread throughout the region, especially with the agency of the nomadic Fulani people (today spreading from Senegal through Mali and Niger to Nigeria, Cameroon and Chad). This group was closely associated with the development of Islamic learning despite their nomadic condition and had developed a high level of normative Islam. This type of normative Islam, however, was not in accord with the syncretistic Islam that was already present among the more sedentary Hausa peoples who dominated the area through fourteen small kingdoms. By the end of the eighteenth century the semi-nomadic Fulani had produced a reformer who would change the religious landscape of the region forever.[40]

---

[38] John Hunwick (trans.), *Timbuktu and the Songhay Empire: al-Sa'di's* Ta'rikh al-Sudan *down to 1613 and other Contemporary Documents*, p. 216.

[39] Ibid., p. 220.

[40] Interestingly, the Fulani claimed to be the descendents of 'Uqba b. Nafi', cf., Hiskett, *The Sword of Truth*, p. 15; and Muhammad Bello, *Infaq al-maysur fi ta'rikh bilad al-Takrur*, p. 107.

This reformer was Shehu 'Uthman Dan Fodio (d. 1817), who, after years of careful preparation starting in the early 1790s, led the Fulani *jihad* of 1804–12 (although most of the fighting was completed by 1808) and founded the network of emirates that still characterize northern Nigeria.[41] Similar to the method of the Prophet Muhammad, Dan Fodio initially preached and gained status as a holy man within the Fulani (but also to some extent the Hausa) community. He regularly summoned the Hausa rulers to repent of their syncretism, and exerted a type of moral influence over the entire region. Thus, when he made his famous *hijra* to Gudu in Febuary 1804, Dan Fodio prepared for a *jihad* after having received a vision from the long-dead Sufi 'Abd al-Qadir al-Jilani. This *jihad* was partially successful. During the course of the campaigns, the Hausa leaders were decisively defeated, and compelled to abandon their free and easy way of interpreting Islam. Henceforth, the region of northern Nigeria and southern Niger was a bastion of normative Islam that continued until the British conquest of the region in 1905. However, 'Uthman Dan Fodio failed to unite all of the Muslims, most significantly the Muslim region of Borno (today northeastern Nigeria and part of Chad), and did not cause Islam to spread very far beyond the boundaries already achieved prior to the *jihad*.

Although 'Uthman Dan Fodio left voluminous Arabic writings behind – John Hunwick in his catalogue of those extant lists 103 authenticated and a number of unverified ones,[42] in addition to his writings in Fulfulde (the language of the Fulani people) – he nowhere addresses the issue of martyrdom. Even his great compendium on the subject of *jihad*, *Bayan wujub al-hijra 'ala al-'ibad* (*Clarification of the Necessity of Hijra for the Servants of God*), unlike other classical or pre-modern *jihad* collections, does not list the rewards of martyrdom. This may have been because of the fact that the Shehu did not take part in the fighting personally, and while concentrating upon the theoretical basis for *jihad*, he ignored the practical exhortations that usually accompany warfare.[43] From his son (and successor) Muhammad Bello's (d. 1837) account, we know of frequent martyrdoms in the Fulani *jihad*, and a number of the poems written during this time commemorate the martyrs.

In general, Bello merely lists the prominent scholars or groups of Muslims who are martyred and does not give many details.[44] Only in one case does he

---

[41] Fundamental works on the life of 'Uthman Dan Fodio include Murray Last, *The Sokoto Caliphate*, pp. 3–60; Ismail Balogun, *The Life and Works of 'Uthman Dan Fodio*; and Hiskett, *The Sword of Truth*.

[42] John Hunwick, *Arabic Literature of Africa*, ii, *The Writings of Central Sudanic Africa*, pp. 52–80.

[43] But his daughter, Nana Asma'u (d. 1864), did enumerate the pleasures of paradise: see Jean Boyd and Beverly Mack (trans.), *Collected Works of Nana Asma'u, Daughter of Usman 'dan Fodiyo (1793–1864)*, pp. 67, 185–86, 258–59, 354.

[44] Muhammad Bello, *Infaq al-maysur*, e.g., pp. 119, 138; similarly 'Abdallah Dan Fodio (brother of 'Uthman Dan Fodio) in his *Tazyin al-waraqat* merely lists off martyrs as well (e.g., p. 60). Other writers like Qadi Muhammad b. Salih, *Taqyid al-akhbar*, trans. Ibrahim Ado-Kurawa, *The Jihad in Kano*, pp. 29, 31 give more details about martyrs.

mention casually that one Ya'qub al-Mujahid was martyred in battle; other than this, he does not give specific details of the martyrdoms. However, occasionally he gives us some poetry commemorating the martyrs, giving the connection to the first Muslim martyr in Africa:

> ... 'Uqba, the grandfather of the Fulani ... O community of Islam! Find and fight, and do not give up for patience is the starting point for victory! Your killed are in paradise, eternally, and the one of you who returns, does so with glory and wealth.[45]

And also,

> From the [battle] Day of Alus, when the mill of war turned; they attained, and we attained, and we bore the glorious deeds;
> Their secret was the martyrdom they gave us – this death that preserves our exploits.
> Whoever they killed, they caused to reach his goal, blessed is he, with grace and excellent musk.
> Spirit, basil, and eternal paradise, together with inheritance of the free women houris.
> Whoever inhabits paradise will be dressed all in silk, brocade and bright gold.[46]

In this still largely oral culture – despite the high level of literacy and culture in the immediate circle of the Dan Fodios and their family – poetry was the best way to communicate the spirit of *jihad*. This message went out far and wide all over the region of northern Nigeria and continues to influence the development of Islam there today.

East Africa

The course of the development of Islam in East Africa was somewhat different. For the most part, there was no early penetration of East Africa by a Muslim conqueror. Two Christian kingdoms, those of Nubia and Ethiopia, dominated, and it took centuries before they had to face serious Islamic penetration of the region. In general, Islam came first to the coastal regions, especially those directly across the Red Sea from the Yemen, and was conveyed to the inhabitants of the Horn of Africa in a peaceful manner. Further to the south, the East African coastline was dotted with trading posts and small towns, usually located on islands, which served as the basis for the spread of Islam through the medium of merchants and sometimes slave traders.[47] By the sixteenth century,

[45] Bello, *Infaq al-maysur*, p. 107; and see also pp. 108–09 for a similar poem.   [46] Ibid., p. 142.
[47] Arthur Strong, "The History of Kilwa. Edited from an Arabic MS," p. 414 details some early conflicts, although those killed in them are not called martyrs; but in Charles Guillain, *Documents sur l'histoire, le géographie, et le commerce de l'Afrique Orientale*, i, pp. 268–69 one ruler killed by the non-Muslim African population is called a martyr.

however, the Islamic civilization in what today is the Ethiopian lowlands, centered upon the city of Harar, was at its peak. In 1529 the great Muslim conqueror, Ahmad Grañ, appeared and initiated a series of conquests called the Ethiopian *jihad*. Fighting a *jihad* in this difficult terrain, it is not surprising that there are a number of prominent and colorful martyrdoms contained within the historical source for these conquests, the *Futuh al-Habasha (Ethiopian Conquests)* of Shihab al-Din ʿArabfaqih. The conquest of the Ethiopian highlands proceeded in 1529–30, after a false start, and Ahmad Grañ quickly defeated a number of the Ethiopian commanders. By 1541 he controlled much of the highlands, and had forcibly converted much of the Christian population to Islam.

The first major martyrdom in the book is of the Zaharbey ʿUthman, who took on one of the Ethiopians patriarchs in single combat in 1531. After ʿUthman pierced him with his spear the point broke inside his opponent, and so ʿUthman took the haft of the spear and proceeded to hit the patriarch with it. Finally ʿUthman managed to wrestle the patriarch off his horse, to the ground, where he finished him off. But then, after the battle was won by the Muslims, largely due to the heroism of Zaharbey ʿUthman, he was killed by an arrow shot by one of the Ethiopians concealed in a tree, while the spoils were being divided up.[48] In a later battle, another prominent commander, Juwayta Allah Majann, was martyred. He had exhorted his troops prior to the fight saying: "I only came for *jihad* and martyrdom from the lands of the Muslims! The Imam [Ahmad Grañ] gave me his standard; am I to retreat without fighting? If you want, flee, but if you want paradise and the houris, then follow me and I will be the first of you, and enter the midst of them!"[49] He killed six of the Ethiopians, before he, like Zaharbey ʿUthman above, had his spear broken in the armor of one of his opponents, who was then killed by a sword-thrust to the stomach. The *Futuh al-Habasha* records other martyrdoms such as that of the Imam's brother, Zaharbey Muhammad, who fell to a poisoned arrow, and the Wazir ʿAdli Kabir Muhammad, who was attacked from behind by an Ethiopian.[50]

However, not all of the martyrdoms recorded from this *jihad* were of Muslims. For example, when the Muslims arrived in the highlands of Tigre, they started discovering the wonderous rock-cut churches that still astound the visitor. The Imam Ahmad kindled a huge fire there, and ordered the monks from one of these churches to enter into it. One of the female anchorites willingly entered the fire and was burned to death, after which the place was destroyed.[51] But we are not given a picture of the martyrdom of Ahmad Grañ

---

[48] ʿArabfaqih, *Tuhfat al-zaman aw Futuh al-Habasha*, pp. 254–55; for chronology and a study see Richard Pankhurst, *The Ethiopian Borderlands: Essays in Regional History from Ancient Times until the 18th Century*, Chapters 19–20.
[49] Ibid., p. 283.   [50] Ibid., pp. 319–20, 334–35.   [51] Ibid., p. 318.

himself, which happened in 1543, after the Portuguese had intervened in the conflict.[52]

Further to the north, along the Nile valley, the spread of Islam had been facilitated by the collapse of the ancient Nubian Christian kingdom in the middle of the 1600s, and the appearance of nominal Muslim dynasties during that time. Islam as usual was spread through the Sufi holy men that are recorded in Muhammad Dayfullah's (d. 1809) *Kitab al-tabaqat* (*Book of Classes*). This volume, which preserves some of the frontier spirit of these early holy men, contains a great many stories of their deaths. Dayfullah does not use the word martyrdom to describe these events, but many of them die in ways consistent with classical martyrdoms, since most of the Sufis that he describes are holy men preaching Islam in a fairly syncretistic or pagan society, and die during the course of their preaching. Some were killed by the people to whom they preach, others died of various diseases (smallpox or plague for example), one was eaten by a lion and several were attacked by tribesmen or robbers. One Sufi who was trying to train a crocodile, became annoyed at its unresponsiveness, tried to shoot at it and was killed when his gun backfired.[53] It is odd that the word "martyr" is not used in the book at all, but it is possible that Dayfullah was not familiar with the types of Islamic martyrology because of the low state of Islamic learning in the area of the Sudan during his time. Most of the classical themes that we have noted thus far appear in this record, such as prognosticatory visions of future death,[54] usually highlighting the fact that a given holy man was killed by non-Muslims or during the course of ministry, and the fact that most of them are said to have had cults surrounding them after their time. Other holy men described from a later time sometimes brought about their own deaths by challenging the rulers or various local groups of outlaws. Examples of such holy men are Shaykh Rajab and al-Hajj Mahmud from the region of Khartoum in approximately 1786–87, who fought and were killed as part of a Sufi band of holy men, and subsequently became known as saints.[55]

By the middle of the nineteenth century, however, the newly aggressive Egyptian state, under the leadership of Muhammad 'Ali (1805–41), had begun to push down the Nile valley to Khartoum, and was also conquering the region bordering upon the Red Sea down to the Horn of Africa. These conquests were facilitated to some extent by the European colonial powers, attempting to both stamp out the slave trade in this region and extend their own influence. For the next half century the Egyptians continued to rule the area of the Sudan, periodically making an effort to fight the slave trade. Because the Egyptian governors were

---

[52] See Philip Caraman, *The Lost Empire: The Story of the Jesuits in Ethiopia 1555–1634*, pp. 8–16 and ff.
[53] Muhammad Dayfullah, *Kitab al-tabaqat*, pp. 29, 34–35, 46, 47f, 51–53, 54, 84, 100, 128.
[54] E.g., ibid., p. 89 (other examples of dreams: pp. 10, 38, 74, 87, 89, 105–07, 127).
[55] P. M. Holt (trans.), *Sudan of the Three Niles: The Funj Chronicle 910–1288/1504–1871*, pp. 26–29.

often part of the problem, gradually during the 1870s the Egyptian government (again under the influence of Britain and France) replaced these governors with those of European extraction (although some had converted to Islam). These latter governors were considerably more energetic in stamping out the slave trade, and created a huge amount of resentment among the Sudanese as well as among the resident Egyptians.

When Muhammad Ahmad al-Mahdi appeared in 1881, making the claim that he was the expected Mahdi who was to usher in the messianic age, and deliver the people from the injustice of the foreigners and Turks (remembering that many of the Egyptian elite were in fact Turkish), this sense of resentment fueled the success of his movement. Al-Mahdi went from victory to victory over the following three years, conquering outposts and towns, until in 1885 he conquered Khartoum. Under mysterious circumstances he died a short time later, and was succeeded by his Khalifa (successor), 'Abdallah, who continued ruling the Mahdist state for the next thirteen years until the British conquered it in 1898. Today the Mahdists continue to have a great deal of political and religious power in the Sudan through the descendents of Muhammad Ahmad al-Mahdi.

The Mahdi established martyrdom as an important part of his movement. From his very first battles he made a special practice of burying the martyrs of his armies in their clothes on the battlefields, just as according to tradition the Prophet Muhammad used to do.

The Mahdi ordered that the martyrs be buried where the battle had taken place with all their clothes, save their weapons. They were buried in the caves of the Mahdi's mosque. As for the dead of the enemy, they were left in the open, prey for the birds and the wild animals.[56]

Large numbers of martyrs are listed specifically in the *Life of the Mahdi*.[57] Since in general, the Mahdi tried as much as possible to emulate the example of the Prophet Muhammad, frequently his battles are compared to those of the Prophet. If they were successes, then they were like the Battle of Badr, if they were not, then like the Battle of Uhud. His followers were said to have been eager to seek out martyrdom, and expressed grief when denied the opportunity, or when a battle went by without their attaining this goal.[58]

The Mahdi's personal behavior confirms this type of martyrdom cult. Two of his brothers are said to have attained martyrdom, and one of his brothers, Muhammad, for example, is called "the martyr Muhammad" long before the time he actually died as if to emphasize this high spiritual rank.[59] When his

[56] Haim Shaked (trans.), *Life of the Sudanese Mahdi* (trans. of Isma'il b. 'Abd al-Qadir, *Kitab sa'adat al-mustahdi bi-sirat al-Imam al-Mahdi*), p. 83.
[57] Shaked, *Life*, e.g., pp. 81, 98, 113, 114, 126, 131, 134, 135, 138–39, 140, 172–73, 184, 186.
[58] Ibid., pp. 96, 110 (when several of the Mahdi's emissaries were put to death by the Turks).
[59] Ibid., p. 100–01, 114.

followers died, the Mahdi was said to have rejoiced at their martyrdom.[60] However, in the end, the Mahdi did not die as a martyr himself, despite having been wounded a number of times (according to the accounts). The manner of his death is unclear, and it is interesting that apparently none of his followers tried to make him into a martyr (perhaps following the example of the Prophet Muhammad himself, who also died a natural death). The later martyrology of the Mahdist state is not as detailed, although of course the Mahdi's successor, the Khalifa 'Abdallah continued to fight his many enemies until he himself perished in 1898.

African Muslim martyrdoms are mostly contained within historical accounts, and like the Indian ones demonstrate a mixture of fighters and ascetic scholars and holy men, all of whom came to be lumped together within the historical memory as martyrs. For the most part, they continue to be revered to this day as part of cults surrounding their *baraka*, or blessing. It is interesting to note that very few of the primary leaders of these various movements, however, attained martyrdom. Despite 'Uthman Dan Fodio's initiation of the Fulani *jihad* neither he nor any of his family actually died as martyrs. Nor were the Mahdi or other prominent leaders of various revivalist-*jihadist* movements during the nineteenth century commemorated in this manner. In general, these people inspired martyrdom and frequently extolled it, but did not serve as personal examples.

Indonesia and Malaysia

Martyrdom of holy men in Indonesia–Malaysia was different from the African experience. In this region we find the cult of martyrs has formed around figures who were significant in the missionization process of the islands of Southeast Asia. Although the process by which the Islamization of the islands that would ultimately become the country of Indonesia is uncertain – perhaps starting as early as the twelfth century, it was much more peaceful than the Islamization of West Africa.[61] By the sixteenth century, when European traders and missionaries began to arrive in the region, the strong Indonesian state of Aceh (on the northern tip of the island of Sumatra) was only one of a number of Muslim states in the region. Like many other areas converted to Islam, the Indonesian–Malay world was heavily influenced by Sufism, most especially by the doctrines of *wahdat al-wujud* (the "unity of being" associated with the great mystic Ibn al-'Arabi, d. 1240). This doctrine, although phrased using Islamic terminology, has close affinities with pantheism, and has been controversial in many places.

[60] Ibid., p. 111.
[61] Cf. al-Attas, *Preliminary Statement on a General Theory of the Islamization of the Malay–Indonesian Archipelago*; and especially Alijah Gordon (ed.), *The Propagation of Islam in Indonesia and Malaysia*, pp. 23–156 .

As scholars from India and especially the Arabian Peninsula began to arrive in Indonesia and to assume high positions within the various Muslim courts during the seventeenth and eighteenth centuries, there was considerable tension between them and the local Sufis because of these semi-pantheistic beliefs.

As will be noted in Chapter 6, there are a large number of Malay and Javanese epics extant, and a striking number of these advocate the doctrine of annihilation after the fashion of al-Hallaj, or tell the dramatic stories of other Muslim martyrs. With this in mind, the sources portray the conflict between foreign-educated Muslim Indonesian–Malay scholars and the local Sufis would be portrayed in the form of martyrdom.[62] This theme is best exemplified in the story of Siti Jenar, who has been tentatively dated to the period of 1490–1500. Siti Jenar is a saint who is traditionally held to have been responsible for the conversion of the region around Mount Merapi on the Indonesian island of Java. The popular story circulated about him (only recorded in the nineteenth century) is that he was in competition with the more orthodox *wali*s and that his teachings were causing people to avoid coming to them.

In addition to this element of competition, Siti Jenar was accused of having Hallajian antinomian leanings. For example, in a (posthumous) poem attributed to him, he says:

> The reason the Law is disregarded is that it is troublesome, and causes continuous work, irresolution, restlessness, one knows not if one can rely upon it.
>
> That Law is to be used (destined) for this world: should one come to death, then it fails.
>
> The most Essential Knowledge is to be unflinching in the contemplation of the Self.
>
> Confirm your conception of it (concentrate on the idea of it), (then) one arrives at the certainty that it is One.
>
> The analysis of the esoteric Knowledge is in the Being, which is perfect Rest.[63]

With this type of attitude towards the Law (the *shariʻa*) it is easy to see why Siti Jenar attracted the dislike of the religious leadership.

After some discussion, according to the story, the *wali*s agreed that Siti Jenar must be summoned to appear before them. If he agreed to stop his teaching, then all would be well, but if not, he must be executed. Emissaries sent to bring him before the assembly of *wali*s were frustrated because after they asked for Siti Jenar, he said to them, "Know, both of you, that Siti Jenar *is* not, at present (only) Allah *is*." Foiled by this statement, they returned empty-handed, where leader of the *wali*s, Sunan Giri, informed them that they must ask for Allah

---

[62] See overall Azyumardi Azra, "Opposition to Sufism in the East Indies in the Seventeenth and Eighteenth Centuries."

[63] D. Rinkes, *Nine Saints of Java*, p. 29 (trans. H. Froger).

(i.e., Siti Jenar had identified himself so closely with God that it was better to ask for Allah). Eventually, Siti Jenar appeared before Sunan Giri, and the latter asked him why he did not perform the Friday service or fulfill the Law. Siti Jenar replied, "There *is* no Friday, and there *is* no *masjid* [mosque], only Allah *is* indeed. Nothing has Existence at present, save He."

After this answer, Sunan Giri ordered one of the others to draw his sword, and asked Siti Jenar what it was. The reply was: "It is Allah, who is to be seen here." Then his head was cut off. His blood flowed red around his body, but then turned to white, while saying the *shahada*: "There is no God, save Allah; Muhammad is the Messenger of Allah." Siti Jenar's body disappeared at that point and he was heard to recite the poem above as well as some other statements of an antinomian nature. All seven of his disciples who had accompanied him chose to be executed as well, and like their master, their bodies disappeared after their deaths (these disciples are not actually the "Nine Saints of Java").[64] Siti Jenar is said to have been the author of prophecies about the coming of the Dutch to Indonesia and the sufferings they would inflict upon the Muslims. Siti Jenar's heresy was partly his antinomian beliefs, but also partly his own success. He spread Islam into places where it had never been before and was not over-concerned by his own adherence to the *shari'a*. This casual attitude towards the law is something that many Sufis, and especially those on the fringes of Islam, shared.

Other Indonesian epics, such as the *Hikayat Malem Dagang* tell the story of the great Acehese ruler Iskandar Muda (d. 1636), who deputed Malem Dagang to fight a heathen ruler named Si-Ujut. Together with his subordinates, Raja Raden and the Panglima Pidie, Malem Dagang brought the heathen to defeat and converted their leaders to Islam. During the course of the final battle, it was said that the Panglima Pidie sought martyrdom. In order to demonstrate this, he took a white cloth, symbolizing the winding clothes of burial, and wore his *shaykh* (respected elder, usually accorded to Sufi Masters) Ja Pakeh's clothing in order to be closely and eternally united with his master after death. Shortly thereafter the Panglima Pidie was shot by Si-Ujut, who thought that he was actually Ja Pakeh. In the end Si-Ujut was captured and executed, and his people converted to Islam.[65]

In general, the number of Sufis and Muslim missionaries over the centuries who have died for their message is rather small. Compared to Christians, Muslims have tended to missionize using syncretistic tactics that did not emphasize the testimonial value of martyrdom to win over a given population. Part of this

---

[64] Ibid., pp. 21–25, also pp. 154–55, 166 (for comparisons with the story of al-Hallaj, see pp. 175–77); and see Achmad Chodjim, *Syekh Siti Jenar*, Chapters 11–12; and on the role of this and other legends in Sufi Indonesia, see Peter Riddell, *Islam and the Malay–Indonesian World*, p. 172f.

[65] Amirul Hadi, *Islam and State in Sumatra: A Study of Seventeenth-Century Aceh*, pp. 194–99 at p. 198.

trend is probably due to the fact that missionization and conversion in Islam has not been (in general) until the present time the result of some group-initiated intensive drive. The overwhelming number of Muslim missionaries throughout history probably did not consider themselves formally to be missionaries, but converted people to Islam through their personal engagement through trade and other social encounters such as education. It is for this reason that regions that have converted to Islam are frequently interwoven with other regions that have not converted in somewhat of a random pattern, especially in Africa, India and Southeast Asia, where the conversion process remains incomplete.

Since there was no organization to "send" Muslim missionaries to a given dangerous location, the missionization remained random and personal. Individual traders or Muslim holy men would come to an area and live, converting some people, while rarely exciting the type of institutional opposition that Christian missionaries did (that created martyrs). In general, Muslims did not make serious attempts to convert peoples that were already possessed of a strong monotheist or semi-monotheist belief system (Christianity, Buddhism) who lived outside the borders of the political control of Islam. Instead, they concentrated upon pagan Africans, Turks and Southeast Asians (Indonesians and Malays), and Hindus. Although Hindus had an arguably high culture, many of these other groups were already predisposed to accept Islam as a result of the fact that they were already attracted to Islam as a culture. From this familiarity it seems that Islam as a faith was not such a huge leap. But then to make the second leap – from syncreticism to normative Islam – was much more difficult, as can be seen from the numerous *jihad*s in West Africa, the martyrdom of Siti Jenar in Indonesia and others.

Ironically, even when discussing Muslim missionization and conversion, many of the martyrs were killed by other Muslims. Missionary martyrdoms, whether as a result of fighting or proclamation, were not so different from other types of martyrdom previously discussed. Knowing the universal love that so many of the Sufis and Sufi orders preached it is not surprising to find them at the forefront of missionization. However, at the same time as this conversion was taking place there were other martyrs of love dying for more mundane reasons.

6   Martyrs of love and epic heroes

Each curling lock of thy luxuriant hair
Breaks into barbed hooks to catch my heart
My broken heart is wounded everywhere
With countless wounds from which the red drops start.   Hafiz[1]

One of the traditions cited by Jalal al-Din al-Suyuti in his book on the circumstances of martyrdom (in Chapter 3) was: "whoever loves passionately (*'ashiqa*),
but exhibits self-control, conceals [it] and dies [as a result] is a martyr."[2] While
one cannot say this tradition has ever acquired canonical status inside Islam
because it is never cited by any of the authoritative collections, it definitely
represents a trend in Muslim martyrology. Stories of the romantic lover, whose
love is pure and passionate yet chaste and denied, and who ultimately dies as
a result of this love, are an extremely popular theme running through much of
the literature of the Muslim world. Many of these stories survived not because
of their mundane character, but because of the possibility that they could be
reinterpreted in a Sufi manner. From the time of the martyrdom of al-Hallaj,
the category of "martyrs of love" (*shuhada' al-mahabba*) had been ambiguous
because of the possibility that these martyrs in their desire for earthly union (usually of a homosexual nature) actually sought union with their divine beloved.
Stories that described their passion for other humans could be allegorically
interpreted in terms of love for God. Given this ambiguity, it is not unusual for
even apparently suggestive or passionate love stories to have several interpretations.[3] For the purposes of analysis, however, two prominent types of non-Sufi
martyrs are included in the category of "martyrs of love." The first is the famous
'Udhri lovers so prominent in the seventh through ninth centuries among the
Bedouin, whose extravagant yet hopeless and chaste variety of love is thematic.[4]

---

[1] From Arthur Arberry, *Fifty Poems of Hafiz*, p. 108 (no. 24).
[2] Al-Suyuti, *Abwab al-sa'ada*, p. 53 (no. 28); see also Ibn Muflih, *Furu'*, i, pp. 537–38; for a
religious critique of this tradition see al-Ghumari, *Dar' al-da'f an hadith man 'ashiqa fa-'affa*.
[3] For example, see al-Sa'di, *Gulistan*, Chapter 5 "Concerning Love and Youth"; also al-Munawi,
Tabaqat al-Sufiyya, iv, p. 507.
[4] The major study on this subject is Lois Giffen, *Theory of Profane Love among the Arabs: The
Development of a Genre*; on pp. 3–50 she discusses the authors, and pp. 99–116 the martyrs of
love. My discussion is indebted to hers.

The second category includes those whose love caused sickness (at least according to the observation of the time) and actually led to death.[5]

The ʿUdhri lovers are by far the more prominent of the two categories. Of all of these couples, probably the Majnun-Layla sequence has had the greatest ramifications for Islamic culture, as this story has achieved popularity in most Muslim societies, although others such as Jamil and Buthayna have also been popular. Strictly speaking there is little martyrdom in ʿUdhri love. Usually the story focuses upon a true romance that for structural reasons cannot be consummated. Either the father of the beloved is unwilling to allow her to marry her lover, who is inappropriate for his daughter for various reasons – mostly low social status or an imbalanced personality – or she is already in a loveless marriage. The lover is not deterred by these impediments and continues to express his love in extravagant ways, sometimes to the beloved's delight, sometimes to her embarrassment. In some stories (such as that of Jamil and Buthayna) friends and relatives generously allow the two lovers to spend some time together (albeit in public), but in most cases there is a bitter hostility between the family/husband of the beloved and the lover. Structural power is almost entirely on the side of the family/husband of the beloved, and the lover is usually an outcast with only poetry to express his hopeless, unconsummated love. ʿUdhri love is always chaste, and even during those few times when the lover and beloved can spend some snatched time together, there is no consummation of their passion. In some ways their love is even beyond the sexual; it has a topical relation to that type of Sufi restrained love for God that led al-Hallaj to make his extravagant declarations about his oneness with the deity. These lovers are so strongly united that even the lack of physical consummation cannot separate them.

The classic story of ʿUdhri love is that of Majnun and Layla.[6] Majnun (crazy, insane) was a name that one Qays (or in alternative versions, Mahdi) took for himself after he fell in love with Layla. There is a considerable amount of controversy surrounding Majnun: concerning his name, his tribal affiliation (which is usually said to have been to Banu ʿAmir, but there are variants) and even how many Majnun(s) there were among his tribe (it is said that several of them were in love with Layla). Whatever the answer to these questions, the cycle of stories concerning Majnun and Layla is cohesive enough that we can speak of what people commonly believed concerning them, even if the actual history of their star-crossed romance is obscured. According to the accounts,

---

[5] Almost all of whom are listed by Mughaltay, *al-Wadih al-mubin fi dhikr man ustushhida min al-muhibbin*.

[6] For interpretations, see Asʿad Khairullah, *Love, Madness and Poetry: An Interpretation of the Majnun Legend*; Andre Miguel, *Deux histories d'amour: de Majnun à Tristan*; biographical material in al-Isfahani, *Aghani*, ii, pp. 3–88; Mughaltay, *Wadih*, pp. 298–312; and Ibn al-Mibrad, *Nuzhat al-musamir fi akhbar majnun Bani ʿAmir*.

Majnun and Layla used to herd lambs together when they were children. As they matured, Majnun became obsessed with her and asked her to marry him. She, however, had turned away from him and rejected him.

This rejection caused him to go insane with love for her,[7] and he began to do irrational things, such as live out in the barren desert, naked, and compose verses about her. Layla's tribe refused any talk of marriage between the two, pointing out Majnun's condition (Layla's feelings in this matter are not revealed), and they received permission from the Umayyad rulers to kill Majnun on sight if he approached her at all. Various solutions to the difficulty were proposed by go-betweens (friendly visitors, Majnun's father, etc.), but they were all rejected. It is difficult to say when Layla's feelings changed but at least at a certain point after this time, when a visitor told her of Majnun's poetry and the fact that he was living with animals and not in human company any more, she described how sad she was and how much she missed him.[8] But by that time her father had married her to another man, and union between Majnun and her was impossible. For a long time Majnun wandered in his madness, and he apparently did not leave the wilderness again. He continually composed poetry about Layla, which according to some of the tales was brought to her by the wild beasts, the birds or even the wind. When Majnun heard of her death, he exclaimed that it was impossible for him to go on living. Later his body was found in a wadi, but it is uncertain exactly how he died.[9]

The story of Majnun and Layla is one of the most popular to be found throughout the Muslim world. Collections of the poetry of Majnun concerning Layla were gathered from a very early stage, and the anecdotal stories about them are legion. From the time of Nizami Ganjavi's (d. 1202–03) epic on Majnun and Layla, as well as Jami's (d. 1492) retelling (and others detailed below), the story passed into Persian and from there into a number of Turkish languages as well as Urdu. Rumi (Chapter 4) in his *Masnawi* used the story of Majnun and Layla to express the totality of the lover's care for his beloved. Even lost in his love-sickness and insanity, Majnun, when a physician comes to bleed him (cupping blood from his arm), protests that:

But my whole being is full of Layla: this shell is filled with the qualities of that Pearl.
I am afraid, O cupper, lest if you let my blood you suddenly inflict a wound with your lancet upon Layla.
The (man of) reason whose heart is enlightened knows that between Layla and me there is no difference.[10]

Despite the fact that people told him Layla was not that beautiful, and there were lots of women with whom he could fall in love,

[7] He was far from being alone in insanity caused by love; see Ibn Qayyim al-Jawziyya, *Akhbar al-nisa'*, pp. 39–86 for other examples.
[8] Mughultay, *Wadih*, p. 306.   [9] Al-Isfahani, *Aghani*, ii, pp. 80–82.
[10] Nicholson, *Mathnawi*, v, p. 121; Rumi, *Mathnavi* (text), pp. 777–79, at 778.

He replied: The (outward) form is a pot, and beauty is the wine. God is giving me wine from her form.

He gave you vinegar from her pot, lest love of her should pull you by the ears.[11]

In Sufi adaptations of popular romances such as that of Majnun and Layla it is possible to see the multiple facets of the basic ʿUdhri love story. Union of the lovers when denied by circumstances is easily translatable into an allegory for the denied union with the divine that has to be put off until the time of death. Or, in certain cases, such as those of al-Hallaj and ʿAyn al-Qudat, this union could be speeded up by the efforts of the lover. This deeper allegorical layer of meaning has certainly contributed to the wide popularity of the Majnun-Layla cycle throughout the Muslim world.

Another equally important ʿUdhri narrative is that of Jamil and Buthayna, whose story took place, according to the sources, during the early Umayyad period prior to 701 (when Jamil is said to have died).[12] Jamil was an accomplished poet, a friend of the romantic poet Kuthayyir ʿAzza (himself known for his love for ʿAzza), and a member of the tribe of ʿUdhra, who lived in Medina. He had loved Buthayna since she was small, asked for her hand when she reached maturity, and was refused. However, Jamil did not accept this rejection, and he began to compose poetry about her, at first secretly, and later openly, which aroused the ire of her relatives and ultimately of the governor of Medina and other officials. She and Jamil would meet secretly, usually as the result of intermediaries facilitating their trysts, and sit together while Jamil recited poetry for her. It is difficult to say whether Buthayna reciprocated his feelings because while occasionally she would meet with him, at other times she avoided him or said negative things about him. Despite this, Jamil's love for her never waned, even though he never received more from her than being able to hold her hand once and put it on his heart. According to the accounts of his death, he fell into a swoon at the recollection of this event and died from it.[13]

While the ʿUdhri love is always chaste, it does not always lead inexorably to death. Majnun and Jamil both lived on past the point at which they were rejected by their beloved, nursing their sorrows and reciting their poetry, although both are given "martyrs'" deaths in the end and are listed as such in the literature. But there are many lovers whose love went unconsummated either because it was unreciprocated or because of misunderstandings between them, and whose subsequent death is portrayed as inevitable. The source of these martyrdoms is the malady of lovesickness, which unlike in contemporary usage, really was a sickness (at least according to the historical and medical sources).[14] When

---

[11] Nicholson, *Mathnawi*, v, p. 198; *Mathnavi*, p. 836.

[12] Biographical sources from al-Isfahani, *Aghani*, viii, pp. 95–164; al-Kharaʾiti, *Iʿtilal al-qulub*, pp. 101, 242, 245, 262; Mughaltay, *Wadih*, pp. 158–68; and al-Antaki, *Tazyin al-aswaq*, ii, pp. 111–25.

[13] Mughaltay, *Wadih*, p. 162; other accounts in al-Isfahani, *Aghani*, viii, pp. 162–63.

[14] See Hans Biesterfeldt and Dimitri Gutas, "The Malady of Love."

a lover first beheld his beloved the former was invariably stricken to the core with desire that when unmet had physical effects. This desire was so deep that it would literally cause sickness and ultimately death. Once stricken the lover becomes helpless, oftentimes listless and confined to bed, while his friends (hopefully) try to persuade the beloved to accept the lover and consummate the passion, which would presumably put an end to the sickness.

But sometimes the passion was too great and could not be consummated, or the sickness too deep, or in other cases the structural factors preventing the union of the two lovers are too great to be overcome. Mughaltay's (d. 1361) composition, *al-Wadih al-mubin fi dhikr man ustushhida min al-muhibbin (The Clear Clarifier concerning Mention of those Lovers who were Martyred)* contains a list of 177 martyrs of love. Of these, 18 are couples (counted separately in the original count); in other words, both partners were martyrs in the fashion of Romeo and Juliet. Most of the martyrs of love are men, but there are a few women separate from the couples.[15] Not all of these lovers were human; at least one died from love of a jinn (a spirit of fire in the Islamic tradition).[16] This lover was named Ja'far, the first-born son of Abu Ja'far al-Mansur (ruled 754–75), the second 'Abbasid caliph. Thus it was possible for very high-ranking people to become martyrs of love (Yazid II, Umayyad caliph 720–24, is also listed).

The circumstances of martyrdom for each of these martyrs differ considerably. Some of the lovers die while touching something sent by the beloved, occasionally a letter or some other item from their possessions. A certain al-Harith b. al-Sharid who was in love with a woman named 'Afra', when he received a letter from her, placed it upon his face, smelled the perfume of her hand, and then died on the spot. She was wooed by other men after his death, but instead chose to kill herself.[17] Certain others died from love of the Qur'an; touching or fondling it, or hearing it recited led to their demise. Yet others, who were devoted to Islam, and tried initially to refuse temptation, were gradually led astray, and then brought back by an admonition from the Qur'an and died because of their intense love for words of God.[18]

Many of the martyrs of love chose, like Romeo and Juliet, to kill themselves after their lover died, or they died naturally of grief or occasionally died together of a surfeit of love.[19] For example, in Medina during the Umayyad period it was

---

[15] E.g., Mughaltay, *Wadih*, pp. 181, 187, 210.

[16] Mughaltay, *Wadih*, p. 158; for intercourse and marriage between humans and jinn see al-Shibli, *Ghara'ib wa-'aja'ib al-jinn*, pp. 85–99; Jalal al-Din al-Suyuti, *Laqt al-marjan fi ahkam al-jann*, pp. 30–37.

[17] Al-Khara'iti, *I'tilal al-qulub*, p. 198; Mughaltay, *Wadih*, p. 180; a similar story is related in Ibn Qayyim al-Jawziyya, *Akhbar al-nisa'*, pp. 62–63 concerning a man who dropped dead while entering his wife on the night of their wedding. She died shortly afterwards clutching his portrait to herself.

[18] Mughaltay, *Wadih*, pp. 170, 195, 202–03; al-Antaki, *Tazyin al-aswaq*, i, p. 94.

[19] Sometimes they even killed their beloved (accidentally), see al-Tanukhi, *Nishwar al-muhadara*, i, p. 338.

said that a young man loved a singing girl, and that the righteous governor 'Umar b. 'Abd al-'Aziz gave her to him when he learned of it. But she died after one year of being together, and he did not last a month after her death (apparently dying of grief). In Medina it was said "Hamza [uncle of the Prophet Muhammad, slain at the Battle of Uhud] is the *sayyid* [lord] of the martyrs, this man is the *sayyid* of lovers."[20] Another story is that of a young man married to his cousin, who was sent with the army to Khurasan during the Umayyad period. When he returned, he found her dead, and died of grief immediately afterwards.[21]

Other martyrs of love were homosexual. For example, according to the accounts, there was a teacher in Hama (today in Syria) named Ibn al-Duri who was tempted by a boy who was his student, and fell in love with him. The boy's father forbade him from going to Ibn al-Duri, and complained to the sultan about the conduct of Ibn al-Duri. When the latter heard about this, he sat down, and "his eyes became reddened, and his face until blood almost dripped from it . . . then he vomited. He then went to the mosque, and there vomited black vomit." After these physical manifestations, blood began to flow from his gullet, and the doctors could not staunch the flow, and finally his liver burst and he died.[22] Yet others were suspected of homosexual tendencies, such as two youths named Muhammad b. al-Husayn al-Dabbi and 'Abd al-'Aziz b. al-Shah al-Taymi. These two companions were always together, and gossips believed that their love was not entirely chaste. When Muhammad died, his companion 'Abd al-'Aziz was desolate and prayed that God would take him as well. After 'Abd al-'Aziz died, he was seen in a dream wearing green clothes and was asked what God had done with the both of them. He said: "He forgave me . . . because of what people used to say concerning that which they did not know, and the false accusations against me." He was asked what had become of Muhammad, and said that God had joined the two of them together, and that they were not separated.[23] This category of lovers is occasionally called the "mutual lovers in God": two males who love each other purely, and will be joined together in heaven (cf. I Samuel 20:17, II Samuel 1:26).[24]

All of these martyrs of love are granted this title because of their essential self-denial, and faithful perseverance in pursuit of their beloved. The cruelties that the existence of the beloved inflict, as in the couplet of Hafiz (d. 1389 or 1390) cited at the beginning of this chapter, are part of their glory and enhance their spiritual stature as well as define the nature of their love. In many cases this love is very one-sided, and despised by the other, beloved, who is embarrassed by the exaggerated obsession of the lover with them. But in some of those cases, such

[20] Mughultay, *Wadih*, pp. 204–05.   [21] Mughultay, *Wadih*, p. 360.
[22] Mughultay, *Wadih*, p. 186; for other stories with homosexual content pp. 248, 337–38; also Ibn 'Asakir, *Ta'rikh madinat Dimashq*, xv, pp. 166–68.
[23] Mughultay, *Wadih*, pp. 239–40.
[24] Ibn Qudama al-Maqdisi, *Kitab al-mutahabin fi Allah*, pp. 51, 54, 57–58.

as with Layla or Buthayna, the beloved comes back to her lover (if only in spirit), and expresses some reciprocal attachment.[25] This type of cruel, one-sided love can easily be interpreted, as previously stated, as an allegorical representation of the Sufi love for God.[26] Since this is the case, it is not surprising to find next to the lists of the martyrs of love described above categories of "martyrs of love through desire for union with the Lord of Worlds."[27] Although these lists contain substantially the same Sufi martyrs already described in Chapters 4–5, the topical connection of these two groups is revealing. But it is also the basis for the romantic (and tragic) epics that were to develop out of these stories and expand their audiences considerably.

Epic heroes: literary and political martyrs

There is a whole class of martyrs that are non-religious but occasionally acquire religious significance after their deaths. Some of these were literary in nature, while others have historical reality to them but are gradually transformed into literary figures. The Islamic world has many epics and folk tales. These stories are part of the sum total of the culture and usually exist in an oral version (or in cases, many versions) as well as a written version. Epics and folk tales are older than Islam in a number of cases (such as the *Shahnamah*), and represent a continuity of culture that both defines the cultural identities of certain regions and spans across multiple cultures. The best-known defining epics – those of ʿAntar for the Arabs, Firdawsi's (fl. ca. twelfth-century) *Shahnamah*, later reworks of the cyle of *Layla and Majnun* (by Nizami and Jami) and al-Tartusi's *Abu Muslimnama* for the Persian speaking world, *Sayyid Battal* for the Turkish speaking world, the *Hikayat Sultan Ibrahim ibn Adham* for the Indonesian–Malay world, and the Swahili stories of East Africa – all contain elements of heroism, tragedy and martyrdom. Indeed, it would be difficult to imagine an epic without these cardinal ingredients.

Arabic epics

These Arabic epics[28] are among the core stories of the Islamic world. They have been passed from culture to culture and continue to inspire creative variations

---

[25] E.g., Ibn ʿAsakir, *Ta'rikh*, lx, p. 276 for an example of this type of love; also Yaqut, *Muʿjam al-udaba*, vi, p. 2528.

[26] According to some interpretations even Satan (rejected by God but affirming His oneness) is also a lover: see Peter Awn, *Satan's Tragedy and Redemption: Iblis in Sufi Psychology*, p. 167f.

[27] E.g., al-Antaki, *Tazyin al-aswaq*, i, pp. 71–90; but sometimes that leads to the murder of the beloved: al-Tanukhi, *Nishwar al-muhadara*, i, pp. 338–39.

[28] For research on the Arabian epic, I am relying upon Peter Heath, *The Thirsty Sword*: Sirat ʿAntar *and the Arabic Popular Epic*, Helen Zimmern, *Epic of Kings: Shahnameh. Stories Retold from Firdusi*, Georgios Dedes, *The Battalname: An Ottoman Turkish Frontier Epic Wondertale*, Russell Jones, *Hikayat Sultan Ibrahim Ibn Adham*, and M. C. Lyons, *The Arabian Epic*.

even today. The story of 'Antara b. Shaddad is probably the best known of all. Historically, 'Antara was an Arab of mixed race (his mother was black), and a slave of the tribe of 'Abs who lived in the pre-Islamic period (sixth century). At a particularly desperate moment in the tribe's history he was given his freedom by his father, allowed to fight (a slave could not fight), and became a champion. His poetry and love for his beloved cousin 'Abla were legendary, and one of his poems even achieved immortality as part of the seven pre-Islamic Odes, the *al-Mu'allaqat*. Moreover, 'Antar (as the legendary 'Antara was usually called) is often seen as the paradigm of the noble qualities that Arabs admire most (generosity and bravery). Unfortunately, due to the extreme length of the story (eight volumes long) it is impossible to touch upon more than a few of the themes recounted in it.

Like the historical figure, the legendary 'Antar is originally a slave who fights to gain his freedom. However, most of the story centers around his star-crossed love for 'Abla, whose father is hostile to their passion. The father repeatedly sends 'Antar on missions to prove his love, favors other suitors and ultimately tries to have 'Antar murdered by any other suitor who can kill him. Despite the hostility of her father, 'Abla is constant in her attachment to 'Antar, and while she is repeatedly kidnapped by various other suitors, she makes it clear that 'Antar is the only man for her. War after war among the Bedouin tribes is precipitated because of various suitors being rejected, and in each one 'Antar is victorious over his enemies. Finally 'Antar and 'Abla are married. However, when 'Antar together with a number of other prominent pre-Islamic Arab heroes decides to take revenge upon the emperor of Persia for the murder of an Arab prince, he overreaches himself and is captured. 'Abla agrees to a liaison with the emperor, who fell in love with her, in order to gain 'Antar back, but then stabs him to death. Shortly thereafter another opponent, Wizr b. Jabir, appears and terrorizes all of the Arab tribes, and 'Abla asks 'Antar to challenge him, which he does, capturing and blinding him. Twenty years later, after 'Antar has had many adventures all over the world (Rome, Constantinople, Spain and mythical islands of the sea), he comes home and Wizr is waiting for him. Even though Wizr is blind, he has learned to shoot arrows quite accurately, and shoots at 'Antar in the dark. 'Antar, though wounded, still managed to kill Wizr. Since his clan (including 'Abla) are at the same time trying to find refuge with their tribe from some raiders, the dying 'Antar mounts his horse one last time and sits guarding their retreat until he dies. The raiders finally realize that he is dead[29] and bury him.[30]

Sirat 'Antar reveals a number of the heroic themes that are important in the discussion of martyrdom: the single-minded focus of the hero upon his beloved,

---

[29] Compare Qur'an 34:14.
[30] This summary is dependent upon that of Peter Heath, *Thirsty Sword*, pp. 168–231; and that of Lyon, *Arabian Epic*, iii, pp. 17–76.

the many structural difficulties that are placed in the way of their romance, and their repeated trials and tribulations even after the marriage ('Abla is kidnapped at least thirty times during the course of the epic, many of them after her marriage). The final martyrdom is part of the double vengeance story that is played out with Wizr, who previously had been blinded by 'Antar, but finally was able to take revenge upon him. 'Antar for his part lives long enough to kill Wizr, and then dies defending his clan. It is small wonder that this story has been popular throughout the Arab world for at least the past 800 years. Many themes and stories in *Sirat 'Antar* anachronistically date from the time of the Crusades, and other popular epics such as *Sirat al-Zahir Baybars* and *The Story of 'Umar al-Nu'man and his Sons* also employ these themes. While *Baybars* lacks any obvious martyrdom themes, *'Umar al-Nu'man*, which is the longest story in the great collection of the *Thousand and One Nights*, is worth reviewing here.[31]

'Umar al-Nu'man focuses upon a family headed by a patriarch of that name who was said to have ruled the Arab world (although nominally set in pre-Islamic times). 'Umar is said to have had one son, Sharr Kana, who was a great champion. Sharr Kana became bewitched by Abrizah, the daughter of the king of the Greeks, who defeated him in single-combat repeatedly, and finally together with her handmaidens actually defeated his entire army.[32] She then fell in love with him, but after he took her back to his father 'Umar in Baghdad, so did the latter. When Abriza refused the advances of 'Umar, the latter drugged her and raped her, from which she became pregnant. During an escape attempt from Baghdad after she was ready to give birth, she was killed by one of 'Umar's black slaves who was also trying to have his way with her. The king of the Greeks vowed revenge upon 'Umar and sent his mother Dhat al-Dawahi (Mother of Calamities) to kill 'Umar in Baghdad. Dhat al-Dawahi managed to ingratiate herself into the entourage of 'Umar al-Nu'man as a Sufi holy woman, and because of her vast knowledge of Sufi lore tricked him into a process of purging himself to achieve purity (by abstaining from food for a whole month). She then had him drink a poison, and he under the impression that it was a potion, gave orders that he was not to be disturbed. Finally, when his servants opened up the door to his chambers by force, they found him "dead, with his flesh torn into strips and bits, and his bones broken."[33] Dhat al-Dawahi had thoughtfully left a note explaining who she was and why she had taken such a horrible vengeance upon 'Umar. The story continues at length, treating themes of incest, betrayal and polemic, but the element of martyrdom in it is

---

[31] *Alf layla wa-layla*, i, pp. 207–379; trans. Richard Burton, *Burton's Arabian Nights*, ii, pp. 77–283, iii, pp. 47–103.

[32] The theme of the warrior women is another popular one in Arabic epics, see Remke Kruk, "Warrior Women in Arabic Popular Romance: Qannasa bint Muzahim and other Valiant Ladies."

[33] Burton, *Arabian Nights*, ii, p. 214.

strikingly amoral. 'Umar and his family, although Muslim, are hardly paragons of virtue. But it is sufficient for 'Umar to have been killed by a Christian for him to have the aura of a martyr about him.

The Persian epic tradition takes a number of pre-Islamic themes and weaves them into the copious story-cycles that we know today. Of these, the *Shahnamah* of al-Firdawsi is undoubtedly the best-known and is a permanent favorite for Persian-language speakers. The story of the *Shahnamah*, like that of the other epics summarized above, is too complicated to be told in-depth here. Basically it is a story that focuses upon a turbulent noble family, and especially upon the heroic figure of Rustam. Living over a period of centuries, Rustam becomes something of a protector of the land of Iran. Although not every fight in which he participates is just, and sometimes like every heroic figure he has temper tantrums, Rustam and his steed Rakush are usually defenders of right. Firdawsi's epic gives the full span of Iranian history from creation down to the Arab conquest, and presents several everlasting conflicts with two malevolent figures: Dahhak (usually identified with the Arabs) and Turan (the Turks). Rustam frequently fights against both, but his end comes as the result of sibling jealousy. His half-brother, Shugdad, married to the daughter of the King of Kabul (Afghanistan), together with his father-in-law decides to take Rustam down by deceit. Together they lure Rustam to their court, where they have planted a trap. After having dug a deep hole, they fill it with sharp spears and cover the pit over lightly so that Rustam can fall into it and be gored to death.

Rustam was completely oblivious to the ruse, but his horse Rakush felt that there was something wrong:

> The next day the King made ready a great hunt, and he led it to the spot where the pits were hidden. Shugdad ran beside the horse of Rustam and showed him the path. But Rakush, when he smelt the soil that had been newly turned, reared him in the air, and refused to go onwards. Then Rustam commanded him to go forward, but Rakush would not listen to his voice. Rustam was angry when he beheld that Rakush was afraid. But Rakush sprang back yet again. Then Rustam took a whip and struck him; before this day he had never raised his hand against his steed. So Rakush was grieved in his soul and he did that which Rustam desired, and he sprang forward and fell into the pit. The sharp spears entered his body, and they pierced also the flesh of Rustam, and steed and rider were impaled upon the irons that had been hidden by the King.[34]

However, this was not sufficient to actually kill Rustam, who managed to hoist himself up out of the pit and begged from the king a bow and two arrows to defend himself as he lay dying. The king gave him these implements, and with them Rustam, at his dying gasp, was able to dispatch Shugdad his faithless brother. In this way the cycle of vengeance is preserved.

---

[34] Helen Zimmern (trans.), *The Epic of Kings*; Firdawsi, *Shahnamah*, v, pp. 461–67.

Persian epics

Some literary figures have achieved some level of cult or hero status, usually because they were representatives of marginal groups who admired and worshipped them, and accorded them the status of martyr after their deaths. Probably the best known of these is the famous 'Abbasid general Abu Muslim (d. 754). Abu Muslim was a slave of unknown origins who was chosen by the 'Abbasid family to lead their propaganda and military machine in the eastern Muslim province of Khurasan (today eastern Iran and western Afghanistan). Together with the pre-existing 'Abbasid missionaries he created an army of both Arabs and Persians, indoctrinated it to be absolutely loyal to the 'Abbasid family, and ultimately lead it to victory against the Umayyad dynasty based in Syria.[35] Abu Muslim probably had no serious designs upon the caliphal throne, but the 'Abbasids, having risen to power, systematically killed most of those who had helped them achieve that victory. Thus Abu Muslim was seen as a threat, and in 754 the caliph Abu Ja'far al-Mansur had him murdered secretly.

In the standard account by the historian al-Tabari (d. 923), the murder of Abu Muslim is portrayed as an inevitable event that everyone sees other than Abu Muslim himself.[36] Abu Muslim had a general attitude of suspicion towards the caliph Abu Ja'far al-Mansur's attempts to separate him from his army (which idolized him), and to appoint him governor of provinces far from his power base of Khurasan. But in the end Abu Muslim could not avoid coming to Abu Ja'far, since the latter was the caliph and had the right to order him to appear before him. When this happened, the caliph spoke to Abu Muslim using rough language, but dismissed him for the night. The next morning, however, the caliph had made arrangements with several of his closest bodyguards, headed by 'Uthman b. Nahik, to kill Abu Muslim. When Abu Muslim arrived, 'Uthman and the bodyguards were hidden in the room, and after the caliph proceeded to work himself into a fury by throwing accusations at Abu Muslim, the bodyguards rushed into the room and began to stab him. Abu Muslim was said to have begged for mercy: "Pardon! And I [the caliph] said: Pardon?? O son of an uncircumcised woman (*ya ibn al-lakhna'*), [is there] pardon, when the swords are taking turns on you? And I said: Slaughter him, and they slaughtered him."[37] In some other versions Abu Muslim is said to have begged for his life saying that he would be a sword against the caliph's enemies, to which Abu Ja'far al-Mansur is said to have replied: "What enemy do I have worse than you?"[38]

While these accounts do not portray Abu Muslim in a very glorious light, his public image of a hero (cultivated by himself) was strong enough that

---

[35] See Moshe Sharon, *Black Banners from the East* and *Revolt: Social and Military Aspects of the 'Abbasid Revolution.*
[36] Taken from al-Tabari, *Ta'rikh al-rusul wa-l-muluk,* vii, pp. 479–94.
[37] Al-Tabari, *Ta'rikh,* vii, p. 489.   [38] Ibid., p. 492.

the opposition to the ʿAbbasid regime adopted him. Shortly after his murder, Abu Muslim was used by a Zoroastrian rebel in Khurasan named Sindibad, who demanded vengeance for him.[39] Within a short while Abu Muslim began to acquire the aura of a martyr among the Persian-speaking population, and a number of messianic cults. Some of these believed that the rights of the imamate should have gone to Abu Muslim instead of the ʿAbbasid family.[40] Many believed that he had not died, but would soon reappear and take vengeance upon the ʿAbbasids.[41] This messianic speculation eventually set the stage for the appearance of wide-scale movements based upon belief in Abu Muslim during the Safavid period (sixteenth–eighteenth centuries) in Persia, and the popularity of the cycle of stories about him, the *Abu Muslimnama* in Persian. Probably most of the population which idolized Abu Muslim and others like him did not know precisely what he stood for or what the nature of his opposition to the ʿAbbasid government was. It was enough that he was a larger-than-life figure, having considerable charisma, and was persecuted by a government perceived to be tyrannical.[42]

From the story of the murder of Abu Muslim there is the spin-off tale of the *Abu Muslimnama*, another heroic cycle that had a profound political and religious influence over pre-modern Iran. During the fourteenth and fifteenth centuries, prior to the time when Iran was converted to Shiʿism, the ancestors of the Safavid dynasty (ruled 1501–1722) used the story of Abu Muslim in order to convey propaganda glorifying the Prophet Muhammad's family. Instead of the historical Abu Muslim, who was the servant of the ʿAbbasid dynasty (747–1258) – an essentially Sunni dynasty that employed extensive Shiʿite themes in order to gain power – the *Abu Muslimnama* (composed approximately 1065) was reshaped into a story of support for the Shiʿite descendents of al-Husayn (the Twelve Imams). Thus, Abu Muslim is presented as having loyalty to the Imams and having received a dream from the Prophet Muhammad in which he was instructed to take vengeance upon the Umayyad dynasty for their murder of al-Husayn.[43] Gradually Abu Muslim, leading a movement of the poor and dispossessed, is said to have created a mass following among the people of Iran. Plying his trade as a blacksmith he goes from one locality to another, and founds communities of lovers of the Prophet Muhammad's family who are ready to die for the cause. Although Abu Muslim was a true servant of the family of Muhammad, the ʿAbbasids betrayed him and used him to arrogate power instead

---

[39] Ibid., p. 495.   [40] Al-Baghdadi, *al-Farq bayna al-firaq*, pp. 242–43.

[41] (Pseudo-) Nashiʾ al-Akbar, *Kitab usul al-nihal*, pp. 31–32 (in van Ess, *Frühe muʿtazilitische Häresiographie*); also Saʿd b. ʿAbdallah al-Ashaʿri al-Qummi, *Kitab al-maqalat wa-l-firaq*, pp. 64–65.

[42] Others similarly in al-Tamimi, *Mihan*, pp. 207, 215, 252–56 lists those crucified, also pp. 258 (burning), 280, 286 (beating).

[43] Kathryn Babayan, *Mystics, Monarchs and Messiahs: Cultural Landscape of Early Modern Iran*, p. 130 (my analysis of the *Abu Muslimnama* is dependent upon that of Babayan).

of letting the descendants of ʿAli and al-Husayn, the rightful rulers of Islam, come into their heritage.

The martyrdom of Abu Muslim is presented in much the same way as in the historical accounts. The ʿAbbasid caliph Abu Jaʿfar al-Mansur is said to have suspected him of wanting to overthrown the dynasty, and had an argument with Abu Muslim. However, the *Abu Muslimnama* details that al-Mansur was surrounded by supporters of the Umayyads, the dynasty that Abu Muslim had worked to overthrow, and had thus betrayed Abu Muslim and the ideals of the revolution he had initiated in the name of the Prophet Muhammad's family. In addition to this change, Abu Muslim is specifically said to have died a martyr (*shahid*), a statement which is not to be found in the historical accounts.[44] Bringing Abu Muslim over to the side of the Shiʿites in this epic retelling of his tragic death was a brilliant move that eventually enabled the Safavid dynasty to ride to power themselves. By comparing the exploits of the historical and legendary Abu Muslim to their own situation they were able to present themselves as the servants of the family of the Prophet Muhammad and thus capture the loyalties of many throughout Iran. The fact that they, like the ʿAbbasids before them, eventually betrayed these followers (the Qizilbash) and had them murdered just as Abu Muslim was murdered closes the circle.[45]

Among the other very influential tales concerning martyrdom in the Persian language Nizami's retelling of the story of Layla and Majnun stands out. Nizami took the basic Arabic story recounted earlier and elaborated on it considerably. First of all, Majnun becomes more visibly insane than he was in the original story, and his efforts to gain Layla are far more practical and violent. After his initial rejection by Layla's father, he is said to have befriended a Bedouin warrior named Nawfal. After recounting his love for Layla, Majnun and Nawfal decide to declare war against her tribe in order to gain possession of her, and gather together a number of tribesmen and ruffians to fight. Eventually Nawfal defeats the members of Layla's tribe – although Majnun is unwilling to participate because of the slaughter of her close relatives – and he demands that her family hand her over. Layla's father comes out and says:

It is now your task to pronounce judgment. If you leave me my daughter, you can be certain of my gratitude. If you are determined to kill her – do! Cut her to pieces, burn her, drown her; I shall not rebel against your decision. One answer alone I will not accept; never shall I give Layla to this demon, this Majnun, a madman who should be tied with iron bands, not with nuptial bonds. Who, after all, is he? A fool, a common muddle-head, a vagrant and homeless tramp, who roams mountains and steppes. And what has he ever achieved? Shall I sit down with a vile versifier who has sullied my good name – and his own? There is not one corner of Arabia where my daughter's name is not bandied about on everyone's lips – and I should give her to him who is the cause of all this? . . . I swear

---

[44] Al-Tartusi, *Abu Muslimnama*, iv, p. 498.   [45] Babayan, *Mystics*, Chapter 5.

to God that I would rather cut off her head with my own hands and feed this moon-like bride to the dogs to save my honor and to live in peace . . . better that the dogs should devour her than this demon in human shape. Better they than he![46]

Despite the friendship between Nawfal and Majnun, he is moved by what Layla's father says and cannot bring himself to force him to hand her over. And so Majnun goes back into the wilds.

However, in Nizami's retelling of the story Layla is secretly in love with Majnun and she envies his liberation from society and its norms, while after this disastrous war precipitated by Nawfal she is given in marriage to a man she does not love. In her heart Layla fixates upon this crazy man who runs with the animals of the field and talks to them, and composes wild, unrestrained poetry about her that is circulated everywhere in Arabia. To punish her husband she would not allow him to touch her; he in turn guarded her night and day so that no one else could get to her. She is the true prisoner, and longed to be free to love who she would. After her husband dies of unrequited love, Layla longs to experience freedom, but instead at that moment she sickens and dies. Her dying thoughts, spoken to her mother, are of Majnun:

When I am dead, dress me like a bride. Make me beautiful. As a salve for my eyes, take dust from Majnun's path . . . I want to be clad in a blood-red garment, for I am a blood-witness like the martyrs. Red is the color of the feast! Is not death my feast? Then cover me in the veil of earth which I shall never lift again.[47]

As Layla knew he would, Majnun came and brought his following of wild animals to Layla's gravesite, where he died shortly thereafter. Since Majnun is usually accorded the title of a martyr of love, his body remained pure according to the tradition and did not decay.[48]

Turkish epics

As previously mentioned, while the Nizami telling of *Layla and Majnun* was very influential within the Persian language world the ending was not entirely satisfactory to all audiences.[49] Perhaps for this reason the Turkish (although Iraqi in origin) poet Fuzuli (d. 1556) retold the story again. In Fuzuli's telling, Layla and Majnun have the opportunity to come together after the death of Layla's husband. She does not die immediately after him, but instead begins

---

[46] Rudolf Gelpke (trans.), *The Story of Layla and Majnun*, pp. 65–66; text in Nizami, *Layla va-Majnun*, pp. 109–14.

[47] Ibid., pp. 167–68; text, pp. 250–51.

[48] Ali Asghar Seyed-Gohrab, *Layli and Majnun: Love, Madness and Mystic Longing in Nizami's Epic Romance*, p. 137.

[49] On this see Mehmed Kalpakli and Walter Andrews, "Layla Grows up: Nizami's *Layla and Majnun* 'in the Turkish Manner.'"

to correspond with Majnun, and attempts to consummate their love. But he rebukes her on the grounds that their union is spiritual alone and is too passionate to be consummated on earth.[50] Therefore, the two of them bound each other to chastity and a mutual love that would be stronger because it denied fleshly desires and could not be destroyed by the ravages of time. After their deaths the two martyrs are seen in a dream, in paradise:

> Within a glad garden two beauties supreme,
> their faces he saw with all pleasure aglow, no fear, grief or trouble did either face show.
> Each countenance spoke of all joy and delight . . . Now Zayd in a swoon,
> All drowned with his slumber said: "Say, who are these bright moons? Are they princes?" . . .
> The answer he had, showed the garden of joy, as the sect field of paradise lovers enjoy,
> While mid all the houris and beautiful boys sweet Leyla and Mejnun did gladly rejoice.[51]

In this Turkish version of *Layla and Majnun* it is possible to see the almost complete spiritualization and even in some ways Islamization of their love.

While others were influential, the best-known Turkish epic harked back to the early Islamic period and focused upon the figure of Sayyid Battal. Historically speaking, Sayyid Battal was an Arab from the Umayyad period (probably early eighth century) who fought against the Byzantines along the coast of what is today Lebanon and Syria.[52] His exploits were those of a borderman, fighting against the Umayyad government almost as much as against his Christian enemies. By the fourteenth and fifteenth centuries the epic of Battal became associated with the Turks of central Anatolia who were fighting against the last remains of the ancient Byzantine Empire as well as some outposts of the Crusaders scattered around present-day Turkey. As with the other epics the stories of Battal are too involved to be recounted here. At the end of his life, Battal, after having fought numerous Christian kings, saw the Prophet Muhammad in a dream, and was told of the dire straights of the Muslims of Malatya (today eastern Anatolia). Although Battal was outnumbered, with supernatural aid (100,000 winged fairies) he was able to slaughter the Christians. However, Battal decided not to sit on his laurels but to continue fighting until he became a martyr. He went on to besiege the fortress of Masiha where the Caesar of the Byzantines was, and behaved so heroically that one of the daughters of the Caesar fell in love with him. While he was sleeping outside the fortress, she threw a stone at him with a message that an army was going to attack him from behind, and that she was willing to betray her father and convert to Islam.

---

[50] See Fuzuli, *Leyla and Mejnun*. Trans. Sofi Huri and Alessio Bombaci, p. 303f.
[51] Ibid., p. 327.   [52] See Ibn 'Asakir, *Ta'rikh madinat Dimashq*, xxxiii, pp. 401–06.

Unfortunately, the stone was thrown so accurately that it killed Battal. The girl then said to her father that she would like to go out and cut off his head, and when she came out she realized that she had killed him.

She saw that he had surrendered his soul, sighed and said, "If in this world I was deprived of him, let me not be without him in the other world. Without him I have no need for this world." With these words she drew the sword, placed its hilt on Sayyid's breast and fixed the cutting edge against her own breast, pronounced the confession of faith and fell on the sword. She lay there on top of Sayyid and offered her soul to God. Then there was a black cloud and a strong wind, it rained and thundered and the two corpses were covered. No one knew anything more about what happened to them.[53]

With this type of ending the Battal romance is given a finale more closely associated with the martyrs of love, even though the historical figure of Battal was known to have been martyred in battle. This theme was very attractive to Turkish audiences just as it had been to Arab and Persian ones previously.

Indonesian–Malay epics

Other common themes of martyrdom can be found in the Indonesian–Malay Sufi romance of *Hikayat Sultan Ibrahim ibn Adham*. This story is based upon the Sufi figure Ibrahim b. Adham whose career as a fighter and a martyr was recounted in Chapter 4. For the most part the *Hikayat* is a Sufi didactic tale that periodically makes digressions into Islamic teachings presumably either to communicate them to a mass audience or to reinforce them. The figure of Ibrahim is bound closely with his spiritual wife Siti Saliha, from whom he initially learns until he decides to leave her when she reveals her love for him. Upon her bewailing his impending departure, he rebukes her, saying: "Do not upset yourself over our parting, my dear; truly the Lord who created heaven sees that two people who serve Him loyally are reunited. Cheer up, in heaven you will be reunited with me."[54] Ibrahim then explains that being with her has prevented him from absolute devotion to God, and that he has to leave.

In essence Siti Saliha is a martyr to love. Like Layla in the version of Fuzuli (Turkish) she is rejected in favor of a greater love that the ascetic has for God, and is made to wait patiently for the time at which she can be reunited with her lover (either Ibrahim or, metaphorically, God). Although she is denied the continued presence of her love, when he leaves her she is pregnant, and in time gives birth to Ibrahim's son Muhammad Tahir. Eventually Muhammad seeks out his father, and communes with him, and finally reproaches him for having abandoned Siti Saliha, who still pines for her husband. When Muhammad Tahir returns to his mother, he bears another message from Ibrahim b. Adham that he

---

[53] Georgios Dedes, "The Battalname, An Ottoman Turkish Frontier Epic Wondertale," p. 438.
[54] Russell Jones (trans.), *Hikayat Ibrahim ibn Adham*, p. 133.

cannot tear himself away from his devotions even a single day to come see her. The final message of the story is to praise Siti Saliha's devotion to her husband, saying "That is how women who love their husbands behave. If Siti Saliha was like this, how much the more should we women believers be devoted to our husbands, in the hope that we shall obtain the mercy of God the Exalted in the hereafter."[55] Sexual and social denial are some of the hallmarks of the Sufi martyr of love, and although in the Malay story Ibrahim b. Adham does not actually die the martyr's death ascribed to him in the Arabic sources, both he and his wife give up everything on the promise of the next world.

East African Swahili epics

Furthest removed from this world of epics are the East African Swahili stories. Two will be referred to here: the story of Hamza, the Prophet Muhammad's uncle, and the death of Muhammad. Hamza, it will be remembered, was killed by the Ethiopian slave Wahshi who threw a spear at him at the Battle of Uhud (625). In the Swahili tale, however, Hamza is far grander. He is a wandering warrior over Iraq and Iran, who fights all sorts of evil creatures. When he comes back to the Arabian Peninsula, he arrives just in time to help Muhammad fight an Indian enemy named Fur. After defeating Fur, who commanded a large army, Hamza was struck down by Fur's mother, who was a witch. The witch then ate Hamza's liver (just as Hind did, historically, at the Battle of Uhud).[56] In another story coming from the Swahili culture, *Utenzi wa-Katawafu Nabii*, the death of the Prophet Muhammad is recounted. However, unlike normative accounts of the Prophet's death, this one is given more of a Christian martyrdom flavor. Muhammad is long aware of his imminent death, and consoles the members of his family. When the Angel of Death, Azriel, arrives he is told to wait patiently – "something he had never done [before] and would not do for anyone else" – so that Gabriel could arrive and accompany Muhammad to paradise.[57] This theme of making Death submit to the authority of the Prophet Muhammad is known from Christian martyrologies, most notably the Coptic version of "the Death of Joseph" (Jesus' father), in which Jesus also rebukes Death and makes him afraid.[58]

In many of these stories it is apparent that fact and fiction blur easily. Stories concerning Sufis and lovers are historical (perhaps) as well as having an epic or folk aspect to them. This is apparent with regard to the story of Majnun and Layla, in which the original core of the story has been fleshed out to such a

---

[55] Ibid., pp. 173, 175.   [56] Jan Knappert, *Islamic Legends*, ii, pp. 401–04.

[57] J. T. W. Allen (trans.), *Utenzi wa-Katawafu Nabii*, pp. 45–51 (the word *kushuhudi* is used on p. 30 but it appears to mean "witness" rather than "martyr") and see Jan Knappert, *A Survey of Swahili Islamic Epic Sagas*, pp. 89–96 for a summary.

[58] P. de Lagarde (ed.), "De morte Iosephi" (The Death of Joseph) in *Aegyptiaca*, pp. 1–37.

degree that it is impossible to separate it into factual and fantastical sections. In the same way, the story of Abu Muslim, while having an originally factual core, flows easily into the narrative of the Abu Muslim epic to the point where one cannot divide the two. Likewise, the narratives of Rumi, themselves reworkings of previous stories, flow seamlessly into a continual narrative of Sufi edification and idealization. Martyrdom is part of this totality. In the end, the symbolism contained within the stories of martyrdom are more important than the facts anyway, because it is the symbolism that inspires people and is remembered generation after generation.

*'Abdallah b. Ghalib al-Harrani . . . broke the sheath of his sword, advanced
and fought until he was killed and was carried from the battlefield while there
was still a breath of life in him, but died short of the army camp. When he was
buried there was a smell of musk emanating from his grave, and his brethren
saw him in a dream, and he said: O Abu Firas, what has happened? He said:
The best!*[1]

Martyrdom, since it is a theme within Islam, has been given a set form by tradition (both the Islamic tradition as well as the martyrdom tradition of religions
that preceded it). This form often demands that the martyr be given knowledge of his or her death just prior to its occurrence, either in a dream/vision by
means of an earthly figure who is privy to divine or supernatural knowledge,
or occasionally by the drama that leads up to his or her death. Sometimes there
are dreams or visions that occur after the martyr's death as well, so that the
audience knows he or she has been suitably rewarded. Usually the martyr must
die in a dignified manner, to the extent that such a death is possible under the
circumstances, with his or her faith untainted, and have the ability or opportunity to speak to the audience before death supervenes. Inside the martyrdom
sequence there are repeated symbols: colors, smells, objects and other commonalities that trigger within the audience the knowledge that the narrative will
be acceptable to God, that the manner of death is a holy one and that the person
will be venerated and perhaps be an intercessor for sinners.

   These symbols speak to the reader – or in the case of oral traditions of
martyrdom, the listener – and communicate an eternal form of pathos that
places the martyrdom within the larger context of suffering for the sake of
a goal, person or cause. When these symbols are related, they highlight the
significance of events, creating a sequence that must be followed. Death is
predestined for all humans by God, but the believer does not know (and cannot
know) when and under what circumstances it will happen. As the Qur'an 31:34
says " . . . nor does any living soul know in what land it shall die." While
this is equally true of the martyr, the symbols that surround his approaching

---

[1] Al-Tamimi, *Mihan*, p. 232; Ibn al-Jawzi, *Sifat al-safwa*, iv, p. 238.

death within the narrative allow the audience to know what is about to happen. Death is unpredictable, but martyrdom is a process in which the communicative symbolism is crucial. From a scholarly point of view, while it is fairly evident that many of the symbols, numbers, colors, etc., are in fact literary *topoi* (tropes lacking historical reality). Muslim martyrdoms, like Jewish, Christian, Buddhist or atheist martyrdoms, are part of a huge family of stories designed to edify and inspire the believers. Without the basic symbols employed by the narrators of the martyrdoms these stories would fail to accomplish that goal.

Symbols

The primary symbol of the martyr is blood or the color red.[2] This is fairly self-evident, but, obviously, it also plays a major role in the formation of the martyrdom narrative. Because the sign that a martyrdom is about to occur is the spilling of blood – at which point the houris are said to be attendant upon the martyr – blood in itself plays a symbolic role. Blood is seen dripping or flowing, prior to death, in visions; sometimes the martyr or others will see him cut or wounded in various ways. The blood signifies expiation as noted below, since "the blood of a Muslim is expiation for his sins." But the color white is almost as important for martyrologies, since it signifies the color of the winding sheets used to wrap a dead body (although not always that of a martyr, who is buried in his clothes), or perhaps the body drained of blood. Heavenly beings – whether angels or houris – are sometimes dressed in white, and white signified various political-religious leanings in early Islam.[3] We are told on occasion that those who sought martyrdom would dress themselves in white, perhaps symbolizing their preparation to depart from this world.

In the martyrologies, blood is often spilled on the ground or on the rocks, symbolizing the loss of life; the end of the usefulness of the blood to the body.[4] In sectarian martyrdom sequences bodily parts are sometimes used for advertisement or remembrance – such as the hand of ʿUthman or the head of al-Husayn – and perpetuate the acquired sanctity of the martyr's body. Unavenged blood, such as that of al-Husayn or other Shiʿite martyrs is said to boil and bubble from the ground as a sign of the unrest of the dead.[5] This unrest is symbolic of the need to sate the dead by achieving the necessary

---

[2] See *Encyclopedia of Religions*[2], s.v. "Symbols and Symbolism" (Peter Struck); and further, Gershom Scholem and Klaus Ottman, *Color Symbolism: The Eranos Lectures*; and see René Guénon, *Symbols of Sacred Science* (primarily on symbols important in European culture; unfortunately there is no good study of symbols important in Islam).

[3] Khalil ʿAthamina, "The Black Banners and the Socio-Political Significance of Flags and Slogans."

[4] Al-Tamimi, *Kitab al-mihan*, p. 188; al-Isfahani, *Maqatil*, p. 240; compare Joyce Salisbury, *The Blood of Martyrs*, Chapter 7.

[5] See, e.g., al-Wasiti, *Fadaʾil Bayt al-Maqdis*, p. 55 (no. 83); Ibn Abi al-Dunya, *Kitab al-manam*, pp. 80, 82 (nos. 132–33, 136); also citation in Chapter 4, note 20.

vengeance for their unjust murder (usually by other Muslims). The boiling blood as a symbol is closely related to the pre-Islamic belief that owls – viewed as harbingers of death – called for avenging the blood of slain innocents (cf. Genesis 4:10).[6] Because this belief was not accepted in Islam, the symbolism of the blood of the unavenged martyr was used for the same purpose.

Without a doubt, the body of a Muslim martyr is in itself holy. This holiness is created by the manner of death or suffering, and it continues to pervade the martyr's body even after the soul has left that body. The bodies of Muslim martyrs are pure and untainted, they continue to manifest a sweet and pleasant smell (usually musk) reminiscent of the smell of paradise the martyr enjoys after death in heaven.[7] This sweet smell stands in contradistinction to the foul, loathsome stench of the bodies of the enemies of Islam, whose rotting corpses are a visual reminder of the fact that they are in hell. It is extremely important for martyrologies to point out this distinction and to maintain it as a literary fiction – something that continues in present-day radical Muslim martyrologies.

Historically, it is difficult to tell when this belief first became prevalent. The idea of the incorruptability of the martyr's body is not cited in the Qur'an but is alluded to in the tradition that states: "The earth is forbidden [to consume] the bodies of the prophets."[8] Although bodies of martyrs are not specified by this tradition, the idea of the incorruptible nature of the martyrs appears widely in the later *jihad* and martyrology literature, and is alluded to in martyrologies from the early Islamic period. For example, the fighter Abu Firas 'Abdallah b. Ghalib (died early Umayyad period: see chapter opening quotation) is described as having had a sweet smell coming from his grave, such that people were actually drawn to it.[9] By the sixteenth century, the tradition of the incorruptibility of the prophets' bodies appears in history books with the addition of the word "martyrs"[10] and it seems that this is the way the tradition was understood popularly. Thus, it appears to be a legend that has grown up around the figure of the martyr, probably in response to the popular Christian veneration of saints and their "uncorrupted" bodies.

One of the most pleasant smells associated with the martyr is that of musk. Musk (mentioned in Qur'an 83:23) is said to be one of the smells of paradise. For example, in the story of the Prophet Muhammad's Night Journey and Ascension into heaven (*al-Isra' wa-l-mi'raj*), the earth of paradise is said to be made of

---

[6] Suzanne Pinckney Stetkevych, *The Mute Imortals Speak*, p. 69.

[7] Al-Isfahani, *Ma'rifat al-sahaba*, ii, p. 124 (no. 694), mentioning Muhammad b. Shurahbil.

[8] Abu Da'ud, *Sunan*, ii, p. 89 (no. 1531); Ibn Maja, *Sunan*, i, p. 524 (no. 1637); this idea is expanded upon by al-Bayhaqi, *Hayat al-anbiya' fi quburihim*.

[9] Al-Tamimi, *Kitab al-mihan*, pp. 232–33; see also al-Ramli, *Kitab nihayat al-muhtaj ila sharh al-minhaj fi al-fiqh 'ala madhhab al-Imam al-Shafi'i*, v, p. 131 (section on leasing out land in which a *shahid* is buried); Ibn 'Abdin, *Hashiyat kitab al-jihad*, iii, p. 238 (citations from 'Abdallah 'Azzam, *Ayat al-Rahman fi jihad al-Afghan*, p. 15).

[10] Al-Qadiri, *Nashr al-mathani*, ii, p. 155.

musk.[11] The bodies of martyrs are repeatedly described as smelling of musk, and it is the scent of the women of paradise (houris) who form part of the reward of the martyr. One of the most common traditions states that "Anyone who is wounded in the path of Allah [*jihad*] comes on the Day of Resurrection when [his] color is the color of blood, [but] his scent is the scent of musk."[12] Other traditions state that the dust on the feet of the martyr will be musk on the Day of Resurrection.[13] This sweet perfume is repeatedly invoked in the *jihad* and martyrdom literature. The smell of musk is often conflated with the sweet smell emanating from the gravesites mentioned previously. Occasionally the sweet smell even emanates from the person prior to his martyrdom in order to indicate that this person is about to become a martyr. Signs such as these are important for the literary construction of the martyrdom process.

Prognostications and posthumous dreams of martyrs

Part of the martyrdom process is the certain knowledge that the martyr has concerning his or her end.[14] (However, inside the literature of dream interpretation, for some reason actually dreaming of becoming a martyr does not indicate that one will become a martyr.)[15] But in the *jihad* literature knowledge is usually conveyed by the prognosticatory dream which is normally symbolic and requires interpretation. One early example from Ibn al-Mubarak's *Kitab al-jihad* (late eighth century) states that the early jihad fighter Nawf al-Bikali was confronted by a man who told him: "I saw you in a dream. Nawf said: Tell it. He said: I saw you leading an army, when you had a long spear with you that had a candle lighting the way for the people at its tip. Nawf said: If you are right, then I will be martyred."[16] Of the martyrs listed in one of the earliest Muslim martyrologies, al-Tamimi's *Kitab al-mihan* (from the tenth century), a substantial number received dreams or foreknowledge of their end. For example, 'Umar b. al-Khattab shortly before he was assassinated is said to have seen a vision of a red rooster that pecked him twice, while 'Uthman saw no fewer than four different visions of his imminent death (of course, 'Uthman's assassination could have been predicted by almost anyone seeing the volatile state of the Muslim community at the time).[17] These dreams involved the literal vision

[11] Al-Bukhari, *Sahih*, i, p. 107 (no. 349).
[12] Al-Bukhari, *Sahih*, iii, p. 269 (no. 2803); al-Tirmidhi, *Al-Jami' al-sahih*, iii, p. 104 (nos. 1707–08).
[13] Ibn Maja, *Sunan*, ii, p. 927 (no. 2775).
[14] See Joyce Salisbury, *The Blood of Martyrs*, Chapter 4.
[15] See, e.g., (pseudo-) Ibn Sirin, *Tafsir al-ahlam*, ii, p. 52 (on the margins of 'Abd al-Ghani al-Nablusi, *Ta'tir al-anam fi ta'bir al-manam*); also al-Qadiri, *al-Ta'bir fi al-ru'ya aw al-Qadiri fi al-ta'bir*, i, pp. 157, 348–49,
[16] Ibn al-Mubarak, *Kitab al-jihad*, p. 110 (no. 135).
[17] Al-Tamimi, *Kitab al-mihan*, pp. 76, 79, 82, 87, 91; also see Ibn Abi al-Dunya, *Kitab al-manam*, p. 105 (no. 178), where the blood of 'Uthman is said to be collected close to the Prophet and that God will take vengeance for it.

of 'Uthman seeing the Prophet Muhammad, Abu Bakr and 'Umar, who told him that he would sup with them that evening. Other dreams led him to point out where he was to be killed and buried. Yet other predictions are ascribed to Muhammad, such as:

When I was taken up into heaven I entered paradise, and I was given an apple. When it fell from my hand it split open and one of the beautiful houris came out from it, as if the eyelashes of her eyes were the length of the wings of eagles. I said: Whom do you belong to? She said: To the caliph, who will be killed unjustly after you, 'Uthman.[18]

While it is obvious that such a tradition is designed to point out that 'Uthman was killed unjustly, it also serves as a sacralization of the martyrdom of 'Uthman.

Descriptions of the fate of martyrs in dreams also constitute an important verification of their high spiritual status. A great many of these dreams are contained within the dream book of Ibn Abi al-Dunya (d. 894–95). For example, one al-Husayn b. Kharija al-Ashja'i (*ca.* end of seventh century), who was perturbed because of the numerous tribulations during the early Islamic period, asked God to grant him a vision that would show him the way of the truth. Among the things that he saw was the following:

. . . It was as if there was a wall between them [people of paradise] and me, and so I said: If I jumped this wall I would meet them and could ask them. So I jumped the wall, and there were people wearing white clothes. I asked them: Are you angels? They said: No, we are martyrs.[19]

The dream vision goes on to describe other elements of heaven, but the citation demonstrates what is apparent from reading Muslim sources: quite a number of individuals had communication with martyrs after the deaths of the latter.

Other examples of dreams' importance in Muslim martyrdom sequences arise when martyrs are interviewed after their deaths and asked about their fate or on what basis they were admitted into paradise. For example, the fighter Abu Firas 'Abdallah b. Ghalib was interviewed in a dream after his death in battle (cited at the chapter heading). The unknown interviewer asked how Abu Firas had been rewarded, for what, and why his tomb was so sweet-smelling (because of his recitation of the Qur'an and the thirst he suffered during the hottest time of the day).[20] Yet others include the Prophet Muhammad's great-great-grandson Zayd, who was crucified in 739. Afterwards one of the onlookers saw the Prophet in a dream standing beside Zayd on the cross, saying, "Is this how you treat my descendants?"[21] Again, this dream is most probably interpreted as a legitimization of the cause for which Zayd died; the temporal proximity

---

[18] Al-Tamimi, *Kitab al-mihan*, p. 91.   [19] Ibn Abi al-Dunya, *Kitab al-manam*, p. 102 (no. 175).
[20] See note 1; and compare the dream of Yunis b. 'Ubayd in Ibn Abi al-Dunya, *Kitab al-manam*, p. 109 (no. 185).
[21] Al-Isfahani, *Maqatil*, p. 139.

to the martyrdom also serves to confirm Zayd's status as a martyr, although this status was generally accepted by the populations of Iraq and the eastern Muslim empire. Another martyr, Ahmad b. Nasr, who was killed by the caliph al-Wathiq (842–47), is said to have related in a dream that God forgave anyone who disliked the fact that he had been killed.[22]

All of these dreams – only a small selection of those available[23] – are common throughout the Muslim martyrdom tradition. The general themes of the martyrdom dream literature serve to confirm the status of the martyrs after their death, to demonstrate their satisfaction with their fate and to influence others to follow them.

Poetry of martyrdom

Poetry has always been one of the most important cultural expressions of the various cultures that constitute Islam; the love of poetry is one common factor that binds different Muslim cultures together. From the pre-Islamic period Arabs fixated upon poetry, while the Persian poetic epics of the eleventh through the sixteenth centuries are magnificent; the Turks composed verse epics later, while verse is characteristic of African Islam, and Indonesia and Malaysia have narratives of their love of poetry.[24] It is impossible to characterize all of this disparate poetry, so this section will merely summarize some of the broader martyrdom themes that appear in the poetic literature. Most of the poetry concerning martyrdom is either contained within collections devoted to *jihad* poetry or is even to be found within the same poems. The themes are very similar to the poetry of *jihad*: defiance of death or occasionally an embrace of it, contempt for this world, love for God, admonishing the cowardly or doubting soul just before fighting or death and praise for the pleasures of paradise as compared to the vanities of this world. These themes are eternal and not necessarily specifically Islamic in nature; they have similarities to pre-Islamic poetry as well as to epic and heroic poetry from all over the world.

As was noted in Chapter 4, the Kharijites of all the early Islamic groups were the ones best known for their noble and martyrdom-seeking poetry. This poetry was cited even by their opponents, and the sect won converts to its side by the recitation of its poetry and the admiration that audiences felt when contemplating the bravery of the sentiments expressed by the poets. The greatest collections of poetry that became normative for Sunni Muslims are found in the collections on the subject of *jihad*. From the early *jihad* collection of Abu Ishaq al-Fazari (d. 802–03), *Kitab al-siyar*, we find war ditties, some of them

---

[22] Al-Tamimi, *Mihan*, pp. 252–53.   [23] See ibid., pp. 242, 279, 281.
[24] For an overview, see Stefan Sperl and Christopher Schackle (eds), *Qasida Poetry in Islamic Asia and Africa*.

allegedly dating to the time of the Prophet Muhammad.[25] These are completely in the tradition of Bedouin war-poems, however, and do not contain obvious Islamic themes.

In the great jihad collection of Ibn al-Nahhas (d. 1411) there is a far more significant collection. Ibn al-Nahhas cites the story of one 'Abd al-Wahid b. Zayd al-Basri who, during a time when an enemy (presumably the Byzantines) was attacking the Muslims, appeared before a group of people in Basra in order to encourage them to go on *jihad*. For this reason he declaimed a poem concerning the houris of paradise, whom he described in the following manner:

> A dainty woman possessed of coquetry and liveliness; the one who describes will find in her what he extemporizes;
> Created from everything beautiful, good; regrets concerning her are flung away;
> God has decorated her with a face in which are gathered together the descriptions of the most beautiful women;
> On her eye her kohl is part of her flirtatiousness; on her cheek musk with sweat;
> Delicate, on his [the martyr's] side runs the splendor of a king and pearls of joy!
> Do you see her suitor listening to her as the cup and flagon is passed once?
> In gardens whose narcissus is pleasant; every time the breeze blows to him it diffuses [its scent];
> She calls him in true love, filling the heart with it until it overflows;
> "O beloved, I do not love anyone other than him!" The opener finishes [opening] the seals;
> "Do not be as one who is dedicated until his need is finished and then leaves!"
> "No, one who is unattentive does not woo the likes of me; only one who presses forward can woo me!"[26]

The response of the crowd to this recitation was said to have been enthusiastic. One of the audience was a certain Umm Ibrahim al-Hashimiyya, who was said to have been among the ascetics of the time. She immediately offered to have her son Ibrahim marry a girl who fit the description of the houri of 'Abd al-Wahid's poem on the condition that he go on *jihad* with 'Abd al-Wahid and be killed as a martyr, in order to act as an intercessor for both her and his father (remembering that a martyr can intercede for seventy of his relatives according to the traditions listed in Chapter 3). To this Ibrahim agreed, and he married the girl his mother offered, leaving his singing career and citing: "God has bought from the believers their lives and their possessions in return for paradise" (Qur'an 9:111). As Ibrahim left for the *jihad* in 'Abd al-Wahid's company, his mother Umm Ibrahim gave him winding sheets and balm as a sign that she expected him to become a martyr.

---

[25] Abu Ishaq al-Fazari, *Kitab al-siyar*, e.g., pp. 180, 286, 302.
[26] Ibn al-Nahhas, *Mashari'*, i, p. 216.

On the battlefield, Ibrahim was one of the first to volunteer to go out and fight, and according to the account, killed a number of the enemy fighters before he himself was killed. On ʿAbd al-Wahid's way back to Basra, he told the other fighters to be careful how they gave Ibrahim's mother the news; they would not want to make it too brutal lest she publicly mourn and lose her reward. But there was no fear of that; Umm Ibrahim said: "O Abu ʿUbayd [ʿAbd al-Wahid's patronymic], was my gift received from me so that I can greet you or was it returned so that I will have to mourn?" (By this she meant, was the gift of her son Ibrahim accepted as a martyr or did he return alive.) He said: "Your gift, by God, was received from you; Ibrahim is alive with the living, sustained" (Qurʾan 3:169). She is said to have fallen to the ground, praying and thanking God for this.[27] This story, although a bit convoluted, is important because it helps us see the practical function of martyrdom poetry and the way in which it encouraged *jihad* fighters to seek martyrdom.

Another collection of *jihad* poetry from Morocco from the tenth through seventeenth centuries contains a great many of these same themes.[28] These themes include aiding God's religion, going forth to victory, praise of courage, descriptions of the flashing swords and spears of warfare, taunts directed at the enemy, descriptions of the Christians' corrupt and infidel practices, and Islamic slogans. Defeat is described in terms of humiliation and disgrace, and the fear of being ruled or dominated by Christians. Although descriptions of martyrdom and paradise are not the themes most dwelt upon within this poetry, they are consistently represented throughout the entirety of the corpus. The poet describes life as fleeting, death as a victory and paradise as being spent in the close company of God and the other righteous ones, such as prophets and martyrs. For example, one poet, al-Tunmarti, from the fifteenth century says:

> O lions of the Moroccans, take heed! For a long time you have been in error and sleep,
> Light and heavy go forth and prepare yourselves,[29] before you glorious victory leads.
> Verily souls from among us are eternalized in the earth; we have a home of blessedness, eternal.[30]

In general, the words are simple, the allusions Qurʾanic or historical, and the slogans quite up-beat and positive. In other poems, we learn that those martyrs who died saving helpless Muslim women, children and elderly from the infidel are part of the blessed going to paradise. "He gains felicity and favor from God, and at the time of the return [to God] he has riches in the Gardens of Eden."[31]

---

[27] Ibn al-Nahhas, *Mas;hariʿ al-ashwaq*, i, pp. 215–18; other poetry is found pp. 212, 579, ii, p. 669.

[28] ʿAbd al-Haqq al-Marini (ed.), *Shiʿr al-jihad fi al-adab al-Maghribi*; see also Hadia Dajani-Shakeel, "*Jihad* in Twelfth-Century Arabic Poetry"; and Carole Hillenbrand, *The Crusades: Islamic Perspectives*, pp. 166, 179–80 on some of the poetry from that period.

[29] Qurʾan 9:41. [30] Al-Marini, *Shiʿr*, ii, p. 61.

[31] Ibid., ii, p. 69 (from the work of one ʿAbd al-ʿAziz al-Gharnati, tentatively dated to 1437).

From the poet we learn how the martyr wishes that he could be slain, resurrected, slain and resurrected in order to gain further reward. This idea is based upon the tradition in al-Bukhari that speaks of the fact that none but a martyr would ever want to come back to this world, since if he were resurrected, he would want to die again as a martyr because of the martyr's high status in heaven.[32]

Other themes include the honor and glory that accompany the *jihad* against the infidels. This theme is usually forbidden in the *jihad* literature, because it is God who grants the true glory and honor to a fighter in the *jihad* (since God alone knows who is truly fighting for the sake of lifting the Word of God to the highest, cf. Qurʾan 9:41) or to the martyr. However, reading over the selections of *jihad* and martyrdom poetry reveals how deep this glory-seeking theme was throughout the early modern period of Islam. For example, from the period of the Algerian fight against the French invasion in the 1830s, we have the poem of Muhammad b. Idris al-ʿUmarawi, who said:

> O dwellers of the west, *jihad, jihad*! Infidelity has joined you (associated with you) in the land.
> Rise to aid your religion, smash the people of *shirk* (associating other deities with God)[33] like locusts;
> Whatever you can, prepare for them – firing power and outstripping [them] with fleet horses;
> Die as nobles in the *jihad* against the enemy, for death for the sake of Allah is life that continues;
> Fight infidelity and its supporters, and liberate country after country from them.[34]

This poet makes a clever use of the Arabic root for associating other deities with God (*shirk*, or *sharaka*), which is the primal sin in Islam, and the idea of associating with the French or allowing the enemy in the land of Algeria. Many of these later *jihad* poems bring up the theme of the destruction of the Spanish Muslim states hundreds of years previously, especially as some of them claimed descent from these refugees who went to North Africa.

Death is often spoken of as a treasure that needs to be claimed, and contempt for the fear of death is a major feature in the *jihad* and martyrdom poetry.[35] But again this theme can hardly be said to be confined to Islam. The poetry of martyrdom in general contains few overtly Islamic references and usually employs these heroic themes.

---

[32] Ibid., ii, p. 70; compare the original tradition in al-Bukhari, *Sahih*, iii, p. 268 (no. 2797).

[33] Originally the epithet of *mushrikun* was only applied to polytheists, but by the eighth century also to Christians.

[34] Ibid., ii, p. 94.

[35] E.g., ibid., i, pp. 94–95, 244, ii, p. 100; for a discussion on these major themes see pp. 295–381; also ʿAbdallah b. Salih al-ʿArini, *Shiʿr jihad al-Rum hatta nihayat al-qarnʿ al-rabiʿ al-hijri fi mawazin al-naqd al-adabi*, pp. 77–88, 117–28.

Apocalypse

One of the methods by which martyrdom narratives are conveyed is to portray them within the genre of apocalypse. Muslim literary apocalypses and apocalyptic fragments contain a substantial number of symbolic martyrdoms, both those typological figures that represent the Prophet Muhammad's family fighting for their rights (not all of Shi'ite provenance) as well as those who are of a pan-Muslim appeal. Apocalypses are, as Franz Rosenthal described them, a "future history"[36] and are designed to provide the believer with control over the future, to give some sense of hope and a possible scenario in which the wrongs of the present will be rectified in the future. These apocalypses are the refuge of the powerless (or those who perceive themselves to be powerless), and for this reason have some topical similarity to martyrdom narratives.

The Muslim apocalyptic scenario is fairly complicated, but it essentially stretches from the present through a series of ever intensifying Signs of the End (*ashrat al-sa'a*) until the destruction of this world and the Resurrection of the Dead for the next. These signs include wars against powers the early Muslims could not defeat (the Byzantines, various Turkish tribes, etc.), the appearance of a malevolent figure called the Sufyani – closely associated with Syria – and his opponent the Mahdi (the Muslim messianic figure). In general, the Sufyani represents the oppressive Umayyad dynasty in its hatred for the Prophet Muhammad's family and is often shown martyring them. For example, in the "Daniel Apocalypse" (from the tenth century Baghdadi work of Ibn al-Munadi), we find the Sufyani's general, the Zuhri conquering Medina, as the Umayyads did several times, and taking members of the Prophet Muhammad's family captive. The following scene will then ensue:

The Zuhri will say to the youth: Who are you? He will reply: My name is 'Ali b. Muhammad b. 'Abdallah, my mother's name was Fatima daughter of Muhammad b. 'Abdallah. He will say to the girl: Who are you? She will reply: I am the sister of the youth. He will say: Your father fought me more than any other [opponent]. Then he will order them to be stretched out before him, and take a spear and stick it in the belly of the girl. Her brother will turn his face away from her, and the Zuhri will say to those holding his head: Turn his face towards his sister, so that he sees the shame and the humiliation! So they will turn his face back towards his sister, but he will lower his gaze and place his hands upon his eyes. He [the Zuhri] will stick the spear into his [the youth's] belly, and then into his rectum, and then in the rectum of his sister, while the youth says: O God! You have the praise! Quickly bring vengeance and shame upon him and his followers and make them know Your power! Then he [the Zuhri] will order them to be thrown beneath the horses so that the horses will trample them . . . [37]

This apocalyptic fragment has all of the classic characteristics of a Muslim martyrdom narrative. The names of the youth from the Prophet Muhammad's

---

[36] Rosenthal, *A History of Muslim Historiography*, p. 23.
[37] Cook, "An Early Muslim Daniel Apocalypse," pp. 75–76.

family and his ancestors are all stereotypical. Torments that the youth and his sister undergo at the hands of the Zuhri, as well as the nobility that the youth demonstrates when he is forced to look at his sister's shame (cf. Qur'an 24:30) are also stereotypical. Prayers of vengeance (which are answered as the apocalypse continues), cried out in the extremity of death, are also part of the Muslim martyrdom sequence.

Other apocalyptic enemies such as the Dajjal (the Muslim antichrist) also create martyrs. Many of these are tortured in even more gruesome ways than previously described, including being boiled alive, dismembered or sawed into pieces. These tortures continue until Jesus returns to lead the Muslim community into ultimate victory and establishes the messianic state. The whole process of apocalypse is one of winnowing out the wheat from the chaff, separating the true and faithful Muslims from those who are false or hypocritical. It is clear that the torments that the Muslims undergo both in the present and in the future constitute an expiation for the community as a whole. As the popular tradition states, "My community is a blessed community – it has no punishment in the next world, since its punishment is in this world, tribulations, earthquakes and killing."[38] For true Muslims, this world is a testing ground, where "Allah may know who are the believers and choose martyrs from among you" (Qur'an 3:140).

Expiation

Part of the attraction of martyrdom for any believer is the fact that suffering in this world insures forgiveness or at least entrance into paradise. This raises the question of the process of expiation for the Muslim martyr. From the early *jihad* book of Ibn al-Mubarak cited in Chapter 3, we read:

... [Then] a believer, committing offenses and sins against himself, who struggles with himself and his possessions in the path of God, such that when he meets the enemy [in battle] he fights until he is killed. This cleansing wipes away his offenses and his sins – behold the sword wipes [away] sins! – and he will be let into heaven from whatever gate he wishes.[39]

It is clear that the fighting process in and of itself, when the intention behind it is pure and solely for the sake of God or to "raise the Word of God to the highest," brings automatically a blanket forgiveness. *Hadith* and legal literature discuss how all-encompassing that forgiveness is, and to which sins it applies. From the *hadith* collection of al-Nasa'i (d. 915–16) there is an often-cited *hadith* to the effect that although evil actions are forgiven, outstanding loans are not

---

[38] Abu Da'ud, *Sunan*, iv, p. 103 (no. 4228).
[39] Cited in Chapter 3, note 6; and see al-Wazir al-Sarraj, *al-Hulal al-sundusiyya*, ii, p. 401 for a similar statement.

absolved by death in battle.[40] Thus, the martyr, while receiving rewards above and beyond other Muslims, is not entirely exempt from the need to set his or her affairs in order as best he can prior to death.

The expiation process happens by means of wounds and blood. It is clear from the *hadith* and *jihad* literature that it is the drops of blood falling from the martyr or the wounds that lead to his or her death which are objective proof for the forgiveness of sins.[41] Without those visual indicators the cleansing does not happen. Extensive citations gathered by the moralist Ibn Abi al-Dunya (d. 894–895) in his *Kitab al-marad wa-l-kaffarat* (*The Book of Sickness and Expiation*) indicate that many Muslims from this time also saw other forms of suffering, which did not necessarily lead to death, such as injustice or physical ailments, as constituting an expiation for sins. Although this line of tradition is comparatively muted in the canonical collections, it is far more important in Muslim popular literature, in which it is related to the traditions about the plague cited in Chapter 2. If Muslims who die in the plague are indeed martyrs then it is easy to see why those who suffer from sickness should also receive forgiveness for their sins as a result of their suffering.[42]

In this popular type of literature expiatory suffering is extended to a number of different types of sicknesses and problems. For example, the famous scholar 'Urwa b. al-Zubayr (son of one of the Prophet Muhammad's closest Companions) is said to have suffered from a growth on the leg. Upon receiving medical advice to take a drug that would kill the pain but render him unconscious and allow the doctor to operate, he preferred to saw off the growth without any painkillers.[43] This operation would be painful, but one that would enable him to continue to remember God in a conscious state and thereby expiate himself. Although such an extreme response does not seem to have been the norm in classical Muslim culture, it certainly represents one possible response to pain and suffering.

The core of the expiation lies in the fundamental attitude of the Muslim martyr and not his or her bodily wounds. Although the issue of suffering, loss of limbs and shedding of blood features prominently in the literature on expiation, the question of intention is always present. There is nothing inherent in suffering, pain or death themselves that is unique to Muslim martyrs. Therefore, the question remains: what is the added element that accords them an expiation for sins that was not accorded to other Muslims or to non-Muslims? It appears that this

---

[40] Al-Nasa'i, *Sunan*, vi, pp. 34–36; also Muslim, *Sahih*, vi, p. 37; Ibn Muflih, *Kitab al-furu'*, iii, p. 430.

[41] For example, Ibn Hanbal, *Musnad*, iv, p. 268, vi, p. 168; al-Tamimi, *Kitab al-mihan*, p. 275.

[42] Especially when they die from plague, see al-Qadiri, *Kitab iltiqat al-durar*, p. 154 where one Muhammad b. Abi Shita' al-Manqushi dies in Istanbul of the plague (in 1661) as a martyr; because of his many sufferings a beam of white light is said to have shone from his tomb.

[43] Ibn Abi al-Dunya, *Kitab al-marad wa-l-kaffarat*, pp. 113–19.

crucial element is intention, which we have already seen to be key in the question of who precisely is or is not a martyr. Since the general trend of the tradition literature is that it is not one's actions that creates the martyr, but one's intentions, it seems logical to assume that the same holds true with expiation of sins.

Expiation is also created by the sense of patience and long-suffering under hardship and torment (*sabr*). One of the many Qur'anic verses cited to support this ideal is 39:10 ". . . the steadfast (*sabirun*) will be paid their wages in full, without reckoning."[44] This patience or steadfastness is one of the most important Muslim virtues, and indicates a willingness to accept that which God has decreed without bitterness. Although it might be easy to confuse this sense of patience with fatalism or even indifference, the Muslim sources do not confuse these various qualities. Patience bred from detachment is not considered a virtue; on the contrary, the Muslim must be fully aware and involved, but focused upon the will of God and the importance of the next world rather than this one. Thus the fortitude that is created is not a brittle shell of indifference, but, rather a cushioned, proactive shield of faith. Patience and intention are intertwined within the martyr because he or she knows that God's will is being fulfilled through the sufferings being endured and indeed, the martyr is able to rejoice and take comfort in that fact.

There are other legal issues connected to this concept of expiation through suffering. Is there some type of exchange that takes place in order to effect this type of expiation? The tradition usually cited to support this doctrine is a controversial one: "A Jew or a Christian will be brought on the Day of Resurrection as well as a [sinning] Muslim, and God will say [to the Muslim]: This is your redemption from the Fire [of Hell]."[45] In other words, the Jew or the Christian will expiate the sins of the Muslim by suffering in hell. This tradition, which belongs to a whole family of similar traditions,[46] is problematic for fairly obvious reasons: it seems to indicate a lack of absolute justice on the part of God and an absence of the need for a Muslim to be concerned about committing sins. If Jews and Christians will spend eternity expiating the sins of Muslims, why should Muslims worry about whether they sin or not?

In general, the question of intercession is one that has proved to be divisive for Muslims, but the consensus appears to be that there will be intercession for Muslims (or substitution), and that no Muslim will actually have to spend eternity in hell, but that some Muslims will have to expiate their sins in hell for a time.[47] Sometimes this expiation is for a long time, and according to

[44] Cited by al-Tamimi, *Kitab al-mihan*, p. 284.

[45] Muslim, *Sahih*, viii, pp. 104–05; cited by al-Tamimi, *Kitab al-mihan*, p. 205.

[46] Compare Ibn Maja, *Sunan*, ii, p. 1434 (no. 4292); al-Bayhaqi, *al-Ba'th wa-l-nushur*, pp. 94–98; and other sources in Wensinck, *Concordance*, s.v., *fida'*, *fikak*; al-Baghawi, *Sharh al-sunna*, viii, p. 390; and al-Hindi, *Kanz al-'ummal*, xii, pp. 159 (no. 34,473), 170–71 (nos. 34,524–25, 34,527–29).

[47] According to the creedal statements in W. Montgomery Watt, *Islamic Creeds*, pp. 36 (Hanbalite), 53 (al-Tahawi), 60 (Abu Hanifa), 65 (a Later Hanafite creed), 71 (al-Qayrawani, Maliki).

some traditions there will be a group of Muslims in heaven who will be known as the *jahanamiyyun* (those who had spent some time in hell).[48] However, there have been equally strong voices against the idea of intercession and pardon for Muslims guilty of grave sins.

The martyr is not the only one who seeks or needs expiation, obviously. All too often the audience is guilty as well, and may seek forgiveness or penance for the shame of having watched and/or participated in the martyrdom of a righteous person, or for not having actively tried to stop it. Probably the best-known example in Islam is that of the *al-Tawwabun*, the Penitents, who appeared in 685, some years after the murder of al-Husayn outside Kufa. These Penitents were drawn from those Muslims who had first invited al-Husayn to come to Kufa, then had betrayed and abandoned him as a result of the intimidation by the governor ʿUbayduallah. After Husayn's murder these people felt an intense guilt and shame over what had happened and sought to expiate these feelings by throwing themselves at the Umayyad army until they were completely wiped out.[49] It is not clear, however, whether this historical instance is a precedent for expiation.

Expiation is also necessary not merely as a result of abandonment and betrayal as in the case of al-Husayn, but also when the death process involves humiliation. The best example of this is the crucifixion of Zayd, the Prophet Muhammad's descendant, in 739. During the course of his torment, his loincloth gradually came loose and exposed his nakedness to the crowds. This was humiliating for him, but doubly so for the audience which acquired extra guilt in seeing this shameful event (until someone retied a cloth around him). Tradition after tradition curses those who gazed upon his nakedness, and many of those who viewed the crucifixion felt they were personally guilty not just for their lack of support for his cause, but also for witnessing him in this manner during his death.[50]

The final exhortation

In general, the martyr's death is given meaning by his final exhortation. Although it often strains historical credulity to believe that lengthy statements were actually made by the dying man or woman or that someone was available to write them down verbatim, these types of exhortations convey the belief of the martyr to the audience and make certain that they know for which cause he died. For example, as ʿUmar died, he not only exhorted the believers to uphold the *sunna* and to keep the faith, but he did so in rhymed Arabic.[51] One difference between Muslim and Christian martyrology appears to involve the last phase: the martyr's relationship towards his or her executioner (or assassin). Whereas

---

[48] Ibn ʿAdi, *al-Kamil fi duʿafa al-rijal*, iii, p. 53.   [49] See *EI²*, s.v. "Tawwabun" (F. M. Denny).
[50] Al-Isfahani, *Maqatil*, pp. 126–28, 138–39.   [51] Al-Tamimi, *Mihan*, p. 75.

in Christian martyrdom there developed a strong sense that one should cry out forgiveness for one's tormentors, assassins or executioners – in accordance with Jesus' last words (Luke 23:34) – the attitude in Islam towards oppressors is a good deal less forgiving. When the caliph 'Uthman was assassinated, his wife is said to have cursed the murderers with the prayer of a wronged person (see Chapter 3).

Part of the purpose of the final exhortation of the martyr is to bring home to the oppressor the true evil of his deeds. As previously stated, it is important in a classical martyrdom that the evil figure realizes (at least in the end or after the martyrdom) the gravity of what he has done. A good example of this *topos* was the behavior of the Umayyad governor al-Hajjaj b. Yusuf al-Thaqafi (ruled Iraq 692–715), who has come down in history as the archetypical cruel governor. Widely hated by Shi'ites, and feared by many of the religious elite, he executed large numbers of Iraqis during his rule (although he is also credited with having achieved vast conquests and having kept public order during his term of office). One of the religious leadership he executed was Sa'id b. Jubayr (in 713). In al-Tamimi's martyrology Sa'id is given a great deal of prominence[52] and allowed to deliver a powerful remonstration to al-Hajjaj, telling the governor precisely what quite a number of those living under al-Hajjaj would have loved to tell him: that he was a tyrant. Al-Hajjaj lost his temper at Sa'id and had him killed, but then suffered pangs of guilt afterwards and could not sleep because of what he had done. Although it is doubtful whether the material about al-Hajjaj and Sa'id is historical, the martyrology is true to type. The persecuted scholar is bold in confronting the tyrant, who in turn eventually comes to recognize the fundamentally unjust sentence he has carried out. There are few available examples of forgiveness being granted to these figures; they will be remembered for all time as tyrants and very little attempt is made to portray them sympathetically or to rehabilitate them posthumously.

Remembrance

Obviously the literary form of the martyrology is designed to commemorate the martyr's sacrifice and to perpetuate his or her legacy in this world, as well as to provide role models for future generations. The manner of this perpetuation is different from culture to culture and from time period to time period. Most of the time Muslim martyrs are described in literary prose or poetry texts. However, there are local martyrs, or martyrs of those communities that are under some oppression or have not achieved full literacy and thus cannot record in writing their experience of martyrdom. For these communities the usual form of commemoration is to generate oral compositions. No doubt most of the

---

[52] Ibid., pp. 216–31.

stories that we have in al-Tamimi's *Kitab al-mihan*, al-Isfahani's *Maqatil al-Talibiyyin* and al-Kashifi's *Rawzat al-shuhada'* were originally of this variety. Over the centuries the traditions contained in these works came to be set down in written form. Some local martyrs even to this day are unrecorded in authoritative sources, and are only known through oral tradition.

Other forms of remembrance involve the preservation of artifacts, usually either the personal possessions of the martyr or more commonly parts of his body. This latter element is problematic in Islam, both because of the sacred nature of the body of the martyr, and because veneration of these relics has traditionally been looked upon with some suspicion by religious authorities. Veneration of bodily relics oftentimes falls into a gray area where Islam and polytheism are not well differentiated, and this ambiguity is unacceptable to many Muslims (especially present-day Wahhabis and strict Sufi orders).

Another form of remembrance is the construction of shrines, usually upon the spot at which the martyr died. Examples of these are numerous – all of the Shi'ite imams have shrines dedicated to them, as do many of the Prophet's Companions. There are numerous local holy men and women whose shrines dot the landscape of the Muslim world; however, not all of these people were martyrs. Local art is also important in preserving the memory of martyrs, although within the context of Islam it is less important than in other faiths because of the partial ban upon depiction of the human form. However, from the Persian, Turkish and Indo-Muslim cultures we have a vast artistic collection of portraits of martyrs, albeit only of the epic or romantic variety (Majnun and Layla especially).[53]

Perhaps the best-known manner in which the martyr is remembered is the *ta'ziya* (the passion play), which is a prominent part of Shi'ite celebrations and commemorations of the martyrdom of al-Husayn.[54] These *ta'ziya*s, which historically have their roots in the tenth century, when Shi'ites became politically dominant in Iraq, are part of a culture of oral recollection and group dramatization of a collective grief and remembrance. Each year on the 10th of Muharram (the 'Ashura') Shi'ites re-enact the events of al-Husayn's martyrdom using one of a number of accepted *ta'ziya* cycles. Each one of these cycles focuses upon a part of the overall events of the martyrdom (since there is no way to include all of them). For example, some of the *ta'ziya*s focus upon the sufferings of several of al-Husayn's children, both male and female, while others dramatize the battles and single-handed combats of that fateful day. Whole villages take part in

---

[53] See, e.g., B. W. Robinson, *Persian Paintings in the John Rylands Library: A Descriptive Catalogue*, pp. 144 (no. 541), 199 (no. 625) (both of the death of Rustam), 276 (no. 818) (Layla's funeral); Ebadollah Bahari, *Bihzad: Master of Persian Painting*, p. 147 (no. 83) (Majnun on Layla's tomb).

[54] For the rites of visiting al-Husayn, see al-Shajari, *Fadl ziyarat al-Husayn*, pp. 39, 50–51, 62; for the *ta'ziya* overall, see *EI²*, s.v. "Ta'ziya" (Peter Chelkowski).

these dramas, and often there is symbolic or commemorative bloodshed (usually done by a person upon his or her own body). The form of these *ta'ziyas* is based to a large degree upon al-Kashifi's (d. 1504) *Rawzat al-shuhada'* (*Garden of Martyrs*), composed in the Safavid period when Iran was converted to Shi'ism. Most of the actual *ta'ziyas* that are used in contemporary Shi'ite communities date from a more recent period, however.[55] Thematically, the *ta'ziyas* are con-flicts between good and evil, and are based upon motifs that are older than Islam (most especially the martyrdom of Siavush, an epic hero of pre-Islamic Iran).[56]

A good example of a *ta'ziya* is, for instance, that quoted by Malekpour, in *The Martyrdom of Imam Husayn* (dating from the 1880s), which shows us the last moments of al-Husayn's life:

> Husayn: (*to angels*): I do not need your help, my friends,
> Leave me to be alone with my God,
> That this is the promised day!
>
> (*All the players and the audience start reciting elegies and beating their chests.*)
> Mourners: Husayn, Husayn, Husayn, Husayn, killed by Ashghya, Husayn.
> Husayn, Husayn, Husayn, Husayn, head separated from the body, Husayn.
> Husayn, Husayn, Husayn, Husayn, tonight, Holy Fatima!
> Husayn, Husayn, Husayn, Husayn, in fear and pity.
> Husayn, Husayn, Husayn, Husayn, coming to the Karbala plain.
> Husayn, Husayn, Husayn, Husayn, asking what happened to my Husayn.
> Husayn, Husayn, Husayn, Husayn.
> Shimr [sub-commander of the Umayyad troops]: Good news, Army of the Devil!
> A hero, Husayn, has arrived. You soldiers, take his life, make his friends mourn.
> Ibn Sa'd [commander of the Umayyad troops]: The soldier from my army who takes this dagger and goes to the field, and cuts the head off this holy Arab will have the land of Rayy as a reward.
>
> (*Silence. No one moves.*)
> Soldiers, do not be afraid, do not panic!
> Husayn no longer has a brother,
> Husayn no longer has a son.
> The soldier from this army who takes this dagger and goes to the field and cuts the head off this holy Arab will have the land of Rayy as a reward.
> Shimr: The reward, sir, is mine.

[55] For a description of the Indian Shi'ite material, including numerous descriptions of the *ta'ziya*, see Saiyid Athar Abbas Rizvi, *A Socio-Intellectual History of the Isna 'Ashari Shi'is in India*, ii, Chapter 4.

[56] Ehsan Yarshater, "Ta'ziyeh and Pre-Islamic Mourning Rites in Iran"; also Malekpour, *The Islamic Drama*, Chapter 3.

Send me, send me, this is my task!

It is I who am going to shake God's pavilion! It is I who am going to cut the
  head of Husayn from his body . . .

Husayn: Shimr, give me kindly a few minutes,

Let me pray for the last time.

Shimr: You are free to pray now,

Put your pleading face to the ground before God.

Husayn: (*praying*) I have kept my promise to You, Almighty God!

Oh Lord, forgive the sins of my Shi'ite followers, for my sake . . .

(*to Shimr*) You miserable man, hurry up and do your job!

Shimr: Husayn, say "There is no God but God" so that I can cut off your head!

(*Shimr cuts Imam Husayn's head off.*)

Bring the banner and play the drum! Display the head of Husayn to all.[57]

As Malekpour states, the themes in this *ta'ziya* are quite straightforward. The
goodness of al-Husayn, his inherent nobility and godliness are readily apparent,
while the evil of his two major opponents, Shimr b. Dhi Jawshan and the overall
commander of the Umayyad forces, 'Umar b. Sa'd, is obvious. As one would
expect, the nuances related in the history books – 'Umar's unwillingness to kill
al-Husayn for example – have no place in the *ta'ziya*. Only the Umayyad soldiers
are somewhat hesitant to take part in this slaughter. Again, this latter tendency
demonstrates that even Husayn's enemies and murderers had to acknowledge
his superior qualities.

Other *ta'ziya*s focus upon the tragedies of al-Husayn's family, such as that of
his brother al-Hasan's son al-Qasim, who was betrothed to al-Husayn's daughter
Fatima. According to the play, the marriage goes forward even as the ghastly and
tragic circumstances of Karbala unfold. Al-Qasim marries Fatima, but of course
is unable to consummate the marriage under these conditions, and so promises
consummation will occur in heaven. Fatima is said to have asked how she will
recognize him, and he says that "she will recognize him by his rent sleeves, his
torn body, bleeding from one hundred wounds and his eyes wet with sorrow,
marching in the service of her father."[58] He then goes out to the battlefield and
is slain after displaying great heroism. This tragedy, which employs to great
emotive force the juxtaposition of the normalcies of life and the joy of marriage
with the horrors of warfare, is rightly popular. Al-Husayn is present, and always
in the background, but is not the focus of this particular *ta'ziya*. However, the
element of good versus evil is maintained due to the appearance of the two
figures of Shimr and 'Umar b. Sa'd at critical points.

One cannot say that the Sunnis have anything remotely so dramatic to aid in
the commemoration of their martyrs. While there are certainly plenty of pilgrimage books and guides from the classical period, and ample evidence that Sunnis,

[57] Malekpour, *The Islamic Drama*, pp. 78–79 (I modified the translation slightly to improve the
English, and to standardize the spelling of Arabic names).

[58] Sadeq Humayuni, "An Analysis of the Ta'ziyeh of Qasem," at p. 14.

like Shi'ites, venerated dead holy men and women, there is little evidence that martyrs were singled out for special recollection. Certain pilgrimage books and narratives, such as that of al-Harawi (d. 1214) list the graves of martyrs, most of whom have been mentioned. For example, al-Harawi mentions Abu Ayyub al-Ansari, the early Muslim fighter who was martyred beneath the walls of Constantinople during the seventh century, but does not mention any particular rites associated with him other than that the Christians venerated him as did the Muslims.[59] As I will note in Chapter 8, not until the rise of radical Islam, which is focused on the *jihad*, have Sunnis started to produce martyrologies in large numbers. The remembrance of martyrdom promotes a political program, and that has been one of the core issues of contemporary radical Islam.[60] Revival of the past, focus upon the suffering and glory of the past has brought out the political program of the future. Manipulation of ancient themes and symbols has been key in gaining new followers for new ideologies and doctrines. All of these matters are grist for the mill of present-day radical Islam.

[59] Al-Harawi, *al-Isharat ila ma'rifat al-ziyarat*, p. 53.
[60] How this is accomplished is best recounted in Peter Chelkowski and Hamid Dabashi, *Staging a Revolution: The Art of Persuasion in the Islamic Republic of Iran*.

8   Martyrdom in contemporary radical Islam

Of the believers, there are men who have fulfilled what they pledged to Allah;
some of them have died, some are waiting, without changing in the least.

Qur'an 33:23

From the first centuries of Islam, martyrdom has been important but not crucial in the growth of the religion. As detailed in Chapters 4 and 5, most Muslim martyrs were martyrs for one particular sect or branch of Islam (and were often demonized by its opponents). There are comparatively few examples of martyrs who actually died in a cause that could represent Islam in its ontological form, other than fighters and Sufi missionaries, which are categories that often overlapped. Muslims rarely had to choose between giving up their faith and torture or death, with the exception of slaves or those captured by Europeans, and most who achieved the title of "martyr" were in fact martyred by those who claimed to be Muslims themselves. Although during this time – from the thirteenth through nineteenth centuries – Muslims continued to expand aggressively, and sometimes used the slogans of *jihad* in order to legitimize this expansion, most of the conquest was achieved by governmental initiative. There was little need to make the call for *jihad*, since in general, at least during the early part of this period, Islam was expanding gradually.

But by the end of the seventeenth century, that trend was reversing, especially in areas bordering upon lands controlled by Europeans or claimed by them. The Ottoman Empire in southeastern Europe was beginning a long, slow retreat from the walls of Vienna (1680–83), the Russian Empire was aggressively expanding through the Ukraine and out into Siberia at the expense of the Muslim Turks and Mongols (sixteenth through nineteenth centuries), and during the eighteenth and nineteenth centuries, the Indian subcontinent came to be dominated by Great Britain. Throughout the nineteenth century large areas of the Muslim world, including North Africa, East Africa and Indonesia, were subordinated to colonial non-Muslim control. Only the core Muslim lands under the Ottomans (until 1918) and Iran under the Qajar dynasty (until 1905) continued to be ruled by Muslims, and both territories were heavily under the influence of foreigners as well. This long litany of military defeat continued during the early part

of the twentieth century with the break-up of the Ottoman Empire in 1918–
22 and the occupation of most of its territories by Great Britain and France.
Although, along with the rest of the territories controlled by European powers,
the Muslim world received its independence between 1948 and 1970, many
Muslims found that independence did not mean the end of foreign control or
cultural domination.

Jihad played a role in the resistance Muslims posed towards European incursions. However, for many elites in Muslim majority countries during the nineteenth and early twentieth centuries, *jihad* with its religious connotations was
not attractive or useful, and while sometimes these elites used the words or
phrases associated with *jihad*, they were usually divorced from its religious
content. Although these elites usually rejected colonialist occupation of their
countries and sometimes actively resisted it, in general they tried to accomplish
this by using nationalistic and non-sectarian ideals. Many of these elites were
themselves Christian or had been educated in Christian missionary schools and
for this reason either lacked the classic foundational training in Islam or desired
that their (future) states be free of sectarian divisions. Prominent Muslim opponents of imperialism did not command broad support and were accused by
secular nationalists of being divisive. Calls for *jihad* were consequently muted
and often seen as subsidiary to a general pan-Arab or nationalist call to unity
against the foreign invader. Many nationalist movements have lists of *shuhada'*
(martyrs), even though the cause in which they died was not Muslim, strictly
speaking.[1] This broad use of the term is descended from the trend discussed in
Chapter 6, where the term is used for political heroes or epic figures accorded
the status of "martyr," at least within the popular memory. In contemporary literature this broadened terminology for martyrdom reaches the ridiculous when
we find secular or even communist parties calling their fallen *shuhada'*. In
general, these secular (or at least not overtly Islamic) martyrdoms do not have
the characteristics of classical Muslim martyrdom, and need not be discussed
further. The muted use of *jihad* held throughout the Muslim world until the rise
of political Islam after the Six-Day War with Israel in 1967.

The problem of Israel is a central one for Arab Muslims specifically, and also
generally for all Muslims. Ever since its establishment in 1948, Israel has consistently defeated its Arab neighbors, for whom its existence was unacceptable,
in battle. However, prior to 1967, the tendency of Arab propaganda concerning
Israel was generally to belittle its prowess, to characterize its soldiers as cowards and to predict its quick demise. This attitude changed considerably after
the Six-Day War, in which the Egyptian, Jordanian and Syrian armies were
all decisively defeated and the Israeli army occupied parts of their territories.

---

[1] For example, Kumar Bharati, *Shahadatnama* (commemorating those who fought the British in
India for independence).

After this defeat, the tendency has been to exaggerate the military abilities of the Israelis, and to make it seem that they are supermen. (This tactic worked quite well; excessive confidence in its own superiority led Israel to almost lose the next war in 1973.) Therefore, the shock of the Six-Day War was very great, and consequently the disillusionment with secular nationalistic systems that had dominated the Arab world was deep. This shock, together with the rise in the importance of the conservative oil-producing states after 1973, especially Wahhabi Saudi Arabia, gave political Islam an attractive quality it had lacked prior to that period. Together with this resurgence of Islam came a heavy emphasis upon *jihad* as a better method of waging warfare, since nationalistic warfare had so clearly failed.[2]

An unfortunate byproduct of this exaggeration of the power of Israel and of the worldwide Jewish community has been the widespread acceptance in the Arab and Muslim world of *The Protocols of the Elders of Zion*. This book, an early twentieth-century Russian anti-Semitic forgery purporting to be the minutes of a program established by Zionists to dominate the world and turn it into a techno-dictatorship, has become extremely important to radical Muslims (as well as to many other religious and secular groups) to establish a paranoid outlook towards the world. Without comprehension of this outlook, much of their writing about *jihad* and martyrdom is difficult to understand. Contemporary popular radical Islamic literature emphasizes the idea that there is a worldwide conspiracy against Islam, usually said to be led by Jews and Christians (with Hindus occasionally), with the ultimate goal of literally annihilating Islam and murdering all Muslims. This analysis of world events goes a long way towards helping one understand the importance of *jihad* for contemporary radical Muslims. Since they feel that they are fighting a battle for their very existence, they fight in a desperate manner. Their list of enemies is not confined solely to non-Muslims, however, as they also believe that Muslims are equally culpable for this grim situation.

Anti-governmental *jihad*

Political Islam has also fed off of the absence of Islam from the public discourse, another by-product of the colonial era that was reinforced by the subsequent secular nationalist regimes. Although nationalist Arab and Muslim leaders strongly opposed the colonialist European order present throughout the world prior to the 1950s, most of these leaders were themselves secular and Western-educated. Their ideal society was a secular (non-Islamic), mostly socialist system, which

---

[2] Note the appearance of a great number of works on *jihad* during this period, and a re-emphasis upon classical Muslim slogans, such as Operation Badr for the Egyptian attack on the Sinai Peninsula in 1973.

would strive to emulate and eventually overtake Western societies. In the Arab world this ideology took the form of pan-Arabism, while in other areas of the Muslim world either forms of socialism, Third-Worldism (such as that of Mu'ammar Gaddafi of Libya) or varieties of pro-Western ideologies reigned supreme. Political Islam had little place in the calculations of these elites, and a number of the regimes (Egypt, Algeria, Tunisia, Iraq and Syria) were overtly hostile to religious Muslims. The same was true in the larger Muslim world, where the nationalistic leaders in Pakistan, Indonesia, Iran and Muslim Africa were for the most part socialist and not very religious. The systems they set up were based ultimately upon Western norms, and usually the *shari'a*, if it was a source of law at all, was confined to the laws of personal status (marriage, divorce, etc.). Traditionally, however, the *shari'a* had been the basis for Muslim society and for the devout Muslim it was unacceptable for their supposedly "independent" societies to ape the West in an attempt to relegate Islam to the private life of the individual.

From this starting point radical Islam began with three intellectual leaders: Sayyid Qutb in Egypt, Abu al-'Ala al-Mawdudi in Pakistan and the Ayatullah Ruhullah al-Khumayni in Iran. Qutb, starting during the 1950s, began to write powerful and devastating critiques of the Egyptian regime, characterizing it as infidel (*jahili*, being equivalent to the pre-Islamic societies against which Muhammad fought), and undercutting its legitimacy. Although Qutb during his lifetime never achieved prominence, after his execution by the Egyptian government in 1966 his writings became the basis for political radical Islam. His most important writings on the subject of *jihad* are to be found in his commentary on the Qur'an, *Fi zilal al-Qur'an* (*In the Shade of the Qur'an*), of which a selection was published in his last book, *Ma'alim fi al-tariq* (*Signposts along the Way*), for which he was executed.[3] Many of these selections detail his attitude towards martyrdom.

For Qutb, the subject of *jihad* was a central one. Since he believed that the anti-Islamic world systems would never allow the free proclamation of Islam, fighting was necessary in order to give people a chance to decide between truth and infidelity. Martyrdom forms one of the key aspects of this process, and indeed the final chapter of *Ma'alim* is devoted to the story of the Companions of the Pit (Qur'an 85:1–9), which was discussed in Chapter 2.[4] This story is one of those few Qur'anic examples of a martyrdom sequence, and by using it Qutb demonstrates that he is perfectly aware that the price of *jihad* is martyrdom. He describes the Companions of the Pit as the paradigmatic believers in God

---

[3] See Ibrahim Abu-Rabi', *Intellectual Origins of Islamic Resurgence in the Modern Arab World*; William Shepard, *Sayyid Qutb and Islamic Activism*; and Suha Taji-Farouki and Basheer Nafi' (eds), *Islamic Thought in the Twentieth Century* for discussions on his ideology.

[4] See translation in Appendix 1.

in an otherwise godless world-system, who are taken and tortured for the sake of their faith.

Qutb asks after these graphic comments, who was the real victor in the battle for truth here? Since all of the Companions of the Pit died in gruesome ways, what is the nature of their victory? To this he answers that they represent a triumph of human dignity and a decisive rejection of the temptations of this world.

All humans embrace death. But the circumstances of death are different and varied. All human beings are not graced with such success, nor can all of them present such a high standard of belief . . . this is God's grace that He selects an august group from amongst His servants, which although it shares death with others is separate and distinctive . . . Their mortal bodies were being burnt in the fire, but this immaculate and sublime principle dictated their success, rather than the fire, by further purifying them and turning them into pure gold.[5]

Thus for Qutb actual worldly victory was not necessary since martyrs by virtue of their sacrifice have already achieved victory over the world. Although martyrdom played but a small role in the achievement of the Muslim state (during the time of Muhammad), Qutb saw it as a necessary role and was careful to portray himself as a martyr during the trial at which he was sentenced to death.[6] Thus, Qutb became the living embodiment of radical Islamic martyrdom.

Abu al-'Ala al-Mawdudi's experience was considerably different than that of Qutb, but he was no less tenacious about the subject of *jihad*. Growing up in British-controlled India, and being a part of the sectarian divide between Hindus and Muslims that would ultimately lead to the creation of a separate Pakistan in 1947, Mawdudi had several equal and opposite imperatives.[7] One is reflected in his small booklet on *jihad*, which was one of his earliest writings (dating from 1927–30). It is almost completely apologetic, and focuses upon the effort to make *jihad* into a simple proclamation of Islam. With this irenic view of *jihad*, martyrdom means persecution of the missionaries proclaiming the message of Islam, and eventually the proclamation of the Islamic state. However, he also clearly believed that the establishment of a Muslim state was also an imperative, and could not be achieved without the use of force. He cites Qur'an 9:43–45, which speaks harshly to the Prophet Muhammad when he allowed some Muslims to stay behind from a raid:

[5] Sayyid Qutb, *Ma'alim fi al-tariq*, p. 176; trans. S. Badrul Hasan, *Milestones*, pp. 262–63 (I have modified the English to make it more readable); see also *Fi Zilal al-Qur'an*, IV, pp. 3871–73; also 'Ukasha 'Abd al-Manan al-Tibi, *al-Shahada wa-l-istishhad fi Zilal al-Qur'an li-l-Shaykh Sayyid Qutb*, esp. pp. 19f, 63f, 133–5, 178f.

[6] Qutb, *Li-ma a'adamuni?* Mamduh al-Dayri stated that when Qutb was in prison he was asked what was the meaning of the word *shahid*, and he said "One who bears witness that the *shari'a* of God is more important than his life." Cited in *Sawt al-jihad* 16 (May 2004), p. 40.

[7] See Seyyed Vali Reza Nasr, *Mawdudi and the Making of Islamic Revivalism*, Chapters 1–2 for his formative influences.

May God pardon you! Why did you allow them before it became clear to you who were the truthful ones and you knew who were the liars. Those who believe in God and the Last Day do not ask you for [exemption from] fighting in the way of God with their wealth and lives. God knows well the righteous. Only those who do not believe in God and the Last Day will ask you [for exemption] when their hearts are in doubt. Thus they vacillate in their state of doubt.

Mawdudi uses this selection of verses to emphasize that spending "lives" is going to be necessary in the grand cause of building the Islamic state, and raising the Word of God to the highest (the basic goal of *jihad*).[8] However, it is also clear that unlike Qutb and Khumayni, martyrdom is not a major theme in Mawdudi's work.

Ayatullah al-Khumayni stands apart from the other two, since as a Shi'ite, his vision of Islam was considerably different. Drawing upon the considerable intellectual and emotional heritage of Shi'ite martyrdom, he crafted a very powerful and attractive radical message. Until the middle of the twentieth century, although Shi'ism had cultivated the commemorative aspect of the *ta'ziya* (Chapter 7), for the most part the Shi'ite religious establishment was not very proactive about martyrdom. Most Shi'ites lived under the control of the Shah of Iran or scattered in communities dominated by Sunni (Iraq, Bahrain and Turkey) or non-Muslim (Lebanon, India and the USSR) political elites. None of these elites had any interest in promoting an activist form of Shi'ism or in encouraging the development of a new doctrine of martyrdom.

Al-Khumayni changed all of that. By focusing upon the figure of al-Husayn, revered by all Shi'ites, as a proactive figure and as a willing martyr rather than merely a tragic figure fated to die, Khumayni was able to change the discourse of Shi'ism from quietist to radical.[9] Part of this change was the re-emphasis upon the role of martyrdom inside Shi'ism. Much of this doctrine was fleshed out during the period of the Iran–Iraq War (1980–88), about which see below. But the emphasis upon martyrdom proceeds naturally from al-Khumayni's doctrine. He is said to have stated: "the action of seeking martyrdom[10] is among the highest forms of martyrdom and sacrifice in the path of religion . . . there is no difference between male and female [in this]."[11]

Other Shi'ite thinkers and leaders followed al-Khumayni's lead. For example, the prominent Shi'ite religious figure Mortaza Motahhery in his book *The Martyr* speaks of the transformative power of the martyr's blood:

---

[8] Abu al-'Ala al-Mawdudi, *al-Jihad fi sabil Allah*, p. 43 (in *Thalath rasa'il fi al-jihad*).

[9] See Khumayni, *Islam and Revolution* (trans. Hamid Algar), pp. 35, 50–51 (trans. of *Vilayat-i faqih*).

[10] In Arabic *al-'amal al-istishhadi*; I am translating in this way in order to avoid confusion with the more contemporary Arabic term *al-'amaliyyat al-istishhadiyya* (martyrdom operations, suicide attacks) which would be anachronistic in Khumayni's time.

[11] *Masa'il jihadiyya*, pp. 27–28.

What does a martyr do? His function is not confined to resisting the enemy and, in the process, either giving him a blow or receiving a blow from him. Had that been the case, we could say that when his blood is shed it goes waste. But at no time is a martyr's blood wasted. It does not flow on the ground. Every drop of it is turned into hundreds and thousands of drops, nay, into tons of blood and is transfused into the body of his society . . . Martyrdom means transfusion of blood into a particular human society, especially a society suffering from anaemia, so to speak, of true faith. It is the martyr who infuses such fresh blood into the veins of such [a] society.[12]

In the Shiʿite communities of Lebanon, just coming into political power during the 1970s and 1980s, al-Khumayni's message of activism was seconded by Musa al-Sadr (disappeared 1978). Al-Sadr, like al-Khumayni, used the example of al-Husayn to promote the development of the Shiʿites, who were held in contempt by the ruling Christian Maronite sect and the Sunni Muslims of Beirut.[13] Although this message did not involve martyrdom, when the Shiʿites of southern Lebanon began to fight the Israeli army after 1983 (culminating in the Israeli withdrawal from Lebanon in 2000) they employed the rhetoric popularized by al-Sadr and al-Khumayni. For example, Shaykh Muhammad Husayn Fadlallah, the spiritual leader of the Hizbullah fighting against the Israelis during most of the 1990s, described martyrdom and its effects in confronting tyrants and oppressors using this rhetoric – straight from the taʿziya.[14] Others compared the fighting in southern Lebanon quite literally to that of Karbala in an effort to promote martyrdom.[15] Perhaps because of its long history of martyrdom and familiarity with martyrdom, Shiʿite Lebanon supported martyrs and their families more systematically than any other area in the Muslim world that has produced martyrs in the recent past. Organizations for families and children of martyrs provided a support network unlike any other in the Muslim world.[16]

Both Qutb and Mawdudi were fated not to see their visions of Islam become a reality. However, their ideological descendants in Egypt (and the larger Arab world) and Pakistan have translated their message into reality. In Egypt, Qutb's primary spiritual descendants were the Gamaʿat al-Islamiyya, a loosely organized group of radicals that first rose to prominence in 1981 when one of its members assassinated President Anwar al-Sadat. The ideology behind this assassination was largely contained in the document known as *al-Farida al-ghaʾiba* (*The Neglected Duty*) written by Muhammad ʿAbd al-Salam Farag (later executed) for the internal purposes of the group. His vision of martyrdom

---

[12] Mortaza Motahhery, *The Martyr* (trans. Yusuf Nafsi), p. 63; for similar ideas see ʿAli al-Khamenaʾi (spiritual successor to al-Khumayni), *ʿItr al-shahada*, pp. 12–22, 91–101.

[13] Fouad ʿAjami, *The Vanished Imam: Musa al-Sadr and the Shia of Lebanon*, p. 141f.

[14] *Masaʾil jihadiyya*, pp. 29–30; and see also Fadlallah, *al-Masaʾil al-fiqhiyya*, pp. 316–17.

[15] E.g., Muhammad Qudusi, *Karbala al-jadida: ayyam maʿ al-muqawama fi janub Lubnan*.

[16] E.g., see the instruction booklet on educating the children of martyrs, ʿAli al-Qaʾimi, *Tarbiyat awlad al-shahid*; and for a study of Shiʿite suicide attacks, Saʿd Abu Diyya, *Dirasa tahliliyya fi al-ʿamaliyyat al-istishhadiyya fi janub Lubnan* (until 1986).

is a powerful one and demonstrates some development beyond that of Qutb. For Farag there are no excuses for Muslims being unwilling to establish a Muslim state. Those who believe that one should merely proselytize in order to achieve a Muslim state, or perform good actions, acquire knowledge, establish political parties or achieve things gradually are deluding themselves. None of these ideological alternatives is a substitute for waging *jihad* against the apostate government. His presentation of the present-day Muslim world is stark: all of the states are non-Muslim. Muslims must fight in order to achieve the ideal just Islamic state. He rejects with contempt the idea that *jihad* is for defensive purposes alone and states categorically that it is a mechanism for the aggrandizement of Islam and to demonstrate its superiority and God's will throughout the world.

With this presentation, martyrdom is important, since Farag realizes that fighting will generate martyrs. He asks whether it is better to be killed or taken in battle and cites the story of Khubayb (Chapter 2). This is interesting, because the story of Khubayb gives the Muslim both options in a desperate situation. In the story of Khubayb, the commander of the detachment, ʿAsim, fought until he was killed, while Khubayb himself was taken captive and then martyred. Unfortunately, Farag does not answer which of these two options is the one he prefers. But he does warn very strongly of one thing: spiritual pride in martyrdom. Repeatedly he notes that one cannot state that so-and-so is a martyr; only God is privy to that knowledge. It is crucial for the martyr to die for the right cause: not for glory, for fame or for any other reason, but for the purpose of raising the Word of God to the highest.[17] Farag is also one of the first Sunnis in the contemporary period to deal with the question of martyrdom operations, at which he hints briefly, citing the classical legal material summarized in Chapter 3.

Later Gamaʿat documents published during the 1990s and beyond, as this group began to fight a war against the Egyptian government, begin to speak more and more of the problems of "martyrdom operations" or suicide attacks, and indiscriminate killing. It has proved impossible for radical Muslims to discriminate between their enemies and innocents during suicide attacks,[18] and as with so many other extremist groups throughout the world, indiscriminate killings of civilians have proved to be the Gamaʿat's undoing. Because it was true to the logic of Qutb's identification of Egypt as a non-Muslim country, the Gamaʿat did not closely differentiate between killing the infidel rulers and innocent bystanders.[19] The Egyptian people were unwilling to tolerate this

---

[17] Abd al-Salam Farag, *al-Farida al-ghaʾiba*, p. 48; trans. Jansen, *The Neglected Duty*, pp. 220, 223–24.

[18] For the most part; of course, that does not mean that radical Muslims do not engage in selected assassinations such as those of Farag Foda in 1992 and Theo Van Gogh in 2004, and many others in order to intimidate their opponents.

[19] "Seven Misconceptions in Fighting the Apostate Ruler and His Regime," sections 2–5 (document taken from *al-Qawl al-qatiʿ*).

attitude and the group was ultimately forced to shut down operations because of popular opposition to the indiscriminate killings of civilians (primarily tourists, but also local Egyptians). However, the document *Imatat al-litham* (*Removal of the Veil*), a manual on tactics written by the *amir* (leader) of the Gama'at, Rifa'i Ahmad Taha, in 2001, proves that for these extremists, the logic of allowing the killing of civilians was not decisively refuted within the group, but has merely fallen into abeyance.[20]

Throughout the 1990s and beyond, radical Muslims have fought their governments and tried to set up Muslim regimes in place of what they consider to be apostate and illegitimate governments. This type of warfare led to civil wars breaking out in Algeria and Sudan, violence in Nigeria, Pakistan, Saudi Arabia and Indonesia, and unrest throughout the Muslim world. For the radical Muslims, those who fall in battle against non- or anti-Islamic regimes are martyrs, but for most of the rest of the Muslim world, these are either misguided people or on the level of common criminals or even murderers. Radical Muslim prestige has suffered immensely because of their willingness to use random and indiscriminate killings in order to achieve their goals. For this reason in many cases radical Muslims have tried to adopt a local resistance movement (or to Islamize an existing one) or to direct their violence away from Muslims towards the more popular non-Muslim targets.

Resistance and *jihad* against occupation

Ultimately the anti-governmental *jihad* in the Muslim world has been a failure (with the exception of Iran). *Jihad*s against occupation of Muslim lands or lands claimed by Muslims, however, have proved to be much more popular and today command widespread support among certain elements of the Muslim world. Among these *jihad*s, several stand out, of which the struggle against Israel is the most important and galvanizes the most widespread support throughout the Muslim world. As was stated previously, this struggle until the late 1980s did not have the character of a *jihad*; until 1975 it was largely spearheaded by neighboring Arab states (Egypt and Syria) all of which were of a secular socialist bent and uncomfortable with Islamic rhetoric. From 1975 until the signing of the Oslo Accords in 1993 the Palestinian Liberation Organization (PLO), a secular non-sectarian group, led the military opposition toward Israel, first through operations from southern Lebanon and then through the First Intifada (1987–93) against Israel through the territories occupied by Israel in the Six-Day War. In general, the PLO also kept Islamic rhetoric out of its proclamations and was usually careful to frame this struggle in terms of a global anti-colonialist, anti-imperialist war. Like other Arab nationalist organizations and movements

---

[20] Rifa'i Ahmad Taha, *Imatat al-litham 'an ba'd ahkam dhurwat sinam al-Islam*, pp. 13–38, 42–68 (where Taha specifically allows the killing of infidel and apostate Muslim non-combatants).

before it, the PLO referred to its fallen as *shahid*s, but did not differentiate between Muslim and Christian in this usage, and divorced the use of this term from its Islamic context.

However, starting in the late 1980s the PLO began to sustain a very powerful ideological challenge from Palestinian radical Muslims in the form of Hamas (Harakat al-muqawama al-Islamiyya). Founded in 1988, at first the group suffered from problems of legitimacy. Since radical Muslims had not been prominent in the struggle against Israel prior to that period and belatedly joined the First Intifada, Hamas had to provide for itself an Islamic martyrology to prove that Islam was the driving force behind this struggle. (As stated previously, the PLO had avoided this message because of the prominence of Christians and secular Muslims in its ranks.) This Hamas accomplished by taking the revolt of 'Izz al-Din al-Qassam, a comparatively minor revolt against the British in 1936, and making Qassam into their paradigmatic martyr. Qassam's revolt was Islamic in nature (although the PLO had also used him), most especially since Qassam himself was Syrian-born and not Palestinian at all.

The Hamas covenant, issued on August 18, 1988, presents part of the radical Palestinian Muslim vision of the entire Palestinian people as fighters and martyrs. Throughout the covenant there are citations of the Qur'an as well as traditional *hadith*s describing martyrdom. This picture is backed up by the repeated references to martyrs and remembering them in the published leaflets of the First Intifada. For example, in the January 1988 leaflet (no. 2 in the collection of Mishal and Aharoni), the movement states:

Every day the earth absorbs the blood of the righteous, [and] kneels in front of the graves and bows before the martyrs of grace. This is part of the price of pride and honor, liberation and salvation. This is the dowry of those with lovely eyes [the houris], a substitute for paradise. "Behold! God had bought from the believers their lives and their wealth in return for Paradise . . . " [Qur'an 9:111].[21]

With this type of comment Hamas skillfully works into traditional Islamic martyrology the popular Arab element of honor and the more contemporary theme of liberation. Many other citations in the leaflets call for commemoration of the martyrs, support of their families after their deaths, and there are calls not to forget their sacrifices when negotiations are held.

Since overcoming its initial struggle with legitimacy, Hamas has developed its martyrology along the lines of Egyptian radical Muslims, and has closely followed the ideological developments pioneered by the latter. Among those developments has been the suicide attack or "martyrdom operation," which since it was first used in 1994 has gradually become the primary violent expression of Palestinian radical Muslims. After the outbreak of the Second Intifada

---

[21] Mishal and Aharoni, *Speaking Stones*, p. 206 (I have modified the English somewhat).

(2000–04), gradually those groups owing allegiance to the PLO (the al-Aqsa Martyrs Brigades) and other secular Palestinian groups have followed Hamas in the use of this tactic, which has become emblematic of Palestinian warfare against Israel. We will examine the Islamic rationale behind the martyrdom operation below.

Other struggles have also been important in the development of radical Islamic martyrology. Of those, the war in Afghanistan against the Soviet occupation (1979–88), and then against the communist Afghan government (1988–92) were the most important. When the Soviet Union invaded Afghanistan in 1979 in order to prop up a failing communist regime, Muslim radicals from all over the world came to join the local Afghan *mujahidin* in order to fight the communists. These *mujahidin* were divided into a number of factions – usually estimated at between seven and thirteen at any given time – but they are best known for the role that these foreign fighters played in the battle. Supported by the Pakistani military regime under General Zia al-Haqq (assassinated 1988) and the covert operation of the CIA, and funded by Gulf states such as Saudi Arabia, much of the money and supplies ended up with the most extreme groups and helped create a school for international *jihad*. One of the key figures in this process was the Palestinian radical 'Abdallah 'Azzam, who had left the fight against Israel because of the hopeless nature of the struggle, and had come to Peshawar (Pakistan). With his publication of *Ilhaq bi-l-qafila* (*Join the Caravan*), he encouraged Muslims from all over the world, but primarily those from Arabic-speaking regions, to come and fight the infidel communists. 'Azzam was key in developing a great many of the foundational teachings of radical Islamic *jihad* as it is now understood, and below we will consider his contribution to the understanding of martyrdom. He himself was assassinated in 1989, but his compatriot Usama bin Ladin, a Saudi radicalized by the Afghan war, with whom he had co-founded the globalist *jihad* organization al-Qa'ida, continued his struggle after the conclusion of the war.

For radical Muslims during the 1990s the war was far from over. Many veterans of the Afghan war went back to their home countries and contributed to the anti-governmental *jihad*s in Egypt (1992–97) and Algeria (1992–2005). However, the primary fields of battle (not including resistance movements already discussed) were the Muslim regions of the former USSR (Chechnya, Uzbekistan and Tajikistan) and other former communist regimes in Eastern Europe (Bosnia-Herzegovina and Albania), and the Kashmir dispute between India and Pakistan. Fighters from Afghanistan and other recruits from the Middle East and the wider Muslim world flocked to all of these destinations throughout the 1990s. Although objectively speaking, as with the foreign *mujahidin* in Afghanistan, it cannot be said that they were decisive in obtaining victory in any one of these locations, their contributions aided in raising the consciousness of the Muslim world to the plight of those Muslims they characterized as persecuted by the global conspiracy to destroy Islam. And this trade in international *jihad* served to create a body of potential fighters who were essentially rootless and country-less, loyal only to globalist radical Islam.

For a brief period toward the end of the 1990s these rootless *jihad*ists were able to establish a few regimes (Afghanistan and Chechnya) or at least find refuge in states that were sympathetic to their cause (Sudan) or had collapsed and could not resist their incursions (Somalia and Tajikistan). But because of the nature of globalist radical *jihad*, which demanded a continual process of fighting the infidels until the Word of God is raised to the highest, these states or refuges proved to be transitory. Globalist radical Muslim fighters could not resist attacking enemies more powerful than they could handle, such as the United States on September 11, 2001, and this proved to be to their detriment. One by one either the states that they had established fell to the power of their enemies, or the refuges were no longer welcoming. While many of these radicals have found a new field of fighting in Iraq it remains to be seen (as many experts fear) whether they can export their newly gained experience into further regions of the Middle East and the rest of the world.

Contemporary *jihad* literature and martyrdom

Contemporary literature on *jihad* has a number of different trends. One trend is apologetic in nature and results from accusations that non-Muslims, especially Christian missionaries, leveled against Muslims. For the most part these swirl around the question of how Islam came to achieve the dominant position it had in history. Historically, for Muslims this success was achieved by the power of God to affirm the truth of Islam. The early conquests were in fact interpreted as a miracle, and the continued ability of Islamic civilization to project power over a period of 1,000 years indicated the abiding nature of this miracle. Because by the eighteenth and nineteenth centuries Muslims were on the defensive all over the world, this close relationship between Islam and victory had begun to seem hollow. It was given a severe intellectual blow by Christian missionaries during the nineteenth and twentieth centuries, who interpreted Islamic history to mean that Islam was at its essence a violent religion and had achieved its success solely through conquest.[22] Because of this claim many Muslims began to reinterpret the whole concept of *jihad* in an apologetic light.

---

[22] I personally reject this interpretation of Islamic history, although I think that to see Islam (in the sense of conversion to the religion) as having spread via conquest is an easy mistake to make since ironically, prior to the modern apologist approach, conquest and domination through conquest was a major theme inside classical Muslim histories. But when a scholar examines the progression of Islam and the pattern of delayed conversion to the faith, while there is a link between the political domination of Islam (usually but not always achieved through conquest) and conversion in some areas of the world, there are just as many areas if not more in which there is no such link.

This apologetic trend took several forms. One form was to claim that *jihad* was an internal struggle against one's lower soul, a doctrine that had been developed in Sufi Islam. It is unclear how prevalent this doctrine was among Muslims prior to the time when apologists seized upon it, but there can be no doubt that its religious and intellectual roots stretch back at least to the ninth and tenth centuries.[23] Thus it is an authentic Muslim doctrine, albeit one that prior to the nineteenth century had never seriously been seen as a challenge to the one promoting actual fighting of *jihad*. In the hands of Muslim apologists it was fashioned into a peaceable proclamation of Islam coupled with internal self-examination and betterment. The principal problem with this apologetic approach is the fact that it has never been successful among Muslim audiences in their languages (Arabic, Farsi, Urdu, etc.), only among Muslims in Western languages (or Western converts and apologists for Islam). It is virtually impossible to find literature in Muslim languages that promotes the idea that militant *jihad* has been superceded by this irenic form of *jihad*, and consequently the whole issue remains one of academic and apologetic interest alone.

However, there are other types of apologetic *jihad* in contemporary Muslim literature. Obviously the question of who is a martyr has attracted a great deal of attention within the *jihad* literature. It is fascinating to note that the definitions supplied by contemporary authors completely ignore any martyrdom that is not death as a result of fighting.[24] There is virtually no acknowledgment of the rich heritage of martyrdom from other, non-military causes, and no one appears to take the "martyr of love" category seriously anymore. Thus, the more common apologetic trend in contemporary Muslim *jihad* literature is to ignore any type of martyrdom known from the classical sources that does not fit into the category of warfare and to grapple with the idea of the martyr in the Qur'an.

One of the major problems for apologetic contemporary radical Muslim writers on martyrdom is the fact that most of them are very Qur'an-centered. Like so many radical Muslims, they would prefer to base their interpretations of Islam as much as possible upon the text of the Qur'an, and cite the *hadith* literature – other than the most authoritative collections of al-Bukhari and Muslim – as little as possible. This attitude creates some difficulties for the development of radical Muslim martyrdom, because as was demonstrated in Chapter 3 the word *shahid* and the derivatives of the root *sh-h-d* (to bear witness, to be a martyr) in the Qur'an do not seem to specify the meaning of "martyr" in an unambiguous manner. For example, the contemporary Saudi writer al-Qasimi,

---

[23] See John Renard, "*al-Jihad al-akbar*: Notes on a Theme in Islamic Spirituality"; and my discussion in *Understanding Jihad*, Chapter 2.

[24] Demonstrating complete ignorance of history Jamal Salim al-Damuni, *al-Shahada wa-l-shuhada': ahham al-shahid fi al-shari'a al-Islamiyya*, p. 25 actually says that there is no such thing as martyrdom in any other faith than Islam.

in his book *al-Jihad* uses three verses (4:69, 39:69, 57:19) in which the word *shuhada'* is used in conjunction with lists of other groups to be rewarded in heaven (prophets, *siddiqin* and righteous ones). Because the word *shuhada'* is not defined in these lists, he is able to point to the Qur'anic use of the word, but only by ignoring the much larger number of verses in which the word is defined and means merely "witness," and by reading later Islamic developments into the meaning of these three verses.[25] In addition to this linguistic problem, there is also the fact that with the exception of the Companions of the Pit there are virtually no references to sequences of martyrdom in the Qur'an. Although it is not difficult to cover this fact up by emphasizing the role of *jihad* (which is described in detail in the Qur'an) reading contemporary books on the subject of martyrdom one senses some desperation on the part of the writers because of this fact.

Other than this linguistic issue there are few interesting developments inside the *jihad* literature with regard to martyrdom.[26] All of the writers accept in accordance with the classical sources that martyrs are distinguished from other Muslims and have an elevated place in heaven, and receive special rewards. Like the classical writers, the contemporary ones see the need to discuss how far one can go in seeking out martyrdom. In the classical material there was considerable hesitation concerning the question of suicidal operations or the legal category of "the single fighter who charged a large number of the enemy." Was this person committing suicide (strictly forbidden in Islam according to Qur'an 4:29)? There was also some danger that a fighter who sought to go on a suicidal operation might do so merely for fame or personal aggrandizement, whereas ideally *jihad* should be an anonymous spiritual endeavor, with the feats and bravery of the individual known only to God.[27] All of these questions continue to swirl around the most controversial group of martyrdoms in contemporary Islam: suicide attacks or martyrdom operations.[28]

---

[25] Al-Qasimi, *al-Jihad wa-l-huquq al-duwaliyya al-'amma fi al-Islam*, pp. 514–15 and ff; also see Muhammad 'Ali Qutb, *al-Shahid wa-awsimatuhu al-'ashara*, pp. 5–11 (where a considerable effort is made to relate the different meanings of the root *sh-h-d*); 'Umar Ahmad 'Umar, *al-Jihad fi sabil Allah*, pp. 120–21; 'Abd al-Baqi Ramadun, *al-Jihad sabiluna*, pp. 154–56; Jum'at Amin 'Abd al-'Aziz, *al-Farida al-muftara 'alayha*, pp. 250–58; al-Qadiri, *al-Jihad fi sabil Allah*, ii, pp. 170–71; Muhammad 'Abd al-Rahim, *Arba'un hadithan fi fadl al-shahid wa-l-shahada*, introduction; al-Damuni, *al-Shahada*, pp. 26–27; Ahmad 'Ali al-Imam, *al-Shahada wa-hayat al-shuhada'*, pp. 9–10; Ibn Mar'i, *Ahkam al-mujahid bi-l-nafs*, i, pp. 233f.

[26] Ibn Mar'i, *Ahkam al-mujahid bi-l-nafs*, i, p. 268 deals with the question of whether a martyr's body can be kept frozen for a time (since usually he is supposed to be buried immediately) and he accepts it.

[27] This idea persists among critics of martyrdom operations: see Ibn 'Abd al-'Aziz, *Risalat al-'umda li-l-jihad fi sabil Allah*, p. 353; and Ibn Mar'i, *Ahkam al-mujahid bi-l-nafs*, ii, pp. 397–99 (who rejects the suicidal charge), 596f.

[28] For further study see my "Suicide Attacks or Martyrdom Operations in Contemporary *Jihad* Literature"; and "The Implications of Martyrdom Operations for Contemporary Islam."

Radical Muslims and martyrdom operations

One of the unusual developments to appear from radical Islam has been the appearance of suicide attacks or martyrdom operations. While self-sacrifice and martyrdom have often been closely associated with Shi'ism, classical Sunnism for the most part has avoided these expressions of warfare. Suicide in general is forbidden in Islam (Qur'an 4:29), and classical legal experts and exegetes of the Qur'an felt that suicidal warfare should be avoided (Chapter 3). However, even in Sunni *jihad* literature there has always been a sub-stratum that has discussed suicide attacks, but rarely beyond academic terms. The general consensus was that one should not undertake these types of operations except in the direst of circumstances and only when there is a clear benefit for Muslims. Otherwise the person who performs a suicide attack is committing suicide. Even Ibn al-Nahhas (d. 1411), the most graphic of medieval Muslim *jihad* writers, discusses the issue but does not encourage suicide attacks, thus leaving the matter open.[29] *Jihad* was open warfare while suicide attacks were seen as a method of warfare that was closer to assassination than *jihad*. Also, prior to the invention of explosives in an easily transportable form it was difficult for a single fighter to accomplish very much by his suicidal charge. Although the sources occasionally list stories of single fighters who supposedly killed dozens or even hundreds of their opponents, these stories are problematic.

In their quest for a self-sacrificial type of Islam that can be used to demonstrate the religious bankruptcy of the Muslim elites, contemporary radical Muslims have used martyrdom operations more than any other single method. To this end they have generated a great many legal discussions on martyrdom operations, hagiographical accounts of the martyrs and analyses of their tactics and the results of the martyrdom. Of these, the most serious is that of Nawwaf al-Takruri, whose (originally) 1997 book, *al-'Amaliyyat al-istishhadiyya fi al-mizan al-fiqhi* (*Martyrdom Operations in the Legal Balance*), which has gone through three editions since that time, marshals almost every conceivable bit of evidence to support the Islamic legality of these operations. It is worth examining his book in full, since almost everyone else writing about the subject cites him.

Al-Takruri is writing primarily to support the use of martyrdom operations against Israel. But, he surprisingly begins with a statement that is globalist radical Muslim to the core (this is surprising because usually material printed in Syria is not pan-Islamic in tone).

From this it was the decree of God during the difficult times in which the Muslims live, that the fruits of the Islamic Revival throughout the world are brought to their maturity, and that their bearers despite the hardship and lack of hope will carry the

---

[29] Ibn al-Nahhas, *Mashari' al-ashwaq*, i, pp. 557–60 (see discussion in Chapter 3).

banner of defense of the honor of the community (*umma*), lifting the flag of *jihad* in order to liberate it from all manner of oppression. The youth have volunteered with their blood without fleeing from life or responsibility, without grief or despair about the circumstances to which the community has fallen, but in belief that *jihad* is the only way to liberate lands and peoples. So it is not strange that these youths who grew up at the table of the Qur'an, and believed that "he who overcomes after being wronged – upon those there is no reproach" (42:39) that they sacrifice in the way of raising the Word of God in the world and glorifying His religion and His servants.[30]

From this and further comments Takruri seems to see martyrdom operations as a panacea for the problems facing the Muslim world and a certain source of pride and victory over its enemies, and cites Bosnia and Kashmir as well as Palestine (in his later editions he adds Afghanistan and Iraq).

The However, Takruri is far from being a cheerleader. He is quite aware of the problems and difficulties facing the writer who seeks to justify contemporary martyrdom operations squarely upon the classical Muslim sources. In order to focus upon the successes that would be achieved, he lists off the advantages of martyrdom operations for the reader:

1) They are a deterrent by means of causing terror among the enemy.
2) They cause the highest number of casualties on the part of the enemy with the fewest number of casualties on the part of the Muslims.
3) They equalize what would otherwise be unequal conflicts (such as that against Israel).
4) They cause the Israelis to think twice before perpetrating crimes against the Palestinians.
5) They cause happiness and fortitude to enter into the hearts of the Muslims, and despair to enter into their enemies.
6) They give the Muslim community the spirit of *jihad* and martyrdom, and cause Muslims to focus upon fighters and martyrs as examples rather than other popular heroes or symbols.
7) They bring non-Muslims to the knowledge of what is Islam.[31]

Some of these points are repeated, since numbers 1, 4 and 5 are more or less the same, as are 2 and 3. Takruri does not seriously answer the question of whether martyrdom operations are indeed effective in actually defeating an enemy. He also does not seem to consider the question of why martyrdom operations are only used against certain enemies, mainly democracies.[32]

Takruri lists sixteen operations that he considers to have been successful, and analyzes their strategic impact. With the exception of the suicide attacks

---

[30] Takruri, *'Amaliyyat al-istishhadiyya*, p. 43; note the references in Imam Samudra (the ideological leader of the October 12, 2002 Bali suicide bombings), *Aku melawan teroris*, pp. 171–72.

[31] Ibid., pp. 49–51.

[32] This point is discussed extensively by Robert Pape, *Dying to Kill: The Strategic Logic of Suicide Terrorism*, Chapter 4.

upon the American and French forces in Lebanon (October 23, 1983), killing 219 Marines and 47 French soldiers, leading to the withdrawal of French and American forces from Lebanon, Takruri is unable to point out specific results to any of these operations. He merely says that the operations lead to a heightened sense of terror or panic on the part of the enemy. Takruri also brings material from the time of the Prophet Muhammad and lists eleven occasions in which he claims that suicide attacks were performed either in Muhammad's presence or with his blessing. Again, when one examines this material it is clear that the line between bravery in battle and suicide is blurred. As in the material cited in Chapters 2 and 3, none of the Muslim fighters cited by Takruri actually committed suicide; they all merely fought until they died at the hands of the enemy.

Takruri also selectively summarizes the legal material from classical Islam, and once again draws all of his conclusions from the category of the "fighter who attacks the enemy single-handedly." He then proceeds to overwhelm the reader with a list of twenty-nine *fatwa*s from a wide range of contemporary Muslim scholars (several of the *fatwa*s are from groups of scholars) on the subject of martyrdom operations.[33] Because the scholars are drawn from all over the Muslim world – especially when one takes Takruri's collection together with that published by the Lebanese Shi'ites in the *Masa'il jihadiyya* and further material on the Internet – this collection effectively shows a level of consensus about the tactic of suicide attacks. (One should remember that as a community Sunni Muslims are quite consensus-driven, and that *ijma'*, consensus, is one of the major bases for Sunni Muslim law and society.) Takruri completes his exposition of the subject by covering several controversial questions such as whether women can carry out martyrdom operations, to which he cites a total of six *fatwa*s in favor.[34] However, Takruri himself is not convinced on this particular point, and says that this section of the book was the most agonizing for him to write and that he could not come to a final conclusion as to whether women can be permitted to carry out suicide attacks.

Other *fatwa*s associated with Saudi radical Muslims have cited additional proofs for the use of martyrdom operations, ironically using the example of a woman who carried out a suicide attack. Of these, the most common on the Internet is the "Islamic Ruling on the Permissibility of Martyrdom Operations: Did Hawa Barayev Commit Suicide?" This *fatwa*, although signed by an anonymous "Council of Scholars living in the Arabian Peninsula" was probably authored

---

[33] Al-Takruri, *'Amaliyyat al-istishhadiyya*, pp. 102–79; other *fatwa*s can be found in Muhammad Tu'mat al-Qudat, *al-Mughamara bi-l-nafs*, pp. 27–36; *Masa'il jihadiyya*, pp. 26–42; Nawaf al-Zarw, *al-'Amaliyyat al-istishhadiyya*, pp. 129–33; and Ahmad 'Abd al-Karim Najib, *al-Dala'il al-jaliyya 'ala mashru'iyyat al-'amaliyyat al-istishhadiyya*. There are approximately (to my count) forty-five different *fatwa*s on the subject on the Internet, but some of those overlap with the ones cited above.

[34] Al-Takruri, *'Amaliyyat*, pp. 208–24; and see my "Women Fighting in *jihad*?"

by Yusuf al-ʿAyyiri, who prior to his death in June of 2003 at the hands of Saudi security forces, was the leader of al-Qaʿida in the Kingdom.[35] The occasion of the *fatwa*'s composition was the martyrdom operation carried out by Hawa Barayev in June 2000 against the Russian forces in Chechnya. Given the fact that this event is well outside the parameters of suicide attacks against Israel, it is an important justification of these types of operations for globalist radical Muslims (al-Qaʿida and its allies).

The author of the "Islamic Ruling" concentrates upon much of the same historical and legal material as did Takruri, but he focuses more on the actual martyrdom. In order to do that, he cites a tradition that it is important to consider, the so-called tradition of the boy and the king, otherwise in the tradition literature known as "The Companions of the Pit" (referred to in Qurʾan 85:1–8, and translated in Section I of the Appendix).[36] In this story we have an example of a classical martyrdom in which the boy, a believer in the one God, is willing to die for his beliefs, and gives the king instructions about how to kill him (turning him into a martyr). After this, many people believe in the Lord of the boy (the true God) and cast themselves into the fires prepared for them by the evil king. As previously stated it is interesting that this story, almost completely ignored for the totality of Muslim history, would achieve some prominence during the recent past. It is still problematic although it is a clear case of a believer dying specifically for his faith (and thus comparatively rare in Muslim accounts), since the boy is not a fighter and he does not kill anyone else (like Samson) when he is killed. Thus, the supportive value of the story is unclear. However, the "Islamic Ruling" uses this *hadith* and three verses from the Qurʾan: 9:111 (cited at the beginning of Chapter 2), 2:249: "How many a small force has overcome a numerous force, by the permission of Allah!" and 2:207: "And some people sell themselves for the sake of Allah's favor. Allah is kind to His servants."

Taking these three verses together, which speak of a salvific covenant between God and man on the basis of fighting and dying for God in return for paradise, small forces overcoming larger ones (from the Qurʾanic story of David and Goliath), and then people "selling" themselves for God's favor, leads the writer to the possibility of suicide attacks. However, unlike Takruri, the writer of the "Islamic Ruling" is concerned with the intent of the would-be suicide attacker. If that person intends to wage *jihad* by blowing himself up in the midst of his enemies, and if this *jihad* is for the sake of raising the Word of God to the highest, then it is to be accepted as such and the person is actually a martyr.[37] Although

---

[35] Al-ʿAyyiri, *Hal intaharat Hawaʾ um ushtushhidat?* trans. "The Islamic Ruling on the Permissibility of Martyrdom Operations."

[36] Cited on p. 3 of the English translation, the very first *hadith* in the selection; for a radical Muslim study on this verse sequence see Rifaʿi Surur, *Ashab al-ukhdud* (37 pages).

[37] Ibid., p. 12.

this is a very thin line – since classically (Chapter 3) we had seen that seeking out martyrdom without a reasonable chance of survival was frowned upon by the exegetes and jurisprudents – it has been sufficient to garner widespread Islamic support for suicide attackers as literal martyrs.

In general, given the weak support for suicide attacks in the classical sources, it is surprising how muted Muslim opposition to them has been. No doubt some of that absence of opposition is due to the fact that suicide attacks have become closely associated with the Palestinian struggle against Israel, and it is rare to find Arab or Muslim voices who would seek to undercut the legitimacy of this struggle. However, there have been several powerful arguments put forward by Muslims against martyrdom operations. Certain scholars, such as the renowned *hadith* expert Nasir al-Din al-Albani (based in Syria), opposed suicide attacks on the grounds that despite the best efforts of their supporters to demonstrate otherwise, they are not different from actual suicide. The well-known and highly respected Saudi jurisprudent Ibn 'Uthaymin opposed suicide attacks on the grounds that their strategic value was nil and that it was impossible to ensure that no civilian or Muslim casualties would ensue as a result of the explosion. Ibn 'Uthaymin also emphasized the fact that Islam suffered from negative publicity as a result of such attacks. Several radical Muslim manuals on *jihad* have tended to oppose martyrdom operations, using the argument that *jihad* is an anonymous spiritual activity[38] known only to God and rewarded by Him. Since the suicide attacker today is well-known after his or her death and often leaves behind a letter or a video testifying to his or her actions, and the families of such people are often rewarded or compensated, it is impossible to free the action from the taint of desire for fame and fortune (even though the individual does not gain).[39]

It is impossible to know at this stage what will be the conclusion of the internal Muslim debate concerning martyrdom operations or suicide attacks. To date those proposing their essential Islamic basis have largely dominated the discussion, and almost all books or *fatwa*s on the subject that are popularly disseminated reflect their pro-suicide attack opinions. However, the arguments of those opposed to martyrdom operations, while lacking the critical mass of distribution in the Muslim world, and being subject to frequent demonization, are persuasive and strongly rooted in Islamic history and law as well. In the end, the argument appears to be resolved by the appeal to emotional issues, such as vengeance for perceived wrongs, restoration of lost honor and admiration for the individual martyrs, the vast majority of whom are not involved in suicide attacks.

---

[38] See Chapter 3 for the classical antecedents to this argument.

[39] For Muslim opposition to suicide attacks, see Muhammad Tu'mat al-Qudat, *al-Mughamara bi-l-nafs*, pp. 37–40; and especially Ergün Çapan (ed.), *An Islamic Perspective: Terror and Suicide Attacks*, pp. 102–18.

Contemporary martyrologies

In order to support the process of fighting the *jihad* contemporary Muslim groups – and also those Palestinian groups that transcend sectarian divisions – regularly publish martyrologies or hagiographical accounts of the so-called martyrs' deaths. From the classical period of Islam we have cited several of these types of publications, the most prominent of which were al-Tamimi's *Kitab al-mihan* and Abu al-Faraj al-Isfahani's *Maqatil al-Talibiyyin*. The contemporary martyrologies share some features with these classical sources, but also add in new themes as well. Among the recent martyrologies, two categories stand out: the more nationalist-religious martyrologies of the Iranians and the Palestinians, and the Islamic-neoclassical martyrologies of radical Muslims from the Afghanistan war (1979–92) and other globalist radical Muslim conflicts. In the first category we find a massive literature in Farsi stemming from the Iran–Iraq War (1980–88) that has been analyzed by Werner Schmucker.[40]

The Iran–Iraq War was precipitated by the invasion of Saddam Husayn of Iraq into Iran (probably to take advantage of the confusion created by the Islamic Revolution at that time and a number of other disturbances inside Iran). Ostensibly the goal of this war was to detach the largely Arab (albeit Shi'ite) province of Khuzistan from Iran, which was presented as a liberation of Arabs from Persian rule. In reality this province contains the concentration of Iran's oil reserves, and so it is more likely that the Saddam Husayn regime was motivated by a desire to corner the world's oil market. Suffice it to say, that the Iraqi forces managed during the months after September 1980 to capture part of the province, a success that prompted desperate Iranian counter-measures. Among these counter-measures was the use of mass waves of poorly trained soldiers (called Bassij) who were essentially sent as suicide battalions to clear minefields and to attack Iraqi outposts.[41] Many of these soldiers were encouraged by the Islamic leaders of Iran to seek out death, and masses of people seemed to be willing to follow this encouragement.[42] In general, these tactics prevailed for the first years of the war, but eventually Iran began to redevelop its professional army (weakened by the revolution) and achieved notable successes. In the end, the war subsided into almost a trench warfare that was deadly for at least a million people (a conservative estimate), crippling and wounding many more and devastating the economies of the two countries. In 1988 the war concluded with a general withdrawal back to the pre-war lines.

By the second year of the war the Ministry of Islamic Guidance of Iran began to issue martyrologies and testaments of martyrs. In general, these documents

---

[40] Werner Schmucker, "Iranische Märtyrertestamente." My treatment of the subject is dependent upon Schmucker.
[41] Analyzed by Farhad Khosrokhavar, "Le martyre révolutionnaire en Iran"; and then in his book, *Les Nouveaux Martyrs d'Allah*, especially p. 124f.
[42] Saskia Gieling, *Religion and War in Revolutionary Iran*, pp. 56–58.

were designed to portray the conflict in terms that the Shi'ite society of Iran would understand. The soldiers were referred to using names familiar to everybody from the *ta'ziya* such as al-Husayn, 'Ali and so forth, while the Iraqi enemy was designated "Yazid" (the Umayyad caliph who had al-Husayn murdered, and who is loathed by all Shi'ites). Consequently the idea of these soldiers being martyred was not so unusual because that is what had happened to al-Husayn.[43] All of this was using traditional Shi'ite motifs, but in a way in which they had not been used prior to the Islamic Revolution. The new martyrs were seen as a continuation of the traditional martyrology of the classical period, and even as a necessary sacrifice in order to usher in the messianic age of the Mahdi (the Muslim messianic figure). Beyond the material collected by Schmucker, during the recent past the trend of personal martyrologies has continued. Large numbers of accounts of personal heroism and martyrdom have been published, and apparently continue to be popular within Iran.[44] Similar martyrologies are to be found among the Hizbullah in Lebanon (from the war against Israel in southern Lebanon 1983–2000).

Since the outbreaks of the First and Second Intifadas (1987–93 and 2000–04) the Palestinians and their supporters throughout the Arab world have been active in publishing martyrologies designed to highlight their plight and galvanize support for their cause. The most complete of these martyrologies is the nine-volume (and as yet incomplete) series entitled *Intifadat al-Aqsa*, which gathers together over 2,700 stories of Palestinians killed, mostly by Israelis, since the outbreak of the Second Intifada in September 2000 until the end of 2004.[45] In general, these martyrologies can be grouped into two categories: the larger group of Palestinians killed by Israeli soldiers in confrontations or as a result of inadvertent (and sometimes questionable) violence, and the smaller group of Palestinian suicide attackers or targeted assassinations. The martyrologies in the former category are usually portrayed as entirely innocent, with the Israelis being put in the worst possible light. These types of martyrologies are clear demonizations, designed to create some moral clarity – the Palestinians being the underdogs and the Israelis being the oppressors – in what would otherwise be a complicated conflict.

Of all the martyrs presented to the reader, the story of Muhammad al-Durra is the most emblematic and has come to symbolize for many Arabs (and others as well) the Second Intifada as a whole. This boy was killed while hiding

---

[43] Schmucker, pp. 200–1, 216–19.

[44] Unfortunately I was unable to obtain these books, but their titles are available: M. Jalali, *Akhirin nasl*; Hamza Va'izi, *Bidrud, khak-i avliya*; *Sayyid, khuda hafiz*; *Surkhjamagan, bamdadi, majmu'a-yi khatirat*; and the series *Majmu'ah-yi khatirat-i sardan-i shahid* (a total of 7 volumes so far); also the *Yadnama-yi shuhada-yi sal-i avval-i difa' muqaddas-i Shahristan va-Qumm*.

[45] One can also find similar lists and stories scattered throughout the Internet. The most complete version appears to be at http://www. palestine-info.info/arabic/palestoday/shuhada/shuhada.htm.

behind a barrel next to his father as Israelis and Palestinians exchanged gunfire near the Israeli settlement of Netzarim (in the Gaza Strip) on September 30, 2000. The sequence was captured on film by the *France 2* news correspondent Talal Abu Rahma, and he verified that it had been the Israelis who had shot the boy. Since that time, however, repeated evaluations of the footage have not removed doubts about whether the incident was staged or who precisely shot Muhammad al-Durra. Despite these questions, Muhammad al-Durra is the paradigmatic Palestinian martyr, and discussion on the circumstances of his martyrdom does not take place in Arab countries. Al-Durra's terrified face as the bullets whiz around him, his father's efforts to protect him, and the general situation of the Palestinians under fire from the technologically superior Israeli forces was sufficient to raise the story of Muhammad al-Durra to the heights of martyrdom. Day after day, and month after month during the period immediately after the beginning of the Second Intifada (throughout Fall 2000) the sequence of Muhammad al-Durra's death was broadcast on Arab news, especially that of al-Jazeera, and the pictures are well-known throughout the region.

This status is reflected in the collection of *Intifadat al-Aqsa*, where not surprisingly the story of Muhammad al-Durra is the first.[46] According to Jamal al-Durra, the boy's father, as the bullets were flying around the pair his son told him that he was doing fine, whereupon Jamal tried by making hand motions to get people to stop firing at the pair of them. These efforts were to no avail, and Jamal al-Durra was himself hit. Then his son said, "Don't be afraid, papa, a bullet hit my leg, but your situation is more important." According to the story, young Muhammad was then hit and killed, but because of the firing going on around them, ambulances could not make their way to the scene and rescue the two of them. *Intifadat al-Aqsa* then lists a number of people who agree that Muhammad al-Durra was a martyr and that he is in heaven.

This religious aspect to the martyrdom of Palestinians is not usually emphasized throughout these volumes, however. In general, this collection is one in which the secular-nationalistic aims of the Palestinian people are played up, not the Islamic motifs. However, in many cases there are notices of the houris,[47] and there are visions of the dead after their martyrdom in close accord with the materials in Chapter 7. For example, the story of one Muhammad Nimr Mahani, who was martyred on January 27, 2001, is related. According to his brother this man had desired to obtain the rank of martyr, and had sought to prove that he was pure of intent to ensure that his martyrdom would be accepted. He would go to the graveyards and read the Qur'an over the graves of martyrs, and he had

---

[46] *Intifadat al-Aqsa*, i, pp. 29–45.

[47] As previously stated the importance of the theme of the houris and their sexual attractions has attracted scorn from certain writers such as Maher Hathout, and recently As'ad Abu Khalil, "Sex and the Suicide Bomber," posted at salon.com (Nov. 7, 2001).

informed his wife that he wanted to be a martyr. (But his wife did not pay very close attention to these remarks at the time.)

On the day of his martyrdom, he bought perfume (*'itr*) from a friend, and said farewell to him, "but [the friend] did not know that this farewell was the final farewell of parting, and that he had an appointment with martyrdom, and that he had taken the perfume because he knew well that he would be led to the houris."[48] Little is said about the circumstances of his martyrdom, other than his family found him in the hospital with a dumdum bullet in his stomach, and that the doctors said that he was bleeding internally. No one could save his life. Mahani's family is said to have greeted his martyrdom with joy, and later his mother saw a vision in which he was carried in paradise by green birds. She called to him, and asked "Where are you going, O Muhammad?" He said: "Leave me, I am in paradise."[49] All of these themes are classical.

Beyond the stories of the innocents, or those who are presented as innocent, there is the second category of the suicide attackers or targeted assassinations. The dominant theme in martyrologies recounting their stories is to emphasize their heroism. (This statement should not be taken to mean that blowing oneself up in the midst of Israeli civilians is actually heroic; on the contrary, such tactics have brought the Palestinian cause into serious disrepute.) These attackers are presented as heroically penetrating Israeli society, taking vengeance upon the oppressor and regaining the honor of the Palestinian (and sometimes the Arab) people. For example, Darin Abu 'Aysha, who carried out a suicide attack on a roadblock near the Israeli town of Modi'in (injuring two soldiers) on February 26, 2002, is said to have been motivated by vengeance for close relatives killed by Israeli soldiers. The Islamic themes that are so prevalent in Muhammad Nimr Mahani's martyrdom have no place in that of Abu 'Aysha. The account says she inquired whether a number of different groups (including Hamas and Islamic Jihad) would accept her, and the only one that would was the al-Asqa Martyrs Brigades (associated with the official PLO). No one saw her in visions and there is no mention of her being conveyed to paradise; she sought only vengeance.[50]

A number of those prominent figures killed by Israeli targeted assassinations are associated with classical Islamic themes. Of those, two stand out: Yehye 'Ayyash (killed January 5, 1996), known as "the Engineer," and Shaykh Ahmad Yasin (killed March 22, 2004). 'Ayyash had been the chief bomb-maker of the radical Islamic Palestinian organization, Hamas, and had been on the run for some three years before his assassination. For many Palestinians, the high-profile suicide attacks he pioneered and honed into a deadly weapon against Israel were the only weapon they had against its trained army. In the end,

---

[48] *Intifadat al-Aqsa*, iii, pp. 137–38 (at p. 138).   [49] Ibid., p. 138.
[50] *Intifadat al-Aqsa*, vii, pp. 29–36; also see Barbara Victor, *Army of Roses*, Chapters 7, 20.

'Ayyash's death was not on the battlefield; he was assassinated when his cell-phone was booby-trapped and blew up next to his head. Since that time his life has been turned into that of a hero by Palestinians.[51]

Ahmad Yasin was a considerably more important figure, having been the founder and spiritual leader of the Hamas. He was also a quadraplegic who had overcome serious structural barriers to gain intellectual and religious renown within Palestinian society and to some extent within the Muslim world as a whole. Although he had been imprisoned by Israel for a time, he was released in 1997 as part of a prisoner exchange. During the period following his release until his assassination in 2004 there is no question that he was the dominant figure within the organization, although he was not in charge of military operations. It was Yasin who had been drawn into the increasing use of suicide attacks by Hamas during the middle of the 1990s and had encouraged their use after the outbreak of the Second Intifada in 2000. Israel viewed him as responsible for these suicide attacks, and although Israelis tried to assassinate him on a number of occasions Yasin was always able to escape.

On March 22, 2004 just after the dawn prayers he was returning from the Mujamma' al-Islami Mosque in Gaza. According to the hagiography, just before he got into his car, one of the youths in the area told him of the Israeli planes circling the area. Yasin's response was classic Muslim: that he would rely completely upon God to protect him. Shortly afterwards there were three major explosions from rockets fired by the planes at Yasin's car and motorcade during the course of which Yasin, his guards and a number of bystanders were killed. In the martyrology of Yasin, no extensive Islamic elements are given, unlike in some of the previous martyrologies. He is described as a Palestinian hero, speeches and eulogies given at his funeral are adduced, and then his life-story is laid out for us. Perhaps the Islamic elements in Shaykh Ahmad Yasin's life were so obvious that there was no need for embellishment on the part of the martyrology.[52]

The martyrologies that conform the most closely to those of the classical period described in Chapters 3 and 7 are those of radical Muslims. During the Afghanistan war, the Palestinian radical Muslim 'Abdallah 'Azzam penned several martyrologies, most notably the *Ayat al-Rahman fi jihad al-Afghan* (*The Signs of the Compassionate One in the Afghani* Jihad).[53] 'Azzam, who had become depressed with the lack of progress in fighting Israel during the late

---

[51] See Mukhlis Yahya Barzaq, *Fada'il al-shahid Yehye 'Ayyash*, and see Appendix 2a for a translation of his martyrdom as he presents it (p. 119f).

[52] *Intifadat al-Aqsa*, ix, pp. 204–16.

[53] All 'Azzam citations are from *Ayat al-Rahman* (partially translated "Signs of ar-Rahman" at www.almansurah.com/articles/2003/jan/140103b.htm), but further materials can be found in his *Basha'ir al-nasr, 'Ibar wa-basa'ir li-l-jihad fi al-'asr al-hadir*, pp. 19–39 unless otherwise noted.

1970s, preached a powerful salvific version of *jihad* that sought to combine traditional Islamic teachings together with folk beliefs about the miracles associated with fighters and radical Islamic messianic theology prophesying the rebirth of the caliphate and the future worldwide triumph of Islam. For ʿAzzam, martyrs and martyrdom, and most especially the example that is set through the process of martyrdom, was crucial for capturing the allegiance of Muslims. In a very powerful and direct statement, "Martyrs: The Building Blocks of Nations," he explains this idea:

The life of the Muslim Ummah is solely dependent upon the ink of its scholars and the blood of its martyrs. What is more beautiful than the writing of the Ummah's history with both the ink of a scholar and his blood, such that the map of Islamic history becomes colored with two lines: one of them black . . . and the other one red . . . History does not write its lines except with blood. Glory does not build its lofty edifices except with skulls. Honor and respect cannot be established except on a foundation of cripples and corpses. Empires, distinguished peoples, states, and societies cannot be established except with examples. Indeed, those who think that they can change reality or change societies without blood sacrifices and invalids, without pure, innocent souls, they do not understand the essence of this *din* [religion] and they do not know the method of the best of Messengers [Muhammad].[54]

For ʿAzzam, in this somewhat Darwinistic view of history, these martyrs provide the foundation for the revival of Islam. As he states further in this article, "as for the one who wants to construct glory, he must be prepared to ascend to the price of glory upon seas of his blood and his sweat, and the blood of those around him."

In order to encourage martyrdom ʿAzzam related dozens of miracle stories centered around the *mujahidin*. Although ʿAzzam was himself a radical Muslim (and thus hostile towards the Sufi hagiography surrounding martyrs and holy men), these stories resemble nothing so much as the type of stories to be found among various Sufi cults of saints and martyrs. The bodies of the martyrs smell sweet, are protected from decay and often radiate a light. For example, ʿAzzam cites a story by one Arslan, who accompanied by another fighter named Fathallah sought the body of one of their companions, ʿAbd al-Basir, who was killed. Fathallah told ʿAzzam that he knew the *shahid* was close by because he could smell a sweet smell, and then he said: "I saw the color of blood in the darkness upon light that proceeded from his wounds." In addition to these post-mortem miracles, martyrs often are described holding onto their weapons in death and even after their deaths causing damage to the enemy. ʿAzzam's colorful and attractive reformulations of Muslim martyrdom have set the standard among Sunni radical Muslims and continue to influence the genre.

---

[54] ʿAzzam, "Martyrs: The Building Blocks of Nations," at http://www.religioscope.com/info/doc/ jihad/azzam_martyrs.htm.

Obviously this group of martyrs is much more self-selecting than are the Iranian or Palestinian ones, and consequently one can distinguish much more of a process of martyrdom, especially in the martyrologies from the 1990s. This process is initiated by the martyr himself (usually) by a gradual departure from this world into the next. First, the martyr cuts himself off from his friends and family and departs for the battlefield. When this battlefield region is a distant or difficult-to-access region the martyr often has to pass through a process of temptations. For example, those fighters going to Bosnia–Herzegovina during the 1992–95 war often had to pass through Europe. While making this transition, they had the opportunities to view the temptations of this world: the women, the easy life of the Europeans, even other Muslims who would advise them to avoid going to fight the *jihad*. Overcoming these types of temptations was the first step into the battle, the spiritual battle.[55]

The next step is harder to discern but often involves cutting the fighter off from his comrade fighters. (Obviously since these martyrologies are all written with the benefit of hindsight, this perception may be anachronistic, but this is the way it is presented.) In other words, the fighter is gradually singled out as someone who is set aside for martyrdom. He begins to talk about being martyred, sees visions or dreams about martyrdom or heaven, or other fighters see these visions about him. Sometimes the commanding officer notes this figure to be one who is either solitary or willing to participate in suicidal missions; occasionally there are physical manifestations of his impending martyrdom (wounds that appear on his body, sweet smells that emanate from him). All of these types of stories are closely in accord with the martyrdom narratives set down by 'Azzam during the Afghan war.

After his death the martyr's comrades remember him to have been the most pious of all of them, the most selfless and the bravest, and construct a hagiographical narrative that presumably is the source of the martyrologies on the Internet.[56] The martyr's body, exuding a sweet smell and resisting decomposition, is often contrasted with the foul stench of infidel bodies, indicating that the martyrdom has been accepted by God. These martyrdom narratives often include visions of the martyr in paradise, with the houris or flying inside green birds (as the *hadith* literature describes the martyr in paradise). It is not unusual for the martyr to continue to influence this world in various ways, sometimes helping out other Islamic fighters: having his body give them his weapons, guiding them sometimes when they are lost or hurting the enemy in various ways.

---

[55] See the list of some eighty-five Arab martyrs from the Bosnian–Herzegovinan conflict (1990–95) at saaid.net.

[56] Note the cyber graveyard detailed by Yassin Musharbash, "Cyber cemetery for mujahideen" at derspiegel.com (November 1, 2005).

The most interesting thing about the martyrological narrative constructed by 'Azzam and his radical Muslim successors is its close topical relationship to Sufi martyrologies. Virtually all radical Muslims have a strong hostility towards Sufism, and most especially towards that aspect of Sufism that venerates dead holy men and women. This veneration of the dead, and especially asking them for intercession from them with God, is one of the bases for the divide between radical Islam and Sufism. From the perspective of radical Muslims this veneration and the intercession that flows from it constitutes *shirk*, associating other beings with God, which is the primal sin in Islam. Therefore, it is all the more amazing to find 'Azzam and his successors creating much the same mythology around the figures of the *jihad* fighters. Only the element of intercession is yet to be introduced. Already, the complete cult of relics of the martyrs has been resurrected by radical Muslims. However, this is not the only irony in contemporary radical Muslim martyrology.

Poetry of martyrdom

As with the classical period, the poetry associated with contemporary Islamic martyrdom is copious, and quite influential.[57] However, just as with classical Muslims, the attitude of contemporary radical Muslims is ambivalent. Poetry is strongly condemned in the Qur'an (e.g., 16:80, 26:224 and 36:69). However, one can hardly deny that a great deal of poetry is included within the classical literature, even the *jihad* literature (Chapter 7). Probably for this reason one finds even very pious radical Muslims (not to speak of the more secular nationalists) using poetry in order to communicate their messages to the masses. Much of this poetry is closely connected to the Israeli–Palestinian conflict and is the outgrowth of considerable sympathy for the Palestinians as well as frustration at being unable to render them practical aid. Poetry readings or recitations on prominent Arabic language news channels, especially al-Jazeera (based in Qatar), were a regular feature of the years of the Second Intifada (2000–04). However, for the most part these poetic selections do not differ in theme significantly from their classical predecessors. Probably one of the most famous is that by the former Saudi Arabian ambassador to the United Kingdom (2002), Ghazi al-Qusaybi called *For the Martyrs* (*Li-l-shuhada'*):

> God bears witness that you are martyrs; the prophets and friends [of God] bear witness.
> You have died so as to glorify the Word of my Lord, in the dwellings glorified by the Night Journey [of the Prophet Muhammad].

---

[57] A great deal of this poetry is collected by Khalid al-Karaki, *Hamasat al-shuhada': ru'iyat al-shahada wa-l-shahid fi al-shi'r al-'Arabi al-hadith*; and note the large collections of radical Muslim poetry on tawhed.ws and other websites (such as alneda.com, now defunct).

Have you committed suicide?? [No,] we are the ones who have committed suicide in life, but our dead are alive.

O people, we have died, so prepare to listen to how they eulogize us.

We were impotent until even impotence complained of us, we wept until weeping had scorn for us.

We prostrated until prostration was disgusted by us, we hoped until hope asked for assistance.

We licked the shoe of [Israeli Prime Minister Ariel] Sharon until the shoe cried: Watch out, you are tearing me!

We repaired to the illegitimate rulers of the White House, whose heart is filled with darkness.

O people! We have died but dust is ashamed to cover us.

Tell Ayat [al-Akhras]: O bride of the highest heavens, [We] ransom all beauty for your pupils.

When champions are castrated, the choice [ones] of my people.

Beauty confronts the criminal, she kisses death and laughs in proclamation – when leaders flee from death.

Paradise opens its gates and is cheerful. Fatima the Splendorous [daughter of Muhammad] meets you!

Tell those who embellished those *fatwas* [against suicide attacks]: Grant a delay. Many *fatwas* have heaven in an uproar.

When *jihad* calls, the learned man is silent, the reed [pen], books, and the jurisprudents.

When *jihad* calls, there is no asking for *fatwas*: the day of *jihad* is [a day of] blood.[58]

This poem is striking for its ability to globalize the issue of martyrdom. For al-Qusaybi those who are still alive are the ones who are really dead. They are dead from shame, from humiliation and from self-abasement. Al-Qusaybi is calling for emulation of the example of Ayat al-Akhras (who blew herself up in Jerusalem on March 29, 2002),[59] and plays on a great many themes of bravery and heroism that are present in the classical and contemporary sources.

Of those themes, no doubt the one that is the most galling to his audience is the loss of manhood. Since the classical Arabic themes stress manhood and bravery very strongly, and abominate cowardice (associated with women), the choice of Ayat al-Akhras as his heroine resonates very strongly with his audience. This resonance is even stronger when one considers that in al-Akhras' final video she asks pointedly: "Where are the Arab leaders?" Her accusation is capable of shaming the larger community into action, and the fact that women, traditionally not associated with bravery, are taking the lead in martyrdom

---

[58] Ghazi al-Qusaybi, *Li-l-shuhada'*, pp. 7–10; see also the translation at memri.org, Special Dispatch series no. 372 (April 25, 2002) (although I referred to this translation, the above is my own and follows the poem in al-Qusaybi's published work, not the *al-Hayat* [April 13, 2002] version.)

[59] Information about her can be found in Barbara Victor, *Army of Roses*, Chapters 17–18.

operations, is both a source of pride as well as shame. Clearly al-Qusaybi is also filled with contempt for scholars who discuss suicide attacks such as that of al-Akhras and question their Islamic legitimacy. Even the Palestinian Hamas leader Ahmad Yasin for a time rejected the idea that women could be suicide attackers (although eventually he relented and several Palestinian female suicide attackers came from Hamas). Moral authority, according to al-Qusaybi, comes from self-sacrifice, and those whose lives are not on the line do not have the right to criticize or belittle the sacrifices of the Palestinians.

But even beyond these accusations, al-Qusaybi is clearly part of a reconstruction of the idea of Muslim martyr. Traditionally the martyr is greeted in heaven by the houris, the women of Paradise. Here, Ayat al-Akhras is welcomed into heaven, even though she does not have the male equivalent of the houri (of which there are none in the classical texts). She is herself the "bride of heaven"; she is going joyfully to her wedding day in heaven, although it is not clear to whom she will be married. This is the more poignant because Akhras was about to be married in her real life before she chose to commit suicide. Thus, in a number of different ways Ayat al-Akhras, through the interpretive lens of al-Qusaybi's poem, poses a challenge to classical Muslim martyrdom.

The challenge of martyrdom for contemporary Muslims

Because radical Islam by its very nature is a challenge to Islam as a whole, what are the challenges that lie before Muslims as they confront this new permutation of Islam, and its persuasive use of martyrdom and martyrdom operations? It must be stressed that radical Muslims, despite their best attempts to demonstrate otherwise and despite the Western media's fixation upon them, do not constitute more than around 10 percent of the total number of Muslims and their numbers may not even be this high. While in a given region or as the result of a given event their support can rise dramatically, their message of rejecting Sufism and conservative Islam has not been successful. Thus, while the tactic of martyrdom has won radical Islam a great deal of prominence, and spiritual influence within the world of Islam, it has not succeeded in actually translating this prominence into mass movements that have accomplished its practical goals.

Perhaps the reason for that failure is the fact that those goals are so grandiose that it is difficult to grasp them. For example, most radical Islamic movements call for the strict enforcement of the *shari'a*; however, from a practical point of view, while this goal is attractive for Muslims, it is difficult to define. What would a *shari'a* state look like? Radical Muslims offered Afghanistan under the Taliban (1996–2001) as an example, and it was not persuasive to the vast community of Muslims. Another goal of radical Islam is the unification of all Muslims under a caliph. Again, this goal seems doomed to irrelevance, as the practical difficulties of selecting a caliph, not to speak of the problems of unifying the multiple cultures making up the worldwide Muslim population, are insurmountable.

But the most painful difficulty associated with radical Islam is its theory of martyrdom. Ideally, *jihad* should be focused outside the community of Islam against the infidel. However, the course that radical Islam has taken over the past thirty years has proven that radical Muslims really prefer to kill each other. Although some groups, usually those associated with national resistance movements, such as Hamas or the Chechens, have tried to avoid killing Muslims, many, such as radical Muslims in Algeria, Morocco, Egypt, Iraq, Saudi Arabia, East Africa, Central Asia[60] and Pakistan, have killed far more Muslims than any infidel ever has. Through the use of suicide attacks, the rise in Muslim deaths has been exponential. And in many cases, the Muslims who have carried out these attacks have been glorified in some place, or by some Muslim group as actual martyrs. This development has had consequences for the unity of worldwide Islam, because these attacks create volumes of hatred between what would otherwise be neighbors (such as in Pakistan and Iraq). While it might be possible for radical Muslims to intimidate certain populations in this manner, these tactics have not demonstrated the ability to create a mass movement or the sympathy for their cause that would lead to a pan-Islamic state.

The challenge for Muslims in the coming years will be to formulate a theory of martyrdom that will enhance the community rather than cause it to slide into endless internecine bloodlettings (such as in Algeria or Pakistan), and to focus perhaps on those martyrdoms that were constructive to the commuity overall. Worship of suicide attackers, which has become endemic in certain parts of the Muslim world, has ended up failing the community of Islam. It may be that there are other alternatives.

---

[60] On the Central Asian movements, see Vitaly Naumkin, *Radical Islam in Central Asia*, p. 114f (on the suicide attacks in Tashkent, Uzbekistan, in March and July 2004).

9   Martyrdom in Islam: past and present

*The Christians and the Muslims who have divided the world between them
fight each other, but every one of them purifies his intent to God – is ascetic,
fasts, prays and goes out determined to kill the other, believing that killing is
the greatest good and sacrifice to God. So they kill each other, and each one
of them believes that he is going to the Garden and Paradise.*

Judah ha-Levi (d. twelfth century)[1]

Martyrdom in Islam is a major theme, although one cannot say that it is a
dominant one. In the end, several issues have most probably contributed to the
comparatively recessive nature of the theme. One of those issues would have
to be that Muhammad, the apostle and founder of the faith, was not personally
a martyr.[2] Although as a result of the absolute nature of the message of Islam
vis-à-vis Arabian paganism that Muhammad preached he suffered in various
ways, this suffering does not stand out within the context of his society nor
in comparison to the martyrs of other faiths (Judaism, Christianity, Buddhism,
etc.) or even in comparison to later Muslim martyrs. Muhammad's experience
is a normative one for all Muslims – both Sunni and Shi'ite – and therefore
perhaps his example is also a normative one with regard to martyrdom. None
of the other major prophets or messengers of Islam, with the exception of John
the Baptist, is said to have been martyred, and there are virtually no martyrdom
narratives in the Qur'an (other than the problematic one of the *Ashab al-ukhdud*,
the Companions of the Pit, in *sura* 85:1–8 discussed in Chapter 2).

Another dominant theme is the close relationship between martyrdom and
persecution. Most Muslims have always lived under either a Muslim dominated
society, even if the majority of the people in it were not Muslim, or one in
which Muslims were widely accepted and tolerated. In general, the Muslim
experience until the twentieth century has not been to live under a non-Muslim
government. Since the early years of Islam, persecution of Muslims has usually

---

[1] Judah ha-Levi, *Kitab al-radd wa-l-dalil fi al-din al-dhalil (Sefer ha-Khuzari)*, p. 6.
[2] Some claim that he was, see Kohlberg, "The Image of the Prophet Muhammad as *shahid*"; this is
continued by contemporary writers such as As'ad Muhammad Sa'id al-Saghirji, *al-Jihad fi sabil
Allah*, pp. 25–28 who makes an effort to claim that the Jews of Khaybar poisoned him so that he
can die a martyr.

been inflicted upon them by other Muslims. Even those societies hostile to Islam, such as medieval Catholic Spain and the communist regimes of the USSR and China, have produced few martyrs that are generally known and venerated by the public. (This does not imply that there Muslims were not martyred *en masse* by these regimes; merely that the stories about them do not seem to have wide currency.) Overwhelmingly, the martyrdom narratives come from within the mainstream of the Islamic community and are not narratives being sent from the fringes.

Martyrdom in Islam is in general not a passive act on the part of the believer, but more of an active action in which the martyr seeks out the circumstances that will lead to his or her own martyrdom. One of the dominant themes, therefore, is the close relationship between martyrdom and *jihad*, rather than between martyrdom and missions, as is the case in other missionary religions such as Buddhism or Christianity. The fact is that there are few prominent Muslim missionary martyrs. Most of the Sufis that were active in missionizing regions bordering upon the core Muslim lands (India, Africa, Central Asia, Turkey and southeastern Europe) did not die for their faith but tended to be venerated by the groups they converted as holy men. The exception to this rule is Indonesia, where there are a number of martyred missionaries from the earliest period of conversion. However, the experience of the Nine Saints of Java is atypical even within this context, and suggests that the initial experience of martyrdom was sufficient to make an impact upon the population. For the most part, conversion to Islam in Southeast Asia was peaceful.

The fighting martyr is the type that stands out in the overall category of Muslim martyrdom. Although one can point to traditions that indicate other types of martyrs, such as those who are drowned at sea, died in childbirth, merchants who die protecting their goods and so forth, there are few concrete examples given in the sources for them. These extra categories seem to be largely shams without a martyrdom tradition to flesh them out. The one obvious exception to that rule are the martyrs of love, who have considerable literary attestation to support their reality. But the number of Muslim martyrs who were killed on the battlefield is quite significant, frequently discussed in the sources and their cults are quite popular in most regional Islamic communities. (It is significant, however, that these martyrs venerated as holy men still constitute only a tiny fraction of the huge number of shrines dedicated to holy men and women throughout the Muslim world.) Other types of martyrs that are popular in the non-Muslim world, for example, the philosopher martyr (Socrates) or the scientific martyr (Archimides and Galileo) are almost entirely absent from Islam.

What is a Muslim martyrdom and how can it be defined after looking at the different types of deaths that Muslims have died, and those classified by the community as martyrs? This is not an easy question to answer, because nowhere in the literature do we actually find an exact, agreed upon definition of martyrdom. The *hadith* and legal literature gives us a sense of the range of martyrdom – collections like al-Suyuti's *Abwab al-sa'ada* give at least forty different circumstances that are considered by elements of the Muslim community to constitute martyrdom. However, from lists like this it is difficult to know where the boundary is to be drawn. Al-Suyuti and others writing on the subject seem to be widening the definitions of martyrdom to the point where they might become meaningless. And no established martyr's calendar or authoritative list to which one can turn exist.

The question of definitions raises the further issue of the process by which one person is declared to have been a martyr and another not. Those who are most easily categorized are those Muslims killed by non-Muslims specifically for their faith, or in battle with non-Muslims during the course of a *jihad*. However, we have seen that relatively few Muslim martyrs actually fall into these two categories and that most were killed by other Muslims. In fact, for the categorization of a given person as a martyr we often have only a few sources to go on, and perhaps the witness of a shrine to that martyrdom that is a testament to continuing popular veneration. Beyond these obvious attested categories we have a great many ambiguous cases that have local, regional or sectarian status, and have never been accepted by the Muslim community overall.

It seems that the rank of the person involved as well as the tragedy or nobility of their death has a great deal to do with their relative martyrdom status and whether their martyrdom is ultimately accepted by the entire Muslim community or at least a significant section of it. For example, one cannot say objectively that the sufferings of al-Husayn at Karbala were qualitatively greater than those of other martyrs detailed in this book. But the fact that he was the grandson of the Prophet Muhammad made these sufferings so much more poignant and guilt-inducing for those who would ultimately become Shi'ites, and even for some Sunnis. The popular perception is that al-Husayn was blameless and not self-seeking, while his opponents, the Umayyad rulers, were the exact opposite. Therefore, the tragedy of Karbala is all the more jarring. Al-Husayn also fought against tremendous odds, and thus projects the image of the hero. In a number of ways, however, the martyrdom of al-Husayn stands out within the Islamic tradition. It is by far the longest martyrdom to be found in the Islamic sources, with a plethora of details that have been embellished over the centuries. In addition to this fact, although al-Husayn is strictly speaking a sectarian figure, venerated by the Shi'ite community, his martyrdom has achieved something of a pan-Islamic character as well. Few Sunnis today believe that killing him was justified or take the Umayyad side of the story, and many have written sympathetically about Karbala (without going so far as to actually become Shi'ites).

Perhaps in order to better understand the definitions of martyr in Islam we can consider some problematic figures. A good example is the figure of Abu

Muslim, killed by Abu Ja'far al-Mansur in 754. Abu Muslim was without a doubt a man who projected the image of piety for his 'Abbasid masters, and was a genuine hero in the battlefield as well as dying a tragic death. Indeed, for a number of groups in Persia he was and continues to be considered a martyr (see Chapter 6). However, given the fact that it is difficult to present him as a martyr who actually died for Islam (as opposed to dying in a power struggle with al-Mansur), the reasons why his martyrdom is problematic are clear. It is possible to compare him to a figure such as the great vizier Nizam al-Mulk, who served the Seljuq dynasty in Iraq and Iran during the eleventh century, and who was never accepted as a martyr. This highly cultured personality, whose loyalty to the dynasty was absolute and whose abilities were legendary, is best remembered as the author of the political tract *Siyasatnama*, a kind of Persian-language type of Nicolo Machiavelli's *The Prince*. Nizam al-Mulk, however, had aroused the anger of the Isma'ili sectarians, the Assassins, who in 1092 sent a pair of assassins to kill him. During this period, the northern-Persia based Assassins were the most feared group of all the sectarians, whose activities targeted a number of prominent personalities at that time. Nizam al-Mulk had made a determined effort to contain them, and thus, from their point of view, he constituted an enemy. As he was coming out of the public baths (*hamam*), he was accosted by two men, who were dressed in the manner of supplicants. They both stabbed him and fled, and he died on the spot.[3] Nizam al-Mulk's assassination was a disaster for the Seljuq dynasty, which until that time had upheld Sunnism in the areas of Iraq and Iran. After his death the dynasty fell apart, and the area remained weakened until it was ultimately devasted by the Mongols two centuries later.

Comparing the murder of Abu Muslim with the assassination of Nizam al-Mulk it is possible to see the reasons why certain personalities were chosen for the figure of martyr while others were not. Both Abu Muslim and Nizam al-Mulk were widely respected during their lifetimes as political and to some extent religious leaders. While Abu Muslim was executed by the caliph he retained the aura of martyrdom, but while Nizam al-Mulk was assassinated by a hated Assassin (and thus could have claimed to be a martyr by virtue of being assassinated by a heretic), he did not. Abu Muslim gained religious stature after his death to the point where he is best remembered in the *Abu Muslimnama* as a religious leader, while Nizam al-Mulk essentially lost all of the aura of religious authority he had during his life and is remembered only as the author of political treatises. While Abu Muslim was killed privately (although later on the circumstances became known), Nizam al-Mulk was killed publicly, and was given a magnificent state funeral. The circumstances of death and the final

---

[3] Sadr al-Din al-Husayni, *Akhbar al-dawla al-Saljuqiyya*, pp. 66–67; 'Imad al-Din al-Isfahani, *Ta'rikh dawlat Al Saljuq*, pp. 226–27; Ibn al-Jawzi, *al-Muntazam fi al-ta'rikh*, xvi, pp. 302–07.

honors accorded each of these two figures were different: Abu Muslim was denied a formal funeral and yet lived on via his supporters (eventually as a martyr) while Nizam al-Mulk was granted the funeral and did not acquire the status of Abu Muslim.

Another group of martyrs that won general acceptance are the Sufi warriors, who were often instrumental in the conquest or conversion of various regions. It is possible to make a comparison between the early proto-Sufi ascetics, such as Ibrahim b. Adham and Ibn al-Mubarak, and later Sufis such as Baba Palangposh (Chapter 5). The early ascetics have achieved something close to community-wide acceptance, as their stories are repeated in numerous literary compositions as well as oral recitations. However, the later ones are usually only venerated by the local regions in which they died. After a certain period Islam was simply too widespread for martyrdom narratives from Africa, Central Asia and Indonesia to circulate, and there was no central hierarchical system to disseminate these stories or to enforce commemoration of them.

For a martyr to be accepted in the Muslim community overall, there are a number of different components necessary. The most widely accepted martyrs are all from the early period of Islam and geographically they were associated with the core areas of Islam (the Middle East). They all died specifically for either Islam or a political-religious cause that came to be identified with the faith (political opposition to unjust rulers or opposition to specific religious trends that were later accepted to be non-Islamic). Usually they are fighters, but in certain cases merely prominent leaders, but always having some previous high status inside the faith. Since there is no process by which martyrs come to be generally accepted other than the consensus of the Muslim community, it is natural that the formula of acceptance is problematic. But for the scholar studying Islam I think that it is useful to consider a tripartite formula: if an individual has an account of his or her death that is consistent with classical martyrologies (as described in Chapter 1), if this account is cited and perhaps embellished over a period of several generations, and if there is a popular cult associated with that individual (with the oral tradition), then it is safe to assume that person has achieved martyrdom status.

From a literary point of view, the genre of martyrdom in Islam remains curiously underutilized. In general, the Shi'ites made the best use of this genre of literature – one thinks of the voluminous *Maqatil* literature – but Sunnis have only rarely published detailed accounts of martyrs. This absence of literary unity does not mean that there are no martyrdom accounts in Sunnism, but that they are only rarely brought together in single useful compositions, like *Foxe's Book of Martyrs*. In addition to this the martyrdom narratives, again with the exception of that of al-Husayn, are only rarely drawn out, usually lack the blood and gore of Jewish or Christian narratives, and sometimes are almost bland and unemotional.

Contemporary martyrologies of political and religious victims, especially those connected with the Palestinian conflict, and the larger world of radical Islam, have changed considerably from these classical norms. In the Palestinian literature, for example, there are all of the elements of emotional and pathos-engendering martyrologies. Radical Muslims also have mastered these techniques in order to marshal sympathy for their cause. And martyrologies are no longer, thanks to modern communications and the Internet, so regional.[4] What is known among the Palestinians, for example, is immediately broadcast around the Muslim world, and remains the subject of intense interest. However, this level of interest is rather uneven, and Muslim martyrs in certain areas of conflict or fighting repressive governments remain virtually anonymous. Even when there is a plethora of material – for example, in the Central Asian republics of the former USSR – there is not necessarily an interest in perpetuating the past persecution of Muslims. (Interviews with Muslim leaders in Uzbekistan and Tajikistan suggest this to be the only cogent explanation for the absence of martyrologies detailing the slaughters of Muslim leaders during the Soviet period.)

After reading about the evidence from the historical, legal and contemporary accounts it is important to consider the place of martyrdom within Islam and the ramifications that it has for the present and the future of this dynamic faith. Since martyrdom is to a large degree advertisement we should ask: how has this advertisement been received? Does martyrdom as a statement actually garner converts to the faith? This question is not one that is easily answered because so few studies of converts to Islam exist (either classical or contemporary), and of those most are of Western converts (who usually convert via Sufism). It may be that conversion because of the testimonials of martyrs is a factor within the overall conversion to Islam, but it is unlikely to be a very significant one.

The more likely testimonial for the martyrs and martyrologies is not to convert people to Islam (although of course such conversion is welcome) but to convert Muslims to a given cause or to highlight its importance or the heroism of those participating in it and willing to die for it. This tendency would again be consistent with classical Islam in which martyrdom at the hands of those outside the faith was a minor factor in the overall martyrologies, while martyrdom was more useful in shoring up support for a sect or cause within Islam. For this reason, Muslim martyrdom may have more of an inward-looking quality than do either Christian or Buddhist martyrologies. They are basically designed to compliment and support those already within the faith rather than to reach out and convince those beyond the boundaries of Islam.

One may reasonably ask what is the future of Muslim martyrology? At present, martyrology is very closely associated with radical Islam (most of

---

[4] Consider the numerous Palestinian, radical Muslim and other cyber graveyards for the fighters.

the formerly nationalist resistance movements that were predominant prior to the 1990s have become Islamized over the past twenty years). In the context of Sunni Islam, this close association will probably continue until radical Islam loses its appeal or becomes quietist. Neither of these two possibilities seems likely at the present, although since 2001 radical Islam has suffered a number of reverses and its ideology of *jihad* has a number of unresolved problems.[5] As long as there are Muslim resistance movements in the world, and as long as radical Muslims continue to attempt to establish a Muslim state or to confront non-Muslims on a global scale, there will be martyrs. Not all Muslims will consider the people who die in these causes to be martyrs – although many will be sympathetic to those of the first category – but enough will so that martyrologies will be perpetuated.

[5] For a discussion, see Oliver Roy, *The Failure of Political Islam* (although I do not necessarily want to write off radical Islam quite yet, the general trends in my opinion point to Roy's hypothesis); for an excellent discussion of the problematics of *jihad* in the contemporary world see Firyal Mahanna, *Ishkaliyyat al-jihad fi 'asr al-ma'lumatiyya*, especially pp. 125–94.

Appendix
The classical story of the *Ashab al-ukhdud* and translated contemporary martyrdom narratives

I. Story of the king, the monk and the boy[1]

There was a king among those prior to you [the Muslims], and he had a magician. When he became aged, he said to the king: I have become aged; so send me a youth (*ghulam*) so that I can teach him magic. So he sent him a youth to teach him, and along the way, he passed a monk, sat down beside him, listened to his words and they amazed him. Whenever he came to the magician he would pass the monk, and sit with him, and when he got to the magician the latter would beat him, and say: "What took you [so long]?" And then when he returned to his family, he would sit with the monk listening to his words, and when he returned to his family they would beat him and say: "What took you [so long]?" He complained about that to the monk, and the latter said: If you fear the magician, say: "My family kept me"; and if you fear your family then say: "The magician kept me."

While they were in this situation, one day a great beast passed by on the road, stopped the people and would not let them pass. The boy said: "Now I will know – is the magician more favorable to God or the monk?" And so he took a rock, and said: "O God (*Allahumma*) if the monk is more beloved to you than the magician, then when I throw my rock, let it kill him [the beast] so that the people may pass." So he threw it and killed [the beast], while the people passed. This news reached the monk, and the monk said to the youth: "You are greater than I am; if you are tortured do not reveal me." The youth would heal those born blind, the lepers and other sicknesses.

The king had a boon-companion who became blind, and it was said to him: "There is a youth who heals the born blind, the lepers and other sicknesses, so maybe you should go to him." So he took gifts for him and said: "O youth, if you heal me, all of these gifts are yours." He said: "I am not a doctor who can heal you, but God heals, and so if you believe then I will pray to God to heal

---

[1] Taken from al-Tabari, *Jami'*, XXX, pp. 133–34; additions and corrections from the version in Muslim, *Sahih*, VIII, pp. 229–31; the commentary in al-Nawawi, *Sharh Sahih Muslim*, XI, pp. 7289–90 is valuable to make sense of this somewhat garbled tradition; also al-Tha'labi, *'Ara'is al-majalis*, pp. 439–42; al-Hindi, *Kanz al-'ummal*, XV, pp. 159–63 (no. 40466).

you." The blind man believed and he [the youth] prayed to God and he healed him. The [formerly] blind man sat with the king as he used to sit, and the king said: "Weren't you blind?" He said: "Yes." He said: "Who healed you?" He said: "My Lord." He said: "Do you have any other lord besides me?" He said: "Yes, my Lord and your Lord are Allah." He said: "Take him to the torture."

He said: "You will show me who taught you that," and he pointed the youth to him. So he called the youth, and said: "Renounce your faith" and the youth refused, so he took him to the torture, then he pointed the monk out to him. Then he took the monk and said: "Renounce your religion" and he refused. So he placed a saw upon his [the monk's] head and sliced him [in two] until he fell to the ground. Then he took the blind man, and said "Verily, if you do not renounce your religion I will kill you!" And the blind man refused, so he put the saw upon his head, and sliced him [in two] until he fell to the ground. Then he said to the youth: "Renounce or I will kill you!" and he refused.

So then he said: "Take him to the peak of a mountain, and if he renounces his religion [then fine] but if not toss him over." They took him to the peak of the mountain but the (mountain shook), they fell off and all died. The youth came seeking the king and entered into him, and he said: "Where are your companions?" He said: "God took care of them for me." He said: "Take him and put him in a barge, and set sail in the sea. If he renounces his religion [then fine], if not drown him." So they took him and when they had set sail to sea, the youth prayed: "O God, take care of them for me [or: protect me from them]!" and the boat flipped them over. The youth came seeking the king and entered into him, and the king said: "Where are your companions?" He said: "I prayed to God, and He took care of them for me." He said: "Verily, I am going to kill you!" He said: "You will not be able to kill me until you do what I command you." The youth then said to the king: "Gather the people into one place, then crucify me (on a beam), then take an arrow from my quiver (and place it in the middle of a bow) and shoot it [at me], saying: In the name of the Lord of the youth! And then you will have killed me."

So he gathered the people into one place, and crucified him, and took an arrow from his quiver, and placed it in the middle of the bow, shot it, and said: "In the name of the Lord of the youth!" The arrow landed in the temple of the youth, and the people said: "We believe in the Lord of the youth!" They said to the king: "What have you done? That from which you were cautioned has come to pass. The people have believed!" So he ordered for them to be taken to the entrances of the streets, to dig trenches (*ukhdud*), and to light fires, and to take them and say: "If you renounce [then fine] if not we will throw you into the fire." They would throw them into the fire, and then a woman came with her boy, and when she went into the fire she drew back because of the heat. Her boy said to her: "Mother, go on, for you are in the right" and she went into the fire.

II.   Contemporary Islamic martyrdom narratives

Palestinian

All of these points we have adduced previously are minor compared with that which we will bring afterwards at the side of the distinction to which the heroic fighter Yehye ʿAyyash attained, and that is it was sealed for him by martyrdom. Not everyone who fights attains martyrdom, even if he is eager for it; it is like God most high told, a selection and an honor: "Such are the times; We alternate them among the people, so that Allah might know who are the believers and choose martyrs from among you. Allah does not like the evildoers!" [Qurʾan 3:139–40] ... how excellent was the one who said concerning him [ʿAyyash] on the day of his martyrdom: "By God, it is not strange that you should be martyred, O ʿAyyash it would have been strange had you not been martyred." Or the one who formed a poem whose beginning is thus:

> My covenant for the likes of you is to die as a martyr, so ascend to your glory, your promised glory.

... [ʾAyyash's] martyrdom was by the shedding of blood, by a bomb charge that exploded next to his head. The day of his martyrdom was Friday, which God has made special above all other days with blessing ... the spirit of our martyr was lifted during this month [Shaʾban] in which the works of the servants are lifted unto God ...

During all the years that the Engineer was a wanted fugitive the Jews were never able to lay their hands on him, and the Shabak, the Shin Bet, the Mossad, the covert "Arab" units[2] ... and ... and ... and they didn't get to him. They were unable to get a hold of him until their international efforts were unified and the United States helped the Jews with superior techniques. They failed to kill him using the newest scientific and technological impliments ... [lists the Palestinians who helped Israel find ʿAyyash] ... for this reason the martyrdom of the Engineer helped reveal to the [Muslim] community all of the most dangerous enemy – the agents and traitors who sold their religion and their conscience to their enemies. They are those concerning whom God said: "They are the enemy, so beware of them. May Allah fight them! How they are perverted" [Qurʾan 63:4].

In his eulogy for the martyr Yehye ʿAyyash, Hilmi al-Asmar wrote: "O Yehye [John] is it coincidence that led you to die in the same way as John [the Baptist] the prophet of God was martyred? Or was this divine planning only known to the believers? John the prophet of God was killed by the Jews by having his

---

[2] Units of the Israeli Army that pretend to be Arabs and often inflict damage upon the Hamas and other Palestinian groups.

head cut off from his body to be given to a low dancer[3] and you had your head cut off from your body by an explosive charge placed by the Jews. This was in order to place this believing head upon the altar of peace. You see what a deep sign there is between your martyrdom and the martyrdom of John the prophet of God in the same way?[4]

Afghani

(The martyrdom of Ahmad Shah Massoud on September 9, 2001, as remembered by Mas'ud [or Masood] Khalili, the Ambassador of Afghanistan to India.)

Masood Khalili, a confidante of the alliance Commander Ahmed Shah Massoud, was there when the camera set up by the assassins conducting the deadly trick blew up. The camera exploded just after the first false question was asked. "It was like a thick curtain of fire rushing though the lens at us. Everything was coming through the lens," Khalili recalled. Khalili, the Northern Alliance's ambassador to India, where the alliance is considered the legitimate government of Afghanistan, was seriously injured. Four other members of the anti-Taliban Northern Alliance who were present perished. Khalili believes that Massoud died in the blast or shortly afterward. He gave his first account of the attack to CNN, filled with emotion as he recalled details of the incident from a hospital in Germany. He is convinced Osama bin Laden – wanted by the United States in the catastrophic strikes on New York and Washington [on September 11, 2001] – was behind it.

Three men posing as journalists wanted to interview Massoud, Khalili said. Two of them came into Massoud's room. Khalili said he was surprised at the aggressiveness of their questioning. Speaking in Arabic, they asked what the Northern Alliance would do if it captured bin Laden and why the Northern Alliance hated him so much. Khalili was meant to translate the questions into Persian, Massoud's tongue.

"That killer, coward man was asking about Commander Massoud's most recent trip to Europe, where he criticized Osama bin Laden," Khalili said. The Taliban regard bin Laden as a guest in Afghanistan and refuse the US demand to turn him over. While in Europe, Massoud had described bin Laden as a "terrorist and a killer, not a guest," Khalili said. "That's why they planned this all. I know it. Osama bin Laden did it," the ambassador said. "Just before the interview started, the two bombers asked Commander Massoud why he had been critical of Osama bin Laden and why he had called him a terrorist and a killer," he continued. "The first question they asked the commander on camera

---

[3] See Matthew 14:6–11.
[4] Mukhallis Yahya Barzaq, *Fada'il al-shahid Yehye 'Ayyash*, pp. 119–35 (selections).

was 'What is the situation in northern Afghanistan?'" I had just translated the question when there was a huge boom. "Then, from the camera, I saw a blue, dark, deep fire coming from the lens. I was screaming, 'This is your last minute, I should say something holy.' Then from this fire I saw Commander Massoud's hand reaching toward me."

"He reached my hand, he touched me. Then I lost consciousness. When I recovered I was on a helicopter and Commander Massoud was just a few inches from me. I saw his beautiful face full of blood. His attractive hair [was] full of blood."

Khalili said he asked someone on the helicopter about Massoud's condition.

"All he could do was cry. And I could not even reach to kiss him (Massoud) goodbye."

The third "journalist" who accompanied the suicide bombers – both "Arab-looking in their mid-20s" – was not allowed in the room. Khalili said that someone present told him that within seconds of the blast, the third man was screaming: "God is great. We have been successful." Unfortunately, said Khalili, the third man was shot before he could be interrogated. Khalili lost the use of one eye and has severe burns on his legs. He said, however, that he has a new mission in life. "God saved me to fight the Taliban. And if I die it will be from the hands of those who are the enemies of humanity," he said. "Even if this holy war takes us twenty years we should all unite to fight against the Taliban." The ambassador said his wife later found his leather-bound passport, embedded with shrapnel, in the pocket of his shirt. "My wife told me 'your passport acted like a shield to your heart. This saved your life.'" His camera also survived the blast, Khalili said, and he has since developed photographs from that last roll – one of them a picture of Massoud reading a book. "I'm proud I have taken this photograph." Khalili said he will never forget Massoud, his friend of twenty-four years, who made the supreme sacrifice for the country he loved. "He took it straight in the heart. Me, I just lost an eye and got injured in the legs." Ambassador Khalili's wife has joined him in Germany. "She can now be my other eye," he said. Khalili has 400 pieces of shrapnel in his legs. He says with amusement that a doctor told him his legs look like the "sky with lots of stars." On Saturday, his spirits were lifted when he was able to walk for the first time since the attack.[5]

Chechen: Khattab (Sami al-Suwaylam)

He began his journey fourteen years ago in Afghanistan, and that was in the year 1988. He was present at most of the major operations of the Afghani *jihad*, and participated in the conquest of Jalalabad and Khost, and in the conquest

---

[5] CNN report (Satinder Bhindra), October 7, 2001.

of Kabul in 1993. One of the *mujahidin* told how he was hit in the stomach by a burst of fire from a 12.7mm rifle. He said: "During one of the operations we would sit in a room in the back of the front line, at night, while the fighting on the front lines was fierce. After a short while Khattab came into the room, and his face was pale, but other than that he acted normally. He came in walking slowly, then sat to one side, near us. He was quiet and did not speak differently than usual. The brothers felt that something was wrong, though he gave no hint and made no movement that would indicate he was feeling any pain. We asked him whether he had gotten hit. He replied that he had gotten hit a little bit during the fighting on the front, but that it was not a bad hit.

One of the brothers came near to him to see his wound, and Khattab refused to show him, saying that it was not bad. But the brother pressured him to show him his wound, and touched his clothing in the area of his belly, and found his clothes soaked in blood which was pumping out fast. We made haste and called him a car, and took him to the nearest hospital, while at the same time Khattab was insisting that his wound didn't require all that attention and that it was a small hit.

In Tajikistan . . . he lost two fingers of his right hand from a grenade . . . when the brothers tried to take him back to Peshawar for treatment he refused and instead put bees' honey on his wound. After two years in Tajikistan, Khattab and his little group returned to Afghanistan at the beginning of 1995, and that was the beginning of the war in Chechnya. Khattab described his feelings when he saw the news of the Chechens on the satellite news channel in Afghanistan. He said: "When I saw the Chechen bands covered in slogans saying: 'There is no God but Allah and Muhammad is the Messenger of Allah, and crying *Allahu akbar!*' I knew that there was a *jihad* in Chechnya and I decided that I would go there."

As for details of his martyrdom the accounts have differed, but the two major accounts agree that he was killed by treachery. The website *wah-islam-ah* related that his death was at the hands of one of those traitorous hypocrites, among those whom Khattab trusted. It happened when one of them slipped Khattab a poisoned letter, and he died as a result. One of the leaders of the Arab groups two weeks ago had sent a messenger to Commander Khattab with an operational letter, and Khattab had sent one of his own messengers to pick up the letter. But this messenger from Khattab was a traitor (an agent whom the *mujahidin* had trusted) and put poison in the letter, and immediately handed it over to Commander Khattab. When he touched the poison with his hand, it only took five minutes for it to affect him and he gave up the ghost.

There is another version from the site qafqaz.com that indicates that he was killed by a poison that was treacherously slipped into his food . . . The *mujahidin* concealed his martyrdom for the benefit of the *jihad* until circumstances were ripe for them to reveal it.[6]

Bosnian–Herzegovinan War

Abu Mu'adh al-Kuwaiti, commander of foreign volunteers, Operation Miracle, July 21, 1995. The son of a governor from Kuwait, and also an Olympic athlete from Kuwait. He went to Afghanistan to join his brothers there for six years. He came to Bosnia in 1994, and became the commander of the Ansar/foreign volunteers. In spite of this, this brother, in Operation Miracle, in July 1995, was not placed in the attack group, and so he was very sad at that. Despite the fact that he was not successful, Abu Mu'adh went to the top of the mountain and began organizing the groups. He was then killed before he got to the top and fell down [as a] *shahid, insha'allah* [if God wills]. Four days later, one brother from Medina in Bosniq saw him in a dream where he was going back to the *masjid* [mosque] of the *mujahidin*. "I saw Abu Mu'adh meeting all the brothers and everone was happy at seeing him. He had a bandage on his head at the place where he was shot. And I was very angry, at Abu Mu'adh when he was meant to be a *shahid*. So I shook his hand and I asked him: Abu Mu'adh! Why are you here? Are you a *shahid* or not?!

He turned away and did not want to say anything. And then when no one was looking he began to make his way out of the *masjid*. I knew that he was going to go so I waited for him at the door of the *masjid*. He left the *masjid* and waited for a plate to come under him, which started to lift him up into the sky. I then ran up to him and I grabbed him on his leg. I said: "Abu Mu'adh. Please tell me what is happening. Why are you here? Are you a *shahid* or not?" And he said: "Yes, I am a *shahid*." I said: "What is it like?" He said: "On the day of the operation, a window opened in the sky from Paradise, and all of the Muslims that would be *shahid*s, all of the *mujahidin* that would be killed that day, they pass through this window, straight into *jannah* [paradise]." I said: "What is the actual mark and what does it feel like?" He said: "You don't feel a thing. As soon as you are killed, you see two beautiful blonde girls, they come and sit beside you in *jannah* with you." I asked him: "What is *jannah* like?" And Abu Mu'adh replied: "It is not *jannah* [one], it is *jannat* [many]." I said: "What about enjoying and pleasure?" He said: "Every day and every place." Then Abu Mu'adh said: "Now let me go." I then said to Abu Mu'adh: "One last thing. Can you tell me when I am going to be *shahid*?" Abu Mu'adh said: "I cannot tell you that." So I asked him: "Can you at least tell me by coming to me in a dream a few days before I am going to be killed?" And Abu Mu'adh said: "I will try. Now, let me go."[7]

---

[6] Materials from jeeran.com (May 5, 2003).
[7] From "In the Hearts of Green Birds, side b, part 1, at almansurah.com (I have modified the English slightly to make it more understandable).

Pakistani–Kashmiri

When they brought me to prison, after spending nearly a year in various torture centers, even the dreadful prison seemed to be a pleasant place. In prison I could no longer hear those screams and sobs which send shivers to the spine, nor could I witness the most degrading, shameful and inhuman scenes which are the daily routine of every torture center. In the prison they subjected me to special treatment and consigned me to an infamous ward, whose harsh and severe regime scares the daylight out of even the most hardened criminals. Actually, this ward is a prison within the prison, where they consign only those prisoners who have committed rioting or some exceptional crime for the maximum period of thirty days. But upon my arrival they consigned me immediately to a cell in this ward. But I still felt like a man who found a shadowy tree after spending the day in the searing heat, because the place where they [had] consigned me previously was a place where every new dawn was accompanied by heart trembling trepidations.

Where every morning used to begin with the removal of the handcuffs and the chains from the feet. Under the shadow of guns, batons and abusive language, we were herded towards the toilets. As this is the only opportunity in twenty-four hours to relieve ourselves, every one of us has to make this journey, staggering, falling on all fours, under the constant lashes of the baton, moaning, groaning and sobbing, we would somehow perform this necessary task. At nine o'clock the whole building starts to vibrate with the ear-piercing screams. Yes! The process of interrogation has started. Some are hanged upside down, they scream, but in the midst of their screams the verses of the Holy Qur'an can also be heard; some are tortured by releasing the electric current to the sensitive parts of their bodies, they yell, they scream, yet the word "Allah, Allah!" is on their lips. Some are forced to the ground while their legs are pulled apart by the torturers. On some naked bodies, incessant whipping is in progress. Someone's beard is pulled out from the skin. Some are trampled upon, in order to force them to drink alcohol. Most of the victims' clothes are removed and [they] are completely naked. Their penises are forced into their colleagues' mouths while the torturers mock them with: "Now, why don't your colleagues help you?" or: "Well now, have you found your independence?" Some are pumped with petrol injections and their gut wrenching screams shake the whole torture center. Some are made to stand on their toes for days.

Among the favorite tortures of these animals are the mixing of urine and excrement into the food of the victims, or putting the victim in the center and forming a circle around him, then punching and kicking him in turn, while taunting him by such words as: "Well now, why are you not talking about the *jihad?*" Then the beating with the iron bars begins amidst this torture, and the victim is forced to swear at his mother, to shout anti-Pakistan and anti-*jihad* slogans ... In such torture centers, though the body is carved and slashed and mutilated, the *iman* [faith] not only remains intact but grows stronger; here the true face of the enemy is observed, here the spirit and the soul are enhanced, here though the blood oozes out of the body, the believers are solidified and heightened.

Here I observed with my own eyes the true nature of the *iman* and the *kufr* [infidelity] described in the Holy Qur'an ... Here the common experience has been that while one of us is going through the unimaginable physical pain and anguish, the rest of us suffer both the physical and mental pain on his behalf. Once when I had been brought back to the cell after a special torture, [when] the colleagues saw my condition, they wept underneath their sheets so much that the whole room was filled with the noise of their weeping. During the physical torture my body was oozing with blood, but my eyes remained dry and not a drop of a tear fell from my eyes, but after witnessing their feelings and their compassion, the dam broke and I started weeping as well. But I offer thanksgiving to Allah that I did not weep because of the violence of [the infidels] but I wept due to the sweetness of *iman*.[8]

"An American Shahid"

(Summarized from the martyrology in Minhaj al-Muslim)

"All I want is *shahada* in Kashmir. I don't want to be famous and well-known." Those were the words of Abu Adam Jibril al-Amriki as we walked around the center in Pakistan. As we strolled around the giant mosque and looked at the horse stable we talked of the difficulties in training and *jihad* in general. Abu Adam was only nineteen years of age when he went to the killing fields of occupied Kashmir. Born into a wealthy family in Atlanta, Georgia, Abu Adam ... had gone with his family to Ebenezer Baptist Church, the church of Dr Martin Luther King, Jr. After graduating from high school he left Atlanta to go to college in Durham, North Carolina, about four hours away. It would be in Durham that he would gain a more detailed understanding of Islam and the reality of the situations faced in many of the Muslim lands ... The burning desire to wage *jihad* against the enemies of Allah soon overtook Abu Adam and thus he began a program of training to prepare himself for the extremely difficult battle conditions.

Perhaps we might pay heed and take benefit from his program: Abu Adam began to spend more and more time in the mosque. He would increase his voluntary prayers and fasting. He began to read the Qur'an daily and memorize supplications of the Prophet for every occasion. He also began to lengthen his prayers (*salat*), and try to build up his humility. Abu Adam even cut back

---

[8] *Zad-e-Mujahid*, pp. 6–10 (I have modified the original slightly to make it more comprehensible).

on food and drink, and his amount of sleep so as to get himself ready for the hardships of *jihad*. He realized that *jihad* is directly connected to the spiritual cultivation of the person. The preparation of Abu Adam for *jihad* was not relegated to the spiritual side alone. He also undertook physical preparation in the form of running, exercise and military tactics ... Allah also blessed Abu Adam with brothers in his area with prior military experience. He benefited greatly from one who was a former US Army Ranger ... after months of spiritual and physical training ... in November of 1997 he went to Kashmir.

Abu Adam began his training in Ramadan of 1997 with the *mujahidin* of Lashkar-i Tayba. Lashkar-i Tayba are the *mujahidin* of *ahl al-sunna* in Kashmir and are the most feared warriors in the occupied valley. He chose to train at the hardest time of the year: mid-winter. I firmly believe that the more difficulties you go through in training, the more *baraka* [blessing] your training will have. The *mujahid* will go through things in the course of training that purify him as the gold is purified by the fire. He will sometimes go through things that cause him to say: "Ya Allah! You know that this is for You alone, and I only continue through this extreme difficulty for Your sake. If you do not help me I will not be able to continue." ... Abu Adam opted for the intense training in winter while at the same time fasting. Abu Adam was known to carry extra weight and march on no matter what ... He would always try harder and make frequent *du'a* [prayer] to Allah for firmness on the path of *jihad*. He would fast in the day while running miles in the cold Kashmiri mountain paths. He would train in military tactics while having numbed limbs from the intense cold of winter. He would continue to shout: *Allahu akbar!* even while his throat was dry and parched for lack of water due to his fast. He would climb through the beautiful snow-covered Kashmiri mountains even while his body lacked nutrients because of his fasting. He would break his fast on dirty brown-colored water taken from a running stream, and he would eat the lentils that always gave him digestive and stomach problems. And it was he that would march out in the dark cold night with his *mujahidin* brothers from 8 pm until the time of the dawn prayers.

... I always admired his determination. After a few weeks of recovery and rest, Abu Adam received the news that he was long waiting for: the *amir* told him: "Pack your bags. You are going to Jammu to launch!" Abu Adam was shining from happiness and delight. "I am finally getting a chance to go and do *jihad fi sabil Allah* [in the path of God]." After two-and-a-half weeks I met back up with Abu Adam at the launching sector to prepare to infiltrate with him into the occupied valley. We were only waiting for our slot to carefully infiltrate the occupied valley of Kashmir to strike down and destroy the enemies of Allah, the vile Hindus and Sikhs ... It was around July 5th that our group of ten brothers received what it was waiting for: the news of its launching into the occupied valley. After two days of preparation, the weapons were test fired, cleaned and sighted. The equipment and gear were distributed. The magazines were loaded and the *iman* was as high as ever waiting for the chance to please Allah. It was time to wage *jihad* and secure some expensive real estate in heaven. And, as always, Abu Adam demanded that he carry more gear and ammo than anyone else in the group. *Allahu akbar*!

Unfortunately some of us were separated from Abu Adam and his group due to external factors, so at this launching point would be the last time I would see my brother Abu Adam. Indeed, he was crying from happiness and at the same time realizing that this would be the last time we would see him for a long while. Abu Yahya said about him: "When we were infiltrating in the pitch black darkness of the cloudy Kashmiri border area he (Abu Adam) was always at the front of the group – never lagging at all. When we stopped for ten minutes of rest he sat next to me and looked to the heavens and sighed: *al-hamdu li-llah* [praise be to God]. I then asked him: "What is it that makes you say that right now?" To which he replied: "All of my life I wanted a piece [a gun] and some grenades, and a blade [a knife], and now I have my piece [a Makarov 9mm pistol] and my rifle [AK-47], and I have my hand-grenades, and it is all *fi sabil Allah*."

After five days of night movement and infiltration, Abu Adam with the rest of the brothers successfully entered into the occupied valley of Kashmir. It was there that Abu Adam would take an active part in laying ambushes and carrying out raids against the Indian oppressors. After two-and-a-half months of guerrilla *jihad* Abu Adam finally achieved that which he strove for: *al-shahada fi sabil Allah* [martyrdom in the path of Allah]. Abu Adam and his team of brothers launched a bloody raid on an army post in the Doda sector in the Jammu region. Reports indicate that out of the thirty-four Indians killed in the action, Abu Adam was responsible for killing seventeen. *Allahu akbar*! It was at the exact time of his *shahada* that I had a dream in which I saw Abu Adam at the launching sector base. He had returned from fighting. His hair had grown out and there was fresh blood on his clothes. He was shining from happiness to see me. I then asked him: "How was it?" to which he replied: "It was hard but worth it." After this dream I received news that my good friend Abu Adam had beaten me to our respective goal – *al-shahada fi sabil Allah*. I remember him saying to me once: "I want to get shot in the chest so that my soul doesn't leave immediately and I can prostrate to Allah on the battlefield before my soul leaves my body." I can't help but wonder if he got his last wish or not.

Abu Adam Jibril al-Amriki never did drugs before Islam and when he left this *dunya* [world] he was still a virgin, something that is very rare for an American youth. His news eventually reached his non-Muslim family in Atlanta. And it was after hearing this news that his older sister Lisa took *shahada* [Muslim confession of faith] and entered into the fold of Islam. May Allah make her like her brother! "And do not think those who have been killed in the way of Allah as dead; they are rather living with their Lord, well-provided for" (Qur'an 3:169).[9]

---

[9] From Minhaj al-Muslim, at maktabah-alsalafiyah.org/English/abuadam.htm (2/28/2002). I have made minor modifications to the original to make it more comprehensible.

Bibliography

'Abbas, Ihsan, *Diwan shi'r al-Khawarij*. N.p., 1982.

Abbott, Freeland, "The *jihad* of Sayyid Ahmad Shahid," *Muslim World* 52 (1962), pp. 216–22, 288–95.

'Abd al-'Aziz, Jum'a Amin, *al-Farida al-muftara 'alayha: al-jihad fi sabil allah*. Iskandariyya: Dar al-Da'wa, 2001.

'Abd al-Rahim, Muhammad, *Arba'un hadithan fi fadl al-shahid wa-l-shahada*. Damascus: al-Halbuni, 1995.

Abu Da'ud al-Sijistani (d. 888–89), *Sunan*. Beirut: Dar al-Jil, 1988 (4 vols).

Abu Diya, Sa'd, *Dirasa tahliliyya fi al-'amaliyyat al-istishhadiyya fi janub Lubnan*. Beirut: Jami'at al-'Ummal al-Matabi' al-Ta'awuniyya, 1986.

Abu Khalil, As'ad, "Sex and the Suicide Bomber," at selon.com (Nov. 7, 2001).

Abu Mikhnaf, Lut b. Yahya (d. 773–74), *Kitab maqtal al-Husayn*. Ed. al-Hasan al-Ghifari, Qumm: Chapkhan-i 'Ilmiyya, 1342/1923.

Abu-Rabi', Ibrahim, *Intellectual Origins of Islamic Resurgence in the Arab World*. Albany, NY: State University of New York Press, 1996.

Ado-Kurawa, Ibrahim (trans.), *The Jihad in Kano: Translation and Analysis of Taqyid al-akhbar of Qadi Muhammad Zangi ibn Salih* (d. 1869). Kano: Kurawa Holdings, 1989.

'Adwan, 'Abd al-Jabbar, *al-Shuhada*. London: Dar al-Intifada, 1989.

Ahmad, Mohiuddin, *Saiyid Ahmad Shahid: His Life and Mission*. Lucknow: Institute of Islamic Research and Publications, 1975.

Ajami, Fouad, *The Vanished Imam*. New York: Cornell University Press, 1986.

Akhir Ayyam Gharnata (*ca.* 1493). Ed. Muhammad Ridwan al-Da'iyya, Beirut: Dar al-Fikr, 2002.

Alf layla wa-layla. Ed. Rushdi Salih, Cairo: Dar Matabi' al-Sha'b, n.d. (2 vols).

Allen, J. T. W. (trans.), *Utendi wa-kutawafu Nabii*. Lewiston, ID: E. Mellen Press, 1991.

Al-'Amaliyyat al-fida'iyya: shahada am intihar? Gaza: Markaz al-Quds li-l-Dirasat wa-l-I'lam wa-l-Nashr, 2001.

Al-'Amaliyyat al-istishhadiyya: Watha'iq wa-suwar al-muqawama al-wataniyya al-Lubnaniyya 1982–85. Damascus: al-Markaz al-'Arabi, 1985.

Amad, Salma, *al-Imam al-shahid fi al-ta'rikh wa-l-aydiyalujiya*. Beirut: al-Mu'assasa al-'Arabiyya li-l-Dirasat, 2000.

Al-Antaki, Da'ud b. 'Umar (d. 1599–1600), *Tazyin al-aswaq bi-tafsil ashwaq al-'ushshaq*. Ed. Ayman 'Abd al-Jabir al-Buhayri, Beirut: Dar al-Kutub al-'Ilmiyya, 2002.

Ante-Nicean Fathers. Grand Rapids, MI: Eerdmanns, 1986 (10 vols).

'Arabfaqih, Shihab al-Din Ahmad (d. *ca.* 1534), *Tuhfat al-zaman aw Futuh al-Habasha*. Ed. Fuhaym Muhammad Shaltut, Cairo: al-Ha'iya al-Misriyya, 1974.

Arberry, Arthur (trans.), *Muslim Saints and Mystics: Episodes from the Tadhkirat al-awliya' of Farid al-Din 'Attar*. Chicago, IL: University of Chicago Press, 1966.

___ (trans.), *Mystical Poems of Rumi*. Chicago, IL: University of Chicago Press, 1968.

___ (trans.), *A Sufi Martyr: The Apologia of 'Ain al-Qudat al-Hamadhani*. London: George Allen and Unwin, 1969.

___ (trans.), *Fifty Poems of Hafiz*. Richmond: Curzon Press, 1970.

___ (trans.), *Mystical Poems of Rumi II*. Boulder, CO: Westview Press, 1979.

Al-'Arini, 'Abdallah b. Salih, *Shi'ir jihad al-Rum*. Riyadh: Wizarat al-Ta'lim, 2002.

Al-'Askari, Abu Hilal al-Hasan b. 'Abdallah (d. 1004–05), *al-Awa'il*. Ed. 'Abd al-Razzaq Ghalib al-Mahdi, Beirut: Dar al-Kutub al-'Ilmiyya, 1997.

Athamina, Khalil, "The Black Banners and the Socio-Political Significance of Flags and Slogans," *Arabica* 36 (1989), pp. 307–26.

'Attar, Farid al-Din (d. *ca.* 428/1036–7), *Tadhkirat al-awliya'*. Ed. Marhum Qazvini, Tehran: Safi 'Alishah, 1380/2001. *See*, Arberry, Arthur.

Attas, Muhammad Naguib Syed, *Preliminary Statement on a General Theory of the Islamization of the Malay–Indonesian Archipelago*. Kuala Lumpur: Malaysian Sociological Research Institute, 1970.

Attwater, Donald, *Martyrs: From St. Stephen to John Tung*. London: Sheed & Ward, 1958.

Avan, Abbas Akhtar, *Karvan-i shuhada: Kabul se Kashmir*. Lahore: Idara-yi Matbu'at-i Tulbah, 1994.

Awn, Peter, *Satan's Tragedy and Redemption: Iblis in Sufi Psychology*. Leiden: E. J. Brill, 1983.

Ayoub, Mahmoud, *Redemptive Suffering in Islam: A Study of the Devotional Aspects of the 'Ashura' in Twelver Shi'ism*. The Hague: Mouton, 1978.

___ "Martyrdom in Christianity and Islam," in Richard Antoun and Mary Elaine Hegland (eds), *Religious Resurgence: Contemporary Cases in Islam, Christianity and Judaism*. Syracuse, NY: Syracuse University Press, 1987, pp. 67–77.

Al-'Ayyiri, Yusuf, *Hal intaharat hawa barayev um ustushhidat?* Trans. "The Islamic Ruling on the Permissibility of Martyrdom Operations." Available at azzam.com.

Azra, Azyumardi Azra, "Opposition to Sufism in the East Indies in the Seventeenth and Eighteenth Centuries," in de Jong and Radtke (eds), *Islamic Mysticism Contested: Thirteen Centuries of Controversies and Polemics*. Leiden: E. J. Brill, 1999, pp. 665–86.

'Azzam, 'Abdallah, *Ayat al-Rahman fi jihad al-Afghan*. Peshawar: Markaz Athar al-Shahid 'Abdallah 'Azzam, n.d.

___ *Basha'ir al-nasr, 'Ibar wa-basa'ir li-l-jihad fi al-'asr al-hadir*. Peshawar: Markaz Athar al-Shahid 'Abdallah 'Azzam, n.d.

Babayan, Kathryn, *Mystics, Monarchs and Messiahs: The Cultural Landscape of Early Modern Iran*. Cambridge, MA: Harvard University Press, 2002.

Al-Baghawi, al-Husayn b. Mas'ud (d. 1122), *Sharh al-sunna*. Ed. Sa'id al-Lahham, Beirut: Dar al-Fikr, 1998 (8 vols).

Al-Baghdadi, 'Abd al-Qadir b. Tahir (d. 1037–38), *al-Farq bayna al-firaq*. Beirut: Dar al-Afaq al-Jadida, 1987.

Bahrati, Kumar, *Shahadatnama: A Saga of Martyrs*. Jaipur: Sanghar Vidya Sabha Trust, 2001.

Al-Baladhuri, Yahya b. Ahmad (d. 892), *Ansab al-ashraf*. Vol. 4, ed. Ihsan 'Abbas, Beirut: Franz Steiner, 1959–.

Balogun, Ismail A. B., *The Life and Works of 'Uthman Dan Fodio*. Lagos: Islamic Publications Bureau, 1981.

Al-Barqi, Ahmad b. Muhammad b. Khalid (d. 887 or 893–94), *al-Mahasin*. Ed. Mahdi al-Raja'i, Qumm: al-Majma' al-'Alami li-l-Ahl al-Bayt, n.d. (2 vols).

Barzaq, Mukhallis Yahya, *Fada'il al-shahid Yehye 'Ayyash*. London: Filistin al-Muslima, 1998.

Bash, Hasan, *al-'Amaliyyat al-istishhadiyya*. Damascus: Dar Qutayba, 2003.

Al-Bayhaqi, Ahmad b. al-Husayn (d. 1066), *al-Ba'th wa-l-nushur*. Ed. 'Amir Ahmad Haydar, Beirut: Markaz al-Khidmat, 1986.

___ *Hayat al-anbiya fi quburihim*. Al-Mansura: Maktabat al-Iman, 1993.

___ *Shu'ab al-iman*. Ed. Muhammad al-Sa'id b. Bassayuni Zaghlul, Beirut: Dar al-Kutub al-'Ilmiyya, 2000 (9 vols).

___ *Sunan al-kubra*. Ed. Yusuf 'Abd al-Rahman al-Mar'ashli, Riyadh: Maktabat al-Ma'arif, n.d. (10 vols).

Bedjan, Paul (ed.), *Acta martyrum et sanctorum Syriace*. Hildesheim: G. Olms, 1968 (7 vols) (reprint).

Behari, Ebadollah, *Bihzad: Master of Persian Painting*. London: I. B. Taurus, 1996.

Bekkenkamp, Jonneke and Sherwood, Yvonne (eds), *Sanctified Aggression: Legacies of Biblical and Post-Biblical Vocabularies of Violence*. London and New York: T & T Clark International, 2003.

Bergman, Susan (ed.), *A Cloud of Witnesses*. London: HarperCollins, 1997.

Bianquis, Thierry, "Ibn al-Nablusi: un martyr Sunnite," *Annales Islamologiques* 12 (1974), pp. 45–66.

Biesterfeldt, Hans and Gutas, Dimitri, "The Malady of Love," *Journal of the American Oriental Society* 104 (1984), pp. 21–55.

Birge, John Kingsley, *The Bektashi Order of Dervishes*. London: Luzac, 1965.

Boyd, Jean and Mack, Beverly (trans.), *Collected Works of Nana Asma'u, Daughter of Usman 'dan Fodiyo (1793–1864)*. East Lansing, MI: Michigan State Press, 1997.

Bukhari, Muhammad b. Isma'il (d. 256/870), *Sahih*. Ed. 'Abd al-'Aziz b. Baz, Beirut: Dar al-Fikr, 1991 (5 vols).

Bunt, Gary, *Islam in the Digital Age: e-jihad, Online fatwas and Cyber Islamic Environments*. London and Sterling, VA: Pluto Press, 2003.

Burton, Richard (trans.), *The Arabian Nights*. London: Burton Ethnological Society, 1885–86 (10 vols).

Buzmee, A. S., "Sayyid Ahmad Shahid in the light of his letters," *Islamic Studies* 15 (1976), pp. 231–45.

Campenhausen, Hans von, *Die Idée des Martyriums in der alten Kirche*. Göttingen: Vandenhoeck & Ruprecht, 1936.

Çapan, Ergün (ed.), *An Islamic Perspective: Terror and Suicide Attacks*. Somerset, NJ: The Light, 2004.

Caraman, Philip, *The Lost Empire: The Story of the Jesuits in Ethiopia 1555–1634*. Notre Dame, IN: University of Notre Dame, 1985.

Çelebi, Elvan (*ca.* fourteenth cen.), *Menakibu'l kudsiyye fi menasibi'l unsiyye*. Eds. Ismail Erunsal and A. Yasar Ocak, Istanbul: Edebiyat Fakultesi Matbaasi, 1984.

Centlivres, Pierre (ed.), *Saints, santeté et martyre: la fabrication de l'exemplarité: Acts du colloque de Neuchâtel. 27–28 novembre 1997*. Paris: Maison des sciences de l'homme, 2001.

Chandler, Andrew, *The Terrible Alternative: Christian Martyrdom in the Twentieth Century*. London and New York: Cassell, 1998.

Chelkowski, Peter (ed.), *Ta'ziyeh: Ritual and Drama in Iran*. New York: New York University Press, 1979.

___ and Dabashi, Hamid, *Staging a Revolution: The Art of Persuasion in the Islamic Republic of Iran*. New York: New York University Press, 1999.

Chenje, Anwar G., *Islam and the West: The Moriscos. A Cultural and Social History*. Albany, NY: State University of New York Press, 1983.

Chittick, William, *The Sufi Path of Love: The Spiritual Teachings of Rumi*. Albany, NY: State University of New York Press, 1983.

Chodjim, Achmad, *Syekh Siti Jenar*. Kakarta: Serambi, 2002.

Colbert, Edward, *The Martyrs of Cordoba 850–59: A Study of the Sources*. Washington, DC: Catholic University of America Press, 1981.

Conrad, Lawrence, "Die Pest und ihr soziales umfeld in Nahen Osten in frühen mittelalters," *Der Islam* 73 (1996), pp. 81–112.

Cook, David, "Muslim Apocalyptic and *jihad*," *Jerusalem Studies in Arabic and Islam* 20 (1996), pp. 66–102.

___ "An Early Muslim Daniel Apocalypse," *Arabica* 49 (2002), pp. 55–96.

___ *Studies in Muslim Apocalyptic*. Princeton, NJ: Darwin Press, 2002.

___ "Suicide Attacks or 'Martyrdom Operations' in Contemporary *Jihad* Literature," *Nova Religio* 6 (2002), pp. 7–44.

___ "The Implications of Martyrdom Operations for Contemporary Islam," *Journal of Religious Ethics* 32 (2004), 129–51.

___ *Contemporary Muslim Apocalyptic Literature*. Syracuse, NY: Syracuse Universiy Press, 2005.

___ *Understanding Jihad*. Berkeley, CA: University of California Press, 2005.

___ "Women Fighting in *Jihad*?" *Studies in Conflict and Terrorism* 38 (Sept.–Oct. 2005), pp. 375–84.

Cormack, Margaret (ed.), *Sacrificing the Self: Perspectives on Martyrdom and Religion*. Oxford: Oxford University Press, 2002.

Dabashi, Hamid, *Truth and Narrative: The Untimely Thoughts of 'Ayn al-Qudat al-Hamadani*. Richmond: Curzon, 1999.

Dajani-Shakeel, Hadia, "*Jihad* in Twelfth-Century Arabic Poetry," *Muslim World* 66 (1976), pp. 96–113.

Dale, Stephen, "Religious Suicide in Islamic Asia: Anticolonial Terrorism in India, Indonesia and the Philippines," *Journal of Conflict Resolution* 32 (1988), pp. 37–59.

Damant, G. H., "Risalat ush-Shuhada," see al-Shattari.

Damuni, Jamal Salim, *al-Shahada wa-l-shuhada: ahkam al-shahid fi al-shari'a al-Islamiyya*. London: Filistin al-Muslima, 2000.

Dan Fodio, 'Abdallah b. Muhammad b. 'Uthman b. Salih (d. 1829), *Kitab tazyin al-waraqat*. Kano: Maktabat Abu Bakr Ayyub, n.d.

Dan Fodio, Muhammad Bello (d. 1837), *Infaq al-maysur fi ta'rikh bilad al-Takrur*. Cairo: Dar wa-Matabi' al-Sha'b, 1964.

Dan Fodio, 'Uthman b. Muhammad (d. 1817), *Bayan wujub al-hijra 'ala al-'ibad*. Ed. F. H. al-Masri, Khartoum: University of Khartoum Press, 1985.

Davis, Joyce, *Martyrs: Innocence, Vengeance and Despair in the Middle East*. New York: Palgrave Macmillan, 2003.

Dayfullah, Muhammad b. Muhammad (d. 1809), *Kitab al-tabaqat*. Beirut: al-Maktaba al-Thaqafiyya, n.d.

Dedes, Georgios, *"The Battalname: An Ottoman Turkish Frontier Epic Wondertale: Introduction, Turkish Transcription and English Translation and Commentary."* Unpublished Ph.D. Dissertation, Harvard University, 1995.

Digby, Simon (trans.), *Sufis and Soldiers in Awrangzeb's Deccan: Malfuzat-i Naqsh-bandiyya*. Oxford: Oxford University Press, 2001.

Dols, Michael, *The Black Death in the Middle East*. Princeton, NJ: Princeton University Press, 1977.

Droge, Arthur J., *A Noble Death: Suicide and Martyrdom among Jews and Christians in Early Antiquity*. San Francisco, CA: Harper San Fransisco, 1992.

Encyclopaedia Iranica. Ed. Ehsan Yarshater, London: Routledge and Kegan Paul, 1982– (13 vols).

Encyclopaedia of Islam[2]. Ed. Bernard Lewis, C. E. Bosworth, *et al.*, Leiden: E. J. Brill, 1960–2002 (12 vols).

Encyclopedia of Religions. Ed. Lindsey Jones, Detroit, MI: MacMillan Reference, 2005 (15 vols).

Ernst, Carl, *Words of Ecstasy in Islam*. Albany, NY: State University of New York Press, 1985.

Ess, Josef van, *Theologie und Gesellschaft im 2. und 3. Jahrhundert Hidschra: Eine Geschichte des religiösen Denkens im frühen Islam*. Berlin and New York: Walter de Gruyter, 1991–95 (6 vols).

—— *Frühe mu'tazilitische Häresiographie* [Pseudo-Nashi' al-Akbar]. Beirut: In Kommission Ergon Wurzburg, 2003 (reprint).

Fadlallah, Muhammad Husayn, *al-Masa'il al-fiqhiyya*. Beirut: Dar al-Malak, 2001 (vol. 2).

Fakhry, Majid (trans.), *The Qur'an: A Modern English Version*. London: Garnet Press, 1997.

Farag, Muhammad 'Abd al-Salam, *al-Farida al-gha'iba*. Amman: n.p., n.d.; trans. Johannes Jansen, *The Neglected Duty*. New York: Macmillan, 1986; also trans. Abu Umama, *The Absent Obligation*. Birmingham: Maktabat al-Ansar, 2000.

Al-Fayruzabadi al-Shirazi, Ibrahim b. 'Ali b. Yusuf (d. 1083), *al-Muhadhdhab fi fiqh al-Imam al-Shafi'i wa-bi-dhayl al-Nazm al-musta'dhab fi sharh gharib al-Muhadhdhab* (Muhammad b. Ahmad b. Muhammad al-Rikabi al-Yamani [d. 1235]). Ed. Zakariya 'Umayrat, Beirut: Dar al-Kutub al-'Ilmiyya, 1995 (3 vols).

Al-Fazari, Abu Ishaq (d. 802–03), *Kitab al-siyar*. Ed. Faruq Hamada, Beirut: Mu'assasat al-Risala, 1987.

Fenech, Louis, *Martyrdom in the Sikh Tradition: Playing the Game of Love*. New Delhi and New York: Oxford University Press, 2000.

Firdawsi (fl. *ca.* 12th cen.) *Shahnamah*. Ed. Jalal Khaliq Mutlaq, New York: Bibliotheca Persica, 1988 (6 vols).

Foxe, John (d. 1587), *Foxe's Book of Martyrs*. Nashville, TN: Thomas Nelson Publishers, 2000.

Freamon, Bernard, "Martyrdom, Suicide and the Islamic Law of War: A Short Legal History," *Fordham International Law Journal* 27 (2003), pp. 299–369.

Fuzuli, Mehmet b. Sulayman (d. 1556), *Leyla and Mejnun*. Trans. Sofi Huri and Alessio Bombaci, London: George Allen and Unwin, 1970.

—— *Hadiqat as-su'eda*. Ankara: Kultur ve Turzim Bakanligi, 1987.

Gelpke, Rudolf (trans.), with E. Mattin and G. Hill, *The Story of Layla and Majnun by Nizami*. New Lebanon, OH: Omega Publications, 1997 (reprint).

Ghayba, Muhammad Sa'id, *al-'Amaliyyat al-istishhadiyya wa-ara al-fuqaha' fiha*. Damascus: Dar al-Maktabi, 2001.

Al-Ghazali, Abu Hamid Muhammad (d. 1111), *Ihya 'ulum al-din wa-yalihi al-Mughni 'an haml al-asfar fi al-isfar fi takhrij ma fi al-Ihya min al-akhbar* (Zayn al-Din 'Abd al-Rahim al-'Iraqi [d. 1403]). Beirut: Dar al-Qalam, n.d. (5 vols).

Al-Ghumari, Ahmad b. al-Siddiq (d. 1962), *Dar' al-duf 'an hadith man 'ashiqa fa-'affa*. Ed. Iyyad Ahmad al-Ghawj, Cairo: Dar al-Mustafa, 1996.

Gieling, Saskia, *Religion and War in Revolutionary Iran*. London: I. B. Tauris, 1999.

Giffen, Lois, *Theory of Profane Love among the Arabs: The Development of the Genre*. New York: New York University Press, 1971.

Goldstein, Jonathan, *II Maccabees: A New Translation with Introduction and Commentary*. New York: Doubleday, 1983.

Gordon, Alijah (ed.), *The Propagation of Islam in the Indonesian–Malay Archipelago*. Kuala Lumpur: Malaysian Sociological Research Institute, 2001.

Gramlich, Richard, *Alte Vorbilder des Sufitums*. Wiesbaden: Otto Harrassowitz, 1995.

Guénon, René, *Symbols of Sacred Science*. Trans. Henry Fohr, Hillsdale, NY: Sophia Perennis, 2004.

Guillain, Charles (ed), *Documents sur l'histoire, le géographie, et le commerce de l'Afrique Orientale*. Paris: A. Bertrand, 1856.

Gunther, Sebastian, "*Maqatil* Literature in Medieval Islam," *Journal of Arabic Literature* 25 (1994), pp. 192–212.

Hadi, Amirul, *Islam and State in Sumatra: A Study of Seventeenth Century Acheh*. Leiden: E. J. Brill, 2004.

Ha-Levi, Judah (fl. twelfth cen.), *Kitab al-radd wa-l-dalil fi al-din al-dhalil*. Ed. David Baneth, Jerusalem: Magnes Press, 1983.

Hammad, 'Isam Jum'a, *Karamat wa-bushriyat fi mutaharrik al-haqq al-yaqin*. Khartoum: I. J. Hammad, 1994.

Al-Harawi, 'Ali b. Abi Bakr (d. 1214), *al-Isharat ila ma'rifat al-ziyarat*. Ed. 'Ali 'Umar, Cairo: Maktabat al-Thaqafa al-Diniyya, 2002.

Harvey, L. P., "Crypto-Islam in Sixteenth Century Spain," in *Actas. Primer Congreso de Estudios Arabes y Islámicos*. Madrid: Comite Permanente del Congreso de Estudios Arabes y Islámicos, 1964, pp. 163–85.

—— *Muslims in Spain 1500–1614*. Chicago, IL: University of Chicago Press, 2005.

Haykal, Muhammad Khayr, *al-Jihad wa-l-qital fi al-siyasa al-shar'iyya*. Beirut: Dar al-Barayiq, 1993 (3 vols).

Heath, Peter, *The Thirsty Sword: Sirat 'Antar and the Arabic Popular Epic*. Salt Lake City, UT: University of Utah Press, 1996.

Hedayatullah, Muhammad, *Kabir: The Apostle of Hindu–Muslim Unity*. New Delhi: Motilal Banarsidass, 1977.

Henten, Jan Willem van, *The Maccabean Martyrs as Saviours of the Jewish People: A Study of 2 and 4 Maccabees*. Leiden: E. J. Brill, 1997.

—— and Avemarie, Friedrich (trans.), *Martyrdom and Noble Death: Selected Texts from Graeco-Roman, Jewish and Christian Antiquity*. London and New York: Routledge, 2002.

Hillenbrand, Carole, *The Crusades: Islamic Perspectives*. Edinburgh: Edinburgh University Press, 1999.

Al-Hindi, al-Muttaqi (d. 1567–68), *Kanz al-ʿummal*. Ed. Bakri Hayyani, Beirut: Muʾassasat al-Risala, 1989 (18 vols).

Hinds, Martin, "The Murder of the Caliph ʿUthman," *International Journal of Middle Eastern Studies* 3 (1972), pp. 450–69.

Hinojosa Montalvo, Jose, *Los Mudejares: La voz del Islam en la España cristiana*. Teruel: Centro de Estudios Mujéjares, 2002 (2 vols).

Hiskett, Mervyn, *The Sword of Truth: The Life and Times of Shehu Usuman Dan Fodio*. Evanston, IL: Northwestern University Press, 1994 (second edn).

Holt, P. M. (trans.), *The Sudan of the Three Niles: The Funj Chronicle 910–1288/1504–1871*. Leiden: E. J. Brill, 1999.

Humayuni, Sadeq, "An Analysis of the *Taʿziyeh* of Qasem," in P. Chelkowski, Taʿziyeh: *Ritual and Drama in Iran*. New York: New York University Press, 1979, pp. 12–23.

Hunwick, John (ed.), *Arabic Literature of Africa*. Leiden: E. J. Brill, 1995 (4 vols).

—— (trans.), *Timbuktu and the Songhay Empire: Al-Saʿdi's* Taʾrikh al-sudan *down to 1613 and Other Contemporary Documents*. Leiden: E. J. Brill, 2003.

Al-Husayni, Sadr al-Din b. ʿAli (d. 575/1180), *Kitab akhbar al-dawla al-Saljuqiyya*. Ed. Muhammad Iqbal, Beirut: Dar al-Afaq al-Jadida, 1984.

Husayniyya, Ahmad, *Bayad raft*. Tehran: Markaz-i Asnad-i Inqilab-i Islami, 2003.

—— *Miyan-i khun*. Tehran: Markaz-i Asnad-i Inqilab-i Islami, 2003.

Ibn ʿAbd al-ʿAziz, ʿAbd al-Qadir, *Risalat al-ʿumda li-l-jihad fi sabil Allah*. Tawhed: n.p., 2002.

Ibn ʿAbd al-Hakam al-Qurashi al-Misri, ʿAbd al-Rahman b. ʿAbdallah (d. 871), *Futuh Ifriqiya wa-l-Andalus*. Ed. ʿAbdallah Anis al-Tabbaʿ, Beirut: Dar al-Kitab al-Lubnani, 1987.

Ibn ʿAbidin, Muhammad Amin b. ʿUmar (d. 1836), *Radd al-muhtar ʿala al-durr al-mukhtar (Hashiyat kitab al-jihad)*. Damascus: Dar al-Thaqafa wa-l-Turath, 2000.

Ibn Abi al-Dunya, ʿAbdallah b. Muhammad (d. 894–95), *Mujabu al-daʿwa*. al-duʿa. Ed. Majdi al-Sayyid Ibrahim, Cairo: Maktabat al-Qurʾan, 1987.

—— *Kitab al-marad wa-l-kaffarat*. Ed. ʿAbd al-Wakil al-Nadwi, Bombay: al-Dar al-Salafiyya, 1991.

—— *Kitab al-manam*. Ed. Leah Kinberg, *Morality in the Guise of Dreams*. Leiden: E. J. Brill, 1994.

—— *Kitab Maqtal Amir al-muʾminin*. Ed. Ibrahim Salih, Damascus: Dar al-Bashaʾir, 2001.

Ibn Abi Shayba, ʿAbdallah b. Muhammad (d. 849–50), *Kitab al-musannaf*. Ed. Muhammad ʿAbd al-Salam Shahin, Beirut: Dar al-Kutub al-ʿIlmiyya, 1995 (9 vols).

Ibn Abi Usaybiʿa, Ahmad b. al-Qasim (d. 1269–70), *ʿUyun al-anbaʾ fi tabaqat al-atibba*. Ed. Samih al-Zayn, Beirut: Dar al-Thaqafa, n.d.

Ibn Abi Ya'la, Muhammad b. Muhammad (d. 1132), *Tabaqat al-Hanabila*. Ed. Henri Laoust, Beirut: Dar al-Ma'rifa, n.d. (4 vols) (reprint).

Ibn Abi Zaminayn, Muhammad b. 'Abdallah (d. 1008–09), *Qudwat al-ghazi*. Ed. 'A'isha al-Sulaymani, Beirut: Dar al-Gharb al-Islami, 1989.

Ibn 'Adi al-Jurjani, 'Abdallah (d. 975–76), *al-Kamil fi du'afa' al-rijal*. Eds Suhayl Zakkar and Yahya Mukhtar Ghazzawi, Beirut: Dar al-Fikr, 1988 (8 vols).

Ibn al-'Arabi al-Ma'afiri, Abu Bakr Muhammad b. 'Abdallah (d. 1148–49), *Ahkam al-Qur'an*. Ed. 'Ali Muhammad al-Bijawi, Beirut: Dar al-Jil, 1987 (4 vols).

Ibn 'Asakir, 'Ali b. Hasan b. Hibbatullah (d. 1175–76), *Ta'rikh madinat Dimashq*. Ed. 'Ali Shibri, Beirut: Dar al-Fikr, 1995–98 (80 vols).

Ibn A'tham al-Kufi, Ahmad (d. 931), *Kitab al-futuh*. Ed. Muhammad 'Abd al-Mu'id Khan, Beirut: Dar al-Nadwa al-Jadida, n.d. (8 vols) (reprint of Haydarabad edn).

Ibn al-Athir, al-Mubarak b. Muhammad al-Jazari (d. 1209–10), *al-Nihaya fi gharib al-hadith*. Eds Tahir Ahmad al-Zawi and Mahmud Muhammad al-Tanahi, Beirut: Dar Ihya al-Kutub al-'Arabiyya, n.d. (5 vols).

Ibn Hamdun, Muhammad b. al-Hasan (d. 1166–7), *al-Tadhkira al-Hamduniyya*. Ed. Ihsan 'Abbas, Beirut: Dar Sadir, 1996 (10 vols).

Ibn Hanbal, Ahmad (d. 855), *Musnad*. Beirut: Dar al-Fikr, n.d. (6 vols).

Ibn Hanbal, Salih b. Ahmad (d. 879–80), *Sirat al-Imam Ahmad b. Hanbal*. Ed. Muhammad al-Zaghli, Beirut: al-Maktab al-Islami, 1997.

Ibn Hisham, Abd al-Malik (d. 833), *al-Sira al-nabawiyya*. Ed. Muhammad Muhyi al-Din 'Abd al-Hamid, Beirut: Dar al-Fikr, n.d. (4 vols).

Ibn Hubaysh, 'Abd al-Rahman b. Muhammad (d. 1188), *Ghazawat*. Ed. Suhayl Zakkar, Beirut: Dar al-Fikr, 1992 (2 vols).

Ibn 'Idhari al-Marakashi, Muhammad (d. *ca.* 1295), *al-Bayan al-mughrib fi akhbar al-Andalus wa-l-Maghrib*. Ed. E. Levi-Provençal, Beirut: Dar al-Thaqafa, 1998 (reprint) (4 vols).

Ibn Isfandiyar, KayKhusraw, Fani, Muhsin (d. 1671–72), *Dabistan-i mazahib*. Ed. Rahim Rizazada-yi Mulk, Tehran: Gulshan, 1362/1983 (2 vols).

Ibn al-Jawzi, Abu al-Faraj 'Abd al-Rahman (d. 1200), *Dhamm al-hawa*. Ed. Ahmad 'Abd al-Salam 'Ata', Beirut: Dar al-Kutub al-'Ilmiyya, 1993.

___ *al-Muntazam fi ta'rikh al-muluk wa-l-umam*. Eds Muhammad 'Abd al-Qadir 'Ata' and Mustafa 'Abd al-Qadir 'Ata', Beirut: Dar al-Kutub al-'Ilmiyya, 1993 (19 vols).

___ *Sifat al-safwa*. Eds 'Abd al-Rahman al-Ladiqi and Hayat Shaykha al-Ladiqi, Beirut: Dar al-Ma'rifa, 2001 (2 vols).

___ *'Uyun al-hikayat*. Ed. 'Abd al-'Aziz Sayyid Hashim al-Ghazuli, Beirut: Dar al-Kutub al-'Ilmiyya, 2003.

___ *Manaqib al-Imam Ahmad b. Hanbal*. Ed. Muhammad Amin al-Khanji, Beirut: Khanji wa-Hamdan, n.d.

Ibn al-Jawzi, al-Sibt Yusuf b. Qizughli (d. 1256), *Mir'at al-zaman (section viii)*. Ed. Richard Jewett, Chicago, IL: University of Chicago Press, 1907.

Ibn Jubayr, Hani b. 'Abdallah b. Muhammad, *al-'Amaliyyat al-istishhadiyya*. Riyadh: Dar al-Fadila, 2002.

Ibn Kathir, Abu al-Fida' b. 'Umar (d. 1372–73), *Qisas al-anbiya'*. Ed. al-Sayyid al-Jumayli, Cairo: Dar al-Sabuni, 1989.

___ *Tafsir al-Qur'an al-'azim*. Beirut: 'Alam al-Kutub, 1993 (4 vols).

Ibn Maja al-Qazwini, Muhammad b. Yazid (d. 888–89), *Sunan*. Ed. Muhammad Fu'ad 'Abd al-Baqi, Beirut: Dar al-Fikr, n.d. (2 vols).

Ibn Mar'i, Mar'i b. 'Abdallah, *Ahkam al-mujahid bi-l-nafs*. Medina: Maktabat al-'Ulum wa-l-Hikam, 2003 (2 vols).

Ibn al-Mibrad, Yusuf b. Hasan (d. 1503), *Nuzhat al-musamir fi akhbar Majnun Bani 'Amir*. Beirut: 'Alam al-Kutub, 1994.

Ibn al-Mubarak, 'Abdallah (d. 797), *Kitab al-jihad*. Ed. Nazih Hammad, Beirut: Muhammad 'Afif al-Zu'bi, 1971.

Ibn Muflih al-Maqdisi al-Hanbali, Muhammad (d. 1362), *Kitab al-furu'*. Ed. 'Abd al-Razzaq al-Mahdi, Beirut: Dar al-Kitab al-'Arabi, 2002 (3 vols).

Ibn al-Munadi, Ahmad b. Ja'far b. Muhammad (d. 947–48), *al-Malahim*. Ed. 'Abd al-Karim al-'Uqayli, Qumm: Dar al-Sira, 1998.

Ibn al-Nahhas al-Dumyati, Ahmad b. Ibrahim (d. 1411), *Mashari' al-ashwaq ila masari' al-'ushshaq fi al-jihad wa-fada'ilihi*. Eds. Durish Muhammad 'Ali and Muhammad Khalid Istambuli, Beirut: Dar al-Basha'ir al-Islamiyya, 2002 (2 vols).

Ibn Qayyim al-Jawziyya, Shams al-Din (d. 1350), *Akhbar al-nisa'*. Ed. Mufid Muhammad Qumayha, Beirut: Dar al-Fikr al-Lubnani, 1990.

Ibn Qudama al-Maqdisi, Muwaffaq al-Din Abdallah b. Ahmad (d. 1223), *al-Mughni wa-yalihi al-sharh al-kabir*. Beirut: Dar al-Kitab al-'Arabi, n.d. (14 vols).

Ibn Qudama al-Maqdisi al-Hanbali al-Jama'ili, Muhammad b. Ahmad b. 'Abd al-Hadi (d. 1343), *al-Mutahabbun fi Allah*. Khayrallah al-Sharif, Damascus: Dar al-Taba', 1991.

Ibn Qutayba al-Dinawari, 'Abdallah b. Muslim (d. 889), *Kitab ta'bir al-ru'ya*. Ed. Ibrahim Salih, Damascus: Dar al-Basha'ir, 2001.

Ibn Rushd, Muhammad b. Ahmad (d. 1126), *al-Bayan wa-l-tahsil aw Sharh wa-tawjih wa-ta'lil fi masa'il al-mustakhraja*. Ed. Muhammad Hajji, Beirut: Dar al-Gharb al-Islami, 1988 (20 vols).

Ibn al-Sari al-Kufi, Hunnad (d. 857), *Kitab al-zuhd*. Ed. 'Abd al-Rahman b. 'Abd al-Jabbar al-Firyawa'i, Kuwait: Dar al-Khulafa' li-l-Kitab al-Islami, 1985 (2 vols).

Ibn Shahrashub al-Mazandarani, Muhammad b. 'Ali (d. 1192), *Manaqib Al Abi Talib*. Beirut: Dar al-Adwa', 1985 (4 vols).

Ibn Sirin, Muhammad (d. 728–29), (pseudo.), *Tafsir al-ahlam*. On the margins of al-Nablusi, *Ta'tir al-anam fi ta'bir al-manam*. Beirut: Dar al-Fikr, n.d. (2 vols).

Ibn Taghribirdi, Yusuf al-Atabaki (d. 1469–70), *al-Nujum al-zahira fi muluk Misr wa-l-Qahira*. Ed. Muhammad Husayn Shams al-Din, Beirut: Dar al-Kutub al-'Ilmiyya, 1992 (16 vols).

Imam, Ahmad 'Ali, *al-Shahada wa-hayat al-shuhada*. Beirut: al-Maktab al-Islami, 2000.

Imam Samudra, *Aku Melawan Teroris*. Solo: Azera, 2005.

Intifadat al-Aqsa 2000. Amman: Dar al-Jalil, 2003–4 (9 vols).

Al-Isfahani, Abu al-Faraj (d. 967), *Kitab al-aghani*. Ed. 'Abd al-'Ali Mahanna, Beirut: Dar al-Fikr, 1986 (25 vols).

—— *Maqatil al-Talibiyyin*. Beirut: Mu'assasat al-A'lami li-l-Matbu'at, 1987.

Al-Isfahani, Abu Nu'aym (d. 1038–39), *Sifat al-janna*. Ed. 'Ali Rida' 'Abdallah, Damascus: Dar al-Ma'mun li-l-Turath, 1986.

—— *Ma'rifat al-sahaba*. Medina: Matkabat al-Dar, 1988.

—— *Hilyat al-awliya'*. Ed. Mustafa 'Abd al-Qadir 'Ata', Beirut: Dar al-Kutub al-'Ilmiyya, 1997 (12 vols).

Al-Isfahani, 'Imad al-Din Muhammad b. Muhammad b. Hamid (d. 1201), *Ta'rikh dawlat Al Saljuq*. Ed. Yahya Murad, Beirut: Dar al-Kutub al-'Ilmiyya, 2004.

Al-Isfara'ini, Abu Ishaq Ibrahim b. Muhammad (d. 1028), *Nur al-'ayn fi mashhad al-Husayn wa-yalihi Qurrat al-'ayn fi akhdh tha'r al-Husayn* (al-Imam 'Abdallah b. Muhammad). Tunis: Matba'at al-Manar, 1960.

Janju'ah, Faridulislam, *Jihad, shahadat, jannat*. Rawalpindi: Markaz-i Matbu'at Kashmir, 2000.

Jawabirah, Basim, *Tafrij al-karb bi-fada'il shahid al-ma 'arik wa-l-harb*. Riyadh: Dar al-Raya, 1993.

Jeffery, Arthur, *The Foreign Vocabulary of the Qur'an*. Baroda: Gaekwar of Baroda's Oriental Series, 1938.

Al-Jihad wa-khisal al-muhajidin fi al-Islam. Beirut: Markaz Baqiyat Allah al-A'zam, 1999.

Jones, Russell (trans.), *Hikayat Sultan Ibrahim ibn Adham: An Edition of an Anonymous Malay Text with Translation and Notes*. New York and London: Lanham, 1985.

Jong, Frederick de and Radtke, Bernd (eds), *Islamic Mysticism Contested: Thirteen Centuries of Controversies and Polemics*. Leiden: E. J. Brill, 1999.

Kalpakli, Mehmed and Andrews, Walter, "Layla Grows up: Nizami's *Layla and Majnun* 'in the Turkish Manner,'" in Kamran Talattof and Jerome Clinton (eds), *The Poetry of Nizami Ganjavi: Knowledge, Love and Rhetoric*. New York: Palgrave, 2000, pp. 29–49.

Al-Karaki, Khalid, *Hamasat al-shuhada'*. Beirut: al-Mu'assasa al-'Arabiyya li-l-Nashr, 1997.

Karamustafa, Ahmad, "Early Sufism in Eastern Anatolia," in L. Lewisohn (ed.), *The Heritage of Sufism*. Oxford: OneWorld, 1992–99, i, pp. 179–83.

Al-Kashifi, Mullah Husayn Va'iz (d. 1504), *Rawzat al-shuhada'*. Ed. Hajj Shaykh Abu al-Hasan Sh'irani, Qumm: Intisharat-i Islamiyya, n.d.

Khairullah, As'ad, *Love, Madness and Poetry: An Interpretation of the Maǧnun Legend*. Beirut: Franz Steiner, 1980.

Al-Khallal, Ahmad b. Muhammad (d. 923–24), *al-Hathth 'ala al-tijara wa-l-sina'a wa-l-'amal, wa-l-inkar 'ala man idda'a al-tawakkul fi tark al-'amal wa-l-jumma 'alayhim fi dhalika*. Ed. 'Abd al-Fattah Abu Ghada, Aleppo: Maktabat al-Matbu'at al-Islamiyya, 1995.

Al-Khama'ini, 'Ali, *'Itr al-shahada*. Trans. Markaz Baqiyat Allah al-A'zam, Beirut: Markaz Baqiyat Allah al-A'zam, 2001.

Al-Khara'iti, Muhammad b. Ja'far (d. 939–40), *I'tilal al-qulub fi akhbar al-ushshaq wa-l-muhibbin*. Ed. Gharid al-Shaykh, Beirut: Dar al-Kutub al-'Ilmiyya, 2001.

Khizri, Farhad, *Bih majnun guftam zindah biman . . .* Tehran: Rivayat-i Fath, 2002.

Khosrokhavar, Farhad, "Le martyre révolutionnaire en Iran," *Social Compass* 43 (1996), pp. 83–100.

—— *Les nouveaux martyrs d'Allah*. Paris: Flammarion, 2002.

Khumayni, Ayatullah Ruhullah, *Islam and Revolution: Writings and Declarations of Imam Khomeini*. Trans. Hamid Algar, Berkeley, CA: Mizan Press, 1981.

Knappert, Jan, *Islamic Legends: Histories of the Heroes, Saints and Prophets of Islam*. Leiden: E. J. Brill, 1985.

—— *A Survey of Swahili Islamic Epic Sagas*. Lewiston, ID: Edwin Mellen Press, 1999.

Kohlberg, Etan, "The Development of the Imami Shiʿi Doctrine of *Jihad*," *Zeitschrift der Deutschen Morgenländischen Gesellschaft* 126 (1976), pp. 64–86.

―― "Medieval Muslim Views on Martyrdom," *Mededelingen der Koninklijke Nederlandse Akademie van Wetenschappen* 60 (1997), pp. 281–307.

―― "Martyrdom and Self-Sacrifice in Classical Islam," *Peʾamim* 75 (1998), pp. 5–26 (in Hebrew).

―― "The Image of the Prophet Muhammad as *Shahid*," in *ʿIyyunim ba-Islam hakadum: Devarim she-neʾemru bi-yom ʿiyyun li-kvod Meir Y. Kister bi-melaot lo tishiʿim shana*. Jerusalem: Ha-Akademiya ha-Leumit ha-Yisraelit la-Madaʿim, 2005, pp. 45–71 (in Hebrew).

Koningsveld, P. S. van, "Muslim Slaves and Captives in Western Europe during the late Middle Ages," *Islam and Christian–Muslim Relations* 6 (1995), pp. 1–23.

Kruk, Remke, "Warrior Women in Arabic Popular Romance: Qannasa bint Muzahim and other Valiant Ladies," *Journal of Arabic Literature* 24 (1993), pp. 213–30, 25 (1994), pp. 16–33.

Lagarde, Paul de, *Aegyptiaca*. Gottingen: A. Hoyer, 1883.

Lahham, Hanan, *Sumayya bint Khayyat: al-shahida al-ula*. Damascus: Dar al-Thaqafa, 1978.

Lahidan, Salih, *al-Jihad fi al-Islam bayna al-talab wa-l-difaʿ*. Riyadh: Dar al-Sumayʿi, 1997.

Laird, Lance Daniel, "Martyrs, Heroes and Saints: Shared Symbols of Muslims and Christians in Contemporary Palestinian Society." Unpublished PhD Dissertation, Harvard University, 1998.

Last, Murray, *The Sokoto Caliphate*. New York: Humanities Press, 1967.

Leemans, Johan and Mayer, Wendy, Allen, Pauline and Dehandschutter, Boudewijn (eds), *"Let us Die that We May Live": Greek Homilies on Christian Martyrs from Asia Minor, Palestine and Syria c. AD 350–AD 450*. London and New York: Routledge, 2003.

Levtzion, Nehemia and Hopkins, J. F. P. (eds), *Corpus of Early Arabic Sources for West African History*. Princeton, NJ: Marcus Wiener, 2000.

Lewisohn, L., "In Quest of Annihilation: Imaginalization and Mystical Death in the *Tamhidat* of ʿAyn al-Qudat al-Hamadhani," in L. Lewisohn (ed), *The Heritage of Sufism*. Oxford: One World, 1992–99, i, pp. 285–336.

Lomack, Margaret (ed.), *Sacrificing the Self: Perspectives on Martyrdom and Religion*. Oxford: Oxford University Press, 2002.

Lorenzen, David, *Kabir Legends and Ananta-Das's Kabir Parachai*. Albany, NY: State University of New York Press, 1991.

Lyons, M. C., *The Arabian Epic*. Cambridge: Cambridge University Press, 1995 (3 vols).

Mahanna, Firyal, *Ishkaliyyat al-jihad fi ʿasr al-maʿlumatiyya*. Beirut: Dar al-Fikr, 2005.

Mahmood, Tahir, "The Dargah of Sayyid Salar Masʿud Ghazi in Bahraich: Legend, Tradition and Reality," in Christian Troll (ed.), *Muslim Shrines in India: Their Character, History and Significance*. New Delhi: Oxford University Press, 2003, pp. 24–43.

Maimonides (d. 1206), *Iggeret ha-Shmad* [Letter on Forced Conversion or the Sanctification of the Name], in Y. Shailat (ed.), *Iggrot ha-Rambam*. Maʿale Adumim: Maʿliot, 1989 (2 vols).

Malekpour, Jamshid, *The Islamic Drama*. London: Frank Cass, 2004.

Al-Maliqi al-Asha'ri, Muhammad b. Yahya (d. 1340–41), *al-Tamhid wa-l-bayan fi maqtal al-shahid 'Uthman*. Ed. Muhammad Yusuf Za'id, al-Dawha: Dar al-Thaqafa, 1985.

Al-Maqdisi, Taqi al-Din 'Abd al-Ghani b. 'Abd al-Wahid (d. 1203–04), *Tahrim al-qatl wa-ta'zimuhu*. Ed. Abu 'Abdallah 'Ammar b. Sa'id Tamalat al-Jaza'iri, Beirut: Dar Ibn Hazm, 1999.

Al-Maqrizi, Ahmad b. 'Ali b. 'Abd al-Qadir (d. 1441–42), *al-Suluk li-ma'rifat duwal al-muluk*. Ed. Muhammad 'Abd al-Qadir 'Ata', Beirut: Dar al-Kutub al-'Ilmiyya, 1997 (8 vols).

Al-Marini, 'Abd al-Haqq, *Shi'r al-jihad fi al-adab al-Maghribi*. Muhammadiyya (Morocco): Matba'at al-Fadala, 1996 (2 vols).

Martyrologium romanum ex decrets sacrosancti oecumenici Concilii Vaticani II instauraotum auctoritate Ioannis Pauli PP II promulgatum. Vatican City: Libraria Editrice Vaticana, 2004.

Masa'il jihadiyya wa-hukm al-'amaliyyat al-istishhadiyya. Beirut: al-Wahda al-Islamiyya, 2002.

Massignon, Louis, *The Passion of al-Hallaj*. Trans. Herbert Mason, Princeton, NJ: Princeton University Press, 1982 (4 vols).

Al-Mawardi, 'Ali b. Muhammad (d. 1058), *al-Hawi al-kabir fi fiqh madhhab al-Imam al-Shafi'i*. Eds. 'Ali Muhammad Mu'awwid and 'Adil Ahmad 'Abd al-Mawjud, Beirut: Dar al-Kutub al-'Ilmiyya, 1999 (20 vols).

—— *Tafsir al-Mawardi*. Beirut: Dar al-Fikr, n.d. (6 vols).

Mawdudi, Abu al-'Ala (d. 1979), *al-Jihad* in *Thalatha kutub fi al-jihad*. Amman: Dar 'Ammar, 1991.

Melchert, Christopher, "The Transition from Asceticism to Mysticism at the middle of the Ninth Century CE," *Studia Islamica* 83 (1996), pp. 51–70.

—— "The Hanabila and the Early Sufis," *Arabica* 48 (2001), pp. 352–67.

Miguel, André, *Deux histories d'amour: de Majnun à Tristan*. Paris: Editions O. Jacob, 1996.

Mishal, Shaul and Aharoni, Reuben, *Speaking Stones*. Syracuse, NY: Syracuse University Press, 1994.

Mishra, Vijay, "Suffering in Union: Kabir's Burning Bride," in Kapil Tiwari (ed.), *Suffering: Indian Perspectives*. New Delhi: Motilal Banarsidass, 1986, pp. 237–61.

Motahhery, Mortaza, *The Martyr*. Trans. Yusufi Nafsi, Houston, TX: Free Islamic Literature, 1980.

Al-Mubarrad, Muhammad b. Yazid (d. 899), *Kitab al-ta'azi wa-l-marathi*. Ed. Muhammad al-Dibaji, Beirut: Dar Sadir, 1992.

Al-Mufid, al-Shaykh Muhammad b. Muhammad al-'Ukbari (d. 1022), *Awa'il al-maqalat*. Vol. 4 in *Mu'allafat al-Shaykh al-Mufid*. Eds. 'Ali Mirsharifi, *et al.*, Beirut: Dar al-Mufid, 1993 (14 vols).

Mughaltay b. Qulayj al-Hakari al-Hanafi (d. 1361), *al-Wadih al-mubin fi dhikr man ustushhida min al-muhibbin*. Beirut: al-Intishar al-'Arabi, 1997.

Al-Munawi, 'Abd al-Ra'uf (d. 1612–13), *al-Kawakib al-durriyya fi tarajim al-sadat al-Sufiyya*. Ed. Muhammad Adib al-Jadir, Beirut: Dar Sadir, 1999 (5 vols).

Muqatil b. Sulayman al-Balkhi (d. 767), *Tafsir Muqatil b. Sulayman*. Ed. Mahmud Shihata, Cairo: al-Ha'iya al-Misriyya, 1983 (reprint: Beirut: Dar Ihya al-Turath al-'Arabi, 2003) (5 vols).

Murtazavi, Ibrahim, *Akhirin nasl*. Tehran: Hawzah-yi Hunari-yi Sazman-i Tablighat-i Islami, 1997.

Muslim b. al-Hajjaj al-Qushayri (d. 875), *Sahih*. Beirut: Dar Jil, n.d. (4 vols).

Musurillo, Herbert, *The Acts of the Christian Martyrs: Introduction, Texts and Translations*. Oxford: Oxford University Press, 2000.

Najib, Ahmad 'Abd al-Karim, *al-Dala'il al-jaliyya 'ala mashru'iyyat al-'amaliyyat al-istishhadiyya*. Aleppo, 2004.

Al-Nasa'i, Ahmad b. Shu'ayb (d. 915–16), *Sunan*. (With commentary of Jalal al-Din al-Suyuti) Beirut: Dar al-Fikr, n.d. (4 vols).

Nasr, Seyyed Vali Reza, *Mawdudi and the Making of Islamic Revivalism*. Oxford: Oxford University Press, 1996.

Naumkin, Vitali, *Radical Islam in Central Asia: Between Pen and Rifle*. Lanham, MD: Rowman and Littlefield, 2005.

Al-Nawawi, Yahya b. Sharaf (d. 1277), *Sharh Sahih Muslim*. Beirut: Dar al-Fikr, 1996 (11 vols).

New International Version: Holy Bible. Nashville, TN: Holman Bible Publishers, 1986.

Nicholson, Reynald (trans.), *The* Mathnawi *of Jalal al-Din al-Rumi*. London: Luzac and Co., 1977 (3 vols).

Nizami Ganjavi, Abu Muhammad Ilyas b. Yusuf b. Zaki Mu'ayyad (d. 1202–03), *Layla va-Majnun*. Ed. Hasan Vahid Dostgirdi, Tehran: Qatra, 1380/2001.

Norris, H. T., *The Arab Conquest of the Western Sahara*. Harlow: Longman, 1986.

O'Callaghan, Joseph, "The Mudejars of Castile and Portugal in the Twelfth and Thirteenth Centuries," in James M. Powell (ed.), *Muslims under Latin Rule, 1100–1300*. Princeton, NJ: Princeton University Press, 1990, pp. 11–56.

O'Kane, John (trans.), *The Feats of the Knowers of God*: Manaqeb al-'Arifin *by Shams al-Din Aflaki*. Leiden: E. J. Brill, 2002.

Pankhurst, Richard, *The Ethiopian Borderlands: Essays in Regional History from Ancient Times until the Eigteenth Century*. Lawrenceville, NJ: Red Sea Press, 1997.

Pape, Robert, *Dying to Kill: The Strategic Logic of Suicide Terrorism*. New York: Random House, 2005.

Pappi, Lionello, *Torment in Art: Pain, Violence and Martyrdom*. New York: Rizzoli, 1990.

Pathan, Mumtaz Husain, "Sufi Shah 'Inayat Shahid of Sind," *Islamic Culture* 59 (1985), pp. 65–70.

Pettigrew, Joyce (ed.), *Martyrdom and National Resistance Movements: Essays on Asia and Europe*. Amsterdam: VU University Press for Centre for Asian Studies Amsterdam, 1997.

Pourjavady, Nasrollah (trans.), *Sawanih: Inspirations from the World of Pure Spirits: Ahmad Ghazali*. London: KPI, 1986.

Al-Qadi, 'Abd al-Rahim (d. eighteenth cen.?), *Daqa'iq al-akhyar fi dhikr al-janna wa-l-nar*. Cairo: Mustafa al-Babi, n.d.

Al-Qadiri, 'Abdallah b. Ahmad, *al-Jihad fi sabil Allah*. Jidda: Dar al-Manara, 1992 (2 vols).

Al-Qadiri, Muhammad b. al-Tayyib (d. 1773–74), *Kitab iltiqat al-durar*. Ed. Hashim al-'Alawi al-Qasimi, Beirut: Dar al-Afaq al-Jadida, 1983.

___ *Nashr al-mathani li-ahl al-qarn al-hadi ʿashara wa-l-thani.* Eds Muhammad Hajji and Ahmad al-Tawfiq, Rabat: Maktabat al-Talib, 1986 (4 vols).

Al-Qadiri, Nasr b. Yaʿqub b. Ibrahim al-Dinawari (fl. *ca.* eleventh cen.), *Kitab al-taʾbir fi al-ruʾya aw al-Qadiri fi al-taʾbir.* Ed. Fahmi Saʿd, Beirut: ʿAlam al-Kutub, 2000 (2 vols).

Al-Qaʾimi, ʿAli, *Tarbiyat awlad al-shahid.* Beirut: Dar al-Balagha, 1999.

Qamar, Muhammad Saghir, *Ashab-i junun.* S.I.: Paira Midiya Publishaz, 1998.

Al-Qasimi, Zafir, *al-Jihad wa-l-huquq al-dawla al-ʿamma fi al-Islam.* Beirut: Dar al-ʿIlm li-l-Malaʾayyin, 1982.

Al-Qayrawani, ʿAbdallah b. Abi Zayd (d. 996–97), *al-Nawadir wa-l-ziyadat ʿala ma fi al-mudawwana min ghayriha min al-ummahat.* Ed. ʿAbd al-Fattah Muhammad al-Hilw, Beirut: Dar al-Gharb al-Islami, 1999 (15 vols).

Qudusi, Muhammad, *Karbalaʾ al-jadida: Ayyam maʿ al-muqawama fi janub Lubnan.* Cairo: al-Lajna al-ʿArabiyya, 1999.

Al-Qummi, ʿAli b. Ibrahim (*ca.* ninth cen.), *Tafsir al-Qummi.* Beirut: Muʾassasat al-Aʿlami li-l-Matbuʿat, 1991 (2 vols).

Al-Qummi, Saʿd b. ʿAbdallah (d. 913), *al-Maqalat wa-l-firaq.* Ed. Muhammad Jawad Shakur, Tehran: Markaz-i Intisharat-i ʿIlmi va-Farhangi, 1360/1982.

Al-Qurtubi al-Ansari, Muhammad b. Ahmad (d. 1272–73), *al-Jamiʿ li-ahkam al-Qurʾan.* Ed. ʿAbd al-Razzaq al-Mahdi, Beirut: Dar al-Kitab al-ʿArabi, 2003 (10 vols).

Al-Qusaybi, Ghazi ʿAbd al-Rahman, *li-l-Shuhadaʾ.* Amman: Dar al-Faris, 2002.

Qutb, Muhammad ʿAli, Muhammad ʿAli Qutb, *al-Shahid wa-awsimatuhu al-ʿashara.* Beirut: Dar al-Qalam, n.d.

Qutb, Sayyid, *Fi Zilal al-Qurʾan.* Beirut: Dar al-Shuruq, 1996 (6 vols).

___ *Maʿalim fi al-tariq.* Riyadh: al-Ittihad al-Islami al-ʿAlami li-Munazzamat al-Tullabiyya, n.d. Trans. S. Badrul Hasan, *Milestones.* Karachi: International Islamic Publishers, n.d.

___ *li-Madha aʿadamuni?* Riyadh: al-Sharq al-Awsat, n.d.

Rajabi, Muhammad Hasan, *Rasaʾil va-fatava-yi Jihadiyya.* Tehran: Wizarat-i Farhang va-Irshad-i Islami, n.d.

Rajaʿi, Ghulam ʿAli, *Lahzahha-yi asmani: karimat-i shahidan.* Tehran: Shahid, 2001.

Ramadun, ʿAbd al-Baqi, *al-Jihad sabiluna.* Beirut: Muʾassasat al-Risala, 1990.

Al-Ramli, Ahmad b. al-Husayn Ibn Raslan (d. 1441), *Kitab nihayat al-muhtaj ila shaʾn al-minhaj fi al-fiqh ʿala madhhab al-Imam al-Shafiʿi.* Cairo: Ahmad Hanafi, n.d.

Al-Razi, Fakhr al-Din Muhammad b. ʿUmar (d. 1209–10), *al-Tafsir al-kabir.* Beirut: Dar Ihya al-Turath al-ʿArabi, n.d. (16 vols).

Renard, John, "*al-Jihad al-akbar*: Notes on a Theme in Islamic Spirituality," *Muslim World* 78 (1988), pp. 225–42.

Reuter, Christoph, *My Life is a Weapon: A Modern History of Suicide Bombing.* Trans. Helena Ragg-Krikby, Princeton, NJ: Princeton University Press, 2004.

Riddell, Peter, *Islam and the Malay–Indonesian World: Transmission and Responses.* Honolulu, HI: University of Hawaii Press, 2001.

Rinkes, D. A., *Nine Saints of Java.* Trans. H. M. Froger, ed. Alijah Gordon, Kuala Lumpur: Malaysian Sociological Research Institute, 1996.

Rizvi, Mehdi Amin, *Suhrawardi and the School of Illumination.* Richmond: Curzon, 1997.

Rizvi, Saiyid Athar Abbas, *A Socio-Intellectual History of the Isna 'Ashari Shi'is in India*. New Delhi: Munshiram Manoharlal Publishers, 1986 (2 vols).

___ *A History of Sufism in India*. New Delhi: Munshiram Manoharlal, 2002 (2 vols) (reprint).

Robinson, B. W., *Persian Paintings in the John Rylands Library: A Descriptive Catalog*. London: Sotheby Parke Bernet, 1980.

Rosenthal, Franz, "On Suicide in Islam," *Journal of the American Oriental Society* 66 (1946), pp. 239–59.

___ *A History of Muslim Historiography*. Leiden: E. J. Brill, 1968.

___ *Knowledge Triumphant*. Leiden: E. J. Brill, 1970.

Roy, Oliver, *The Failure of Political Islam*. Trans. Carol Volk, Cambridge, MA: Harvard University Press, 1994.

Rumi, Jalal al-Din Muhammad Mawlana (d. 1274), *Masnawi ma'nawi*. Ed. Reynald Nicholson, Qazvin: Intisharat-i Sayih Gustar, 1379/2000. *See*, Nicholson, Reynald.

Al-Sa'di, Muslih b. 'Abdallah (d. *ca.* 1388–89), *Golestan of Shaikh Sa'di*. Trans. Major R. P. Anderson, Tehran: Intisharat-i Mugstan, 1380/2001 (reprint).

Al-Saghirji, Muhammad Sa'id, *al-Jihad fi sabil Allah*. Damascus: Maktabat al-Ghazali, 1997.

Salisbury, Joyce, *The Blood of Martyrs: Unintended Consequences of Ancient Violence*. London and New York: Routledge, 2004.

Al-Samarqandi, Muhammad b. Yusuf al-Husayni (d. 1161), *al-Fiqh al-nafi'*. Ed. Ibrahim b. Muhammad b. Ibrahim al-'Abbud, Riyadh: Maktabat al-'Ubyakan, 2000 (3 vols).

Al-Sarraj al-Qari, Ja'far (d. 1106–07), *Masari' al-'ushshaq*. Beirut: Dar al-Kutub al-'Ilmiyya, 1998.

Sawt al-jihad (monthly journal of al-Qa'ida in Saudi Arabia, 2003–05). Available at e-prism.com.

Sayim, Muhammad, *Shuhada al-da'wa al-Islamiyya fi al-qarn al-'ishrin*. Cairo: Dar al-Fadila, 1992.

Schmucker, Werner, "Iranische Märtyrertestamente," *Die Welt des Islams* 27 (1987), pp. 185–249.

Scholem, Gershom and Ottmann, Klaus, *Color Symbolism: The Eranos Lectures*. Putnam, CT: Spring Publications, 2005.

Seven Misconceptions in Fighting the Ruler and the Apostate Regime. Available at azzam.com.

Seyed-Gohrab, Ali Asghar, *Layli and Majnun: Love, Madness and Mystic Longing in Nizami's Epic Romance*. Leiden: E. J. Brill, 2003.

Shahid, Irfan (ed. and trans.), *The Martyrs of Najran: New Documents*. Brussels: Société des Bollandistes, 1971.

Al-Shajari, Muhammad b. 'Ali b. al-Hasan (d. 1053), *Fadl ziyarat al-Husayn*. Ed. Ahmad al-Husayni, Qumm: Maktabat-i Ayatallah al-'Uzma al-Mara'shi, 1403/1982.

Shaked, Haim (trans.), *The Life of the Sudanese Mahdi: A Historical Study of* Kitab Sa'adat al-Mustahdi bi-sirat al-Imam al-Mahdi. New Brunswick, NJ: Transaction Press, 1976.

Sharbasi, Ahmad, *Fida'iyyun fi al-ta'rikh al-Islam*. Beirut: Dar al-Ra'id al-'Arabi, 1982.

Sharon, Moshe, *Black Banners from the East*. Jerusalem: Magnes Press, 1983.

___ *Revolt: Social and Military Aspects of the 'Abbasid Revolution*. Jerusalem: Magnes Press, 1990.

al-Shattari, Pir Muhammad (*ca.* 1633), *Risalat al-shuhada*'. Ed. G. H. Damant, "Risalat ush-Shuhada' of Pir Muhammad Shattari," *Journal of the Asiatic Society of Bengal* 1874, pp. 215–40.

Al-Shaybani, Muhammad b. al-Hasan (d. 805), *Kitab al-athar*. Ed. Abu al-Wafa' al-Afghani, Beirut: Dar al-Kutub al-Ilmiyya, 1993 (reprint of Haydarabad edn) (2 vols).

Shepard, William, *Sayyid Qutb and Islamic Activism: A Translation and Critical Analysis of Social Justice in Islam*. Leiden: E. J. Brill, 1996.

Al-Shibli, Muhammad b. 'Abdallah al-Dimashqi (d. 1367–68), *Ghara'ib wa-'aja'ib al-jinn*. Ed. Ibrahim Muhammad al-Jamal, Cairo: Maktabat al-Qur'an, 1983.

____ *Mahasin al-wasa'il fi ma'rifat al-awa'il*. Ed. Muhammad al-Tanukhi, Beirut: Dar al-Nafa'is, 1992.

Sijill al-nur. Beirut: al-Wahda al-I'lamiyya al-Markaziyya, 1998.

Smith, Lacey Baldwin, *Fools, Martyrs, Traitors: The Story of Martyrdom in the Western World*. New York: Alfred A. Knopf, 1997.

Sperl, Stefan and Shackle, Christopher (eds), *Qasida Poetry in Islamic Asia and Africa*. Leiden: E. J. Brill, 1996.

Stetkevych, Suzanne Pinckney, *The Mute Immortals Speak*. Ithaca, NY and London: Cornell University Press, 1993.

Strong, Arthur, "The History of Kilwa. Edited from an Arabic MS," *Journal of the Royal Asiatic Society* 1894, pp. 385–430.

Al-Subki, Taqi al-Din 'Ali b. 'Abd al-Kafi b. 'Ali b. Tamam (d. 756/1355), *Fatawa al-Subki*. Ed. Husam al-Din al-Qudsi, Beirut: Dar al-Jil, 1992 (2 vols).

Suhaybani, 'Abd al-Hamid b. 'Abd al-Rahman, *Siyar al-shuhada*. Riyadh: Dar al-Watan, 1999.

Al-Sulami, 'Abd al-Malik b. Habib (d. 852), *Wasf al-firdaws*. Ed. Muhammad 'Ali Baydun, Beirut: Dar al-Kutub al-'Ilmiyya, 2002.

Al-Sulami, Muhammad b. al-Husayn (d. 1021), *Tabaqat al-sufiyya wa-yalihi dhikr al-niswa al-muta'bbidat al-sufiyyat*. Ed. Mustafa 'Abd al-Qadir 'Ata', Beirut: Dar al-Kutub al-'Ilmiyya, 1998.

Al-Surabadi, Abu Bakr 'Atiq Nishaburi (d. 1100–01), *Tafsir-i Surabadi*. Ed. Sa'idi Sayr Jani, Tehran: Farhang-i Nashr-i Naw, 1381/2002 (5 vols).

Surur, Rifa'i, *Ashab al-ukhdud*. Available at tawhed.ws.

Suvorova, Anna, *Muslim Saints of South Asia*. London: RoutledgeCurzon, 2004.

Al-Suyuti, Jalal al-Din (d. 1505), *Abwab al-sa'ada fi asbab al-shahada*. Cairo: al-Maktaba al-Qiyyama, 1987.

____ *Laqt al-marjan fi ahkam al-jann*. Ed. Mustafa 'Ashur, Cairo: Maktabat al-Qur'an, 1988.

____ *al-Budur al-safira fi ahwal al-akhira*. Ed. Muhammad Hasan Muhammad Hasan Isma'il, Beirut: Dar al-Kutub al-'Ilmiyya, 1996.

____ *Ma rawahu al-wa'un fi akhbar al-ta'un*. Ed. Muhammad 'Ali al-Baz, Damascus: Dar al-Qalam, 1997.

Al-Tabarani, Sulayman b. Ahmad (d. 971), *Kitab al-du'a*. Ed. Muhammad Sa'id b. Muhammad Hasan al-Bukhari, Beirut: Dar al-Basha'ir al-Islamiyya, 1987 (3 vols).

____ *Musnad al-Shamiyyin*. Ed. Hamdi 'Abd al-Majid al-Silafi, Beirut: Mu'assasat al-Risala, 1996 (4 vols).

Al-Tabari, Muhammad b. Jarir (d. 923), *Jami' al-bayan*. Beirut: Dar al-Fikr, n.d. (15 vols).

___ *Ta'rikh al-rusul wa-l-muluk*. Ed. Muhammad Abu al-Fadl Ibrahim, Beirut: Rawa'i' al-Turath, n.d. (11 vols).

Taha, Rifa'i Ahmad, *Imatat al-litham 'an ba'd ahkam dhurwat sinam al-Islam*. Available at tawhed.ws.

Taji-Farouki, Suha and Nafi', Basheer (eds), *Islamic Thought in the Twentieth Century*. London: I. B. Tauris, 2004.

Al-Takruri, al-Nawwaf, *al-'Amaliyyat al-istishhadiyya fi al-mizan al-fiqhi*. Damascus: N. al-Takruri, 2003 (4th edn).

Taliqani, Mahmud, Jihad wa-Shahadat: *Struggle and Martyrdom in Islam*. Houston, TX: Institute for Research and Islamic Studies, 1986.

Al-Tamimi, Muhammad b. Ahmad (d. 944–45), *Kitab al-mihan*. Ed. Yahya al-Juburi, Beirut: Dar al-Gharb al-Islami, 1988.

Al-Tanukhi, Abu 'Ali al-Muhassin b. 'Ali (d. 994), *Nishwar al-muhadara wa-akhbar al-mudhakhara*. Ed. Abood Shalochy, Beirut: Dar Sadir, 1995 (8 vols).

Al-Tartusi, Abu Tahir (d. *ca.* 1065), *Abu Muslimnama*. Ed. Hossein Esmaili, Tehran: Institut Français de Recherche en Iran, 2001 (4 vols).

Thackston, W. M. (trans.), *The Mystical and Visionary Treatises of Suhrawardi*. London: Octagon, 1982.

Al-Tha'labi, Ahmad b. Muhammad (d. 1035–36), *'Ara'is al-majalis*. Ed. 'Abd al-Fattah Murad, Cairo: Maktabat al-Jumhuriyya al-Misriyya, n.d.

Al-Tibi, 'Ukasha 'Abd al-Manan, *al-Shahada wa-l-istishhad fi Zilal al-Qur'an*. Cairo: Maktabat al-Turath al-Islami, 1994.

Al-Tibrizi, Yahya b. 'Ali al-Khatib (d. 1108–09), *Sharh Diwan al-Hamasa*. Beirut: Dar al-Qalam, n.d.

Al-Tirmidhi, Muhammad b. 'Isa (d. 892), *al-Jami' al-sahih*. Ed. 'Abd al-Wahhab 'Abd al-Latif, Beirut: Dar al-Fikr, n.d. (5 vols).

Tortel, Christiane, "Loi islamique et haine imperiale: Sarmad Shahid Kashani, poete mystique et martyr (d. 1659)," *Revue de l'histoire des Religions* 214 (1997), pp. 431–66.

Tu'mat al-Qudat, Muhammad, *al-Mughamara bi-l-nafs fi al-qital wa-hukmuha fi al-Islam*. Amman: Dar al-Furqan, 2001.

Al-Tusi, Muhammad b. al-Hasan (d. 1067–68), *al-Tibyan fi tafsir al-Qur'an*. Ed. Ahmad Habib Qasir al-'Amili, Beirut: Maktab I'lam al-Islami, n.d. (10 vols).

'Ubaydi, 'Ali 'Aziz, *Shuhada' bi-la akfan*. Baghdad: Dar al-Hurriyya li-l-Tiba'a, 2000.

Al-'Ulaymi al-Maqdisi, Mujir al-Din al-Hanbali (d. 1522), *al-Minhaj al-ahmad fi tarajim ashab Ahmad*. Ed. Muhammad Muhyi al-Din al-Hamid, Beirut: 'Alam al-Kutub, 1984 (2 vols).

'Umar, 'Umar Ahmad, *al-Jihad fi sabil Allah*. Damascus: Dar al-Maktabi, 1999.

Vaudeville, Charlotte, *A Weaver Named Kabir: Selected Verses with a Detailed Biographical and Historical Introduction*. New Delhi: Oxford University Press, 1993.

Victor, Barbara, *Army of Roses: Inside the World of Palestinian Women Suicide Bombers*. Rodale, 2003.

Vilawi, 'Ali Muhammad, *Shahidan-i shahadat*. Tehran: Nashr-i Shahid, 2000.

Waltz, James, "The Significance of the Voluntary Martyrs of Ninth-Century Cordoba," *Muslim World* 60 (1970), pp. 143–59, 226–36.

Al-Wasiti, Muhammad b. Ahmad (fl. *ca.* 1021), *Fada'il Bayt al-Maqdis.* Ed. Yitzhak Hasson, Jerusalem: Magnes Press, 1979.

Watt, W. Montgomery (trans.), *Islamic Creeds: A Selection.* Edinburgh: Edinburgh University Press, 1994.

Al-Wazir al-Sarraj (d. 1736–37), *al-Hulal al-sundusiyya fi akhbar al-Tunisiyya.* Beirut: Dar al-Gharb al-Islamiyya, 1985 (3 vols).

Weiner, Eugene and Weiner, Anita, *The Martyr's Conviction.* Atlanta, GA: The Scholar's Press, 1990.

Wensinck, A. J. (ed.), "The Oriental Doctrine of the Martyrs," *Mededeelingen der Koninklijke Akademie van Wetenschappen, Afdeeling Letterkunde* 53 (1921), pp. 147–74.

___ *Concordance et indices de la Tradition Musulmane.* Leiden: E. J. Brill, 1936–64 (8 vols).

Westcott, G. H., *Kabir and the Kabir Panth.* New Delhi: Munshiram Manoharlal, 1986 (reprint).

Wheeler, Brannon, *Prophets in the Quran: An Introduction to the Quran and Muslim Exegesis.* London: Continuum, 2002.

Al-Yafi'i al-Shafi'i, 'Abdallah b. As'ad b. 'Ali (d. 1366–67), *Dhikr madhahib al-thinatayn wa-saba'in al-mukhalifa li-l-Sunna wa-l-mubtadi'in* in al-Sakasaki, 'Abbas, *al-Burhan fi ma'rifat 'aqa'id al-adyan.* Beirut: Dar al-Kutub al-'Ilmiyya, 2004.

Yaqut al-Hamawi (d. 1229), *Mu'jam al-udaba'.* Ed. 'Umar al-Tabba', Beirut: Dar Ibn Hazm, 1999 (7 vols).

Yarshater, Ehsan, "*Ta'ziyeh* and Pre-Islamic Mourning rites in Iran," in Peter Chelkowski (ed.), Ta'ziyeh: *Ritual and Drama in Iran.* New York: New York University Press, 1979, pp. 88–94.

Zad-e Mujahid. Available at azzam.com.

Zarw, Nawwaf, *al-'Amaliyyat al-istishhadiyya: 'awamil, dawafi', khalfiyyat, hasad, tada'iyyat, ta'thirat.* Amman: al-Mu'tamar al-Sha'bi li-l-Difa' 'an al-Quds, 2003.

Zimmern, Helen, *Epic of Kings: Shahnameh. Stories Retold from Firdusi.* New York: E. Hill, 1906. Available at classics.mit.edu.

Index